BRITAIN

1–2000

The Institute of Contemporary British History, University of London

Editor: Derrick Murphy

Contributors: *Lawrence Black, Simon Fowler, Graham Goodlad, Harriet Jones,
Derrick Murphy, Helen Parr, Virginia Preston, Gillian Staerck
and Marietta Stankova*

Collins Educational

An Imprint of HarperCollinsPublishers

Published by Collins Educational
An imprint of HarperCollins Publishers Ltd
77–85 Fulham Palace Road, Hammersmith
London W6 8JB

First published 2000

ISBN 0 00 327131 5

Lawrence Black, Simon Fowler, Graham Goodlad, Harriet Jones, Derrick Murphy, Helen Parr, Virginia Preston, Gillian Staerck and Marietta Stankova assert the moral right to be identified as the authors of this work.

20 01000 172

British Library Cataloguing in Publication Data
A catalogue record for this book is available from the British Library.

Cover Photograph:
The Corporate Rope (acrylic on board) by Alfred Daniels RWSRBA (1993)
Private Collection/Commissioned by Manya Igel Fine Arts Ltd., London, UK/Bridgeman Art Library, London/New York

Edited by Joanne Stone and Lucy Nicholson
Design by Derek Lee
Cover design by Derek Lee
Map artwork by Tony Richardson
Picture research by Caroline Thompson
Index by Gillian Beare
Production by Kathryn Botterill
Printed and bound by Bath Press

www.CollinsEducation.com
On-line Support for Schools and Colleges

> *We have needed a book like this for a very long time.*
> *It will be a godsend to both the teachers and the taught.*
> *The Institute of Contemporary British History has brought*
> *together a vibrant group of contributors and created a*
> *fascinating whole.*
>
> Peter Hennessy
> *Professor of Contemporary History*
> *Queen Mary & Westfield College, University of London*

The Institute of Contemporary British History (ICBH)
The ICBH was founded in 1986 by Professor Peter Hennessy and Dr Anthony Seldon to promote study and research on Britain since the Second World War. In 1999, the ICBH joined the Institute of Historical Research at the University of London.

For more information on the ICBH, see http://ihr.sas.ac.uk/icbh/

About the Contributors

Derrick Murphy is Head of Sixth Form in a school in Altrincham; Chief Examiner at GCE A Level with AQA/NEAB, and Consultant Editor of the *Modern History Review*.

Dr Lawrence Black teaches history at the Universities of London and Sussex. He is a specialist in postwar British political history, and has written widely on the politics of affluence in the 1950s and 1960s.

Simon Fowler is an archivist and historian currently studying for a PhD at University College, London

Graham Goodlad is Director of Sixth Form Studies at St John's College, Southsea, and a regular contributor to *Modern History Review*.

Dr Harriet Jones is the Director of the ICBH, and is an authority on the history of the Conservative Party in the twentieth century.

Helen Parr teaches history at Queen Mary & Westfield College, University of London, where she is completing her doctorate on Britain's second application to join the European Economic Community.

Virginia Preston is Deputy Director of the ICBH and editor of *Survey of Current Affairs* for the Foreign and Commonwealth Office.

Gillian Staerck is the Editorial Research Officer of the ICBH, where she edits *Modern History Review* and *The Electronic Journal of International History*.

Dr Marietta Stankova teaches history at the London School of Economics and the University of Sussex. She is a specialist on Britain's Cold War relations with Eastern Europe.

ACKNOWLEDGEMENTS

The publishers would like to thank the following for permission to use their text extracts: Addison Wesley Longman Ltd for extracts from *The Conservative Party and British Politics 1902–1951* by Stuart Ball (Longman Seminar Studies, 1995); Blackwell Publishers for extracts from *The Labour Party since 1979* by Eric Shaw (1994) and *The Labour Party since 1945* by Eric Shaw (1996); BBC Radio WM for extracts from the series *The Century Speaks* produced by Helen Lloyd (1999) (accompanying book *The Century Speaks Birmingham Voices* published by Tempus, 1999); Curtis Brown Ltd, London, on behalf of the Estate of Sir Winston Churchill, copyright Winston S.Churchill; the Fabian Society for an extract from *Election '45: Reflections on the Revolution in Britain* by Austin Mitchell (1995); Fourth Estate Ltd for an extract from *Labour Rebuilt: the New Model Party* by Colin Hughes and Patrick Wintour (1990); HarperCollinsPublishers for extracts from *Another Heart and Other Pulses* by Michael Foot (Collins, 1984), *An Appetite for Power: A History of the Conservative Party since 1830* by John Ramsden (1998) and *Parliamentary Socialism* by Ralph Milliband (George Allan and Unwin, 1973; Bill Hamilton as the Literary Executor of the Estate of the Late Sonia Brownell Orwell, Martin Secker & Warburg Ltd for an extract from *The Road to Wigan Pier* by George Orwell, Copyright © George Orwell, 1937; the Labour Party for extracts from Labour Party manifestos; Little, Brown for an extract from *The Unfinished Revolution* by Philip Gould (1998); Macmillan Press Ltd for extracts from *British Political Facts 1900–1994* by David and Gareth Butler (1994), *The Labour Government 1974–1979* by Martin Holmes (1985) and *The Lost Victory* by Corelli Barnett (1995); Orion Group for an extract from *From Blitz to Blair* by Nick Tiratsoo (Weidenfeld and Nicolson, 1997); Penguin UK for an extract from *British Society 1914–1945* by John Stevenson (1984); the Public Record Office for an extract from the summary of De Gaulle's Press Conference, January 14 1963 (PRO PREM 11/4413); Random House for extracts from *Twopence to Cross the Mersey* by Helen Forrester (Jonathan Cape, 1974) and *Ramsay Macdonald* by David Marquand (Jonathan Cape, 1977); Routledge for extracts from *Modern Britain: An Economic and Social History* by Sean Glynn and Alan Booth (1996); Sutton Publishing Ltd for an extract from *Generating Socialism: Recollections of Life in the Labour Party* by Daniel Weinbren (1995); Verso for an extract from *The Age of Insecurity* by Larry Elliott and Dan Atkinson (London, 1998); Yale University Press for extracts from *Baldwin and the Conservative Party: The Crisis of 1929–1931*, by Stuart Ball (1988).

Every effort has been made to contact the holders of copyright material, but if any have been inadvertently overlooked the publishers will be pleased to make the necessary arrangements at the first opportunity.

The publishers would like to thank the following for permission to reproduce photographs:

AP Photo/David Crosling, 216;
Associated Press, 199, 208;
By kind permission of the Belfast Telegraph Newspapers Ltd, 262, 268;
© Steve Bell – The Third Way – first published in the *Guardian* 23 September 1998, 158;
Eurostar (UK) Ltd, 389;
By kind permission of the *Evening Standard*/Solo Syndication – Tour de l'Europe by Vicky Photo from: The Centre for the Study of Cartoons and Caricature, University of Kent, Canterbury, 372;
By kind permission of the *Evening Standard*/Solo Syndication – Tramsay by David Low – first published in the *Evening Standard* 10 February 1930, 97;
Express Newspapers, 93;
Fotomas Index, 27, 66;
Hulton Getty Collection, 18, 42, 46, 50, 51, 68, 69, 76, 77, 80, 82, 89, 130, 140, 160, 169, 177, 226, 231, 238, 246, 258, 264, 283, 286, 296, 310, 323, 328, 329, 350, 355, 377;
© Imperial War Museum, London, 30, 178;
National Museum, Dublin, Ireland, 256;
'PA' News Photo Library, 297, 305;
Popperfoto, 272;
Popperfoto/Reuter, 333;
Punch Ltd, 63, 132, 141;
Rex Features Ltd, 385;
Reproduced from the Spectator – cartoon by Trog published 16 October 1959, 318.

Contents

Study and examination skills

- Differences between GCSE and Sixth Form history
- Extended writing: the structured question and the essay
- How to handle sources in Sixth Form History
- Historical interpretation
- Progression in Sixth Form History
- Examination technique

This chapter of the book is designed to aid Sixth Form students in their preparation for public examinations in History.

Differences between GCSE and Sixth Form History

- **The amount of factual knowledge required for answers to Sixth Form History** questions is more detailed than at GCSE. Factual knowledge in the Sixth Form is used as supporting evidence to help answer historical questions. Knowing the facts is important but not as important as knowing that factual knowledge supports historical analysis.

- **Extended writing is more important in Sixth Form History.** Students will be expected to answer either structured questions or essays.

Structured questions require students to answer more than one question on a given topic. For example:

1. In what ways did the Labour governments of 1945 to 1951 try to improve social conditions?

2. To what extent did the Labour governments of 1945 to 1951 bring about a transformation in social conditions?

Each part of the structured question demands a different approach.

Essay questions require students to produce one answer to a given question. For example:

How successful were the Thatcher governments of 1979 to 1990 in dealing with trade union problems?

Similarities with GCSE

- Source analysis and evaluation

The skills in handling historical sources which were acquired at GCSE are developed in Sixth Form History. In the Sixth Form sources have to be analysed in their historical context, so a good factual knowledge of the subject is important.

● Historical interpretations

Skills in historical interpretation at GCSE are also developed in Sixth Form History. The ability to put forward different historical interpretations is important. Students will also be expected to explain why different historical interpretations have occurred.

Extended writing: the structured question and the essay

When faced with extended writing in Sixth Form History students can improve their performance by following a simple routine that attempts to ensure that they achieve their best performance.

Answering the question

What are the command instructions?

Different questions require different types of response. For instance, 'In what ways' requires students to point out the various ways something took place in history; 'Why' questions expect students to deal with the causes or consequences of an historical event.

'How far' or 'To what extent' questions require students to produce a balanced, analytical answer. Usually, this will take the form of the case for and case against an historical question.

Are there key words or phrases that require definition or explanation?

It is important for students to show that they understand the meaning of the question. To do this, certain historical terms or words require explanation. For instance, if a question asked 'how far' a politician was an 'innovator', an explanation of the word 'innovator' would be required.

Does the question have specific dates or issues that require coverage?

If a question mentions specific dates, these must be adhered to. For instance, if you are asked to answer a question on British policy towards Ireland it may state clear limits, such as 1914 to 1922. Also questions may mention a specific aspect such as 'domestic policy' or 'foreign policy'.

Planning your answer

Once you have decided on what the question requires, write a brief plan. For structured questions this may be brief. This is a useful procedure to make sure that you have ordered the information you require for your answer in the most effective way. For instance, in a balanced, analytical answer this may take the form of jotting down the main points for and against an historical issue raised in the question.

Writing the answer

Communication skills

The quality of written English is important in Sixth Form History. The way you present your ideas on paper can affect the quality of your answer. Since 1996 the government (through SCAA and QCA) has placed emphasis on the quality of written English in the Sixth Form. Therefore, punctuation, spelling and grammar, which were awarded marks at GCSE, require close attention. Use a dictionary if you are unsure of a word's meaning or spelling. Use the glossary of terms you will find in this book to help you.

The introduction

For structured questions you may wish to dispense with an introduction altogether and begin writing reasons to support an answer straight away.

However, essay answers should begin with an introduction. These should be both concise and precise. Introductions help 'concentrate the mind' on the question you are about to answer. Remember, do not try to write a conclusion as your opening sentence. Instead, outline briefly the areas you intend to discuss in your answer.

Balancing analysis with factual evidence

It is important to remember that factual knowledge should be used to support analysis. Merely 'telling the story' of an historical event is not enough. A structured question or essay should contain separate paragraphs, each addressing an analytical point that helps to answer the question. If, for example, the question asks for reasons why the Second World War began in 1939, each paragraph should provide a reason for the outbreak of the Second World War. You may also mention links between reasons. You may also explain why some reasons are more important than others. In order to support and sustain the analysis evidence is required. Therefore, your factual knowledge should be used to substantiate analysis. Good structured question and essay answers integrate analysis and factual knowledge.

Seeing connections between reasons

In dealing with 'why'-type questions it is important to remember that the reasons for an historical event might be interconnected. Therefore, it is important to mention the connections between reasons. Also, it might be important to identify a hierarchy or reasons – that is, are some reasons more important than others in explaining an historical event?

Using quotations and statistical data

One aspect of supporting evidence that sustains analysis is the use of quotations. These can either be from an historian or a contemporary. However, unless these quotations are linked with analysis and support-ing evidence, they tend to be of little value.

It can also be useful to support analysis with statistical data. In questions that deal with social and economic change, precise statistics that support your argument can be very persuasive.

The conclusion

All structured questions and essays require conclusions. If, for example, a question requires a discussion of 'how far' you agree with a question, you should offer a judgement in your conclusion. Don't be afraid of this – say what you think. Students who write an analytical answer, ably supported by factual evidence, under-perform because they fail to provide a conclu-sion that deals directly with the question.

Source analysis

Source analysis forms an integral part of the study of History. In Sixth Form History source analysis is identified as an important skill in Assessment Objective 3.

In dealing with sources you should be aware that historical sources must be used 'in historical context' in Sixth Form History. Therefore, in this book sources are used with the factual information in each chapter. Also, a specific source analysis question is included.

Assessment Objectives
1. knowledge and understanding of history
2. evaluation and analysis skills
3. a) source analysis in historical context
   b) historical interpretation

How to handle sources in Sixth Form History

In dealing with sources a number of basic hints will allow you to deal effectively with source-based questions and to build on your knowledge and skill in using sources at GCSE.

Written sources

Attribution and date

It is important to identify who has written the source and when it was written. This information can be very important. If, for instance, a source was written by Harold Wilson, the Labour Party leader, during the 1964 general election campaign, this information may be of considerable importance if you are asked about the usefulness (utility) or reliability of the source as evidence of Labour Party policy during the general election campaign.

It is important to note that just because a source is a primary source does not mean it is more useful or less reliable than a secondary source. Both primary and secondary sources need to be analysed to decide how useful and reliable they are. This can be determined by studying other issues.

Is the content factual or opinionated?

Once you have identified the author and date of the source it is important to study its content. The content may be factual, stating what has happened or what may happen. On the other hand, it may contain opinions that should be handled with caution. These may contain bias. Even if a source is mainly factual, there might be important and deliberate gaps in factual evidence that can make a source biased and unreliable. Usually, written sources contain elements of both opinion and factual evidence. It is important to judge the balance between these two parts.

Has the source been written for a particular audience?

To determine the reliability of a source it is important to know at whom it is directed. For instance, a public speech may be made to achieve a particular purpose and may not contain the author's true beliefs or feelings. In contrast, a private diary entry may be much more reliable in this respect.

Corroborative evidence

To test whether or not a source is reliable, the use of other evidence to support or corroborate the information it contains is important. Cross-referencing with other sources is a way of achieving this; so is cross-referencing with historical information contained within a chapter.

Visual sources

Cartoons

Cartoons are a popular form of source used at both GCSE and in Sixth Form History. However, analysing cartoons can be a demanding exercise. Not only will you be expected to understand the content of the cartoon, you may also have to explain a written caption – which appears usually at the bottom of the cartoon. In addition, cartoons will need placing in historical context. Therefore, a good knowledge of the subject matter of the topic of the cartoon will be important. To test your ability to analyse cartoons successfully use the *Punch* cartoon on page 66.

Photographs

'The camera never lies'! This phrase is not always true. When analysing photographs, study the attribution and date. Photographs can be changed so they are not always an accurate visual representation of events. Also, to test whether or not a photograph is a good representation of events you will need corroborative evidence.

Maps

Maps which appear in Sixth Form History are predominantly secondary sources. These are used to support factual coverage in the text by providing information in a different medium. Therefore, to assess whether or not information contained in maps is accurate or useful, reference should be made to other information. It is also important with line written sources to check the attribution and date. These could be significant.

Statistical data and graphs

It is important when dealing with this type of source to check carefully the nature of the information contained in data or in a graph. It might state that the information is in tons (tonnes) or another measurement. Be careful to check if the information is in index numbers. These are a statistical device where a base year is chosen and given the figure 100. All other figures are based on a percentage difference from that base year. For instance, if 1920 is taken as a base year for the level of unemployment within the British economy it is given the figure of 100. If the index for British unemployment in 1922 is 115 then unemployment had risen 15% on the 1920 figure.

An important point to remember when dealing with data and graphs over a period of time is to identify trends and patterns in the information. Merely describing the information in written form is not enough.

Historical interpretation

An important feature of both GCSE and Sixth Form History is the issue of historical interpretation. In Sixth Form History it is important for students to be able to explain why historians differ, or have differed in their interpretation of the past.

Availability of evidence

An important reason is the availability of evidence on which to base historical judgements. As new evidence comes to light, an historian today may have more information on which to base their judgements than historians in the past. For instance, a major source of information about 20th-century political history is the Public Record Office (PRO) in Kew, London. Some of the information held at the PRO has remained confidential, in some cases, for 50 to 100 years. Therefore, it is only recently that historians have been able to analyse and assess this evidence. Some material will not be available until later in the 21st century.

'A philosophy of history?'

Many historians have a specific view of history that will affect the way they make their historical judgements. For instance, Marxist historians – who take the view from the writings of Karl Marx the founder of modern socialism – believe that society has been made up of competing economic and social classes. They also place considerable importance on economic reasons in human decision making. Therefore, a Marxist historian of the causes of the Slump of the 1930s might have a completely different viewpoint to a non-Marxist historian.

The role of the individual

Some historians have seen past history as being moulded by the acts of specific individuals who have changed history. Lloyd George, Churchill and Thatcher are seen as individuals whose personality and beliefs changed the course of 20th-century British history. Other historians have tended to 'downplay' the role of individuals; instead they highlight the importance of more general social, economic and political change. Rather than seeing Clement Attlee as an individual who changed the course of political history, these historians tend to see him as representing the views of a broader group of individuals, such as the supporters of socialism and the introduction of a Welfare State.

Placing different emphasis on the same historical evidence

Even if historians do not possess different philosophies of history or place different emphasis on the role of the individual, it is still possible for them to disagree because they place different emphases on aspects of the same factual evidence. As a result, Sixth Form History should be seen as a subject that encourages debate about the past based on historical evidence.

Progression in Sixth Form History

The ability to achieve high standards in Sixth Form History involves the acquisition of a number of skills:

● **Good written communication skills**

● **Acquiring a sound factual knowledge**

● **Evaluating factual evidence and making historical conclusions based on that evidence**

● **Source analysis**

● **Understanding the nature of historical interpretation**

● **Understanding the causes and consequences of historical events**

● **Understanding themes in history which will involve a study of a specific topic over a long period of time**

● **Understanding the ideas of change and continuity associated with themes.**

Students should be aware that the acquisition of these skills will take place gradually over the time spent in the Sixth Form. At the beginning of the course the main emphasis may be on the acquisition of factual knowledge, particularly when the body of knowledge studied at GCSE was different.

When dealing with causation students will have to build on their skills from GCSE. They will not only be expected to identify reasons for an historical event but also to provide a hierarchy of causes. They should identify the main causes and less important causes. They may also identify that causes may be interconnected and linked. Progression in Sixth Form History will come with answering the questions at the end of each sub-section in this book and practising the skills outlined through the use of the factual knowledge contained in the book.

Examination technique

The ultimate challenge for any Sixth Form historian is the ability to produce quality work under examination conditions. Examinations will take the form of either modular examinations taken in January and June or in an 'end of course' set of examinations.

Here is some advice on how to improve your performance in an examination.

- **Read the whole examination paper thoroughly**
  Make sure that the questions you choose are those for which you can produce a good answer. Don't rush – allow time to decide which questions to choose. It is probably too late to change you mind half way through answering a question.

- **Read the question very carefully**
  Once you have made the decision to answer a specific question, read it very carefully. Make sure you understand the precise demands of the question. Think about what is required in your answer. It is much better to think about this before you start writing, rather than trying to steer your essay in a different direction half way through.

- **Make a brief plan**
  Sketch out what you intend to include in your answer. Order the points you want to make. Examiners are not impressed with additional information included at the end of the essay, with indicators such as arrows or asterisks.

- **Pace yourself as you write**
  Success in examinations has a lot to do with successful time management. If, for instance, you have to answer an essay question in approximately 45 minutes then you should be one-third of the way through after 15 minutes. With 30 minutes gone you should start writing the last third of your answer.

Where a question is divided into sub-questions make sure you look at the mark tariff for each question. If in a 20-mark question a sub-question is worth a maximum of 5 marks then you should spend approximately one-quarter of the time allocated for the whole question on this sub-question.

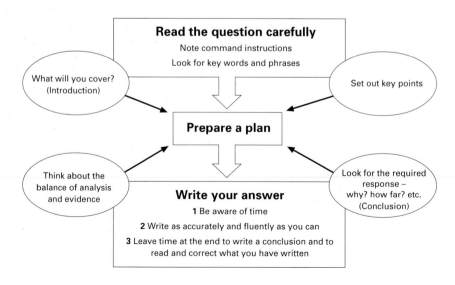

Read the question carefully
Note command instructions
Look for key words and phrases

What will you cover? (Introduction)

Set out key points

Prepare a plan

Think about the balance of analysis and evidence

Look for the required response – why? how far? etc. (Conclusion)

Write your answer
1 Be aware of time
2 Write as accurately and fluently as you can
3 Leave time at the end to write a conclusion and to read and correct what you have written

Britain 1914–2000: a synoptic assessment

Key Issues

- *How did Britain's position in international affairs change between 1914 and 2000?*

- *To what extent was the British economy and society transformed between 1914 and 2000?*

- *How far did the British political system change between 1914 and 2000?*

1.1 Why did the Commonwealth develop out of the British Empire between 1914 and 2000?

In 1914 Britain possessed the largest empire in world history. It covered a quarter of the land surface of the earth and contained about a third of the world's population. The Empire reached its greatest extent in 1933 with the inclusion of a large part of Antarctica – but by the end of the century Britain's overseas possessions were limited to small groups of islands such as the Falkland Islands. Although the British Empire has all but disappeared, large parts of the former Empire remain together in an international organisation, the Commonwealth. By 1999 this also included states that had never been part of the Empire such as Mozambique. So why did the Empire disappear to be replaced by the Commonwealth?

Parts of the British Empire had internal self-government by as early as 1914. These were Canada, New Zealand, Australia, South Africa and Newfoundland, territories ruled by white populations. Between 1914 and 1931 two other territories received internal self-government: the Irish Free State in 1922, and Southern Rhodesia in 1923. By 1931, the Statute of Westminster gave these states virtual independence. They were linked to Britain through a common head of state, the British monarch. Their degree of independence was shown at the outbreak of the Second World War: Canada declared war on Germany one day later than Britain to emphasise that this was a Canadian not a British decision; Eire (the former Irish Free State) remained neutral throughout the war.

Dominion: Up until 1931 this meant a part of the British Empire with internal self-government. After that date dominions had control over their foreign policy.

The transition of the 'white' **dominions** from territory to full independence under the British monarchy was the role model for the development of the Commonwealth. It reflected a view of empire held by the 19th-century Liberal leader, W. E. Gladstone. He thought that the 'white' parts of the British Empire should be a free association of states held together by common allegiance to the monarchy with common historical and racial roots.

During the inter-war period the idea of empire was affected by the development of two political movements, nationalism and democracy. The creation of the Irish Free State can be seen as the success of these two political ideas. More importantly the inter-war period saw the steady and rapid rise of the Indian nationalist movement. Founded in 1886, the Indian National Congress became the main advocate of Indian self-government. In 1918 its leaders were demanding Home Rule for India. By 1939 they were demanding full independence. Under the guidance of M. K. Gandhi, the Indian National Congress used a variety of strategies to force the British to accept Indian independence. Civil disobedience through strikes and non co-operation became a central feature of Gandhi's strategy. He also advocated self-reliance and the encouragement of Indian industry.

From 1909 to 1947 the British tried a number of policies to limit the demand for independence. Reforms of the Indian political system in 1909, 1919 and 1935 increased the participation of Indians in the administration of the British Indian Empire. This policy of reform was combined with repression and imprisonment of nationalist leaders. The most notorious incident came in 1919 in Armritsar in the Punjab where General Dyer ordered the massacre of unarmed demonstrators. Although Dyer was relieved of command after the incident it did create considerable bitterness in India.

By 1947 the British government had come to the decision to give independence to its Indian Empire. However, under the last Viceroy, Lord Mountbatten, the Indian Empire was divided between India and Pakistan. In 1948 independence was granted to Ceylon (Sri Lanka) and Burma (Myanmar). These developments stand as a major turning point in British imperial history. Not only was independence granted to non-white territories but India was allowed to remain a part of the Commonwealth after it declared itself a republic in 1950.

From 1950 to 1970 Britain gave most of its Empire independence, with the vast majority of former territories deciding to stay within the Commonwealth. However, the independence of Black African territories was bitterly opposed by the white supremacist government in South Africa. In 1961 South Africa became a republic and left the Commonwealth. In 1965 the decision of the white government of Southern Rhodesia to declare a UDI (unilateral declaration of independence) added to the racial conflict. From 1965 until the creation of Zimbabwe in 1980 the Rhodesian problem was a major issue within the Commonwealth.

From the 1960s the Commonwealth became a loose collection of states sharing a common history within the Empire. In 1948, 1965 and 1971 two Commonwealth states, India and Pakistan, fought a series of short wars against each other. The Commonwealth also supported an anti-racist policy directed against South Africa and Rhodesia. The creation of Zimbabwe from Rhodesia led to the new state's inclusion in the Commonwealth. Only with the release of Nelson Mandela and the granting of full democracy in South Africa was that state allowed to rejoin.

The loss or transformation of the British Empire seems to have been an inevitable process. Britain lacked the military and financial power to maintain such a large trans-global empire. The speed at which Britain handed over power was due to factors such as the advance of nationalism and democracy in Asia and Africa.

1. What were the main changes that affected the British Empire between 1914 and 2000?

2. Why do you think these changes took place?

1.2 How far did British foreign and defence policy change between 1914 and 2000?

Britain's foreign and defence policy is directly linked to Britain's decline as an imperial power. Throughout the period 1914 to 1939 Britain aimed to defend its Empire. To do so it needed to keep command of the sea. As part of this global aim Britain wanted to prevent any one state dominating the European continent. These inter-connected aims were central features of British foreign policy during the 19th century.

When Britain went to war with Germany in 1914 it was an attempt to prevent German domination of the European continent. Britain also feared the threat posed by the huge German sea fleet to the British Empire. By 1918 Britain had broken German ambition and its naval power but at great cost: about 960,000 British imperial troops had died in the war, 750,000 from Britain itself.

In the inter-war period defence of the Empire was the prime consideration. The decision to build a major naval base at Singapore was a major political issue in the late 1920s and 1930s. Unfortunately for Britain, the 1930s saw the appearance of three major threats to its global position. In the Mediterranean and East Africa Mussolini's Italy was following an expansionist policy, conquering Abyssinia (Ethiopia) in 1935–36. From 1931 Japan followed an expansionist policy towards China in the Far East. Finally, from 1933 Hitler followed a similar policy in Central Europe.

The dilemma facing British policy makers during a period of economic depression was apparent. Britain's lack of military and financial resources greatly limited her ability to meet the potential threats of Italy, Japan and Germany simultaneously. Attempts were made by prime ministers Baldwin and Chamberlain to curb these threats through a policy of appeasement. This was first used towards Italy, where an attempt was made to appease Mussolini with the Hoare-Laval Pact, but the pact was never implemented due to widespread opposition within Britain. Secondly, it was used towards Germany. The most notable example of this policy was the Munich Agreement of 1938. Chamberlain had little room for manoeuvre when Hitler threatened European war over the Sudetenland of Czechoslovakia. Fear of massive aerial attack when the RAF had yet to rearm fully, the fear that South Africa and other dominions might not join the fight against Germany, and the possibility of heavy casualties all affected Chamberlain's judgement. When Britain finally abandoned appeasement, in the spring of 1939, the decision was made because of the genuine fear that Germany again wanted to dominate the European continent.

Britain's involvement in the Second World War highlights the major problems facing British foreign and defence policy makers. Britain lacked the ability to fight Germany and Italy alone after July 1940. Without considerable financial assistance from the United States through the **Lend-Lease** programme Britain would have gone bankrupt. In addition, from December 1941 Britain's war effort against Germany, Italy and Japan was heavily dependent on the USA and the Red Army of the USSR.

Lend-Lease: An American policy introduced during the Second World War where military aid was given to Britain, and other allied countries, with the aim of acquiring payment for such aid after the war.

Although Britain was regarded as one of the 'Big Three' of the Grand Alliance it was clear by 1945 that Britain's role as a world power was rapidly coming to an end. From 1945 to 1991 Britain was a secondary player in a bi-polar world dominated by the USA and USSR. As part of the NATO alliance from 1949, Britain has been an ally of the USA in its global fight against communism. In 1950 British troops were sent to aid the USA in the Korean War. More significantly Britain has since then been a major base for US air and naval forces, including US nuclear forces. Britain was also a member of the South East Asia Treaty Organisation (SEATO).

Although the Atlantic alliance has been the main feature of British foreign and defence policy since 1945 there were occasions when Britain attempted to defend its imperial and global interests independently from the USA. In 1956 the Eden government engaged in the humiliating Suez operation against Egypt. In 1982 the Thatcher government was successful in retaking the Falkland Islands following an Argentine invasion.

However, for most of the period Britain has worked together with the USA. This was shown most clearly by the deployment of British army and air forces in Germany. It was also shown through the development of a British nuclear deterrent which has relied heavily on USA nuclear technology. Even following the collapse of the Soviet Union Britain continued to work closely with the USA. In 1991 both states, as part of a broader UN force, were involved in the Gulf War against Iraq. In 1999, acting on behalf of NATO, both states were involved in an air war against Yugoslavia over the situation in Kosovo.

Why did Britain decline as one of the world's major powers between 1914 and 2000?

In 1999 Britain lacked the military and financial power to act independently on the world stage. As a result, British foreign and defence policy at the end of the 20th century was inextricably linked to the USA. There have been limited attempts to develop a British defence establishment through joint European ventures such as the Tornado aircraft and the Eurofighter but this has been on a very limited scale. Attempts by EU politicians to advance the cause of an EU foreign and defence policy have not been popular within Britain.

1.3 To what extent did Britain experience economic decline between 1914 and 2000?

A constant feature of British history throughout the period has been the relative decline of the British economy. In 1914 Britain was a world economic power. London was the world's financial and banking centre. The British merchant navy was the largest in the world and Britain dominated trade in textiles and coal. By 2000 Britain had lost this position. For the first time since the Industrial Revolution in the 18th century, per capita income in Britain was below that in France and Italy. Even the relatively new Republic of Ireland had surpassed Britain in this respect by 1998.

Why did Britain lose its strong world economic position? Firstly, the two world wars had a major effect on world trade and with it Britain's economic prosperity. During both wars Britain lost markets, mainly to the USA. In addition the development of textiles, shipbuilding and steel industries in countries such as Japan and other Asian countries reduced demand for British goods.

In a recent study, the historian Geoffrey Owen has attributed Britain's economic decline to a lack of competition within industries. However it can also be attributed to poor industrial relations. Weak management and militant trade unionists have both been blamed for a decline in Britain's ability to compete internationally. The General Strike of 1926 and the Miners' Strikes of the early 1970s were seen as part of this trend. Poor productivity and lack of investment in British industry have contributed to a loss of competitiveness.

The decision to join the European Economic Community in 1973 gave Britain the opportunity to participate in a large European market. In addition, structural reforms during the Thatcher years increased productivity, reduced government debt and increased flexibility in the labour market. However, it also saw a major decline in the manufacturing sector (almost 30% between 1979 and 1984) and a shift towards the tertiary or service sector of the economy. Britain's attempt to retain the City of London as a world financial centre led to deregulation in 1987.

1. *In what ways did Britain experience economic decline between 1914 and 2000?*

2. *What do you regard as the main reason for the change in Britain's economic position in this period? Give reasons for your answer.*

Demand Management Economics

as put forward by the economist J. M. Keynes. It formed the basis of post Second World War government economic policy until 1976.

Keynes believed that when the British economy faced economic depression in the 1930s this was due mainly to a lack of demand within the economy. Demand could be increased by the government spending money in the economy through financing factory building or improvements in the economy's infrastructure.

This money would lead to an increase in employment. The newly employed workers would have money to spend so this, in turn, would increase demand within the economy.

Direct government intervention in the economy could, therefore, help to reduce unemployment. Through changing the amount of direct taxation and government spending the government could also affect the rate of inflation (a rise in prices).

By these methods governments between 1945 and 1976 attempted to keep unemployment and inflation low. Unfortunately, in 1973, the quadrupling of the world price in oil caused a large increase in business costs, which resulted in high inflation and growing unemployment.

Keynesian economic policy was replaced by monetarist economic policy, which placed greater emphasis on using interest rates and a control of the money supply to achieve low inflation and unemployment.

By 2000 Britain had one of the lowest unemployment rates in the European Union. It also had low, stable inflation. The economic policies followed under Thatcher, Major and Blair seemed to have laid the foundations for future sustainable economic growth.

1.4 How significant were changes in the mass media, 1914–2000?

The 20th century was a period that saw considerable advances in the mass media. The mass media includes books and film but is usually associated with the press, television and radio. These are important institutions for the spreading of information about the political system. As a result, they can also help form or influence people's opinions about politics.

Major factors in the development of the mass media have been the growth of literacy and the advance of technology. The Education Act of 1902 extended government involvement in education to cover provision of secondary as well as elementary education. By the end of the century the government was involved in pre-school years (nursery education) through to university education. This massive rise in literacy caused by statutory education in turn led to a rise in demand for information in various forms.

Newspapers

Until 1896 newspapers were read primarily by a small number of educated people. In that year, Alfred Harmsworth, later Lord Northcliffe, founded the *Daily Mail*. At one ha'penny (0.2p) the *Daily Mail* became the first mass circulation newspaper with a daily sale of over one million copies. In 1900 it was followed by the *Daily Express* and, in 1904, the *Daily Mirror* was refounded as a mass circulation cheap daily paper.

With a wide readership these newspapers began to have influence in society. In 1898 the so-called 'Yellow Press' in the USA were regarded as having whipped up popular opinion in favour of the Spanish-American War. In Britain during the First World War the mass circulation papers followed a strongly patriotic line. This was partly due to DORA (the Defence of the Realm Act) which censored newspapers.

In 1918 the *Daily Mail* ran the 'Hang the Kaiser' campaign supporting candidates in the 1918 general election on this issue. In the 1924 general election the publication of the **Zinoviev Letter** in the *Daily Mail* helped the Conservatives beat Labour. In 1930–31 the *Mail* and *Express* ran a campaign against the Conservative Party leader, Stanley Baldwin. He accused the press of having power without responsibility, an accusation that has lasted until today. By 1937 the sale of daily newspapers reached 10 million copies.

In 1949 the first Royal Commission on the Press was set up. One of its recommendations, the creation of a Press Council to deal with complaints from the public, took place in 1953. The issue of press infringement of personal privacy has been a major complaint. This issue reached its height in 1997 with the death of Princess Diana and her brother's criticism of **freelance** journalists.

With the advent of independent television in the 1950s newspapers faced a rival in advertising. The effect was to lead to the closure of several national and local papers. In 1960 the *News Chronicle* closed. By the 1970s London possessed one evening paper, the *Evening Standard*, when in the 1950s it had had three (the *Standard*, *Evening News* and *Star*).

Nevertheless, newspaper circulation continued to grow. In 1979 total daily sales reached 14 million. This was due in part to the development of tabloid newspapers. The acquisition of the *Sun* by Rupert Murdoch in the early 1970s started a press revolution in both the production and content of popular newspapers. With its concentration on sensational stories and sport the *Sun* became the most popular daily paper with over 4 million sales by the 1990s. Its style was emulated by the *Mirror* and the Express group of newspapers with the launch of a new newspaper the *Daily Star*.

Zinoviev Letter: A letter apparently from Grigori Zinoviev, President of the Communist International, asking British Communists to encourage subversion among the armed forces. It caused distrust of the political left.

Freelance: A journalist who works independently of a specific newspaper.

To what extent does this photograph suggest that radio was an important method of communication in the 1920s?

Men listening to a commentary on the Grand National horse race in the 1920s.

Radio

The development of the radio led to the creation of the British Broadcasting Company in 1922. By 1926 the government had created the British Broadcasting Corporation (BBC). Under the leadership of Lord Reith the BBC offered radio broadcasting. It had a monopoly on public service broadcasting. Lord Reith believed that the BBC had the responsibility of educating and informing the public rather than offering popular entertainment.

The BBC's monopoly of radio within Britain continued until the 1960s. Beginning with Radio Caroline, a number of pirate radio stations based on ships outside the three mile limit began broadcasting popular music. By 1968 the Labour government had decided to declare these stations illegal, but to cater for a wider range of taste BBC radio was reorganised with the creation of Radio 1 and Radio 2 for popular music, Radio 3 for classical music and Radio 4 for public service broadcasting.

In 1972 the Sound Broadcasting Act ended the BBC monopoly. From 1973 it faced competition from commercial radio stations, which were funded by advertising. By the end of the century Britain had a network of national and local BBC radio stations as well as commercial stations.

Television

Of all the forms of mass media the television has had the greatest impact on British society. Although the BBC began television broadcasts as early as 1936, television did not begin to have a major impact until the 1950s. However, by the end of the 20th century virtually every household possessed at least one television.

A major breakthrough came with the end of the BBC's monopoly on television in 1954 with the Television Act. From 1955 the Independent Broadcasting Authority (IBA) regulated independent television companies such as Granada in northwest England. The start of independent television resulted in a major fall in the BBC's viewing figures. Quiz shows, game shows and soap operas made independent television very popular. 'Coronation Street', a Granada production, began broadcasting in 1960 and has remained one of television's most popular programmes.

Television not only entertained, it also informed: news and current affairs programmes became the main source of news for the bulk of the population. National events such as the Coronation in 1953 and the funeral of Princess Diana 44 years later were shown live on television. Television also helped popularise sport: the FA Cup Final, the Five Nations rugby championship, Wimbledon and the Grand National were all viewed by millions.

The BBC and IBA involvement in television was increased in 1964 with the creation of BBC 2 and, in 1982, with Channel 4. However, the late 1980s saw a major technological development with satellite and cable television. Rupert Murdoch's BSkyB network made financial deals with major sports organisations such as football and rugby union about the exclusive broadcasting of sports features. By the end of the century virtually all the major sporting fixtures in Britain could be found on satellite and cable television. It has also led to specialist channels for popular music and shopping. In addition, technological advances have led to the advent of digital television.

By the start of the new millennium Britons had the opportunity of receiving in excess of 100 TV channels. This has raised serious issues about the quality of broadcasting, its financing and whether public service broadcasting will survive.

The political influence of the mass media

In 1993 a survey revealed that 69% of people regarded the television as their most important source of political information. However, throughout most of the century newspapers had this role. Therefore, the ownership of mass circulation newspapers has had an influence on the political process. The *Daily Mail* and *Daily Express* have both been supporters of the Conservative Party. More recently so has the *Sun*. These newspapers have been credited with helping the Conservatives win political power regularly since 1945. The decision of the *Sun* to switch allegiance to Tony Blair's New Labour Party in 1997 was a factor in Major's landslide defeat.

Attempts to influence the mass media have also been a goal of politicians. Over the years the BBC has been accused of having either a pro-Labour or pro-Conservative bias by the other party. Political leaders employ press secretaries (spin doctors) to hand out information to the press. Occasionally politicians deliberately leak information to try to influence the media. Today the media image of politicians has become at least as important as their views.

In what ways has the mass media changed between 1914 and 2000?

Conclusion

The advance of technology has led to a wider and wider choice of media for the British people. By the end of the century the widespread use of personal computers and the Internet has led to the globalisation of the media. The British public has the opportunity to acquire information from around the globe with or without government approval. Attempts to control or limit public access to the media is becoming increasingly difficult.

1.5 In what ways did British society change between 1914 and 2000?

British society has been transformed during the 20th century. In 1914 the population of the United Kingdom was approximately 43 million, with 36 million living in England and Wales. Shortly afterwards about 3 million people were deducted from that figure when the Irish Free State/Eire left the United Kingdom. Even so by 2000 the population had reached about 60 million.

Not only has the British population increased, its age profile has also changed. During the second half of the century the average age of the population began to increase. The rate of population increase also began to fall. By the end of the century about one-third of the population were in retirement. At the same time the time spent in full-time education also increased. Britain now faces the problem of an increasingly elderly population with a shrinking labour force available to pay for pension and health benefits in old age for the older generation. This is because when the pension scheme was set up in 1948, it was not funded in perpetuity, each worker's payments were immediately paid out in pensions for other people.

The change in Britain's population profile has been considerably affected by the introduction of the National Health Service in 1948. The improvement in the nation's health has been a main feature of the second half of the century. Programmes of infant immunisation have resulted in a dramatic drop in infant mortality. Improved diet has also helped increase longevity, but junk food has led to more obesity among the population and other health problems.

The ethnic make-up of Britain has also changed. In 1914 the population comprised English, Welsh, Scots and Irish with small Jewish, Afro-Caribbean and Chinese communities. Overall immigration was outweighed by emigration from Britain, mainly to North America and Australia.

After the Second World War the immigration of significant numbers from the Caribbean and the Indian sub-continent has led to the establishment of thriving immigrant communities. In turn British society has become a multi-cultural society of different races and religions.

Long before 1914 Britain had seen a marked decline in religious attendance, but with a greater cultural mix Britain became a multi-faith society. Catholics, Jews, Muslims, Hindus and Sikhs had all established sizeable religious communities. In 2000 although the Church of England was still the official state religion it was supported by only a small minority of the population (about 5 million out of 60 million).

During the 20th century the role of women within society changed dramatically. In the two world wars women played a major role in the work force. From 1918 they received the vote. In addition, the idea that a 'woman's place was in the home' changed significantly after the Second World War. With more political and social freedom women became more independent. The development of the contraceptive pill and legalised abortion in England, both during the 1960s, greatly aided this process. The social change in the status of women helped fuel the women's movement.

The change in status for women was part of a broader change in social attitudes towards minorities. In 1967 homosexuality was legalised. From a society dominated by men in 1914 Britain had become, by the end of the century, a more diverse and socially liberal state.

The period also witnessed the rise and decline in the power of trade unionism. In the period 1918–1926 trade union membership was high enough to enable the threat of industrial action to affect government policy. This happened on Red Friday, in 1925, and in 1926 the power of trade unionism and the government met head on with the General Strike. It wasn't until the 1970s that trade unionism again began to threaten government authority. The Miners' Strike of 1973–74 led to a three day working week and the fall of the Heath government. In 1978–79 the 'winter of discontent' undermined the Callaghan Labour Government. It wasn't until the Thatcher administration that trade union political power was broken. Through legislation and the defeat of the Miners' Strike of 1984–85 the Thatcher government greatly reduced trade union influence in politics and society.

In what ways has Britain become a more tolerant and diverse society between 1914 and 2000?

1.6 How did British democracy develop between 1914 and 2000?

Householder franchise: The right to vote based on ownership of a house. A house would only have one owner.

During the course of the century British democracy has changed considerably. In 1914 the right to vote was limited to adult males over the age of 21. It was based on a **householder franchise**. However, registration and other restrictions meant that around 40% of adult males did not vote. In addition, plural voting existed: if an adult male owned property in more than one constituency he had more than one vote. For example Joseph Chamberlain MP had 26 votes in 1900. Also there were a number of university seats (e.g. Oxford and Cambridge): graduates of these universities also had an extra vote.

The major change in the electoral system before the Second World War was the achievement of full democracy for adult males and the inclusion of women in the national political process. In the Franchise Act 1918, women over 30 years received the vote. In 1928 the vote was given to all women over 21 years. In addition, women entered Parliament and government. Lady Astor (Conservative) became the first woman MP to sit in the House of Commons. Margaret Bondfield (Labour) became the first woman minister in 1929.

Since the Second World War plural voting and university seats have been abolished (both in 1948). In 1969 all adults over 18 years received the vote. As a result, today Britain is a democratic state based on one person, one vote. However, the method of voting was an issue throughout the period. Britain has traditionally used the single-majority or 'first past the post' system of voting. This has usually guaranteed one party government, but it discriminates against some third parties such as the Liberals. The most glaring example was the 1983 general election: Labour won 27.6 % of the vote and 209 seats while the Liberal/SDP alliance won 25.4% of the votes but just 23 seats.

Ireland has also experienced a major problem with this democratic system. In 1914 Irish nationalists wanted internal self-government within the United Kingdom (Home Rule). Following the political changes of 1920–22 Ireland was partitioned: 26 southern counties received independence within the British Empire, and Northern Ireland received Home Rule. Within Northern Ireland since 1920 the issue of democratic rights has been a major source of conflict: about 60% of the population want to stay within the United Kingdom and about 40% would like to unite with southern Ireland.

Demands for a form of proportional representation (PR) have met with some success. In the early years of the Northern Ireland parliament PR was used. More recently it has been used for European Union elections and elections to the Scottish Parliament and Welsh and Northern Ireland Assemblies.

A central feature of the period has been the dominance of the House of Commons in the political process. The Parliament Act of 1911 removed the **absolute veto** from the House of Lords. In 1949 the delaying veto was reduced to one year. In 1958 and 1963 acts of Parliament altered the membership of the Lords: life peerages were created and hereditary peers could renounce their peerage. Most recently, the Blair government has removed hereditary peers from the House of Lords. If the new House of Lords were chosen by election it could cause a political clash between two elective houses of Parliament.

Since 1973 British democracy has been part of a larger political and economic unit, now called the European Union. Elections to the European Parliament began in 1979. Now the EU Parliament and Brussels administration of the EU have raised serious questions about the power of democracy within Britain. The issue of greater European centralisation has seriously split the Conservative Party.

At the same time Britain, as a political unit, has undergone change. In the 1974 general election nationalist parties in both Scotland and Wales gained seats at Westminster. By 1979 referendums were taking place to decide on whether these two areas should receive devolution. The referendums failed to achieve the majority of votes necessary. During the Thatcher–Major years (1979–97) the issue of Scottish and Welsh **devolution** was not a political priority. However, since 1997 both Scotland and Wales have received devolved assemblies and governments. The addition of Northern Ireland to this process has meant that the United Kingdom both internally and within the EU is increasingly becoming a federal political structure.

Absolute veto: The right of the House of Lords to reject a proposal for change (a bill), so preventing it from becoming law.

Devolution: Power for an area is removed from central government and given to regional assemblies.

1. *In what ways has the power of the government at Westminster been weakened between 1914 and 2000?*

2. *What do you regard as the most important development of the British political system between 1914 and 2000? Give reasons for your answer.*

1.7 To what extent did political parties change between 1914 and 2000?

The British political party system between 1914 and 2000 has seen the dominance of the Conservative Party. In that period the Conservatives either ruled directly by themselves or as a major member of a coalition for 61 out of 86 years. The Conservative Party has attracted a wide base of support. It has received support from the upper and middle classes and around one-third of the working classes for much of the period. Its main regional base has been England, mainly south and central England. In some ways it could be described as the English national party.

In 1914 it was a party centred on Parliament with a national organisation based on local Conservative Associations. As the electorate grew to incorporate women in 1918 and 1928, the party organisations expanded and developed to incorporate women's organisation within the party. Following the major election defeat of 1945 Lord Woolton reorganised the party structure, which helped the Conservatives to regain power in 1951. Although the party had a mass membership of nearly one million by the early 1950s, its following has since declined. In addition, it failed to attract younger voters. By the 1997 general election the average age of membership was over 60 years. Under William Hague a major reappraisal of organisation has been launched in an attempt to attract new and younger members.

In its policy the party has also changed considerably. In 1914 the Conservatives were a party of economic protection, defending British business interests. It was also a party that placed great emphasis on defending British imperial interests. Increasingly, however, the party began to develop a social policy, which involved major health reforms in the late 1920s and aid for areas of high unemployment in 1934. With the establishment of the Welfare State after 1945 the Conservatives adopted policies similar to Labour in terms of health and education. It was only with the arrival of Margaret Thatcher as party leader in 1975 that a distinct break with post-war Conservative economic and social policy was made. The Thatcher years (1979–90) were closely associated with the abandonment of Keynesian demand management economics and a renewed emphasis on free market economics. Privatisation and deregulation of the British economy were Thatcher's main economic legacies.

A major change in party policy occurred over the Empire and Europe during the 1950s and 1960s. The Conservative governments of 1951 to 1964 organised the withdrawal of British control of much of Africa and South-east Asia. It also saw Britain's first attempts to join the European Economic Community. Membership was achieved finally by Edward Heath in 1973. However, since 1979, the Conservative Party has become increasingly divided on Britain's role within Europe. The split on this issue helped lead to its landslide electoral defeat of 1997.

The Labour Party in 1914 was a small radical party that generally supported the Liberal Government in Parliament. By 2000 it had transformed into a government party with the largest parliamentary majority since the Great Reform Bill of 1832. However, the Labour Party had held power for relatively short periods since 1914. Before 1945 it held power only with the support of the Liberal Party. The Labour Party's greatest achievements in power took place between 1945 and 1951 when it established the Welfare State. It also nationalised important sectors of the economy. Although the party held power again between 1964 and 1970 and between 1974 and 1979 it became increasingly divided between its right and left wings. By the early 1980s the party split with the creation of the Social Democratic Party in 1981. Under the leadership of Neil Kinnock, John Smith and then Tony Blair the party reorganised itself, adopted less radical policies and reduced its links with the trade unions. By the 1990s the party was able to increase its support from beyond traditional working class areas. Tony Blair's New Labour was able to win its greatest electoral victory in 1997.

In 1914 the Liberal Party had won three successive general elections and had become the 'natural party' of government. Since 1914 the Liberal Party has declined into the position of a third party behind both Labour and the Conservatives. The split between Asquith and Lloyd George during the latter stages of the First World War destroyed its prospects of returning to government. It was only in the 1970s that the Liberals began to reassert themselves as a growing party, mainly in local government. The creation of the Liberal/SDP alliance and then the Liberal Democrat Party has re-established Liberalism as a force in British politics. However, its breakthrough into government is only likely through the introduction of proportional representation in national elections.

A major force in British politics in 1914 was the Irish Nationalist Party. From 1918 Irish nationalist MPs withdrew from Parliament. However, since the 1970s nationalist politics has again begun to have an impact on the British political system. The rise of the Scottish and Welsh nationalist parties in the 1970s placed devolution in the centre of British politics. Since 1997 the Welsh and Scottish nationalists have achieved part of their aims with Scottish and Welsh devolution.

The main area of contention involving nationalist politics is in Northern Ireland where the political troubles since 1969 have split the community into Unionist/Loyalist and Nationalist/Republican factions.

1. In what ways was Britain's position in the world different at the beginning of 2000 from its position at the beginning of the First World War in 1914?

2. Why did British society change so much between 1914 and 2000?

3. What do you regard as the most important change in British politics and society between 1914 and 2000? Give reasons for your answer.

The political, social and economic impact of the First World War, 1914–1918

Key Issues

● *What was the impact of the First World War on political parties?*

● *How did the First World War lead to a change in the role of the State?*

● *Was the First World War a turning point in British history?*

Framework of Events

1914	Kitchener becomes Minister of War
	Defence of the Realm Act
	State control of the railways
1915	Asquith forms a coalition government
	Lloyd George is made Minister of Munitions
	Lord Derby's recruiting scheme
	Treasury Agreements with the unions
1916	Lloyd George becomes Prime Minister
	Shipping Controls set up
	Conscription
1917	Food Controller is appointed
	Rationing introduced
	Industrial unrest
	Ministry of Reconstruction created
1918	Education Act
	Representation of the People Act
	Armistice

Overview

The 19th-century Russian novelist Leo Tolstoy said, 'War is the locomotive of change'. More recently the historian Arthur Marwick entitled his study of the impact on the war on British society as *The Deluge*. Both these views are apt in describing the impact of the First World War on Britain.

By 1914 the Liberal Party had won three successive general elections and was confident of another victory in the expected 1915 general election. The outbreak of war in 1914 changed the political scene completely. The main political parties supported the idea of a national coalition government. However, in December 1916 the Asquith coalition government fell from power. It was replaced by a new coalition government under the Liberal Lloyd George, splitting the Liberal Party into Asquithian and Lloyd George factions. Asquith's Liberals opposed the coalition government. In the general election of 1918 the two Liberal factions fought each other. The Liberal Party never formed a government again.

During the war the Irish Parliamentary Party also collapsed. From 1910 to 1915 it held the balance of power in the House of Commons between Liberal and Conservative. However, in 1916 an armed uprising in Dublin radically altered the political situation in Ireland. Although the rising failed it led directly to the rise of a separatist republican party, Sinn Fein, which in 1918 won 73 of the 105 seats in Ireland. The Irish Parliamentary Party won only 7. The war however revived Conservative Party, which because of the Liberal split ended the war as the dominant party in the coalition government. Perhaps more surprisingly the Labour Party benefited from the war. In 1914 the party had split into pro and anti war factions, but from 1917 it reorganised, taking a new constitution in 1918. In 1918 the party greatly increased its vote in the general election, winning 63 seats.

The war also led to an increase in the power of the British state. A Defence of the Realm Act (DORA) reduced individual freedom and introduced censorship. The government also took over the running of the railway network and coal mines. In 1916 compulsory military conscription was introduced into Britain for the first time. By 1918 the government had introduced rationing.

1. In what ways did the First World War affect Britain?

2. What do you regard as the most important change brought about by the First World War in Britain? Give reasons for your answer.

With millions of men in the armed forces large numbers of women entered the workforce for the first time, working in munitions production and transportation. This change in the social status of women was followed in 1918 with a change in their political status. The Franchise Act of 1918 gave the vote to all women over 30 years of age. In the general election later that year Countess Markiewicz became the first woman elected to parliament, but as a Sinn Fein MP she refused to take her seat. Instead Lady Astor became the first woman to sit in the House of Commons.

In industry and commerce the war boosted trade unionism. The number of workers in trade unions increased. By 1915 the war had also affected the internal structure of trade unions. Beginning on Clydeside in Scotland shop stewards were created. These were trade union officials elected by ordinary union members to represent separate factories and businesses. As a result, central control of unions weakened. Shop stewards became an important feature of British trade unionism.

2.1 How far did the war and coalition government affect the political parties?
A CASE STUDY IN HISTORICAL INTERPRETATION

When war broke out the Liberal Party had been in power since December 1905. However, the ideas and policies that were followed by the Liberal government were not suited to fighting a major European War. The Party dislike compulsory military service, restrictions on personal freedom and government intervention in the economy. On the other hand, the Conservative Party had traditionally supported the idea of strong armed forces. Such a long and costly war had a major impact on both political parties. In addition, the war had an important impact on the two main 'third parties', the Labour Party and the Irish Parliamentary (Home Rule) Party. At the beginning of the war the Labour Party was relatively small and divided in its view towards the war. The Irish Parliamentary Party, at the beginning of the war, had just seen Home Rule become law. (The Home Rule Act was suspended for the duration of the war and was never put into practice, see chapter 11.)

In May 1915 it was decided to create a coalition government, led by the Liberal Leader, Herbert Asquith, but to include Conservatives. The person who turned out to be the driving force of the coalition government was the former Liberal Chancellor of the Exchequer, David Lloyd George. He became Minister of Munitions. His energy and determination boosted the production of armaments.

Lloyd George may well have given impetus to munitions production, but the central direction of the war was still muddled. Decisions were made so slowly that Sir Maurice Hankey – who had been Secretary of the Imperial Defence Committee and was secretary of an unofficial war committee from November 1915 onwards – was moved to exclaim that the Constitution should be suspended and a dictator appointed. He was impatient with the size of the committee (it had nine members), with the fact that final decisions still lay with Cabinet and that no one seemed to have 'access to all the necessary information on which plans were to be based'. Nobody really liked the Coalition Cabinet; the Liberals felt betrayed by the intrigue that had let the Conservatives into government, while the Conservatives felt that they had been deceived into joining a government which was seen to be making little headway in the war.

Events in 1916 were no better – the Easter Rising, Kut, the Somme, the German U-boat campaign – on top of which political storm clouds were gathering as Liberal sensitivities were injured by the ever-expanding tentacles of government control. The battle over conscription in early 1916 showed reluctant Liberal attitudes at their worst. Twenty-seven Liberals voted against the Conscription Bill and the Home Secretary, Sir John Simon, resigned. At least three other Cabinet Liberals threatened to do the same, fearing the dangers to individual liberty posed by a 'dicta-torial' state.

At least Kitchener was on his way to Russia in July, enabling Lloyd George to become Minister of War. Rejecting President Wilson's sugges-tion of American mediation, Lloyd George allowed himself to be convinced that a final 'knock-out blow' was needed against Germany. However, in his view, it required a more energetic approach than Asquith was providing. At the end of 1916, Lloyd George organised a campaign with Bonar Law and Edward Carson for a small War Committee to take over the running of the war. Lloyd George would be its chairman. In the intrigue and double dealing which followed, nobody could escape accusa-tions of treachery, not even the eventual victim, Asquith.

On 3 December 1916 Asquith apparently agreed to the establishment of a War Committee, although he would have final control over policy. *The Times* then published an article the next day that criticised Asquith, saying that he was being pushed to the sidelines on war policy. Asquith assumed Lloyd George was behind this and announced that the War Committee would not be chaired by Lloyd George but by himself.

Lloyd George resigned and the Conservatives said that they would no longer serve in the Cabinet. A meeting of party leaders, held on 6 December, recognised that Bonar Law was the natural successor to Asquith. It was Asquith who made the next decisive step; he said that he would not join a government led by the Conservative leader.

By the following day though, Lloyd George had managed to form a government that the Conservatives agreed to join. Asquith and all the Liberal Ministers resigned, and none of them found themselves back in government. They promised support to the government but loyalty to Asquith; the ensuing feuding between Asquith and Lloyd George would divide and destroy the Liberal Party. It also placed the Prime Minister's destiny in the hands of the Conservatives; despite Lloyd George's apparently powerful position at the head of the coalition, he could not guarantee carrying the Liberal Party with him (many considered him a traitor) and the Conservatives tolerated him, exploiting his popularity but never really trusting him. Lloyd George had built his support on shifting sands.

Along with Arthur Henderson (Labour), Lloyd George formed a small War Cabinet made up of Bonar Law, Lord Curzon and Alfred Milner. This was a most important change to the rather chaotic working practices of government. Sir Maurice Hankey became the first Cabinet Secretary ever appointed, and he instituted proper records of decisions taken so that these could be communicated to the relevant departments. As the historian L.C.B. Seaman notes, 'It is strange to recall with what lordly amateurism the politicians had hitherto controlled the nation's affairs'.

The decline of the Liberal Party

A fatal blow had been delivered to the Liberal Party, which has been the subject of much debate. There is an argument that the Liberal Party had failed to adapt to Edwardian class-based politics and that the 'Strange Death of Liberal England' was already apparent before the First World War. Historian Trevor Wilson argued in his book *The Downfall of the Liberal Party, 1914–35* (1966) from a different standpoint; that Liberalism was still sound in 1914 but then it was knocked down by a 'rampant omnibus' – the war – from which it never recovered. In the December 1910 election, the Liberals had 272 MPs; in 1918, after the 'Coupon election', Asquith's section of the party had 28 MPs, while Lloyd George's had 133. Why did the Liberal Party decline? Was there an acceleration of processes at work before the war? Was it due to the actions of leading Liberals during the war? Or, as Trevor Wilson emphasises, is there a case for arguing that the long-held ideals of Liberalism were incompatible with the conduct of the war?

Firstly, let us examine the record of the Liberal leadership. Lloyd George was traditionally cast as the villain; here was the self-seeking opportunist who was behind the intrigues that made him leader of the coalition with the Conservatives. As historian Martin Pugh notes in *The First World War in British History* (1995), recent verdicts have been less harsh: 'In the early years of the war, Lloyd George's conspicuous success at Munitions was an asset to the Liberals when under attack over the handling of the war. It is now clear that he did not plot to deprive Asquith of the premiership.' Pugh goes on to argue that Asquith should take more of the blame since he neglected Bonar Law and refused to serve in the wartime coalition. By 1918 it was too late; Lloyd George fought the election with

A NON-PARTY MANDATE.

Punch cartoon, 13 December 1916 entitled 'A Non-Party Mandate'. John Bull is saying: 'I don't care who leads the country so long as he leads it to victory.'

? *John Bull represents Britain in this cartoon.*

a) What reasons are given in the cartoon to explain the formation of the Lloyd George Coalition Government of December 1916?

b) Using information in this chapter, how far does this cartoon explain the reasons for the formation of the Lloyd George Coalition Government?

the Conservatives and 526 government MPs, endorsed by the 'Coupon' signed by Bonar Law and Lloyd George, had been returned. The division in Liberal ranks had been underlined.

Secondly, is there evidence that the Liberals were uneasy with their interventionist role during the war? On the one hand, the Liberals' welfare reforms before the war had shown a willingness to shift away from *laissez-faire* policies. Why should more State action bother them? On the other hand, some Liberals, such as Arthur Ponsonby, were uncomfortable with how the State was threatening civil liberties through the Defence of the Realm Act and, in particular, the introduction of conscription. Ponsonby, like others, joined the Union of Democratic Control, which had been formed at the start of the war to bring about peace by negotiation. Historian A. J. P. Taylor does point out that these views on more state intervention won support at first from middle-class intellectuals and the Independent Labour Party (ILP). It is doubtful, then, if such concerns about the undermining of truly Liberal values really concerned the rank-and-file in the country when voting. The party remained split into groups led by Asquith and Lloyd George.

On balance, the division between Asquith and Lloyd George, confirmed by the 1918 election, was to prove more decisive.

Other divisions?

It was not the only division that took place though. In 1915, Labour MP Arthur Henderson joined the government as President of the Board of Education, but with a particular brief covering industrial relations. This did much to enhance Labour's standing in the country. However, in 1917, Henderson was convinced that Labour Party delegates should attend a peace conference organised by socialists in Stockholm. The Cabinet was furious and Henderson was forced to resign. His departure had two major effects.

Firstly, it ended the 'Lib–Lab' electoral pact which had contributed so effectively to several Conservative general election defeats before the war. Now the Conservatives could engage in straight fights with a divided opposition made up of Liberal and Labour candidates, rather than just one opponent. It helped their chances at the ballot box enormously.

Secondly, Henderson set about severing links with the Liberals by reforming Labour as a fully-fledged independent party. There were a number of factors which helped this process. Full employment during the war increased the power and membership of trade unions; they rose from 4 million in 1914 to 6 million in 1918. Labour was bound to derive extra support and funds from this expansion. Membership of the government gave them not only credibility but also the confidence to strike out on their own. The Representation of the People Act of 1918 – which gave universal male suffrage to those over 21 and to women over 30 – increased the number of voters from 8 million to just under 22 million. It is true that many of these new electors were women, but, many were working-class men and possibly Labour voters. However, the extent of the effect of the changes on Labour's election results continues to be the matter of debate.

Henderson, meanwhile, was busy improving the organisation of the ILP. Branches were set up in many more constituencies; there was a drive to boost membership and select more candidates. A new National Executive Committee of 23 members was to be elected by annual conference and by the block vote system, giving more influence to the larger unions. A new socialist programme, 'Labour and the New Social Order', was adopted. The policies it contained, such as State control of industry (Clause Four) and a minimum wage, enabled Labour to fill the gap left by

Radical Liberals in many parts of the country. In 1918, just under 400 candidates stood for Parliament, whereas in December 1910 the figure was just short of 80. In all, 61 Labour MPs were elected in the 1918 election – not a huge increase, but this was the 'Coupon' election and patriotic loyalty to Lloyd George was decisive. However, their share of the vote increased from 7% in 1910 to 22% – the foundations had been laid; in 1922 Labour secured 142 seats.

In Ireland foundations of a different sort had been not laid but undermined. John Redmond, the leader of the Irish Home Rule Party, found that the start of the war prevented the implementation of the 1914 Home Rule Act. Then events during the war, particularly the influence of Conservatives in the Coalition (who would be certain to oppose Home Rule) and the violent nationalist uprising in Dublin at Easter 1916, led to rapid growth in support for Sinn Fein. In 1918, Sinn Fein won 73 seats, while Redmond held on to only six. The upheaval on the political scene was complete. Was there a similar upheaval in the relationship between State and society?

If contemporary evidence is to be believed, Lloyd George was adept at large-scale organisation as well as showing great resolve to mobilise the resources of the nation. Under him, state control and direction moved ahead at unprecedented speed and into new areas of control.

2.2 How far did the State increase its role in the economic life of Britain?

The defence of the realm

The government faced the huge task of mobilising the resources of the State to meet the demands of a conflict, the scale of which was so completely outside Lloyd George's previous experience. Throughout the war piecemeal measures were taken at particular times to meet specific emergencies – these occurred in two distinct phases. Under Asquith, government interference was more limited. But Lloyd George rapidly expanded the government apparatus after December 1916, transforming the State's involvement beyond recognition.

The problems they faced were enormous: how to mobilise manpower, how to maintain resources for the army and how to feed the population. And it had to be paid for, preferably avoiding national bankruptcy.

The Defence of the Realm Acts formed the basis of government interference. The first one in August 1914 gave the Cabinet the power to 'issue regulations as to the powers and duties of the Admiralty and Army Council, and other persons acting on their behalf, for securing the public safety and defence of the realm'. Later Acts gave wide powers beyond economic control into such areas as censorship and control of the press.

Mobilising the economic resources of the State

From the outset of the war, rapid action was taken to place the railways under government control. A Railway Executive Committee, made up of the ten General Managers of the larger companies, would run the system. The government approach to shareholders was followed elsewhere – the profits were fixed at their 1913 rates, while the 130 companies affected would share the profits from a pool. Central direction allowed the rapid movement of troops and war materials between regions.

Essential commodities had to be guaranteed, and not only were reserves of wheat built up but meat was purchased overseas in bulk. By 1916, the government was buying the entire Indian **jute** crop and the

Jute: This was needed for sandbags, used by the army, for example in the trenches on the Western Front.

Flax: Used to make tents.

Russian **flax** crop. In Britain, measures were taken to guarantee wool supplies for blankets and uniforms. The majority of imported sugar came from Central Europe, and a Royal Commission was established in 1914 to oversee supplies.

Historian Sidney Pollard notes how government purchasing was hampered by a continuing faith in a market economy as well as in the cycle of supply and demand. Habits were difficult to shift; it was only slowly accepted that government intervention on such a scale would drastically alter normal trading conditions. Government demand for certain goods would so upset prices that their control was essential.

The alleged shell shortage in 1915 brought about a great extension of control from Lloyd George's Ministry of Munitions. Lloyd George gathered new people around him, like Eric Geddes, selected from business rather than the Civil Service. They also had to set about finding skilled workers to swell the labour force. The Treasury Agreement of 1915, which was later contained in the Munitions of War Act, laid down an agreement with the unions. In return for guaranteed good wage levels and profits linked to the 1913 level, the unions gave up the right to strike in favour of arbitration. The government also persuaded the unions to agree to 'dilution' (the use of semi or unskilled men and women in skilled positions), while restrictive practices would be put aside until the end of the war when they would be restored.

The Ministry then extended its controls to the supply of raw materials required in the production of armaments. The success of these measures was clear: between May 1915 and July 1916, shell production rose from 20,000 a month to 1,000,000. By 1918 the Ministry had 65,000 staff to administer production and supply. None of this avoided tensions and strife within associated industries.

Food supplies (apart from sugar) were generally satisfactory until the end of 1916 when U-boats were taking their toll. What was done? The civilian population was particularly sensitive to price rises and profiteering, but it took some time: indeed until July 1917, when the prices of meat, sugar and wheat were fixed. By then a Food Controller had been appointed to ensure that food was distributed fairly.

A munitions poster, April 1917

The Board of Agriculture assisted in boosting productivity and thereby reducing the reliance on imports. Prisoners of war and the Women's Land Army provided extra labour; tractors and fertilisers were distributed and mechanisation of farming forged ahead. Pasture was converted to arable, such as wheat and potatoes, so much so that by 1918, 3 million more acres [1.2 million hectares] of arable were under cultivation. Calculations were based on how many people 100 acres of land could feed; only 9 if given over to meat production, but 415 people if it grew potatoes. Hence some food-stuffs were never in short supply – such as potatoes and bread. Bread prices were kept low through subsidies. Rationing only became necessary at the end of 1917 when Lord Rhondda, the Food Controller, introduced rationing in tea, cheese, bacon, butter, margarine and fresh meat.

The threat of shortages often led to hoarding – far more dangerous to food supplies than U-boats. There was much talk of only weeks' supply of wheat and sugar left in the country in 1917, but the reality in Britain was so different from the starvation that was rife in Germany because of the effects of the British blockade on German ports.

In industry, despite losses of manpower, production was maintained and considerable advances were made in engineering, scientific research and in the rationalisation of production. However, shipbuilding experienced diffi-culties in meeting demand. Persistent U-boat activity led to the formation of a Shipping Control Committee and the appointment of a Shipping Controller to divert imports towards essential items. A Controller of the Navy was placed in charge of construction and the requisitioning of nearly all merchant ships. By 1917 building capacity had been enlarged (here and abroad, especially in the USA). Helped by expanding steel production, as well as the convoy system, building outstripped losses.

Coal supplies were maintained, despite mass enlistment into local 'pals' battalions such as those in Barnsley or Accrington. Tight government con-trols were needed to maintain output and, more importantly, to keep prices down. By the middle of the war, central government was dictating to the old managers who ran the pits. In 1917 and 1918 national wage agreements tried to keep wages rising with the cost of living, in an attempt to avoid industrial action. Profits were again fixed at pre-war levels, but a Coal Controller claimed most of the excess profits in taxes.

Sidney Pollard comments on how the war had taught the government much about central planning and the organisation of national resources; railways were more integrated, supplies of steel and coal were rational-ised to meet need, resources were used more efficiently – there was even talk of a 'national grid' for electricity supply. It was a world apart from 1913: collectivism, beginning to be evident before the war, had been given its head.

2.3 What impact did the State have in mobilising the human resources of Britain?

The Armed Forces

Initially volunteers responded to the call to arms, but by 1915 recruiting figures were tailing off. In October 1915 Lord Derby, who had become Director of Recruiting, introduced The Derby Scheme, by which all men between the ages of 18 and 41 would be asked to place their names on a voluntary register. Single men would be enlisted first and if that proved insufficient, married men would follow. The Scheme did not work, as bachelors failed to register; neither did it adequately differentiate between men in essential and non-essential occupations. To fill the gap and to provide more cannon-fodder for an army that was looking ahead to one more 'big push' (this time on the Somme as it turned out), in January 1916 all single men aged 18–41 were conscripted. In May the decision was taken to extend this to married men.

The distribution of manpower was not without its political dangers. **Conscription** was opposed by some Liberal MPs. Asquith survived the crisis, albeit temporarily.

Conscription: Compulsory military service.

In May 1918 Lloyd George was accused by General Sir Frederick Maurice of misleading the House of Commons. The Prime Minister had said that troops had not been kept back in England and that the numbers in the reserve sectors of the Western Front were greater at the beginning of 1918 than a year earlier. Asquith seized on this, but to no effect; Lloyd George had in fact misquoted the figures but the ex-Liberal leader was unable to make capital out of it. It proved to be a temporary moment of embarrassment, but it underlined that Lloyd George's hold on power was not as firm as it might be, especially since he relied on Conservative support to maintain his position in the House of Commons.

The impact of war on the labour force

To imagine that trade union members sacrificed all thoughts of industrial action as they patriotically placed their might behind the war effort is an over-simplification. Shortages of labour were apparent by 1915; not only had enlistment drained industry of crucial workers, but the apparatus of exemptions from military service was not put in place until it was too late. Women were soon drafted in: the Treasury Agreement of 1915 allowed for dilution, whereby unskilled women (and men) were allowed to fill vacancies left by skilled workers. In all, women's employment increased from three million in 1914 to five million in 1918. Many came from domestic service to which they never returned; but one and a half million were new workers.

In the short term, women's employment in factories sharply declined after the war when men reclaimed their previous employment. However, in the long term some occupations came to be monopolised by women after the war, particularly in shops, hotels and offices. One million more people drew salaries after the war than before it; some of these were professional men, but women in white-collar jobs contributed significantly to the increase.

Wage rates during the war barely kept pace with rises in the cost of living, and workers had to rely on piece rates or overtime to keep up with price inflation. Trade unions had given up their right to strike and TUC leaders had begun to develop a working relationship with some government departments as part of the war effort. This didn't mean that there was no discontent among the rank-and-file. South Wales miners went on strike in 1915 and there was trouble among engineering workers on the Clyde. In general, though, serious trouble was avoided until 1917. War weariness had by then combined with anger at price rises, black marketeering and food shortages. The rich still seemed able to buy luxuries. Dilution angered skilled men; they not only witnessed unskilled people just minding machines which undermined generations of craft skills, but also had to accept fixed wage rates when unskilled workers were able to earn more because they were paid on piece-rates. By 1917 dilution was being applied to all trades without restriction. If a craft worker wished to change jobs, he could not do so unless he received a leaving certificate from his employer. Conscription was badly handled; men who had exemptions certificates were sent to France and then had to be recalled.

Shop stewards: Shopfloor trade union activists who played an important role in local organisation of their members.

1. **What changes did the British government make to improve Britain's chances of fighting the war effectively?**

2. **How successful were the government's attempts to mobilise the workforce for the war effort?**

Days lost to strikes rose from 2.5 million in 1916 to just short of 6 million in 1918. For instance, Coventry, Sheffield and Manchester were all hit by strikes in the engineering industry in May 1917. Ironically, trade union membership doubled to 8 million by 1919. Rank-and-file members who felt vulnerable turned to **shop stewards** to defend their interests. At a local level, shop stewards spoke for the workers, established factory works committees, intervened in disputes and took an active role during unrest. Some had a syndicalist background; those in the munitions industry were particularly important because it was there that industrial recruitment had taken place on a vast scale and where the problems were greatest. Shop stewards played key parts in the strikes on the Clyde in 1915 and 1916. In Sheffield, munitions workers withdrew their labour when exempt workers were conscripted. A serious engineering strike in 1917 was sparked off by more extensions of the 'dilution' principle.

The government was suitably alarmed, and responded with a commission, with the result that controls on prices and profits were strengthened, key foodstuffs were subsidised and national wage rates were improved and imposed by arbitration.

2.4 What was the impact of financing the war and planning for reconstruction?

National Debt: Money borrowed by a government and not yet repaid.

Death duties: A tax payable on a dead person's property and money.

Excess profit tax: Tax on profit over and above a limit set by the government.

The cost of prosecuting the war to a conclusion was staggering; one economist put the figure at just under £4 million a day. How would it all be paid for? Principally, by increasing the **National Debt**. Some of the costs were borne by bank borrowing, although a significant amount was raised by taxation. Income tax rose from 9d [less than 4p] in the pound in 1914 to 6 shillings [72p] in 1918. **Death duties** rose sharply, and **excess profits taxes** were imposed on a range of goods. The increased National Debt did contribute to the inflationary spiral and, given the unrest in key industries, some thought was given to reconstruction. In 1916 a new Ministry of Pensions planned to provide benefits to widows and those disabled in the fighting. Dr Addison's Ministry of Reconstruction (1917) prepared measures, inadequate by later standards, to improve health provision and build 'homes fit for heroes to live in'. Herbert Fisher's Education Act of 1918 raised the school-leaving age to 14 and planned to expand tertiary education.

1. **What methods were used by the government to raise revenue for the war effort?**

2. **What changes were made by the Representation of the People Act, 1918?**

3. **Why do you think women over 30 were given the vote in 1918?**

Most dramatically, the Representation of the People Act extended the vote to women over 30 and to all men over 21. It was the most democratic reform of the franchise so far and it became part of the mythology of the First World War that women's contribution to the war effort was being rewarded by the granting of the vote. If women had established parity, why were so many displaced by men reclaiming their jobs in industry when the war was over? Had attitudes to women really changed? Martin Pugh argues not; it was still felt that their place was in the home, just as before the war. What politicians really wanted to do was to enfranchise more men; the inclusion of so many women, probably over eight million, was not considered to be a great advantage to any particular party, so there seemed no point in resisting their demands. Pugh argues that it was thought that confining the vote to women over 30, who were more likely to be married housewives, would add stability to society which had lost a whole generation of men. Hence, Pugh argues, women were enfranchised by politicians who 'felt satisfied it was safe to do so'. Gail Braybon also argues that for many women things had not changed significantly:

Study the whole chapter.

What do you regard as the most significant change to occur within Britain as a result of the First World War?

Give reasons to support your answer.

'One can recognise the devastating emotional … consequences of the First World War, and note the dramatic effect of war work on women's skills, self-confidence and income, yet still be aware that for millions of women life offered limited opportunities for employment, combined with low pay and household drudgery, before, during and after the war.'

Historians continue to debate the extent of the impact of the First World War. Did it mark a break with the past or did it accelerate trends which were clearly identifiable in the era before 1914? In the final reckoning, a whole generation had been lost, around 700,000 members of the armed forces. Few families escaped the sense of loss. The 'Great War for Civilisation' would cast its shadow over generations to come.

Source-based questions: The impact of the First World War

SOURCE A

Government regulations have to be suspended during the war because they are inapplicable in a time of emergency. The same thing applies to many Trade Union regulations and practices … I should like to call attention to those rules which had been set up, for very good reasons, to make it difficult for unskilled men to claim the position and rights of men who have had training … If all the skilled engineers in this country were turned on to produce what is required, if you brought back from the front every engineer who had been recruited, if you worked them to the utmost limits of human endurance, you have not enough labour even then to produce all we are going to ask you to produce during the next few months. Therefore we must appeal to the patriotism of the unions to relax these particular rules … to enable us to turn out the necessary munitions of war to win a real and speedy triumph.

From a speech made in Liverpool on 14 June 1915 by Lloyd George, in which he asked for the support of workers and trade unions for munitions manufacturing.

SOURCE B

The chloroforming pill of patriotism is failing in its power to drug the mind and consciousness of the worker. The chains of slavery are being welded tighter upon us … The ruling classes are over-reaching themselves in their hurry to enslave us … Comrades, I appeal to you to rouse your union to protect the liberties of its members. An industrial truce was entered into by our leaders behind our backs … Away with the industrial truce! We must not stand by

and allow the workers to be exploited and our liberties taken away.

A. J. Cook, a miners' leader, April 1916. Quoted in Britain: Industrial Relations and the Economy 1900–39 by Robert Pearce, 1993.

SOURCE C

Industrial unrest worried the government enormously in 1917 and 1918. The Bolshevik revolution in Russia seemed to give a fillip to revolutionary groups in Britain … There were rumours of a possible general strike, and a workers' soviet was set up in Glasgow, before its leader was sentenced to five years' imprisonment with hard labour. A. J. Cook was also prosecuted, in March 1918, for preaching revolution. Nevertheless, despite these fears and isolated incidents, enough was done by the end of the war to remove grievances and so to blunt the edge of militancy.

From Britain: Industrial Relations and the Economy 1900–39 by Robert Pearce, published 1993.

1. Study Source A.

How does this source help historians to understand the crisis in munitions production during 1915?

2. Study Sources A and B.

How do Sources A and B differ in their views of industrial relations? Explain your answer.

3. 'The First World War had only a limited impact on industrial relations.' Is there sufficient evidence in Sources A, B and C to prove the accuracy of this statement? Explain your answer.

Social and economic history, 1918–1939

Key Issues

● *Was decline or growth more significant as a feature of Britain's inter-war economic performance?*

● *What was the impact of government policy on the inter-war economy?*

● *How was the trade union movement affected by industrial conflict?*

3.1 How serious were Britain's economic problems in the inter-war period?

3.2 What were the causes and consequences of the General Strike?

3.3 Historical interpretation: How severe was the impact of the Depression on British society in the 1930s?

3.4 Could the governments of the inter-war period have done more to alleviate the problems of the British economy?

Framework of Events

1919	Suspension of Britain's membership of the gold standard. Wave of industrial conflict; miners demand pay increase and seven-hour day. Sankey Commission recommends nationalisation (state ownership) of mines; rejected by Lloyd George government
1920	Collapse of post-war economic boom; slump begins. Unemployment Insurance Act extends cover for the jobless
1921	Black Friday: miners' strike defeated when rail and transport unions refuse support. Control of mines (transferred to the government in wartime) is returned to private hands
1925	Return to the gold standard: sterling restored to the pre-war exchange rate. Samuel Commission investigates problems of mining industry
1926	General Strike lasts for nine days in May. Miners' strike continues until November and ends in the miners' defeat
1927	Trade Disputes Act makes general strikes illegal and attempts to restrict trade union funding of the Labour Party
1929	October: Wall Street Crash in the USA signals start of world-wide economic depression
1930	Coal Mines Act reduces miners' working day and attempts to rationalise the industry
1931	Second Labour government breaks up over its failure to agree on cuts in unemployment benefit and is replaced by a Conservative-dominated National Government. Britain leaves the gold standard and spending cuts are introduced. Means test introduced to gauge eligibility for unemployment benefit
1932	Import Duties Act imposes general tariff of 10%, except for food and raw material imports and imperial products entering Britain. 'Cheap money' – interest rates reduced from 6% to 2%. Ottawa agreements establish preferential trading arrangements for self-governing Empire countries

1934	Unemployment Assistance Act restores benefit cuts made in 1931. Unemployment Assistance Board set up. Special Areas Act tries to direct investment into designated areas of high deprivation
1935	Rearmament programme begins
1936	Jarrow Crusade – the best known protest march by the unemployed
1938	Nationalisation of coal royalties (mineral rights in mining areas)

Overview

As a result of the First World War, Britain's role in international trade had diminished. This adversely affected the British economy. It was not merely that Britain had accumulated £1 billion of debt, owed mainly to the United States. During the war the disruption of trade had led former overseas customers to reduce the amount of imports they bought from Britain. In the Far East, markets for British goods had been penetrated by new competitors such as Japan. In the post-war years the problems of British exporters worsened as foreign countries protected their economies with tariffs (taxes on imports) and government subsidies.

These developments made life harder for Britain's old, established **staple industries** of coal, cotton, shipbuilding and iron and steel. This sector, which had formed the basis of the industrial revolution, was already vulnerable because of its dependence on ageing plant and technology, and its association with inefficient managerial methods and working practices. After a brief post-

Staple industries: The older, heavier industries, on whose exports the British economy had traditionally depended – coal, textiles, iron and steel, shipbuilding.

How useful is this map for a study of unemployment in the inter-war period?

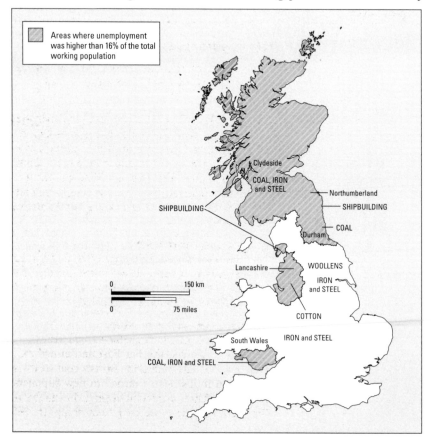

Areas where unemployment was higher than 16% of the total working population

Clydeside
COAL, IRON and STEEL
Northumberland
SHIPBUILDING
SHIPBUILDING
COAL
Durham
Lancashire
WOOLLENS
IRON and STEEL
0   150 km
0   75 miles
COTTON
South Wales
IRON and STEEL
COAL, IRON and STEEL

The staple industries and regional unemployment in Britain in 1931

Boom: A period when the economy expands and demand for goods and services is high.

Slump: A serious decline in demand for agricultural and/or industrial products, leading to a fall in prices and to business failures.

war **boom**, in 1920 a **slump** set in as world demand contracted. The result was large-scale unemployment in the regions (primarily northern England, South Wales and south-west Scotland) where the older factories, mines and shipyards were concentrated. This situation was appreciably worsened by the onset of world depression following the Wall Street Crash (the collapse of the United States stock market) in October 1929. Unemployment persisted in Britain's traditional industrial heartlands, even after the beginning of national recovery from the slump in the mid-1930s.

At the same time a number of newer industries and services managed to escape the worst effects of the depression and expanded in the 1930s, generating new jobs. These industries, which included electrical engineering and motor vehicle manufacture, were based mainly in the south-east and the Midlands. As a result inter-war Britain was a country of strong regional economic contrasts.

Another theme of this chapter is the changing fortunes of the trade union movement. Trade union membership had doubled during the First World War, increasing from just over 4 million to 8.3 million. The onset of mass unemployment, however, weakened the unions' bargaining power and membership grew very slowly during the 1920s. The decade also saw the most dramatic example of industrial conflict in British history, the General Strike of May 1926. The failure of the Strike forced union leaders to adopt a more moderate approach in their dealings with the employers for the remainder of the inter-war period.

3.1 How serious were Britain's economic problems in the inter-war period?

The impact of war

The effects of the First World War upon the British economy can be divided into four main categories:

Physical losses

The First World War was far less physically destructive than the conflict of 1939–45, with the major exceptions of lost manpower (745,000 men were killed and 1.6 million were seriously wounded) and the sinking of approximately one-fifth of the merchant shipping fleet. Nonetheless one should also note the way in which the war increased the rate of depreciation of industrial plant. In wartime, key resources such as railways and mines were used more intensively, while their maintenance tended to be neglected.

Distortion of the economy

The war stimulated industries such as engineering, chemicals and shipbuilding, which had a direct relevance to the needs of the armed forces. Those that were less important in wartime (for example textiles and building) were relatively neglected.

Disruption of the export trade

Britain's staple industries, which relied heavily on exporting, found their old markets in Russia, the Far East and elsewhere closed to them during the war. Former customers for British coal, textiles or steel either developed their own industries or turned to new suppliers such as the United States and Japan. The contraction of trade during the war also reduced the income Britain traditionally derived from shipping. Before 1914 this had been a

Balance of payments: The difference between a country's income from foreign countries and its payments to those countries.

Inflationary effect: An increase in the general level of prices caused by an event or situation.

Gold standard: A monetary system under which a national currency has a fixed value in gold.

Speculative investors: People who invest money in businesses, running risks because they expect to make an unusually large profit.

Primary producer: Producer of raw materials, e.g. raw cotton, coffee beans.

Rationalisation: Reorganisation of an industry in order to improve its efficiency.

major component of Britain's 'invisible income' – earnings derived from services rather than goods, which had ensured a healthy **balance of payments** in peacetime. The decline of invisible income was a serious difficulty for a country facing an uncertain international financial situation.

War debt

To pay for the war the British government sold off foreign assets and borrowed heavily, both at home and abroad. This increased the size of the National Debt and had an **inflationary effect** in Britain. The accumulation of debt placed the country at a disadvantage in relation to its main creditor, the United States. The situation was compounded by the loss of investments in Germany, Austria-Hungary and Turkey (with whom Britain was at war) and in Russia (after the 1917 revolutions). The problems of wartime finance forced Britain off the **gold standard**, under which the value of the pound had been linked to gold. Post-war governments, supported by the orthodox thinking of the banking establishment, favoured a return to gold on the grounds that it was essential for the revival of financial confidence. It is now generally agreed that the 1925 return to the pre-war exchange rate of £1: $4.86 left the currency overvalued, and thereby damaged the prospects of Britain's export industries.

Boom and slump

In the immediate aftermath of the war the economy experienced a short-lived boom, as **speculative investors** responded positively to rising prices and to an optimistic assumption that pre-war 'normality' would return. By 1920, however, demand for goods had begun to decrease as overproduction caused prices to fall and government borrowing rates were raised in preparation for an eventual return to the gold standard. At the same time a world-wide fall in the price of primary products (food and raw materials) took effect. This meant that countries that were **primary producers**, concentrated in the British Empire, Latin America and the Far East, were in a weaker position for buying British manufactured goods.

A less favourable trading environment was bad news for Britain's traditional export-based industries. Exports of cotton textiles, for example, were less than half the 1913 figure in 1922. Coal exports were a third of the pre-war statistic. The world slump worsened the organisational and technological problems of heavy industries, which were dependent on outdated machinery and made extensive use of skilled labour. These industries badly needed to reduce excess capacity, to re-equip and re-locate to new areas. Yet these were costly undertakings for enterprises whose profit margins were falling because of adverse world conditions. Should the management of these old industries be blamed for failing to take strategic decisions in the interests of long-term survival? One possibility was for an industry to amalgamate numerous small, less efficient units and to scrap excess capacity. The leaders of the cotton industry were slow to do so in the 1920s, since they tended to believe that the slump would give way to a revival, in the manner of earlier fluctuations in the trade cycle. After 1929 the Bank of England sponsored the Lancashire Cotton Corporation and Combined Egyptian Mills, which undertook some **rationalisation** of spinning, but this did not go far enough. In the shipbuilding industry, reorganisation was hampered by weak management and by traditional shipyard organisation, which protected counter-productive working practices.

The problems of the 'old staples' were intensified by the United States stock market crash of October 1929, heralding four years of economic depression during which world trade slumped by 35%. In Britain the clearest indicator of depression was the persistence of unemployment at

Insured population: Those workers covered by the National Insurance scheme, begun in 1911.

levels not seen prior to the First World War. Between 1921 and 1940 unemployment never fell below 1 million, or 10% of the **insured population**, reaching almost 3 million in 1932–3, the worst point of the slump. Throughout the inter-war period the areas with the highest figures for joblessness were northern England, Scotland and South Wales – the parts of the country that depended most heavily on the traditional export industries. Nor did the recovery that began in the mid-1930s enable these trades to return to their pre-war levels of prosperity. Whereas Britain's share of world manufacturing exports stood at just under 30% in 1913, it was little more than 22% in 1937.

⟨?⟩ *What do these statistics reveal about the fortunes of Britain's staple industries in the inter-war period?*

United Kingdom staple industries: exports, 1910–38

(Annual averages per decade, prices are adjusted to remove the impact of inflation.)

The exports of individual industries are shown in terms of their value (in millions of pounds) and as a percentage of total United Kingdom exports.

	Textiles		Iron and steel		Coal	
	£m	%	£m	%	£m	%
1910–19	200.2	40	62.9	12	50.0	10
1920–29	288.9	37	96.5	12	65.2	8
1930–38	106.0	24	54.1	12	37.7	9

(Source: *Abstract of British Historical Statistics* by B.R. Mitchell and P. Deane, 1962)

Grounds for optimism?

Gross domestic product (GDP): The total value of goods and services produced within a country.

Integrated works: A factory where all parts of the production process are performed on a single site.

In spite of this decline, historians have often emphasised the more positive aspects of the British economy's inter-war performance. It is noteworthy that on the eve of the Second World War, Britain's **gross domestic product** was half as great again as it had been in 1913. The steel industry, which had been hard hit in the 1920s by a combination of foreign tariffs and cheap imports from abroad, staged a convincing recovery in the ensuing decade. From 1932 British steel was protected by a 33.3% tariff imposed by the government on foreign competition. Existing plant was improved, and efficient, **integrated steel works**, such as the one at Corby in Northamptonshire, were built. In the shipbuilding industry a modest revival of output was facilitated by a reduction of capacity, together with government subsidies and new contracts in the mid-1930s. The position of coal and textiles could be said to have stabilised by the end of the decade. Such developments allowed the historian John Stevenson, writing in *British Society 1914–45* (1984), to conclude that 'in spite of the problems of the traditional sectors, the inter-war years were marked by substantial economic growth, representing a significant improvement on the Edwardian era and in comparison with most other European countries'. The last point is particularly important. Historians such as R. Lewchuck, author of *American Technology and the British Vehicle Industry* (1987), have unfavourably compared British industrial performance with that of the United States. It should be noted that the greater size and purchasing power of the American population created a much larger internal market than in Britain, thus making large-scale capital investment possible.

It is the newer industries that provide the strongest case for an optimistic reading of the period. Industries such as motor-vehicle manufacturing, electrical engineering, plastics and artificial fibres (such as rayon) took advantage of the fact that, especially in the south and the Midlands, the majority of the population remained in work. A combination of steady wage levels and falling food prices meant that, for those who escaped the curse of unemployment, living standards tended to improve in inter-war Britain. Together with the availability of **hire purchase**, these factors created a buoyant market for consumer goods. Technical developments, such as mass production and the application of electricity, boosted the manufacture of cars and consumer durables such as radio sets. Goods were increasingly subject to standardised packaging and pricing. The growth of motor transport enabled new **chain stores**, such as Marks and Spencer, to receive supplies, while the local delivery van became a familiar sight in suburban and rural areas.

Government policy assisted the growth of some of the newer industries. By creating the Central Electricity Board in 1926, for example, it made possible the building of new power stations connected through a national grid of power transmission lines. The consequent fall in electricity prices had clear beneficial effects. Whereas in 1920 there were only 730,000 consumers, by 1939 there were almost 9 million. Similarly certain industries, such as motor vehicles and dyestuffs, gained from the selective imposition of protective tariffs during the First World War and the early 1920s. The aircraft industry, which had enjoyed only modest growth in the 1920s, was one of the main beneficiaries of rearmament in the late 1930s.

Inter-war economic developments

The newer industries managed to avoid some of the problems faced by the traditional export staples by exploiting the home market. Their success should not, however, be exaggerated. As Peter Dewey points out in his study, *War and Progress: Britain 1914–1945* (1997), the only 'new' industries with above average growth rates in the 1930s were motor-vehicle manufacturing, electrical engineering and rayon production. The enormous expansion of house building during that decade reminds us that the new, high technology industries were not the only ones to display evidence of vitality. Rising **real incomes**, together with cheaper mortgages, encouraged the building of 2,723,000 houses in England and Wales between 1930 and 1939. This should deter us from excessive generalisation about the contrasts between older and newer industries. Any study of the inter-war economy needs to recognise the great variety of experience during the period.

Hire purchase: A system that enables a customer to purchase an item by making payments in a series of instalments.

Chain store: One of a large number of shops, under the same ownership and located in different places.

Real income: The value of wages when set against changes in prices – i.e. an individual's purchasing power.

1. How did British industry change during the inter-war period?

2. To what extent were the problems of the 'old staple' industries due to poor management and organisation?

3. Explain why 'new industries' developed in inter-war Britain.

3.2 What were the causes and consequences of the General Strike?

The problems of one of the great staple industries, mining, were the root cause of the General Strike of May 1926. The events of that month stand alone as the only occasion in British history when the trade unions resorted to a general stoppage of work. Approximately 3 million people responded to an appeal from the **Trades Union Congress** (TUC) to strike in support of the coal miners, who were involved in a long-running dispute with their employers. Dockers, railwaymen, bus drivers and printers, together with workers in the building trade and the electricity, gas, steel and chemical industries, were among those who answered the call for working class solidarity. Stanley Baldwin's Conservative government treated the strike very seriously, condemning it as a challenge to constitutional government. With the help of the army and of civilian volunteers, the authorities operated

Trades Union Congress: The central organisation in which Britain's trade unions were represented, established in 1868. The General Council was its governing body.

well-laid emergency plans and managed to maintain the flow of essential supplies. After nine days, the General Council of the TUC called off the strike without securing assurances from the government as to the outcome of the miners' dispute. The miners alone remained on strike for another seven months before succumbing to defeat and returning to work.

Not surprisingly, the episode has attracted a great deal of interest among historians. The defeat of the unions has often been seen as a turning point in the development of the labour movement, a graphic illustration of the limitations of the strike as a weapon in industrial disputes. It is therefore important to be clear about the issues that led to the General Strike and the wider implications of these events.

What were the problems of the coal industry?

The dispute that developed into the General Strike had its origins in the problems of the coal industry. As we saw in Section 3.1, in the post-war period coal was one of the staple export industries worst hit by the adverse conditions of world trade. As new fuels, notably oil, increased in popularity, demand for coal grew at a slower rate than before 1914. The private owners, whose management of the industry had been interrupted by government intervention during the First World War, recovered their control in 1921. They have traditionally been viewed as exceptionally unimaginative and reactionary. In the memorable phrase of L.C.B. Seaman, author of *Post-Victorian Britain 1902–1951* (1966), 'the coal industry was certainly "**private**"; but it was not enterprising'. It is true that the owners were slow to amalgamate small colliery firms in the interests of greater efficiency. However, this view of the industry should not be overdrawn. The amount of coal cut by machinery increased from 8% of output in 1914 to 14% in 1921. Yet as Barry Supple points out in his *History of the British Coal Mining Industry* (1987), the benefits of mechanisation were offset by **deteriorating geological conditions**, a factor outside the owners' control.

Nonetheless the fact remains that the coal owners' most characteristic response to declining profits was to reduce the cost of production, primarily by cutting wages. The pressure to do so was increased by the Baldwin government's decision to return to the gold standard in 1925 at the pre-war exchange rate. The decision had the effect of making British exports more expensive and thus further weakened the position of the coal industry in world markets. In June 1925 the coal owners announced their decision to cut their employees' wages while requiring them to work for longer hours. The stage was set for a confrontation with the leaders of the miners' union, who were determined to defend the living standards of the workforce.

Why did the General Strike begin in 1928?

In 1925 the miners were led by an uncompromising president, Herbert Smith, and a union secretary with a militantly **Marxist** outlook, A. J. Cook. Their intransigent stand against the threatened pay cuts induced the TUC to approve an embargo on the movement of coal from the end of July. Rather than face industrial action, the Conservative government agreed on 'Red Friday' to appoint a royal commission under the Liberal politician, Sir Herbert Samuel, to examine the problems of the coal industry. It also announced a **state subsidy** to maintain the miners' current wage rates for nine months.

At the time, the Red Friday decision was greeted by the miners as a victory, and regarded by the coal owners as a surrender. In retrospect, it seems more likely that the government was seeking a breathing space in which to make preparations for a showdown with the miners, should a compromise settlement prove unattainable. It divided the country into areas

Private enterprise: Ownership of an industrial company by a private individual or group of individuals; the opposite of state ownership.

Deteriorating geological conditions: Physical problems in gaining access to deeper seams in the older coal mines.

A. J. Cook (1885–1931)
General Secretary of the Miners' Federation of Great Britain from 1924. An inspiring speaker, he stood for a policy of refusing all concessions in dealings with the employers.

Marxist: A follower of the ideas of the Communist thinker Karl Marx (1818–83), who argued that history developed through a series of struggles between social classes.

State subsidy: A grant of government money, awarded to support a particular industry.

Events of the General Strike

1 May   Miners are locked out by their employers, following breakdown of negotiations between the government and TUC representatives.

3 May   The General Strike begins.

5 May   In its first issue the government's official newspaper, the *British Gazette*, condemns the Strike as 'a direct challenge to ordered government'.

12 May   The TUC leaders call off the General Strike following a meeting with the Prime Minister.

under the authority of nominated civil commissioners, and established a body known as the Organisation for the Maintenance of Supplies to train volunteer strike-breakers. By the time the Samuel Commission reported in March 1926, the government was well equipped to resist a general strike. By contrast the TUC made few preparations, pinning its hopes on the Commission. The Samuel Report contained recommendations that were carefully balanced, condemning both the subsidy and the owners' demand for longer hours. For the longer term it proposed a reorganisation of the coal industry; in the short term, it accepted the need for wage cuts. The miners' leaders rejected these proposals, A.J.Cook summing up their position as 'not a penny off the pay, not a minute on the day'. When the subsidy ran out at the end of April, the coal owners locked the miners out.

The miners' case was now put to the government by the TUC General Council. Although they set up a committee to prepare a plan for strike action on 27 April, it seems that the TUC leaders believed that the government would give way. Large-scale industrial action began on 3 May, after the Cabinet abruptly broke off negotiations on the grounds that printers at the *Daily Mail* had refused to publish a leading article attacking the idea of a general strike. This has often been interpreted as an act of deliberate provocation, the work of Conservative ministers who were intent on facing down the unions. On the other hand, even if the talks had continued, it is unlikely that the miners would have agreed to any concessions on the issue of wages.

An armoured car escorts a food convoy through London's East End during the General Strike, May 1926

? *How useful is this source for a study of the General Strike?*

What were the consequences of the strike?

Although the response of working people to the strike call was an impressive achievement, the TUC had no reason to welcome a prolonged conflict. Their intention throughout was to put pressure on the government to re-open talks. A long strike would drain union funds and a resort to revolutionary violence was against their traditions. Indeed, with a few exceptions, the strike was remarkable for the orderly way in which it was conducted. The government, however, stood by its claim that the strike was an unjustifiable attempt to **overawe** legal authority. Its access to the broadcasting services of the BBC enabled it to win publicity for its position.

On 12 May the TUC leaders sought a settlement in return for calling off the strike. This was, in effect, an admission that they had been beaten by the government's superior organisational and financial resources. The TUC's failure to secure a definite commitment to the reinstatement of dismissed strikers indicated the extent of their defeat. This left the field open for the victimisation of strikers by their employers when the men returned to work. It took an unofficial resumption of the strike, the following day, to compel the government to intervene in the interests of fair play.

The General Strike did not help the miners, who stayed out until starvation drove them back to work on the owners' terms. By refusing to accept the Samuel Report's proposals, which Baldwin was prepared to implement, they unintentionally relieved the government of the obligation to persuade the owners to compromise. The result was an intensification of class feeling on the coalfields. In the long run, as A. J. P. Taylor argues in *English History 1914–1945* (1965), the owners' 1926 triumph sealed their fate. It made sure that, when the first majority Labour government was formed in 1945, nationalisation of the mines was an early priority.

The events of 1926 discredited the belief, common in trade union circles after the First World War, that employers and government could be coerced by means of large-scale direct action. The average number of workers involved in strikes and **lock-outs** in each of the years 1919–21, was 2,108,000; in 1926 it was 2,751,000. In each of the years 1927–39, it fell to 308,100. As Alan Bullock argues in the first volume of his *Life and Times of Ernest Bevin* (1960), union leaders came to appreciate the need to restrict the use of the strike weapon. The events of 1926 showed that industrial action on a national scale was likely to entail political conflict, of a kind that most leaders were not prepared to contemplate. The result was a move away from direct confrontation, towards a more pragmatic approach to industrial relations. An early example was the **Mond-Turner talks** of 1928–29, which involved employers and TUC representatives in discussions on improving the efficiency of industry.

On the other hand, the cause of reconciliation was not best served by the Baldwin government, which succumbed in the aftermath of the General Strike to pressures from the Conservative right. The 1927 Trade Disputes Act made **sympathetic strikes** illegal, banned civil servants from joining unions affiliated to the TUC and changed the system of trade union members paying their **political levy** to the Labour Party from one of 'contracting-out' to 'contracting-in'. The latter provision reduced Labour's income from affiliation fees by a third.

The General Strike was not a total defeat for working people. It played a part in discouraging employers from cutting wages in general (with the important exception of the mining industry) in the late 1920s. With hindsight the events of May 1926 appear as the final expression of a militant style of trade unionism, which was now being superseded. It is hard not to endorse A. J. P. Taylor's conclusion that 'the General Strike, apparently the clearest display of the class war in British history, marked the moment when class war ceased to shape the pattern of British industrial relations'.

Overawe: To intimidate by fear or superior influence.

Lock-out: A tactic used by employers during an industrial dispute. Employees cannot enter the work place unless they accept the employer's conditions.

Mond-Turner talks: Discussions between the two sides of industry, led by Sir Alfred Mond, head of Imperial Chemical Industries (ICI) and Ben Turner, chairman of the TUC General Council.

Sympathetic strikes: A strike by workers in one industry in support of a strike by workers in another.

Political levy: A subscription to the Labour Party, paid by individual trade union members as part of their union dues. From 1913–27 a worker had to 'contract out' (i.e. positively to opt out of paying) if he did not wish to help fund Labour. 'Contracting in' meant that to contribute to the levy, a worker had to signify a positive wish to do so.

1. Which side was more to blame for the General Strike, the Baldwin government or the trade unions?

2. Why did the General Strike fail?

3. How significant was the General Strike for the future of the trade union movement?

3.3 How severe was the impact of the Depression on British society in the 1930s?
A CASE STUDY IN HISTORICAL INTERPRETATION

One, two or three Englands?

In 1934, as Britain began to emerge from the worst years of the inter-war depression, the celebrated writer J.B. Priestley published a travel book entitled *English Journey*. In this book Priestley related that he had seen not one but three distinct Englands in the course of his travels across the country. The first he termed 'old England', a place of picturesque country-side, inns and historic cathedral cities. The second was the smoky, depressed world of nineteenth-century heavy industry, typified by slum housing, mills, railway stations and Victorian town halls – 'this England makes up the larger part of the Midlands and the North … but it is not being added to and has no new life poured into it'. Thirdly, in southern England, he found a vibrant suburban world of 'arterial and bypass roads, of filling stations and factories that look like exhibition buildings, of giant cinemas and dance halls and cafés'. In this England a consumer culture modelled on American tastes had developed: here were 'miles of semi-detached bungalows and all with their little garages, their wireless sets, their periodicals about film stars, their swimming costumes and tennis rackets and dancing shoes'.

Historians continue to debate the enormous social contrasts that characterised 1930s Britain. The earliest accounts tended to emphasise the social deprivation of 'the devil's decade', a time of mass unemployment and of alleged missed opportunities on the part of successive governments. Since the 1970s, however, a more positive re-evaluation has taken place. Historians such as D.H. Aldcroft, author of *The Inter-war Economy 1919–1939* (1970) detected impressive growth in certain sectors of the economy. The most comprehensive statement of the 'optimistic case' has been *The Slump* (first published in 1977, re-published in 1994 as *Britain in the Depression*) by John Stevenson and Chris Cook. They stressed the rise in living standards for the majority of the population and drew attention to the limited nature of public support for a radical political solution to the depression.

This interpretation of the 1930s has not, however, gone unchallenged. Detailed research into the issues of health and nutrition has led some historians to question the extent to which the working classes escaped from poverty between the wars. Labour historian Jack Laybourn's 1990 study, the significantly titled *Britain on the Breadline*, shifts the focus back on to the human tragedy of large-scale unemployment and the waste of resources that it entailed.

It is important to be aware of the arguments on both sides, and of the passion with which the debate has often been conducted. This section presents some of the evidence for these contrasting interpretations.

What were the indicators of prosperity?

The main cause of stable or rising living standards was the fact that, for those in work, real incomes remained consistently higher than before 1914. Certainly, wages tended to fall during the depression and did not rise significantly until economic recovery was under way in the late 1930s. Prices, however, fell faster than wages during the slump. This was particularly true of food prices. As a result, the cost of living fell by more than a third between 1920 and 1938.

A further factor was the decline in average family size in inter-war Britain. Whereas a woman who married in the 1880s was likely to have an average of 4.6 children, by the late 1920s the equivalent figure was 2.19. This was partly due to the wider availability of artificial methods of contraception, which had been largely confined to the upper and middle classes before the First World War. Knowledge of birth control diffused down the social scale in the 1920s. At the same time, the official disapproval of contraception that had prevailed in Victorian and Edwardian times began to lift. This trend, which was to be continued after 1945, meant that a higher proportion of a family's income could now be spent on non-essential consumer goods.

The main beneficiaries of inter-war prosperity were the salaried middle classes, whose financial security stimulated the great suburban house-building boom of the 1930s. The introduction of mass-production methods, together with low running costs, brought motoring within the grasp of many: the number of private cars rose from 1,056,000 to 1,798,000 in 1930–37. Radio sets were another consumer item that experienced an enormous surge in popularity between the wars. In 1922, the year that the British Broadcasting Company – forerunner of the British Broadcasting Corporation – was founded, 36,000 licences were granted. By 1938 that number had swelled to 8.97 million. As Peter Dewey reminds us in *War and Progress*, this was mainly due to the growth of middle-class purchasing power; in the 1930s a valve radio set would have cost the equivalent of two weeks' wages for an unskilled worker. Moreover the formal 'public service' ethos of the pre-1939 BBC, under its high-minded Director-General, Sir John Reith, may have limited its cross-class appeal.

Nevertheless it is clear that large sections of the working classes experienced a general rise in living standards. The expansion of the motor vehicle, chemical and electrical industries, and of the retail trade, led to the creation of better-paid jobs, especially in the south and the Midlands. Food processing, canning and pre-packaging brought access to a greater variety of foodstuffs. It seems clear that standards of nutrition and health were generally improving. Even John Boyd Orr, author of a critical 1936 study, *Food, Health, and Income*, concluded that the national diet was better than it had been before 1914. Improvements in housing and sanitation helped to reduce the incidence of infectious diseases such as typhoid, which had been major killers in earlier generations. It is significant that a higher proportion of army volunteers was judged fit to fight in 1939 than in 1914.

On average, hours of work were reduced after the First World War, so that opportunities for leisure increased. For the first time day trips to the seaside came within the reach of large numbers of working people, as it became common to hire open-topped charabancs, the predecessor of the motor coach. It was less common, although by no means unknown, to take a week's holiday away from home. The first Butlins holiday camp was opened at Skegness in Lincolnshire in 1937. Professional football and cricket retained their mass appeal between the wars, aided by press and radio coverage. The presence of members of the royal family at the Cup Final match helped to enhance the image of football as a national game. The 1930s were also the golden age of cinema, which replaced the Edwardian music hall as a source of cheap entertainment. A survey of Liverpool audiences in 1937, for example, found that 40% of the city's population went to 'the pictures' at least once a week. Cinema offered not only escapism from urban routine, but also a comfortable environment and opportunities for young courting couples to enjoy some privacy. The popularity of classless open-air activities such as cycling, hiking and rambling in the 1930s was another indicator of relative affluence for the many.

Sir John (later Lord) Reith (1889–1971)
As Director-General of the BBC, from 1927–38, he insisted that public service broadcasting must not only entertain but also inform and educate its audience. Reith established a mixture of news, serious discussion, music and drama, which contrasted strongly with the 'lighter' output of commercial channels. He set the tone for the inter-war BBC by instructing announcers to wear evening dress, even in day time.

How useful are these statistics for the study of living standards in inter-war Britain?

Index of wages, prices and real incomes in inter-war Britain

(The index for 1930 is 100)

	Weekly wage rates	Retail prices	Average annual real wage earnings
1920	143.7	157.6	92.2
1925	102.2	111.4	91.7
1930	100.0	100.0	100.0
1935	98.0	90.5	108.3
1938	106.3	98.7	107.7

Source: *The Inter-war Economy: Britain 1919–1939* by D.H. Aldcroft (1970)

New leisure opportunities in inter-war Britain

Radio: The British Broadcasting Company was founded in 1922, becoming the British Broadcasting Corporation four years later.

Films: The arrival of 'talking pictures' in the late 1920s increased the popularity of the cinema. Between 1914 and 1939 the number of cinemas in Britain increased from 3,000 to almost 5,000.

A magnificent 1930s cinema. The interior imitated the luxurious surroundings of an ocean liner.

Gambling: This expanded in the inter-war years, with the organisation of national football pools and greyhound racing.

Football: The sport retained its pre-1914 popularity. The first Cup Final was played at the new Wembley Stadium in 1923. Other spectator sports, such as cricket and boxing, maintained a popular following, aided by press and radio coverage

> **Motor cars and coaches:** These provided new opportunities for day trips and family holidays. By the 1930s the Bank Holiday traffic jam was an established part of national life. The first holiday camps were opened, with accommodation for half a million people by 1939.
>
> **Hiking and rambling:** These became popular as townspeople discovered the countryside. The Youth Hostels Association and the Ramblers' Association were founded in this period.
>
> **Dance Halls:** Influenced by developments in the United States, dance bands and 'big bands' became a popular form of evening entertainment. Radio broadcasts brought the music of well-known band leaders, such as Henry Hall and Lew Stone, into people's homes.
>
> **Popular reading:** The first paperback books, Allen Lane's Penguin series, appeared in 1935. They were priced at sixpence each – said to be the amount a bank clerk could earn in 20 minutes.

The pessimistic case: the 'wasted years'

The persistence of mass unemployment is, of course, the main reason for a pessimistic reading of the social history of the 1930s. Indeed, as John Stevenson acknowledges in his study of *British Society 1914–45*, the problem of unemployment stands out because it has to be seen against a background of generally rising living standards for the majority. This is what made it appear so scandalous to many contemporaries, and it explains above all the lasting popular perception of the 1930s as 'the wasted years' or 'the devil's decade'.

It should be noted that it is hard to be precise about the extent of unemployment. Most statistics refer to those groups of workers who were covered by the **National Insurance** scheme, begun by the pre-war Liberal government in 1911 to cover workers in trades that were most vulnerable to unemployment. Although insurance provision was extended in 1920 to cover the great majority of manual workers, the self-employed, domestic servants and agricultural labourers remained outside the scheme. The latter were not included until 1936. For the greater part of the inter-war period, we are therefore dependent on estimates of the number of uninsured workers who suffered unemployment.

Unemployment was not a new phenomenon in Britain. Before the First World War it was quite common for workers to experience a number of short spells of unemployment in the course of their lives. This was particularly common for those engaged in trades such as building, which were affected by seasonal factors, or in industries such as shipbuilding, where employment depended on a firm receiving a contract. What made the inter-war years different was the sharp rise in longer-term unemployment. Stephen Constantine, author of *Unemployment between the Wars* (1980), notes that in September 1929, on the eve of the world slump, less than 5% of applicants for relief had been out of work for more than a year. By August 1932 the figure had risen to 16.4%, which was equivalent to more than 400,000 people. One month before the outbreak of the Second World War, there remained 244,000 long-term unemployed.

It was not the case that workers in the newer and generally successful industries were completely immune from unemployment. Seasonal

National Insurance: A scheme devised by Lloyd George as Chancellor of the Exchequer in 1911, intended to save certain categories of worker from the workhouse if unemployed. The idea was that weekly contributions by an employee, his employer and the state would build up a fund on which the former could draw for support when out of work. Benefit was limited to 15 weeks in any one year.

unemployment affected the prosperous motor vehicle manufacturing towns such as Oxford and Coventry, where workers were sometimes laid off in winter, when demand for their products was lower. A regional analysis of Britain, however, reveals that unemployment was most persistent in northern England, South Wales and Scotland, where the older, declining staple industries were located. William Beveridge, author of the 1944 study *Full Employment in a Free Society*, calculated that 84.9% of long-term unemployment was to be found in these areas. Although the rapidly-growing industries of the 1920s experienced unemployment during the slump, they recovered from it more easily than the old staples. To take two examples, in motor vehicle production, insured unemployment ran at 20% in 1932 and at 4.8% in 1937. The corresponding figures for shipbuilding were 62.2% and 23.8%. The underlying issue was one of structural unemployment – in other words, pools of localised but enduring unemployment associated with industries facing long-term problems of adaptation to economic change. For victims of this problem, the recovery of the late 1930s made sense only as a very relative concept.

Unemployment in the United Kingdom, 1929–39

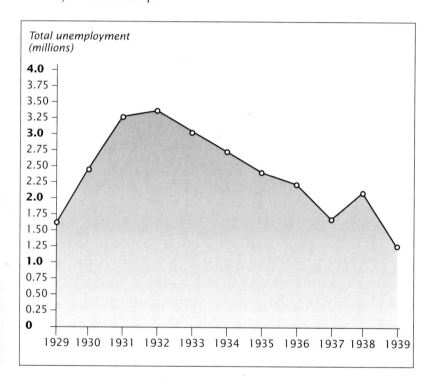

What are the strengths and weaknesses of graphs as a means of showing information?

What was the social and economic impact of unemployment on Britain?

Post-war governments recognised the problem of long-term unemployment by allowing claimants to draw benefit beyond the period to which they were entitled by their past contributions. These additional payments, known as 'uncovenanted' or 'transitional' benefits, showed an intention on the part of government to spare the unemployed the harshness of the **Poor Law**. From 1929 the administration of these benefits was placed in the hands of local authority Public Assistance Committees. As the financial crisis of 1931 deepened, the National Government decreed that applicants

Poor Law: The system of poor relief, dating back to 1834, under which able-bodied applicants for assistance were meant to enter a workhouse administered by a local Board of Poor Law Guardians. Conditions in workhouses were deliberately made unattractive to encourage the poor to be self-reliant.

Means test: An assessment of an unemployed person's economic reserves, carried out by the authorities to decide how much benefit the person was entitled to have.

for relief must submit to a 'means test' designed to gauge the level of need in individual households. The means test was widely resented by the unemployed for its perceived intrusiveness and lack of generosity. An unemployed man could find his entitlement to benefit – popularly known as 'the dole' – reduced if another member of his family was in work. Local variations in the way in which the rules were interpreted led the government to transfer responsibility for transitional payments to a central Unemployment Assistance Board in 1934. The idea was that the new body would ensure that uniform scales of relief would be applied, regardless of local political pressures. When the new scales were revealed, there was an outcry as these were often lower than the ones provided by local authorities. The government was obliged to intervene to maintain the old levels, delaying the introduction of the Unemployment Assistance Board until 1937.

As Stevenson and Cook point out in *Britain in the Depression* (1994), the dole enabled the unemployed to afford the necessities of life and thus helped to defuse popular discontent. Provision for the unemployed in 1930s Britain was more generous than in many countries at the time, including the United States. It is hard to generalise about the impact of unemployment on living standards. A great deal depended on whether a family unit contained dependent children or secondary earners, such as grown up children living with their parents. A number of social surveys were conducted in different areas during the slump, but the criteria for judging what constituted an unacceptable level of poverty varied considerably. Some studies, such as that undertaken by Dr M'Gonigle into mortality rates in Stockton-on-Tees, have been criticised for being based on relatively small samples. It is also difficult, when studying historically deprived areas, to isolate the effects of unemployment from more generalised poverty.

Even more subjective are the works of contemporary writers such as George Orwell, whose account of a visit to depressed north-west England, *The Road to Wigan Pier*, became a classic after its publication in 1937. In an important article in the journal *History* (July 1997), Robert Pearce has cast serious doubt on the book's authenticity as a social document. By comparing the finished work with an unpublished diary kept by Orwell at the time, Pearce shows how the writer often lifted events out of sequence, exaggerated for dramatic effect and presented individual people and incidents as representative types without real justification. This underlines the fact that we should be cautious in appraising even the most prestigious of historical sources.

Nonetheless it is important to recognise the value of first-hand accounts of the effects of unemployment. A number of its victims wrote eloquent and moving memoirs depicting their experiences. Among the most widely read is Helen Forrester's account of Liverpool in the early 1930s, *Twopence to Cross the Mersey*. The book, first published in 1974, describes the descent into extreme poverty of a middle-class family, following the bankruptcy of the author's father. One of its strengths is its implicit acknowledgement of the greater psychological difficulties faced by a once-moneyed family in adapting to unemployment. The working-class people in whose company they found themselves were far more resourceful in coping with the problems of joblessness.

None of this should be interpreted as an attempt to minimise the suffering of the unemployed and their families in the 1930s. There can be no doubt of the very real hardship experienced by people whose horizons were determined by steadily diminishing expectations of a return to work. There is clear evidence that unemployment had an adverse effect on standards of nutrition, as families replaced relatively expensive foods with cheap 'fillers', producing an ill-balanced, unhealthy diet. Interviews with the unemployed, carried out by organisations such as the Pilgrim Trust, convey the equally serious psychological effects of their situation. The sense of powerlessness in the face of overwhelming economic forces, the gradual loss of hope and self-respect, are no less significant for being impossible to quantify. The most characteristic response to unemployment seems to have been a gloomy, fatalistic acceptance of one's lot. Thus a Carnegie Trust study of attitudes among young unemployed men in South Wales concluded that 'unemployment is not an active state; its keynote is boredom'. In the longer term the inter-war experience left a deep sense of waste and injustice, which led post-1945 planners to work for a better and more equal society.

? *What do these sources reveal of the social contrasts of 1930s Britain?*

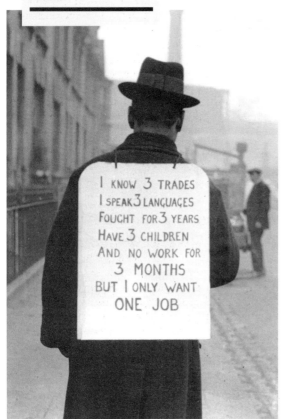

Depression and affluence: contrasting images of the 1930s

Did the depression lead to political extremism?

The refusal of the unemployed to turn in large numbers to extreme remedies for their plight has often been noted. Sir Oswald Mosley's British Union of Fascists failed to make a major impact, even in the East End of London, where it concentrated its activities. Fascist violence and anti-semitism repelled the decent, law-abiding majority, while the movement's adoption of political uniforms seemed alien to British tradition. At the other end of the political spectrum, working-class support for Communism was limited to a handful of localities, such as the 'little Moscows' of the South Wales coalfields, where there was an historic tradition of militancy.

The one pressure group to concern itself exclusively with the problems of the workless, the left-wing National Unemployed Workers' Movement, was unable to overcome widespread apathy and suspicion of its Communist associations. Significantly, the organisers of the 1936 Jarrow Crusade, the best known demonstration by unemployed people in the period, refused to join forces with a NUWM protest. The Crusade, which was prompted by the closure of Palmer's shipyard, a major Tyneside employer, was a model of restraint. Supported by Jarrow's MP, Ellen Wilkinson, and by both Labour and Conservative councillors, the marchers went to London to present a moderately worded plea for state assistance in regenerating the local economy. After their appeal for an audience with government leaders was turned down, they quietly returned home. The episode drew public sympathy for the tragedy of mass unemployment, while underlining the fact that most of its victims were far from embracing revolutionary politics. The re-election of the Conservative-dominated National Government in 1935, together with the evident popularity of the monarchy, suggest that in broad terms the population shared similar values. The slump failed to undermine fundamental assumptions about constitutional government. In spite of the persistence of obvious contrasts, it seems that Britain in the 1930s remained a well-ordered and essentially cohesive society.

1. How and why have historians differed in their views of the British economy in the 1930s?

2. Why was there so little support for extreme political movements in Britain in the 1930s?

3.4 Could the governments of the inter-war period have done more to alleviate the problems of the British economy?

Treasury orthodoxy and the Keynesian alternative

The inter-war experience of unemployment and industrial stagnation has stimulated a lively debate about the policies pursued by the governments of the time. The post-1945 generation overwhelmingly took the view that the pre-war decade constituted a missed opportunity of tragic dimensions. Had the National Government undertaken an ambitious programme of public investment, the argument ran, Britain's recovery from depression would have begun at an earlier stage. Such a policy would have increased the purchasing power of consumers and thus encouraged a revival of economic activity and employment. This approach was associated with the followers of the economist John Maynard Keynes, whose ideas found favour with governments after the Second World War. In the depression years, however, an expansionary economic policy was proposed by a mere handful of public figures. Those who advocated radical initiatives, such as Lloyd George and Oswald Mosley, were largely excluded from the corridors of power.

Instead, the inter-war political establishment remained wedded to a collection of ideas known as the 'Treasury view' and derived from Victorian traditions of public finance. This view placed great emphasis on the importance of a balanced budget, which was seen as vital to the maintenance of confidence in trade and industry. The aim of budgetary policy was to keep taxation at a relatively low level, so that it did not place an undue burden on productive enterprise. This placed limits on the permissible level of government expenditure. Orthodox thinking ruled out the idea of governments running a deficit to finance extensive programmes of state intervention. It was held that this would involve a risk of undermining private initiative and weakening business confidence. In conditions of depression, therefore, the natural tendency of governments was to abstain from large-scale manipulation of the level of demand in the economy. This

John Maynard Keynes (1883–1946)

A brilliant Cambridge economist, Keynes resigned his position as a Treasury civil servant in 1919 because he disagreed with the severity of the peace settlement with Germany. In the 1920s he became associated with the Liberal Party and developed radical ideas for government action against economic depression. He became a respected government adviser during the Second World War and was a major influence on the economic thinking of post-1945 British governments.

was believed to be counter-productive and likely to exacerbate the contraction of economic activity.

Governments and the economy

There are two approaches that a government can take towards the economy. It can pursue a fiscal policy or a monetary policy:

Following a fiscal policy means a government raising revenue through taxation and deciding on the level and pattern of government expenditure. The budget, prepared by the Chancellor of the Exchequer, is an annual statement of government income and spending plans.

If a government pursues a monetary policy it regulates the level of money in the economy and thus the general level of economic activity. A government could use a reduction in the **bank rate** to make money cheaper (i.e. through lower interest rates, which lowers the cost of repaying a loan to a commercial bank) and thus encourage businesses to borrow and invest. Higher interest rates, on the other hand, make borrowing more difficult and are a means of restraining price rises. Decisions about fixing the rate at which one currency exchanges for another (or, alternatively, allowing them to find their own levels) are also part of monetary policy. These decisions will affect the balance between a country's imports and exports.

Bank rate: The interest rate at which the Bank of England lends to the commercial banking system

How could fiscal policy affect the problem of unemployment?

Since the 1970s there has been a greater awareness of the limitations of the 'Keynesian' approach to public finance. In particular, there has been a keener appreciation of the inflationary consequences of government spending – a dimension often ignored by those who have claimed that the governments of the 1930s could have done more. Moreover, historians now demonstrate a closer understanding of the constraints within which governments operated. One of the main arguments for government-funded public works was the concept of the 'multiplier', according to which demand would be generated as a multiple of the original expenditure. The idea would not, however, find full expression until Keynes' publication of his masterpiece, *The General Theory of Employment, Interest and Money* in 1936. The case for an expansionary programme of investment was not, therefore, fully formulated until recovery from the depression was well advanced. In any case, as the historian Ross McKibbin has pointed out, the small scale of pre-war British budgetary operations would have made such a strategy impossible. It would have called for a revolution in the machinery of government, to bring a greater volume of investment under state control, which would have been unacceptable to mainstream political opinion at the time.

The fact that governments did not use their fiscal (i.e. taxation) policies to 'prime the pump' of economic activity does not mean, on the other hand, that they pursued orthodox remedies with consistent rigour. A strict interpretation of the 'Treasury view' would have dictated a deflationary response to the depression – in other words, the raising of taxes and cutting of public spending, to reduce prices and costs, thus restoring **competitiveness**. In practice a balanced budget remained an unrealised ideal for both Conservative and Labour administrations. Philip Snowden,

Competitiveness: The ability of an industry to produce goods at a price that will attract purchasers.

Labour Chancellor from 1929–31, raised taxation without reducing expenditure, to maintain the existing level of social provision for the unemployed. The onset of the 1931 financial crisis made necessary more restrictive measures, with the raising of direct taxation and of unemployment insurance contributions, together with cuts in public sector salaries. As the economic situation stabilised from the mid-1930s, there was a

---

Classical and Keynesian views on managing the economy

- Classical economic ideas were well established in government and academic circles by the early twentieth century. Economists such as the Cambridge professor, Alfred Marshall, viewed the economy as a self-regulating mechanism, which did not need large-scale government intervention. It was subject to trade cycles, in which a period of downward movement in the level of output was followed naturally by an upturn or boom. Prices were determined mainly by the cost of labour (wages and in some cases National Insurance). In a slump wages and interest rates would fall, bringing down the level of prices, until a point was reached at which businessmen would be able to start investing again. This would enable economic recovery to begin; prices would rise and full employment would return.

- Keynes argued that a general reduction of wages would have serious side effects. It would reduce wage earners' ability to consume (purchase) goods and services, thus keeping demand down. If interest rates continued to fall, there would be no incentive for people with spare money to invest it. The result would be a prolonged depression. Instead governments should focus on ways of increasing investment and consumption. They should spend money on public works schemes, to create jobs. Employed people would have money to spend on goods and services, which would stimulate economic activity.

- Classical economists argued that government spending on this scale would create a budget deficit (i.e. spending would exceed income). This was as bad for a government as it was for a private household. An unbalanced budget would hold up the revival of business confidence. Spending on government run public works would reduce the amount of money available for private investment.

- In response to these criticisms, by 1936 Keynes developed the concept of the 'multiplier'. According to this theory, a stimulus to demand could occur as a multiple of the original amount invested. By putting people back to work and increasing their purchasing power, the original investment would have a 'knock-on' effect on demand, encouraging activity in other areas of the economy.

- In the early 1930s Keynes likened himself to Cassandra, the prophetess in Greek mythology who was fated never to be believed. His ideas did not find wide acceptance until the Second World War. In the inter-war period, the 'Treasury view' was heavily influenced by the assumptions of classical economics.

general liberalisation of government policy; income tax rates were reduced and the salary cuts were restored.

From 1937 increased spending on rearmament indicated a shift of emphasis, away from the pursuit of strictly balanced budgets. Nonetheless the National Government was reluctant to accept the need for borrowing as a means of financing rearmament. Traditional fears of the inflationary implications of government borrowing, and the need to reassure the financial markets, had a restraining influence. The eventual abandonment of these inhibitions was a measure of the seriousness of the international situation in the late 1930s. In short, inter-war fiscal policy was neither rigidly orthodox nor consciously radical, but a pragmatic response to changing pressures.

What impact did monetary policy and the gold standard have on the British economy?

The decision to return to the gold standard in 1925 at the pre-war parity has been widely blamed as a cause of economic hardship. As Chancellor of the Exchequer, Winston Churchill was formally responsible for re-establishing a **fixed exchange rate**. This was considered essential for the re-creation of conditions of pre-war 'normality'. The United States dollar was the only acceptable currency for a return to the gold standard, since it was the only one to have maintained its old parity unchanged. The price to be paid for restoration was a high one. To maintain the value set for the pound, interest rates had to be kept high. This made it expensive for businesses to borrow money from the banks. It also depressed the level of demand in the home market, with adverse consequences for both the manufacturing and the service sectors.

Fixed exchange rate: A set rate (or price) at which currency is exchanged for another or for gold.

The case against the decision was put by Keynes in his 1925 essay on *The Economic Consequences of Mr Churchill*. According to Keynes, the Treasury had been misled by advice from the banking community into taking a step that left sterling overvalued by 10%. Keynes predicted that this would reduce the competitiveness of British exports, leading to a general reduction of wages and to serious job losses in staple industries. The decision therefore sacrificed the interests of industry to those of the City of London as an international financial centre.

Historians such as Donald Moggridge, author of *The Return to Gold* (1969), have endorsed this critical attitude to the decision to adopt the pre-1914 exchange rate. They argue that post-war governments ignored the fundamental changes in Britain's world position that had occurred since the beginning of the First World War. The authorities had tied themselves to a single remedy and lacked the flexibility to change course in the late 1920s, when it became clear that British exports were lagging and unemployment remained at a high level. As Peter Dewey reminds us in *War and Progress: Britain 1914–1945*, policy makers failed to appreciate that British competitiveness had deteriorated during the war in relation to that of the United States. The exchange rate should have been determined by the realities of relative international efficiencies, and not the other way round.

In mitigation of the 1925 decision, it should be noted that there was nothing inherently unreasonable in wanting a system of fixed exchange rates, which would win the confidence of international traders and investors. British policy was based upon a widely anticipated rise in United States prices, which failed to materialise. Had this occurred, it would have reduced any gap between British and foreign prices and costs. Nor can the British authorities be held responsible for the fact that some countries, notably France and Belgium, returned to the gold standard after

1925 at much lower exchange rates than pre-1914. It is likely that these countries would have sought a competitive rate, regardless of the level chosen by the British authorities.

In his survey of *The British Economy since 1914* (1998), Rex Pope argues that an emphasis on government decision-making has distracted attention from more fundamental problems of British exporters. He identifies these as changes in global demand, continuing private investment in old technologies and a revival of competition following Germany's re-entry into world markets in the mid-1920s. This line of argument diminishes the responsibility of the government for economic difficulties.

Did 'cheap money' and the abandonment of the gold standard help the British economy?

It took the international financial crisis of July-August 1931 to force Britain off the gold standard. The National Government was formed to protect the position of the pound, after the second Labour government had failed to agree on a package of economy measures designed to achieve that end. Within a month of the new government's formation, a mutiny at the Invergordon naval base, sparked by news of spending cuts, caused a financial panic and compelled the abandonment of the gold standard.

It was ironic that it was the pressure of external events, rather than a deliberately considered government policy, that facilitated Britain's emergence from the 1931 crisis. The value of the pound stabilised at $3.40, thereby confounding the doom-laden predictions of those who had maintained that 'going off gold' would produce roaring inflation, on the scale of Germany in 1923. Instead the abandonment of the gold standard introduced a new flexibility to monetary policy, enabling a reduction of interest rates and thus helping to boost business confidence. The introduction of 'cheap money', with interest rates at 2%, seems to have been at least a **permissive factor** in the economic recovery of the 1930s. Although interest rates were irrelevant for many firms, whose investment was derived from reinvested profits, it certainly encouraged an expansion of the private house-building industry. The consequent growth of suburban Britain must have had a beneficial effect on other aspects of the economy by stimulating, for example, the road building and motor car industries. In this way government policy, modified by circumstances, had a generally positive effect.

Permissive factor: A factor, which among others, allows an economic change to occur.

Did the introduction of protective tariffs in 1932 help the economy?

Protective tariffs had been imposed on specific goods during the First World War to save shipping space when imports were menaced by German submarine warfare. In the immediate post-war period, measures such as the 1921 Safeguarding of Industries Act targeted certain industries which were deemed to be the victims of 'unfair' foreign competition. The success of the British dyestuffs and motor vehicle industries in the 1920s owed a great deal to the placing of tariffs on the products of overseas competitors.

Nonetheless, at the beginning of the 1930s more than four-fifths of imports remained untaxed. The defeat of the Conservatives, Britain's only major protectionist party, in the 1923 general election, indicated continuing popular support for free trade. The opportunity for a frontal attack on free imports was provided by the August 1931 financial crisis. The Conservative-dominated National Government's overwhelming electoral victory in October enabled it to introduce a general tariff of 10%, with exceptions for Empire goods and food and raw materials. The duties therefore bore most heavily on manufactured goods produced by Britain's European competitors.

The government failed, however, to realise the vision of a system of imperial preference, to which a large section of the Conservative Party had become converted 30 years earlier. The idea was that Britain would sell its manufactured goods to the Empire countries, which in turn would sell their food and raw materials cheaply to the mother country. By raising tariffs against other producers, this would convert the Empire into a self-sufficient trading bloc. This dream did not correspond with the economic realities of the inter-war period. By then countries such as Canada and Australia had developed their own industries, and their priority was to protect them. Moreover in the 1930s the British government was committed to protecting its own farmers, which ruled out the free admission of large quantities of agricultural produce from the Dominions. Government subsidies enabled Britain's wheat farmers to enjoy guaranteed prices for their crops. Barley, oats and horticultural products were protected by import duties, while **marketing boards** were set up to aid other sectors. As a result the Ottawa agreements, negotiated in the summer of 1932, consisted of a series of **bilateral** deals and did not amount to an over-arching scheme of imperial protection.

Was protection worthwhile? It is hard to give a categorical verdict, since the effect on imports depended on the level of duty, the nature of demand for the product and the response of the overseas seller to its imposition. Protection helped to stabilise the position of the old heavy export industries such as steel, where the grant of a protective tariff was linked to an agreement to undertake reorganisation. Tariffs were a useful bargaining tool in negotiations to induce other countries to sign bilateral trade agreements with Britain. However, they were a blunt instrument that protected the inefficient and the efficient alike. The imposition of retaliatory tariffs by foreign competitors further limited the effectiveness of the policy.

What were the origins of government planning in the inter-war period?

The inter-war period also witnessed the first hesitant steps towards government planning for depressed industrial areas. The Industrial Transference Scheme, introduced by the Conservative government in 1928, was an attempt to improve the prospects of those living in areas of high unemployment, especially in the coal mining industry. The scheme's effect was marginal, largely because it failed to pay sufficient attention to aggregate demand for labour; in many cases miners were transferred to areas where unemployment was already problematic. The National Government devised a new regional policy in 1934, when it identified four 'special areas' – South Wales, north-east England, west Cumberland and Clydeside – where unemployment was particularly high. The intention was to encourage investment in these areas, although the level of funding allocated to the project was not high enough to have more than a limited effect on unemployment.

Governments fought shy of outright state ownership of industries, but were increasingly prepared to intervene where market forces failed to promote necessary rationalisation. For example in the late 1930s there were government initiatives to deal with over-capacity in the cotton industry. The chief effect of government intervention was to reduce competition, as in the case of civil aviation and road transport. The device of the **public corporation**, a compromise between private

Marketing boards: These were set up after 1933 to help producers of specified products, by controlling prices and output. They covered milk, potatoes and bacon.

Bilateral: Involving two parties only.

Public corporation: A body run by a board nominated by the government, but operating largely on business principles and independent of day-to-day government control. The British Broadcasting Corporation, established in 1926, is an example.

1. What policies were available for governments to deal with Britain's economic problems between the wars?

2. What were the main differences between the Treasury and the Keynesian approaches to Britain's economic problems between the wars?

3. How damaging to the British economy was the return to the gold standard in 1925?

4. 'Cheap money and protection were vital to Britain's recovery from depression in the 1930s.' Do you agree? Use the information in this section to support your answer.

and state control, was used to establish monopolies in certain activities, for example in electricity generation and broadcasting.

However, neither these policies, nor the variety of subsidies and tax concessions awarded to industry and agriculture in the early 1930s constituted a coherent approach to economic planning. The machinery of government prior to 1939 was not adapted to a major expansion of the role of the state. The prestige and power of the Treasury enabled it to sustain its traditional function as a brake on government spending. The more 'interventionist' Ministries of Health, Labour and Transport, all relatively recent creations of the Lloyd George Coalition government, lacked the status to push for innovative policies. The result was that government aid and protection in the inter-war period tended to reduce competition and stabilise prices, without tackling the fundamental problems of the old industries, the twin challenges of inefficiency and excess capacity.

Conclusion

A comprehensive response to the problems of inter-war Britain would have entailed a planned overall approach to the stimulation of economic growth, migration of labour and location of industry. As Richard Middleton, author of *Towards the Managed Economy* (1985) has argued, this would have required a radical transformation of the existing political and administrative system. Perhaps the consequent erosion of democratic choice would have been too high a price to pay for the anticipated economic benefits. Instead, by the 1930s governments were moving in a pragmatic and piecemeal way towards greater intervention. Although this did not amount to a truly managed economy, it nonetheless provided a basis for more substantial departures in the field of planning after 1939.

Source-based questions: Reactions to unemployment in the 1930s

SOURCE A

When people live on the dole for years at a time they grow used to it, and drawing the dole, though it remains unpleasant, ceases to be shameful. Thus the old, independent, work-house fearing tradition is undermined, just as the ancient fear of debt is undermined by the hire-purchase system. In the back streets of Wigan and Barnsley I saw every kind of privation, but I probably saw much less conscious misery than I should have seen ten years ago. The people have at any rate grasped that unemployment is a thing they cannot help. It is not only Alf Smith who is out of work now; Bert Jones is out of work as well, and both of them have been 'out' for years. It makes a great deal of difference when things are the same for everybody.

So you have whole populations settling down, as it were, to a lifetime on the P.A.C. And what I think is admirable, perhaps even hopeful, is that they have managed to do it without going spiritually to pieces. A working man does not disintegrate under the strain of poverty as a middle-class person does ... Life is still fairly normal, more normal than one really has the right to expect. Families are impoverished, but the family-system has not broken up. The people are in effect living a reduced version of their former lives. Instead of raging against their destiny they have made things tolerable by lowering their standards.

From The Road to Wigan Pier *by George Orwell,*
Copyright © George Orwell, 1937.

Source-based questions: Reactions to unemployment in the 1930s

SOURCE B

Eventually I lived under a menacing cloud of fear that darkened my whole existence ... There was no immediately obvious cause for it, no objective happenings or surroundings to which it could be immediately traced. It was a hellish brew, compounded of crushing despair, an abysmal sinking of the heart, and a mental distress so acute as to be well-nigh indistinguishable from physical pain.

I grew to an attitude of life that was entirely morbid. I sank deeper and deeper into a vortex of fear, depression and despair.

From I was One of the Unemployed *by Max Cohen, 1945.*

SOURCE C

One morning, however, the wait at the employment exchange was particularly long and chilly, and the ragged queue of weary men began to mutter rebelliously, and Father was drawn into sympathetic conversation with his fellow sufferers. They were, for the most part, respectable working men many of whose jobs were dependent upon the ships which went in and out of the port of Liverpool in normal times. They were curious about my father, because he spoke like an educated man ... They were friendly and, as Father met them again and again, they began to fill him in on how to stay alive under almost impossible circumstances ...

There were agencies in the town, he was told, which would provide the odd pair of shoes or an old blanket for a child. There were regimental funds willing to provide a little help to old soldiers ... An open fire, he was assured, could be kept going almost all day from the refuse of the streets, old shoes, scraps of paper, twigs, wooden boxes, potato peelings ... One could travel from Liverpool to London by tramcar, if one knew the route, and it was much cheaper than going by train. Some of the men had done it several times in an effort to find work in the more prosperous south-east of the country.

From Twopence to Cross the Mersey *by Helen Forrester, 1974.*

1. *Using the information contained in this chapter, explain the following terms:*

a) *the 'hire-purchase system' (Source A)*

b) *the 'P.A.C.' (Source A)*

c) *the 'employment exchange' (Source C).*

2. *Study Sources A and B.*

How different are these sources in the impressions they give of working-class reactions to unemployment?

3. *Study Source C.*

How useful is this source as evidence for the impact of the Depression on people's lives?

4. *Study all the sources and the information contained in this chapter. Do the sources give a complete picture of the effects of unemployment on British society in the 1930s? Give reasons to support your answer.*

4 The Conservative Party, 1918–1939

Key Issues

- *Why did the Conservative Party occupy such a strong political position after the First World War?*

- *How did the Conservatives manage to hold office for most of the inter-war period?*

- *What part did Stanley Baldwin play in inter-war Conservative politics?*

Framework of Events

1918	Conservatives agree to fight the December general election as members of a Coalition headed by David Lloyd George: 382 Conservative MPs are elected, together with 133 Lloyd George Liberals. They are opposed by 28 independent Liberals (followers of H.H. Asquith) and 63 Labour MPs
1920	March: proposals for the 'fusion' (amalgamation) of Conservative MPs with their Coalition Liberal partners are defeated
1921	March: Andrew Bonar Law retires as leader of the Conservative Party and is succeeded by Austen Chamberlain.
	November: the party conference at Liverpool approves the settlement of the Irish question negotiated by the Coalition government and Sinn Fein representatives
1922	October: growing backbench and junior ministerial opposition to Lloyd George's leadership culminates in a meeting held at the Carlton Club. The meeting votes, by a majority of 185 to 88, to end Conservative participation in the Coalition. A purely Conservative government, headed by Bonar Law, wins the ensuing general election: 344 Conservatives are elected, as against 142 Labour MPs, 53 Lloyd George Liberals and 62 Asquithian Liberals
1923	May: Bonar Law resigns as Prime Minister and is succeeded by Stanley Baldwin. The latter makes a surprise declaration in favour of a tariff policy at the October party conference, precipitating an election in December, at which the Conservatives lose their overall majority. With 258 seats, they are outnumbered in the Commons by 191 Labour MPs and 158 Liberals. This makes possible the formation of a minority Labour government in January 1924
1924	October: general election – the Conservatives return to office, with 412 MPs facing 151 Labour and 40 Liberal MPs. Baldwin forms a strong government, with Winston Churchill at the Exchequer, Austen Chamberlain as Foreign Secretary and Neville Chamberlain as Minister of Health

1929	The Conservatives lose the general election, winning 260 seats to 287 for the Labour Party and 59 for the Liberals. Ramsay MacDonald forms the second Labour government
1930	Baldwin's leadership is challenged by the 'United Empire Party', organised by Lord Beaverbrook, owner of the *Daily Express*, and Lord Rothermere, owner of the *Daily Mail*. Baldwin's moderate line on the future of Indian government also attracts the hostility of right-wing diehards in the Conservative ranks, led by Churchill
1931	March: the Beaverbrook/Rothermere campaign comes to an end. In August, a major financial crisis leads to the formation of a National Government with MacDonald as Prime Minister and Baldwin as his deputy. Conservatives work alongside Liberals and National Labour (former members of the Labour Party).
	October: general election – the National Government wins 554 seats out of 615. With 470 Conservatives returned, the party is the dominant force within the government. Labour wins only 52 seats
1932	The resignation of the free trade Liberal members of the government, in protest at its tariff policies, further strengthens the Conservatives' hold on power
1934	Baldwin defeats right-wing opposition within the Conservative Party to his policy on India.
1935	June: Baldwin succeeds MacDonald as Prime Minister.
	November: the National Government is confirmed in office, winning 429 seats (387 of these being Conservatives), to Labour's 154
1936	December: Baldwin achieves a final success, through his handling of the abdication of King Edward VIII. The King wanted to marry a divorced woman, Wallis Simpson; public opinion in Britain and the Empire countries will not accept her as Queen
1937	May: Baldwin retires and is succeeded as Conservative leader and Prime Minister by Neville Chamberlain
1938	The appeasement of Nazi Germany becomes a controversial issue within the party, with the debate over Chamberlain's Munich settlement in October
1939	September: Chamberlain takes the country to war, following Hitler's invasion of Poland. He is forced to give ministerial posts to the two most important critics of his appeasement policies, Churchill and Anthony Eden

Overview

Bᴙ 1918 the Conservative Party had developed a distinctive identity and a broad base of support. In the second half of the 19th century it had evolved beyond its traditional land-owning roots, becoming the party of property in general – small as well as large, middle-class and urban as well as aristocratic and rural.

Leaders of the inter-war Conservative Party

November 1911 – March 1921	Andrew Bonar Law
March 1921 – October 1922	Austen Chamberlain
October 1922 – May 1923	Andrew Bonar Law (also Prime Minister)
May 1923 – May 1937	Stanley Baldwin (Prime Minister May 1923 – January 1924, October 1924 – June 1929, June 1935 – May 1937)
May 1937 – October 1940	Neville Chamberlain (Prime Minister May 1937 – May 1940)

Conservatives believed in the following ideas:

Tariffs: Taxes on goods imported into a country. The opposite of the policy of free trade, followed by British governments from the mid-19th century to the early 1930s. Supporters of tariffs were known as protectionists.

- Free enterprise: The government was to interfere as little as possible in the economy. There were some exceptions to this: by the 1920s most Conservative politicians supported the introduction of protective **tariffs** against foreign competition. During the First World War, Conservatives had called for state intervention to organise manpower and materials for victory.

- Moderate social reform: Conservatives accepted the need to remove some of the hardships faced by the working population, partly in order to discourage support for the 'socialist' policies of their opponents.

- The defence of historic institutions: Conservatism was traditionally identified with the monarchy, the Empire and the Union with Ireland. Stability was the hallmark of British Conservatism; change was justified only when the alternative was judged to be worse.

Coalition government: A government containing representatives of more than one party.

The Conservative Party was the dominant force in British politics between the wars. Either on its own or as the most important element in a **coalition government**, it was in office continuously, with the exception of nine months in 1924 and just over two years in 1929–31. Even when the party lost a general election (in 1923 and 1929) its Labour opponents were denied a parliamentary majority. One of the main purposes of this chapter is to provide explanations for this remarkable success in apparently unfavourable conditions of mass democracy, unemployment and growing trade union organisation. One of the enduring themes of the period – and, arguably, of the party's whole history – is the Conservatives' ruthlessness in pursuit of political power. In 1918 the Conservative leaders judged that the party's interests would be best served by an alliance with the charismatic figure of David Lloyd George, who had made a reputation as a victorious war leader. Four years later the party was no less resolute in deciding to fight a general election independently of Lloyd George, whom it had come to regard as a political liability. In 1931 the Conservatives once again joined a coalition, when they entered a National Government with the Liberals and a small number of 'National Labour' MPs, led by Ramsay MacDonald.

The Conservatives proved resourceful and imaginative in campaigning for the votes of a democratic electorate. They were ahead of their opponents in exploiting the new media of radio and film to put across their message. They were also fortunate in the divisions that plagued their Labour and Liberal opponents. In Stanley Baldwin, who led the party for a total of 14 years, the Conservatives possessed a leader who was effective in generating a reassuring popular image and in maintaining unity through a series of crises and shifts of policy. Notwithstanding the conflicts over foreign policy issues under his successor, Neville Chamberlain, there is every reason to believe that, but for the political upheavals produced by the Second World War, the Conservative Party could have continued to hold centre stage. Most historians agree that there was little chance of Labour winning a peacetime election in 1939–40.

Leading Conservative ministers of the inter-war period

Lloyd George's Coalition Government, 1918–22

Andrew Bonar Law	Lord Privy Seal to March 1921
Austen Chamberlain	Chancellor of the Exchequer to April 1921; Lord Privy Seal to October 1922
A.J. Balfour	Lord President of the Council
Lord Birkenhead	Lord Chancellor
Lord Curzon	Foreign Secretary

Stanley Baldwin's Conservative government, 1924–29

Stanley Baldwin	Prime Minister
Winston Churchill	Chancellor of the Exchequer
Austen Chamberlain	Foreign Secretary
Neville Chamberlain	Minister of Health

Ramsay MacDonald's National Government, 1931–35

Stanley Baldwin	Lord President of the Council and also (from September 1932 to December 1933) Lord Privy Seal
Neville Chamberlain	Minister of Health, August to November 1931; then Chancellor of the Exchequer
Sir Samuel Hoare	Secretary for India

Baldwin's National Government, 1935–37

Stanley Baldwin	Prime Minister
Neville Chamberlain	Chancellor of the Exchequer
Sir Samuel Hoare	Foreign Secretary to December 1935; returned as First Lord of the Admiralty, June 1936
Anthony Eden	Minister for League of Nations Affairs to December 1935, then Foreign Secretary
Lord Halifax	(formerly Lord Irwin, Viceroy of India 1926–31) Secretary for War June to November 1935, then Lord Privy Seal

Neville Chamberlain's National Government, 1937–39

Neville Chamberlain	Prime Minister
Sir Samuel Hoare	Home Secretary
Anthony Eden	Foreign Secretary (resigned February 1938)
Lord Halifax	Lord President of the Council to February 1938, then Foreign Secretary

4.1 Why did the Conservatives fight the 1918 general election in partnership with David Lloyd George?

The political background

From December 1916 Britain was ruled by a Coalition headed by David Lloyd George, the most dramatic personality in the Liberal Party. In forming this government Lloyd George had split his own party, causing a severe breach with the followers of the former Prime Minister, H.H. Asquith. The latter lost the premiership but retained the leadership of the Liberal Party. Lloyd George took charge of the country's destinies, supported by a minority of the Party's MPs. Between the

**Andrew Bonar Law
(1858–1923)**
As party leader before the First World War, Bonar Law earned a reputation as a fierce opponent of the Liberal government's policy of Irish Home Rule. He accepted office in the Asquith Coalition in 1915 and served as Chancellor of the Exchequer and Leader of the House of Commons in the Lloyd George government. He was, in effect, deputy premier until poor health compelled his retirement in March 1921. In October 1922 he returned to active politics as a leading opponent of the Coalition. He served as Prime Minister until driven from office by terminal cancer seven months later.

Manifesto: A declaration of a party's intentions, published before a general election.

followers of the two men no accommodation was possible. The new Prime Minister's political survival depended on the continuing co-operation of the Conservatives. They occupied three out of the five posts in the new, streamlined War Cabinet (the other two were Lloyd George himself and the leader of the Labour Party, Arthur Henderson). In the House of Commons, Lloyd George relied on the voting strength of Conservative MPs to maintain himself in office. It is therefore unsurprising that, as the war drew to an end in the autumn of 1918, he should seek to negotiate an agreement with their leaders to fight the coming general election together. Without such a deal he could not hope to continue as Prime Minister.

It is less easy to explain why the Conservatives should have wanted to continue their wartime arrangements with Lloyd George into the peacetime period. Why should they not feel confident of winning an election under one of their own leaders and thus having a chance of placing a Conservative Prime Minister in Downing Street? Before the First World War they had clashed repeatedly with Lloyd George, who had earned a reputation as a radical, high-taxing Chancellor of the Exchequer. With his relatively humble origins and Welsh nationalist background, he was an unlikely ally for the party of traditional institutions and inherited wealth. Yet in November 1918 he agreed a joint election **manifesto** with the Conservative leader, Andrew Bonar Law. Both leaders signed a letter of support – dubbed the 'coupon' by an embittered Asquith – addressed to Conservative and Coalition Liberal candidates of whom they approved. The ensuing general election was fought by the two groups working in close partnership.

What did Lloyd George have to offer the Conservatives?

To a large extent the Prime Minister's image as a decisive and successful war leader compensated for his pre-1914 radicalism. Lloyd George had proved his underlying patriotism by working with the Conservatives to demand essential wartime measures such as conscription. In 1918 the Conservatives were reluctant to abandon a man who was popularly known as 'the man who won the war'.

Beyond this, it seemed likely that Lloyd George would have an open mind on controversial questions such as tariffs or Ireland. In spite of his pre-war image as a left-wing firebrand, at high political level there were clear indications that he could be flexible in practice, and that his

Of what value is this cartoon to a historian writing about the role of Lloyd George in British politics between 1918–22?

Lloyd George depicted in *Punch* as a conquering hero after the Paris peace settlement, 1919. He is attended by prominent Conservatives: Bonar Law and Arthur Balfour (in Roman helmets), Austen Chamberlain (the drummer) and Lord Birkenhead (with sponge and towel).

attachment to Liberal ideology was superficial. He could be relied upon to adopt a realistic approach to issues of power politics.

Nor was this all. In the final year of the war all parties had agreed on a reform of the electoral system. The 1918 Representation of the People Act had given the vote for the first time, with minor exceptions, to all men over the age of 21 and to women over 30. The December general election was thus the first contest to be fought in truly democratic conditions. In the past the Conservatives had had to fight elections under a restricted franchise, which had excluded up to 40% of the adult male population and the whole of the female population from the vote. In 1918 the size of the electorate was virtually trebled. In these circumstances many Conservatives despaired for their future as an independent political force. Bonar Law gloomily reflected that 'our party on the old lines will never have any future again in this country'. In contrast with the leaders of traditional Conservatism, Lloyd George was a **populist** politician who could speak to the working classes in their own language. It made sense to exploit his appeal and to cling to power through association with him.

Populist: Someone with a gift for winning the support of ordinary people.

The fear of Labour

Perhaps the most important concern for the post-war Conservative Party was the need to devise a strategy with which to meet the growth of **socialism**. According to the historian Maurice Cowling, author of *The Impact of Labour* (1971), British political history between 1920 and 1924 can be written in terms of the efforts of traditional politicians to resist this new threat to the established order. During the war trade union membership had increased from 4 million to 8.3 million and there had been worrying examples of **organised working class militancy**. In its 1918 manifesto the Labour Party had, for the first time, adopted a formal commitment to the state ownership of industry. When set against a background of Communist success in Russia's 1917 Bolshevik Revolution, the threat of social disturbance did not seem so exaggerated. The imminent **demobilisation** of hundreds of thousands of servicemen, coupled with the likelihood of further industrial disputes, provided powerful arguments for a united political front against Labour.

For many Conservatives, then, partnership with Lloyd George was an essential guarantor of political survival. Bonar Law told his followers that he 'commands an amount of influence in every constituency as great as has ever been exercised by any Prime Minister'. To face the new challenges of the post-war world without him seemed an unjustifiably risky step to take.

Socialism: The extension of the role of the state in the economy, with the intention of creating a more equal society. After 1900 socialism was associated mainly with the outlook of the Labour Party, although Conservative propaganda sometimes pinned the label on the party's Liberal opponents.

Organised working class militancy: Strikes by industrial workers, sometimes started without the approval of official trade union leaders.

Demobilisation: The process of returning servicemen to civilian life after a war.

A new partnership

It should be noted that enthusiasm for co-operation with Lloyd George was always strongest at the highest levels of the party. As John Ramsden, author of *The Age of Balfour and Baldwin* (1978) points out, most Conservative MPs accepted the advice of their leaders, that they should support the Coalition, but they did so in a detached way, without committing themselves to it permanently. Those who were most committed to the new regime were the party leaders, who tended to see the advantages of putting old party divisions behind them in order to tackle complex issues of peacetime reconstruction. Men such as A.J. Balfour, Foreign Secretary in Lloyd George's wartime administration, developed a personal regard for the Prime Minister through working with him in government. They came to envisage a new political environment in which sophisticated men of both the Conservative and the Liberal traditions could overcome their differences. Typical of this approach was the **Lord Chancellor**, Lord Birkenhead, who

Arthur James Balfour, Earl Balfour (1848–1930)
Prime Minister from 1902–5 and leader of the Conservative Party until November 1911. Balfour enjoyed a second political career as a member of the wartime coalition governments and remained a committed Lloyd George supporter until the downfall of the Coalition in 1922.

Lord Chancellor: Britain's most important judge. He serves also as a Cabinet minister and as chairman of debates in the House of Lords.

warned that the electors would reject 'those who try to marshal the dying forces of extinct controversies'.

In time this attitude would encourage some senior Conservatives to depend too heavily on personal association with Lloyd George, making them dangerously detached from the concerns and prejudices of the Tory rank-and-file. This approach therefore carried with it the seeds of the eventual disruption of the Coalition. In 1918, however, the attractions of an escape from pre-war party controversies seemed overwhelming.

1. 'An unnatural alliance.' Is this a fair description of the partnership between Lloyd George and the Conservative Party?

2. Was fear of Labour the main reason for the continuation of the Coalition Government in 1918?

General election results, 1918–1939

	Number of Conservative MPs	Share of total vote (%)
December 1918	382	38.6
November 1922	344	38.5
December 1923	258	38.0
October 1924	412	46.8
May 1929	260	38.1
October 1931	470	55.0
November 1935	387	47.8

4.2 What factors brought about the disintegration of the Lloyd George Coalition in 1922?

The continuation of party loyalties

In the first 18 months of the peacetime Coalition it was often suggested that the Conservative Party should permanently combine with the Lloyd George Liberals to form a new, dynamic centre party. Such a combination, it was argued, would be best equipped to tackle the challenges of the post-war economic and industrial situation and to exclude Labour permanently from power. Proposals for the 'fusion' of the two parties were not finally buried until March 1920, when Coalition Liberals voted against the idea.

Support for such a project was always strongest at governmental level, where the experience of working with former opponents had become an everyday habit by the early 1920s. Lower down the party structure the advantages were far less obvious. Rank-and-file Conservatives could not forget that, while their side provided 70% of the Coalition's parliamentary strength, they occupied only 12 of the 21 Cabinet seats. Talented Conservatives such as Leopold Amery and William Bridgeman found their careers artificially halted at junior ministerial level by the need to find offices for their Liberal partners. **Conservative Central Office** loyally supported the party's participation in the Coalition, yet resented the need to stand aside at by-elections that they stood a good chance of winning outright.

MPs and party workers were well aware of the organisational weakness of the Coalition Liberals. They were cruelly but accurately described by the Conservative MP, J.C.C. Davidson, as a 'stage army' – a collection of prominent senior figures, such as Lloyd George and Winston Churchill, unsupported by a proper **party machine**. By contrast the Conservatives had a well-established and professionally-run national organisation. They enjoyed the advantage of a secure base in constituencies where more than

Conservative Central Office: The professional organisation of the Conservative Party, established in London in 1870 and controlled from 1911 by a chairman appointed by the party leader. Its main role was to support the party organisation in the constituencies, to assist parliamentary candidates and provide publicity material and speakers.

Party machine: A political party's organisational base.

20% of the population was engaged in farming or middle-class occupations. According to the historian Michael Kinnear in *The Fall of Lloyd George* (1973), throughout the 1920s the Conservatives had the support of 22.8% of all agricultural constituencies and 43% of the middle-class ones. Although this was not in itself sufficient for an independent majority, it provided a solid basis for negotiations with other parties. Knowledge of the strength of their grassroots support gave the Conservatives confidence in dealings with their Coalition partners.

Lloyd George as captain of the ship 'Coalition' with Conservative leader Bonar Law as his mate. March 1920.

WHAT'S IN A NAME?

Mate. "While we *are* doin' her up, what about givin' her a new name? How would 'Fusion' do?"

Captain. "'Fusion' or 'Confusion' – it's all one to me so long as I'm skipper."

What does this Punch cartoon reveal about changing views of Lloyd George in the post-war years?

Differences of policy and governing style

It was well known that many Coalition Liberals continued to think in terms of eventual reunion with the Asquithians, from whom they had been separated as recently as 1916. Their need to demonstrate their Liberal credentials antagonised the Conservatives. One example of conflict is the case of the Housing Minister, Christopher Addison, a radical Liberal who was later to join the Labour Party. He aroused Conservative anger through the high cost of his council-house building programme, forcing the Prime Minister to drop him in July 1921. The Addison case was part of a long-running concern about government expenditure, popularly known as 'waste', which underlined the differing priorities of social-reforming Liberals and economy-conscious Conservatives.

National Union: Founded in 1867, this body represented the Conservative Party's voluntary membership outside Parliament. It did not have a direct influence on policy making but Conservative MPs could not ignore its views.

Local Conservative activists, whose collective voice was heard in the annual conference organised by the party's **National Union**, were most vocal in demanding that government policy be given a more distinctively Tory emphasis. The June 1920 conference heard demands not only for reduced government expenditure, but also for protective tariffs and reform of the House of Lords. The weakness of the latter had been an issue for Conservatives ever since the 1911 Parliament Act had deprived the Lords of the right to veto legislation. Rank-and-file Tories believed that it was essential to restore some effective power to the Lords in order to provide a defence against a future Labour government. This issue helps to explain the determination of the party chairman, Sir George Younger, and of the National Union's ruling executive, to frustrate Lloyd George's attempt to force the Coalition into a further general election in January 1922. Party organisers drew a clear distinction between support for the Coalition in the present and its indefinite continuation.

Conservatives admired Lloyd George's skill in resolving national problems, without really warming to him as an individual. His success in handling post-war industrial disputes persuaded many Conservatives that they no longer needed him as a barrier against left-wing revolution. At the same time his flexible approach to policy-making earned him a dangerous reputation for inconsistency. His response to the tangled problems of Ireland is a good example. At the end of the First World War British authority in Ireland faced a determined challenge from **Sinn Fein** and its armed allies in the newly-formed Irish Republican Army (see Chapter 11). Initially Lloyd George tried to defeat republican terrorism by force, reinforcing the British army with the violence of the Black and Tans. In the summer of 1921, however, he reversed the policy, embarking on negotiations with Sinn Fein representatives. The search for a settlement with open foes of the British Empire aroused the fury of the Conservative Party's right wing. It took all the authority of the Conservative Coalition ministers to persuade the party's November 1921 conference to accept the idea of a compromise solution. When Lloyd George sought to capitalise on his Irish settlement by holding a snap election, the Conservative Party organisation in the country rebelled. In this way the Prime Minister discovered the limits of his power as head of a mixed team.

In the autumn of 1922 Lloyd George's policy towards Turkey caused further offence to Conservative feeling. The Prime Minister and a handful of senior colleagues took Britain to the brink of war in order to resist the advance of a Turkish nationalist army towards the coast of Asia Minor. British forces at Chanak, a defensive point on the eastern side of **the Straits**, were instructed to stand firm after other European countries had withdrawn from the area. The policy ran counter to average Conservative opinion for a variety of reasons. Although the crisis was ultimately resolved without fighting, it seemed that Lloyd George had adopted a risky course. Bonar Law, who had retired as Conservative leader the previous year, sent a letter to *The Times* in which he declared that 'we cannot alone act as the policeman of the world'. Moreover the Prime Minister's support for Greek interests in the Mediterranean angered a party whose traditional sympathies lay with the Turks. The Minister of Agriculture, Sir Arthur Griffith-Boscawen, wrote that 'Conservatives generally would prefer to see the Turks there rather than the Greeks. A good understanding with Turkey was our old policy and it is essential having regard to the enormous Mahommedan [Muslim] population of the British Empire'.

Lloyd George's tendency, in the Chanak affair, to conduct policy with the assistance of a few like-minded individuals underlined another anxiety about his style of government. To many it seemed that he saw himself as a presidential leader rather than a traditional Prime Minister. His employment of a collection of unofficial advisers – the so-called Downing Street garden suburb – alarmed the conventionally minded. Moreover, in September 1921 he summoned the Cabinet to a meeting in Inverness Town Hall, in order to suit his personal convenience during a Scottish holiday.

Sinn Fein: The Irish republican party, which at this period campaigned for the removal of Ireland from the United Kingdom. In 1921 the Lloyd George government reached a settlement with the Sinn Fein leaders, Arthur Griffith and Michael Collins. Southern Ireland, now known as the Irish Free State, would receive Dominion status – a form of self-government similar to that enjoyed by, for example, Canada and Australia. Northern Ireland would remain in the United Kingdom, with its own Parliament in Belfast.

The Straits: The narrow stretch of water between Europe and Asia Minor (modern Turkey), linking the Mediterranean and the Black Seas.

'Lloyd George's government was destroyed more by his style than by the content of his policies.' Is this a fair comment on the record of the post-war Coalition?

Perhaps the most objectionable of Lloyd George's methods was his abuse of the political honours system. It was accepted practice for governments to offer titles in return for donations to party funds, and the Conservatives themselves benefited from such transactions. What caused offence was the cynical way in which Lloyd George allocated honours, with a price list apparently being circulated in the London clubs. Some of the proposed recipients were hardly suitable and in the summer of 1922 one of them, a shady South African financier named Sir Joseph Robinson, became the subject of a parliamentary debate. The air of corruption stained the Coalition's image, leading over 200 MPs to support a demand for all-party control of the honours system. It led a number of Conservatives, including the President of the Board of Trade, Stanley Baldwin, to feel that the government could not meet their expectations of high standards of honesty.

The growth of Conservative opposition

The most persistent Conservative opponents of Lloyd George came from the party's 'diehard' or traditional right wing. These people often had aristocratic or military connections and tended to view any liberal policy as a dire threat to national life. They had some success in 1921 when they became involved in a campaign run by the owner of the *Daily Mail*, Lord Rothermere, for the control of government expenditure. On their own, however, the diehards had little chance of unseating the Prime Minister. In *The Fall of Lloyd George* (1973) Michael Kinnear identified only 42 MPs who were unreservedly in their camp. Until the summer of 1922, when they found a more convincing spokesman in the form of Lord Salisbury, son of the Victorian Prime Minister, they lacked effective parliamentary leadership. Many of them held unreasonable and extreme positions, which prevented them from being taken seriously.

The revolt that brought down the Coalition in October 1922 succeeded because by then it extended far beyond the party's right wing. It involved the centre of the parliamentary party and was supported by the bulk of the Conservative organisation in the country. The fundamental issue was the determination of a cross-section of the party to recover its freedom of action. There was a growing feeling that, since Bonar Law's retirement from the party leadership in March 1921, the leading Conservative Coalitionists had become divorced from the feelings of their own supporters. They had fallen increasingly under the spell of Lloyd George and were accepting methods and policies that threatened the unity of the Conservative Party. The readiness of many Conservative candidates to run as independents at the next general election underlined their distrust of the Coalition government.

At the centre of the controversy was Bonar Law's successor as party leader, Austen Chamberlain. He allowed his judgement to be clouded by his loyalty to Lloyd George and by his personal belief that the survival of the Coalition was of overriding importance. He was a poor communicator, remote from his followers, who attended only three of the 26 major meetings of the party organisation held during his time as leader. As a result he tended to underestimate the depth of rank-and-file concern about the dominance of Lloyd George. The majority of Conservative MPs in 1922 would have been satisfied had Chamberlain assured them that after the next election, the Coalition would be restructured to reflect their party's importance – in other words, that Lloyd George would be replaced by a Conservative Prime Minister. At times Chamberlain seemed to indicate his support for this position, but in the end he failed to persuade his followers that he would place the party's

Austen Chamberlain (1863–1937)
The elder half-brother of Neville Chamberlain. He had long experience of high politics, having first entered the Cabinet as Chancellor of the Exchequer in 1903. Apart from William Hague he was the only 20th-century Conservative leader not to become Prime Minister. His identification with Lloyd George put him in the political wilderness for a short time after the fall of the Coalition in 1922. In 1924–29 he served as Baldwin's Foreign Secretary. He was briefly First Lord of the Admiralty (in charge of the Navy) in the National Government of 1931.

Lord Birkenhead (1872–1930)
As F. E. Smith, he made his name before the First World War as a barrister armed with a devastating wit and later as a Conservative MP. He served as Attorney-General during the war and as Lord Chancellor from 1919–22, becoming a close personal associate of Lloyd George.

long-term interests first. The arrogant attitude of another member of the Prime Minister's inner circle, Lord Birkenhead, made the situation worse. One eye-witness, Lord Winterton, later recalled how Birkenhead taunted a gathering of junior ministers: 'Who is going to lead you to victory if you smash the Coalition? Some one like Bonar [Law] or Baldwin? You would not stand a chance.'

By September 1922 almost 200 MPs had informed their constituencies that they would stand at the next election as Conservatives pure and simple. Nevertheless, Chamberlain persisted in his preferred strategy of fighting the next election in partnership with Lloyd George and then attempting to determine the precise composition of the government. With the National Union conference scheduled for November, Chamberlain tried to stifle rank-and-file opposition by summoning a meeting of MPs at the Carlton Club on 19 October. He anticipated that the outcome of the Newport by-election, timed for the previous day, would support his claim that only the Coalition could halt the rise of Labour. With an independent Conservative running against the official Coalition Liberal candidate, he expected the anti-socialist vote to split, handing the seat to Labour. In fact Chamberlain's arguments were exploded by the result of the contest, where the independent Conservative enjoyed a clear victory. In addition, the government's opponents found a convincing champion in the form of Bonar Law, who was now partially restored to health. He was persuaded to attend by the news that a meeting of almost 80 backbenchers had called for 'independent Conservative action, an independent programme and an independent leader'. Both he and Baldwin spoke at the meeting, concentrating on the threat posed by Lloyd George's leadership to Conservative unity.

The Carlton Club rebellion

The Carlton Club gathering voted decisively to end the Coalition. Within hours Lloyd George had resigned from the premiership and Chamberlain

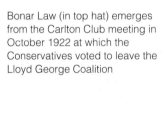
Bonar Law (in top hat) emerges from the Carlton Club meeting in October 1922 at which the Conservatives voted to leave the Lloyd George Coalition

1. Draw a spidergram showing the main problems faced by Lloyd George's Coalition between the end of the First World War and the fall of the government.

2. 'A dynamic force can be a very terrible thing.' How far did the experience of Coalition government between 1918 and 1922 bear out Baldwin's description of Lloyd George?

from the leadership of his party. The events of 1922 highlighted the risks that lie in wait for government leaders who persuade themselves that they are indispensable. Some of those who attended the meeting considered that Chamberlain could have survived if he had accepted a compromise proposal, in favour of informal co-operation with the Lloyd George Liberals rather than outright coalition. D.H. Herbert, MP for Watford, later recalled that 'the uncompromising and somewhat aggressive attitude adopted by Austen Chamberlain surprised many of us, and even before Bonar Law's speech, tended to make us support the break up of the Coalition'.

The Carlton Club rebels were voting not to repudiate all notions of coalition government, but to recover the independence of their party from the stranglehold of this particular ministry. Baldwin's description of Lloyd George as 'a dynamic force … a very terrible thing', who had shattered the Liberal Party and might do the same to the Conservative Party, rang true. The vote marked the rejection of the style of government associated with Lloyd George and his cronies. Those who sided with Bonar Law showed that they valued honesty above brilliance, stability above unpredictability.

4.3 Why did the Conservatives lose the 1923 and 1929 general elections?

1923: an unnecessary contest?

In order to understand the Conservative defeat in the December 1923 general election, it is important to be clear why the contest was held in the first place. Stanley Baldwin's dissolution of Parliament, only six months after he had inherited the premiership from the dying Bonar Law, puzzled contemporaries and has also been a source of historical controversy. The Conservatives had won a clear majority in November 1922, a month after the fall of the Lloyd George Coalition. Parliament had four years to run and the Liberal Party remained split between followers of Asquith and Lloyd George. Then, at the Conservative Party's Plymouth conference in October 1923, Baldwin announced that he was considering the introduction of a policy of tariffs, in order to protect industry and combat rising unemployment. Bonar Law had ruled out such a move the previous year and so a further appeal to the voters was needed before protection could be brought in.

The Plymouth announcement did not commit the government to an immediate election, but it took the party and the country by surprise and led to furious speculation about what would happen next. The result was that Baldwin called an election for 6 December. The Conservatives remained the largest party but lost their majority over Labour and the Liberals, who had unanimously declared themselves for the continuation of free trade. When Parliament met in January 1924 the Liberals, with 158 MPs, joined the 191 Labour representatives to turn the Conservatives out of office. Baldwin was widely criticised for having recklessly sacrificed a position of strength. His action had made possible the installation of the first Labour government. Only the fact that there was no agreed alternative candidate saved him from being ousted from the Conservative leadership.

In later years Baldwin devised his own justification for his behaviour in the autumn of 1923. He claimed that the tariff declaration had been a ploy to attract Austen Chamberlain and the other Conservatives who had remained loyal to Lloyd George in 1922. Protection was, he claimed, the one issue that could reunite the party. Even if the Conservatives lost the ensuing election, this was a price worth paying for having detached the pro-Coalition Conservatives from Lloyd George.

The main points of this rather subtle version of events were for long accepted by most historians, with the notable exception of A.J.P. Taylor. In *English History 1914–1945* (1965), he adopted the more straight-forward explanation that Baldwin was seeking to tackle the problem of unemployment. By 1923 unemployment stood at more than one million, a figure equivalent to 12% of the insured workforce, and it was thus becoming a serious political issue. The fullest study of the episode was published in the journal *Twentieth Century British History* (1992). In an article on 'Conservative reunion and the General Election of 1923', the historian Robert Self demonstrated convincingly that the re-absorption of the pro-Coalition Conservatives was not Baldwin's primary concern. He took up tariffs as a positive weapon with which to resist the Labour Party, and in order to pacify both right-wing diehards outside the government and more moderate protectionists within. Baldwin needed a new policy that would revitalise the government and give it a clear sense of direction. A close examination of contemporary evidence suggests that reunion with Austen Chamberlain and his followers became a serious consideration only in November, shortly before the decision to call the general election.

Self's study also makes clear how the Plymouth episode demonstrated Baldwin's inexperience as a leader. In making his announcement on tariffs, Baldwin seems to have believed that he could avoid committing the government to a general election before the following spring. Unfortunately the speech created such uncertainty that the only possible course of action was to dissolve Parliament at once. The decision took the party's grassroots by surprise. Local organisers had no time to prepare a professional campaign, and many MPs resented having to appeal to the electors little more than a year after the previous contest. Some had publicly committed themselves to free trade in 1922, and were thus highly embarrassed by the expectation that they should now support the opposite position. There had been no time to win over the press and the two most popular Conservative newspapers, the *Daily Mail* and the *Daily Express*, felt that Baldwin's statements on tariffs did not go far enough.

One of the sharpest analyses of the defeat is by the historian Stuart Ball, writing in *How Tory Governments Fall* (1996), a collection of essays edited

---

Key reforms of the 1924–1929 Conservative government

1925   Pensions for widows and orphans and for insured workers and their wives at the age of 65.

1926   Electricity Act transferred the distribution of electricity from numerous private companies to a Central Electricity Board. Creation of the British Broadcasting Corporation (BBC). (See Chapter 3, section 3.)

1928   Representation of the People (Equal Franchise) Act extended the vote to women aged 21 to 30.

1929   Local Government Act transferred responsibility for the poor from the old Boards of Guardians (created in 1834) to county and county borough councils. De-rating exempted agricultural land from rates (local authority taxation) and relieved industrial property and railways of three-quarters of the rate imposed on them.

by Anthony Seldon. He argues that 1923 represented a serious failure of leadership on Baldwin's part. The policy was poorly worked out and left the Conservatives vulnerable to the charge that they would impose taxes on food. This claim had contributed to the Conservatives' loss of the 1906 election and was revived by a reunited Liberal Party in 1923. In defence of the historic Liberal principle of free trade, followers of Lloyd George and Asquith were able to come together for the first time since 1916. The accusation that the Conservatives planned to raise the cost of food for ordinary people in order to benefit the wealthy few also gave the Labour Party a useful card to play. In the circumstances, the Conservatives were fortunate not to lose more heavily. By entering an electoral campaign with a confused and unprepared party behind them, the leadership deserved to be beaten.

1929: the 'Safety First' campaign

The Conservative defeat of May 1929 is less easy to understand than that of 1923, since it came near the end of a full parliamentary term for Baldwin's second government and the party had plenty of time to prepare for it. Baldwin was personally popular and, although there had been clashes between ministers, he had led a remarkably united Government. The only resignation on a matter of policy (the Government's failure to achieve more extensive **disarmament**) had been that of Lord Cecil in 1927. He was a figure of marginal importance in the party. Moreover under the management of J.C.C. Davidson, Party chairman from 1926–30, Conservative organisation improved, with an expanding membership, healthy finances and new methods of publicity.

Nevertheless historians have generally been critical of Conservative preparations for the 1929 contest. According to John Ramsden's study, *The making of Conservative Party policy: the Conservative Research Department since 1929* (1980), little work was done on reviewing and formulating positive policies. Too much responsibility was handed to civil servants, who were not used to fighting elections. Partly because no alternative strategy had been worked out, and partly because Baldwin wanted to avoid potentially divisive issues, the party was forced to concentrate on attacking the programmes of Labour and the Liberals.

A great deal of criticism has focused on the Conservatives' electoral slogan of 'Safety First'. By contrast with Liberal proposals, in the so-called 'Yellow Book', for dynamic measures to deal with rising unemployment, it sounded unduly cautious and uninspiring. The Conservative campaign has received more generous treatment from the historian Philip Williamson, writing in *The Historical Journal* (1982). Williamson's article, '"Safety First": Baldwin, the Conservative Party, and the 1929 General Election', shows that the slogan was in fact a calculated attempt to exploit the strengths of the government's record. It was designed to contrast the solid performance of the government, and its reputation for responsibility, with the superficial glamour of opposition promises. Williamson points out that at the time this approach commanded broad support within the Conservative camp. Even Neville Chamberlain, the government minister most associated with constructive reform, regarded it as an adequate basis for electoral victory.

Nonetheless, the fact remains that the government did not convince the electorate that it had a clear sense of direction. By 1929 its most positive achievements, such as Neville Chamberlain's introduction of contributory pensions and benefits for widows and orphans, lay several years in the past. After the defeat of the General Strike in 1926, the Government had seemed to shift towards a more right-wing stance, thus losing its early appeal as a broad-based, moderate administration. The

Disarmament: The reduction of a country's stock of weapons.

Neville Chamberlain (1869–1940)
Entered national politics in 1918, after a career in business and local administration in Birmingham. As Minister of Health from 1924–29, he earned a reputation as a social reformer. In the early 1930s he emerged as Baldwin's eventual successor, serving as Chancellor of the Exchequer from 1931–37 before becoming Prime Minister. He will forever be linked with the policy of appeasement, which reached its climax in the Munich agreement of 1938.

1927 Trade Disputes Act, which attacked trade union funding of the Labour Party, seemed vindictive. The severing of relations with the USSR, following a police raid in 1927 on Arcos, the Soviet trade delegation, marked a break with earlier moves towards conciliation abroad.

Conservative Party workers were not enthusiastic about the lead given by the government. In economic policy the government had not gone beyond a cautious policy of 'safeguarding' certain industries against foreign competition, so that full-blooded protectionists were dissatisfied. Changes such as the granting (in 1928) of the vote to women between the ages of 21 and 30 – popularly known as 'flappers' – were not calculated to stir Tory hearts. Many ministers, with the important exception of Baldwin himself, seemed old and tired. When the government revealed its master-plan in 1928 for dealing with unemployment, it came too late to take effect. De-rating – a proposal to reduce the rate burden imposed by local government on industry and agriculture – was intended to lower the costs of productive enterprise. Yet in the words of Cuthbert Headlam, a junior minister who sat for a marginal seat in north-east England, 'it is too complicated and revolutionary a series of proposals to be popular however good its effects may be going to be'. Moreover, shortly before the election, many householders found themselves facing rises in the rates that they were expected to pay.

In explaining the defeat Philip Williamson shifts the spotlight on to the increased scale of the Liberal challenge. Stuart Ball agrees with him in his essay on the 1920s in *How Tory Governments Fall* (1996). In 1926 Lloyd George had finally become leader of the Liberal Party, bringing with him not only new ideas about reviving the economy but also an influx of much-needed funds. As a result the Liberals were able to field 513 candidates, compared with 339 in 1924. There were no fewer than 447 three-cornered contests in 1929. In many cases this enabled the Liberals to take votes away from the government, allowing more Labour candidates to win. Labour was also a more convincing alternative to the Conservatives than it had been in 1924. It was no longer widely viewed as an extreme party – an image which the decline of industrial militancy, following the failure of the General Strike, had helped it to shed. With rising unemployment denting the government's claim to economic competence, Labour was in a position to make some gains. In Ball's words, Labour and the Liberals were 'the twin rocks upon which the Conservative vessel foundered'.

1. To what extent was the leadership of Stanley Baldwin responsible for the Conservative defeats of 1923 and 1929?

2. How far were the Conservative defeats of 1923 and 1929 caused by similar factors? Use all the evidence in this section to support your answer.

Source-based questions: The Conservative election defeat of 1929

SOURCE A

Proportion	Item mentioned
78.9%	Criticism of the de-rating policy and the reassessment of rateable values
73.6%	Absence of any 'positive', i.e. protectionist, policy, and criticism of the 'Safety First' strategy
57.9%	Criticism of the granting of the 'flapper' vote
57.9%	Attacks on the Party by a hostile press
42.1%	Leadership out of touch with the rank-and-file, and the ignoring of policy resolutions sent up through the Party organisations
36.8%	Intervention of a Liberal candidate
26.3%	Safeguarding not sufficiently emphasised
26.3%	Failure to modify the Defence of the Realm Act, and criticism of the Home Secretary
26.3%	Effects of the 'swing of the pendulum'
21.0%	Misrepresentation by opposition parties
21.0%	Failure to economise & reduce local and national government expenditure
15.8%	Failure to reform the House of Lords
15.8%	Criticism of the petrol tax
15.8%	Criticism of reforms in local government
10.5%	Criticism of the betting tax

The results of a survey of local Conservative Association opinions on the causes of the party's 1929 defeat. The survey was conducted by the Conservative National Union in July 1929. Quoted in Stuart Ball, Baldwin and the Conservative Party: the crisis of 1929–1931, *1988.*

SOURCE B

I had originally contemplated an election in November 1928, but two factors affected the mind of the Cabinet. One was the large majority we still had in the House of Commons, which, having had since 1924, gave a sense of false security; and the other was a plot hatched by Neville Chamberlain and Winston Churchill by which they would scratch each other's backs on valuation and de-rating. Those of us who were in the professional side of politics knew perfectly well that the Labour local authorities would in March 1929 put in the new assessment figures in red ink on the return which they circulated to the ratepayers, and would feed the press with the news of the great increase of rates on small private people compared to the diminution [reduction] of rate on industrial concerns.

J. C. C. Davidson, Conservative Party chairman in 1929, quoted in Robert Rhodes James, Memoirs of a Conservative: J. C. C. Davidson's Memoirs and Papers 1910–37, *1969.*

SOURCE C

The election was lost, not I think from any wave of resentment against the Govt. [Government] & certainly not against Baldwin, nor on any one particular piece of policy or legislation. Of the items which together produced our defeat I put the love of change common to all democracies or the swing of the pendulum as some call it as the first; after that the coincidence of reassessment with the derating bill which greatly prejudiced the latter, the cry of 'Safety First', the rather lukewarm action of past years in Safeguarding, the failure of most candidates to explain the Derating Bill, and put it forward as it ought to have been, as a winning card, and the wild promises of Liberals & Labour. Of course the money of L[loyd] George & his insistence on fighting every seat gave Socialism a victory which they could not have won, if arrangements had been made to avoid three-cornered fights where it was sure to lose the seat to a Socialist.

A diary entry for July 1929 written by W. C. Bridgeman, First Lord of the Admiralty from 1924–9 and a close friend of Baldwin. Quoted in Philip Williamson (ed.), The Modernisation of Conservative Politics: the Diaries and Letters of William Bridgeman 1904–1935, *1988.*

---

1. **Study Source A. Using information contained in this chapter, explain what is meant by the following:**

a) **the 'de-rating policy'**

b) **the '"Safety First" strategy'**

c) **the '"flapper" vote'.**

2. **Which is more useful to the historian of this period, Source A or Source B? Explain your answer.**

3. **Study Sources A, B and C and information contained in this chapter. Why did the Conservatives lose the 1929 election?**

4.4 Account for the Conservative Party's electoral dominance between 1918 and 1939

A CASE STUDY IN HISTORICAL INTERPRETATION

The ability of the Conservative Party to retain power for so much of the inter-war period was not wholly due to the skill of its leaders or the devotion of its followers. External circumstances helped the party in this period to a quite unusual extent.

The electoral system after 1918

Although many Conservatives privately feared the arrival of full democracy, the extension of the vote in 1918 was balanced by the maintenance of some traditional features, which favoured the party of property. John Ramsden emphasises the importance of these in his study, *An Appetite for Power* (1998). He argues that technical changes to the electoral system denied Labour the chance of a parliamentary majority in 1929 and may have helped the Conservatives to remain the largest party in 1923. Plural voting enabled a businessman who lived in one constituency and owned property in another to have more than one vote. The university constituencies (including Oxford, Cambridge, London and the Scottish Universities), which were invariably won by the Conservatives and their allies, were not abolished until 1948. More importantly, the boundaries between constituencies were redrawn in 1918 to reflect population movements, giving middle-class suburbs a greater share of parliamentary representation. This alone was probably enough to give the Conservatives thirty more seats in 1918 than they had won in 1910.

Nor should the importance of changes in Ireland be underestimated. The Irish Nationalist Party, which had sustained Liberal governments in office since the days of Gladstone, was virtually wiped out in the 1918 election. Sinn Fein MPs, who won former Nationalist votes, refused to come to Westminster because of their extreme republican views, and thus played no part in British parliamentary politics. On the other hand the Unionist MPs, who dominated Northern Ireland, were firm allies of the Conservatives in this period. The 1921 Irish settlement guaranteed their position within the United Kingdom. Overall, Ramsden calculates that the Conservatives could count on approximately 200 safe seats, which gave them a solid advantage in the three party politics of the inter-war period.

The weakness of the opposition parties

The Liberals were plagued by splits within the parliamentary leadership and by weaknesses at grassroots level. Although Asquithians and Lloyd George Liberals reunited to fight the 1923 general election, the bitter split of 1916 had already done its damage. The Liberals were temporarily revitalised by Lloyd George after he took over the leadership of the reunited party in 1926, but even the 'Welsh wizard' could not reverse the party's long-term organisational decay. Many conservative-minded Liberal voters, who had been alarmed to see the party leadership support a Labour ministry in 1924, found a new and more appealing political home in Baldwin's moderate Conservative Party. Lloyd George's flirtation with the Labour government of 1929–31 encouraged a number of right-wing Liberal MPs to find common ground with the Conservatives. These '**Liberal Nationals**' became close partners of the Conservatives in the National Governments.

Although the inter-war years witnessed the steady growth of Labour, the party found it hard to win seats outside its traditional working-class industrial base. The second Labour government was badly divided over

Liberal Nationals (later known as National Liberals): Liberal MPs who agreed with the Conservatives on the need for government spending cuts and tariffs to tackle the economic depression. A total of 35 Liberal National MPs were returned in the 1931 general election. Their leader, Sir John Simon, was successively Foreign Secretary, Home Secretary and finally Chancellor of the Exchequer in the National Governments. The party was formally amalgamated with the Conservatives from 1947.

the August 1931 financial crisis (see Chapter 5, section 3). In the ensuing general election, it was vulnerable to accusations that it had 'run away' from making tough decisions on spending cuts.

The Conservatives themselves suffered from divisions in the inter-war period – over the Lloyd George Coalition in 1922–23, tariff policy in 1929–31, the advance towards Indian freedom in the first half of the 1930s and **appeasement** at the end of the decade. Yet, in spite of violent clashes between leading figures, none of these issues damaged the Conservatives fundamentally. In the end, however heated the argument, the Conservative instinct for unity reasserted itself. Over India, for example, the liberal line taken by the leadership was opposed by approximately one-sixth of the parliamentary party and by a strong movement in some of the constituency parties, especially in southern England. Right-wingers feared that an extension of self-government might lead to the end of British rule in India. However, the National Union Executive remained loyal to Baldwin and, at Westminster, the backbench **1922 Committee** helped to keep MPs in touch with the leadership. Whatever misgivings rank-and-file Conservatives may have felt about concessions to Indian nationalism, there was a general feeling that the issue was best handled by their own side. Baldwin and his colleagues could be relied upon to include safeguards for continued imperial control in the 1935 Government of India Act. In these circumstances the rebels, who had no spokesman of national standing apart from Winston Churchill, were bound to appear outdated and unnecessarily alarmist.

Appeasement: A policy, commonly associated with British governments of the 1930s, of making concessions to a potentially hostile power in order to secure peace. The 1938 Munich settlement, under which the German-speaking part of Czechoslovakia (the Sudetenland), was transferred to Hitler's Germany, is an example of appeasement in action.

The 1922 Committee: This began as a small club of MPs elected in the 1922 General Election. By the 1930s it had evolved into a committee whose membership consisted of all Conservative MPs who were not ministers. It provided a forum where Conservative leaders could meet their followers, in order to explain policy and gauge the opinion of the parliamentary party.

Winston Churchill (1874–1965)
Churchill had been a Liberal MP since abandoning the Conservative Party in 1904. He became a close associate of Lloyd George and held several Cabinet posts in the Coalition. In 1924 he returned to the Conservatives, serving as Chancellor of the Exchequer in Baldwin's second administration. He spent most of the 1930s as a backbencher because he disagreed with the party leadership's liberal line on India and its appeasement of Nazi Germany.

The Conservatives and Indian constitutional change

In 1929 the Viceroy of India, Lord Irwin (later Lord Halifax) responded to Indian nationalist pressure with a declaration that the sub-continent's destiny was to evolve towards Dominion status. In other words, it would become self-governing within the framework of the British Empire, like Canada, Australia and New Zealand. This line was supported by Baldwin and by the leadership of the Labour Party, but was violently opposed by diehards in the Conservative ranks. Churchill condemned it as a betrayal of Britain's imperial mission and resigned from the Conservative front bench team. The rebels staged a powerful show of opposition at the October 1934 party conference but were defeated two months later at a meeting of the Central Council of the Conservative National Union. They were unable to prevent the passage of the 1935 Government of India Act, which extended responsibility to Indians in the provinces and proposed a new federal authority at the centre.

Effective organisation

As Stuart Ball observes in *The Conservative Party and British Politics 1902–1951* (1995), 'the Conservatives were more truly a national party than either the Liberals or Labour'. The party had an organisational framework in all types of constituency and was particularly strong in rural, suburban and small town seats, where Conservative social events were an established part of the local fabric. The growth of a women's organisation was an encouraging sign. Apart from in 1922–23, funding was not a problem. The party was thus able to field more candidates than its opponents and to build up a network of professional constituency agents.

Using the new technology: Stanley Baldwin (on the left) making an open air broadcast during the 1931 general election with his National Government partners, Ramsay MacDonald (centre) and Sir John Simon (right)

How successfully did the Conservatives use new forms of communication in gaining support between the wars?

Superior resources also enabled the party to distribute its publicity material widely and to exploit new methods of putting its message across to the electorate. For example, the Conservatives were the only party before 1939 to use cinema vans to attract audiences who might not have attended a traditional political meeting. They also developed close links with the commercial newsreel companies of the period. Although the latter were not mere tools of the party, in the 1930s the Conservatives and their National Government partners undoubtedly benefited from film coverage.

Policy formulation was another area in which the Conservatives developed a more professional approach between the wars. Under Neville Chamberlain's guidance the party leadership prepared carefully for the 1924 Election, establishing a policy secretariat to review options. The outcome was a document entitled *Looking Ahead*, the party's first comprehensive policy document. After the 1929 defeat a more permanent organisation, the Conservative Research Department (CRD), was created. The CRD proved its worth in gathering information for front bench figures, drafting speeches and helping to prepare the election manifesto. Thanks to the patronage of Chamberlain, the department acquired influence at the highest levels in the 1930s.

A reassuring image

Under Baldwin's leadership the Conservatives had remarkable success in projecting an image which was at once strong and moderate. In 1924 the party played on 'red scare' stories, contrasting itself with a Labour Government that seemed too friendly towards the Soviet Union. In 1931, participation in the National Government enabled the Conservatives to associate themselves with the theme of patriotic unity in the face of economic crisis. They offered a stable yet democratic alternative to the extremism of continental dictatorships. With the first signs of economic recovery by 1935, the Conservative-dominated National Government was well placed to win a further term of office. Prudent financial management, together with moderate reform in areas such as slum clearance and factory conditions, enabled the party to generate a responsible yet mildly progressive image.

As the historian Ross McKibbin argues in an essay on 'Class and conventional wisdom', published in *The Ideologies of Class* (1990), the Conservatives strengthened their position by depicting Labour as the party of a particular sectional interest, the organised working class. By contrast the Conservatives persuaded a solid core of middle-class supporters, together with many uncommitted working-class voters, that they alone were fitted to rule in the interests of the nation as a whole.

On the political right there were no credible challengers. Sir Oswald Mosley's British Union of Fascists (BUF) remained a marginal party of protest, discredited by its attachment to 'un-English' political uniforms and violent methods. In Britain the impact of economic depression was never severe enough, over the country as a whole, to make people turn in large numbers to the radical right. A steady rise in living standards for those who were in work enabled a large section of the population, especially in the south and the Midlands, to benefit from the house-building boom of the 1930s and from the growth of new consumer industries (see Chapter 3, section 3.) Although diehard Tories might protest against 'liberal' National Government policies, few were prepared to support so obviously extreme and unconstitutional a movement as the BUF. Ingrained loyalty led the majority to stay in the Conservative Party, in the hope that they could influence it from within. Throughout the inter-war period the party included a broad range of views, with a secure hold on the centre-right of the political spectrum.

> **Sir Oswald Mosley (1896–1980)**
> A member of the 1929 Labour Government, Mosley resigned in 1930 and founded the New Party. In 1932 he started the British Union of Fascists, who imitated the authoritarian ideas and theatrical displays of Mussolini's Italian blackshirts. The BUF's activities were restricted by the 1936 Public Order Act, passed by the National Government to curb the wearing of political uniforms.

1. *Why have historians disagreed about the reasons for Conservative electoral success between the wars?*

2. *Why did the extreme right prove such a failure in inter-war British politics?*

3. *How far was Conservative electoral success due to good party management?*

> **Social reforms of the National Governments, 1931–1939**
>
> 1933   Slum Clearance Act sets targets for local authorities to re-house people living in inner city poverty.
>
> 1934   Administration of unemployment relief is transferred from local authorities to a national Unemployment Assistance Board. Special Areas Act attempts to attract investment into areas where unemployment levels are highest.
>
> 1937   Factory Act reduces working hours for women and young people.
>
> 1938   Holidays with Pay Act extends paid holidays to 11 million workers.

4.5 How can Stanley Baldwin's long tenure of the Conservative Party leadership be explained?

The unexpected Prime Minister

In some respects it is surprising that Stanley Baldwin should have led the Conservatives for 14 years and have been able to stamp his own personality on the character of the inter-war party. H. Montgomery Hyde aptly subtitled his 1973 biography 'the unexpected Prime Minister'. Although Baldwin had been in the Commons since 1908, when he succeeded his father as MP for the Bewdley Division of Worcestershire, he had not had long experience of high office when he became Conservative leader and Prime Minister in May 1923. He had entered the Cabinet, as President of the Board of Trade, as recently as March 1921. He did not become a recognisable public figure until October 1922, when he spoke out against the Lloyd George Coalition at the famous Carlton Club meeting. The arrival in Downing Street of his patron and friend, Bonar Law, led to Baldwin's appointment as Chancellor of the Exchequer. Even then his succession to the premiership was not a foregone conclusion: in January 1923 he came into conflict with the Prime Minister over the terms of the American debt settlement, and revealed his lack of experience by disclosing the deal to journalists before it had been submitted to the Cabinet.

On several occasions there was a question mark over Baldwin's political future. It was his miscalculation that plunged the Conservative Party, without adequate preparation, into the December 1923 general election. In 1929–31, following a second electoral defeat, his leadership was threatened by a prolonged challenge from the two great newspaper owners, Lord Beaverbrook and Lord Rothermere. In early March 1931 key Shadow Cabinet colleagues prepared to abandon him and he came close to resignation. He was often criticised for not being sufficiently aggressive in opposition and the Conservative right wing never warmed to him. As Prime Minister he lacked a detailed grasp of many policy matters and seemed uninterested in the foreign and defence issues of the 1930s. In retirement during the Second World War, he was savagely criticised by many commentators for Britain's lack of military preparedness. How then are we to explain Baldwin's long period at the summit of British politics?

> **Sir Max Aitken, Baron Beaverbrook (1879–1964)**
>
> The owner of the *Daily Express*, Beaverbrook was a lifelong political intriguer. In 1929–31 he worked with Lord Rothermere, owner of the *Daily Mail*, against Baldwin's leadership. He held government posts in both world wars and was a close associate of Winston Churchill.

> **George Nathaniel Curzon, Marquess Curzon (1859–1925)**
>
> The most distinguished and experienced Conservative figure of the early 1920s. Curzon had served as Viceroy of India from 1898–1905 and had been a member of Lloyd George's five man War Cabinet. He was Foreign Secretary from 1919–23 and considered himself the inevitable choice for Prime Minister when Bonar Law retired.

Good fortune

Luck, the simplest of explanations, takes us some way in analysing Baldwin's success. He gained the premiership in 1923 largely because the only credible alternative, Lord Curzon, was too difficult and pompous to be acceptable to his colleagues. Moreover it was generally accepted that, with Labour now the main party of opposition, it was inappropriate for the Prime Minister to sit in the House of Lords. Baldwin was fortunate in the timing of Bonar Law's retirement. It came too soon after the Carlton Club meeting for Conservatives such as Austen Chamberlain, who had been identified with the Coalition, to be considered. The lack of an obvious alternative also helped Baldwin to survive criticism of his leadership following defeat in the December 1923 general election.

Baldwin also benefited from the 'image problems' of his leading opponents in the 1930s. Churchill's attacks on his party leader over India were weakened by the violence of his language, which suggested that he was exaggerating his case for self-interested reasons. Memories of this episode also limited the impact of Churchill's warnings over Nazi Germany later in the decade.

A great communicator

Baldwin would not, however, have survived as long as he did without positive qualities of his own. Perhaps his greatest asset was a capacity to sense the public mood and to express it. He embodied his age in a way that few other politicians have done. With his baggy suits, country tweeds and trademark pipe, he was a figure with whom the general public could readily identify. His homely, down-to-earth style made it hard to remember that he was, in fact, both the inheritor of a large personal fortune and a highly-professional politician.

The titles of Baldwin's published collections of speeches give a clue to the nature of his appeal: *On England, Our Inheritance, This Torch of Freedom, Service of Our Lives, An Interpreter of England*. Through his public utterances, which were often addressed to non-political gatherings, Baldwin evoked a vision which was in tune with the instincts and feelings

Two photographs of Stanley
Baldwin

*What impression of
Baldwin's political style
and image do these
photographs give?*

of his audience. He spoke nostalgically of a rural way of life which, by the
1920s, was fast disappearing. Sections of his 1924 address to the Royal
Society of St George have become well known: 'the tinkle of the hammer
on the anvil in the country smithy, the corncrake on a dewy morning, the
sound of the scythe against the whetstone, and the sight of a plough team
coming over the brow of a hill…' Linked to this romantic portrayal of the
English landscape were the enduring virtues of the national character: an
instinct for compromise, a basic kindliness and common sense, an ability
to reconcile freedom and individuality with order and responsibility.
Baldwin created an image of a nation at ease with itself, of a community in
which people of all backgrounds shared a common ideal of service. 'There
is only one thing which I feel is worth giving one's whole strength to,' he
declared in 1925, 'and that is the binding together of all classes of our
people in an effort to make life better in every sense of the word.'

In a country which had recently experienced the horror of the First
World War, and which now faced considerable economic and political

uncertainty, Baldwin's public image was immensely reassuring. As Neville Chamberlain once acknowledged, he had a unique gift for communicating with the politically uncommitted 'floating voter'. Baldwin's talent for words was deployed to great effect, not only in traditional public meetings but also through the new media of radio and film. He was the first major politician to grasp the importance of speaking to the radio microphone as if addressing individuals rather than a mass meeting. The introduction of sound newsreels in 1930 enabled him to reach a larger audience than ever before; at that time approximately 20 million people regularly watched cinema films. As John Ramsden observes in *An Appetite for Power*, Baldwin was 'the first British politician ever to become truly familiar to the voting public'. When he said, at the close of his 1935 general election broadcast, 'I think you can trust me by now', Baldwin was accurately reflecting the nature of the relationship that he had built with the ordinary voter.

A skilled politician

Baldwin's image as a plain-spoken countryman was deceptive. Churchill paid tribute to him as 'the greatest party manager the Conservatives ever had'; Beaverbrook, with more feeling, described him as 'the toughest and most unscrupulous politician you could find'. Although passive by nature, Baldwin could hit his opponents hard when the occasion demanded. The fact that he normally avoided excessive partisanship made him more effective when he chose to exert himself. His condemnation of the 1926 General Strike as 'a challenge to Parliament and … the road to anarchy and ruin' is a good example of his toughness in a crisis.

In the more subtle arts of political management Baldwin had few equals. In his 1924–29 administration, for example, he showed skill in maintaining the unity of a diverse ministerial team. He successfully combined keen protectionists such as Leopold Amery, the Colonial and Dominions Secretary, with the pro-free trade Winston Churchill. By offering the Exchequer to Churchill he surprised many observers, since the latter had so recently returned to the Conservative fold. Nonetheless the decision made sense politically, since the post absorbed the energies of a potentially troublesome colleague.

Baldwin's survival of the campaign orchestrated by Beaverbrook and Rothermere in 1929–31 showed him at his most skilful. The press lords' call for a policy of 'Empire Free Trade' struck a chord with large sections of Tory opinion. It was a re-packaging of the historic Conservative idea of imperial preference – the call for a comprehensive system of tariffs, designed to turn the British Empire into a self-sufficient trading bloc. With the 1929 electoral defeat a recent memory, Baldwin's position was vulnerable. The *Express* and the *Mail* possessed a combined daily circulation of 3.5 million and thus provided their owners with an influential platform. By 1930 Beaverbrook and Rothermere had formed their own United Empire Party, which opposed official Conservative candidates at by-elections. As the campaign increased in intensity, Baldwin showed flexibility in gradually moving closer to the Empire Free Trade position, while avoiding unqualified support for a policy which might prove an electoral liability. When the campaign against his leadership revived in the spring of 1931, he chose the right moment to retaliate against his press critics. Speaking in support of the official Conservative candidate in the St George's, Westminster by-election, he presented the issue as one of press versus people. In a famous phrase, he described the newspaper owners as aiming at 'power without responsibility – the prerogative of the harlot throughout the ages'. The attack helped to ensure the victory of the pro-Baldwin candidate, Alfred Duff Cooper, and to bring the Beaverbrook-Rothermere crusade to a close.

The Abdication Crisis, 1936

Edward VIII came to the throne in January 1936 on the death of his father, King George V. He was determined to marry his American-born mistress, Wallis Simpson. Already a divorcee, she was divorced from her second husband in the autumn of 1936. The government, together with majority opinion in both Britain and the self-governing Dominions, regarded her as an unsuitable choice. The King was the official head of the Church of England, which was opposed to divorce. Edward could not disregard conventional ideas of morality and expect to have Mrs Simpson as his

Edward VIII with Mrs Simpson

Queen. The crisis was resolved in December, with Edward's decision to abdicate the throne in favour of his younger brother. Edward took the title of Duke of Windsor and went to live in France, where he married Mrs Simpson in 1937.

Baldwin's handling of the issue was universally regarded as a personal triumph. As the King's first minister he avoided antagonising Edward, while ensuring that abdication was the outcome of the crisis. In so doing Baldwin demonstrated once again his feel for the middle ground of public opinion. Churchill and Beaverbrook, who attempted to start a movement in favour of Edward retaining the throne, were left in an isolated position. Baldwin was able to retire in May 1937, following the coronation of King George VI and Queen Elizabeth, in a glow of popular goodwill.

Conclusion

Lord Kilmuir, who served in the Conservative Cabinets of the 1950s, once described loyalty as the Tories' secret weapon. As Stuart Ball shows in *Baldwin and the Conservative Party: the crisis of 1929–1931* (1988), during the Empire Free Trade episode Baldwin strained that loyalty to the limit. In his anxiety not to commit himself to an electorally risky policy, he nearly alienatied those who most wanted a distinctively Conservative stance. He was fortunate that, as the Depression deepened in the course of 1930, protection became increasingly acceptable to business. This enabled Baldwin to adjust his economic policy to satisfy his own activists, without appearing to give in to pressure from the Empire Crusade.

Baldwin saw himself as educating his party in the need for a moderate, pragmatic approach to new problems. In his speeches he presented this as a characteristically Conservative position. As he declared in 1924, in tackling questions of social reform Conservatives were 'following the very traditions of Disraeli himself, adapted to the present day'. By generating a reassuring image of continuity, Baldwin persuaded the loyal centre of his party to accept change as a necessary part of life. This meant frustration for those who looked for a more confrontational style of politics.

The course of inter-war politics vindicated Baldwin rather than his critics. The creation of the National Government in 1931 isolated those who demanded a more aggressive Conservatism. Baldwin's instinct for consensus made him an ideal leader for the party at such a time. He was able to articulate a sense of national unity in face of the twin threats of economic crisis at home and political extremism abroad. In so doing he consolidated his hold on public opinion and made his position as party leader secure from further challenge. In 1937 he retired at a time of his own choosing, one of only three 20th-century Prime Ministers to leave office without being forced to do so by ill health, electoral defeat or a party revolt. This in itself was a considerable achievement.

'Baldwin owed his survival as Conservative leader solely to the absence of credible alternative candidates.' Do you agree? Use the information in this section to support your answer.

The Labour Party, 1918–1939

Key Issues

● *How did Labour change from being a trade union pressure group to a national party of government?*

● *Did the Labour governments of the inter-war period achieve anything worthwhile?*

● *What was the impact of the financial and political crisis of 1931 on the Labour Party?*

Framework of Events

1918	Labour adopts a new constitution, *Labour and the New Social Order*, containing a commitment to socialism for the first time. In the December general election, Labour wins 57 seats
1921	Trades Union Congress forms the General Council, which formally associates with the Labour Party in a new National Joint Council
1922	November: general election, Labour wins 142 seats, becoming the main alternative to the Conservative government
1923	December: general election, Labour wins 191 seats, and is able to take office for the first time with the support of the Liberals
1924	Ramsay MacDonald's minority Labour government holds office from January to October. It is then defeated in the House of Commons and in a further general election, losing 40 seats
1926	Failure of the General Strike. Conservative government's 1927 Trade Disputes Act inhibits trade union financing of the Labour Party
1929	May: general election. MacDonald forms his second minority government after winning 287 seats
1931	The Labour government breaks up because of divisions over how to respond to a severe financial crisis in August. It is replaced by a Conservative-dominated National government headed by MacDonald. Labour is heavily defeated in the October general election (46 seats compared with the government's 554). George Lansbury takes over as Labour Party leader
1935	Clement Attlee replaces Lansbury as leader of the party. Labour is heavily defeated in the November general election (154 seats, compared with 429 for the National Government)
1937	Labour's immediate programme outlines policies for a centrally planned economy
1939	Expulsion from the Labour Party of Stafford Cripps and other advocates of a 'popular front'. Labour supports the National Government's declaration of war on Germany

Overview

THE inter-war years witnessed Labour's replacement of the Liberals as the main progressive party in British politics. Labour gained only slightly more seats in the 1918 general election than it had done in the last pre-war contest in December 1910. Nonetheless, with more than two million votes, it had secured a larger share of the popular vote. Steps had been taken to lay the foundations of a more effective organisation and a new constitution had committed the party to the 'common [i.e. state] ownership' of industry as a long-term aspiration. These were significant developments for a party, created as recently as 1900 by a group of trade unions and socialist societies, to win parliamentary representation for working-class people.

Ramsay MacDonald, who was elected leader in 1922, was determined to establish Labour as a respectable and responsible party of government. In office in 1924 and 1929–31, this meant the deliberate pursuit of moderate policies to reassure the electorate that Labour was not a revolutionary faction. A clear-cut socialist approach, advocated by the party's left-wing associate body, the **Independent Labour Party**, was to be avoided. The fact that both administrations were minority governments, kept in office with the tolerance of the parliamentary Liberal Party, provided a practical obstacle to the adoption of a radical socialist agenda. In any case Labour's Chancellor, Philip Snowden, was firmly wedded to an orthodox understanding of finance based upon free trade, a cautious attitude towards public spending and the importance of a balanced budget. This effectively ruled out imaginative policies to tackle the problem of unemployment, which worsened appreciably following the onset of world depression in 1929.

In 1931 Labour faced a severe test of its credibility as a governing party. Faced with an international financial crisis, which threatened the stability of the pound, the second MacDonald government was unable to agree on a package of spending cuts. Acceptance of these was necessary if rescue loans from foreign bankers were to be obtained. The argument centred on the demand for a 10% cut in unemployment benefit. A section of the Cabinet, led by the Foreign Secretary, Arthur Henderson, insisted that Labour's historic responsibility for working-class living standards should take priority. Rather than consent to the proposed cuts, nine ministers resigned, bringing down the government. MacDonald then caused lasting resentment in the Labour movement by accepting reappointment as head of a National Government, in which the Conservatives were the dominant group. He was joined by a handful of supporters, who took the label 'National Labour'.

Defeat in the ensuing general election and in the further contest of 1935 condemned the Labour Party to spend the remainder of the 1930s in the political

Independent Labour Party: Founded in 1893, this body advocated the 'common' [state] ownership of industry. In 1900 it joined with representatives of the trade unions and other groups to form the Labour Representation Committee, which took the name 'Labour Party' six years later.

Philip Snowden (1864–1937)
Snowden began his career as an activist in the Independent Labour Party in Yorkshire. His reputation as the Labour Party's financial expert earned him the post of Chancellor of the Exchequer in the first two Labour governments. He stayed with MacDonald when the latter formed the National Government in 1931, resigning a year later in protest at the abandonment of free trade.

Arthur Henderson (1863–1935)
The embodiment of Labour's trade union roots, Henderson served as party secretary for more than twenty years. He was the first Labour MP to acquire governmental experience, serving in both the Asquith and Lloyd George coalitions. After his resignation from the War Cabinet in 1917, he initiated a major overhaul of the party organisation. He was a key figure in the first two Labour governments.

wilderness. The 1931 crisis was a defining moment in the party's history, leaving a bitter memory of alleged betrayal by its leadership. Only the political transformation effected by the Second World War would make it possible for Labour to return to the corridors of power.

Leaders of the Labour Party, 1918–1939

1918–21   William Adamson

1921–22   J.R. Clynes

1922–31   Ramsay MacDonald

1931–32   Arthur Henderson

1932–35   George Lansbury (led the parliamentary party from 1931, after Henderson lost his seat at the general election).

1935–55   Clement Attlee

(The leader of the Parliamentary Labour Party was known as 'chairman' until 1922.)

5.1 How and why did Labour become a potential party of government after the First World War?

The Labour Party was no less divided than the Liberals by the experience of the Great War. Ramsay MacDonald, the most outstanding of the pre-war chairmen of the Parliamentary Labour Party, had resigned his post in August 1914, in protest at Britain's involvement in the war. The majority of the party followed the new leader, Arthur Henderson, in qualified support for British intervention. A minority of Labourites outdid the Conservatives in passionate support for a vigorous prosecution of the conflict. Yet Labour emerged from 1914–18 united, with an increased parliamentary representation, ready to forge ahead as a potential party of government in its own right. By contrast the Liberal Party, which had been indisputably the senior partner in the pre-war progressive alliance, was weak, divided and in no position to provide national leadership. Why were the fortunes of Britain's two parties of the left so divergent?

The preservation of fundamental unity

The most influential study of this topic remains Ross McKibbin's *The Evolution of the Labour Party 1910–1924* (1974). McKibbin argued that Labour's emergence as a contender for power was a product of deep-seated socio-economic changes, which had begun before the First World War. The rise of the party reflected the growth of a strong sense of class consciousness among the industrial workforce, which found expression in the trade union movement. This meant that, far more than the Liberals, the party could claim to speak for the great masses of organised labour. Its foundation on the bedrock of class loyalty gave it an inherent strength, which divisions at parliamentary level could not seriously undermine.

Throughout the war Labour leaders maintained an essential unity on issues that affected the wellbeing of the working classes. The War Emergency Workers' National Committee, which concerned itself with everyday issues such as prices, rents and widows' pensions, was a practical example of this. Chaired by Arthur Henderson, it included MacDonald and other anti-war figures among its members. In any case, wartime differences of opinion in the Labour movement did not have the personal bitterness of the rivalry of Asquith and Lloyd George. The Liberal Party traditionally accorded a more prominent role to individual leaders and was thus harmed more seriously by divisions at high political level.

As his biographer, Chris Wrigley, has shown, Henderson's effectiveness as Labour leader derived largely from his capacity to reflect the consensus view of the Labour movement. His acceptance of Cabinet posts under both Asquith and Lloyd George enabled him to defend working people's interests at the highest level. Thus by declining to oppose military conscription in 1916, he was in a position to resist future moves towards compulsion in industry. His involvement in government enhanced Labour's confidence and laid down an important marker for the post-war period.

The growth of grassroots organisation

While the Liberal organisation contracted during the war, the Labour Party's began to expand and improve. In 1914 the Labour Party was still in essence a federal structure, whose membership was based upon affiliations through trade unions and socialist parties. This limited the party's ability to field candidates outside the small number of constituencies where it could rely upon the co-operation of a powerful affiliated body.

Henderson's resignation from the Lloyd George government in August 1917, following a dispute over his proposed attendance at an international socialist conference, provided an opportunity to overhaul this primitive organisation. Henderson encouraged the growth of local party branches, which, for the first time, would make possible large-scale individual membership. By 1924 only 19 constituencies lacked a branch of the Labour Party.

Nonetheless, one should not exaggerate the importance of this development. The continued growth of trade union affiliations was more significant for the party's electoral strength, since in most constituencies the unions remained the basis of local organisation. In the 1918 general election, no fewer than 25 of the successful Labour candidates were sponsored by the Miners' Federation of Great Britain. It was an accurate reflection of the unions' importance that, under the constitution adopted by the party in February 1918, they commanded 13 of the 21 places on the expanded executive body. Their continued control of party funding prevented the Labour leadership from carrying out a more equal distribution of resources across the constituencies. The overall result was that Labour consolidated its organisation in already winnable seats, which were typically in strongly working-class areas of the industrial north.

The franchise factor

The extent to which Labour benefited from the extension of the franchise, under the 1918 Representation of the People Act, remains controversial. The Act virtually trebled the size of the electorate, giving the vote to large numbers of women and working-class men. In an important article published in the *English Historical Review* (1976), H. C. G. Matthew, Ross McKibbin and J.A. Kay argued for the centrality of the 'franchise factor' in the post-war rise of Labour. They maintained that the Act's most important feature was the enfranchisement of a mass working-class population, whose predisposition to vote Labour could now find expression.

This view has not gone unchallenged. In 1983 Duncan Tanner, writing in *Bulletin of the Institute of Historical Research*, drew attention to the socially diverse nature of the new electorate. He pointed out that the pre-1918 voting rules had also excluded from the franchise middle-class sons living with their parents, domestic servants and soldiers resident in barracks. None of these groups could be viewed as automatic Labour voters. Moreover research into voting patterns among women suggests that they have exhibited a general tendency to vote in a Conservative direction.

As Martin Pugh points out in *The Making of Modern British Politics 1867–1939* (1982), the patriotic fervour of 1918 affected the outcome of the first post-war election. Those Labour candidates who won, such as the railwaymen's leader, J.H. Thomas, were often those who took a populist anti-German line. Those with a **pacifist** background, such as MacDonald and Snowden, suffered heavy defeats.

Pacifist: A person who believes all war to be wrong.

One incontestable reason for Labour success in 1918 was the straightforward fact that the party ran more candidates than in December 1910 – 388 as opposed to 78. This trend was continued in the post-war years; in the 1922 election there were 414 Labour candidates.

The drive towards independence from the Liberals

New Liberalism: The social reforming ideas associated with the pre-1914 administrations of Campbell-Bannerman and Asquith. These governments took a more positive view than their 19th-century predecessors of the role of the state in society.

In the Edwardian period the relationship between the Liberal Party and Labour had clearly been one of patron and client. The latter had few distinctive policies of its own and had been heavily dependent on the goodwill of the Liberal administration for the passage of such measures as the trade union laws of 1906 and 1913 and the payment of MPs. In many respects the post-1914 Labour Party offered a safe haven to radical Liberals who had become disenchanted with the internal wrangling of their own party. Labour stood for free trade, internationalism and social reform in a manner wholly consistent with pre-war '**New Liberalism**'. The Union of Democratic Control, a wartime society that campaigned for a popular voice in foreign policy making, provided a forum in which representatives of both parties worked together. Its members included the idealistic Liberal, Charles Trevelyan, who was shortly to join the Labour Party in protest at the vindictive nature of the Versailles peace settlement.

Nationalisation: The idea of state or common ownership of industry, expressed in clause four of Labour's 1918 constitution.

Capitalist: A supporter of the system of private enterprise.

National Executive: The Labour Party's governing body, especially important in periods of opposition, on which the trade unions, the constituency parties and the parliamentary party were represented.

Yet the younger party was also concerned with carving out for itself a new, clearly defined identity. This was one of the main reasons for the adoption, in its 1918 constitution, of a commitment to 'the common ownership of the means of production'. The espousal of **nationalisation** as a long-term aspiration for industry enabled the party to distinguish itself from the essentially **capitalist** Liberal Party.

The drive to independent status was also reflected in the party's electoral strategy. Henderson's approach as leader was to contest by-elections wherever the local Labour organisation made a challenge feasible. Asked in December 1917 whether he would spare the seats of radical Liberals, he replied that 'discrimination would be difficult and that broadly he thought the policy would be to run a Labour candidate wherever there was a tolerable chance of carrying him'. This strategy was demonstrated in two Lancashire by-elections in the autumn of 1919. At Widnes, where he was a candidate, Henderson was happy to accept Liberal support. Yet shortly afterwards, in the Rusholme division of Manchester, a largely middle-class seat in which the Liberals had expected a free run, Labour's **National Executive** ran its own candidate.

1. Which of the factors discussed in this section do you think was most important in making Labour a potential party of government? Give reasons for your answer.

2. 'Labour's success in the period 1914–22 owed more to the mistakes of the party's opponents than to the skills of the Labour leadership.' Do you agree? Give reasons for your answer.

Labour displayed its new-found ruthlessness most effectively in the 1923 general election, when the party ignored the fact that it shared obvious common ground with the Liberals on the central issue of the contest – free trade versus protection. With the possibility of power at last in sight, Labour's leaders could not afford the luxury of sentimentality towards their former partners. After 1918 they seized the opportunity to polarise politics between themselves and the Conservatives, so that the Liberals were gradually squeezed out as an effective rival.

5.2 Did the Labour government of 1924 fail both the party and the country?

The appointment of the first Labour government in January 1924 was widely regarded by contemporaries as an event of great political and social significance. King George V wrote in his diary, 'Today 23 years ago, dear Grandmama [Queen Victoria] died. I wonder what she would have made of a Labour government!' The new Prime Minister, Ramsay MacDonald, lacked the governmental experience of his predecessors and had risen from obscure origins, the illegitimate child of Scottish fisherfolk. One of the Labour ministers, J. R. Clynes, later recalled 'the strange turn in Fortune's wheel which had brought MacDonald the starveling clerk, Thomas the engine driver, Henderson the foundry labourer and Clynes the mill-hand' to the Cabinet room. Many on the political right expressed alarmist expectations of attacks on private property and established institutions. Among the more extreme predictions was a claim that women would be nationalised and free love proclaimed as official government policy. Winston Churchill, at that time shifting his allegiance from the Liberal Party to the Conservatives, wrote that 'the enthronement in office of a Socialist government will be a serious national misfortune such as has usually befallen great States only on the morrow of defeat in war'.

Notwithstanding such apocalyptic pronouncements, the government's behaviour proved to be so moderate that its most radical supporters were to be gravely disappointed. After less than ten months in office, no significant steps had been taken towards the achievement of socialist goals. The party suffered a heavy defeat in the general election of October 1924, winning 151 seats to the Conservatives' 419. Labour was not to form another government for almost five years. In the eyes of the left wing and of many trade unionists, the MacDonald administration had failed to justify the confidence placed in it a short time earlier. How are we to assess the record of that government today?

The decision to take office

The performance of the first Labour government was to be affected to a large extent by the circumstances in which it took office. It is important to remember that it was a minority administration, which had come to power because of the peculiar outcome of the December 1923 general election. Stanley Baldwin's Conservative government had dissolved Parliament in an abortive attempt to secure a mandate for the introduction of protective tariffs. Although the Conservatives, with 258 seats, remained the largest party in the Commons, they were outnumbered by the Liberals (159 seats) and Labour (191 seats), who had both campaigned in defence of free trade. Since the contest had turned on one issue, it could legitimately be argued that Labour, as the largest pro-free trade party, had the right to form a government. On the other hand, this would mean forming a ministry with the acquiescence of the Liberals, who could withdraw their support at any time.

J. R. Clynes (1869–1949)

He came from the party's trade union wing. Clynes served as Lord Privy Seal in 1924 and as Home Secretary in 1929–31.

J. H. Thomas (1874–1949)

A leading figure in the National Union of Railwaymen, Thomas was a friend of MacDonald. He served in both inter-war Labour Cabinets and in the National Government, until his disgrace in 1936 for revealing budget secrets. The cartoonist David Low invariably depicted him as 'the Rt. Hon. Dress Suit' on account of the enthusiasm with which he participated in high society.

Leading members of the 1924 Labour Government

Prime Minister and Foreign Secretary	Ramsay MacDonald
Chancellor of the Exchequer	Philip Snowden
Home Secretary	Arthur Henderson
Colonial Secretary	J. H. Thomas

Members of the first Labour Government arrive at Buckingham Palace to receive the seals of office. Left to right: Ramsay MacDonald, J.H. Thomas, Arthur Henderson, J.R. Clynes (January 1924).

How important were Ramsay MacDonald and Arthur Henderson for the rise of the Labour Party between the wars?

In these circumstances Labour's term of office was unlikely to be more than a rather unsatisfactory apprenticeship in power. Some on the left were uneasy about the idea of taking office at all, fearing that the party would be hopelessly compromised by the institutions of capitalist society. The left-wing MPs elected for the Clydeside region of Scotland, supported by the Independent Labour Party, argued that MacDonald should deliberately court parliamentary defeat with an uncompromising socialist programme. The ensuing election would then enable the party to rally support in the country for a revolutionary transformation of society.

MacDonald risked the anger of committed socialists by declining to 'ride for a fall' in the manner recommended by the class warriors of the left. Instead he resolved that a policy of moderation was essential, to give the party a chance to prove its capacity to govern responsibly. If Labour was to establish itself as something more than a party of protest, it needed to win the confidence of the ideologically uncommitted outside the ranks of the movement. If Labour could exercise authority with dignity, it could consolidate its lead over the Liberals, which it had won since the end of the Great War. As MacDonald's biographer, David Marquand, points out, such an approach was dictated both by the circumstances of 1924 and by the nature of the Labour Party. Extreme care in demonstrating Labour's respectability was 'the price they paid for belonging to a working-class party which aspired to govern a class-divided and hierarchical society'.

The composition of the Cabinet was at one with this strategy. To compensate for his colleagues' lack of ministerial experience, MacDonald filled many posts with former members of the Conservative and Liberal Parties. The new ministers were schooled in constitutional practice by the Lord Chancellor, Lord Haldane, who had held the same office under Asquith. Only the Minister of Health, John Wheatley, was clearly drawn from the Labour left. Even in such an apparently minor area as the decision to wear traditional Court dress on ceremonial occasions, Labour's representatives emphasised their conformity to social convention.

The government's record

In domestic policy the government was consistent in its avoidance of radical departures. Perhaps its most creative action was Wheatley's Housing Act, which allocated state subsidies to local authorities, enabling them to build houses for rent. This was an extension of council housing policies initiated by Christopher Addison as Minister of Health in the post-war Lloyd George Coalition. On the central problem of unemployment, the Labour government offered no action beyond the uncontroversial funding of public works schemes. Faced with the threat of strikes by dockers and London transport workers, the government showed a readiness to use emergency powers bequeathed by the Lloyd George administration. MacDonald's insistence on the need to govern in the national interest effectively ruled out any particular sympathy for the trade union movement.

Continuity was also the hallmark of the government's imperial policy. Although work on the costly Singapore naval base was halted, there was certainly no indication that Labour stood for the abandonment of imperial commitments in general. Only in the field of foreign affairs could the government be said to have developed something approaching a distinctive line. Here Labour's emphasis on the reconciliation of post-war Germany bore fruit in negotiations for the withdrawal of the French army of occupation from the Ruhr. This was followed by MacDonald's chairmanship of a conference in London, at which the Dawes Plan, an attempt to alleviate Germany's reparations burden, was launched. This, the first successful attempt to mitigate the rigours of the Versailles settlement, set the tone for the policies of Governments of both parties over the next decade and a half. The emphasis was on making concessions to Germany, in the interests of wider European security. MacDonald's attempt, in the so-called **Geneva Protocol**, to widen the power of the League of Nations to settle international disputes, was less successful. The Protocol had not been ratified before the fall of the government and it was allowed to drop by the incoming Conservative administration.

Decline and fall

The manner in which the government met its end casts grave doubt on the political sensitivity of its leading figures. MacDonald's attempt to negotiate treaties with the Soviet Union gave the opposition parties a perfect opportunity to label the government as pro-Communist. The proposal to offer a loan to the Soviet regime, in return for a vague agreement to compensate British investors who had lost their claims in the Bolshevik revolution, was particularly damaging to Labour.

The government's mishandling of a law case involving J. R. Campbell, the acting editor of the Communist *Workers' Weekly*, gave Labour's opponents a further handle for criticism. After Campbell wrote an article calling on troops not to allow themselves to be used against strikers, the Attorney-General, Sir Patrick Hastings, started a prosecution. When the government decided to withdraw the charges, it laid itself open to opposition claims that it was being manipulated by extreme left elements. Conservatives and Liberals then united to defeat the government in the Commons.

In the ensuing general election campaign Labour was again identified in the public eye with the 'red menace'. This was through the publication of the notorious Zinoviev letter, an incitement to **sedition** apparently written by the president of the Communist International in the Soviet Union. The letter probably had a limited impact on the outcome of the election, which would have resulted in a Conservative victory even had it never appeared. In 1999 an official investigation suggested that the letter was forged by an exiled opponent of the Russian Revolution and leaked by members of MI5 and MI6, Britain's security services, to tarnish Labour's image. Historians agree, however, that the real significance of the letter was the way in which it gave Labour a plausible explanation for its defeat. Labour spokesmen maintained that it was a forgery and that they had been the innocent victims of a capitalist conspiracy. In this way the

Geneva Protocol: A document promoted by MacDonald at the League of Nations. The signatories promised to accept a peaceful settlement of all international disputes and to disarm by agreement. They also agreed to offer support to each other if faced with unprovoked aggression.

Sedition: An attempt, by speech or writing, to encourage disorder and disobedience to legal authority.

episode served to distract attention from an honest examination of the party's real weaknesses.

1924 and the future of Labour

Labour's defeat in the 1924 contest obscured the fact that the real losers were the Liberals, whose share of the poll had fallen from just under 30% to less than 18% since the previous contest. The strain of fighting three general elections in the space of two years had placed a considerable strain on the resources of a party denied the solid financial backing of the trade union movement. Moreover it seems likely that, influenced by the 'red scare' atmosphere of 1924, many moderate Liberal voters had turned to the more reassuring Conservative Party. By completing the destruction of the Liberal Party as a credible instrument of government, the election had fulfilled the most important purpose of MacDonald and his colleagues.

On the other hand, the experience of 1924 left many unresolved problems for Labour. In *The Making of Modern British Politics* Martin Pugh argues that MacDonald welcomed the coalescence of Conservative and Liberal opposition to the government in the autumn of 1924. Had the government not been released from office at that point, the passage of more time would simply have made the simmering conflict with the party's left harder to contain. Nine months was long enough to demonstrate Labour's capacity to govern. An extended term of office would have exposed the latent tensions within the Labour movement.

Two questions in particular would have to be faced if Labour were to have a chance of forming a more successful second administration. Serious thinking about unemployment, the dominant social issue of the decade, would have to be done. Further, the relationship between a Labour government and the trade unions would have to be properly defined. The real tragedy of 1924 was that a party that could claim to have been sabotaged by external forces was unlikely to undertake a thoroughgoing appraisal of its own shortcomings.

1. Did the Labour government of 1924 have any worthwhile achievements to its credit? Give reasons to support your answer.

2. 'The author of its own downfall.' Is this a fair verdict on the first Labour government? Give reasons to support your answer.

? *Source-based questions: The Labour government of 1924*

SOURCE A

It would seem that the immediate future is now settled; that Baldwin is to resign and Ramsay to come in. I doubt whether either of them is right. Baldwin could easily have snapped his fingers at the no confidence amendment and announced that, as leader of much the largest section of the House, he had better moral authority than anyone else to carry on the King's Government until he was absolutely blocked, and Ramsay might well have declined to start the first Labour Government under impossible parliamentary conditions.

A letter from H.H. Asquith to a Liberal MP, W.M.R. Pringle, 10 January 1924. Quoted in Asquith *by Roy Jenkins, 1964.*

SOURCE B

It is possible for a Labour Government to exaggerate the limitation imposed upon it by the difficult position, to distrust its own power, and to forget that it has a far firmer hold on the mind of the country than on the mind of the House of Commons … the I.L.P. believes a minority Labour Government even now can advance Socialism by its legislative and administrative acts …

Why should we not at once devote the vast resources of the Government and the ability of its loyal and disinterested advisers, and of other representatives of the community to enquire into the application of Socialist principles to the reorganisation of industry and our economic life?

From Clifford Allen's chairman's address to the Easter conference of the Independent Labour Party, 1924. Quoted in Clifford Allen: the open conspirator *by Arthur Marwick, 1964.*

Source-based questions: The Labour government of 1924

SOURCE C

It is no part of my job as Chancellor of the Exchequer to put before the House of Commons proposals for the expenditure of public money. The function of the Chancellor of the Exchequer, as I understand it, is to resist all demands for expenditure made by his colleagues, and, when he can no longer resist, to limit the concession to the barest point of acceptance.

From a speech by Philip Snowden in the House of Commons, 30 July 1924.

1. Study Source A. How useful is this source to a historian studying the circumstances in which the first Labour government took office?

2. Study Source B. In the context of this source, explain the reference to 'the application of Socialist principles to the reorganisation of industry and our economic life'.

3. Study Sources B and C. How and why do these sources differ in their respective attitudes to the aims of the first Labour government?

4. How complete a picture do Sources A to C give of the problems facing the first Labour government? Use the information in Section 5.2 to help answer the question.

5.3 How far was the failure of the 1929–31 MacDonald government the result of fundamental fissures in the Labour movement?

The period of recriminations following the fall of the first Labour government was short-lived. In the mid-1920s the grip of MacDonald on the party was confirmed. The failure of the General Strike in May 1926 seemed to endorse his moderate, constitutional approach to politics. The party's 1928 programme, *Labour and the Nation*, avoided specific proposals for progress towards a socialist economy.

In the May 1929 election Labour increased its representation in London and the industrial areas of England. The party won 287 seats, while the Conservatives won 260 and the Liberals 59. This meant that once again Labour took office as a minority administration. As Andrew Thorpe points out in his *History of the British Labour Party* (1997), the party's success was partly due to the unusually high number of Liberal candidacies, which helped to split the anti-Labour vote.

Although the new government included the first woman Cabinet minister (Margaret Bondfield at the Ministry of Labour), its overall political complexion was similar to that of its predecessor five years earlier. At the Treasury, Philip Snowden's conventional outlook on financial affairs remained unchanged. Given that the fortunes of the ministry would be dominated by the onset of world depression in the autumn of 1929, this would prove to be MacDonald's most crucial appointment. Faced with rising levels of unemployment, the government resisted calls from Sir Oswald Mosley, a junior minister, for an expansionary economic policy based upon loan-financed public works, industrial protection and social reforms designed to reduce the size of the labour market. Mosley's resignation in May 1930 reflected the triumph of orthodox financial thinking.

In July 1931 a European banking crisis started a dramatic withdrawal of funds from the Bank of England, calling into question the position of the pound. These events coincided with the publication of a report from a

The caption reads:

Rᴛ Hᴏɴ Dʀᴇss Sᴜɪᴛ (Checking the unemployment figures) – 1,739,497 – 1,739,498 – 1,739,499 – 1,739,50**1** !

J. H. Thomas, the minister responsible for unemployment policy, watches as Sir Oswald Mosley resigns from the second Labour government, following the rejection of his proposals for economic regeneration.

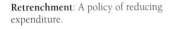

What does this cartoon reveal about the debate on unemployment during the second Labour government?

Retrenchment: A policy of reducing expenditure.

government-appointed committee chaired by Sir George May, secretary of the Prudential Insurance Company. The May Committee predicted a budget deficit of £120 million and called for government economies amounting to £96 million, including a major cut in unemployment benefit. MacDonald and his colleagues accepted the broad thrust of this argument, that spending cuts were necessary to balance the budget. Only such a strategy could enable the government to secure credits from banks in New York and Paris, upon whose support the pound depended.

Acceptance of the principle of **retrenchment** did not, however, translate into Cabinet agreement on the level of the proposed cuts. Ultimately, it proved impossible to settle on a programme of cuts that would satisfy not only Labour ministers but also foreign bankers and the Opposition party leaders, whose approval was necessary for the passage through Parliament of any proposals. The full Cabinet would agree on only £56 million of cuts, a figure well short of that demanded by the Conservative and Liberal leaders. On this issue the second Labour government broke up in August, to be succeeded by a National Government headed by MacDonald but dominated by the Conservatives.

Leading members of the 1929–1931 Labour government

Prime Minister	Ramsay MacDonald
Chancellor of the Exchequer	Philip Snowden
Foreign Secretary	Arthur Henderson
Lord Privy Seal	J. H. Thomas (moved to Dominions Office, June 1930)

Labour and the crisis of 1931

The collapse of the second Labour government has assumed a unique position in the history of the party. To Labour loyalists, the crisis of August 1931 has acted as a grim warning of the dangers of betrayal by untrustworthy leaders. According to this interpretation, Ramsay MacDonald and a handful of senior figures succumbed to the temptations offered by a manipulative capitalist establishment. Labour was undone by the treachery of its leaders, who placed the prospect of continuation in office ahead of their responsibilities for the rank-and-file of the movement. This interpretation perpetuates the sense of bitterness felt at the time by those who believed that a Labour government should resign rather than consent to economies, which would harm the unemployed masses. It reflects the contemporary belief that a capitalist conspiracy or 'bankers' ramp', assisted by the Conservative and Liberal leaders, had been allowed to prevail.

By focusing on the role of personalities, this view tends to divert attention from the deeper issues raised by the crisis. Could the final crisis of the government have been avoided, had different economic policies been pursued? How far did tensions within the Labour movement influence the options open to the government, and thus help to determine the events of 1929–31?

The views of historians

Scholarly debate on the policies of the second MacDonald government continues to be heavily influenced by the work of Robert Skidelsky in the late 1960s. His study, *Politicians and the slump: the Labour Government of 1929–1931* (1970), is a powerful presentation of the case for a radical alternative strategy to tackle the problem of mass unemployment. Skidelsky presents in a positive light the figure of Sir Oswald Mosley, whose unorthodox economic proposals bear comparison with the 'new deal' policies pursued by Franklin Roosevelt in the United States and with the interventionist outlook of Sweden's social democrat government. The rejection of the 'Mosley memorandum' in May 1930 is viewed as a tragically missed opportunity. The MacDonald government could have reversed the contraction of the economy with an imaginative programme of state investment, financed by deficit budgeting and designed to stimulate demand and generate employment. Instead, the Labour leaders' vague belief in 'socialism' as a future goal prejudiced them against the adoption of new initiatives to save the capitalist system. According to Skidelsky, in the circumstances of the slump 'socialism was impossible and capitalism was doomed: there was nothing to do but govern without conviction a system [the Labour Party] did not believe in but saw no real prospect of changing'.

Skidelsky's work reflects assumptions widely held in the 30 years after the Second World War, when it was generally accepted that **Keynesian economic management** had made depressions avoidable. The reappearance of large-scale unemployment a generation after 1945 meant that it was now harder to see government manipulation of demand as a remedy. Attention was focused instead on underlying problems of competitiveness, productivity and business management. This in turn promoted a more sympathetic view of the problems faced by the Labour government in 1929–31.

The most important contribution to the debate was by Ross McKibbin. In an article published in the journal *Past and Present* in 1975, he argued that the experience of the USA and Sweden in the 1930s indicates that expansionary economic policies were hardly an unqualified success. Moreover, the size of the British state's budgetary operations was too small to permit the kind of deficit financing advocated by Mosley and others. The level of government intervention necessary for the direction of investment would not have been acceptable to the conventional wisdom of the time. Only wartime conditions were capable of persuading the political and business world that such a revolution in the machinery of government was

Keynesian economic management: Policies associated with the economist John Maynard Keynes (see Chapter 3). The idea was that governments could stimulate recovery from a depression by investing in public works schemes, thereby generating employment and reviving demand for manufactured goods. To finance such a policy, government would run a deficit – in other words, expenditure would be allowed to exceed revenue. In the inter-war period such thinking ran counter to the trend of orthodox opinion.

feasible. McKibbin's argument is a salutary reminder of the importance of seeing events through the eyes of contemporaries.

Decision-making in 1931

In any case, one should not exaggerate the extent to which the Labour government followed the strict principles of orthodox finance. Although Chancellor Snowden emphasised the importance of a balanced budget, the political and humanitarian need to protect the unemployed meant that the rules were bent in practice. Until the summer of 1931, he continued to allow borrowing from the Treasury to replenish the unemployment insurance fund, from which benefits were financed. He was persuaded to change direction by the need to restore confidence in sterling, in face of the financial crisis that began seriously to drain the Bank of England's gold reserves in July 1931.

It is possible to question the economic sense of the contemporary obsession with the value of the currency. Nonetheless, at the time it was almost universally agreed – even by Labour ministers who regretted its implications – that Britain must maintain its commitment to the gold standard. It was widely believed that the alternative would be a catastrophic collapse in the value of the pound, reminiscent of the German inflation of 1923. The former Labour minister, Sidney Webb, expressed amazement when the National Government later took Britain 'off gold': 'nobody told us we could do that'. In August 1931 the whole Labour Cabinet accepted the need to maintain the **parity of sterling**. To do so, the flow of gold from London must be staunched with the aid of credits supplied by foreign bankers. The only way to obtain these credits was for the government to provide hard evidence of its intention to balance the budget by means of spending cuts.

Parity of sterling: A fixed value for the pound against the United States dollar.

The argument within the Labour Party, then, was about the consequences of deciding to retain the current value of sterling. As was seen earlier, Labour ministers accepted the principle of spending cuts but failed to agree on the precise level. In particular, the fact that the unemployed would be called upon to bear a heavy share of the sacrifices aroused controversy. The idea of cutting unemployment benefit struck at the deepest instincts of the Labour movement. Historically the working classes had been seen as the victims of the capitalist system and as such they were considered entitled to 'work or maintenance'. In the summer of 1931 this case was put most forcibly by the leaders of the TUC General Council, who saw themselves as the legitimate spokesmen of the unemployed. The trade union bosses' conception of their role was essentially defensive; their responsibility was to prevail upon the Labour government not to allow the living standards of working people to be further driven down. Accordingly they mounted a campaign against the proposed cuts and made recommendations that would have penalised the property-owning classes. They called for the replacement of unemployment insurance by a graduated levy, the taxation of fixed interest bearing securities and a possible revenue tariff.

Trade union pressure exercised a decisive influence on a section of the Cabinet led by the Foreign Secretary. For Arthur Henderson, a politician committed to maintaining the unity of the Labour movement, it was inconceivable to go against the explicit wishes of the party's trade union allies on such an issue. Rather than carry out an economy programme prescribed by bankers, Labour must leave office united and transfer responsibility for policy to the Conservative and Liberal Parties. The Lord Chancellor, Lord Sankey, noted in his diary on the day that the Labour Cabinet broke up, 'the result due to Henderson changing his mind. At

1. What were the main problems facing the Labour government in the years 1929–31?

2. Were there realistic alternatives to the policies pursued by the second Labour government?

3. Is there any truth in the accusation of the Labour Party's opponents, that it 'ran away' in the crisis of 1931?

Llandrindod [where the two had met on holiday a few weeks earlier] he and I agreed to equality of sacrifice and cuts in the dole … The TUC won't agree so Henderson gave way.' Not surprisingly Sankey joined MacDonald in helping to form the National Government, whereas Henderson led the bulk of the Labour Party into opposition.

The nature of the rift revealed an underlying difference of priorities between the MacDonald and Henderson camps. The former believed that his long-term strategy of making Labour into a credible party of government required him to accept the advice of the banking community and the Opposition leaders. Labour must be seen to act in the national interest, as defined by the consensus view of informed opinion. Following the publication in 1977 of David Marquand's biography of MacDonald, it has become clear that the formation of a National Government was not for him a first choice. This option emerged only when it became clear that the Prime Minister was unable to find agreement among his colleagues on a package that could command broad parliamentary support. On the other hand, Henderson felt an overriding sense of accountability to the trade unions, with which the Labour Party was inextricably intertwined. In the summer of 1931 his sense of responsibility to the extra-parliamentary forces that had given Labour birth took precedence over other considerations. The crisis was more than a dispute over economic policy: it was a question of Labour's identity as a party and a movement.

5.4 Does Ramsay MacDonald deserve to be remembered as the great betrayer of the Labour Party?

A CASE STUDY IN HISTORICAL INTERPRETATION

Rentier: One who lives on income derived from rents or investments.

The career of Ramsay MacDonald has been overshadowed by his role in the formation of the National Government. Former colleagues in the Labour Party viewed the events of August 1931 as an instance of gross misjudgement at best and as outright treachery at worst. Hugh Dalton, a junior minister at the time, scornfully told journalists that 'for a handful of panic he left us'. Clement Attlee, a man not given to exaggeration, characterised MacDonald's action as 'the greatest betrayal in the political history of this country'. In the wake of the crisis, many writers sympathetic to Labour began to question the whole of MacDonald's political record down to that date. Attention focused on his alleged insecurity, as an outsider to the establishment, which led him to succumb to the superficial attractions of high society. Sidney Webb, who served in the first two Labour governments, wrote ruefully that 'the willingness to use the weapon of seduction will be the last ditch in the defensive position of the British **rentier** class'. For more than a generation, MacDonald's name became a byword for vanity, snobbery and lack of fidelity to socialist ideals.

The process of rehabilitation began in earnest with the publication of David Marquand's biography, the first full-length study to be based on MacDonald's private papers and on Cabinet records. Marquand's scholarly approach did a great deal to correct the worst distortions of party political polemic. Nonetheless, an understanding of 1931 remains central to any appraisal of MacDonald's career. Even a commentator as judicious as the historian Kenneth Morgan concludes that 'in spite of everything, he remains doomed, perhaps damned, by his fatal miscalculation in August 1931'.

The case for MacDonald

Much of the positive work done by MacDonald for the Labour Party falls outside the strict chronological confines of this book. He played a key role in the founding in 1900 of the Labour Representation Committee, the body which later evolved into the Labour Party. He exploited working-class dismay at the Taff Vale case in 1901, a legal judgement that left trade unions liable to be sued for damages incurred by strike action. The case enabled MacDonald, as secretary to the LRC, to obtain a significant increase in the number of trade union affiliations to Labour. Two years later he negotiated a pact with the Liberals, which gave the LRC a free run in 35 working-class constituencies. The deal made it possible for Labour to establish an electoral foothold in the contest of 1906. It also laid the foundations of the 'progressive alliance' between Labour and the Liberal governments, which set the agenda for politics up to the outbreak of the First World War.

As chairman of the parliamentary party from 1911–14, MacDonald was, by common consent, the most effective of Labour's pre-war leaders. He was a prolific writer and an inspiring speaker, both in the House of Commons and on the public platform. His principled opposition to Britain's entry into the war reinforced his radical credentials, giving him a standing with the Labour left that would not wholly dissipate until his second ministry. He sensibly avoided a division of the party, while building links with both Labour and radical Liberal figures through the anti-war Union of Democratic Control.

MacDonald's re-election as leader of the parliamentary party in 1922 enabled him to make his most important contribution to the rise of Labour: the creation of an image, respectable yet radical, that enabled the party to appeal beyond the ranks of its own faithful followers. MacDonald saw that Labour now had an unprecedented opportunity to replace the divided and impoverished Liberals as the main party on the left of British politics. In 1929 the German writer, Egon Wertheimer, memorably described him as 'the focus of the mute hopes of a whole class'. By demonstrating Labour's competence to govern in 1924, and by maintaining a distance from the 'direct action' tactic of the General Strike, MacDonald helped to turn it from a party of protest into one of government. Although MacDonald personally would be attacked by his former comrades, this would broadly be the path followed by the Labour leadership in the 1930s. There are strong grounds for describing Labour's strategy in that decade, with its emphasis on parliamentary action, as 'MacDonaldism without MacDonald'.

More than a year before the formation of the National Government, the left-wing cartoonist David Low, suggests that Ramsay MacDonald is working along lines determined by the Conservative and Liberal Parties.

How useful is this cartoon as a source for studying the second Labour government?

Reflation: A policy designed to increase economic activity by means of government expenditure. See *Keynesian economic management*, p. 94.

In defence of MacDonald's economic policies in 1929–31, it should be recalled that few, if any, of his critics were capable of providing a coherent alternative strategy. A dramatic policy of economic **reflation** would merely have antagonised the business community and worsened the collapse of confidence in the pound. MacDonald's opponents in the August 1931 political crisis objected, not to maintaining the parity of sterling, but to the policies necessary to maintain that parity. Henderson and the eight other ministers who resigned had previously accepted the principle of spending cuts. Even if he was mistaken in his policies, MacDonald was at least consistent in his view of what constituted the national interest. He formed the National Government with reluctance, following strong appeals to his sense of duty from King George V. Far from actively plotting to abandon his Labour colleagues, he initially expected the National Government to be a temporary measure, designed to deal with an exceptional situation.

The case against MacDonald

MacDonald's excessive sensitivity to criticism, his clumsy handling of relations with senior colleagues and his inability to delegate limited his effectiveness as Prime Minister. In January 1924, for example, he almost denied Henderson a Cabinet post on the grounds that the latter would be better occupied in organising the party. This was a highly tactless way of dealing with Labour's second most important figure. Long before 1931, MacDonald's liking for aristocratic society had aroused the suspicions of many in his party, who came to feel that his radicalism was superficial. In his essay on MacDonald in *Labour People* (1987), Kenneth Morgan emphasises his subject's lack of an overtly passionate commitment to fighting social injustice. Personally aloof, he led the party as if from a lofty vantage point, a style against which his successors in the 1930s seemed consciously to react.

MacDonald must bear a large part of the blame for Labour's failure, while in opposition from 1924–29, to evolve a distinctive strategy for tackling unemployment. The party's 1928 statement, *Labour and the Nation*, was frustratingly vague. In *A History of the British Labour Party* Andrew Thorpe suggests that it was the production of a leadership that did not expect to win the next election. MacDonald's appointment of the intellectually limited J.H. Thomas as the minister responsible for unemployment policy in June 1929 was particularly uninspired. Even David Marquand acknowledges that MacDonald could have sought solutions with more energy and imagination. He did not try, for example, to introduce protectionist measures, which might have been a partial remedy and which would have commanded the confidence of business interests.

Before the 1931 crisis, MacDonald demonstrated a wish to put the search for consensus ahead of his loyalties to the Labour movement. On taking office in 1929, he appealed to the different sides in the House of Commons to see themselves 'more as a Council of State and less as arrayed regiments facing each other in battle'. It is hard to resist the conclusion that this statement reflected MacDonald's personal preferences and was more than an acknowledgement of the second Labour government's minority status. In August 1931 he listened to the arguments of foreign bankers and of his political opponents, rather than seeking to understand the perspective of the trade union leadership. In the general election of October 1931 he widened the breach with his ex-colleagues by denouncing them for their alleged irresponsibility. The National Labour group that he led after 1931 proved to be a numerically weak parliamentary force, with a negligible grassroots following. Until his resignation in June 1935 MacDonald served as the uncomfortable figurehead of a predominantly Conservative adminis-tration. He ended his career isolated from his old party and with scant influence over the counsels of his new allies.

Conclusion

Which of the two cases, the one for or the one against MacDonald, do you consider the more persuasive? Use the information in the rest of this chapter to support your answer.

David Marquand considers that MacDonald's career demonstrates the need for a radical party to have not only 'high ideals and skilful leadership' but also 'intellectual coherence and a willingness to jettison cherished assumptions in the face of changing realities'. It was MacDonald's tragedy that his conception of Labour's role in the state led him into a position from which his reputation would never fully recover. Nonetheless it would be unfair to lay the blame for the party's 1931 debacle exclusively at his door. The fact that he was twice chosen as Labour's representative figure, in 1911 and again in 1922, says a great deal about the nature of the party. It can be argued that his tenure of the leadership reflects the struc-tural and ideological weaknesses of the Labour movement as much as the limitations of one individual.

5.5 How convincing was Labour's recovery from the disaster of 1931?

Arthur Henderson gravely underestimated the significance of the events of August 1931 when he assured a Labour gathering that 'this is only an interlude in the life of the party, like the war'. Two months after this pro-nouncement, Labour suffered the greatest electoral defeat in its history. It lost 21% of its 1929 share of the poll, winning only 46 seats to the massive 554 secured by National Government candidates. Most of Labour's leading figures, including Henderson himself, lost their seats: some would never return to the Commons again. A significant minority, including Ramsay MacDonald and his son Malcolm (himself a minister in the National Government) formed the National Labour Party. Their support for a Conservative-dominated administration ensured the permanence of the breach with their former colleagues. The memory of MacDonald's 'betrayal' of Labour in 1931 would haunt the party for a generation.

Although Labour recovered its standing a little in the November 1935 general election, winning 154 seats, the National Government enjoyed a majority of over 250. These results did not merely represent the cancella-tion of the tentative gains made by Labour in non-industrial areas during the 1920s. It was even more galling that many of the depressed parts of the country had declined to return Labour MPs. It was hard for the party to overcome the popular perception that it had 'run away' when faced in 1931 with financial crisis. With a Conservative-dominated administration firmly entrenched in power, and an electorate apparently impervious to Labour's appeal, the party's situation seemed bleak.

This section will assess the extent of Labour's problems in the 1930s. To do this it will examine the experience of the party in four key areas: leader-ship, organisation and discipline, the formation of policy and electoral prospects on the eve of the Second World War.

Leadership

The electoral holocaust of 1931 marked the effective end of Arthur Henderson's career as a front-line politician. After MacDonald's defection, he was a natural choice for the position of party leader, but his removal from the Commons made it impossible for him to perform the role adequately. By the time that he returned, as a result of a by-election in 1933, he was an ageing and increasingly irrelevant figure, with only two years to live.

George Lansbury (1859–1940)
The historian A. J. P. Taylor, in his book *English History 1914–1945*, described Lansbury as the 'leader of the emotional Left'. Lansbury had edited the Labour newspaper, the *Daily Herald*, in the early 1920s. He was popular in the Labour movement for his evident sincerity, but lacked governmental experience.

Ernest Bevin (1881–1951)
Bevin rose from humble origins to lead the Dockers' Union. He created and led the Transport and General Workers' Union from 1921–40. In Churchill's wartime coalition he served as Minister of Labour and National Service. As Foreign Secretary from 1945–51 he was one of the key figures in the Attlee governments.

Clement Attlee (1883–1967)
Of middle-class background, Attlee became a socialist to combat the kind of poverty that he witnessed in London's East End before the First World War. He was Chancellor of the Duchy of Lancaster and then Postmaster-General in the second Labour government, and became leader of the party in 1935. He acted as Deputy Prime Minister in Churchill's wartime coalition. In 1945 he led Labour to its first outright electoral victory, serving as Prime Minister until 1951.

Arthur Greenwood (1880–1954)
A schoolmaster by background, Greenwood was Minister of Health in the second Labour government. He was Labour's deputy leader from 1935–45 and held Cabinet posts in both the Churchill coalition and the post-war Labour government. A drink problem soured his later years and his career ended in 1947.

The decimation of Labour's senior figures in the 1931 general election placed the leadership of the parliamentary party in the hands of the only ex-Cabinet minister to secure a place in the Commons. George Lansbury had served in a relatively modest capacity, as First Commissioner of Works, and in normal circumstances would never have been considered for the leadership. Although he stood out as a principled individual, with a strong ethical commitment to social improvement, he was ill-equipped for the exercise of the political arts. His leadership was abruptly terminated during the 1935 party conference, as a result of his uncompromisingly pacifist attitude towards Fascist Italy's threatened invasion of Abyssinia (modern Ethiopia). Publicly denounced for his conscience-driven politics by the movement's most important trade union figure, Ernest Bevin, Lansbury at once retired.

His successor was his former deputy, the almost equally unlikely figure of Clement Attlee. Like Lansbury, the new leader had been projected to the party's front rank by the events of 1931. Dry and uncharismatic, Attlee was widely viewed as a caretaker leader and had little opportunity to make his mark before the party was caught up in the 1935 election. Although Paul Adelman attributes his subsequent confirmation as leader to the feelings of trust that he inspired in the parliamentary party, it is also true that he benefited from the perceived defects of his two rivals. Arthur Greenwood was respected by the rank-and-file but not regarded as a potential leader. Herbert Morrison's inability to win the confidence of Labour's trade union wing made him an inherently more divisive figure.

Hugh Dalton, a junior minister in the 1929–31 government, commented acidly on Attlee's election in his diary, 'and a little mouse shall lead them'. This was a private comment by a notoriously prejudiced observer. Nonetheless it is true that Attlee failed to make a definite impression in the country at large before the outbreak of war four years later. It would take the experience of the war, during which he served as Deputy Prime Minister, to establish him as a potential national leader. Few people in 1935 could have predicted that he would lead Labour until 1955, becoming the longest serving leader of any major British political party in the 20th century.

Organisation and discipline

From an organisational perspective there were grounds for optimism in the 1930s. The continuing rise in individual membership, with some 419,000 members by 1935, was an encouraging sign.

Nevertheless this development brought its own problems for the leadership, with the growth of a constituency parties movement, intent on securing a greater say in policy making. An increased representation for the constituency section on the party's National Executive was pushed through in the face of trade union resistance at the 1937 conference. As Paul Adelman points out in *The Rise of the Labour Party 1880–1945* (1996), individual spokesmen who were elected to the Executive found themselves entrapped there by the trade union majority.

Perhaps the most striking feature of Labour politics in the 1930s was the further strengthening of the trade union movement's influence at the highest levels of the party. In 1934 the National Joint Council, on which the TUC, the National Executive and the Parliamentary Labour Party had enjoyed equal representation, was transformed into the National Council of Labour. On this body the TUC, whose dominant figure was the Transport Workers' chief, Ernest Bevin, secured seven of the thirteen available seats. One should not, however, exaggerate the role of this new body. As Ben Pimlott, author of a major study of *Labour and the Left in the*

1930s (1977) argues, the main function of the National Joint Council was not to determine policy but to give weight to the pronouncements of the party as a whole. The National Executive remained the most important component in the party's structure; in May 1940 it would take the crucial decision to commit Labour to membership of the wartime coalition.

One of the major themes of the decade was the failure of the left to make a lasting impact on Labour politics. Superficially the aftermath of the 1931 crisis, with the future of capitalism apparently in question, offered an unprecedented opportunity to the advocates of radical socialism. Sir Stafford Cripps, who had served as Solicitor-General under MacDonald, emerged as the champion of the left, declaring in October 1931 that 'the one thing that is not inevitable now is gradualness'. The following year the Independent Labour Party, disgusted with the ineffectual 'reformism' of the leadership, disaffiliated from the party. Some of its members formed the Socialist League, a left-wing pressure group calling for a militant response to any institutions that might try to hamper the programme of a future Labour administration.

Nevertheless the party as a whole remained firmly committed to parliamentary, rather than revolutionary, methods. In particular mainstream Labour opinion refused to be attracted by Socialist League demands for a 'united front' with other left-wing groups, including the Communist Party, to resist the growth of fascism. It was widely believed that such a strategy was 'a trap for innocents', a cover for Communist infiltration of the Labour movement. Conflict within the party came to a head in 1937, when the Socialist League agreed, under pressure from the National Executive, to dissolve itself.

In 1938, with Nazism on the march in Europe, Cripps attempted to build a wider 'popular front'. This was intended to embrace not only Socialists and Communists but also dissident Conservatives and Liberals who were opposed to the appeasement policies of the National Government. The scheme was ruined partly by the refusal of all except a handful of Conservative mavericks to rebel against their own leaders. It was also doomed by the belief of Labour Party managers, that it was simply another version of the discredited 'united front'. As Attlee later recalled, 'Labour leaders were very conscious of how many democratic socialist parties on the Continent had been given the kiss of death by the Communist Party'. Cripps' refusal to abandon the project led to his expulsion, together with that of his leading supporters, a decision that was endorsed by the Labour conference in May 1939.

At one level Labour was damaged by its absorption in internal disputes on the eve of a major international conflict. Nonetheless it is worth noting that the expulsions were a temporary disciplinary measure. Cripps had a long and respectable career ahead as a minister in the wartime coalition and as a post-war Chancellor of the Exchequer. Not for the last time in Labour's history, a former rebel was to be transformed into a pillar of the party establishment. As Andrew Thorpe argues in *A History of the British Labour Party*, the party leadership correctly perceived that the benefits of pacts with Communists and other groups were minimal. In the political conditions of the late 1930s, Labour could not have regained power by such means. The hard left, with its ideological zeal, its underdeveloped economic ideas and ambivalence towards parliamentary government, represented a political dead end.

The formation of policy

The TUC had initiated a reappraisal of economic policy before the crisis of 1931 made such an exercise essential. Although Labour maintained its rhetorical allegiance to 'socialism', in practice the party's dominant ideas in the 1930s owed more to Keynesian concepts of managed capitalism. This was certainly the inspiration behind plans for public works, financed out of national credit and linked to proposals for a maximum working week and the raising of the school leaving age. The purpose was to revive employment by using the resources of the state to stimulate the level of demand in the economy.

By contrast with the MacDonald era, Labour paid close attention to the details of policy making. Policy committees utilised the talents of young economists such as Evan Durbin and Hugh Gaitskell, a future leader of the party. *Labour's immediate programme*, adopted in 1937, detailed a five-year-plan for state-directed investment, together with the public ownership of key industries and services. The underlying assumption was that capitalism was not, as expected earlier in the decade, doomed to final collapse in the near future. Labour's pragmatic thinkers were prepared to accept this reality, while laying plans to make the national economy work in the interests of the people as a whole. Under the influence of Herbert Morrison, the model for the new nationalised industries would be the public corporation. This meant that policy-making for each major industry would be in the hands of a board appointed by a government minister. The notion of 'workers' control' was downplayed in favour of an essentially statist approach to economic management. This concept would be the blueprint for the nationalisation programme pursued by the 1945–51 Labour governments.

By contrast it took much longer to evolve a coherent and agreed position on foreign affairs. The challenge of fascism presented Labour with a difficult set of choices. Although only a minority shared the uncompromising pacifism of Lansbury, a large section of the parliamentary party felt that a capitalist government could not be trusted with responsibility for rearmament. This meant that for much of the decade, the party maintained an illogical stance. While proclaiming its support for collective security through the agency of the League of Nations, until 1937 Labour voted annually in the Commons against the funding of rearmament. A minority, typified by Ernest Bevin and Hugh Dalton, took the straightforward view that fascism, which was responsible for the suppression of free trade unions on the Continent, must be resisted at all costs.

From 1937 the worsening of the international situation, together with the election of Bevin as chairman of the TUC General Council and of Dalton as chairman of the National Executive, served to undermine the case against rearmament. By the time of the 1938 Munich conference, Labour had at last united in opposition to the appeasement of Hitler. Even then, the conscription measures introduced by the Chamberlain administration in April 1939 met with hostility from the party. Nonetheless the party was unequivocal in its support for the declaration of war later in the year.

Electoral prospects

In a sense, the policies adopted by a party in opposition are an irrelevant issue. Elections are more commonly lost by the government of the day than won by the opposition. What, then, can be learned regarding Labour's prospects of power from the electoral record of the 1930s?

Between the general elections of 1931 and 1935, Labour made ten gains in by-elections, a development that was parallelled by a modest recovery at municipal level. In the 1935 contest Labour made a net gain of 94 seats. Tom Stannage, author of *Baldwin thwarts the opposition* (1980), a study of the election, has calculated that in the 450 constituencies where valid statistical comparison is possible, this represented a nationwide swing of 9.4% in the party's favour. The swing was strongest in London and in areas such as Lancashire, west Yorkshire, north-east England and southern Scotland, where the most marginal recovery from the slump had been experienced. The limits of Labour's success are perhaps just as significant. In industrial South Wales the party won 16 seats, compared with 22 in 1929; in the Midlands, the respective figures were 11 and 35. Rising wages in many occupations, together with a drop in the cost of living and a widespread expectation of a continuing decrease in unemployment, meant that many working-class voters were generally satisfied with the National Government.

Labour fought the 1935 general election under the severe handicap of a recent change of leadership, following a public display of disunity at the party conference. Moreover, as Stannage emphasises, the party was far behind the National Government in the handling of the new media of wireless and newsreel. Ironically for the party of change, Labour seemed most at home with traditional campaigning methods, which were not best suited to courting the votes of an uncommitted mass electorate. Labour spokesmen simply could not compete with the sophisticated mastery of broadcasting technique displayed by the Prime Minister, Stanley Baldwin.

Between the 1935 general election and the outbreak of war, Labour won 13 by-elections and lost none. However, the overall impression by 1939 was one of a party that had reached, in Andrew Thorpe's words, an 'electoral plateau'. Labour failed to regain five parliamentary seats, which it had won in 1929 but had subsequently lost. In English and Welsh municipal elections, the party's gains were far from dramatic. In 1936 it lost five of its 19 Scottish burghs; by 1938 the total had recovered to a modest 14. It seems hard to escape the conclusion that, had a peacetime general election been held in 1939–40, Labour would have stood little chance of victory. The electoral hill to be climbed was simply too steep. It would take the transforming effect of the Second World War on British society to make possible the change in popular attitudes from which issued Labour's 1945 triumph.

1. Why did the Labour left fail to take control of the party's destiny in the 1930s? Use the information given in the section to answer this question.

2. Did the 1935 general election represent a significant revival for the Labour Party? Give reasons to support your answer.

British foreign and imperial policy, 1918–1939

Key Issues

● *In what ways did British policy towards Europe change between 1918 and 1939?*

● *How was Britain able to maintain its position as a world power between 1918 and 1939?*

● *How did British policy towards the Empire change in the period 1918 to 1939?*

Framework of Events

1917	November: Balfour Declaration on the creation of a Jewish homeland in Palestine
1918	November: Germany and Austro-Hungary accept US President Wilson's Fourteen Points as a basis for an armistice
1919–1920	Paris peace conferences
1919	League of Nations Covenant is approved
	April: Amritsar massacre
	Government of India Act, introducing Montagu-Chelmsford reforms
	Introduction of Ten Year Rule
1921	Imperial Conference
1921–22	Washington Naval Conference
1922	Chanak crisis
	Genoa Conference on European economic reconstruction
1924	Dawes Plan
1925	Treaty of Locarno
1928	Kellogg-Briand Pact, outlawing war
1929	Young Plan
	New York Stock Exchange collapse
1931	Statute of Westminster
1932	Geneva Disarmament Conference
	Imperial Economic Conference, Ottawa
1933	January: Hitler becomes German Chancellor
	Germany leaves League of Nations and Disarmament Conference
1935	Stresa agreements between Britain, France and Italy
	Anglo-German naval agreement
1936	Hitler remilitarises the Rhineland and denounces Locarno Treaty
1937	Neville Chamberlain becomes Prime Minister
1938	Germany annexes Austria and declares *Anschluss*
	Munich Agreements between Britain, Germany and France on Czechoslovakia

1939	March: Germany occupies Bohemia and Moravia in Czechoslovakia
	March: Anglo-French guarantee of Poland
	August: Nazi-Soviet pact
	1 September: Germany invades Poland
	3 September: Britain and France declare war on Germany

Overview

AFTER the First World War British governments continued to believe that they had a right to guide world affairs, preferably to the benefit of British interests. This belief derived from Britain's international role in the 19th century. Britain's security seemed assured after the First World War:

- As a victor in the First World War, Britain had a major hand in drawing up the peace settlements.

- The League of Nations appeared to provide a means of maintaining peace.

- The Royal Navy was pre-eminent in Europe, with the dismantling of the German fleet.

There were, however, problems ahead:

- Germany was politically, socially and economically unstable. Its extremist politicians were already preaching **revisionism and revanchism**.

- A growing fear of **Bolshevism**. This proclaimed itself in conflict with all non-Communists and posed a threat which was very well understood by Lloyd George and Winston Churchill.

- France feared renewed German aggression but at the same time was causing problems in the Near East **mandated territories**.

- Colonial nationalism threatened violent opposition to British rule, especially in India and Ireland.

- Economic difficulties created major problems and limited diplomatic and strategic options.

Britain's foreign policy in the interwar period was much concerned with attempts to deal with what were seen as Germany's legitimate complaints by revising the terms of the Versailles Treaty, but without alarming the French. The **League of Nations Covenant** was called upon to limit aggressive intent by **arbitration**, for example the French occupation of the Ruhr. Germany's problem of debt was tackled by means of the Dawes Plan of April 1924 and the Young Plan of June 1929. Germany's borders in the west were settled by the Locarno Pact of December 1925.

Additionally there were problems within the Empire. The **White Dominions** (see section 6.4) wanted complete independence. Indian Nationalists were actively agitating for the same. These problems were met by Britain as they arose and addressed in longer-term strategy, with the White Dominions' demand being granted and the Indians being given some self-government. While some of the problems of the 1920s were being settled, new ones were arising. During the

---

Revisionism: Seeking to revise unpopular treaty provisions, in this instance the Treaty of Versailles.

Revanchism: Policy directed towards regaining lost territory.

Bolshevism: The revolutionary communist wing of the Russian Social Democratic Party, led by Lenin, which seized power in October/November 1917.

Mandated territories: Colonies which formerly belonged to Germany and non-Turkish areas of the Ottoman empire that were administered by First World War Allies (e.g. Britain and France) on behalf of the League of Nations.

League of Nations Covenant: The constitution (the formal guiding rules and principles) of the League of Nations, adopted at the Paris Peace Conference in April 1919.

Arbitration: Settling a dispute where the parties involved agree to accept the decision of another person or organisation to act as judge.

White Dominions: Self-governing countries of the British Commonwealth: Australia, Canada, New Zealand and South Africa.

1930s the League of Nations Covenant was called upon to settle disputes, but arbitration proved unsuccessful against the increasingly bellicose 'dictators' Hitler and Mussolini, and Japanese aggression in China.

Failures of the League included:

Annexation: To take possession of a territory, particularly without right to do so.

- League of Nations' condemnation of Japanese **annexation** of Manchuria provoked Japan to leave the League.

- The Geneva Disarmament Conferences were abandoned in 1933 when Hitler flatly refused to take part. Germany also left the League of Nations. His intentions were not disarmament but the strengthening of Germany's armaments to pursue his aggressive and **expansionist** foreign policy aims.

Expansionist: Seeking to enlarge the state, not always by internationally acceptable means.

- Hitler's revisionism and revanchism aroused the envy of Mussolini. He abandoned his stance as international guarantor of peace to become Hitler's ally, and followed an expansionist foreign policy similar to Hitler's.

- The limited ability of the League of Nations to punish aggression was further demonstrated by ineffective enforcement of sanctions against Mussolini after his invasion of Abyssinia.

Ten Year Rule: The Chiefs of Staff did not anticipate Britain becoming involved in a war within ten years.

Britain could read the warning signs and abandoned the **Ten Year Rule** in 1932. The possibility of appeasing Hitler proved to be an illusion because his 'reasonable' demands grew increasingly less so, until they reached the point where they moved from Treaty revision to outright aggression. For example, in March 1939 Hitler occupied Bohemia and Moravia, the Czech part of Czechoslovakia. Slovakia became a puppet state, but was still technically independent.

Collective security: The idea was that future war could be prevented if all members of the League of Nations acted together against a potential aggressor.

Collective security proved to be unrealisable because Britain and France did not feel strong enough to oppose Hitler, but would not confront Hitler by forming an alliance with the Soviet Union because they mistrusted Bolshevism. Thus Britain's apparent security after the First World War was reversed as its position as world leader and mastery of the Empire came to be challenged by nationalism within the Empire and from Europe and the Far East.

6.1 What limits were there on Britain's ability to pursue an independent foreign policy between 1918 and 1939?

Britain had run the Empire on limited means. Nevertheless, it had possessed the largest navy in the world and had widespread influence from running a large Empire. Some independence in its foreign policy direction had been maintained before the First World War. But after bearing the huge cost of the war and owing war debts to the United States, which had to be repaid, the advantages of following an independent foreign policy had to be calculated against the difficulty of finding the money to pay for it. This had the effect of limiting Britain's freedom of action.

What were Britain's main foreign policy aims between 1918 and 1939 and how far had they changed since 1900?

Britain's foreign policy aims remained broadly consistent with those followed between 1900 and 1918. What altered was how they could be achieved in the changed world circumstances after the First World War. The aims were to:

- re-establish a peace which would enable Britain to pursue the commercial interests which were essential for the health of the British economy. This was to be achieved by securing peace settlements which were not unfavourable to British interests, to be maintained through the League of Nations;

- maintain Britain's status as a world power. This would involve safeguarding economic, defence and foreign policy interests around the world;

- maintain the Empire as far as was possible, while limiting opposition;

- prevent the spread of Bolshevism (communism);

- in the 1920s, to avoid involvement in expensive continental commitments, such as guarantees of French security against Germany;

- in the 1930s, to maintain peace, in order to buy time for rearmament.

What were the limits on foreign policy?

Liquidated: The results of assets sold off to pay for something.

Solvent: Having sufficient assets to pay any debts.

The government had an obligation to fund social reforms at home, police the Empire and maintain a world position built on pre-war power and influence. Although far from bankrupt, Britain's financial resources had been seriously drained by the effort to achieve victory in the First World War because vital assets had to be **liquidated**. Beginning the war rich and **solvent**, during its course Britain built up enormous debts (£959 million) to the United States. These limits underpinned the formulation of British foreign, Empire and defence policies, obliging Britain to make hard budgetary choices.

Prime Minister Andrew Bonar Law, in a letter to *The Times* dated 7 October 1922, suggested that 'we cannot alone act as policeman of the world. The financial and social condition of this country makes it impossible'. If Britain were not supported, then it would be unable 'to bear the burden alone but shall have no alternative except to imitate the government of the United States and to restrict our attention to the safeguarding of the more immediate interests of the British Empire'.

The Lloyd George government of 1916 to 1922 had fed the expectation of demobilising forces that they would return to social reforms and 'homes fit for heroes' (see chapter 3). These too would have to be funded out of depleted resources. End-of-war exhaustion was masked by the optimism which followed the war's end, but a brief post-war boom (1919–21) was swiftly followed by an economic slump (from 1921). Unemployment increased in Britain's staple industries, coal, cotton, ship-building and engineering. Because these industries were running down, demand for materials from the Empire to feed them decreased. Without the income from export of their raw materials, the Empire could not afford to buy back finished goods, increasing the effect of the downward spiral.

Main Foreign Secretaries 1918–1939

Marquess Curzon	October 1919 – January 1924
Ramsey MacDonald	January – November 1924
Austen Chamberlain	November 1924 – June 1929
John Simon	November 1931 – June 1935
Samuel Hoare	June 1935 – December 1935
Anthony Eden	December 1935 – February 1938
The Earl of Halifax	February 1938 – May 1940

With financial resources reduced by war debts and economic slump, Britain's commitment to manage and police the Empire nevertheless remained undiminished. The task was increased by responsibility for Egypt. It also involved responsibility for Palestine and Iraq, which were mandated territories, that had formerly been part of the Ottoman Empire. Additionally, the war had re-enforced the White Dominions' and India's desire for increased independence. Independence for the White Dominions was conceded during the war. Indian nationalist agitation required careful handling because the British government did not feel ready to give independence at that stage (see Section 6.4).

How did Britain deal with budgetary limitations on the formulation of defence policy?

Britain coped with this problem by cutting back on defence expenditure to balance budgets. Military commitment on the continent of Europe was potentially too costly to be considered. It was side-stepped at the Paris peace conference of 1919–20, but by doing so, Britain fed French fears about being left to meet potential German aggression alone. Savings were made by cutting the number of men in the armed forces from 3.5 million to 370,000 between the end of the war in 1918 and 1920. Defence cuts were justified by a Ten Year Rule, introduced in 1919, by which war was not foreseen for ten years ahead. Lloyd George justified cuts in defence spending when he told Service chiefs that 'they need not prepare for war as it was not foreseen for at least ten years'. The rule was renewed annually until 1932.

By 1930 British defence spending had been reduced below the level spent in 1910 and armed forces manpower was below the 1914 level, with the army bearing the brunt of the cutbacks. The army's chief role was colonial policeman, and defence responsibilities had been increased by addition of the mandates of Palestine and Iraq. Britain had therefore effectively lowered its standard of security in the Mediterranean, India and the Far East, despite the threats to stability posed by Bolshevism and unrest in Ireland, India and China.

1. What were Britain's foreign policy aims after 1918?

2. What were the factors that affected Britain's ability to pursue an independent foreign policy?

3. How effectively did Britain cope with a wide range of foreign and defence policy commitments?

6.2 How did Britain deal with the problems created by the post-war settlements of 1919–20?

What were Britain's aims in the Paris peace settlements?

At the Paris peace conference that began in January 1919, Lloyd George negotiated for Britain. He aimed to create a lasting settlement that would require no active British participation in European affairs. The British public rejected **pre-1914 diplomacy**, and the Paris peace settlements aimed to keep Britain out of entangling continental alliances. Britain refused to satisfy the French need for guarantees against future German aggression. The League of Nations was set up to contain conflict and keep the peace world-wide at low cost. Reparations (a war indemnity) were sought from Germany to finance payment of war debts to America and social reforms. But how much was to be forthcoming, given the scale of German war debts, and post-war political and economic turmoil?

Of all the settlements reached at the Paris Peace Conference, it was the Treaty of Versailles with Germany that was the most controversial and posed the greatest difficulty for Britain. Writing the peace settlements was a problem of balance, and the negotiators were faced by too many conflicting rights and demands. In his Fontainbleau memorandum of 25 March 1919

Pre-1914 diplomacy: This refers to the series of treaty arrangements and secret deals which preceded the First World War and which, in effect, tripped Europe into war rather than negotiation.

Dichotomy: Separation of ideas into two mutually exclusive classes.

Weimar Republic: The German government between the abdication of the Kaiser and Hitler becoming Chancellor (1918–1933).

Fait accompli: Something that has already been done.

Diktat: A German word meaning a treaty imposed upon the defeated.

Armistice: Truce; cessation of arms for a stipulated time.

Lloyd George summed up the **dichotomy**. The twin aims of France and Britain were to crush Germany and prevent the spread of Bolshevism. But, if Germany was crushed too hard, this might encourage the spread of Bolshevism. He thought that a harsh settlement would undermine the **Weimar Republic** and possibly bring more war to Europe. But he had also to bear in mind the claims of France. A large part of French industry was located in the north-east, near the coal fields. which for four years had been the site of the battlefront. French industry had been largely destroyed and its industrial manpower seriously depleted by the enormous amount of its war dead (1,357,800 against losses of 908,371 from the British Empire, not just Britain).

The allies spent four months considering peace terms. Presented to Germany in May 1919 as a *fait accompli*, they were regarded by the Germans as a *diktat* because they considered that the **armistice** terms had entitled them to negotiate a settlement.

What were the main terms of the Treaty of Versailles?

- Reparations of £6,600 million, plus interest, to be paid to the First World War victors, decided by an Inter-Allied Reparations Commission in 1921;

- Union (*Anschluss*) of Germany and Austria prohibited;

- Acceptance of a war guilt clause (Article 231);

- The German military to be reduced, for example the army to be limited to 100,000 men, with few military supplies (weaponry and ammunition) permitted. The navy was similarly restricted; and the air force abolished.

German territorial losses included:

- Surrender of German colonies – German East Africa (Tanganyika), German South-West Africa. The Cameroons, Togoland – to be mandates of the League of Nations (see page 105);

- Alsace-Lorraine to be returned to France;

- Eupen-Malmedy to be given to Belgium (after a plebiscite – national vote – in 1920) and Memel to Lithuania (1923);

- Northern Schleswig to Denmark (after plebiscite in 1920);

- Danzig to become a free city under League of Nations control;

- Poznan, part of Upper Silesia (after 1921 plebiscite) and parts of East Prussia to Poland;

- The Saar to enjoy special status under the control of the League of Nations for 15 years until a plebiscite to decide its future (1935) – France in the meantime to control the Saar coalmines;

- The Rhineland to be demilitarised and under Allied occupation for 15 years;

The Treaty also contained the Covenant of the League of Nations. The American Congress refused to ratify the Treaty and Germany signed it only under protest, thereby increasing Britain's difficulties.

Why was the League of Nations formed after the First World War?

The League of Nations Covenant was signed in February 1919 to set up an international organisation that aimed to settle disputes by arbitration and so preserve the peace. It had been put forward by US President Wilson as one of his **Fourteen Points**. The League's Constitution was adopted at the Paris Peace Conference and incorporated into each of the four peace treaties: Versailles with Germany, St. Germain with Austria, Sèvres with Turkey and Trianon with Hungary.

Fourteen Points: US President Woodrow Wilson's war aims, which were published in January 1918.

The League of Nations Covenant also provided for disarmament, but this aim was never achieved. A series of conferences were held at Geneva between 1928 and 1934. Sixty nations participated, including the United States and the Soviet Union. They failed because the French insisted that a general security scheme should come before disarmament. Before agreement on disarmament could be reached, Hitler withdrew Germany from the League in October 1933. This effectively ended plans for disarmament.

Why did Britain support the idea of the League of Nations?

The League was seen by Britain as an ideal way of achieving some of Britain's foreign policy aims. The League would spread the burden and cost of keeping world peace. Britain's defence position was undermined by spending cuts which had the effect of limiting Britain's ability to defend its world-wide interests.

The League provided Britain with an excuse to avoid giving a guarantee of security to France against German aggression. This would have bolstered French confidence and underpinned the Treaty of Versailles.

What were the problems that faced the League?

In order for the aims of the League to be achievable every state would have to either join or remain a member. But, the United States never became a member. Germany adopted membership only between 1926 and 1933. The Soviet Union was a member only between 1934 and 1940. The Japanese left the League in 1933, after the League imposed **sanctions** against them for invading Manchuria. Similarly, Italy left in 1937 after sanctions were imposed because of their invasion of Abyssinia (Ethiopia).

Sanctions: Penalties imposed on one country by another or by a group of countries. For instance the refusal to trade.

Arthur Balfour, chief British representative at the League of Nations in 1920, was aware of the potential weaknesses of the League. He reminded the British Cabinet that the 'chief instruments at the disposal of the League are: Public Discussion; Judicial investigation; Arbitration; and, in the last resort … some form of Compulsion. These are powerful weapons but the places where they seem least applicable are those … where nothing but force is understood …' The greatest weakness of the League lay in the fact that its only agreed method of compulsion was the imposition of sanctions. Methods of exerting compulsion by the use of force were never agreed and remained unspecified. Thus, in the last resort, the League had no method of enforcing its decisions.

Why was Britain involved in the Chanak crisis in 1922?

Another difficulty for Britain arising from the Paris Peace settlements was the Chanak crisis of 1922. An Allied army (which included British forces) was occupying the Straits (the Dardanelles) to safeguard the eastern Mediterranean after the end of the First World War. In 1920 the Turkish nationalist leader, Kemal Ataturk, rejected the terms of the Treaty of Sèvres of 1920 with the Ottoman (Turkish) Empire. A war

1. In what ways did the Paris Peace Settlement meet Britain's war aims?

2. How fair were the terms of the Treaty of Versailles? Give reasons for your answer.

3. How far did the League of Nations go to meet Britain's security aims?

began between Turkey and Greece in 1920 over Turkish territory occupied mainly by Greeks and given to Greece under the Sevres Treaty. The Chanak crisis of September–October 1922 began when it was feared that the Turks would attack the Allied army occupying the Straits. The crisis was settled by discussion between local commanders who agreed the terms of the Convention of Mudania of October 1922. The Convention stated that the Straits would remain neutral (to suit Britain) in return for Eastern Thrace and Adrianople being returned to Turkey. In 1923 the Treaty of Lausanne was agreed with the Turks, to replace the Treaty of Sèvres.

The crisis highlighted Dominions' discontent with the current situation concerning who should formulate their foreign policy, with the Canadians seeking first to place the problem before the Canadian Parliament rather than instantly answering Britain's appeal for support, as had Australia and New Zealand.

6.3 What problems did Britain face in the 1920s in dealing with European affairs?

The French occupation of the Ruhr

In the hope of making the Germans deliver quotas of Ruhr coal to France, as part of the reparations agreed under the Versailles treaty terms, France occupied the Ruhr from 1923 to 1925. The idea was for France to seize Ruhr coal and put pressure on the Germans to pay up.

Isolation: In diplomatic terms, isolation means not being tied into a treaty or having diplomatic obligations.

Entente Powers: Britain, France and Russia, who were allies between 1907 and 1917

Ratify: To approve a treaty.

The European foreign policy problems facing Britain in the 1920s were:

● French distrust of Germany and need for a guarantee for France against renewed German aggression;

● America's withdrawal into **isolation**, after having set the agenda at the Paris Peace Conference, and unwillingness either to take responsibility for problems caused by its withdrawal, or compound war debts until faced with the economic consequences of such refusal;

● Germany's economic crises and suspension of reparations payments;

● French occupation of the Ruhr in pursuit of financial compensation;

● Germany's aim to revise the terms of the Treaty of Versailles.

What problems for Britain and Europe arose from the American policy of isolation?

The United States of America, whose participation in the First World War had swung the balance in favour of victory for the **Entente Powers**, retired into isolationism in 1919. The United States refused to **ratify** the Treaty of Versailles and consequently did not join the League of Nations. Britain was left with the problem of maintaining peace in Europe after the Paris peace conference.

US President Wilson's Fourteen Points had provided a basis for the German agreement to an armistice in November 1918. The Fourteen Points also set the principles on which the peace negotiations were based. The British and the French believed the Americans would join with them in guaranteeing the peace settlement. The Americans did not keep their assurances to France that they, with Britain, would guarantee French security against Germany. The French therefore regarded some of terms of the Treaty of Versailles as invalidated by US non-participation and British unwillingness to give a unilateral guarantee. France was further worried by British willingness to accept the possibility that the settlement of Germany's eastern frontiers might be renegotiated at some future date.

What economic crises were caused by the issue of reparations payments?

Reparations from Germany were demanded as part of the peace settlement, in compensation for all damage to the Allied civilian population and their property, for example destruction of civilian shipping by German submarines. Lloyd George also pressed for compensation for war wounded, war widows and orphans: 'Germany must pay the cost of the war up to the limits of her capacity'.

Because of British and French war debts to America, reparations had been set too high at 50 million golden marks (£6,600 million). The justification for reparations was the decision that Germany was to blame for the First World War. Article 231 of the Treaty of Versailles assigned war guilt to Germany. However, Germany was not in a position to pay the reparations without facing social unrest in a country already affected by political extremism. John Maynard Keynes saw the potential problems, which he explained in *The Economic Consequences of the Peace* (1919), deploring the exclusion of 'provisions for the economic rehabilitation of Europe'.

The United States had emerged from the First World War richer, because the war had increased their gold reserves and industries. But they were unwilling to take on the role of world policeman. They further made it difficult to achieve fair and just peace settlements by insistence on repayment of war debts in full. Lloyd George saw that improvement in the German economy could help Britain's post-war revival. Britain had suggested that they might accept cancellation of German war debts to them, if the Americans would cancel debts owed to them by the Allies. The United States was hostile to this suggestion.

What problems arose from Franco-German distrust during the 1920s?

In the 1920s Britain was thus left to deal with two international relations problems arising from the peace settlement. On the one hand Britain sought to avoid involvement in guaranteeing French security, while at the same time calming French fears about the prospects of being at the receiving end of further German aggression. On the other hand, Britain was unwilling to make **unilateral** concessions to Germany to defuse social and political unrest, despite a growing feeling that the terms of the Treaty of Versailles were undeservedly harsh. This feeling was fostered by political agitators, such as Adolf Hitler and Wolfgang Kapp, as well as the German military High Command. They all rejected the idea that Germany had actually been defeated, instead placing the blame for accepting the armistice terms on the German civilian Social Democrat (SPD) government.

Politicians in Britain realised very early in the 1920s that some of the terms of the Treaty of Versailles would probably need to be revised. Winston Churchill, for instance, saw that Britain had commercial motives for wanting to see the revival of the German economy. For this reason he was not only 'anxious to see friendship grow up and the hatred of war die' but equally 'anxious to see trade relations develop with Germany'. But he saw that 'any friendly relations which grow up in time between Britain and Germany will be terribly suspect to France' for fear 'England is more the friend of Germany than of France'. He therefore suggested that Britain should give the French a Treaty which 'bound the British Empire to protect France against unprovoked aggression by Germany. This would then give Britain 'greater freedom to establish new relations, new co-operation with Germany'.

The French desire to keep Germany down and enforce the terms of the Treaty of Versailles, especially where they concerned territory and

Unilateral: One sided, without anything being done in return.

reparations was potentially destabilising to European peace, as were German economic instability and social unrest. British diplomats recognised that the Versailles settlement was likely to provoke war unless two particular sources of German dissatisfaction were lessened: territorial losses to Poland and Czechoslovakia in the east and the economic consequences of reparations.

In 1922 France and Britain differed over reparations again. Britain was willing to agree to suspend reparations payments but France insisted on full repayment on schedule. The Germans stopped reparations payments and in 1923 France occupied the German Ruhr region, seeking to force Britain and the United States to support a new reparations scheme. But Britain could see that French actions were making German instability worse.

Under the Dawes Plan of April 1924, Germany's finances were restructured, although this involved a large US loan to Germany. At the London Reparations Conference of July and August 1924, Britain got Germany and France to accept the Dawes Plan. On that basis the Germans agreed to resume reparations payments and the French to withdraw from the Ruhr. But the incident had demonstrated an underlying weakness of post-war settlements. It showed that the reparations payments to be made by Germany had to be based on a realistic assessment of what Germany could afford to pay. To ignore this fact risked undermining the German economy and causing social and political unrest.

Why were Anglo-Soviet relations so unsatisfactory during the 1920s?

After the October/November 1917 Revolution, the Bolsheviks had announced that Communist Russia was in a state of war with every other non-communist state, including Britain. Only agreement of a Treaty of Mutual Non-Aggression between Britain and the Communist Russians could end this state of war. Anglo-Soviet hostility also derived from three other issues:

● The British resented the fact that the Bolsheviks had withdrawn from the First World War and made a separate peace treaty with the Germans at Brest-Litovsk in 1918. This meant that the Bolsheviks had freed the part of the German army that had been fighting on the Eastern front to fight on the Western Front. As a result Communist Russia was given no role at the Paris Peace Conference.

● Anglo/Russian hostility had been made worse in 1919 by British intervention in the Russian Civil War of 1918–21. Against the advice of Lloyd George, Winston Churchill had sent an expedition of British forces to Archangel (North Russia, near north Finland) to fight on behalf of the White Russians (non-communists).

● The British government also resented the activities in Britain of the Comintern (the Communist International), which the Bolsheviks had established in March 1919. The Comintern's role was to try to create political unrest and possibly Communist revolution in non-communist states. A Communist Party of Great Britain was set up in 1920. The British government was especially concerned about Communist exploitation of economic depression and unemployment in Britain in the 1920s and 1930s (see chapter 3).

How successful was Britain in attempts to improve Anglo-Soviet relations?

Lloyd George was keen to establish peace with the Bolsheviks in order to restore commercial trading relations with the new regime, but only if 'Communistic principles are abandoned'. Then he would be ready to 'assist in the economic development of Russia', which he thought would also help the British economy. When the Soviet Union abandoned the 'War Economy' of 1918–21 and embarked upon a more liberal economic policy in 1921 (the New Economic Policy) this was seen as a potential change of heart in Bolshevik political, economic and social policies. Lloyd George was unsuccessful because the Bolsheviks had not really abandoned 'communist principles'.

Lloyd George tried to get the Soviet Union diplomatically **recognised**. He was unsuccessful because mistrust of Bolshevism prevailed. Lloyd George also tried to tie the '**pariah**' nations, Germany and the Soviet Union, into the European power system. In 1922, at the Genoa conference on European Economic Reconstruction, not only was he unsuccessful in this aim, but Germany and the Soviet Union drew closer together, by means of the 'secret' Rapallo Treaty of 1922. Under its terms Germany and the Soviet Union established diplomatic relations, agreed mutual renunciation of financial claims and also agreed to co-operate on military training. This enabled the German **Reichswehr** to side-step the terms of the Treaty of Versailles by training on Soviet territory. This did not improve Anglo-Soviet relations.

In 1924 the incoming Labour government was more successful in improving Anglo-Soviet relations. It recognised the Soviet Union and attempted to establish mutually beneficial commercial relations. However, links with the Bolsheviks were seen as discrediting the Labour party, who were compromised by the '**Zinoviev Letter**', which confirmed **Reds-under-the-bed** phobia. They were further compromised by the 1926 General Strike.

In 1927 Anglo-Soviet diplomatic relations were severed, after the 'Arcos' raid on a Soviet trade mission by the British secret service. The results of the raid were inconclusive but relations were still damaged. Anglo-Soviet relations were also damaged by British fears about Soviet intentions in China, where the activities of Comintern agent Michael Borodin were encouraging Communists and Nationalists to strikes and riots which were damaging British trading privileges and interests. Fears were also raised about Soviet interests in, and intentions towards, Indian nationalists. Nevertheless, on its return to power in 1929, the Labour government succeeded in restoring diplomatic relations with the Soviet Union.

How far did Britain's foreign policy go to meet French fears and Germany's grievances in the 1920s?

It was recognised that the League of Nations could not guarantee peace and that efforts would have to be made to reconcile Franco-German distrust. Although Germany had signed the Treaty of Versailles, many Germans did not accept that they had thoroughly lost the war. The scale of Germany's defeat had little impact because German territory had not been occupied by the victors, and Germany had not been physically damaged by the war in the way that France and Belgium had suffered. The German illusion that they had not been defeated underpinned Germany's unwillingness to accept the territorial settlements imposed at Versailles and its determination to seek renegotiation of these settlements. It was this determination that made France nervous about the Franco-German borders and necessitated the meeting at Locarno in the autumn of 1925 which produced the Locarno Treaty.

A solution to the problem of French security put to Prime Minister Ramsey MacDonald in 1924, which he was willing to pursue, was a 'Geneva **protocol**'. Under this protocol the League of Nations would

Recognise: In the diplomatic sense, to recognise signifies the establishment of formal diplomatic relations, which involves the opening of an official Embassy, staffed by accredited diplomats, with the ambassador being received by the ruler.

Pariah: Social outcast, e.g. Russia or Germany after the First World War.

Reichswehr: The German armed forces. From 1934 the word Wehrmacht is used.

Zinoviev Letter: A letter said to have been sent to British communists by Grigory Zinoviev, who was Chairman of the Comintern, pressing them to promote revolution by acts of sedition (agitation and rebellion). Published in British newspapers four days before a general election, it is credited with having persuaded middle-class opinion to vote Conservative. The Labour Party, which lost the election, considered it to be a forgery, planted for the purpose of increasing Conservative support.

Reds-under-the-bed: A term expressing the fear that Communist spies were to be found everywhere (even under your bed).

Protocol: Original draft of treaty terms forming part of a diplomatic document that has been agreed after negotiation at a conference.

oversee disarmament and compulsory arbitration between disputing nations. The idea was dropped by incoming Foreign Secretary, Austen Chamberlain, who had a different agenda.

What were the main aims of the Locarno Treaty of December 1925?

Aristide Briand (1862–1932)
Politician of the French Third Republic and Prime Minister eleven times (briefly) between 1909 and 1929. During the 1920s he was the most influential voice in French foreign policy formulation. A strong supporter of the League of Nations, he favoured improved Franco-German relations. Briand shared with Gustav Stresemann the 1926 Nobel Peace Prize and instigated the Kellogg-Briand Pact of 1928 on the renunciation of war as an instrument of national policy.

Gustav Stresemann (1878–1929)
German Chancellor for three months in 1923 and thereafter served as Foreign Minister until his death in 1929. Stresemann believed that Germany should gain the trust of former enemies by fulfilling the Versailles peace terms, which might then be renegotiated. By this means he reduced German reparations, confirmed Franco-German borders at Locarno and gained German admission to the League of Nations and League Council in 1926.

Austen Chamberlain, who was Foreign Secretary from 1924 to 1929, wanted to 'remove or allay French fears' and 'bring Germany back to the concert of Europe', both of which he saw as 'equally vital. Neither by itself will suffice and the first is needed to allow the second'. Chamberlain wanted to find alternatives to the Geneva Protocol binding the countries which had signed the Covenant of the League of Nations to resist aggression world-wide. He thought the Protocol would be an additional burden to Britain, given the number of existing commitments. Chamberlain recognised French fears of Germany. He also recognised that the failure of Britain and the United States to guarantee French security after the Paris peace settlements provoked France to pre-emptive acts against Germany, such as the occupation of the Ruhr.

Historian Richard Grayson argues, in *Austen Chamberlain and the Commitment to Europe: British Foreign Policy 1924–29* (1997), that Chamberlain recognised the need to stabilise Europe in order to safeguard Britain's security. Therefore he engaged Britain in a search for European stability by pacifying both France and Germany. This challenges the view that Britain was isolationist in respect of Europe and favoured France in preference to Germany. Grayson argues that Chamberlain was in favour of peace, forcing both to make concessions.

Chamberlain, French foreign minister Aristide Briand and German Foreign Minister Gustav Stresemann, together with Italian leader Mussolini, met in the autumn of 1925 at Locarno in Switzerland, near the border with Italy. They settled the following:

- Germany recognised the border with France and Belgium made in the Treaty of Versailles.

- British and French occupation troops in the Rhineland were to be reduced, the first reduction to be in January 1926 and the final in 1930. The Rhineland was to remain demilitarised.

- Britain and Italy were to act as guarantors, agreeing to act against an aggressor should the borders be violated by any party to the agreement.

However:

- Germany's eastern frontiers were not guaranteed. Chamberlain remarked that 'no British government ever will or ever can risk the bones of a British grenadier' for the Polish corridor (or any Eastern European issue considered to be outside British interests).

Little Entente: A series of bilateral security agreements between East European states, Yugoslavia, Czechoslovakia and Romania, mainly against Hungarian revanchism.

- Britain would not join with France in guaranteeing the '**Little Entente**', because Chamberlain did not feel that Britain had any interests to secure in Eastern Europe.

In 1926, resulting from the Locarno agreements, Germany rejoined the League of Nations.

How successful was Austen Chamberlain's foreign policy?

At the time, the Locarno agreements were seen as the path to lasting peace in Europe, stabilising the continent. Chamberlain's aim was to work on both France and Germany to accept changes in the Treaty of Versailles, giving both some gains in return for some concessions.

**Austen Chamberlain
(1863–1937)**
Conservative MP and son of
Joseph Chamberlain and half-
brother of Neville Chamberlain,
he served as Chancellor of the
Exchequer 1903–5, Secretary
of State for India 1915–17,
Minister without Portfolio
1918–19, Chancellor of the
Exchequer 1919–21, Lord Privy
Seal 1921–22 and Foreign
Secretary 1924–29 in Baldwin's
administration. Chamberlain
felt that rehabilitation of
Germany was the path to
peace in Europe and actively
engaged Britain in negotiations
with France and Germany to
this end. He received the 1925
Nobel Peace prize for his work
on the Locarno Pact.

Realpolitik: Realism in politics,
especially applied to international
relations.

1. *In what ways were
the security problems
of the 1920s the
outcome of the Paris
peace settlements?*

2. *Were friendly
relations with the
Soviet Union possible?*

3. *Assess the
achievements of
Austen Chamberlain
as Foreign Secretary
1924–29.*

● Chamberlain solved the major problem of the Franco-German border. By successfully reducing tensions between France and Germany, Chamberlain introduced a climate of mutual trust and co-operation. He introduced 'Geneva tea parties' (regular informal meetings of senior diplomats) outside the League of Nations to settle disputes.

● In 1927, Allied military controls in Germany were lifted. Chamberlain wanted to encourage Germans to feel trustworthy. To review German compliance with the disarmament clauses of the Treaty of Versailles, Chamberlain persuaded the French to accept regular League of Nations inspections in Germany instead of the permanent presence of the Inter-Allied Military Commission of Control (IAMC). This policy removed the ability to check German disarmament (which would prove crucial in the next decade).

● Chamberlain did not believe that Stresemann's intentions were aggressive, so he supported Stresemann in seeking some revisions of the Treaty of Versailles. Chamberlain also encouraged Stresemann to initiate discussion of the issue of German minorities in Poland, in order to satisfy German public opinion.

● In December 1927 Chamberlain encouraged informal German involvement in settling the issue of difficulties being faced by Poles living in Lithuania.

● In 1928 the Kellogg-Briand Pact, renouncing war, was signed by 65 states. Theoretically desirable, the Pact ignored the principles of **realpolitik**, but was popular at the time.

● In 1929 the Young Plan reduced German reparations by one-third of the original sum demanded. Also in 1929 the former Allies agreed to evacuate all their troops from Germany by the mid-1930s (which would prove significant in terms of Hitler's reoccupation of the Rhineland in 1936).

● Outside European affairs, Austen Chamberlain increased control of foreign policy by the Dominions.

Not all peace initiatives were successful though. For example, in 1928 preliminary discussions were held on disarmament. Britain was willing to discuss limitations on 'reduction in size and power of capital ships' and to 'establish a basis of equality between principal Air Powers of Europe'. But only if limitations on trained (manpower) reserves were agreed at the same time. France disagreed and the issue was adjourned for some months. The Foreign Office further noted in January 1928, 'it is true that we are pledged to disarm – it is not so clear that we are pledged, anywhere, to sign an agreed disarmament convention'.

Failure to disarm was crucial because Germany was meant to be disarmed, not only as part of the Treaty of Versailles but as part of the general European movement to disarmament. The same Foreign Office memorandum suggested that 'the League has chosen to act as if it were bound to produce a general disarmament convention. The Germans have seized on this and sought to connect general disarmament with their own disarmament in such a way that they can claim to be freed from their part of the bargain if the Allied governments do not perform theirs.' It was the arrival in power of Hitler that removed any potential willingness of European powers to consider disarmament.

6.4 What were the aims of Imperial policy between 1918 and 1939?

Britain wanted to preserve as much of the Empire as circumstances and budgetary limits permitted. Britain also wanted to delay granting independence, for example to India, until such time as preparation had been adequately put into action for Indians to take over all aspects of the government of their country.

What were the problems?

● The White Dominions wanted complete independence from Britain. Especially they wanted freedom of foreign policy formulation so that they would no longer have to participate in a British war not of their making, unless they chose to do so. At the Imperial War Conference in 1917 they had demanded a post-war conference to change their constitutional relations with Britain.

● The growth of nationalism in India, in particular, giving rise to demands for independence, which were accompanied by political agitation and violence.

● There was growth of Irish Nationalism, arising from demands from the mainly Southern Irish Nationalists for complete independence. The Nationalists rejected the terms of the Government of Ireland Act of 1920, which offered only Home Rule. However, the Ulster Protestants of Northern Ireland wanted to remain part of Britain. Satisfying Ulster's demands would effectively have divided Ireland, but this was not acceptable to the Republicans. Britain became involved in a vicious conflict with the Irish Republican Army (the IRA) between 1919 and 1921 (see chapter 11).

● The 1920s saw a struggle for power in South Africa between moderate Afrikaaners, like the pro-British Jan Smuts of the Union Party, and more extreme nationalists, like General Hertzog, who had left the government in 1912 to form a National Party, with a policy of South Africa first. When it came to power in 1924, Hertzog's National Party was unwilling to make concessions to the growing force of African Nationalism, represented by the African National Congress, (founded 1912). The National Party brought in segregation of blacks and whites in their 'civilised labour' policy.

By what steps did the Dominions achieve the level of independence they wanted?

The British Empire, and especially Canada, Australia, New Zealand and South Africa, had given tremendous support, both military and economic, to Britain's war effort. Two-and-a-half million men had fought for the Empire, notably the Australians and New Zealanders at Gallipoli in 1915. The Dominions were disillusioned by lack of consultation with the British during the war and decided to seek a greater measure of independence afterwards. At the 1917 Imperial War Conference, the Dominions called for a post-war conference to settle their constitutional relations with Britain, pressing for a redefinition of Dominion status. In particular they wished to become **sovereign** nations and exercise freedom in foreign policy formulation. Moreover, they were unwilling to become involved in wars of Britain's making and the demanded reforms would provide means to refuse. Additionally they insisted on representing themselves at the Paris peace conference. These concerns were not addressed at the 1921 Imperial Conference because Britain was more involved with trying to

Sovereign: A sovereign nation has control over itself and is not ruled by the government of another nation.

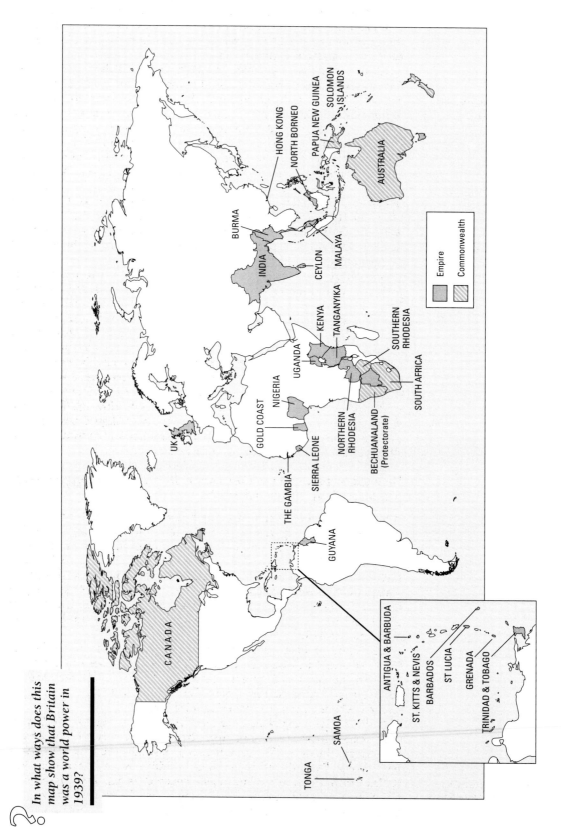

In what ways does this map show that Britain was a world power in 1939?

The British Empire and Dominions in 1939.

solve other imperial dilemmas, such as producing an Irish settlement acceptable to both the Nationalists and the Ulstermen of the North. The Dominions did not support Britain in the 1922 Chanak crisis and ignored the provisions of the 1925 Locarno Pact, although Austen Chamberlain had not bound them to this anyway.

Autonomous communities: Self-governing communities.

At the Imperial Conference of 1926, Arthur Balfour defined the Commonwealth as an idea developed to associate the concept of Empire with the practical reality of Dominions becoming '**autonomous communities** within the British Empire'. The White Dominions were to be 'equal in status and in no way subordinate one to another in any aspect of their domestic or external affairs'. But they were to be 'united by common allegiance to the Crown and freely associated as members of the British Commonwealth of Nations'. The significance of the Balfour Declaration lay in its provision of a means by which Britain hoped to project a semblance of Imperial unity abroad. This was important as it permitted British influence to seem undiminished. At the same time the Dominions were offered a route to achieve the level of independence they were seeking, including exercise of the **prerogative** to conduct an independent foreign policy.

Prerogative: An exclusive right or privilege.

A conference of constitutional experts met in 1929 to consider the problem of Westminster Parliamentary legislation being applied to the Dominions, which undermined their sovereignty. Its recommendations were considered at the Imperial Conference of 1930 and finally enacted in the 1931 Statute of Westminster. The 1931 Statute of Westminster provided a legal framework for the Dominions to be completely self-governing, confirming that they need no longer be bound by British laws if they did not so wish. Equally, the British Parliament could not invalidate Dominion legislation. The Dominions were in free association with Britain and each other within the Commonwealth, although the British monarch remained head of state, represented by a High Commissioner. The Statute covered Australia, New Zealand, Canada, South Africa, and added in the Irish Free State and Newfoundland.

How did Britain and the Commonwealth respond to the economic problems of the 1920s and 1930s?

Protectionism: Economic system of protecting home industries and commerce, usually by imposing taxes on imported goods.

While the Dominions could associate freely, there were no institutions to facilitate mutual co-operation, especially in commerce. During the 1920s Britain had clung to the ideal of free trade. The Dominions, on the other hand, favoured **protectionism**, and a system whereby they traded with each other and imposed lower or no duties on Commonwealth goods while tariffs were imposed on foreign goods. In 1924 an Empire Exhibition was held at Wembley to encourage the purchase of Empire goods and in 1926 an Empire Marketing Board was set up, but it was abandoned in 1932.

Economic problems affecting the Empire were made worse by the Depression that followed the 1929 Wall Street Crash (see chapter 3). In 1931 Britain abandoned the gold standard and set up the Sterling Area as the monetary standard throughout the Empire, with the exception of Canada, whose currency was the Canadian dollar.

Crown Colonies: Those colonies that did not have self-government.

In 1932 Britain abandoned free trade. A conference was held in Ottawa in 1932 and agreements were set up for Imperial preference, a series of bilateral agreements on tariffs between Commonwealth members. This was a revised version of tariff reform enabling the British Dominions (and in 1933 British **Crown Colonies**) to form a self-contained trading unit that was protected by high tariffs against foreign competition. It provided a means for Commonwealth countries to assist each other in the Depression (see chapter 3). Imperial preference was behind an Import Duties Act introduced in 1932 imposing first a duty of 10% then 20% on most foreign goods, but with exemptions on food, raw materials and Commonwealth produce. But it had only limited success because national self-interest prevailed. All Commonwealth countries wanted to sell their goods rather than to buy. They wanted to protect their own industry and agriculture against outside competition. Even so, by 1938, Commonwealth countries sold almost 50% of their export goods to each other.

India

Secretaries of State for India (from 1937 Secretary of State for India and Burma)

E. Montagu	July 1917 – March 1922
V.T. Peel	March 1922 – January 1924
Earl Birkenhead	November 1924 – August 1929
S. Hoare	August 1931 – June 1935
M. Zetland	June 1935 – September 1939

What were the problems Britain had to face in India?

Large sections of the Indian people did not want to be governed by Britain. They wanted complete independence. By the outbreak of the First World War, the Morley-Minto reforms of 1909 had increased Indian representation in the administration and the legislative councils. But authority was still firmly in British hands, exercised through the **Viceroy**, and Indian nationalist aspirations for complete independence remained unsatisfied.

In 1917 Edwin Montagu, the Secretary of State for India, announced the aim of 'gradual development of self-governing institutions, with a view to progressive realisation of responsible government in India as an

> **Viceroy**: A ruler acting with royal authority within a colony or dependency.

Indian Councils Bill 1909 (Morley-Minto Reforms)

- Increased power of legislative councils.

- Majority of members to be elective.

- Increased Indian representation.

- Elected members given greater share in government.

- Members eligible to sit on Viceroy's Executive Council in India; and Secretary of State for India's Councils in London.

- Indians formed a majority on provincial councils, though a minority on the all-Indian legislative council.

Montagu-Chelmsford Reforms, March 1919 (formed basis of Government of India Act 1919)

- Eleven autonomous provinces created.

- Indian ministers to have control of public health, education and agriculture.

- Viceroy to be responsible for public order, finance, diplomatic relations and foreign policy.

---

integral part of the British Empire', embodied in what became known as the Montagu-Chelmsford reforms. These formed the basis of the March 1919 Government of India Act.

The British government felt an obligation to give in to many nationalist demands. During the First World War India had contributed 500,000 fighting men and donated £100,000 towards the cost of the war. However Britain did not want to meet all demands for independence, feeling that India was not capable of responsible self-government. This was because there was hatred and rivalry between the many and various Indian religions and castes, which too often led to violence.

Despite the reforms begun in the 1919 Government of India Act, too much government remained in the British Viceroy's hands. This left unsatisfied demands for independence of the Indian nationalists: the Hindus in the Indian National Congress and the Muslims in the Muslim League. A civil disobedience campaign was launched by the Indian National Congress in 1919, lasting until 1922.

Anglo-Indian relations were embittered in April 1919 in what became known as the Amritsar massacre. A British army officer, Brigadier General Dyer, ordered his forces to open fire on unarmed Sikh, Hindu and Muslim demonstrators who wanted an end to Britain's special powers of imprisonment of agitators without trial, killing 379 demonstrators. It was claimed that the British authorities feared a mutiny, but the 379 deaths increased Indian nationalist fervour. In 1921 Indians boycotted the visit of the Prince of Wales to show their displeasure with the British.

Gandhi's campaign of civil disobedience continued through the 1920s. He called the British government in India 'satanic' and said that paying taxes was subsidising British repression of Nationalist agitation. The continued unrest called for a response from the British.

How did the British government deal with Indian nationalist agitation?

Large sections of the British government did not feel that India was ready for full self-government. The British government instead offered only limited self-government measures. These were unacceptable to the Indian nationalists because they fell short of the complete independence demanded. In 1927 Baldwin set up the Simon Commission to report on how the 1919 Government of India Act was working ten years on, and its prospects for the future. Gandhi and the Indian National Congress party boycotted the Commission. They saw the Commission's exclusion of Indian representatives as insulting. Wherever the Commission travelled in India it was met with riots and mass demonstrations.

In October 1929, before the Simon Commission reported, Viceroy Irwin announced the intention of the British government to give Dominion status to India and speed up **devolution** of powers into Indian hands. This outcome satisfied Gandhi but not Nehru, the Congress Party leader, and his deputy, Subhas Chandra Bose, who demanded complete independence. Gandhi, not to be outdone, led 'Salt marches'. These were against the salt tax and prohibition against unlicensed manufacture of salt – but they led to violence, which Gandhi abhorred. Gandhi was gaoled, but soon released and invited to discussions with Viceroy Irwin. Beginning in 1931 three Round-Table Conferences were held, to discuss further concessions on independence. These included Indian representatives (unlike the Simon Commission). Even so, many Indians boycotted the conferences and they achieved little.

In 1935 the Government of India Act gave control of provinces to Indians, although India was still subject to the Viceroy. This was a success, but not with central government where the problem revolved around the exclusion of Muslims, who were a minority. The Congress

Mohandas Karamchand Gandhi (1869–1948)
Known as 'Mahatma' (Great Soul), Gandhi was an Indian nationalist and leader of the Congress movement. He was a lawyer who led a campaign of passive resistance and civil disobedience, such as boycotts, strikes and non-co-operation, in pursuit of Indian independence.

Edward Wood, Viceroy Irwin (later Earl of Halifax) (1881–1959)
Becoming Baron Irwin in 1925, he served as Viceroy of India from 1926 to 1931, during a period of increasing nationalist agitation. Nevertheless, he succeeded in winning the confidence of Gandhi. Irwin became Earl of Halifax in 1934 and served as British Foreign Secretary from 1937 to 1941.

Devolution: Formal grant of permission to rule from Parliament to the regions.

Party participated and won eight out of the eleven provinces. However, the British had failed to satisfy the hard-line Indian nationalist demands for complete independence because the Viceroy still retained control of defence, foreign affairs, tariffs on British imports and protection of minorities.

In the 1937 provincial election the Indian National Congress Party gained power but the Muslim League received only 5% of the vote. Therefore the Muslim League was regarded as not representing the Muslim vote. The Muslim leader Jinnah feared that Hindu rule would replace British rule, with Muslims still excluded from government.

Despite all the reforms enacted before the outbreak of the Second World War in 1939, the British government still had not succeeded in appeasing hardline Indian nationalist demands for full independence of central government. What they had succeeded in obtaining so far was devolved powers to the provinces.

Source-based questions: Britain's policy towards India between 1918 and 1939

SOURCE A

They are autonomous Communities within the British Empire, equal in status, in no way subordinate one to another in any aspect of their domestic or external affairs, though united by a common allegiance to the Crown …

The rapid evolution of the Overseas Dominions during the last fifty years has involved many complicated adjustments of old political machinery to changing conditions. The tendency towards equality of status was both right and inevitable. Every self-governing member of the Empire is now the master of its destiny.

From The 'Balfour definition' of the Commonwealth, 1926.

SOURCE B

Whereas it is the declared policy of Parliament to provide for the increasing association of Indians in every branch of Indian administration, and for the gradual development of self-governing institutions, with a view to the progressive realisation of responsible government in British India as an integral part of the empire:

And whereas the time and manner of each advance can be determined only by Parliament, upon whom responsibility lies for the welfare and advancement of the Indian peoples:

And whereas the action of Parliament in such matters must be guided by the co-operation received from those on whom new opportunities of service will be conferred, and by the extent to which it is found that confidence can be reposed in their sense of responsibility.

From The Government of India Act 1919.

SOURCE C

His Excellency the Governor of Bengal said that in his province there is good reason to believe that the movement is definitely on the decline. Picketing is giving a certain amount of trouble … It is, however, generally recognised that the failure of the civil disobedience movement will be followed by an increase in terrorist activities.

His Excellency the Governor of Bombay said … the measures so far taken by His Government have had the effect of keeping down the level of enthusiasm, but on the other hand have increased the size of the movement so far as the numbers of adherents and sympathisers is concerned …

From Report on Indian provincial governors discussion on the civil disobedience campaign, 23 July 1930.

---

1. Study Source A.

What does this source tell a historian about the differences in treatment by the British government of the White Dominions and India?

2. Study Source B.

How useful is this source as evidence of British policy towards India after 1918?

3. Study Sources A, B and C and use information contained in this chapter.

Using your knowledge of the political situations in the White Dominions and India in the period 1918–1939, explain the reasons for the differences in the way Britain treated them.

The Middle East

What problems did Britain face in Palestine?

In 1919 Britain and France had divided up the German and Ottoman Empires on behalf of the League of Nations. In Palestine Britain was faced with the consequences of having made promises to the Jews in the Balfour Declaration of 1917 promising a Jewish homeland in Palestine. In the course of fighting the First World War Britain had also made promises to the Arabs about an independent homeland. These promises and obligations were mutually exclusive. As a consequence, there was hostility between Jews and Arabs. They clashed in April 1919, obliging Britain to guarantee the rights of the Palestinian non-Jews.

The hostility of the Arabs grew with increased Jewish immigration into Palestine. Between 1919 and 1929 the Jewish population in Palestine had doubled and the Palestinian Arabs protested. The Jews retaliated, and in August 1929 200 people were killed in the fighting. The Arabs felt that their position in Palestine had been weakened because the Jewish population increased from 4,075 in 1931 to 61,854 in 1935, and they comprised one third of the population of Palestine. Jewish immigration, especially from Germany after 1933, sparked off an Arab Rebellion lasting from 1936 to 1939.

How did Britain try to solve the problem?

White Paper: A report published by the government on aspect of policy often with a recommendation for action.

A Labour government **White Paper** of 1930 threatening to limit Jewish immigration provoked such widespread Jewish protests that the government backed down. Following the deaths of British soldiers in the Arab Rebellion in 1936 the Peel Report was commissioned. Published in 1937, its chief recommendation was partition of Palestine into separate Jewish and Arab states. The British would supervise a corridor from Haifa inland to include Jerusalem, Bethlehem and Nazareth. Partition was rejected by most Arabs and **Zionists**. The Report's recommendations were never implemented.

Zionism: The political movement that wanted to create a separate homeland for Jews in Palestine. This new state would be called Israel.

Unable, by the terms of the mandate, to hand over to the Jews a Zionist homeland, the government were obliged both to attempt to keep the peace and find a solution acceptable to Jews and Arabs.

Iraq was the scene of a revolt in July 1919. It was crushed, but the Iraqis were given a degree of self-government, although with a British adviser and retention of a large British airfield at Habbaniya.

In 1922 Egypt was declared independent, although Britain remained in charge of foreign policy and maintained a garrison there to protect the Suez Canal. The 1936 Anglo-Egyptian Treaty gave Egypt a greater measure of independence and promised withdrawal of the British garrison in 1956.

With defence expenditure cut and force levels reduced, Britain had 'bitten off more than it could chew' by taking on administration of the Middle East mandated territories. Then why take them on? At the time, their addition to the British Empire nearly completed Curzon's hoped-for land bridge stretching from the Mediterranean to India. The effects were either unforeseen or ignored.

How successfully did Britain handle problems arising from administration of African territories?

To save the cost of administration the British government planned to incorporate Southern Rhodesia into South Africa. Frustrated by rejection of this plan in the November 1922 referendum the British government dropped it, not wishing to antagonise the settlers. Instead, in October 1923, Britain successfully saved administrative costs by handing over Southern Rhodesia to a legislative assembly. In effect Southern Rhodesia was from then governed by white settlers, but they were denied Dominion status.

In 1927 a White Paper produced by Colonial Secretary Leo Amery proposed a 'Great White Dominion' in East Africa composed of Kenya, Uganda, Tanganyika, the Rhodesias and Nyasaland, to be held in trust for Britain. Supported by white settlers, it was resisted by Indian immigrants and Africans.

A problem British administrators of African territories had to deal with was the issue of African rights conflicting with the demands of white and Indian interest groups for self-government. This problem was highlighted by the growth in organisation of African nationalist groups. In Kenya native Africans outnumbered settlers by 10,000 to one. In 1922 the Kikuyu tribe of Kenya rioted against the imposition of increased taxes and requirements for African males to carry an identity card. Twenty-five Africans died in the riots. The 1929 Young Commission Report argued for African interests to be paramount because white settlers were not the best trustees of African interests. The Labour government of 1929–31, which appointed Sidney Webb as Colonial Secretary, reasserted the Devonshire Declaration. This stated that only agents of imperial government were to act on behalf of Africans rather than white settlers. Webb argued for adequate representation for all interest groups. However, the Labour government of 1929–31 was too short-lived to achieve change in this aspect of colonial policy.

British governments were also uncertain of how to deal with colonial welfare reforms. Most colonial administrators argued that colonial policy should aim to improve the educational standards of colonial inhabitants in addition to exploiting the wealth of the colony for the benefit of Britain. However, between the wars economic and social improvements were neglected. Less than 15% of black Africans in British-administered Africa went to school, health care was primitive and housing inadequate. The Labour government in 1929 introduced improvements in a Colonial Development Bill. However, with the Depression of the 1930s there was little enough government money made available for investment in social welfare programmes in Britain and even less was allocated to Colonial development. At the same time the Colonies were badly affected by the world recession, opening Colonial trade unions to targeting by the Comintern. The government could not agree on colonial policy, trying to decide whether it should deal with India or Africa first.

1. How did Britain cope with unrest in India and demands for independence?

2. Did Britain treat the White Dominions more favourably than other parts of the Empire? Explain your answer.

3. How successful were Britain's policies towards the Empire between 1918–39?

6.5 What were the problems facing British foreign policy during the 1930s?

Gunboat diplomacy: Diplomatic negotiations carried out with the backing of military action if negotiations do not progress in the right way.

Why did Britain feel unable to take too strong a line with Japanese, German and Italian aggression in the 1930s? Britain had given priority to obligations to legislate for social reforms during the 1920s, at the expense of defence requirements (under the Ten Year Rule). Budgetary limits were compounded by the Depression, which eroded the financial base that underpinned defence spending. Britain was simply unable to operate the **gunboat diplomacy** that had characterised the era of Palmerston. Thus, the British government was obliged to temporise and to negotiate agreed settlements, based on the notion of collective security through the medium of the League of Nations.

Successive governments have been blamed for seeking electoral popularity by adopting economic measures to maintain the standard of living. They did so at the cost of lowering the defence posture of a country whose overseas trade was fundamental to economic survival and whose interests must be defended and be seen to be capable of defence. Cabinet Secretary Sir Maurice Hankey believed that to safeguard trade (vital to the economy) it was necessary to 'preach to the people that they must pull in their belts and economise' as 'fighting strength has been reduced by repeated "cuts" and there has been an orgy of extravagance on social reform'.

The desire for peace was typified by the Peace Pledge Union and the East Fulham by-election results of June 1935, which portrayed the British public not only as anti-war, but willing to negotiate rather than fight, whatever the issue of principle involved. Appeasement was popular.

These were key issues in confirming Hitler's growing belief that Britain could be persuaded to allow him to go on revising the Treaty of Versailles.

How did Britain and the League of Nations deal with Japanese aggression in Manchuria?

From 1931 Britain had to deal with Japanese aggression and territorial expansion in China, which threatened British commercial interests. Attempts to solve the problem through the League of Nations failed when Japan left the League.

Japanese aggression in Manchuria

- The early 1930s saw a rise in extreme and aggressive nationalism among the Japanese military.

- They began to take control of foreign policy from the Japanese civilian government.

- The Japanese army, stationed in Manchuria (Northern China) to protect Japanese commercial interests, seized control of the South Manchuria Railway on the excuse that China was weak and unstable and that Chinese aggression posed a risk to Japanese commercial interests.

- China took the issue of Japanese aggression to the League of Nations.

- League of Nations action to sanction Japan was postponed to see if Japan and China could settle South Manchurian Railway treaty rights between themselves.

- In October 1931, the Japanese Army annexed Manchuria, after the Mukden incident.

Open Door: A policy for economic development in China, whereby all states were to enjoy equal commercial and tariff rights and equal rights of access to commercial opportunities.

Britain and the United States both had important commercial interests in China. They considered that the Japanese annexation of Manchuria violated the Washington Nine Power Treaty of 1921, which guaranteed the '**Open Door**' to trade with China. The League of Nations sent a Commission of Enquiry to Manchuria, led by Lord Lytton. The Lytton Commission reported in September 1932. The Report condemned Japanese military action as unjustifiable, but also called on China to respect Japanese and other foreign rights.

Japan withdrew from the League of Nations in March 1933 following censure of its aggression in China. Lack of a firm response from the League of Nations and failure to impose sanctions after the report of the Lytton Commission of Enquiry demonstrated the fundamental weakness of the League – its inability to punish transgressors, to a point where they desisted from aggressive behaviour, because the League lacked an agreed method and means of punishment and/or coercion.

In 1932, Japanese aggression was extended to Shanghai, threatening British commercial interests. Britain feared that the Japanese would take control of the International Settlement, making it a Japanese concession. If that happened, Britain would have to retire from the Far East because the only way to check Japan was by force. Britain's depleted defence capacity would not stretch to the defence of commercial interests in China.

How did Britain deal with Mussolini's ambitions for an Italian Empire in 1935–36?

Benito Mussolini (1883–1945)
Formed right-radical group which became the Italian Fascist Party and came to power in 1922 to forestall a communist revolution. As Italian Prime Minister he was also known as *Il Duce* – the Leader. During the 1920s he posed as a peacemaker but became jealous of Hitler's successes and desired to emulate him by acquiring an Italian 'empire'. Following the war with Abyssinia and imposition of League of Nations sanctions, Mussolini collaborated with Hitler, forming the Rome-Berlin Axis in 1936.

In the 1930s Britain and other members of the League of Nations proved as powerless to check the territorial ambitions of Mussolini as they had those of Japan. In October 1935 Mussolini invaded Abyssinia, both to avenge Italy's defeat at Adowa in 1898 and to establish an Italian 'empire' in the region. The League of Nations condemned the invasion. The British and French governments wanted to appease Mussolini's desire for African territory. This had been promised to Italy in 1915 under the terms of the Secret Treaty of London should Britain and France gain German territory in Africa. The promise was not kept. British Foreign Secretary Samuel Hoare and French Foreign Secretary Pierre Laval met in Paris in December 1935 and devised the Hoare-Laval Plan. They agreed to give Mussolini two-thirds of Abyssinia. The French were anxious to do nothing that would provoke Mussolini to leave the League. The House of Commons and the British public were enraged when these arrangements became public knowledge, believing the agreement to be a reward for aggression.

Effectively, the Stresa Front had been destroyed by Mussolini's actions and France and Britain's refusal to accommodate him. Although the League of Nations imposed oil sanctions upon Mussolini, they were neither effectively incapacitating nor properly enforced. But they provoked Mussolini to tell Hitler that he would no longer uphold the Locarno Agreements, opening the way to Germany's reoccupation of the Rhineland.

How successful was Britain's policy towards Italy in the mid-1930s?

- Britain's policy of working with Mussolini to contain Hitler through the Stresa Front failed in 1936.

- So too did Britain's policy of working through the League of Nations to contain aggression, because the League had no means to enforce punishment of aggression.

- The British government did not connive with Mussolini to permit him territory in Abyssinia, as had Laval. Their chief interest was to keep Mussolini working with Britain and France and bound by the Stresa Front agreements. But the tone of the Maffey Report of June 1935 suggested that no British interest would be served by keeping Italy out of Abyssinia.

- However this opinion was not shared by the British public, which was attached to the idea of the League of Nations and collective security. Public disgust with the terms of the leaked Hoare-Laval plan ensured that the British government would support the League of Nations' decision to impose sanctions on Italy.

- In turn, this reinforced Mussolini's desire to improve Italy's relations with Germany. The Stresa Front collapsed.

How did Britain respond to Hitler's unilateral actions to revise the Treaty of Versailles?

Britain's policy towards Hitler between 1933 and 1939 was reactive. Hitler 'made all the running' in reversing the terms of the Treaty of Versailles and Britain (and France) responded to his actions. Large numbers of British policy-makers considered that many of the Versailles Treaty terms were harsh and little was done to check Hitler until March 1939. Instead they followed a policy of gradual revision of the Versailles Treaty terms. This was known as appeasement. Appeasement was abandoned from March 1939, when the Germans occupied the remainder of Czechoslovakia. Britain and France then began a period of international negotiation in an effort to get together a coalition of nations willing to stand against Hitler and stop him.

The British government had some sympathy for Hitler's treaty revision ambitions. They had also approved his anti-communist stance when he first became Chancellor of Germany in 1933, elected by legitimate democratic process. But Britain and France were dismayed in October 1933 when Germany left the League of Nations and withdrew from the Geneva Disarmament Conference. This was done on the basis that, if the Allies had not disarmed (now 14 years after the Peace Conference), Germany was entitled to rearm. Furthermore, Hitler reintroduced conscription in 1934, also in contravention of the Versailles Treaty terms.

In order to get Hitler back into the Disarmament Conference, Britain wanted to negotiate with him, being willing to accept a limited German navy, airforce and military, on the basis that it was better to agree limited German rearmament than continue to argue about who was to blame for the failure of the Disarmament Conference. Britain had suggested to Hitler that a German military would be accepted if he returned to the League of Nations and agreed levels of air rearmament. The 1935 Anglo-German Naval Treaty was excused on the grounds that Hitler was going to rebuild the German navy anyway, and it would be better to agree some limitation on its size than to allow it to develop unchecked.

Early in 1934, the British government had decided that Germany was a potential enemy. In 1934 Hitler had attempted a coup to take power in Vienna, but it failed after Mussolini moved troops to the Italian borders with Austria, thereby 'dissuading' him. At that time Mussolini, one of the guarantors with Britain of the Locarno Treaty, was still posing as a peacemaker. Because Britain had run down its defence capacity, standing up to a rearming Germany seemed too risky an option. Hitler's actions and his hatred of communism persuaded the Soviet Union in 1934 to join the League of Nations, in the belief that collective security would provide protection.

In 1935, at Stresa, the Prime Ministers of Britain, Italy and France, (MacDonald, Mussolini and Flandin respectively) met to discuss a common front against German unilateral revision of the Treaty of Versailles: the Stresa Front. Meanwhile Britain connived to allow Germany to rearm.

Britain and France were appalled in 1936 when Hitler reoccupied the Rhineland. This was in violation not only of the Treaty of Versailles but also of the Locarno Treaty. But Britain did not have troops available to tackle Hitler, because they were in India and Palestine. German military capabilities were overestimated, but even so the French were unwilling to invade the Rhineland alone, in the teeth of German opposition. Therefore, it was decided to accept the remilitarisation as a *fait accompli* and try (unsuccessfully) to negotiate with Hitler.

A German **Anschluss** with Austria in April 1938 was also seen as a legitimate revision of Versailles Treaty terms, to deal with a German grievance. After all, in terms of Wilson's Fourteen Points, Hitler was only seeking a right of **self-determination** for Germans. A similar case was put forward for the Sudeten Germans in Czechoslovakia to join Germany in September 1938.

Anschluss: Union of Germany and Austria. In February 1938 Hitler had submitted an ultimatum to the Austrian Chancellor, demanding his resignation after he had attempted to forestall Anschluss by holding a plebiscite. His replacement, Seyss-Inquart, a Nazi, invited the German Army to occupy Austria, and proclaimed Union with Germany on 13 March 1938. A month later, on 10 April, a Nazi-controlled plebiscite voted by 99.75% for Anschluss.

Self-determination: The political right of a group of people to determine the future of their own nation, through a referendum.

Why did Britain rearm in the 1930s?

Britain's defence capacity had been deliberately run down to save money during the 1920s. (See section 6.2.) In 1933 Hitler left the League of Nations and the Disarmament Conference. He also began to rearm Germany. Having concluded that Hitler was potentially a major enemy, Britain decided it was imperative to rearm. However, there was a lot of lost ground to make up, based on government assumptions about Germany's superior military capability.

- 1932, the Ten Year Rule was abandoned and Baldwin expressed the fear that 'the bomber would always get through'. But in 1933, defence spending was only 3% of gross national product (GNP), about £100 million. By 1939 defence spending had grown to £700 million, 18% of GNP, but weapons manufacture lagged behind Germany's.

- 1936, a Joint Services Planning Committee expected that Germany's first attacks would be 'knock-out blows' and Britain should plan accordingly.

- February 1937, the Chiefs of Staff in reported '… our naval, military and airforces … are still far from sufficient to meet our defensive commitments, which now extend from Western Europe through the Mediterranean to the Far East'.

- In September 1938 a record of a meeting by Defence adviser Hastings Ismay suggested that Britain's air defences were insufficient. 'If war with Germany has to come, it would be better to fight her in, say, six to twelve months time …'

- Also, the new Radar system would not be complete before 1939.

What other steps did Britain take to prepare for a possible war?

- 1935 the government took on the organisation of civil defence.

- 1936 an Air Raid Precautions Department was set up.

- 1937 Sir Thomas Inskip, the Minister for the Co-ordination of Defence, produced a major review of defence. A major rearmament programme commenced because its pessimistic view of Britain's defence capacity reinforced calls from the Chiefs of Staff for increased production of fighter aircraft and naval capability. The Munich Agreement of September 1938 was partly inspired by Neville Chamberlain's concern for the effect on London of a bombing campaign because he thought Britain's defences insufficient to stop German bombers.

- 1937 a call for air raid wardens attracted over a million volunteers.

- 1938 an Air Raid Precautions Bill charged local authorities with drawing up detailed contingency plans, including mass evacuations from major industrial and urban centres. Fifty million gas masks were distributed.

- 1939, June, 120,000 volunteers joined the Auxiliary Fire Service.

Why did Neville Chamberlain agree that Sudetenland should be annexed by Germany?

Neville Chamberlain regarded the Munich Agreement of 29 September 1938 to settle the Sudeten question as a diplomatic success. He thought he had obtained 'peace in our time'. Czechoslovakia was under German threat of war over alleged mistreatment of the Sudeten Germans. Chamberlain was not interested in saving Czechoslovakia and had never given the Czechs the guarantee they desired. Czech security was based on the 1922 Little Entente alliance with France, which would hold Germany in the west and in that way divide German military efforts. But in 1938, when put under German pressure, the French decided that the alliance with Britain was more important and adopted the British line. Chamberlain reasoned that, if the French had treaty obligations to the Czechs and Britain was an ally of France, then if the French supported the Czechs, Britain was likely to be drawn into a fight in which no British interests were at stake.

Why was Czechoslovakia under threat from Germany?

- Hitler's real aim was to attack the Soviet Union. For this he would need access through Czech territory.

- Therefore he needed to cripple Czech defences by detaching the well-fortified frontier area bordering Germany.

- The Czech frontier with Germany included German Bohemians (known as Sudeten Germans). They inhabited an important economic and strategic area on the border with Germany. There was longstanding conflict between the Czechs and the Germans, which strengthened Hitler's case.

- Hitler used the Sudeten German Party (Nazis), led by Konrad Henlein, as his agents. Sudeten German Nazi agitation increased after 1935. In April 1938, under Hitler's orders, they demanded self-government for Germans in Czechoslovakia and subordination of Czech foreign policy to German interests. A German press campaign against Czechoslovakia orchestrated these demands and heightened tension.

A British mediator, Lord Runciman, was sent to Czechoslovakia in August 1938, without telling the French, to 'persuade' the Czechs to accept whatever demands were made in order to keep the peace. Runciman reported unfavourably on the Czechs. Neville Chamberlain wanted to avoid another European war at all costs. To try to avoid war, he flew to see Hitler three times during September (see section 6.6).

The Munich crisis

15 September 1938: Chamberlain and Hitler met at Berchtesgaden. They agreed that the Sudetenland should be detached from Czechoslovakia. Neither Chamberlain's Cabinet nor the French were informed of his intention to persuade Hitler to accept the territory demanded rather than go to war with the Czechs.

22 September 1938: Chamberlain flew to meet Hitler at Bad Godesberg. Hitler really wanted war with Czechoslovakia, so the territorial demands escalated to what Hitler thought would be a British, French and Czechoslovakian sticking point.

23 September 1938: Czech forces were mobilised.

23 September: Hitler's show of anger increased, because he was trying to push the British, French and Czechs to go to war.

Chamberlain attempted to persuade the British Cabinet to appease Hitler. This met with Cabinet opposition. Mobilisation of the British navy was authorised.

Mussolini convened a Four Power conference.

30 September 1938: Hitler backed down and allowed himself to be persuaded by the heads of governments of Britain, France, and Italy (Chamberlain, Daladier and Mussolini) to accept the territory demanded. Czechoslovakia was not represented at the meeting. Neither was the Soviet Union, an ally of the Czechs.

The situation in Europe after the Munich Agreement, September 1938

Legend:
- Annexed by Germany in October 1938
- Annexed by Germany in March 1938
- Remilitarised by Germany March 1936
- Recovered by Germany after a plebiscite in 1935
- Annexed by Germany in March 1939
- Annexed by Hungary in March 1939

The terms of the Munich Agreement, 30 September 1938

- The Czechs gave 10,000 square miles of the Czech-German border to Germany, the Sudetenland;

- They gave up 5,000 square miles to Hungary on the Czech-Hungarian border;

- Later, Teschen was given to Poland;

- The Four Powers, Britain, France, Italy and Germany guaranteed the remainder of Czechoslovakia against further unprovoked aggression.

1. How far can the territories given up by the Czechoslovak state to Germany, Poland and Hungary be justified?

2. Why was the event in the photograph significant in Chamberlain's subsequent fall from power in May 1940?

Neville Chamberlain at Heston Airport, London, on his return from the Munich Conference on Czechoslovakia

Purges: The systematic removal of an individual's or group's political enemies.

1. What circumstances persuaded the British Government to start a rearmament programme?

2. Why did Neville Chamberlain agree that the Sudetenland should be German rather than Czechoslovakian?

On 30 September 1938, while taking leave of Hitler, Chamberlain produced a 'piece of paper', confirming Anglo-German friendship and a determination not to go to war against each other, which Hitler signed. On his return to Britain Chamberlain declared that he had secured 'peace in our time'.

Chamberlain dismissed the principle of Soviet support because British and French officials believed that the Soviet military was seriously weakened by the **purges**. He was also reluctant to involve them because he was opposed to communism. Exclusion of the Soviet Union from the Munich meeting had grave consequences. Soviet leader Stalin's belief in the value of collective security and his adherence to the League of Nations were undermined. Peter Calvocoressi and Guy Wint in *Total War* (1979) suggest that Stalin, in accordance with his treaty with the Czechs, would have mobilised and could have overflown a corner of Romania to reach Germany. Soviet mobilisation would have heartened the French and faced Hitler with war on two fronts.

6.6 *Was appeasement justified?*
A CASE STUDY IN HISTORICAL INTERPRETATION

In his *Dictionary of Political Thought* (1996) Roger Scruton defines appeasement as denoting 'policies aiming to remove by common agreement the grievances generated by the peace settlement of 1919 – especially those felt in Germany … Appeasement involves concessions in response to explicit or implied threats; it acts to the detriment of a power that doesn't threaten, and to the benefit of a state which makes non-negotiable demands.'

Appeasement began at the Paris peace conference. Lloyd George saw the Treaty of Versailles as 'a temporary measure of a nature to satisfy public opinion'. He had supposed that the League of Nations would be used as the medium to renegotiate the harsher terms of the Treaty of Versailles: 'No-one supposes that the terms are eternal and immutable … they will be sensibly modified'.

Rapprochement: Reconciliation.

Neville Chamberlain, who became Prime Minister in May 1937, was obsessed with the need to seek a **rapprochement** with Germany because he abhorred war and wanted to avoid another war in Europe. Chamberlain's views were underpinned by a movement among Liberal and Labour politicians and the British press to agree modification of the Treaty of Versailles.

But Chamberlain misread Hitler, believing that appeasement would work because Hitler was reasonable. Documents in the Public Record Office at Kew show Hitler to have been intent on attacking communism via war with the Soviet Union (not unpopular as communism was regarded as the greater menace) and regaining lost territory and uniting the German 'volk'.

Volk: The 'pure-blood' German people.

As Ruth Henig suggested in a *Modern History Review* article (Volume 10, issue 3, February 1999), many historians argue that only an alliance of Britain, France and the Soviet Union in the late 1930s could have deterred Hitler and prevented the outbreak of war, and that the only feasible alternative to appeasement was a strategy of deterrence and alliances. But deterrence by alliance was unpopular because alliances had been discredited by the outbreak of the First World War and deterrence needed rapid rearmament and accretion of trained and equipped military manpower. Chamberlain ignored the claims of the Soviet Union to be consulted at Munich as a participant in collective security, and was

GOOD HUNTING

Mussolini. "All right, Adolf – I never heard a shot"

> **How useful are these cartoons in explaining events in Europe in 1938?**

STILL HOPE

lukewarm about pursuit of a treaty with Stalin afterwards. The result of this was confirmation of Stalin's distrust of British and French intentions towards the Soviet Union and negotiation of the Nazi-Soviet Pact of August 1939. This became a trigger to the Second World War as it released Germany from fear of war on two fronts until it was ready.

In an article for the *Electronic Journal of International History* (2000) Patrick Finney has examined the **historiography** of appeasement and placed it in the context of Britain's **geopolitical** strategic and economic dilemmas. Britain's global strategic dilemma was too little defence and too much to defend; there were other uses for money needed to provide an

Historiography: Different historical views by historians. Another term for historical interpretation.

Geopolitical: The political opportunities and limits determined by a nation's geographical position and natural resources.

adequate defence posture for all commitments. Thus Finney perceives appeasement as the outcome of decline. He divides the historiography into three periods:

The orthodox 'Guilty Men' period

The *Guilty Men* view blames Neville Chamberlain, assuming that Britain still had great power and sufficient clout and resources to take on Hitler. Therefore policy-makers were free to choose resistance and confrontation rather than appeasement.

Written in 1940 by Michael Foot (writing under the name of Cato), Peter Howard and Frank Owen, who were not in a government in power, *Guilty Men* accuses the Chamberlain Cabinet of blindly misjudging Hitler's capacity to fight by overestimating it and of appeasing him by giving in to his demands.

The problem was of gauging Hitler's intent. Winston Churchill in *The Gathering Storm* (1948), concludes that Hitler had a plan of conquest of Eastern Europe and advanced inexorably towards it. This should have been obvious and Britain lost opportunities to stop him.

The revisionist view

Revisionist: An interpretation that revises or changes a widely held point of view.

In the late 1950s and in the 1960s **revisionist** views appeared. A.J.P. Taylor's *Origins of the Second World War* (1961), exposed defects in the orthodox view. Although Taylor is ambivalent about appeasement, and his book cannot truly be considered revisionist, it did make historians re-evaluate the events of the 1920s and 1930s. Historians such as Martin Gilbert in the *Roots of Appeasement* (1966) examined the disparity between resources and commitments, suggesting that Chamberlain had little alternative. But examination of newly-opened British archives suggested that Britain was reluctant to take a stronger stance against Hitler because its defences were too weak. Additionally, the government feared to destabilise economic recovery from the Depression by embarking upon too accelerated a rearmament programme. Therefore, as Richard Overy points out, appeasement was the only rational policy in the circumstances because Britain's decline was apparent in the 1930s.

The counter-revisionist view

Counter-revisionist: Against the policy of revisionism or modification of Marxist-Leninist doctrine.

In the 1980s **counter-revisionist** interpretations appeared, admitting decline and constraint but casting doubt on Neville Chamberlain's motives. Was he driven by events or did he use events to justify his pre-determined course? R.A.C. Parker in *Chamberlain and Appeasement* (1993) suggests that the appeasers were neither fools nor cowards but misread Hitler and underestimated Nazi expansionism and its menace. Chamberlain had unreasonable hopes of satisfying Hitler. Also, the policy of appeasement was popular with the British electorate. Nevertheless Chamberlain was too conciliatory and did not apply sufficient counter-pressure.

Other views

The work of other recent historians suggests that Hitler was an opportunist. He had a programme but no detailed long-term plans of how it could be achieved. Therefore he kept pushing at the open door of appeasement, and was successful while he was revising the harsher terms of the Treaty of Versailles. But he misjudged France and Britain. Once he went beyond Treaty revision by occupying the Czech rump and demanding Polish territory, he obliged them to oppose him. With these acts of aggression Hitler had broken his promise to Neville Chamberlain, convincing him of his bad faith and incidentally turning the tide of Dominions' reluctance to stand by Britain and undermining the pacifists.

Another interpretation is offered by the Intentionalist/Functionalist view outlined by Martin Housden in *Modern History Review* (Volume 10, issue 2, November 1998). The Intentionalists believe that Hitler had a plan and some idea of how to achieve it. The Functionalists suggest that he had a plan and achieved it on an *ad hoc* basis as opportunities arose. Additionally, they suggest that much of Nazi policy was the unintentional outcome of an over-bureaucratised system, with competing departments, which was run by a lazy man (Hitler) who would not devote himself to work.

Britain and France are criticised for giving in to German demands. But there were reasons for doing so:

- There was a public dislike of war. Democratically elected politicians cannot ignore the wishes of the electorate; either they will not be voted into power or they will not remain there for more than one term. This view was reinforced by the Peace Pledge Union, set up by Dick Shepherd, Vicar of St. Martins in the Fields. Moreover, it was claimed that the East Fulham by-election of June 1935, had been lost because of pacifist votes. The League of Nations Union (a peace movement) had over 400,000 members in 1931.

- The British government believed German demands for Treaty revision were reasonable. It did not understand Hitler's intentions, especially as he could be personally charming. Neville Chamberlain believed that Hitler's territorial demands were limited and that 'he was a man who could be relied upon when he had given his word'. Therefore Chamberlain believed after Munich that he had achieved 'peace in our time'. However, others, such as Winston Churchill and Michael Foot, were less gullible.

There were other reasons which made appeasement seem an attractive option:

- It had proved impossible to stop Hitler rearming. Europe did not disarm during the 1920s. This provided an excuse for German rearmament and some politicians felt it difficult to argue with.

- Unification of Germans could be interpreted as being in line with national self-determination, as per Wilson's Fourteen Points, for the Rhineland, Austrians, Sudeten Germans in Czechoslovakia, Danzig Free City – again, difficult to argue with.

- Britain and France saw themselves as being in no position to stop him anyway.

- The threat of communism was seen as a worse evil than a potentially Nazi-dominated Europe. But, having had a Mutual Assistance Treaty with Czechoslovakia, Stalin felt insulted by exclusion from the Munich settlement.

- Germany was seen as a buffer zone against the Soviet Union.

- The British government feared further damage to the British economy would result from engaging in another war.

- Britain had problems to deal with in the Far East, the Mediterranean and in India.

1. How far was Neville Chamberlain personally responsible for the policy of appeasement?

2. Why have historians differed in their views of appeasement? Give reasons for your answer

6.7 Why did Britain go to war in 1939?

Britain went to war with Germany because Germany invaded Poland. In March 1939 Britain and France had given a guarantee that, if Poland was attacked and it fought back, Britain and France would go to war with the aggressor. However, despite having given the guarantee, both Britain and France began intensive diplomatic negotiations on ways to avoid fulfilling the obligation.

Why did Britain and France decide it was necessary to try to stop Hitler's aggression and territorial expansionism?

When Hitler occupied the Czech regions of Bohemia and Moravia in March 1939 it was apparent to the British government that:

● The policy of appeasement had failed, because Hitler would not be satisfied with revision of the Treaty of Versailles, as demonstrated by his occupation of Bohemia and Moravia, the existence of Czechoslovakia not being a term of the Treaty of Versailles;

● Hitler was therefore likely to endanger the security of other states in the path of his territorial expansionism to find 'living space' (Lebensraum), his hostility to Slavs, for example Poland, and desire to exterminate Bolshevism.

● Hitler could not be trusted because he had broken his word about Czechoslovakia. Neville Chamberlain, however, had thought he was a man 'with whom he could do business'.

● Britain must stand up to Hitler or permit him to conquer Europe unchallenged. It was feared that, once master of Europe, he would eventually pose a threat to Britain.

Why did Britain and France feel it necessary to offer a guarantee of security to Poland in March 1939?

Britain and France offered Poland a guarantee on 6 April 1939 because Poland was under threat from Hitler, who demanded the return to Germany of Danzig and a German road across the Polish corridor. Poland was chosen by Britain and France as the 'sticking point' beyond which Hitler would not be appeased. They gambled that the Poles would give in to Hitler's demands.

What was the international situation between March and September 1939?

● The Poles resisted the urgings of Britain and France to behave as the Czechs had done and refused Hitler's March 1939 demands. They also refused Hitler's invitation to join the Anti-Comintern Pact.

● After March 1939 Britain seemed to be standing alone. The Dominions did not wish to support Britain. France was weak and Eastern Europe was unstable.

● The United States was isolationist and neutral, although there was an equally appalled Anglo-American stance in the face of Japanese aggression in China from 1937.

● The British guarantee strengthened Polish resolve to hold out against Hitler over Danzig. The Poles did not want to suffer the fate of the Czechs, who had relied for security on the Western powers. They felt that, when it had come to the point, the Western Allies had not defended Czechoslovakia.

- Hitler was enraged and denounced the Anglo-German Naval Treaty of 1935 (see section 6.5) and his 1939 Non-Aggression Pact with Poland.

- A defence evaluation prepared by Defence adviser Hastings Ismay for the government suggested that Britain did not feel ready in September 1938 to oppose Hitler's demands.

Why did Britain and France fail to reach an alliance against Hitler with the Soviet Union in the summer of 1939?

Britain, France and the Soviet Union seemed to be obvious allies against Hitler, being the three strongest powers willing to stand up to him. Why did they fail to agree?

- Britain and France ignored Stalin's March 1939 proposal of a six-power conference to discuss collective action to prevent further German aggression. This was because they did not trust the Soviet Union. Britain and France were more concerned to gain Soviet help to defend Poland and Romania, than to defend the Soviet Union.

- Britain and France gave a lukewarm response to Stalin's proposal of a tripartite pact, involving an explicit military convention.

- An invitation to British Foreign Secretary Halifax to go to Moscow for negotiations was declined. Instead, negotiations commenced in June 1939 between Soviet Foreign Minister Molotov and the British Ambassador in Moscow. Molotov was empowered to make an alliance (provided Stalin agreed). The Ambassador was not so empowered to make an alliance for Britain. This could be seen as insulting to the Soviet Union.

- Britain and France dragged their feet on joint Soviet, British and French military talks. The British and French sent a low-level delegation by the slow train whereas Soviet Defence Minister Voroshilov had plans for military co-operation and was empowered to conclude an agreement.

- The Russians therefore did not believe that the British and French were serious about negotiations.

- The Russians did not trust the British, believing that they were secretly negotiating with Hitler to conclude an anti-Soviet pact with them. This view was reinforced by British and French failure to negotiate agreements with Poland and Romania for Soviet troops to cross their territory en route to Germany. German approaches to the Russians from May 1939 began to seem an attractive alternative. German Foreign Minister Ribbentrop met Molotov in Moscow on 23 August and the Nazi-Soviet Pact was negotiated and signed that day.

- On 1 September Hitler invaded Poland and on the morning of 3 September Britain and France issued an ultimatum to Hitler to depart Poland. He did not reply and on the same day Britain and France declared war on Germany.

1. Why did Britain abandon appeasement in 1939?

2. To what extent was the British government responsible for the signing of the Nazi-Soviet Pact of August 1939?

7 The Liberal Party, 1918–2000

Key Issues

- *Why did the Liberal Party's influence in British politics decline so sharply in the 1920s?*

- *How effectively did the Liberal Party adapt to the changing political situation from the 1920s to the present day?*

- *What are the difficulties for a third party in the British electoral system?*

Framework of Events

1918	Liberals compete against each other in the 1918 general election. 'Coupon' Election sees Lloyd George triumph and 133 of his Coalition Liberals elected, but only 28 Independent (Asquith) Liberals
1920	Several Coalition Liberal MPs forced to withdraw from National Liberal Federation General Meeting at Leamington Spa
1922	End of Lloyd George Coalition government
1923	Asquith and Lloyd George Liberals reunite in opposition to Baldwin's protectionism. Divisions re-emerge after election
1924	Only 40 Liberal MPs returned at general election
1926	Asquith resigns as party leader and is succeeded by Lloyd George
1928	Publication of *Britain's Industrial Future* (the 'yellow book')
1931	Most Liberals (except Lloyd George group) enter National Government. Herbert Samuel becomes leader
1932	Samuel group leaves National Government over issue of Free Trade. John Simon's group remains
1935	Archibald Sinclair becomes leader
1940	Liberals enter Churchill coalition, Sinclair at the Air Ministry
1945	12 MPs returned at the general election. Clement Davies becomes leader
1951	Davies rejects Churchill's offer of the Ministry of Education
1956	Jo Grimond becomes party leader
1957	Loss of Carmarthen seat in a by-election to Labour (represented by Megan Lloyd George) reduces the number of Liberal MPs to five, the lowest ever
1958	By-election victory at Torrington
1962	Orpington by-election victory represents peak of 'revival'
1967	Jeremy Thorpe replaces Grimond as leader
1972	Series of by-election victories marks second 'revival'
1976	May: Thorpe resigns in the wake of the revelations of the Norman Scott affair. Grimond returns to lead the party until David Steel is elected leader by party members in July

1977	March: Party enters into Lib–Lab pact with the Callaghan government (until 1978)
1981	March: Formation of Social Democratic Party (SDP)
	September: Formation of Liberal-SDP Alliance
1983	SDP/Liberal Alliance gain 25% of the vote but only 3% of seats in the general election
1988	January: Liberals and SDP vote for merger
	March: merged party (without Owenites) launched as Social and Liberal Democrats jointly led by Steel and Robert Maclennan
	July: Paddy Ashdown becomes leader
1989	Party changes its title to Liberal Democrats
1994	Big advances in local elections take Liberal Democrats ahead of the Conservatives
1997	40 MPs returned at general election. Ashdown sits on Cabinet Committee in the Blair government
1999	Charles Kennedy succeeds Ashdown as leader

Overview

I N 1935 George Dangerfield argued in *The Strange Death of Liberal England* that the roots of the Liberal Party's rapid decline after 1918 lay in the array of problems – Lords Reform, Ireland, Suffragettes and labour unrest – that it had failed to deal with before the First World War. By the mid-1930s the Liberal Party was on its death bed, and in many ways it is remarkable that it did not fade away before the close of the 1950s. Since then the party has struggled to exert influence, surviving on a diet of impressive by-election triumphs, but little more substantial. Even by the 1990s, with a significantly expanded role in local government and 46 MPs (the most since 1929) elected to parliament in 1997, the Liberal Democrats remained resolutely the third party in Britain with limited prospects of witnessing a rebirth of Liberal Britain.

But in other ways it is unhelpful to talk of the death of Liberal Britain. **Liberalism** has remained intellectually strong and Britain has become a more Liberal society – it has been the tragedy of the Liberal Party not to be able to make political credit out of this. Liberalism was associated with two of the most influential thinkers of 20th-century Britain: William Beveridge, the architect of the post-war Welfare State, and John Maynard Keynes, who helped to design the International Monetary Fund, the World Bank and to shape the way governments approached economic thinking. Lloyd George's Liberal Party after 1926 was full of ideas. Even today much New Labour thinking is more Liberal than socialist in its origin – especially in areas such as devolution and constitutional and electoral reform.

The history of the Liberal Party is also important in illustrating the nature of the first-past-the-post electoral system in British politics. Caught between the two main parties, the Liberal vote has rarely turned into a proportionate number of parliamentary seats. Thus while the Liberals have been able to score remarkable by-election victories, attracting protest and tactical votes from both Labour and the Conservatives, it has proved difficult to turn this occasional level of support into anything more permanent. Largely because of this Liberals have strongly supported **proportional representation** (PR) as a way of improving their situation. Yet before they were replaced by Labour as the main opposition to the

Liberalism: A set of political ideas based on the ideas of minimal government intervention in the economy and individual freedom. During the early 20th century Liberal ideas changed to include the intervention of the state to help the 'deserving poor' to achieve individual self-advancement. This was called New Liberalism.

Proportional Representation: An electoral system in which seats in parliament are distributed in proportion to votes rather than constituencies won.

Conservative Party, the Liberals had twice, in 1912 and 1918, rejected the introduction of PR into the electoral system. Support of PR has been a condition of coalitions and pacts that the Liberals have agreed with Labour, for example in 1930 and 1977. The coalitions and pacts made by the Liberals have been a result of their inability to turn votes into seats. Yet the problems of appearing as either progressive (anti-Conservative) or as anti-socialist have threatened to upset committed supporters and confuse the image of the party in voters' minds.

The history of the Liberal Party after the 1920s is essentially that of how a third party adapted to a two-party system. Its lack of success and the failure of experiments like the SDP Alliance in the 1980s amply illustrate the resilience (for good or ill) of that system. However, this failure should not be deemed inevitable. In local government, the Liberal Democrats can no longer be considered a third party. However, their limited prospects of victory, and in the two-party system the idea that a vote for their party is a 'wasted vote' have prevented this leading to a similar level of support in general elections. The Liberals did not, however, see themselves to be battling with third-party status in the 1920s. Instead they saw the problem as coming to terms with a vastly expanded and mainly working-class electorate. It was in part the chronic divisions between Lloyd George and Asquithian Liberals in the 1920s that enabled Labour to make the jump from third-party status. The Liberals were to this extent architects of their own downfall. This is a problem with which Charles Kennedy's Liberal Democrats continue to grapple. The history of the Liberal Party, to be read together with those of the Labour and Conservative Parties, has rarely been happy. Titles like *The Strange Death of Liberal England*, *The Downfall of the Liberal Party* (Trevor Wilson, 1966) and *The Rise and Fall of British Liberalism 1776–1988* (Alan Sykes, 1997) dominate.

Study the statistical data below.

How far does the information support the view that the first-past-the-post system of election seriously disadvantaged the Liberals between 1918 and 1997?

The Liberal Party's general election results

		Seats	Total Vote	% share of vote
1918	Coalition Liberals	133	1,455,000	13.5
	Liberal	28	1,298,000	12.1
1922	National Liberal	62	1,672,000	11.6
	Liberal	54	2,516,000	17.5
1923	Liberal	159	4,311,000	29.6
1924	Liberal	40	2,928,000	17.6
1929	Liberal	59	5,308,000	23.4
1931	Liberal National	35	809,000	3.7
	Liberal	33	1,402,000	6.5
	Independent Liberal	4	106,000	0.5
1935	Liberal	21	1,422,000	6.4
1945	Liberal	12	2,252,430	9
1950	Liberal	9	2,621,000	9.1
1951	Liberal	6	730,000	2.5
1955	Liberal	6	722,000	2.7
1959	Liberal	6	1,638,000	5.9
1964	Liberal	9	3,092,000	11.2
1966	Liberal	12	2,327,000	8.5
1970	Liberal	6	2,117,000	7.5
February 1974	Liberal	14	6,063,000	19.3
October 1974	Liberal	13	5,346,000	18.3
1979	Liberal	11	4,313,000	13.8
1983	Liberal/SDP	23	7,341,000	25.4
1987	Liberal/SDP	22	7,341,000	22.6
1992	Liberal Democrats	20	5,998,000	17.8
1997	Liberal Democrats	46	5,242,000	16.8

7.1 Why did the Liberal Party decline after 1918?

Free trade: International trade free from import or protective tariffs. Historically Liberals judged this vital both for the British Empire and to maintain peace.

Herbert Asquith (1852–1928)
Prime Minister 1908–16 and leader of the Liberal Party 1908–26. A firm advocate of Liberalism, but increasingly ineffectual as party leader in the 1920s.

David Lloyd George (1863–1945)
MP for Caernavon Boroughs 1890–1945, Chancellor of the Exchequer 1908–15, Prime Minister 1916–22 and Liberal Party Leader 1926–31. Lloyd George was both a radical thinker and wily political fixer.

Whip: MPs of a party responsible for ensuring MPs support that party's position in the House of Commons.

As the First World War drew to a close the conflicts within the Liberal Party intensified. Many of these were long-standing, but most arose immediately from the war itself. Several principles of Liberalism were victims of 'total war'. Censorship, for instance, offended the party rank-and-file. Conscription, both industrial and military, extended the coercive role of the state at the expense of Liberal belief in individual liberty. Asquith's reluctant acceptance of the need for military conscription provoked the resignation of his Home Secretary, Sir John Simon, early in 1916. **Free trade**, the guiding principle of 19th-century Gladstonian Liberalism, had also fallen foul of the war. McKenna's 1915 budget not only increased taxation, but introduced tariffs on luxury goods.

Above all, tensions within the Liberal Party came to a head in December 1916, when Lloyd George replaced Asquith as Prime Minister. Along with many Conservatives, Lloyd George had long argued that Britain needed a more efficient, concerted war effort and that Asquith was not providing the necessary leadership. A historical view, blaming Lloyd George for conspiring with the Conservatives to remove Asquith and thereby splitting the Liberal Party into two factions, developed around the events of December 1916. Besides crediting Lloyd George with a foresight beyond even his undoubted skill at weighing up the political mood, this neglects both the extent to which parts of the party supported Lloyd George and the extent to which Asquith and his supporters were actively opposed to the government. While refusing to serve under Lloyd George and sitting on the opposition benches, Asquith initially promised the Coalition an attitude of 'general support'. Nonetheless, from 1917, as the historian Alan Sykes has argued, the Liberals were split between 'a leader who was no longer prime minister, and a prime minister who was not leader of the party'.

What impact did the 'Coupon' election of 1918 have on the Liberal Party?

When the first general election since 1910 was declared for December 1918, there were, effectively, two Liberal Parties in existence. The differences that emerged in 1916 had hardened into opposition. Broadly the Liberal idea of individual freedom was in conflict with the desire to fight the war effectively. During the war there were sharp clashes over the extension of duties on Indian goods, extending conscription to Ireland and excluding conscientious objectors from the franchise under the new Representation of the People Act. Most historians consider that the Maurice Debate of May 1918, when Asquith (for the only time) led opposition to the Coalition over the inaccuracy of War Office troop figures, cemented the divide within the party. Treating it as a vote of confidence in his government, Lloyd George won backing from 71 Liberals, but 98 voted against. In parliament separate **whips** operated for each group, but local Liberal Associations were increasingly partisan – mostly backing the Asquithians.

The allegiance of the local associations was important in Lloyd George's calculations in 1918. With an electorate expanded threefold from 1910 to some 21 million, constituency organisation was essential. Despite some negotiations for reunion with the rest of the Liberal Party, the Prime Minister decided to continue the Coalition, issuing a coupon, signed by himself and Conservative leader Bonar Law, to approved candidates. Seats were divided between 374 Conservatives and 159 Lloyd George Liberals. In some seats Coalition Liberals backed Conservatives against Liberals and likewise Liberals backed Labour rather than Coalition candidates. In this election, with war having ended only a month earlier, the coalition won a landslide with 332 Conservatives and 133 Coalition Liberals returned. By contrast only 28 Asquithians won: John Simon, Reginald McKenna, Herbert Samuel and Asquith himself, in East Fife, were all defeated.

The Conservatives were the main beneficiaries of the 'coupon' election. However, the coalition programme had been radical in its proposals for social reform and reconstruction, and had gained Asquith's approval. Liberal ministers, notably Fisher at Education and Addison at Housing, acted on this programme and fought against the 'Geddes Axe' of 1922. This cut public spending after recession took hold late in 1920. As a result the position of the **'wee free'** Independent Liberals seemed uncertain. Even when Asquith returned to parliament in 1920 he provided only weak leadership. The differences between Liberals, to most voters, seemed more a question of personality than policy.

The electoral position of the Coalition Liberals was no more certain however. In Parliament they depended upon Conservative support and lacked real party and constituency organisation. Their successes in 1918 had come on a wave of patriotism at the victorious end of the war and by avoiding Conservative opponents in the election via the 'coupon'. These were conditions unlikely to last for long.

Lloyd George was aware of this problem. Through 1919 and 1920 there was discussion of a formal union with the Conservatives to form a 'centre party', a large anti-socialist grouping. This further split the Liberals. At the 1920 National Liberal Federation General Meeting in Leamington Spa, Coalition Liberals who attended were denounced and forced to withdraw. In the aftermath of Leamington Spa the Lloyd George constituency organisations, as many as 220, supported from the Prime Minister's own fund, were created. Competing magazines, the *Liberal Magazine* and *Lloyd George Liberal Magazine* were published. Division was now spread throughout the party.

'Wee free': Nickname of the Independent Liberal MPs after 1918 – opposed to the Coalition and its Liberal supporters.

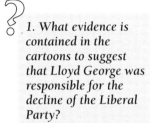

1. **What evidence is contained in the cartoons to suggest that Lloyd George was responsible for the decline of the Liberal Party?**

2. **Of what value are these cartoons to a historian writing about the decline of the Liberal Party in the early 1920s?**

INTO THE LIMELIGHT.

THE COLOSSUS: A TALE OF TWO TUBS.

Two cartoons from *Punch* magazine from the early 1920s

Why did Liberal support erode?

This question needs to be addressed in relative terms and over the broad inter-war period. It was the party's failure to expand its support that was crucial and failure was often due to the number of candidates it could field. In the 1924 election (the third in three years) the party could only afford to run 346 candidates. In itself this suggested its third-party status. The party's proportion of the electorate fell dramatically, from 29% in 1922 to 10.7% in 1931. Only in 1929 did it receive more than 5 million votes, still a smaller volume than Labour in its heavy defeat of 1931.

The divisions within the Liberal Party were not solely responsible for the party's declining support. The expansion in the size of the electorate in 1918 meant effective local organisation was now vital for political parties. Compared with Labour, Liberal local organisation was poor. Labour in 1918 had reorganised its constituency structure and had the financial support of the trade unions. The organisational and financial strength of the Conservatives was also strong. Besides the lack of morale caused by divisions among the party leaders this lack of funds meant that fewer candidates could be fielded. Herbert Gladstone at the party HQ reported that organisers and activists were drifting away into the Conservative and Labour parties. Survival was achieved in cases such as Sheffield and Bristol through the creation of local alliances with Conservatives. Elsewhere Liberal local government representation, especially after the disastrous 1919 elections, went into rapid decline.

Without resources of finance and personnel the Liberals struggled to appeal to the new working-class and women voters. To many historians the rise of class politics in this period signalled the decline of the Liberals, caught between Labour and the Conservatives. Certainly, the Conservative and Labour votes were more geographically concentrated, in Southern and suburban, and industrial working-class constituencies respectively. This was vital in the first-past-the-post British electoral system. The Liberals had more even distribution.

The rise of Labour, especially in the industrial working-class areas, eroded the Liberal vote; it was against Labour opponents more than Conservatives that the Liberals struggled in the inter-war period. Mining areas which Liberals had held were solidly Labour by 1922. The Liberals were also less at ease with the growing influence of trade unionism than Labour. However, since the Conservatives also polled heavily among many of the new voters and Labour struggled in cities such as Liverpool and Bristol, class was clearly not the only factor behind voting behaviour.

Labour was increasingly able to pose as the alternative to the Coalition government. Lloyd George took a heavy-handed attitude. He used the force of the state against Labour unrest in the 1920 miners' strike. This contributed to the impression that Liberalism was neglecting the working class. On issues such as housing, unemployment, foreign and Irish policy, Labour benefited from the absence of distinctive Liberal leadership by Asquith. In by-elections against the Coalition, Labour picked up 14 seats between 1918 and 1922. The Asquith Liberals were not always able to field candidates and after 1919 only picked up two seats in Louth and Bodmin, the rural, **non-conformist**, Celtic fringes of Britain, which remained the party's only firm strongholds.

Non-conformist: A Protestant who is not a member of the Church of England. Religious groups include Methodists, Baptists and Quakers.

1. **What factors contributed to the divisions in Liberalism in the 1920s?**

2. **Why did Labour replace the Liberals as the main opposition to the Conservative Party?**

7.2 Why did Lloyd George fail to revive Liberal fortunes in the 1920s?

In 1922 the Conservatives withdrew from the Coalition. A central figure in this was Stanley Baldwin, the Conservative leader from 1923 to 1937.

Sale of honours: Allowing individuals to buy hereditary peerages and knighthoods.

Baldwin was concerned that if the coalition continued the Conservatives would be associated with the corruption of Lloyd George's **sale of honours** (see chapter 4) and that Lloyd George might split the Conservatives just as he had done the Liberals. Baldwin's suspicion of Lloyd George's conspiring, historian Maurice Cowling has argued, led him to enter into a loose agreement with Labour leader Ramsay Macdonald to keep Lloyd George out of government.

The 1922 election exposed the weakness of the National (ex-Coalition) Liberals under Lloyd George. He was out of government for the first time in 16 years. The Liberals were reduced to 62 seats, despite the fact that most (and especially those in Scotland) were spared Conservative opposition. It also showed the divisions within Liberalism: National and Independent Liberals fought each other in several seats and in some there were even three Liberal candidates. The Independent Liberals increased their representation to 54, winning 32 seats from the Conservatives, but only one from Labour. Labour now outnumbered the Liberals and included some former Liberals within its ranks.

Reunion and revival?

The defeat of 1922 placed the possibility of reunion back on the agenda of Liberal politics. There were moves towards this, although they were strictly limited. This was due to Asquith's mistrust of Lloyd George and his overtures towards Labour and the continuing links between ex-Coalitionists and the Conservatives. By 1923, while the competing magazines had ceased publishing, Lloyd George was still reluctant to free up his fund for the Liberal Party or his separate HQ. What succeeded in uniting the Liberals was Baldwin's declaration in favour of protection at the end of 1923.

Liberal leaders were able to unite in defence of Free Trade. It says something about the condition of Liberal politics that it took a Conservative leader to achieve what two Liberal Prime Ministers could not. Local associations were revived by the old battle-cry of Free Trade. Substantial finance was forthcoming from the Lloyd George Fund. Despite this, Lloyd George allowed Asquith to lead the united party. This was because his supporters lacked a national constituency organisation. The Liberals defended the status quo and promised unspecified social reforms. Asquith argued that protection would push up food prices. Various schemes such as the extension of unemployment insurance and state investment in the economy were proposed to tackle unemployment. While Labour also defended Free Trade, Liberals criticised its ideas for the nationalisation (state ownership) of industry.

The Liberals won 158 seats, polling well in many of its traditional and nonconformist regions – the west country and the industrial north-west. Some 69 seats were won from Conservatives, but only 13 from Labour, with voting in northern England, South Wales and the Midlands (Derby, Leicester) demonstrating the Liberals' diminishing working-class support. Baldwin's protectionism had suffered a clear rebuff, with 258 Conservatives in the new parliament weighed against the Liberals and 191 Labour MPs after the Free Trade election.

The Liberal leadership was once more divided over its course of action. With the balance of power within the Liberal Party in Asquith's favour, the prospect of co-operating with the Conservatives was unpopular. Equally, outright alliance with the Labour Party was feared. Ultimately, a policy of independence was pursued, supporting Labour with the hope of influencing the policy of Macdonald's inexperienced administration. For such a strategy the Liberals required a united leadership to put pressure on Labour. Asquith adopted a rather passive attitude, awaiting Labour's failure. Lloyd George, on the other hand, while hoping that Labour would push reform (including electoral reform) forwards, was also hoping for an anti-socialist coalition with the Conservatives. Neither Baldwin nor Macdonald looked favourably upon such manoeuvring, and divisions between the Liberal leaders were reinforced. Yet the Liberal factions needed each other. Lloyd George and his supporters were increasingly aware that given limited prospects for coalition, they needed the party machine as a base. Under Asquith's control, the party organisation remained poverty-stricken and in need of the Lloyd George Fund.

The division meant that for the 1924 election (the third since 1922), Lloyd George was prepared to give only £50,000 to the party (compared with £160,000 for the 1923 contest). The upshot of this was that the Liberals fielded only 346 candidates, received less than 3 million votes and were reduced to a mere 40 MPs. Beyond the Celtic Fringe (North Wales, Scottish Highlands) the Liberals were decimated – losing 63 of the 67 English county seats won in 1923.

Lloyd George and new policies?

The 1924 result suggested that the Liberals were not seen as an alternative to Labour or the Conservatives. During the campaign, historian Chris Cook argues, 'the Liberals said nothing not being said already by Labour or Conservative'. The lack of a distinctive identity and original policies had blighted Liberal prospects since 1918. In 1923 this had been obscured by the defence of Free Trade, but by 1924 with the Conservatives abandoning protectionism and securing a landslide victory, the shortcomings of Liberal thinking and policy were more evident. Too easily Liberals in the 1920s resorted to outdated Victorian Liberal ideas in the absence of thoughts on the modern world. In addition, there was the lack of leadership provided by Asquith, who was defeated in 1924. Lloyd George, for good or ill, was a 'dynamic force' and one recognised as bringing ideas into the party, while being in no sense bound by them.

From 1921 the Liberal **Summer School movement**, founded by radicals like E. D. Simon and Ramsay Muir of the Manchester Liberal Federation, had served as a forum for debate and new policies within Liberalism. They had attempted to build upon pre-war New Liberalism and its belief in the positive, interventionist role of the state in securing the 'common good', an idea that came out of **John Stuart Mill**'s thinking. They also supported more traditional Liberal ideas of individual liberty and choice. The war had emphasised the more coercive role of the state. In the 1920s the competing interests of capitalism and labour (especially in industrial conflict and unemployment) made it more difficult for Liberal policy to claim to represent the 'common good'. New thinking was necessary to revive both the party and Liberalism itself.

From 1924 Lloyd George chose to appoint expert officials on inquiry panels to devise new policies. Such panels drew from the personnel of the 'summer schools'. The Land Inquiry Committee in 1925 published *Land and the Nation*. (Because of the colour of its cover it was known as the 'Green Book'.) It advocated state purchase of land. This would be leased to those who would use or cultivate it wisely and productively. *Coal and Power* (1924) had proposed a similar scheme for the mining industry.

However, re-thinking was inevitably linked to in-fighting within the Liberal Party. Such proposals were seen as too close to socialist nationalisation or too interfering on the part of the state for many Liberals. The fact that Lloyd George kept these panels independent of official Liberal organisation and funded them himself, also provoked opposition. Lloyd George was reluctant to release his fund to an inefficient party machine. To critics

Summer School movement: A forum for Liberal policy discussion, independent of the party, founded in 1921. Intellectuals such as Keynes and Beveridge were among the participants. It was influential on Lloyd George's policy in the later 1920s.

John Stuart Mill: Liberal philosopher, 1806–73.

it seemed that Lloyd George, through these committees and organisations like the Land and Nation League, formed late in 1925, was creating a powerbase at the expense of the Liberal Party. As ever, lack of finances, after the failure of the 1925 'Million Fund', was central to Liberal problems. Lloyd George had offered to fund the party for three years in return for it adopting his land policy and this had deepened inner-party conflicts. By early 1926, when the land proposals were limited to acquisition of land for sale, some compromise had been reached.

However, by mid-1926 divisions had arisen once more. The Liberal position on the General Strike of May 1926 was to condemn the TUC for a constitutional challenge to the government. Lloyd George, now in more radical mood, argued that the government as much as the unions was worthy of condemnation and that a negotiated settlement was needed. Asquith turned on his old enemy. While Lloyd George's position as party chairman was secure, his position in the Liberal shadow cabinet was not. However, a stroke forced Asquith to resign as party leader in October and only Lloyd George had the qualities of leadership and wealth to help the party. With Lloyd George as leader, the old-guard followers of Asquith in the party, especially those who ran its organisation, such as Vivian Phillips, Herbert Gladstone, and Walter Runciman, withdrew. Herbert Samuel, not only an effective operator, but a neutral figure in party factionalism, was appointed chair of the organisation committee in 1927. Re-organising the party and promising to finance it for three years put the Liberal Party firmly under Lloyd George's control.

The Yellow Book and the 1929 general election

From 1925 the Liberal Industrial Inquiry, which included such luminaries as E.D. Simon, Ramsay Muir, Seebohm Rowntree, economist John Maynard Keynes, Herbert Samuel and Lloyd George himself, had been considering questions of industry and unemployment. In 1928 their conclusions, *Britain's Industrial Future* (the 'Yellow Book') were published. Its proposals were for government loans (more than £200 million) for public works such as electrification and road-building, a national investment board to direct resources into home industries, and expert staff to advise the government on economic matters. In terms of industrial relations, the hope was that a voluntary framework into which labour and management could enter would reduce conflict. Less than two years after the General Strike this did not, however, seem entirely realistic.

Broadly speaking, the state was to play a supervisory role, guiding and aiding, but not interfering with the economy. The document reflected the influence of the radical economics of Keynes in which the state acted to iron out the ups and downs of the trade cycle and unemployment. It also drew from Lloyd George's belief in the positive role and responsibility of the state, a theme of his pre-war New Liberalism that continued through the 1920s. Keynes had been a critic of Lloyd George's role in negotiating the Versailles treaty of 1919. That year he published *The Economic Consequences of the Peace*, arguing that the treaty was too harsh on Germany. But he was active in the 'summer schools' and owner of the influential Liberal magazine, *The Nation*.

Certainly Liberal thinking from the mid-1920s influenced what the historian Arthur Marwick termed 'middle opinion' in the 1930s. Figures like Harold Macmillan shaped moderate 'one nation' Conservatism. Hugh Dalton and Hugh Gaitskill shaped moderate Labour thinking in the post-war world. Keynes and Beveridge (also involved in the summer schools) were responsible for shaping much of the post-1945 economic and social framework. Some historians, notably Robert Skidelsky, have judged *Britain's Industrial Future* a bold, radical document, addressing social problems and setting the agenda for future politicians. Others, like Sykes, consider the policy initiatives of the 1920s to have lowered the emphasis on Liberalism's popular, moral appeal to the strengths of individual character in favour of an emphasis on the technical management of the economy. This was understood only by an elite of experts.

In March 1929 *We Can Conquer Unemployment* (the 'Orange Book') put forward more concrete policy proposals. Politically, Lloyd George had always stressed the need to deal with the question of unemployment. *We Can Conquer Unemployment* proposed a self-financing two-year programme of road- and house-building that would reduce unemployment to 'normal' proportions, without leading to inflation. With Keynes as co-author of the accompanying *Can Lloyd George Do It?*, which explained the plans to solve unemployment, this was the centrepiece of the 1929 election campaign.

Hopes were high of Liberal success in 1929, prompted by a series of by-election victories (mostly in Conservative rural seats) through 1927 and 1928. *We Can Conquer Unemployment* had widespread support within the party and with the backing of the Lloyd George Fund there was an increase of no fewer than 167 candidates in 1924. The results were very disappointing. Only a mild recovery was registered, with 59 seats won. Mostly these had been rural Liberal strongholds prior to 1924, while further ground was lost to Labour in working-class areas like the north-east, East London and Lancashire. Only in South Wales did the plans for tackling unemployment win working-class constituency seats.

Despite these efforts, the Liberals found themselves (as after the 1923 election) supporting a minority Labour administration. If, as Trevor Wilson wrote in 1966 the Liberals had presented the most 'far-sighted and responsible party programme' put before British voters, why had it been rejected?

It seems doubtful that many voters considered the Liberal programme in such a light. After all, for much of the 1920s the Liberals had been more anxious to squabble among themselves than address the problems of the people. Having defended Free Trade in 1923 the party now seemed more pro-intervention, if not protectionist. Labour rather than the Liberals seemed in tune with working-class interests. For instance, *Britain's Industrial Future* showed a reluctance to side with the trade unions against employers. The state remained a force to be used against the unions and the stress put upon economic efficiency invariably seemed to favour management. Nor, in truth, was unemployment the problem in 1929 that it had been in the earlier 1920s or was to be by 1930. The programme was in many ways very technical, lacking in immediate popular appeal. It was also untried in practice, a set of theoretical ideas. This may well have prevented many voters taking an interest and put off (like those who voted against Baldwin's protectionism in 1923) many of those who did. Ideas could not win an election unless turned into popular policies. Caught as the third party in a two-party system (as Lloyd George feared in 1929), this was less a vote against Liberalism than against the Liberal Party and its track-record throughout the 1920s.

1. Was Lloyd George the Liberal Party's only hope for revival or the cause of many of its problems in the 1920s?

2. Why did the Liberal Party do so poorly in the 1929 election?

7.3 Why were the Liberals in the political wilderness from 1931 until the 1950s, and why did the revival of the early 1960s prove to be a 'false dawn'?

After 1929, an all too familiar descent into division developed. MPs deserted to other parties. In June 1930, the deal with the Lloyd George Fund expired, leaving the party in financial difficulty. This opened divisions with the

Asquithian Liberal Council (formed in 1926 when Lloyd George became leader). Holding on to Free Trade often left the Liberal Council more in sympathy with Labour chancellor Phillip Snowden (a staunch Free Trader) than Lloyd George's more middling stance. At the other end of the spectrum, a group around John Simon saw Labour as a socialist threat and moved towards the Conservatives, despite their growing interest in tariffs. In September 1930, in return for assistance in combatting rising unemployment, Lloyd George was able to get support from Labour for electoral reform. While this was popular, the issue of how far the Labour government should be supported further divided the party. Both Liberal policy and the party were in disarray. In that situation, part of the reasoning for supporting Labour was simply to avoid a general election.

 ## Source-based questions: The Liberal Party and the second Labour government 1929–1931

SOURCE A

We have every confidence that within three months of a Liberal government being in power, large numbers of men at present unemployed could be engaged on useful work of national development; and that within twelve months the numbers unemployed would be brought down to normal proportions. We should not, of course, rest satisfied with that, but should resume that policy which Liberalism was pursuing up to the outbreak of war, designed to reduce still further the burden of normal unemployment.

To summarize: unemployment is industrial disorganisation. It is brought to an end by new enterprise, using capital to employ labour. In the present stagnation the Government must supply that initiative that will help to set going a great progressive movement.

From We Can Conquer Unemployment *by David Lloyd George. This was the manifesto on which the Liberals fought the 1929 general election.*

SOURCE B

At first Lloyd George aimed at a policy of parliamentary independence, judging Labour's proposals on their merits, and if necessary abstaining or even voting against them. Above all, party unity was to be maintained. This policy soon collapsed when the Parliamentary Liberal Party twice voted three ways over the government's Coal Bill in 1929–30. From mid-1930 Lloyd George began to move towards a policy of real cooperation with Labour in order to achieve an agreed policy on unemployment and electoral reform.

From The Decline of the Liberal Party 1910–1931 *by Paul Adleman, 1981.*

SOURCE C

Broadly speaking the position is that the vast majority of the Party are working well together under Mr Lloyd George's leadership. Nevertheless there are certain members of the party – and among them some of the best known Liberals in the country such as Simon and Hutchinson – who are definitely bent on turning out the Government and those who follow them believe that they will have no Tory opponent at the next general election. They constitute a nucleus of disloyalty and disaffection in the Party; their interventions in debate and constant opposition in the division lobby weaken the influence of the Party in the House of Commons, while their criticism of our policy, as unprincipled as well as unwise, bewilders and discourages our supporters in the country.

From a letter by Sir Archibald Sinclair, Chief Whip of the Liberal Party, to H. A. L. Fisher, March 1931, during the second Labour government.

SOURCE D

Fresh splits completed the ruin of a once great party. As in 1924, how far to support a Labour government caused much soul-searching among Liberals. Lloyd George pushed for a comprehensive deal involving electoral reform to remove the first-past-post system. Sir John Simon and a group of Conservative-minded Liberals declared war on the Labour Government and denounced Lloyd George's dialogue in November 1930.

The crisis of August 1931 completed the fragmentation. Lloyd George was ill and Sir Herbert Samuel as acting leader of the party took the Liberals into the National Government that emerged. The party faced the 1931 election split three ways: Simonite Liberal Nationals who gained 35 seats; Samuelite Liberals who gained 33; and Lloyd George Independents who gained 4.

From British Political History 1867 to 1990 *by M. Pearce and G. Stewart, 1992.*

1. Using information contained in this chapter explain the meaning of the phrases highlighted in the sources above:

a) *using capital to employ labour (Source A)*

b) *electoral reform (Source C)*

2. *Study Source A.*

Of what value is Source A to a historian writing about the Liberal Party and the 1929 general election?

3. *Study Sources B, C and D, and use information from this chapter to assess 'To what extent was the decline of the Liberal Party between 1918 and 1931 due to internal divisions within the Party?'*

National Government and the Liberal journey into the wilderness: the 1930s

The collapse of the Labour government in economic crisis in August 1931 led to the formation of a National Government. This the Liberals warmly welcomed, not least as it at first appeared to reduce the chances of an election. Two Liberals, Herbert Samuel (Home Secretary and party leader in Lloyd George's absence through illness since July) and the Marquis of Reading (Foreign Secretary) joined the cabinet. Others served at the Education, War and Scottish offices. The chance of a split in the Labour Party, since Macdonald headed the National Government, further pleased the Liberals. However, by October the Conservative group, which was dominant in the government, had forced an election.

The Liberals entered the election with a hopeless variety of positions. Lloyd George and his family group of four North Wales MPs, opposed to the election, had withdrawn from the National Government. The official Liberal Party backed Labour's Free Trade position. Lacking the Lloyd George Fund and being in a coalition government restricted the opportunities for other Liberal candidates. Most of the 160 Liberals chose to support the National Government, despite its Conservative, and therefore protectionist, character. The group around John Simon (Liberal Nationals) were mostly spared Conservative opposition and returned 35 MPs. Herbert Samuel's official party took an anti-Labour, Free Trade position. Although supporting the National Government, they were faced with substantial Conservative opposition and only 33 were returned. Compared with 1929, the Liberal vote had fallen by over 3 million. Little wonder that in the aftermath of 1931 Lloyd George talked about the Liberal Party being 'annihilated'.

The Liberal Nationals, while distancing themselves from the Liberals, merged with the Conservatives and were duly rewarded. John Simon became Foreign secretary and Walter Runciman headed the Board of Trade. The Liberals (Samuelites) resigned from the government in September 1932. The Ottawa Imperial Economic Conference had introduced a system of imperial preference (privileged terms for trade within the British Empire), signalling the end of Free Trade. By the end of 1933, with support from the National Liberal Federation, this group of around 30 MPs had moved into opposition.

As leader Samuel faced a dire situation: by-elections, if they were contested, were lost heavily; organisation, membership and morale were collapsing. Liberals had little to say in criticism that was different from Labour and in other cases agreed with the moderate course the National Government pursued from 1934. Some proposed a revival of **Lib–Labism**. Lloyd George supported occasional Labour candidates and early in 1935 launched the 'New Deal' campaign, reviving parts of the 1929 Liberal Programme that echoed the efforts of F. D. Roosevelt in the USA and was aiming to unite all those opposed to the National Government.

The 1935 election saw just 159 Liberal candidates take the field. Only 21, including Lloyd George's family group that rejoined the party, were returned (although 33 Liberal Nationals were elected without Conservative opposition in their constituencies). Only 6.4% of voters supported the Liberals. Herbert Samuel lost his seat at Darwen in Lancashire, and was succeeded as leader by the MP for Caithness, Sir Archibald Sinclair. The prospect of the utter collapse of the party, sparked some efforts at rejuvenation. A reorganisation committee (a device also used in 1946 and 1969) under Lord Meston reported in 1936. While replacing the National Liberal Federation with a Liberal Party Organisation, the report did not address local organisation, the party's real weakness and reason for its poor performance in parliamentary and local government elections.

Not unlike Labour, the Liberal Party's real difficulty in the 1930s was the majority enjoyed by the National Government, which made opposition almost impossible. Talks aimed at reuniting with the Liberal Nationals collapsed in 1938 – Free Trade was, as ever, the sticking point. As within the Labour Party one option, a United Front of all opinion opposed to the National Government, was considered by the Liberals, but ultimately rejected. The Labour Party was uninterested in the proposal, and even the prospect of electoral reform could not induce many Liberals to work with Labour. Where Labour differed from the Liberals was in the recovery it had started in 1935 and in its re-thinking of policy that gave it a unique voice. Even though the Liberal policy documents of the 1920s exercised influence over 'middle opinion' in the 1930s, the Liberal Party itself was too small to be an important part of that opinion.

The Liberals were divided over the Munich Settlement and conscription (from 1939), but joined Churchill's coalition after May 1940. Archibald Sinclair served as the Secretary of State for Air. While the deferring of a general election came as a relief to the impoverished Liberal organisation, the electoral truce that all parties entered into did not please activists. Since Liberal MPs were meagre in number and the party could not contest seats it did not already hold, there was little for the Liberals to gain from the truce. In 1941 the Liberal Action Group, opposed to the truce, was formed and some of its members – like Honor Balfour at Darwen in 1943 – resigned from the party to contest by-elections as Independents. In 1942 the Commonwealth Party, which also side-stepped the truce, was formed by the Liberal MP for Barnstaple, Sir Richard Acland. Division and defections and the failure to unite with the Liberal Nationals left the party in a wretched condition by the close of the war.

From 1945 to 1962: talk of a revival

Poorly prepared for the 1945 election, the Liberals fielded 307 candidates, but received only 9% of the vote and returned only 12 MPs. Despite a programme written by William Beveridge, the architect of the post-war welfare state and a recent (July 1944) Liberal recruit, the party received

Lib–Labism: The idea that the two progressive, left of centre parties in British politics should work together.

Jo Grimond (1913–1993)
Liberal Party leader 1956–67 and 1976. MP for Orkney and Shetland 1950–83. Part of a great Liberal dynasty through marriage to Laura Bonham-Carter, Grimond was an effective, charming and cultured leader.

little support. Beveridge headed the campaign, but was defeated at Berwick-upon-Tweed (a seat he had only won in October 1944), Sinclair lost his seat and even Caernarvon Boroughs, Lloyd George's old constituency, fell to the Conservatives.

Clement Davies, MP for Montgomeryshire, succeeded Sinclair. His task was a near impossible one. The Liberal Party's very existence was hanging by a thread. It was estimated that there were only 200 local Liberal associations functioning in 1946. In the local government elections of 1945 and of the early 1950s the party was left without a single councillor in cities such as Birmingham and Liverpool. Less than a third of by-elections during the Attlee government were fought by a Liberal and in most of those the deposit was lost. In 1947 a formal renewal of the Conservative-Liberal National alliance posed an additional setback.

On the other hand, while quality candidates were hard to find, reorganisation was proceeding more successfully. A committee reported in 1946 and established a 'Foundation Fund' and revived many local associations. This at least enabled the Liberals to field 475 candidates in the 1950 election. Over 300 of these lost their deposits and only 9 won. Only in the old strongholds of south-west England and rural Wales and Scotland had the party received any size of vote (like Jo Grimond in Orkney and Shetland). In 1951, with the party only able to put forward 109 candidates, Liberal representation in the Commons fell to a mere 6. Only 2.6% of the votes in 1951 were for the Liberals.

Churchill, returning to office in 1951 with a small majority, offered the Liberals a coalition – with Davies taking a cabinet post. This appeared to offer the party some influence – however the fear remained that the Conservatives would simply absorb anything distinctly Liberal as they had done with the Liberal Nationals. Davies rejected Churchill's offer. The Liberal's dilemma as a third party from the 1920s to today was that to gain office or influence it would have to co-operate with other parties, thereby almost inevitably compromising its principles and its independence.

Nor was it clear in the mid-1950s to which party the Liberals inclined – Labour or Conservative. Liberalism itself was an increasingly ill-defined creed. During the 1955 election, in which only 110 Liberals stood, some urged Liberal voters to side with the Conservatives in seats without a Liberal candidate, others (notably Lady Megan Lloyd George) urged support for Labour. The party retained the six seats won in 1951, but under Davies' lacklustre leadership the party was lost in the wilderness.

In September 1956 Davies made way for the more dynamic Jo Grimond. His leadership had a troubled start. In the Carmarthen by-election in February 1957 the Liberal candidate, despite facing no Conservative opposition, lost the seat to Labour. This reduced the number of Liberal MPs to an all-time low of five. Otherwise the Liberals performed better at by-elections through 1957. In Rochdale in 1958 Ludovic Kennedy, a young and well-known face on TV, almost won for the Liberals. Finally, Mark Bonham-Carter recorded a by-election victory at Torrington. Admittedly the seat had been held by a Liberal National until 1958, but nonetheless the victory boosted the morale of the party. On the other hand, it was indicative of the Liberals' decline and desperate condition that a single victory in a by-election, rarely a representative gauge of the political mood, was invested with such importance.

At the 1959 election the revival stalled. While the Liberal vote and number of candidates doubled, only six seats were won. Torrington was lost, but Jeremy Thorpe won North Devon. Since Labour had lost ground to the Conservatives and was quarrelling bitterly over issues like **Clause Four** and nuclear disarmament, there was some justification (admittedly limited) for Grimond's musing on some realignment of the left. These

Clause Four: The part of the 1918 Labour Party constitution, that put forward the idea that the state should control the economy.

hopes were beginning to gather some evidence. Local government and by-elections through 1960 and 1961 showed a growth in Liberal support. In by-elections in March 1962 the Liberals almost won Blackpool North and Middlesbrough East and Eric Lubbock won Orpington in Kent.

What was the extent of the 1962 revival and why did it not last?

Lubbock's victory, turning the 1959 Conservative majority of almost 15,000 into a Liberal majority of almost 8,000 suggested the Liberals could break out of their remote rural strongholds and attack suburban, middle-class Conservative seats. Orpington was a commuter town and the Liberals profited from disaffection at economic slow down from later 1961. In the local government elections of May 1962 the Liberals continued to poll heavily in the Home Counties and middle-class seaside towns like Blackpool. Certainly such losses sent shock waves through the Conservative Party, although solid Labour areas witnessed little Liberal advance. In mid-1962 opinion polls put the Liberals on an even footing with Labour and Conservative, and besides the retention of Davies' old seat of Montgomeryshire there were other impressive by-election results.

Yet by the close of 1962 the Liberal advance was slowing. By-election results returned to the familiar tale of lost deposits – as at Luton in late 1963. The Liberals could not retain support at the levels they had enjoyed in 1962. Labour under Wilson was rising in the opinion polls, capturing the anti-government protest votes. With an imminent general election, votes were becoming divided between the two main parties, and the Liberals were squeezed downwards in the polls. At the 1964 election, while the Liberals increased their proportion of the vote to 11%, they returned only nine MPs. Although they polled heavily in the Home Counties and other suburban areas, no new middle-class seats were won. The four seats they did win were in Bodmin and the Scottish Highlands – only Lubbock, returned in Orpington, did not have a seat in the 'Celtic Fringe'. In short, 1962 demonstrated the volatility of Liberal support and was, as Chris Cook argues, more of an 'Indian Summer' for the Liberal Party than a revival.

The youthful, modern, classless appeal of the Grimond Liberals had seemed well-tailored to the 'affluent' Britain of the late 1950s and early 1960s. In 1959 Grimond toured the country in a helicopter, and he and candidates like Ludovic Kennedy and Robin Day came across well on television. However, the old problem of being the third party in a two-party system remained. Liberalism itself, except for its support for the European Economic Community, seemed to be making its limited advance mostly at Conservative expense. The failure of 'Orpington' Liberalism was clear by 1966. In the election the Liberals ran fewer candidates than in 1964 and won only one new suburban seat, Cheadle in Manchester.

1. How did the Liberal Party survive during the 1930s?

2. To what extent was there a Liberal Revival in the early 1960s?

7.4 What factors limited the influence of the Liberal Party in the 1970s?

Jeremy Thorpe (1929–)
Party leader 1967–76 and MP for North Devon 1959–79. A talented speaker and debater, Thorpe was out of touch with some parts of his party. He fell in 'disgrace' in 1976.

In 1966, with 12 MPs returned, Grimond stood down as Liberal leader. Jeremy Thorpe came to the job with a reputation as a talented speaker as well as being something of a television joker and political lightweight. Growing disillusion with the Wilson government might have presented the Liberals with an opportunity to advance, but it was the Conservatives and even the occasional Scottish Nationalist that picked up protest votes. Internal problems contributed to Thorpe's difficulties. Finances were short and local organisation was crumbling after the hopes of 1962 had been dashed. Conflict with the radical Young Liberal wing of the party, which had adopted policies more closely associated with the extreme left such as nationalisation, withdrawal of US troops from Vietnam and British withdrawal from NATO embarrassed the Liberal leadership.

The Young Liberals had also devised a method termed 'community politics' for local campaigning. Drawing from the radical movements this aimed to involve local people in local decision making and grassroots campaigning. For the Liberals it brought success in local government elections in Liverpool, Leeds and Birmingham. In 1969, one of the originators of this tactic, Wallace Lawler, won a by-election in the previously Labour Ladywood division of Birmingham.

However successful, community politics was a technique requiring many activists and good local organisation – and in the approach to the 1970 election the Liberals had those resources only in a few centres. Indeed, only 17 Liberal constituencies had agents two months prior to the election. Further clashes with the Young Liberals, over the militant action they had taken against the South African Rugby tour of 1970, had secured the party some unwelcome press. Although more candidates stood than in 1966, the Liberal vote fell. Ladywood, Cheadle and Orpington were among seven Liberal casualties. With only six MPs returned, Thorpe's party was back in the position of 1959.

Why did Liberal fortunes revive in 1972–73?

At the 1970 Liberal conference a Young Liberal motion was passed urging the development of 'community politics'. The leadership remained indifferent to the new radicals, and most thought the motion had been passed in the absence of any alternative. Unexpectedly the strategy began to reap rewards. In local government elections in 1971 Liberals made gains: in Liverpool, with Trevor Jones a leading proponent of 'community politics', the Liberals advanced from having a single seat in 1968 to being the largest party on the city council in 1973. By 1972, Jones was president of the party and the radicals were beginning to achieve a parliamentary breakthrough. In the 1972 to 1973 by-elections, supporters of 'community politics', such as Graham Tope in Sutton and Cheam (a suburban, Surrey seat) and David Austick in Ripon (a middle-class market town), scored impressive victories. By the end of 1973 the Liberals had also captured the Isle of Ely and Berwick-upon-Tweed, and while local government gains in industrial Labour heartlands were limited, there was no denying that this Liberal 'revival' was greater than that of 1962.

What really boosted Liberal confidence was the hope of a new type of 'centre' politics. Disillusionment with the Conservative government and within the Labour Party seemed to explain the Liberal revival. The rise of the Welsh and Scottish Nationalist parties (the SNP won 11 seats in October 1974) put third-party politics nearer the centre of the political arena than at any time since the 1920s. In another 1973 by-election at Lincoln, Dick Taverne defeated the official Labour candidate. He stood in protest at Labour's move to the left and its control by trade unions, under the banner 'Democratic Labour'. The Liberal Party entered the February 1974 election optimistically, with a distinctive programme promising a strict prices and incomes policy, a minimum wage, profit-sharing, a Bill of Rights and increased pensions. It won 19% of the vote, but only 14 seats. Yet with Labour having a majority of only five MPs, the question of coalition or realignment remained at the centre of the political agenda.

By now Liberals were of course well used to talking of revival based on by-election results, and skilled at living off the hope of a realignment in the two-party system. In reality, they remained caught in the trap of the two-party system. Core Liberal voters, party members and activists were not keen on losing Liberal political ideas in a coalition with either Labour or Heath's Conservatives. Party leaders were conscious that, given the likely chance of another election soon, it was important to keep the party's identity clear. However, the protest votes that underpinned the revival of 1972–73 were based on the belief that the Liberal Party could influence the major parties. Without this they were likely to remain protest votes rather than a permanent electoral base for the Liberals.

Nor was it clear with whom the Liberal voters or those Liberal leaders prepared for coalition might side. Just as in the 1920s, the Liberals struggled, ultimately unsuccessfully, with the complexities of 'centre' politics in the 1970s. Heath's initial approach to Thorpe to maintain the Conservatives in office was unpopular within the party. Later David Steel, Liberal chief whip, discussed a similar deal with Roy Jenkins, the rightward-leaning, pro-EEC Labour Home Secretary. Christopher Mayhew, Labour MP for Woolwich, joined the Liberals between the February and October 1974 elections. Yet after the Liberals proposed a 'Government of National Unity' in June, it was Heath who expressed some interest.

Criticism of the failure to deal with industrial relations in the 1970s could, after all, be directed at both Labour and Conservative administrations, and so it was in the October 1974 manifesto, *Why Britain Needs Liberal Government*. In fact, while another close result left the party with some influence, it could not hide a disappointing result. Fielding more candidates than in February 1974, the party's vote fell heavily and it lost two seats to the one gained at Truro.

The 'disgrace' of Thorpe and the Lib–Lab Pact

Thorpe campaigned with Heath and Jenkins for a 'yes' vote in the EEC referendum in March 1975, but after the poor result in 1974 and with a run of poor by-election results in 1976, pressure began mounting on his leadership. In addition, Thorpe suffered from his association with a collapsed bank and the allegation by a male model, Nicholas Scott, that they had had an affair. Thorpe denied it, but more seriously he was charged with conspiracy to attempt to murder Scott. The chief prosecution witness in this increasingly embarrassing affair was John Bessell, formerly Liberal MP for Bodmin. In May 1976 Thorpe resigned and Grimond took over for three months while a new leader was chosen.

David Steel, the victor, was known to favour a co-operative strategy. With the Labour government's thin majority eroded by by-election losses, Steel was anxious to avoid an election so soon after the fall of Thorpe. Both Labour and the Liberals were keen to keep an increasingly right-wing Thatcher-led Conservative Party at bay. The logic of a Lib–Lab pact was strong. It was agreed in March 1977 to save the government from a no-confidence vote. The Liberals were given regular meetings with Prime Minister Callaghan and Chancellor Healey, and were promised a system of direct elections to the European Parliament (possibly by a system of proportional representation, PR) and devolution for Scotland and Wales. By November 1977, when the Labour Party rejected a PR system for European elections, Steel was under pressure to withdraw from a pact that had saved Labour but delivered little for the Liberals. Nor was devolution achieved, and in August 1978 Steel abandoned the pact, although with the Scott case continuing (Thorpe was acquitted in 1979) the Liberals did not move to directly oppose the ailing Callaghan administration.

Under Steel and the pact by-election results held out few prospects for a forthcoming election. Council elections in 1977 brought dismal results and the Lib–Lab pact meant that the party was linked with an increasingly unpopular Labour government. The 1979 election was approached with low expectations. They were realised, with a fall in the Liberal vote of one million and three of 14 seats lost – among these was Jeremy Thorpe's.

David Steel (1938–)
Party leader 1976–88. A controversial leader who made pacts with Labour in 1977, the SDP in 1981 and was influential in the merger that created the Liberal Democrats in 1988.

Roy Jenkins (1920–)
Labour Home Secretary 1965–67 and 1974–76 and Chancellor 1967–70. The 'father figure' of the SDP and leader 1981–83. Headed the Commission on Electoral Reform from 1998. Jenkins' autobiography was titled, *A Life at the Centre* (1991).

1. How did the Liberal Party respond to its third party status in the 1970s? Consider the following:

a) Community politics.

b) Attempts at cross-party Coalitions and Pacts.

2. What damaged the Liberals more – Thorpe's 'disgrace' or the Lib–Lab pact?

7.5 How and why did the Liberal Party become the Liberal Democrats?

Thatcher's strong victory in 1979 brought to a close the hope of a coalition or pact with the governing party. What it did not destroy was the Liberal hope for some realignment of 'centre' politics. With the Thatcherite Conservative Party moving to the right and the Labour Party of the early 1980s led by Michael Foot moving sharply to the left, the centre ground of politics was being left open by the two major parties.

Centrists in both the Labour and Conservative parties eyed the centre ground. After Thatcher's purge of the cabinet moderates ('wets') in September 1981, Conservatives were anxious at the right-wing direction and unpopularity of the government. Roy Jenkins, who had resigned from the Labour government to become President of the European Commission, had considered the possibility of a new 'centre party'. The merits of coalition and PR were made in his televised Dimbleby Lecture, 'Home Thoughts from Abroad', at the end of 1979. It was from the Labour ranks that moves for realignment came. Many were unhappy with Labour's leftward drift, its opposition to nuclear armaments and involvement in the EEC. After the special January 1981 conference had confirmed the role of the trade unions in selecting the leader, a group of leading social democrats openly broke with the party. Jenkins, David Owen, Shirley Williams and Bill Rodgers issued the 'Limehouse Declaration' putting forward their differences with Labour in January 1981. By March, with Jenkins as leader, they had established the Social Democratic Party (SDP).

The SDP's 'gang of four' had all been influential Labour figures – Owen, Williams and Rodgers had been Foreign Secretary, Education Secretary and Transport Secretary respectively in the last Labour administration. In parliament Owen and Rodgers were joined by ten Labour MPs and one Conservative, and across the country many Labour councillors joined the new party. The creation of the SDP might be seen to signal the failure of the Liberals to occupy the centre ground, but in fact Jenkins and Steel had begun to discuss an electoral agreement and (so far as it is possible to precisely tell) the Liberals benefited from the creation of the SDP.

Certainly the 1981 local elections brought Liberal gains. With the alliance between the parties supported by their respective conferences, the Liberal William Pitt was the first to secure what was to be one of many Alliance by-election victories, winning Croydon north-west from the Conservatives in October 1981. In November Williams won Crosby, a safe Conservative seat in Liverpool, and by March 1982 Jenkins was back in parliament having won Glasgow Hillhead, also from the Conservatives. Not all Alliance victories came at Conservative expense – Bermondsey was won by Liberal Simon Hughes early in 1982 against a divided and acrimonious Labour campaign. Riding high in the opinion polls, Steel was encouraged to suggest to the 1981 Liberal conference delegates that they ought to 'go back to your constituencies and prepare for government'.

In fact by the time a general election was set for June 1983, not only had Conservative fortunes picked up, but the Alliance's advance had halted. Equally, hopes that the Alliance might win enough Conservative votes to allow Labour to sneak a win and introduce policy without the restriction of its right-wing leaders, were misplaced. The Liberals and the SDP divided the constituencies and fought on a rather indistinct programme promising a reduction of unemployment, membership of the EEC, multilateral disarmament, devolution and proportional representation. The result confirmed the difficulties of third-party politics and, coming second in so many constituencies, reaffirmed the Liberal's desire for proportional representation. In votes the Alliance polled less than a million behind Labour. But only 23 Alliance MPs were returned (6 SDP

David Owen (1938–)
Labour Foreign Secretary 1977–79 and SDP founder and leader 1983–90. Opposed the full merger of the Alliance after 1987.

and 17 Liberal). The Alliance had received 25% of the vote, but only 3% of the seats while Labour with 27% had more than 30% of the seats. The Conservatives won a landslide victory.

The disappointment of 1983 was lessened by the impressive vote that the Alliance had recorded. This allowed the Alliance to survive the defeat. With Owen replacing Jenkins as leader of the SDP, the joint leadership of 'the two Davids' was born. Ridiculed on TV programmes like *Spitting Image* (in which the 'Owen' puppet kept a tiny 'Steel', as his junior, in his pocket), their differences were about policy as much as personality. Certainly, where Steel seemed amicable and easy-going, Owen took a more superior tone which verged on arrogance.

Perhaps most damaging was the fact that the shared leadership contributed to doubts about the Alliance's rather indeterminate, opportunistic image. For Owen, the SDP was a distinct party and the alliance one of electoral sense. Steel, on the other hand, was keener for the parties to ally more permanently and deeply. In terms of policy, the persistence of a strong opposition to the place of nuclear weapons in British and European defence policy among many Liberal members exposed strains within the Alliance. Since Owen and the SDP were convinced of the need for Britain to have a nuclear deterrent, a pact with Labour in a **hung parliament** was seen as impossible. For Steel, however, it was the idea of co-operating with the Conservatives that was ruled out. Thus, whatever the 1987 manifesto *Britain United* promised, the role the Alliance would adopt in holding the balance of power was uncertain.

Otherwise the Alliance trod a familiar path after 1983, with periodic by-election results exciting hopes of revival and the question of the true nature of the unity of the SDP and Liberals being avoided. Certainly the Alliance achieved some remarkable by-election results. Penrith and Borders in 1983 saw a swing of 15% to the Alliance, Portsmouth South was won in 1984, Brecon and Radnor in 1985, West Derbyshire and Ryedale in 1986 and Greenwich (the only gain from Labour) in 1987. Yet there was little consistency and the Alliance's performance elsewhere, such as the 1984 European elections or 1987 council elections, was disappointing. Steady advance and only periodic breakthroughs suggested that Steel's comment for Liberals to 'seriously prepare ourselves for government' was a little optimistic. The 1987 election saw the Alliance take some 22.5% of the vote, but secure only 22 seats (5 SDP and 17 Liberal).

The end of the Alliance and the end of the Liberal Party

To many, after 1987 it seemed pointless to maintain the machinery of two parties when the space for a third party was in itself so limited. Steel was the first to call for a formal merger of the SDP and Liberals. In many constituencies the two parties were already united. Most Liberals backed their leader, but the SDP leaders and members were less certain. David Owen was strongly opposed. Among his fellow SDP MPs Charles Kennedy and Robert Maclennan backed the idea, but Rosie Barnes and John Cartwright stood with Owen. A ballot of the SDP's members in August 1987 showed nearly 26,000 in favour of merger and 19,000 opposed. Owen resigned as SDP leader. Maclennan replaced him, but at the party conference it was clear that Owen was thinking about a breakaway 'fourth party' and that many members continued to see him as leader.

The Liberal conference duly voted for merger talks to begin in September. There were numerous difficulties – the party name, the new constitution, and NATO. In particular the question of support for NATO threatened to divide Liberal leaders and activists. There was also concern at the proposed new name, Alliance, and the absence of the word 'Liberal'

Hung parliament: A situation, after a general election, when no one party has a majority over the others combined.

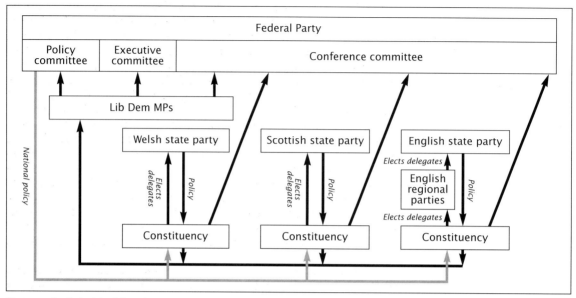

The organisation of the Liberal Democrat Party

from this title. By January 1988 the merger talks were at breaking point. Many of the Liberal negotiators had resigned (over the NATO and name questions) and Steel had agreed a policy statement with Maclennan that shocked most Liberals in proposing an extension of VAT to food and children's clothes and a pro-nuclear policy. Maclennan was forced to back down on these policy commitments, thereby angering many SDP members. A reformulated merger and policy statement, condemned by the Owenites, was agreed by the special Liberal assembly and by an SDP meeting at the close of January.

Whatever the activities of their leaders, party members had the final say. The ballot results of March 1988 endorsed a merger, with just over half the memberships of the Liberals and SDP turning out. Two-thirds of SDP members either rejected a merger, or did not vote. This result delighted the Owenites as they relaunched the SDP. Nevertheless, in March 1988 the awkwardly named Social and Liberal Democratic Party (SLD), with Maclennan and Steel as joint leaders, presented itself to the political world. It marked the historic end of the Liberal Party.

1. Why did the Liberal Party ally itself with the SDP?

2. Why was the merger that created the Liberal Democrats so difficult to achieve?

7.6 *The fate of the Liberal-SDP Alliance*
A CASE STUDY IN HISTORICAL INTERPRETATION

Since new political parties rarely have the impact of the SDP (however short-lived) it was the subject of much debate and commentary. Not least because its rise was so rapid. Within weeks of March 1981 the party had some 50,000 members. Before its birth, its creators were confident of its potential. In a speech delivered six months after 'Home Thoughts From Abroad', Jenkins – himself a biographer of Asquith and Gladstone – considered 'that in a few years time someone may be able to write ... convincingly of The Strange and Rapid Revival of Liberal and Social Democratic Britain'. Also pursuing the Dangerfield analogy, Jeremy Josephs argued in *Inside the Alliance* (1983) that it was 'all well and good ... if, as it appeared, the SDP had helped to bring about an equally strange rebirth of liberal England'. Certainly the SDP, via the Alliance, seemed to breathe life into the Liberal Party. More controversially, one might argue that in the longer-term it helped to revive the Labour Party.

Militant: An extreme left-wing group within the Labour Party. Controlled the Liverpool City Labour group in the early 1980s. Expelled from the Labour Party, under the leadership of Neil Kinnock, from 1985.

Ethical socialist: People who believe that a fair distribution of wealth is either religiously or morally correct.

The SDP's rise was discussed in terms of the decline of working-class politics and the crisis in the Labour Party, which was attacked both from the right by the SDP and the left by **Militant**. Historian Raphael Samuel, in a 1982 essay in *New Society* (now reprinted in *Island Stories*, 1998) suggested that the SDP might be the product of a new middle class that in itself was something of a new political class. Samuel was no fan of the SDP and a scathing critic of its claim to be working in the tradition of **ethical socialists** like R. H. Tawney, in the form of its think-tank, the Tawney Society. But, he argued, it was a party in which the new values of the professional and managerial middle class, such as lawyers, doctors, bankers, accountants, dentists and lecturers, were accepted. The party's self-proclaimed image was youthful and professional. It was launched (or marketed) with the aid of a variety of public relations techniques and new members could pay their party membership by credit card. The party's largest single branch, Samuel noted, was in the affluent south-west London suburb of Richmond. A survey of members at the close of 1981 found 57% to be from the professional classes compared with 7% from the manual working class.

This perhaps provides some clues to the tensions within the SDP and between it and the Liberals. Shirley Williams might have proclaimed in the title of her book *Politics is for People* (1981), but the SDP seemed uneasy in the presence of the working class or trade unions. No trade unions left the Labour Party with the 'gang of four' or the Labour MPs that followed, and David Owen was strongly critical of the miners' union during the 1984–85 strike. It was the influence the trade unions enjoyed within the Labour Party that had been a large part of the reason for the Social Democrats' departure. In the SDP's desire for a new politics, overcoming the old divisions and interests of capital and labour, the unions seemed an entrenched, reactionary force in society. This was important because compared to the advances it made against the Conservatives, the make-up of the SDP limited its ability to win working-class Labour votes.

Merger talks from 1987 revealed differences between the parties: in its structure and relationship with members the SDP was centralised and elitist in some respects; the Liberals were a more federal body, attaching considerable influence to their councillors. Where the SDP was professional, cautious, but prolific in its policy formulation and presentation, the Liberals were rather more improvised and free-thinking. It was the hope of the Liberal Democrats to merge all that was best from the Alliance. Nor was the Alliance always solid at constituency level. In 1981 the Liberal Association in Croydon refused to stand down their candidate in favour of Shirley Williams, despite the wishes of David Steel.

Relations within the leadership, for all the show of unity, often caused problems. The issue of a full merger caused friction between Owen and Steel. In his memoirs, *Time to Declare* (1991), Owen described his relationship with Steel as 'edgy but civil'. Steel's open support for a merger after 1987 angered Owen, who considered it an attempt to force change on the SDP. But Owen also suggests that the SDP might have benefited from not forming an Alliance with the Liberals in 1981 and going it alone. After all, the Liberals were not in themselves strong opponents, the SDP might have polled as heavily as it did in any case and been able to negotiate a merger from a stronger position. Des Wilson, who was President of the Liberal Party 1986–87 and chair of the Liberal election campaign committee in 1987, offers an inside account of relations within the Alliance in *Battle for Power* (1987). Wilson's account is sympathetic towards Steel's position. He describes working with Owen as 'difficult' and argues that the 'sheer practical benefits of merger' – not least in avoiding a lengthy post-mortem on the election defeat of 1987 – outweighed any philosophical differences between the parties. The latter were real enough, but for Wilson, the continuing hope of forging a new centre party remained.

Despite bright prospects for a new politics at that time, with Labour and the Conservatives abandoning the centre ground of politics from 1979, the SDP and Alliance story, like so much in 20th-century Liberal history, is ultimately one of disappointment. Ivor Crewe and Tony King's *The History of the SDP* (1993) includes an **obituary** of the party entitled 'A Study in Failure'. The SDP could not break the mould and realign British politics. But Crewe and King suggest that this 'does not necessarily mean that it had no consequences for British politics'. In fact the SDP, in its failure, serves as a useful case study in third-party politics and in understanding the changes in British politics in the 1980s and 1990s.

Crewe and King explained the Alliance's failure to break the party alignment of British politics. The last time the party system realigned was during the 1920s when Labour replaced the Liberals as the main anti-Conservative Party. Three factors, they argue, were decisive in this process: Labour's class-based appeal, the expansion of the electorate after 1918 (mostly working-class voters) and the split in the Liberal Party from 1916. In 1981 none of these factors was present to help the Alliance achieve a breakthrough. Its appeal lacked focus. It had to win voters from other parties, and thus win on the first-past-the-post system. Also the Labour Party did not split again after 1981.

Indeed for all the talk of splitting in 1981, the majority of Labour's social democratic wing – figures like Denis Healey, Roy Hattersley and John Smith – remained within Labour. At most 28 MPs left Labour for the SDP, and when the majority of these failed to retain their seats in 1983, the career-sense as well as principles of staying with Labour were clear. Social democracy remained strong within the Labour Party.

Besides Labour's failure to split further, it was clear that the electoral system weighed against the Alliance. Whatever its difficulties of leadership, policy or tactics in dealing with the Liberals, the SDP faced major structural barriers in the electoral system to its advance. In 1983 it had around 200 seats fewer than it would have won in a system of PR. Because of the system, the Alliance struggled to turn votes into seats in Parliament, thus appearing unlikely to wield power after the election – and through the notion of 'wasted votes' or tactical voting to keep either Labour or the Conservatives out, it may have been deprived of additional voters. The Alliance's pro-PR views were democratic as well as self-serving.

Obituary: A summary of a person's life written shortly after their death.

What message is this cartoon trying to give about the Liberal Democrat Party under Paddy Ashdown? Explain your answer.

From the *Guardian*, 23 September 1998

In addition, Crewe and King suggest that the Alliance's advance was limited by this system, giving the Labour Party time to change and modernise its image and policies. By 1987 Labour's renewal and the recovery of its vote had put an end to talk of realignment across the centre-left of British politics. Many within Labour had argued that the breakaway of the SDP helped to maintain the Conservatives in office and delay Labour's return. This is, however, difficult to support. Most Alliance by-election victories (as tended to be the case with the Liberals in the 1960s and 1970s) were from the Conservatives and served to limit their majority. Had the 'gang of four' stayed, the in-fighting within Labour would most probably have got worse. Moreover, was not the New Labour Party influenced by the SDP in its modernisation under Kinnock, Smith and most recently Blair?

By 1991, when Labour had abandoned unilateral nuclear disarmament and nationalisation and was more pro-EEC and free market and more image-conscious, Bill Rodgers suggested that 'the SDP showed the way ... the Labour Party has been re-made in the image of the SDP'. This undoubtedly claims too much influence for a policy rethink in the Labour Party that was most rapid after 1987. By that time the SDP was involved in merger talks. Yet, in New Labour's thinking on combining the welfare state, redistribution and the free market economy there were traces of the SDP's Social Market Foundation, of Crosland's revisionist socialism of the 1950s. Crosland was a close friend of Jenkins and leading thinker of Labour's social democrats. Certainly Blair's notion of a new politics (the 'Third Way') seems to involve working with Liberal Democrats like Ashdown and Jenkins. Even David Owen, the SDP's most fervent defender, has expressed admiration for Blair.

1. What were the chances of political success for the SDP in 1981?

2. Was the Alliance a failure?

3. Why have historians and political scientists differed in their views on the impact of the Alliance on British Politics?

7.7 Why did Paddy Ashdown's Liberal Democrats prove more successful in local elections than general elections?

Neither Maclennan nor Steel gained much credit from the merger process and a new leader promised to confirm the break from the past that the SLD represented. In July 1988 Paddy Ashdown took sole charge of the party. This was no easy task, not least because the existence of Owen's SDP both confused voters and proved a problem to SLD candidates at by-elections. The SDP out-polled the SLD at the Richmond by-election in February 1989, but it was poaching votes that the SLD might reasonably expect to gather. Splitting the 'centre' vote seemed to reduce the point of voting for a 'centre' party, either to elect the party itself, or as a tactic to defeat the major parties. In other respects the party's electoral performance was worsening. The May 1989 council elections saw a loss of seats. The European elections a month later again saw the SLD, the self-proclaimed party of Europe, gain not one seat. It received only 6% of the vote. Even third party status seemed in doubt, because the Scottish Nationalists had gained a seat and the Green Party some 15% of the vote. Even the party's name was a continuing problem. The 1988 conference took the informal title 'Democrats' before Liberal Democrats was adopted in 1989. After the blood-letting of 1987–88, both morale and finances were low.

Only by 1990 was the gloom lifting. By June the Owenite SDP had dissolved itself. A month earlier it had polled below the Monster Raving Loony Party in the Bootle by-election. Owen did not stand in the 19??
election. Only the 'old' Liberal Party, reconstituted in 1989, wa?
Although it put up 70 candidates in the 1992 election and ?
European elections, it was no real threat. Support for the Gree?
dropped from the peak of 1989. By-election victories in th?
seats of Eastbourne in 1990, Ribble Valley and Kincardi?

Paddy Ashdown (1941–)
Leader of the Liberal
Democrats 1988–99, MP for
Yeovil since 1983. A successful
leader, he increased the party's
local and national
representation.

the Liberal Democrats to have inherited the Alliance's ability to achieve large swings in the vote. In the local elections of 1991 the Liberal Democrats registered a gain of over 500 council seats, mainly at Conservative expense. Ashdown himself was an increasingly popular and assured leader. The 1991 policy document, *Shaping Tomorrow, Starting Today*, reflected his stress on electoral reform and PR, a strong pro-Europe policy, devolution and an increase in income tax to fund education.

Thus the 1992 election was approached with some optimism. The prospect of a hung parliament as usual focused attention on what course of action the third party would adopt. Ashdown underlined his demand for electoral reform as the condition for any cross-party agreement, and underlined the Liberals' distance from both main parties. The Conservatives however, won a comfortable victory, and the Liberal Democrats were reduced to 20 seats. With almost 18% of the vote this was disappointing. All the by-election gains since 1987 were lost. In a sense the Liberal Democrats remained on the Celtic fringe. Their main strongholds in terms of seats were those of the old Liberals (with the exception of Wales), south-west England and the Scottish Highlands. In south-east England, despite gaining 23% of the vote, the party won no seats.

Progress after 1992 was swift. In 1993 two sensational by-election victories were won at Newbury and Christchurch. Both were safe Conservative seats and in the latter the Liberal Democrats registered the biggest swing (35.4%) in post-war politics. More impressive was the party's advance in local government. In the 1993 county elections, the party made sweeping gains against the Conservatives. Of the Home Counties only Buckinghamshire remained in Conservative control. While only gaining outright control of Cornwall and Somerset, the Liberal Democrats had vastly expanded their role in local government. This was due in part to Lib–Lab pacts in counties like Essex and Berkshire. Neither Labour nor Liberal Democrats were content with such coalitions, but the party was now simply too large to be ignored. In May 1994 the Liberal Democrats advanced to be the second party in local government. In terms of council seats and councils controlled they had reduced the Conservatives to third place. Gains included Kingston-upon-Thames, Bath and Eastleigh. Even Labour inner-city strongholds were under pressure from the Liberal Democrats. Despite the racist scandal in Tower Hamlets which saw three councillors resign and the loss of the council, the Liberal Democrats advanced strongly in Lambeth and Southwark.

Much more than the SDP, the Liberal Democrats were serious and practical in their pursuit of local issues. The old Liberal strategy of 'community politics' remained within the party. While Ashdown was criticised for his interest in foreign affairs (especially the Bosnian crisis) and contrast with the euro-apathy or scepticism attitude of many voters, the party was popular at the local level. By 1994 the Liberal Democrats had made such an important breakthrough as a governing party that they had to hope it could be repeated at parliamentary level.

This was helped by a by-election victory at Eastleigh, but rather diminished by the June 1994 European elections. While the Liberal Democrats returned their first two European MPs in Somerset and Devon North, and Cornwall and Plymouth West, the party trailed behind both Conservative and Labour. With Tony Blair appointed as new leader, Labour's hopes in particular were looking far-reaching.

Labour's resurgence raised problems for the Liberal Democrats. History appeared to have come full circle, with Blair abandoning Labour's historic Clause Four, which had distinguished it from the Liberals in 1918. Labour was no longer committed to nationalisation, central planning, unilateral disarmament or withdrawal from the EEC, and was returning to other radical interests. The prospect arose of re-building the pre-1918 progressive alliance of Labour and Liberals, a sort of 'centre' party.

On the other hand, it seemed that this political 'centre' was being built around Blair more than the Liberal Democrats. New Labour threatened the Liberal Democrats by moving to the centre and adopting many of their policies, most notably constitutional reform. To survive meant the Liberals had to either distance themselves from Labour or set clear terms for any cooperation. With further local election advances in 1995, Ashdown abandoned the policy of distance from the two main parties in favour of Labour. There was considerable disquiet among activists and MPs, especially in northern and inner-city areas where Labour was the Liberal Democrats' main opponent. The move was also unpopular among those fighting New Labour in the Littleworth and Saddleworth by-election, although a narrow victory seemed to support Ashdown's stance.

This was confirmed at the 1995 conference, although Ashdown also stressed the distinctive tax, environment (curbing private motoring, taxing pollution) and electoral reform proposals his party represented. At the close of the year the party was joined by Emma Nicholson, Conservative MP for Devon West, gaining a little media attention from that directed towards New Labour. Further advances in the 1996 council elections (the party now had over 5,000 councillors) could not allay the problem of relations with New Labour. Many Liberal Democrats recognised the common ground between the two. Some saw this as way for the two to work together, others feared, and some like Bill Rodgers urged, that Liberal Democrats might vote tactically (meaning for Labour) to ensure the Conservatives were defeated after 18 years. By October 1996 a joint committee, headed by Maclennan and Labour's Robin Cook, was created to discuss constitutional reform. As Labour-sceptic Liberals had warned, the Conservatives denounced this as a revival of the Lib–Lab pact.

The 1997 election was eagerly awaited. Almost half of the Liberal Democrat candidates had experience as councillors. There were 50 special target seats that the party believed were within its reach. This was a sensible strategy as on a reduced percentage of the vote the Liberal Democrats returned 46 MPs, the largest number since 1929. In particular south-west England, Scotland and suburban south-west London (Sutton and Cheam, Kingston and Surbiton) turned **yellow**. Overwhelmingly these seats were won from the Conservatives, while in northern and inner-city areas the Liberal Democrats made little impact on Labour support. Certainly, many Liberal Democrat gains were marginal; Winchester was won by two votes. The party benefited from tactical voting: 1997 was a celebrated achievement for the party.

The size of the New Labour majority meant there was no hope of coalition. Nevertheless, Liberal Democrats had reason to welcome the Blair government. It was quickly declared that PR would be used for the next European elections, devolution legislation was introduced for Scotland and Wales and by July 1997 Ashdown had been invited to sit on a cabinet committee on constitutional reform. In addition a Commission on Electoral Reform, headed by Roy (now Lord) Jenkins, was to look at the question of PR more carefully. By 1999 a Freedom of Information Bill, a long-standing Liberal demand, had been promised. The party's prospects looked bright, but there was the continuing fear that Blair and New Labour might absorb the Liberal Democrats, depriving them of a distinct identity. By January 1999 the question of relations with Labour was obscured by Ashdown's announcement that he would resign in the summer. He was succeeded in August by Charles Kennedy, an SDP supporter of merger in 1987. (He was the only surviving former-SDP MP.) He had steered a more cautionary line towards working with Labour.

Yellow: The party colour of the Liberal Democrats.

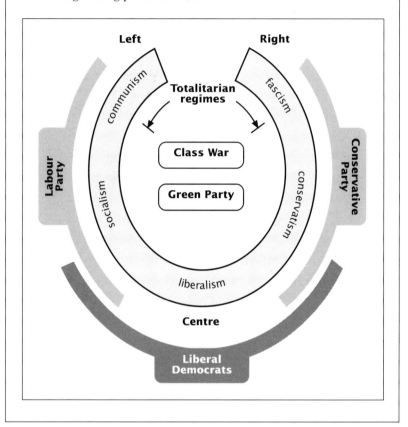

Liberal Democrat ideas

A diagram of the relationship between British political parties and left and right wing political ideas.

1. To what extent does the Liberal Democrat advance in local government mark a significant breakthrough for the third party?

2. What problems do the Liberal Democrats share with their Liberal predecessors?

'The best is yet to come', Ashdown proclaimed at the party's 1997 conference – a familiar, hopeful rallying call sounded often during the years of Liberalism had endured in the wilderness. Ashdown's Liberal Democrats, whatever their successes in local government, remained very much the third party in Parliament. If new prospects were born out of 1997, it was clear that old, historic problems and questions remained.

The road to 1945: the impact of the Second World War

Key Issues

- *What were Britain's war aims and how and to what extent were they achieved?*

- *How and why did the Second World War change Britain's status as a world power?*

- *To what extent did the Second World War bring political, social and economic change to Britain?*

Framework of Events

1939	September: Britain declares war on Germany
1940	May: Winston Churchill replaces Neville Chamberlain as Prime Minster
	June: evacuation of British troops from Dunkirk
	July to September: Battle of Britain
	July: beginning of Blitz
1941	March: Lend-Lease Act
	Atlantic Charter
	June: Soviet Union allies with Britain after German invasion
	Clothes rationing introduced
	December: United States allies with Britain and Soviet Union after Japanese attack on US fleet in Pearl Harbour
1942	Fall of Malaya and Singapore base to Japanese
	Beveridge Report on Social Insurance and Allied Services
1943	January: meeting of Roosevelt and Churchill at Casablanca
	Ministry of Town and Country Planning created
	November: meeting of Churchill, Roosevelt and Stalin at Teheran
1944	June: Allied invasion of Normandy, D-Day
	White Papers produced on a National Health Service, Employment Policy and Social Insurance
	Butler Education Act passed
	Moscow, 'Spheres on Influence' agreement between Churchill and Stalin
1945	February: meeting of Churchill, Roosevelt and Stalin at Yalta
	Family Allowances Act passed
	May: Victory in Europe (VE) day
	July: meeting of Churchill, Roosevelt and Stalin at Potsdam
	Attlee replaces Churchill as Prime Minister during Potsdam meeting
	August: atom bombs dropped on Hiroshima and Nagasaki
	Japan surrenders: Victory in Japan (VJ) day
	America ends Lend-Lease agreement

Overview

Status quo: Things as they were, i.e. without any change happening.

THE Second World War involved Britain in an unprecedented fight for survival. The First World War had been a war to maintain the military, economic and territorial **status quo**. The Second World War was more than a fight to maintain the status quo. It was also seen as a just war against a military dictator who viciously pursued the implementation of extreme racial theories and political oppression. If Britain had been defeated, it would have risked becoming subjected to these extreme practices. It therefore became a war with few 'holds barred'. Britain had to win, and much was sacrificed to the achievement of victory. One of the principal adjustments to be made was a change in Britain's status as a great power.

Before the war Britain had been the leading global power. By the end of it the United States and the Soviet Union had become the most significant world leaders and Britain was relegated to a supporting role. Britain retained its status as a power, with global commitments and responsibilities due to the Empire, but had neither sufficient military nor economic might to act against other great powers. The United States possessed military and economic might and the atomic bomb, having built up all three during the war. The Soviet Union possessed enormous military might, and by the end of the war the Red Army occupied most of Eastern and Central Europe. Thus, by the end of the war, it was a **bipolar** world, and Britain was not one of the poles. This state of affairs had developed as both the United States and the Soviet Union had learned to flex their diplomatic and military muscles during the course of the war, and had emerged from the comparative diplomatic isolationism each had preferred pre-war. On the other hand, as the war progressed, Britain's threadbare defences were revealed by its difficulty in overcoming Germany, and the ease with which the Japanese had over-run the Far East and South-East Asia. These were the issues that relegated Britain to a supporting role in comparison with the United States and the Soviet Union. By the end of the war it was apparent too that Britain would find it easier to achieve its diplomatic and strategic aims as an ally of the United States.

Bipolar: The split between the two superpowers the United States (capitalist) and the Soviet Union (communist). Ideologically opposed, they came to dominate and Western and Eastern power blocs in world politics.

One of Britain's principal problems was that it was nearly bankrupted by the Second World War. Having fought Germany alone for nearly two years, it had relied heavily on American informal aid, in the form of **Lend-Lease**, and continued to do so during the remainder of the war. But lend-lease, and all the other aid, had to be paid for after the war.

Lend-Lease: An American policy introduced during the Second World War where military aid was given to Britain, and other allied countries, with the aim of acquiring payment for such aid after the war.

British society changed too. Rationing and the losses and fears caused by the bombing raids had been shared by all, high and low. Even the King and Queen in Buckingham Palace were bombed. The government took control of people's lives in an unprecedented way, organising industrial and agricultural production, directing people into industries or the forces, evacuating children and using women to support the war effort. Mass acceptance of increased government interference bred a corresponding expectation that the government would interfere equally as much to improve welfare provision. The Beveridge Report, which advocated specific welfare reforms, was received with enthusiasm by many people. The Labour Party's promise to introduce its proposals improved its chances of electoral success, as was seen in the 1945 general election.

In 1940 Parliamentary practice had been adjusted by a move to all-party Coalition government. This remained in place until the 1945 general election. This election changed the political scene in Britain, passing power to the Labour Party from the Conservative Party, which had dominated the National Government from 1931 to 1945. Enthusiasm for the Labour Party's political platform signified a change in British political expectations from what might be called 'laissez-faire' Conservatism to an acceptance of an almost socialist programme.

The relationship between Britain and the Commonwealth changed too. Colonial territories no longer saw Britain as a natural '**trustee**' of their best interests. Britain had proved not to be invincible, as Japanese conquests in the Far East and South-east Asia had demonstrated. The loyalty of Australia and New Zealand had been stretched to the limit by the easy loss to the Japanese of Malaya and Singapore, where **ANZAC** forces, sent to reinforce the defence facilities there, had been taken prisoner. Britain had encouraged both Dominions to look to the United States for their defence, and this position did not entirely retrieved after the war. Indian Nationalists too stepped-up demands for full independence. Although they did not achieve them during the war, they extracted promises of post-war independence from a British government that was obliged to concentrate on winning the war. India was important to Britain, but the military strategies that were to lead to the defeat of Germany were more immediate problems.

Trustee: Someone given the responsibility of overall care.

ANZAC: The forces of Australia and New Zealand.

8.1 What were Britain's main war aims, and how did the conduct of the military campaigns affect the international settlements at the end of the Second World War?

What were Britain's main war aims?

The immediate cause of Britain declaring war on Germany on 3 September 1939 was Hitler's invasion of Poland on 1 September. But Britain and France had no strategy to save Poland by fighting for that country, once Hitler had invaded. They feared that they would also have to fight the Soviet Union, under the terms of the Nazi-Soviet Pact of August 1939.

At the outbreak of war, Britain and France had failed in their aim of stopping Hitler attacking Poland. They still thought it necessary to oppose him in order to prevent him from gaining mastery of Europe. Hitler made peace offers to Britain from the end of September 1939. The British government rejected them all. Hitler asked, 'Why do they fight? They have no definite objective … I want England to retain her empire and its command of the seas unimpaired. But I must have the continent. A new age is dawning in Europe.' But Hitler had not grasped the point. It was to prevent his gaining mastery of Europe and the institution of a 'new age' that Britain fought on. Hitler had broken his word so many times that his statements could not be trusted. By standing up to him, Britain aimed also to keep its Empire intact, its naval superiority (over all but the United States navy) and preserve its status as a global power. Even so, the government understood very well from the experience of the First World War that going to war risked upsetting the status quo and would be very expensive.

US President Franklin Delano Roosevelt (1882–1945)
Democrat President of the United States from 1932 to 1945. Roosevelt is known for his 'New Deal' programme, which drew the United States out of the Depression. He unofficially helped Britain to fight the war until December 1941 because he recognised that Hitler would eventually turn on the United States if Britain were to be defeated.

Fall of France: The surrender of France to Germany, which resulting in German domination of French strategy and diplomacy during the Second World War.

- By December 1941 Roosevelt and Churchill had agreed that the defeat of Germany took precedence over defeating Japan in the Pacific war.

- At Casablanca in January 1943, Churchill and Roosevelt agreed to press for unconditional surrender of Germany and Japan. This policy was extended in May 1943 to cover the expected Italian surrender.

- As the war wore on, and Hitler's treatment of Jews, gypsies and disabled people became public knowledge, a moral dimension was added to Britain's war aims.

How was Britain involved in the early stages of the war?

The period between the start of the Second World War and the **Fall of France** is known as the 'phoney war' because very little happened to Britain. Britain and France set up a Supreme War Council, for policy co-ordination, and each agreed not to conclude a separate peace with Germany. Britain assumed the war would last three years and instituted a naval blockade in the belief that this would cause Germany to surrender. The naval blockade was completely undermined by Hitler's conquest of Eastern Europe, from which he obtained the mineral resources and agricultural produce Germany needed.

- The 'phoney war' ended in May 1940 when Hitler invaded Holland, Belgium, Luxembourg and then France. The British expeditionary force was sent to fight alongside the French, but they were encircled by the Germans and had to make a run for the coast. Although much valuable military equipment was lost, 200,000 British and 140,000 French troops escaped to the coast, at Dunkirk. Between 26 May and 6 June 1940 they were rescued by an 'armada' of mainly privately-owned little ships which the Royal Navy had organised to sail from Britain, with RAF cover.

The Blitz: The word by which the British public referred to the German bombing. It especially relates to the period September 1940 to May 1941.

- In July 1940 Germany launched an intensive bombing campaign from Northern France on the British mainland, known as 'the **Blitz**' (see section 8.2). The Blitz continued until May 1941.

- German Bombers flew with fighter-plane cover. British fighter-planes (Spitfires and Hurricanes) needed to destroy both German fighters and bombers to prevent their arrival over targets in Britain to release their bombs. These German attacks were countered by British fighters in aerial combat, celebrated as 'The Battle of Britain', of which Winston Churchill said 'Never in the field of human conflict has so much been owed by so many to so few'. He also said, 'The Navy can lose us the war, but the Air Force can win it'. By maintaining control of the skies over Britain, the Royal Air Force frustrated the launch of Hitler's 'Operation Sealion' to invade Britain from Northern France, for which German mastery of the skies would have been a key factor. In June 1941 Hitler turned his attention from Britain to the invasion of the Soviet Union.

Why did Britain's involvement in the war spread from Europe to North Africa?

Axis: The name given to the alliance between Germany, Italy and Japan during the Second World War.

It was Mussolini's entry into the war on 10 June 1940 which extended its geographical location. Once French defences had been put out of action, Mussolini thought it safe to enter the war on the **Axis** side. He was jealous of Hitler's conquests in Northern Europe and wanted an Empire running from the Red Sea to the Atlantic including the

Main events and military theatres of war

1939
1 September Start of 'phoney war'. Although France and Britain had declared war on Germany, no fighting began between them.

1–27 September German conquest of Poland.

14 September Soviet occupation of Poland.

November Soviet invasion of Finland.

1940
March End of Soviet/Finnish war.

April German occupation of Norway and Denmark; a British expeditionary force sent to help failed.

May German attack on Belgium, Holland and Luxembourg.
Germany attacked France, and the British Expeditionary Force in France was nearly cut off and lost. 26 May-4 June a fleet of small ships from Britain evacuated British troops cut off in France through the port of Dunkirk.

June Mussolini declared war on France and Britain. France capitulated and the northern half and western coast was occupied by Germany. The southern half was governed from Vichy (in central France) by supporters of Germany under Marshal Pétain.

July German bombing raids on Britain commenced (the Blitz).

August Battle of Britain commenced.

November Churchill and Roosevelt agreed Lend-lease scheme.

1941
March Germany invaded the Balkans to assist Italy's unsuccessful attempts at conquest.

May The Blitz ended.

June Germany invaded the Soviet Union (Operation Barbarossa).

August Churchill-Roosevelt meeting at Placentia Bay (Canada) agreeing Atlantic Charter.

December On the 7th Japan attacked the United States navy at Pearl Harbour in the Hawaiian Islands, after which Japan declared war on the United States. Germany and Italy also declared war on the United States. On the 8th Britain declared war on Japan.

1942
February The Japanese occupied Malaya, Singapore and Thailand

Spring The Japanese went on to occupy Indonesia, the Philippines, parts of Burma and New Guinea and many Pacific Islands.

June In the Far East the United States fleet destroyed the Japanese fleet at the Battle of Midway and then began to re-take all the Pacific Islands the Japanese had occupied.
Germany and Italy fought British, Commonwealth and eventually United States forces for control of North Africa and the Mediterranean.

November Great Allied victory at El Alamein.

1943
January Soviet Union defeated Germany at the Battle of Stalingrad.

June Axis powers (Germany and Italy) defeated in North Africa.

July Soviet Union defeated Germany at Battle of Kursk.

August Britain and United States took Sicily and invaded Southern Italy. Italy capitulated, Mussolini was arrested and imprisoned, Germany took up the fight against United States and British forces.

1944
Germans driven out of Soviet Union.

June Normandy landings opening second front in West.
New German weapon introduced, the V1 flying bomb – an unmanned jet, known as the doodlebug. Battle of Leyte Gulf, United States reoccupied the Philippines.

September Another new German weapon introduced, the V2, an unmanned rocket.

November Russians delayed relief of Warsaw ghetto. Poland liberated by Soviet Union. Romania and Finland surrendered.

1945
January Burma liberated and Hungary surrendered.

April Russians outside Berlin, Hitler committed suicide on 30th.

May On 7th Germany surrendered and 8th Victory in Europe (VE) day.

June United States recaptured Japanese island of Okinawa.

August United States dropped atom bombs: on Hiroshima on 6th and on Nagasaki on 9th. On 15th Japan surrendered (Victory in Japan – VJ day). Second World War officially ended.

Key

- Areas controlled by the Allies
- Neutral countries
- Germany and areas under German control or occupation
- Italy and areas under Italian occupation
- Axis co-belligerents

Europe in 1942, the period of Hitler's greatest expansion.

Why was Germany able to acquire so much territory in Europe by 1942?

Mediterranean islands of Malta, Corsica, Sardinia, Crete and Cyprus. Because Britain had key interests to defend in the Eastern Mediterranean, for example, Egypt and the Suez Canal, Cyprus and Libya, the war moved to North Africa. In September 1940 the Italians invaded Egypt in an attempt to take the strategically important Suez Canal, which was a vital Allied communications and supply route. The battle for North Africa was fought between September 1940 and January 1943, principally between the Italian Army and the German Afrika Korps, commanded by General Rommel, on the one hand, and the British Eighth Army, which included Commonwealth forces, mostly Australians and New Zealanders, commanded by a succession of generals, ending with General Montgomery. The battle ended when the Germans and Italians were caught in a pincer movement between the British Eighth Army and an Anglo-American force invading Algeria (Operation Torch) under General Eisenhower. Allied forces then effectively controlled the south coast of the Mediterranean.

Why did Britain's forces move onto the European mainland?

Strategically, Britain was unwilling to open up a second front in Europe, and refused to invade France in 1942, because the British did not believe that the Allied forces were ready. Britain, with experience of fighting the Germans, believed that they needed to be worn down first before they could be defeated, otherwise deaths and casualties would be very high. The Americans thought there was no military problem that sufficient resources and men could not overcome. The British thought the Americans too rash and the Americans thought the British too cautious. This difference caused diplomatic and strategic problems between the Allies throughout the war.

The Americans had promised Stalin a second front in Europe to relieve German pressure on the Soviet Union. Churchill argued, successfully, for a Mediterranean strategy. The United States would have preferred an invasion of France. The Western Allies would not be ready to invade Northern France for another year (Operation Overlord).

The Allied forces, therefore, moved on to Italy (which Churchill called 'the soft under-belly of Europe'), taking Sicily in July 1943 and invading the Italian mainland in September 1943. Mussolini was overthrown but escaped to Northern Italy. His successor, Marshall Badoglio, surrendered, but the Germans took over the defence of Italy against the Allied forces from a line just north of Naples. Thereafter the Allied forces were bogged down, taking one year to fight their way through Italy and north of the Alps.

Why did Britain become involved in a war in the Far East?

The war in the Far Eastern theatre was fought for control of valuable resources, which the Japanese needed and the United States and Britain sought to deny them. Britain was involved because its extensive commercial interests in China had brought it into conflict with the Japanese, who were intent on bringing China under Japanese control. Japan was seen as an aggressor nation. Germany and Italy were Japan's allies, through the 1937 Anti-Comintern Pact and the 1940 Tripartite Axis, and they were at war with Britain. Though not actually at war until 8 December 1941, Britain and Japan were nevertheless hostile to each other.

The European war was a catalyst to the outbreak of war in the Far East. German occupation of France and the Netherlands left their South-east Asian colonial territories, Indo-China and Indonesia, vulnerable to Japanese control. In 1941 the French Vichy government and the Japanese set up a joint protectorate over the whole of Indo-China, which permitted immediate Japanese occupation. In retaliation, the United States and Britain cancelled trade agreements, and the Americans stopped selling oil, copper and scrap metal to the Japanese. As the United States tightened its trade embargo, so Japan intensified its plans to seize South-east Asia to gain access to Indonesian oil and Malayan metals. Moreover, the Japanese had always maintained that they would not fight both the Royal Navy and the United States Navy simultaneously. With the fall of France, Britain had to withdraw the bulk of its ships in the Pacific region to the Mediterranean, leaving the way clear for the Japanese to take on the United States Navy. Negotiations between Japan and the United States over Japanese withdrawal from occupied territories failed. The Japanese attacked the United States fleet in Pearl Harbour, Hawaii on 7 December 1941. Japan, Germany and Italy then declared war on the United States. Britain declared war on Japan on 8 December 1941. With the United States officially in the war, Britain was no longer fighting alone.

Josef Stalin (1879–1953). Soviet Leader from 1928. He stayed in power by operating a reign of terror. His cruelty in establishing the collectivisation programme (1931–33) and the purges (1935–38) was only exceeded by his inhumane treatment of his forces and the Soviet people during the war. However, he did drive the Red Army and the Russian people to achieve a tremendous victory over Hitler's Germany.

The Far East and and Western
Pacific showing the greatest
extent of Japanese control

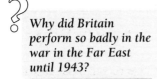

*Why did Britain
perform so badly in the
war in the Far East
until 1943?*

What was the extent of Britain's involvement in the Pacific war?

Involvement in the Far Eastern theatre of war was a nightmare situation
for Britain, whose Chiefs of Staff throughout the 1930s had warned that
Britain would be unable to fight simultaneous wars in Europe, the
Mediterranean and the Far East. Japanese forces invaded the Malayan
peninsular on 7 December 1941. Non-implementation of the British
defence plans permitted the Japanese to gain air superiority and by
31 January 1941 Malaya had fallen. Britain's main defences were concentrated on the Singapore naval base, which commanded strategically key
sea routes through the region. Insufficiently funded to achieve its defensive purpose, Singapore fell to the Japanese on 15 February 1942. Nearly
100,000 British troops and reinforcements from Australia, New Zealand
and India were captured.

Churchill's objective was to recover Burma, Malaya, Singapore and
Hong Kong, but the United States and Britain had taken the decision that
priority would be given to the European war. Japan's territorial expansion
throughout the Pacific area was checked by the United States Navy at the

Battle of Midway in June 1942. At the Casablanca meeting in January 1943 a counter-offensive was planned. Britain's role was to re-take the Burma Road to facilitate overland delivery of supplies to the Chinese ally, Chiang Kai-shek, whose Nationalist (Kuomintang) regime, based inland at Chungking in South China, was cut off by Japanese occupation of the coastal region.

Churchill was not keen for British forces to be committed to operations in conditions favourable to the Japanese. Moreover, he regarded relief of Chiang Kai-shek and the retaking of Burma as of secondary importance to European military operations. By this stage of the war, however, United States strategic planning dominated the alliance and the Americans were inclined to over-estimate the importance and capabilities of Chiang Kai-shek and his forces. Churchill's objections were over-ruled, and the first Chindit operation was launched into Burma in February 1943. British forces finally entered Rangoon on 3 May 1945 but Churchill's fears about heavy losses in jungle warfare were proved correct: combined British and Commonwealth casualties amounted to 71,244.

How did Churchill try to safeguard British interests during the Second World War?

To safeguard British interests Churchill needed allies, because Britain did not have the resources to fight alone, especially after the Fall of France. In pursuit of alliance diplomacy, Winston Churchill embarked upon a remarkable series of wartime conferences, meeting other Allied leaders to discuss war aims, strategy and the post-war settlements. These conferences involved Churchill flying several times between the United States, Canada, the Soviet Union and North Africa. By paying such close attention to wartime strategy and diplomacy Churchill was better placed to try to guard Britain's interests.

The alliance with the Soviet Union and the United States was put together over six months. Once the Germans had attacked the Soviet Union on 22 June 1941 the British signed an agreement with the Soviets on 12 July 1941. They promised to give one another material support and not to sign an armistice with Germany, except by mutual consent. The formal alliance with the United States began after the Japanese attack on the American fleet at Pearl Harbour on 7 December 1941. Britain declared war on Japan on 8 December. On 11 December Germany and Italy declared war on the United States.

Britain, the Soviet Union and the United States then came together in what Churchill called a 'Grand Alliance'.

The main meetings of the Grand Alliance

☐ **Placentia Bay, Newfoundland (Canada)** 9–14 August 1941 (Churchill and Roosevelt only)

They agreed the terms of the Atlantic Charter. This set out basic principles for the post-war world and the ideals for which Britain was fighting.

- Opposition to territorial enlargement or changes contrary to the expressed wishes of the peoples concerned.

- The right of people to select their own forms of government and the right to live without fear and want.

- Post-war collaboration: the Charter proposed that aggressor states should be disarmed pending the establishment of a security system.

The Soviet Union signed the Charter reluctantly.

☐ **Moscow, Three Power Conference**, September 1941 (Beaverbrook for Britain, Averell Harriman for the United States, and unnamed Soviet representatives)

They discussed the distribution of lend-lease military supplies to the Soviet Union from October 1941 to June 1942. Ideologically hostile to Britain and the United States, Stalin thought the offer insufficient for his needs, but took the goods anyway. As the Soviet Union was almost surrounded by Axis forces, the convoys of goods were shipped by Britain and the United States by the North Cape (Arctic) route at considerable danger to themselves, or through Iran (then called Persia).

☐ **Washington Conference**, December 1941 (Churchill, Roosevelt and their military advisers)

They hammered out military strategy and co-ordination of their war efforts, including bombing, blockade and subversion. A Combined Chiefs of Staff Committee was set up to operate from Washington. They also discussed:

● military assistance to US South-west Pacific Commander-in Chief, General MacArthur, fighting against the Japanese in the Philippines;

● the possible invasion of North Africa and conquest of the entire coastline;

● further lend-lease for the Soviet Union;

● US War Production Board manufacturing targets.

☐ **Casablanca**, January 1943 (Churchill and Roosevelt)

Stalin refused the invitation. Churchill met Roosevelt and they agreed the policy of unconditional surrender. They also decided to launch a Combined Bomber Offensive against Germany.

General de Gaulle was persuaded to work with General Giraud in opposing the French Vichy regime, leading to the formation of the French National Committee for Liberation. The Americans were pressing for a second front in France. Britain urged a Mediterranean strategy to weaken Italy believing this would draw German forces from Northern France and the Soviet Union. The Americans reluctantly agreed.

They also discussed strategy for the Pacific War. The Americans agreed to help the British attack the Japanese occupying Rangoon, in Burma, in an attempt to free up the Burma Road to assist Chiang Kai-shek. This proved impossible for another two years.

☐ **Quebec**, August 1943 (Churchill, Roosevelt and their American and British diplomatic staff)

This meeting outlined the plans for the Normandy landings, planned for 1944.

They agreed to set up South-east Asia Command, with Lord Louis Mountbatten as Supreme Commander. Brigadier Orde Wingate outlined his plans for guerrilla warfare behind Japanese lines in Burma. His men were known as Wingate's Chindits.

Churchill and Roosevelt signed the secret Quebec Agreement regulating Anglo-American co-operation in nuclear research and development (R&D). They agreed that mutual consent was required for use of the atomic bomb and for passing on details of its manufacture. (The existence of this agreement was unknown to the United States Congress, which enabled them to pass the McMahon Act of 1946 prohibiting further Anglo-United States nuclear R&D collaboration.)

☐ **Washington**, May 1943 (Churchill, Roosevelt and their military and diplomatic advisers)

In this discussion of future strategy they decided to invade France in May 1944, although Churchill had wanted to delay the invasion to maintain pressure on the Mediterranean. They also agreed that unconditional surrender should be pursued with Italy.

☐ **Teheran**, 28 November to 1 December 1943 (Churchill, Roosevelt and Stalin and their military advisers)

This was the first summit meeting of the 'Big Three', Churchill, Roosevelt and Stalin. They agreed future strategy for the conduct of the war and the political shape of post-war Europe. The meeting highlighted the growing domination of the United States and gradual eclipse of Britain as chief power-monger of the Alliance. Roosevelt made it plain to Churchill that he regarded Stalin as the key ally of the United States. It also became clear that the Soviet Union would dominate Eastern and Central Europe after the war, and that Roosevelt saw no need to adopt military strategies that might prevent it because he seemed not to share Churchill's mistrust of Stalin's intentions. In *The Turning Point* (1985), Keith Sainsbury suggests that Teheran was 'the turning point' in international relations, which foreshadowed the bipolar nature of the post-war world. The Big Three discussed:

● the opening of the second front in Europe (the Normandy landings, which had been scheduled for May 1943 but eventually took place on 6 June 1944);

● the progress of the Soviet offensive against Germany on the Eastern front;

● the possible entry of the Soviet Union into the Far Eastern war against Japan;

● the need to establish a post-war international peacekeeping organisation;

● the possibility of bringing Turkey into the war;

● the future political orientation of Poland and Finland, the post-war division of Germany and support for Yugoslavian partisans and their leader General Tito.

☐ **Quebec**, September 1944 (Churchill and Roosevelt)

● They drew up plans for the post-war division of Germany into occupation zones, and the Allied Control Commissions in Germany and Austria.

● They discussed the Morgenthau plan for the post-war de-industrialisation of Germany.

● Churchill offered Royal Naval forces to assist the United States Navy in the Pacific war.

☐ **Moscow**, October 1944 (Churchill and Stalin and their diplomatic and military advisers)

This was the conference at which the Percentages Agreement – the so-called 'naughty document' – was agreed, to settle the degree of influence the Western or Eastern blocs would have in the Balkans.

In subsequent negotiations between Sir Anthony Eden and Soviet Foreign Minister Molotov, the percentages for both Hungary and Bulgaria were amended to 80%-20% in favour of the Soviet Union.

☐ **Yalta**, 4 to 11 February 1945 (Churchill, Roosevelt and Stalin)

Four main issues were under discussion:

● **Allied strategy to complete the defeat of Germany** and the terms and ground-rules for the occupation and denazification of Germany;

● **Defeat of Japan.** Secret agreements between the United States and the Soviet Union covered the status quo in Mongolia, and extension of Soviet interests to cover the Kurile Islands and South Sakhalin, in return for Stalin's commitment to enter the war against Japan. Churchill was excluded from this agreement.

● **The 'Declaration on Liberated Europe'** was issued to cover the future settlement in Eastern Europe concerning territory 'liberated' and/or 'occupied' by the Soviet Red Army. Agreements were reached on the constitution of a Polish Government of National Unity (a combination of the Lublin Committee of Stalin-controlled communist Poles together with the London-based Polish government-in-exile) and Polish frontiers. Britain felt a sense of obligation to Poland, arising from the failure to stop Hitler's invasion in September 1939. Stalin's failure to keep his Yalta promises on the constitution of the Polish government resulted in the new United States President Harry Truman showing his displeasure on Soviet Foreign Minister Molotov in April 1945.

● Establishment of a peaceful world order based upon the United Nations, in which both the United States and the Soviet Union would participate, and which should, therefore, be better constituted for its purpose than the League of Nations had been.

There was broad agreement between the Allies on the future of Germany, and approval was given to the plans prepared by the Three Power Commission for occupation zones, different sections in Berlin and for the setting up of the Allied Control Commission. The intention was that Germany and Austria should maintain their national unity. Reparations were to be discussed by Foreign Ministers.

☐ **San Francisco** Conference, 25 April to 26 June 1945

Molotov refused to attend this conference, which was the inaugural conference of the United Nations (United Nations Conference on International Organisation). It was attended by delegates from 50 nations, of which 45 had signed the United Nations Declaration of January 1942. Agreements were signed concerning refugees, regional collective security and the use of the veto in the United Nations Security Council, which was to comprise five permanent members: China, France, Britain, the Soviet Union and the United States, together with six temporary members. A Trusteeship Council was created to administer former Axis territories.

The Potsdam conference

The European war ended on 8 May 1945. Hitler had committed suicide on 30 April 1945 and his successor as head of state, Admiral Doenitz, offered Germany's unconditional surrender on 7 May 1945.

The Potsdam Conference (Berlin), 16 July to 2 August 1945 was the final meeting of the Grand Alliance. It was attended by Churchill, Stalin and Truman. Attlee accompanied Churchill, who left the conference on 26 July after his electoral defeat. Attlee attended all meetings, which facilitated a smooth hand-over of power on Churchill's departure. Issues covered included:

Harry S. Truman (1884–1972)
Became United States President on the death of Roosevelt. He assumed responsibility for the final stages of the Second World War, attended the Potsdam conference, and authorised the dropping of atomic bombs on Japan. Truman soon recognised that Stalin's intentions in Eastern Europe did not accord with the Atlantic Charter. He determined that he would endeavour to stand up to the Soviet Union.

- Allied Control Commission for Germany – Germany was intended by Britain and the United States to be treated as an economic entity, meaning unified control of the German economy, with free exchange of goods and services between zones.

- Reparations – The British zone was principally industrial and could not feed itself. The Soviet zone was agricultural but the Soviets needed industrial reparations and, having stripped the Soviet Zone and wiped out German industry there, demanded more from the British and American sectors. Churchill feared that the Soviet Union might withdraw leaving Britain, after years of domestic rationing, to feed the Russian sector too.

- Poland's government and borders – Britain and the United States accepted the Western Neisse as Poland's border with Germany, (which involved the transfer of German refugees). In return they extracted pledges from the Polish government on free elections, press freedom and the repatriation of Polish forces.

- The Potsdam Declaration on surrender terms for Japan. Terms were agreed for Soviet intervention in the Pacific war.

- The existence of the atomic bomb was revealed to Stalin (who already knew, but Churchill and Truman did not know that he knew).

- Britain sought Austrian independence although the Red Army occupied Austria.

- Britain also wanted an early settlement with Italy, and to retain influence on the future of South Eastern Europe.

The Allies failed to agree at Potsdam:

- A basis for a future European peace treaty;

- An accepted settlement on the future of Poland;

- A settlement on the future of Germany.

But much was sacrificed in order to maintain a semblance of the wartime alliance.

Why were two atomic bombs dropped on Japan during the Second World War?

The wartime collaboration of British, American, Canadian and European refugee scientists in nuclear research and development (R&D) was known as the Manhattan Project. They succeeded in producing an atomic bomb, which was successfully tested in the United States at Alamogordo, New Mexico on 16 July 1945 (while the Potsdam Conference was in progress). It is alleged that the allies calculated that Japan would be induced to seek an early surrender, and many allied lives would thus be saved, if an atomic bomb were to be dropped on Japan. Controversy still exists about the reasons for which the bombs were dropped. The city of Hiroshima was selected as the first target and a bomb was dropped on 6 August 1945, killing 78,000 people and injuring 90,000. A second bomb was dropped on the city of Nagasaki on 9 August 1945 and the Japanese surrendered on 14 August 1945.

1. Why was Britain victorious in the Second World War?

2. How did the International Conferences at

a) Placentia Bay, Newfoundland

b) Tehran

c) Yalta and

d) Potsdam

plan to deal with the post-war world?

3. Why did Britain's status as a global power change during the Second World War?

Source-based questions: British war aims during the Second World War

SOURCE A

We seek no material advantage for ourselves; we desire nothing from the German people which should offend their self-respect. We are not aiming only at victory, but rather looking beyond it to the laying of a foundation of a better international system which will mean that war is not to be the inevitable lot of every succeeding generation …

The peace which we are determined to secure, however, must be a real and settled peace, not an uneasy truce interrupted by constant alarms and repeated threats.

Either the German government must give convincing proof of the sincerity of their desire for peace by definite acts and by the provision of effective guarantees of their intention to fulfil their undertakings, or we must persevere in our duty to the end.

From a speech by the Prime Minister, Neville Chamberlain to the House of Commons, 12 October 1939 on German peace proposals.

SOURCE B

The President of the United States of America and the Prime Minister, Mr Churchill … deem it right to make known certain common principles in the national policies of their respective countries …

First, their countries seek no aggrandisement, territorial or other.

Second, they desire to see no territorial changes that do not accord with the freely expressed wishes of the peoples concerned.

Third, they respect the right of all peoples to choose the form of government under which they will live; and they wish to see sovereign rights and self-government restored to those who have been forcibly deprived of them.

Fourth, they will endeavour … to further the enjoyment by all States, … of access, on equal terms, to the trade and to the raw material of the world which are needed for their economic prosperity.

From The Atlantic Charter *12 August 1941. The Charter was an agreement signed by Churchill for Britain, and Franklin D. Roosevelt, the President of the United States.*

SOURCE C

The Premier of the USSR, the Prime Minister of the United Kingdom and the President of the USA have consulted with each other in the common interests of the peoples of their countries and those of liberated Europe. They jointly declare their mutual agreement to concert during the temporary period of instability in liberated Europe.

The establishment of order in Europe and the re-building of national economic life must be achieved by processes which will enable the liberated peoples to destroy the last vestiges of Nazism and to create democratic institutions of their own choice. This is a principle of the Atlantic Charter.

The three governments will consult the other United Nations and provisional authorities in Europe when matters of direct interest to them are under consideration.

When, in the opinion of the three governments, conditions in any European liberated state make such action necessary they will immediately consult together on the measures necessary to discharge their joint responsibilities set forth in this declaration.

By this declaration we reaffirm our faith in the principles of the Atlantic Charter, our pledge in the Declaration by the United Nations, and our determination to build in co-operation with other peace-loving nations world order under law, dedicated to peace, security, freedom and general well-being of all mankind.

From The Declaration on Liberated Europe *made at the Yalta Conference in February, 1945 between Britain, the USA and USSR.*

---

1. Study Source B.

How, by its use of language and style, does this source suggest it is an official international declaration?

2. Study Source A and use information contained within this chapter.

How reliable is this source to a historian writing about the British government's attitude towards war with Germany during 1939?

3. Study Sources B and C and use information contained within this chapter.

Of what value are these two sources to a historian writing about British war aims between 1941 and 1945?

4. Study Sources A, B and C and use information contained within this chapter.

To what extent did Britain's war aims change between 1939 and 1945?

8.2 What was the impact of the Second World War on the British people?

Food in wartime

- Meats, bacon, butter, sugar and sweets were rationed.

- People were encouraged to eat more vegetables.

- A 'Dig for victory' campaign encouraged people to grow their own vegetables; parks were turned into allotments so that people without gardens could grow their own food.

- People were also encouraged to keep rabbits and chickens to provide additional meat for the table.

In what ways did war affect people's lives?

By means of the Emergency Powers Act, introduced in May 1940, the government intervened in people's lives on an unprecedented level, mobilising the economy and population towards war production and imposing controls, such as rationing of food distribution and consumption, to ensure fair shares for all. A Ministry of Supply oversaw food distribution. An allowance of 3,000 calories per day was introduced, guaranteed to everyone, so that people were healthy and well fed. There were few consumer goods available for purchase, and clothes and household goods were also controlled. Ration books for food and coupons for clothes and consumer goods were issued.

The civilian population was involved in waging war on the home front. A call for volunteers went out in May 1940 which brought forward one-and-a-quarter million men and women by July 1940. The Local Defence Volunteer Reserve (the Home Guard) practised defensive manoeuvres designed to halt or impede invading German forces. Air Raid Protection Wardens (ARP) patrolled the streets, both to ensure that no light could be seen through blackout curtains, which could help a German bomber locate an urban or industrial centre, and to give assistance to the fire fighters and other rescue and relief services after bombing raids.

Maintenance of civilian morale was considered to be essential and the government organised the production and distribution of propaganda posters to encourage people to be sensible and cheerful about their hardships.

Using information in this chapter, do you think the Home Guard were an important part of Britain's defence against German invasion? Give reasons for your answer.

Members of the Local Defence Volunteers (the Home Guard)

People's lives were not completely disrupted. Some attempts were made at maintaining normality and radio broadcasting by the British Broadcasting Corporation (BBC) assumed increased importance. Cinema attendance increased; audiences went to see films that offered them an escape from the fear and drudgery of the war. Some films were blatantly propagandist, promoting the ideals of patriotism and bravery, for example *In Which We Serve* and Laurence Oliver's *Henry V*.

In general many family incomes improved but research gives mixed results. There is little evidence of **upward mobility** based on savings and capital accumulation. Wages in key industries such as aircraft production did rise, but this was not true of all sectors of the war economy.

Upward mobility: The process of increasing personal wealth and social status, for example someone born into the working class joining the middle class.

What was the impact of the Second World War on people's working lives?

In spite of a general public perception that everyone should pull together to win the war, this did not mean that there were no labour problems.

There was competition between employers for skilled engineers because war service depleted the work force. In June 1940 a Restriction on Engagement (Engineering) Order introduced universal recruitment of key workers through Labour Exchanges or trade unions.

In 1941 labour mobility was further limited and the government directed the labour force into war work. Training programmes were introduced to overcome skill shortages. Near full employment was achieved. Average wage rates rose and so did the tax revenue payable to the government, although this was inevitably directed to the war effort rather than to reconstruction.

Despite maintenance of morale there were increased outbreaks of industrial unrest. There was poor time keeping, absenteeism and lack of commitment. By October 1941 there had been one thousand illegal strikes, but the government feared to take harsh measures to control them at a time of national emergency. Trade union membership rose by 1.5 million and Joint Production Committees were set up in firms engaged in war production, where decision-making was based on consultation between management and employees of the firm.

Why do you think posters such as this were issued by the government during the Second World War? To what extent did they help the 'war effort'?

How did war affect women's role in society?

Social and economic emancipation of women followed new employment opportunities arising from the need to replace men on active service or transferred to war work. Additionally, labour shortages benefited many women who were called on to supplement the workforce. Over 97% of women agreed that they should undertake war work in the auxiliary services and industry, resulting in the number of women employed in commerce, industry and the armed forces, rising by almost 50% to 2,250,000 between 1939 and 1943. The National Service No.2 Act of December 1941 conscripted unmarried women into women's auxiliary services such as the WAAF (Air force), WRNS (Navy) and ATS (Army). Although not allowed to engage in active service, women made very good 'backroom boys' in collating information in air force, naval or army operations rooms and in fighter control.

The war promoted a sense of independence, and many women enjoyed increased responsibility previously only accessible to men. Nevertheless the trades unions sought to maintain male privileges and pay for some manual work dropped. Even so, the number of women who remained at home, to bring up children for example, exceeded those who were employed in the forces in industry and in civil defence.

What were the effects on the British public of the German bombing campaign?

On 4 September 1940 the Blitz began on the East End of London, causing wholesale destruction of buildings and services, with over 1,000 casualties. Badly hit areas included major ports, such as Southampton, Plymouth, Liverpool, Portsmouth, together with key industrial areas, such as Coventry, Birmingham, Manchester and Newcastle. Between 1940 and 1941, 44,000 people died in bombing raids. Propaganda in the press promoted a 'Britain can take it' spirit and King George VI, Queen Elizabeth and Winston Churchill visited bombed-out areas and casualties to maintain morale. But not all was bravery and defiance. Mass Observation (an agency who surveyed and published public opinions) reported shortages of bread, milk, electricity, gas and telephones. People were disoriented by shock, discomfort, disruption, dislocation, loss of sleep and confusion. People became accustomed to hearing air raid warnings, then leaving their beds to go and sleep in an air raid shelter under the stairs of their house or in their garden. In London many families slept on platforms in Underground stations.

At the outset of the war Hitler had declared that he would not make war on women and children. His aim was to attack industrial and naval targets to disrupt imports of food supplies and British arms production. However, women and children inevitably became the victims of the Blitz because their homes were clustered around the docks and centres of industrial employment, and in the 1940s bombs could not be aimed accurately.

Over a million children were evacuated in the early stages of the war in 1939 because it was thought that a German bombing campaign would commence immediately. Evacuation brought home to the public the scale of child poverty and deprivation. It also reinforced middle-class determination to accept the potential bonus offered by the introduction of a **welfare state**. However, the culture clash between classes made many evacuees unhappy and they returned to their parents in 1941 as soon as the worst effects of the Blitz eased.

Welfare State: State provision for all citizens of a basic level of income and services through a social security system, a health service, housing, education and maintenance of full employment. This would create a new social order based on equality and a sense of community.

Attrition: Gradual wearing down, through loss of shipping.

Hitler's bombing campaigns did not bring Britain to its knees because the Luftwaffe (German Air Force) lacked the capacity to mount attacks over sufficiently wide areas to knock out all major industrial centres and port facilities. Moreover, despite the high rate of **attrition** achieved by German U-boats (submarines) targeting the Atlantic convoys bringing goods to Britain from the United States, sufficient supplies were delivered to keep Britain going. Domestic production of coal and arms were maintained. The Minister of Food, Lord Woolton, set up a Salvage Branch. This ensured that waste food was collected regularly to feed pigs. Domestic pots and pans and iron railings were sacrificed to provide scarce minerals for weapons production. The wartime slogan 'Britain can take it' seemed appropriate.

How did the war alter public perceptions of government control of people's lives?

The difficulties and hardships of war encouraged an expectation of reduction in social inequalities and that state interference would be applied to social reform. These expectations inclined the public towards support for the Labour Party, which was seen as more likely to introduce them.

Government interference in the conduct of people's lives increased, for example, the introduction of food rationing, evacuation of children, especially from major industrial centres, and the re-housing of bombed-out families. Social legislation enacted included free milk and dinners for children at school, and nurseries for women engaged in war work

The war reinforced the debate on state provision of welfare services by highlighting the inadequacies of pre-war social welfare provision. For example, civilian casualties on the scale of occurrence arising from the Blitz could not be treated in the pre-war system of voluntary and local authority hospitals. This inspired the creation of a wartime emergency hospital service with central government funding of beds in voluntary hospitals.

Economic and industrial controls were also introduced, permitting government direction of resources to maximise the war effort. Wartime discussions about the reconstruction of Britain, at national and local level, accustomed the British public to the idea of planning for the future.

What were the main proposals of the 1942 Report on Social Insurance and Allied Services by William Beveridge?

Universalism: The paying out of government welfare assistance to everyone, regardless of need.

The *Report on Social Insurance and Allied Services* was written by Sir William Beveridge, Master of University College, Oxford. It was published on 1 December 1942. In his report, Beveridge proposed the elimination of what he called the five giants: 'Want, Disease, Ignorance, Squalor and Idleness'. Beveridge's proposals were seen as a 'blue-print' for a welfare state and moved away from the principle of selectivity towards **universalism** of entitlement to national insurance.

The Coalition government's response to Beveridge was predictable. Winston Churchill and the Conservatives, despite their reservations, thought the Report too popular to reject. The Conservative Party was alarmed by the financial implications of some sections of the Beveridge Report. They thought it would be dangerous to encourage expectations which might not be realisable, especially the commitments on post-war reconstruction. In January 1943, the Conservative Party set up a Beveridge Report Committee, which sought to scale down the extent of the proposed reforms. The Committee suggested, for example, that compulsory health insurance should not apply to the higher paid and that unemployment benefit should be less attractive than the lowest paid employment. The lukewarm Conservative response provoked the Labour Party to vote against the Coalition government for the first time. Thus, the Coalition accepted Beveridge's unified universal scheme but rejected the idea of subsistence as unworkable.

White Paper: A government document outlining proposals for changing the law.

A series of **White Papers** was issued in 1944 on provision of a National Health Service, employment policy and social insurance. A White Paper on employment policy recommended a steering committee with five subordinate working parties on manpower, investment, statistics, balance of payments and economic survey.

In 1941 the Family Means Test was abolished. A Family Allowance Act was introduced in 1945, because a quarter of all family incomes were too small. It introduced a payment of five shillings (25p) per week for the second and all following children.

The government also introduced one single universal contribution from earnings, allowing each insured worker to claim maternity, unemployment, sickness and disability benefits, old age pensions and a funeral grant, thereby providing 'cradle to grave' welfare as a right rather than as a reward for good behaviour.

How far did Beveridge's proposals build on Britain's existing welfare policies?

Selectivity: The principle of giving government welfare assistance according to people's needs. This resulted in people being subjected to the 'means test', which wanted to know every detail of their financial circumstances. Many people considered this to be degrading.

On the eve of the Second World War Britain was a country with the most advanced provision of social welfare services. However, the provision was patchy and many aspects of welfare were insufficiently covered or not covered at all. Pre-Beveridge welfare provision was based on a principle of **selectivity**. That is, state provision of welfare benefits was based on the means test. This identified what financial means a prospective recipient already had so that state handouts could be tailored to the recipient's needs.

Beveridge rejected the idea of selectivity in favour of universal entitlement. He believed that social insurance would only succeed in providing a welfare safety-net if it was part of a comprehensive social policy covering family allowances, a national health service and prevention of mass unemployment.

What were the provisions of the Education Act of 1944?

Brought in by a Conservative MP, R.A. Butler, the Act created a new Ministry of Education and 146 local education authorities. It brought in a system of secondary education for everyone based on aptitude. Pupils were sent to grammar schools, technical schools or secondary modern schools. The Act also maintained the system of grant-assisted independent schools and schools which were the responsibility of the local authority.

The Act raised the school leaving age to 15 and made non-denominational worship and religious education compulsory, but with a 'conscience' clause to permit exclusion of anyone who objected on religious grounds.

1. How did the Second World War change the way people lived?

2. Why was the Beveridge Report so well received when it was published in 1942?

8.3 What was the effect of the Second World War on the British economy?

What was the impact of the Second World War on the British economy?

The Second World War nearly bankrupted Britain. The war cost £28,000 million. Britain was obliged to borrow heavily because government revenue was inadequate to cover the cost of the war. Thus, in order to finance the war, Britain disposed of pre-war overseas assets of at least £1,000 million and lost its pre-war creditor position.

The United States provided $47 billion in Lend-Lease goods between 1941 and 1943, of which the bulk went to the UK and the Soviet Union. But, while Lend-Lease meant that no charge was levied on Britain for United States aid and goods supplied during the war, this facility ended when hostilities ceased and Britain then had to make good its promises of payment.

While UK net output rose by 20% between 1938 and 1944, this did not meet the requirements of the war effort, which at its peak absorbed 50% of total national income. The shortfall was made up by disposal of foreign assets, debt accumulation, capital depletion and a fall of 22% in personal consumption. Britain's invisible earnings were seriously impaired through the decline in trade and shipping losses (much of them resulting from German U-boats attacking Atlantic convoys bringing food and military supplies to Britain from the United States). These losses were made good by buying American shipping, and thereby increasing Britain's indebtedness.

At the end of the war Britain's net reserves amounted to $1.8 billion, but there were overseas liabilities against these reserves of approximately $13 billion. Between 1939 and 1940, 45% of public spending was on defence. By 1944–45 this had risen to 83%.

War damage was another burden on the public purse. Britain lost approximately 7% of pre-war housing as a result of German bombing raids.

Post-war credits: A savings scheme introduced during the war. The public bought certificates, thereby loaning the money to the government. The government bought the certificates back after the war.

What part did the British public play in helping to finance the war?

Post-war credits were launched to attract wartime earnings into savings, but purchase of these was not compulsory. The economist John Maynard

Keynes had advocated the introduction of compulsory wartime savings at a time when few consumer goods were available for purchase. His idea was that, when these savings were paid back after the war, money would be released to refloat the economy and to alleviate post-war depression.

What were the principles of Lend-Lease and how was it agreed?

On 3 November 1940 United States President Roosevelt outlined a scheme which enabled Britain to acquire United States weaponry on favourable terms. Roosevelt wanted to help Britain by all means short of war and was prepared to compromise United States neutrality to do so.

The Aid to Democracies Bill was passed by Congress on 11 March 1941, enabling Roosevelt to lend or lease equipment to any nation 'whose defense the President deems vital to the defense of the United States'. The Act worked by permitting Britain to order arms and military supplies from the American government, which ordered and paid for goods from American producers. These goods were then lent or leased to Britain on promise of payment when the war was ended. The Act permitted Britain, and later China and the Soviet Union, to acquire arms, warships, military supplies and other goods immediately. The goods were brought from the United States across the Atlantic in convoys of merchant ships escorted by destroyers. These were targeted by German U-boats, which initially inflicted enormous losses on British shipping. When Britain was able to break the German codes (Ultra and Enigma) and pinpoint submarine positions, the U-boats themselves became targets. In the first half of 1943 over 100 were sunk. Britain acquired $11.3 billion worth of American goods by the end of the war, which made the United States 'the arsenal of democracy'. Without this American effort, it is doubtful that Britain could have continued to fight. It also ensured that the United States would have a predominant say in strategy once it entered the war. Lend-lease was swiftly terminated on 17 August 1945, once Japan had surrendered.

What did Britain agree to at the Bretton Woods Conference in July 1944?

An international monetary and finance conference was held at Bretton Woods in New Hampshire USA in July 1944. Twenty-eight nations, including Britain, participated and agreed to the establishment of an International Monetary Fund (IMF) and a World Bank.

The IMF was intended to operate a cash reserve system on gold and currency that member countries could draw on to meet balance of payments deficits. This was intended to ease world trade. The IMF also provided for the restoration of exchange stability with adjustments in exchange rates only occurring when there was fundamental inequality in the balance of payments. Britain wanted to establish an international currency and a variable volume of credit to facilitate the expansion of trade. Britain also wanted to underpin the IMF with larger reserves than the $25 billion with which it started. Britain's exchange rate, however, was set at too high a rate, to the detriment of the British economy in the following decades.

The World Bank was set up for the advancement of loans to finance important viable projects in the development of a country.

Britain and the United States agreed to apply the principles of free trade, no discrimination and stable rates of exchange to the international economy. It was hoped at Bretton Woods that an international trading organisation would be set up to clear tariffs and quotas. The organisation was not set up in 1944 but what evolved instead, in 1947, was the General Agreement on Tariffs and Trade.

1. What impact did the Second World War have on the British economy?

2. How did Britain cope with the economic problems posed by the Second World War?

8.4 How did Commonwealth members respond to Britain's call to arms, and what effect did the Second World War have on Britain's relationship with the Commonwealth?

How did Commonwealth countries respond to Britain's declaration of war on Germany in September 1939?

Although on the outbreak of war there was massive mobilisation of imperial resources, the response of Commonwealth countries was mixed.

Among the Dominions, Australia and New Zealand offered immediate support. Mindful of Japanese aggression in China, no doubt their decision was influenced by their reliance on the British defence system in the South Pacific and South-east Asia.

The Canadians waited until their House of Commons had had an opportunity to debate the issue, then agreed (unanimously) to enter the war.

Views in South Africa were more mixed. The South African Nationalist Prime Minister, J. B. M. Hertzog wanted to remain neutral. A resolution on neutrality was put to the South African Parliament. In response, the pro-British General Smuts put forward a pro-British and anti-German amendment, which was passed by a majority of thirteen. Failing to obtain a dissolution of parliament, Hertzog resigned. Smuts assumed the premiership and took South Africa into the war. Nevertheless, there was considerable Afrikaner opposition to supporting Britain. The Nationalists, led by Daniel Malan, were pro-Nazi and some of their extremists were interned, as were the communists.

Eire declared itself neutral. It remained neutral throughout the war, denying to the Royal Navy use of its bases. These would have been helpful in combating German U-boats in the Battle of Atlantic (see section 8.1) by reducing the distance to be travelled to reach Atlantic target zones. Thousands of Eire citizens, however, joined the UK forces. Because of Catholic and Republican sympathies in Ulster, the six northern counties did not have conscription.

In total the White Dominions spent £36,000 million on the war between them.

In India Viceroy Lord Linlithgow simply informed the people that Britain was at war with Germany. India was angered by involvement in war without prior consultation, despite the broadening of self-government implemented before the war. Congress leader Nehru and the non-violent protester Gandhi both pointed out that, if India was to fight to defend democracy, India too should have a democracy to defend. Britain did not respond to Indian demands for a statement of Britain's future plans for India. The provincial governments resigned. Section 93 of the India Act was invoked so that Britain could rule by decree, with the Indian Civil Service carrying on the administration. The Indian National Congress began a campaign of non-co-operation with the British, insisting on attainment of immediate self-government. Although anti-Nazi, they resented Britain's high-handed assumption that India would fight for a European cause which was beyond the knowledge and experience of most Indians. In contrast, the Muslim League was willing to support Britain.

In the Middle East the response to Britain's involvement in the war was also mixed. Egyptian nationalists resented the presence of a British garrison under the terms of the 1936 Anglo-Egyptian Treaty, and would have welcomed Axis forces. Nevertheless, the Egyptian government remained nominally neutral and the Suez Canal was safe for Britain's use during the war.

Zionism: The political movement that wanted to create a separate homeland for Jews in Palestine. This new state would be called Israel.

In Palestine also, response to Britain's declaration of war was mixed, with pro and anti-Nazi sympathies splitting along national lines. The Jews hated the Nazis for their anti-Semitic atrocities in Germany, and the Arabs, feeling threatened by militant **Zionism** and ever-increasing Jewish immigration into Palestine, were not completely unsympathetic to German anti-Semitism.

What effect did the Second World War have on Britain's relationship with the Commonwealth?

There was a wave of disaffection among those countries that did not share close ties with Britain.

In the British mandated territory of Iraq an anti-British regime, set up in 1941, sought to deny Britain the use of the Habbanniya Air Force base. Its position at the Eastern end of the Mediterranean gave it strategic importance for the defence of the region and the Suez Canal, which were potentially under threat from Axis presence in the Balkans and North Africa. Britain was also unwilling to relinquish an invaluable source of oil and a route for communication with its ally, the Soviet Union. In 1943 Britain invaded Iraq, and that country subsequently entered the war on the Allied side.

In the Far East and South-East Asia theatre of war (see map on page 170), the British ships *Prince of Wales* and *Repulse* were sunk by the Japanese on 10 December 1941 and Hong Kong was conquered by them on Christmas Day 1941. Singapore, and Burma fell in 1942. The loss of Singapore was both humiliating and devastating, because Britain's defence of the Pacific was based on Singapore. Moreover, by taking Burma, Japan was able to cut off the Burma Road. This was the route along which supplies were delivered to Chiang Kai-shek. The Japanese went on to take possession of British (as well as Dutch, American and French) territories and businesses in the Pacific. These events were enormously damaging to British morale and prestige. In the long term they were damaging to colonial perceptions of Britain's role at the head of the Commonwealth.

Japanese-controlled colonial inhabitants of the Far East and South-east Asia were at first inclined to listen to plans for them to become part of Japan's 'Greater East Asia Co-prosperity Sphere'. But the Japanese did not treat them well and initial enthusiasm for promises of freedom from colonial rule soon dissipated.

Although close to Britain, Australia was very worried by the loss to Japan of Singapore and the remainder of British interests in the Far East. Both Australia and India were vulnerable to Japanese penetration and the Japanese bombed the Australian mainland. Distressed by the capture and imprisonment of large numbers of Australian forces sent to defend Singapore, and losing confidence in Britain's ability to defend Australia, they looked instead to the Americans, encouraged by the British.

Canada also looked to the United States for security. The Ogdensburg Agreement was negotiated with the United States in August 1940. United States President Roosevelt and Canadian Prime Minister Mackenzie King informally agreed to form a Permanent Joint Board for Defence.

Waves of violent protest supporting demands for Indian independence were a source of ongoing concern to Britain. Churchill stood firm that the future of India would not be discussed until the war was over. Embarrassed by American criticisms of Britain's empire policy and aware of the need to keep India loyal to British interests, the government sent the Lord Privy Seal, Sir Stafford Cripps, to India to offer concessions to nationalists. He was authorised to promise self-government after the war, with the equivalent of opt-out clauses for the Muslim provinces, and immediate inclusion of nationalists on the Viceroy's Council. Rejected by Congress as too little and that little not soon enough, a widespread 'Quit India' campaign was organised, calling for the British Raj to be immediately dismantled. In 1942, in the middle of a war, this would have been an impossible step for Britain to take. A wave of protest and demonstrations provoked Britain to ban the Congress Party and detain its leaders. Not to be outdone, Jinnah's Muslim League passed a 'Divide and Quit' resolution. This was to reinforce their 1940 Lahore resolution calling for the creation of a separate state, to be named 'Pakistan', and consisting of principally Muslim provinces: Punjab, Afghania, Kashmir, Sind, Baluchistan, Bengal, Assam and the Muslim regions of the North East. Cripps supported Jinnah's secessionist scheme. So did Churchill, who saw it as a means to upset the Congress Party and reinforce the support of the large number of Muslim soldiers fighting for Britain. Nevertheless, Viceroy Linlithgow and General Wavell, the Commander-in-Chief in India, had reservations about Muslim secession from an independent India. Cripps also reported to Churchill that Hindus in particular were keen not to offend the Japanese, who might win the Pacific war, by active participation in a war effort. In 1943 Viceroy Linlithgow was replaced by Field Marshal Sir Archibald Wavell, who was much more sympathetic to the idea of Indian independence.

One extreme example of Indian anti-British resentment was Chandra Subhas Bose, a former Congress president. He supported the cause of Indian nationalism, which he thought could be served best by allying with Japan and Germany. Bose went to Germany in 1941 and offered his services. Hitler gave Bose propaganda facilities, including 'Free India' radio on which he denounced democracy. He went into exile in Singapore and proclaimed a new Indian government, the Azad Hind (Free India). Bose was also given the opportunity and the means to organise Indian, Tamil and Ghurka prisoners of war into an Indian National Army (INA) and encouraged him to co-operate with the Afghanistani Fakir of Ipi, who was anti-British. However, the INA proved to be an ineffective fighting force and Bose's propaganda equally so. The Japanese soon grew as tired of Bose as had the Germans, and while escaping to Moscow he was killed in a plane crash. Although Bose had nuisance value, he did not gather much support in India, where the most ardent nationalists could not bring themselves to ally with Britain's enemies. Even so, the government of India took the INA seriously and made Bose and his supporters the subject of surveillance, counter-intelligence and counter-propaganda initiatives.

Why did Britain undertake a major reappraisal of colonial policy during the Second World War?

The collapse of British control in Asia undermined the concept of 'trusteeship', the basic doctrine underpinning Britain's colonial administrations. The government recognised that partnership in colonial affairs should replace paternalism and that more than lip-service should be paid to the aspiration of Commonwealth members for self-government.

Debates were initiated by Lord Hailey to determine whether self-government should mean internal autonomy, with Britain controlling foreign policy and defence, or whether it should mean attainment of Dominion status. Hailey also initiated a debate to establish what were the criteria by which readiness for self-government should be determined. He recognised that some colonies were not ready for the responsibility of self-government and needed to be taught the basic principles of honest

Lord Hailey (1872–1969)
Lord Hailey was a retired Indian civil servant. He was a former Governor of the Punjab and the United Provinces.

and impartial government. The idea of federation was promoted to get round this problem. Hailey wrote on imperial and commonwealth affairs. His ideas re-awoke concern for progressive welfare reforms and were increasingly favoured by some sections of the Conservative Party.

Another idea under discussion was decolonisation. This was not meant to represent independence, but rather a change of status within the Empire. The British government felt that most of the smaller colonies would be unable to defend themselves adequately, and would need the security umbrella of the British Empire.

The British government also recognised the need to retain the loyalty of colonial subjects and humanitarian concern to rehabilitate captured peoples after the war. Plans were considered to raise colonial living standards, develop economies and social institutions and provide welfare services after the war. A Colonial Development and Welfare Act was introduced in 1940, setting aside £5,000,000 for the promotion of colonial welfare schemes. A series of colonial reforms were put in hand. Moreover, new constitutions were given to the Gold Coast and Jamaica, where the franchise was extended in preparation for post-war independence. Regional councils were set up in Northern Rhodesia and a number of universities were established in Africa, to train an elite for the administrative responsibilities of self-government.

The need for colonial welfare reforms was underpinned by raised expectations of post-war improvements among the colonial forces that were fighting for Britain. These expectations were reinforced by nationalist unrest in Africa. The Kikuyu Central Association of Kenya was banned for allegedly conspiring with the Italians. In the Northern Rhodesian copper mines there was a violent strike. In Nigeria, Nyasaland and the Cameroons, nationalist political parties were formed in 1944.

The Atlantic Charter (see section 8.1) could be read more than one way. Churchill's priority was given to the re-establishment of British control of enemy-occupied colonies. The Charter was interpreted by Roosevelt as an intention to extend American ideas of democracy and independence to the colonies of the British Empire, but Churchill had applied the terms of the Charter only to ensuring the freedom of Nazi-occupied Europe. The Americans were morally anti-imperialist. In response to sustained American criticism, Britain created a new concept of colonial rule, with the emphasis on partnership rather than domination and presented in constructive and positive terms. Roosevelt advocated that British colonies, especially those in Asia, should be placed under international control to prepare them for independence, inspiring Churchill to retort in November 1942, 'I have not become the King's First Minister to preside over the liquidation of the British Empire'. British government officials believed that the United States wanted to prise open the imperial market, which was closed to them under the terms of imperial preference. The Americans applied pressure for the elimination of imperial preferences, wanting instead a free-trading (multilateral) post-war world economic order. But Churchill was unwilling to sacrifice imperial preference, as to do so would conflict with his ideal of Empire. This attachment was shared by the British government and senior civil servants.

1. What was the impact on the Commonwealth of Britain's declaration of war on Germany?

2. How did the Second World War change Britain's relationship with the Commonwealth and Empire?

8.5 How did British politics adapt to the conditions of a world war?

Why did Winston Churchill replace Neville Chamberlain on 9 May 1940?

In May 1940 the National Government was in crisis. This was because the Labour and Liberal Parties and some Conservatives had lost confidence in Prime Minister Neville Chamberlain. His foreign policy was seen to have failed. He was blamed for the policy of appeasement and complacency in believing that Hitler could be trusted to keep his word. He was also blamed for his failure to achieve an alliance with the Soviet Union during the summer of 1939. The British people had been frustrated by Britain's inability to assist Poland and resist the combined forces of Germany and the Soviet Union. The British government feared the likelihood of fighting the Soviet Union as well as Germany.

Chamberlain's leadership was fatally undermined by the Soviet attack on Finland in November 1939 and the German attacks on Norway and Denmark in April 1940. Scandinavian resources would be valuable to the Nazi war effort, but Britain's short-lived attempt to defend Norway was bungled. Additionally, Neville Chamberlain's hatred of war meant that he was seen as a man of peace. It was therefore feared that he would not wage war 100% to win. Chamberlain had hoped for a short and limited war: he thought it would be possible to undermine Germany with a naval blockade. He underestimated the Nazi regime and did not appreciate the amount of public support for Hitler. This added to his unpopularity.

In the Parliamentary debate of 7 and 9 May 1940 the Labour and Liberal parties attacked Chamberlain and the National Government. The government just survived a **vote of no confidence**, but its majority fell from 200 to 81.

Vote of no confidence: The House of Commons is asked if it has confidence in the government. If the votes prove that it doesn't, the government falls.

Chamberlain realised that he needed to create a true Coalition administration involving Conservatives, Labour and Liberals. But Labour refused to serve under him because they considered him to be discredited by the failure of appeasement and the military reverses in Norway. Alternative leaders proposed were Winston Churchill, then serving at the Admiralty, and Lord Halifax, the Foreign Secretary. But Halifax refused to compete against Churchill for the leadership. On 10 May Winston Churchill was asked to form a Coalition Government with the Labour Party, and he accepted the role the day the Germans invaded Luxembourg, Belgium and the Netherlands.

Winston Churchill (1874–1965)
Wartime leader famous for his inspirational, and morale-lifting, rhetoric. Preferred dealing with defence and foreign affairs, management of which he took on in the absence of Foreign Minister Sir Anthony Eden. An ardent imperialist, he was oblivious to the growth of nationalism in the Empire. Churchill is credited with forging the close wartime collaboration with the United States.

How did war affect parliamentary government?

To cope with the problems posed by the war, Leo Amery MP had suggested a change from peacetime government. He believed that wartime government would need men of resolution, daring and thrust for victory, with clear authority.

The adoption of Coalition government, composed of Conservative, Labour and Liberal MPs, involved setting aside confrontational Parliamentary procedures and political differences between the parties, as far as possible, to help the conduct of wartime government. In addition an all-party truce was agreed in the conduct of by-elections (see section 8.6).

Churchill set up a five-man War Cabinet, with himself as Prime Minister and Minister of Defence. Labour's Clement Attlee served as Lord Privy Seal (until 1943 when he became Lord President of the Council) and Arthur Greenwood as **Minister without Portfolio**. Neville Chamberlain served as Lord President of the Council and Lord Halifax as Foreign Secretary. Chamberlain was retained in the Cabinet because

Minister without Portfolio: A minister without a specific departmental responsibility.

he could command a substantial number of Conservative followers in a way that Churchill could not. This was because the new prime minister had been unpopular during the 1930s when he had opposed the government's policies of appeasement and increased self-government for India. Churchill needed to minimise his unpopularity, both within the Conservative Party and within the Coalition government. In October 1940 Chamberlain resigned due to ill health. With Chamberlain out of government, Churchill's position began to strengthen. Sir Anthony Eden replaced Halifax as Foreign Secretary in December 1940.

In *The Road to 1945* (1975), historian Paul Addison saw the Second World War as a melting pot for politics. Conservatives and Labour, governing together, put together a system of wartime agreements, which formed the basis of consensus politics and the welfare state.

How did the Coalition Government tackle the problems associated with post-war reconstruction?

By late 1943, when it had become clear that the Allies would win the Second World War, the Coalition Government became concerned about examining the problems of post-war **reconstruction**. In November 1943 Lord Woolton became Chairman of the Cabinet Joint Party Reconstruction Committee. Proposals examined included:

Reconstruction: This meant both planning for the future welfare of the country after the war and the rebuilding of buildings, shipping, aircraft and other materials damaged by enemy action.

- a Town and Country Planning Act, to control how and where offices, factories and houses were built;

- post-war housing policy;

- White Papers on the principles of a national health service, post-war sickness and pension schemes, unemployment benefit, workmen's compensation (see Chapter 12, section 1).

All parties were committed to achieving and maintaining a high level of employment.

Conservative MP R. A. Butler maintained that the work of this Joint Committee laid foundations that the Labour Party had only to finalise, after they had won the 1945 election, and 'in some cases bring forward Bills already drafted' by the wartime Coalition Government.

Another issue requiring discussion was the possibility of state ownership (nationalisation). The Conservatives would have preferred to avoid discussing this subject before the election, despite Labour MP Herbert Morrison's skilful presentation of a case for electricity nationalisation.

Why did the Labour Party's approach to domestic policy gain greater public support during the war?

Contemporary commentators noticed a public swing to the left, an impatience with class privileges and a belief that statism (state control of the staple industries), the solution Labour offered, would be beneficial. Labour sought to appear moderate in its proposals. In this they were helped by the extension of wartime controls over the economy and industry, so that Labour's nationalisation proposals did not appear so radical. The Labour Party Manifesto 'Let us Face the Future' promised to nationalise the Bank of England, fuel and power, transport, iron and steel. Labour promised to put the Beveridge Report into immediate effect (see section 8.3). It also promised economic planning and full employment. Labour was 'winning the peace' while Churchill was involved in war strategy and diplomacy.

As the Prime Minister and Minister of Defence, Churchill had overall responsibility for war strategy. He had very little time (or inclination) to concentrate on party politics or post-war domestic strategy. Other

Conservatives took responsibility for foreign, imperial and defence policies, but, in the eyes of many of the public, they were responsible for failing to solve the problems of the 1930s. In contrast to Labour, the Conservative Party was seen to have reservations about implementing the Beveridge Report's proposals. The Conservative Party's manifesto incorporated the Joint Coalition Committee's plans on key issues, for example full employment and a national health service. But they refused to be explicit about policies concerning the extent of state economic controls. The Conservatives were divided between those who were cautiously enthusiastic and those who were suspicious and negative. Some saw welfare reform as creeping socialism and others recognised that it was 'an idea whose time had come' and were willing to accept it as necessary. The public were aware of these Conservative reservations and therefore preferred to vote for the party, which would bring in the reforms they wanted.

Why was the wartime Coalition abandoned?

Winston Churchill wanted to keep the Coalition going until Japan had been defeated, which was expected some time in 1946. The Labour Party felt that this was too far away. They had been ahead in the opinion polls since 1943 and in 1944 had decided not to prolong the Coalition any longer than was absolutely necessary to ensure victory in Europe and the Far East. The Conservatives too were becoming tired of Coalition government. Churchill felt that the shadow of a general election would make parliamentary government unworkable, thus making the Coalition a lame duck administration. Therefore he decided to dissolve Parliament sooner rather than later. On 23 May 1945 Parliament was dissolved and Churchill appointed a caretaker government, which took over until 26 July when the election results were known.

How successful was the Coalition Government?

The Coalition had a keen and dynamic drive to win the war, and the mixture of parties seemed to work. However, Britain *had* to win the war; the alternative was a German victory with the likely subordination of Britain's interests to those of Nazi Germany. This unacceptable alternative seemed to concentrate minds wonderfully on the job in hand.

The Coalition government successfully tackled the problems involved in gearing British society, the economy and industry to the needs of winning the war. Once victory seemed attainable, they produced White Papers to cover proposed post-war reconstruction and welfare reform legislation. The wartime Coalition gave members of all political parties experience of government; when the Labour Party won the July 1945 election, the hand-over of power was smooth because so many Labour MPs were experienced in government.

Churchill's success as wartime leader of the Coalition Government resulted from his personal style of management. He was interested in many aspects of the conduct of the war. He distrusted large departments, fearing they would fail to act swiftly and effectively, preferring to establish a special relationship with a small and loyal staff. He preferred them to take personal responsibility for getting things done (and done quickly) and sent correspondence to ministers headed 'Action this day'. Moreover, Churchill's wartime leadership and his stirring speeches improved public morale.

1. What changes did the Second World War impose on the way Britain was governed?

2. How far was the success of the Coalition Government due to Churchill's wartime leadership?

8.6 *Why did the Conservative Party lose the 1945 election?*
A CASE STUDY IN HISTORICAL INTERPRETATION

The Conservative Party was in power for two-thirds of the 20th century. The Conservative-led National Government of 1931–45 was very successful, staying in power for 14 years. So what were the circumstances that led it to lose the 1945 election?

The 1945 general election

● The general election took place on 5 July 1945 but results were not available until 26 July because time was needed to collect and count votes from overseas servicemen.

● Labour was consistently in the lead from 1943 in by-elections, and opinion polls were suggesting that they had a substantial lead over the Conservatives.

● On 26 July the results showed that Labour had won 393 seats, a gain of 227. The Conservatives had won 189 seats but lost 185 to Labour.

Why did the Conservative Party lose?

Had they lost touch with the public mood for welfare reform, which Labour had understood so well? And linked to this, had their policy development section been allowed to decline during the war so that they failed to develop welfare reform policies which suited the public mood, but which were framed to be acceptable to Conservative traditional supporters?

Problems of policymaking were fundamental to the Conservatives' defeat:

● There was a lack of official policy-making on home affairs – the Conservative Party fell back on 'trust the government' and 'let's win the war first'. The Conservatives were preoccupied with Churchill, his vision of internationalism and new world order and concern for Soviet intentions, at the expense of welfare reform and reconstruction.

Collectivism: Increased involvement of the government in social and economic affairs.

● Churchill himself had no message, apart from warnings about the dangers of **collectivism**, and remained aloof from policy-making, being too concerned with wartime diplomacy and defence. This created a vacuum at the top.

● The Conservatives were not identified with welfare reforms and there was a split within the party between those who were pro- and anti-welfare reforms.

● A case in point was the party's response to the Beveridge Report. This was embraced enthusiastically by the Tory Reform Group, which favoured collectivism, but there were others who treated it with suspicion, such as Churchill, who feared an extension of state intervention and higher taxation.

● This split produced a lack of party policy-making, which did not address reconstruction, whereas the Labour Party fervently adopted the welfare reform programme outlined in the Beveridge Report.

● The 1944 Health White Paper highlighted divisions in the Coalition, which was falling apart over welfare policy, although it held up over wartime diplomacy and strategy. The Town and Country Planning Bill provided for land procurement, which was perceived by the Conservatives as robbery. But Labour would not accept any alterations to it and threatened to withdraw from the Coalition in March 1945.

Had Conservative Party organisation declined so far during the war that it proved impossible to galvanise organisers efficiently to consolidate the Conservative vote in time for the 1945 election?

● Area Offices and Constituency Associations were closed down as staff enlisted or were drafted into the forces. By 1945, 170 agents and 30 women organisers were engaged in war work.

● The co-ordination and direction of the Conservative campaign was almost non-existent in the few months before the 1945 general election. It lacked central direction and carefully composed policies. Those policies that were put together were rushed or delivered late.

● The campaign was principally based on Churchill's wartime leadership. It was not understood that the public would differentiate between Churchill as the effective wartime leader and Churchill the peacetime Prime Minister.

● Too little was spent on publicity, only £3,000. This was less than one-tenth of the £30,000 spent in 1935.

● Local Conservative Party activism was virtually non-existent up to a few months before the 1945 general election.

Were the Conservatives electorally disadvantaged supporting the 'electoral truce'?

An electoral truce had been signed by the Conservatives, Labour and the Liberals on 26 September 1939 requiring each of the parties not to 'nominate candidates at by-elections … against the candidate of the party who held the seat at the time of vacancy'.

● The Labour Party at local level did not endorse replacement Conservative candidates in accordance with the terms of the truce, and in defiance of Labour Party HQ instructions. Conservative seats were often fought by independent left-wingers who ignored the instructions of the Labour National Executive to implement the truce.

● On the other hand, the Conservatives never disobeyed party orders because there was no Party Organisation as such in existence to order conduct one way or another. Only in 1944 did Central Office propose more explicit political battle. Nevertheless, Churchill had refused to make speeches in support of Conservative candidates as being against the spirit of the truce. But even when this ruling was reversed, Conservative by-election defeats continued.

Was there a failure of leadership from Churchill?

There was a leadership vacuum because:

● Churchill was not a good party man. He had been in the political 'wilderness' until the war and had no power base within the party.

● At the time, he was identified as a war leader. This was fine for war but not for peace. He was totally involved with strategy and wartime diplomacy.

● He did not have close relations with the party organisation hierarchy and tended to listen more to his cronies, Beaverbrook and Bracken.

Conclusion

What accounted for the size of the Labour majority?

Labour strategy:

- Attlee was calm and statesmanlike. Churchill's 'Gestapo' speech in March 1945, which warned the electorate that socialist government would lead to dictatorship.

- For sections of the electorate, the reforms promised by the White Papers were important and the Labour Party looked as if it would deliver reform pledges whereas the Conservatives did not.

- The Labour Party blamed the Conservatives for appeasement and unpreparedness for the war effort in a pamphlet entitled 'The Guilty Party', which associated the Conservatives with appeasement.

Other factors involved included:

- The British electoral system had inequalities in constituency sizes i.e. small urban electorate – which Labour won. The average Labour seat contained nearly 6,000 electors fewer than the average Conservative seat. Thus Labour received 48% of the poll but two-thirds of the seats. Although the Conservatives obtained 40% of the vote they were severely disadvantaged by the inequality of constituency sizes.

- The Conservatives' underestimation of lingering memories of 1930s unemployment and paying little heed to a public desire for new men and new policies.

- The National platform being seen as out of date. The public had had fourteen years of National Government and besides it could not be 'National' if it did not include Labour, so it did not ring true.

Contemporary Conservative interpretations of defeat focused on:

- Criticism of Churchill's election campaign. His campaign speeches were described as 'confused, woolly, unconstructed and wordy'.

- Lack of policy development and want of a clear policy. The Conservative Manifesto had been hurriedly produced in two or three weeks.

- The belief that the war had radicalised the forces, whose vote had gone 'en bloc' to Labour.

- The maintenance of party machinery at local level which had became divorced from central direction of National Union and Conservative Central Office.

- Failure of the Party organisation to run an effective campaign, caused by military service of party organisers and the party machine not revived in time for the election campaign. Michael Kandiah suggests in *Contemporary Record* (1995) that this last factor was central to election defeat.

Interpreting the results

What did the 12% swing to Labour represent? Did Labour win or did the Conservatives lose the 1945 election?

- The scale of defeat was exaggerated by the electoral system.

- The evidence suggests that Labour was supported by new voters and benefited from Conservative abstentions. The Conservatives did not get the traditional middle-class vote or traditional female vote.

- The Conservatives themselves agreed that the public was steadily radicalised during the war.

- Service votes were mostly pro-Labour – probably because young men were more attracted to Labour and many were worried about how long the war in the Far East would continue.

- The public was more concerned with issues of post-war reconstruction and welfare reform than theoretical socialism. Therefore Labour gathered support, and the public was not repelled by collectivist aspects of Labour's political platform. The middle classes were attracted by the health schemes and the alliance with the Soviet Union, its battle successes and the avuncular portrayals of 'Uncle Joe' Stalin inclined voters to a more favourable view of the Russians.

- There was tactical voting against the Conservatives and an anti-Conservative vote deriving from: 14 years in government, memories of Munich, unemployment and dole of the 1930s.

- Conservative Party organisation was depleted and in disarray, their election campaign was fudged and publicity and propaganda were misdirected.

Did the Labour landslide constitute a political revolution?

On the one hand, the Conservatives and their political allies retained 40% of the votes cast. On the other hand, the election gave the Labour Party a large majority for the first time and a clear mandate for them to implement considerable change, which they subsequently did.

1. What impact did the Second World War have on the Conservative Party?

2. Did the Labour Party win the 1945 election or did the Conservative Party lose it?

From Empire to Commonwealth, 1945–2000

Key Issues

- *Did the Second World War make decolonisation an inevitability?*

- *How successfully did Britain manage the process of decolonisation?*

- *In what ways did the end of empire affect British society and politics?*

Framework of Events

1947	Partition of India into India and Pakistan
	Independence given to India and Pakistan
	Communist insurrection begins in Malaya
1948	Ceylon (Sri Lanka) given independence
	British withdraws from Palestine mandate
1949	India becomes a republic
	London Declaration allows India to stay in Commonwealth
1951	Anglo-Iranian oil company nationalised
1952	Mau Mau rebellion in Kenya
1953	Shah of Iran restored to power by Britain and United States
1955	State of emergency declared in Cyprus
1956	Suez Crisis
1958	Malayan emergency ends
1960	Nigeria given independence
1961	South Africa becomes a republic and leaves the Commonwealth
	Zambia and Malawi given independence
1962	Uganda given independence
	Tanganyika given independence
1963	Kenya given dependence
1965	Rhodesia's Unilateral Declaration of Independence
1972	End of sterling area
	East Pakistan gains independence as Bangladesh after war with West Pakistan
1979	Rhodesian Settlement in Lancaster House Agreement. Ceasefire in Rhodesian civil war
1980	Zimbabwe created – it joins the Commonwealth
1982	The Falklands war
1984	British-Chinese agreement on future of Hong Kong. Britain to hand over Hong Kong to China in 1997
1985	Britain isolated in Commonwealth over Thatcher government's attitude towards sanctions against South Africa
1987	Fiji leaves Commonwealth after military takeover

1990	Namibia becomes independent and becomes 50th member of the Commonwealth
1994	Multi-racial South Africa rejoins Commonwealth following end of Apartheid
1997	Hong Kong returns to China
1998	Mozambique, a former Portuguese colony joins Commonwealth
	Nigeria's membership of Commonwealth suspended following military takeover

Overview

Dominions: By 1931 the Dominions – Australia, Canada, New Zealand, South Africa and the Irish Free State were legally independent in all internal and external matters, though economic and other ties remained. Egypt and Iran were legally independent but Britain retained control over their foreign policy and had a military presence. The rest of the countries in the Empire were colonies, not Dominions.

ALTHOUGH countries such as Australia had become self-governing **Dominions**, at the end of the Second World War Britain still had a large Empire, and even the Dominions retained strong trade links with Britain and almost all had joined Britain to fight during the war. Twenty-five years later this Empire had almost entirely gone. Decolonisation was not simply the 'end of empire'. The creation of the Commonwealth shows that Britain regarded the process as an adjustment in the nature of the relationship between itself and its former colonies while it still kept its influence over them. The Commonwealth has survived – in 1999 there were 54 member countries, all except one once part of the Empire – because it suits the interests of its member states.

After 1945 Britain's political relationships with its colonies had to change. This was due to various factors. Internally Britain faced economic difficulties. Internationally the situation was changing, as the United States and the Soviet Union became the dominant world powers. The growth of nationalist movements in the colonies also forced change. But Britain still believed that it was possible to retain a 'special relationship' with former colonies, by managing change carefully. In many ways this failed – yet the Commonwealth remains a live and often lively organisation, informal but with influence over its member countries.

Although it had to give India independence immediately after the war, Britain attempted to develop other parts of its Empire as a source of power, prestige and (more easily measured) US dollars. This caused some of the discontent that grew during the 1950s, as nationalist movements took hold in many countries. Britain had seen decolonisation as a leisurely stroll towards independence, followed by continued strong links between Britain and the newly-independent colonies. In practice the processes turned to rapid withdrawal from the colonies, for example from Africa between 1959 and 1964. White settlers, once a key part of Britain's policy of self-government, became an international embarrassment and problem to be solved. The Suez crisis of 1956 demonstrated that Britain could not act independently, when the United States and almost all the countries of the United Nations were against its foreign policies, even when Britain was allied with another European power – France – and (secretly) with Israel.

Commonwealth Secretaries General

Arnold Smith (Canada) 1965–75

Sir Shridath Surrendranath Rampal (Guyana) 1975–89

Chief Emeka Anyaoku (Nigeria) 1989–

The Commonwealth never developed into the profitable trading area that the British had hoped, and from the 1960s Britain began to turn instead towards Europe. However, the Commonwealth has, perhaps unexpectedly, survived. As an informal group of countries, which at least attempts to promote and support democracy, and allow industrialised and developing countries to meet and exchange views, it has become a useful organisation and shows every sign of continuing well into the 21st century.

9.1 How did the Second World War affect Britain's imperial policy?

Closed economy: The deliberate protection of trade through taxation.

Free trade: A system that encourages the free flow of imports and exports.

Freely convertible: Allowing one currency to be traded for another without restrictions.

Zionists: Supporters of the creation of an independent Jewish state called Israel.

During the Second World War, it seemed possible that Britain might emerge with a much-reduced Empire. Burma, Singapore, Hong Kong and Malaya were all occupied by the Japanese in 1942, and although one of Britain's war aims was the preservation of Empire, both its principal allies, the United States and the Soviet Union, were, in principle, opposed to colonialism. The United States periodically suggested that British colonies, especially in Asia, should be placed under international control prior to independence, and was keen that the **closed imperial economy** should be opened up to **free world trade**. President Roosevelt was a committed anti-colonialist. In fact, all Britain's colonies were restored at the end of the war, and although Britain then withdrew from India and Ceylon (Sri Lanka), this was done to improve the running of the Empire as a whole and not to abandon it.

Clinging on to the Empire was intended to support both the British economy and its influence abroad, resisting American attempts to redefine Britain as a European power only. The costs of the war had left Britain dependent on loans from the United States; by the end it was overspending by £2,000 million each year and exports had lost two-thirds of their value. An American loan of $3.75 billion was made in 1945 on condition that sterling became **freely convertible** with dollars in July 1947, which would open up imperial markets to the United States. The formation of the United Nations, although Britain was a member of the security council, reflected the new situation in which the United States and the Soviet Union were the main players in world politics. Both these countries were officially opposed to colonialism.

The postwar Labour government remained committed to the Empire – in 1948 the Prime Minister, Clement Attlee, said to the House of Commons that Britain was 'not solely a European power but a member of a great Commonwealth and Empire'. Ernest Bevin, the Foreign Secretary, said in October that year, 'if we only pushed on and developed Africa, we could have the United States dependent on us and eating out of our hands in four or five years'. They saw Britain as offering a middle way between the American capitalism and Soviet communism, which were both disliked by the Labour Party. The desire to keep Britain's importance in the world is underlined by the decision in 1947 to build an independent nuclear deterrent. The development of nuclear weapons, however, was leading to a world in which possessing an empire was not the way to military greatness. This is underlined by the way that when the Soviet Union was ready to test an atomic bomb in 1949, the importance of the relationship with the United States was stressed again, and the North Atlantic Treaty Organisation was formed, linking the United States permanently with Europe.

Events in Palestine demonstrate how important US influence had become. The British, running Palestine under the UN's mandate, wanted to restrict Jewish immigration to 1,500 people a month, in order not to alienate the Arab population, thus threatening Britain's role elsewhere in the Middle East. But the Americans, responding to a strong Jewish lobby at home, suggested initially that 100,000 Jews be allowed into Palestine and then went further in support of the **Zionists**. An Anglo-American Committee of Inquiry failed to produce a solution acceptable to either Jews or Arabs, and a UN Special Committee recommended partition. In mid-1948, Britain left Palestine rather than be involved in putting the UN plan into practice; this departure was followed by the war which led to the establishment of the Jewish nation-state, Israel.

The development of the Commonwealth was one way of achieving continued British influence. Colonial policy had been redefined during the war, partly in response to American pressure, and the Colonial Office now began to talk of developing colonies' self-governing potential and guiding them along the way to independence. After independence, however, the idea was that the former colonies should join the Commonwealth and continue to co-operate with Britain in the **sterling area** and in defence.

Sterling area: The group of countries that held the pound sterling as their reserve currency after the war.

Originally the Commonwealth (then 'the British Commonwealth') had been restricted to the 'white' Dominions – Australia, New Zealand, Canada, South Africa and the Irish Free State (Eire). These recognised the King as the head of the Commonwealth (though Eire did so only as a convenience and left the Commonwealth altogether in 1949). All except Eire fought with Britain in the Second World War. After the war the Commonwealth came to be seen as a way to set up a flexible, multi-racial community through which Britain would exercise influence. For Britain to build up a 'third force' in the world, separate from the Soviet Union and the United States, the Commonwealth needed to be as large and inclusive as possible. This meant India and Pakistan must be part of it, and since India wanted to become a republic, the Commonwealth was changed with the 1949 London Declaration to allow both Crown Dominions, which had the British monarch as their head of state, and Republican Dominions, which did not. The monarch remained the overall head of the Commonwealth. As described in a Colonial Office paper of 1950 the aim was for the new Commonwealth to be a 'circle of democratic nations exerting a powerful stabilising influence in the world'.

Within the colonies, the aim was 'to guide the colonial territories to responsible self-government within the Commonwealth in conditions that ensure to the people both a fair standard of living and freedom from oppression from any quarter' (a Colonial Office paper, May 1950). In 1946 the head of the Africa Division in the Colonial Office proposed a local government policy that would eventually transfer power to Africans, increasing democracy and bringing 'literates and illiterates together, in balanced and studied proportions, for the management of local finances and services. Failing this we shall find the masses apt to follow the leadership of **demagogues** who want to turn us right out very quickly.'

Demagogue: A charismatic and authoritarian leader.

Although the United States was officially opposed to colonialism, for both ethical and economic reasons, the development of the Cold War meant it was more worried about containing Soviet influence. Protectionist policies, such as the sterling area, were accepted because they could speed European recovery, and in a healthy economy communist parties had less influence. The American military were also anxious that British withdrawal from colonies would create instability and leave those countries open to Soviet influence. As the Cold War spread to Asia, with communist China intervening in Korea in 1950, Malaya became a frontline state. The British army went in to fight during the 'Emergency' caused by a communist insurrection, believed to be backed by the Soviet Union and China. Elsewhere, the United States and Britain co-operated in the 1953 coup in Iran that restored the Shah to power. US influence in the Middle East was increasing, but it was not particularly interested in Africa. The Bureau of African Affairs was not set up at the State Department until 1958. By the time US loans and grants were being made to African countries, British decisions on decolonisation had already been made. Nevertheless, the possibility of American intervention in colonial affairs was one of the reasons for modernising and democratising colonial government.

Elites: Ruling groups or classes.

The British attempted to nurture moderates and create **elites** within the colonies who would work to modernise them, co-operating with the British and acting against communism. These elites would be made up of the

Western-educated middle class who would, according to the plan, become involved first in local government, gradually moving towards self-government modelled on the Westminster Parliament. This was what they had attempted to do in India, where their efforts were upset by the Second World War, but they were more successful in some of the African colonies.

Such change had to happen, partly to avoid international pressure for change, partly in order to promote social and economic development, partly in response to nationalist aims stimulated by the war and partly to block Soviet imperialism. Pressure from within the colonies could produce surprisingly quick effects; in 1948 there were riots on the Gold Coast, and by 1950 there was a new constitution, guaranteeing an African majority in the legislative council. Where there was no significant group of white settlers, it was much easier to set up this system successfully.

1. How did Britain attempt to restructure the Empire after 1945 and why?

2. How did the Cold War affect British colonial policy?

9.2 Why did Britain have to leave India in 1947?

How does this map help show how the British Empire declined in these areas?

The simple answer is that the Indians had been promised self-rule when the war ended. This had long been an aim – the 1935 Government of India Act had promised eventual self-government for India as a Dominion, and the new constitution, introduced in 1937, allowed the Indian National Congress, the main nationalist party (and mainly Hindu), to take control of most of the Indian provinces. Defence and

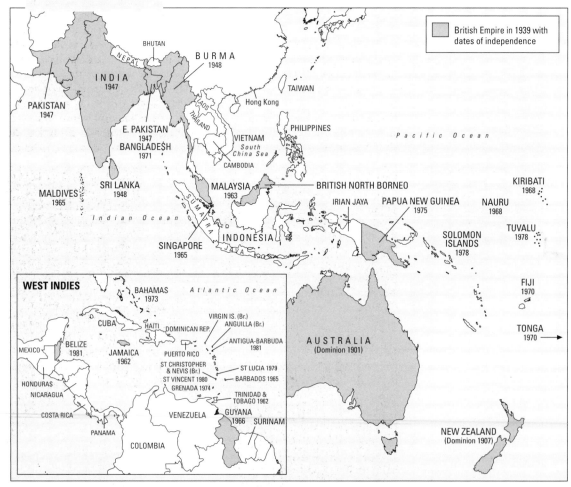

Britain's former colonies in Asia and the Pacific and the Caribbean

foreign policies were still controlled by the Viceroy on Britain's behalf, and the army and police were still under British command.

The British government thought that India could be given self-rule as a united country, still relying on British defence co-operation and with many Britons still working there. Defence was a key issue. The Indian Army, with mainly British officers, could mobilise as many troops as the British Army and had been stationed throughout the Empire, defending the whole – so once war was declared India was vital to the British effort. After the humiliating fall of Singapore, Malaya, Hong Kong and Burma to the Japanese in early 1942, India, along with Australia, was very vulnerable to Japanese attack. At the same time the political handling of the war exposed the limits of what Britain had granted. Britain declared war with Germany on India's behalf, and the Congress Party ministers all resigned over this action being taken without consulting the wishes of the Indians. The subsequent mobilisation, shortages, inflation and disruption of trade, as well as British defeats, meant the government became more and more unpopular. Attempts to gain co-operation from Congress in 1942 failed, despite the promise of self-government immediately the war was over and instead the **Quit India** movement was started. However, the Muslim League, committed to a separate Muslim state since 1940, did work with the British government, and so became more important in Indian politics – making partition more likely.

The promise of postwar independence remained, however, and the Labour government was committed to fulfilling it. American criticism of Britain's rule in the subcontinent had been very embarrassing, but in any case, by 1947 India was in deficit to the United States in **visible trade** and so did not bring additional hard currency to the sterling area. It was clear that Britain needed to focus on parts of the Empire that were likely to be assets, and withdraw from more problematic places. Africa was thought to be more adaptable than India.

At first, the British government hoped to establish a friendly government in India, co-operating with Britain in the Commonwealth. It was thought that Britain could retain access to military bases and manpower in India – as was agreed with Ceylon in 1947. Stafford Cripps proposed in 1946 that the Indian provinces should form a federation where foreign policy, defence,

Quit India: Led by Gandhi, this campaign of civil disruption began in 1942, and was suppressed by the British. All the Congress leaders were jailed for the rest of the war.

Visible trade: Trade in goods (e.g. cars and textiles) rather than services (e.g. insurance).

Gandhi, leader of the Indian National Congress since 1914 and of civil disobedience campaigns, with Lord Mountbatten, last Viceroy of India

**Mohammed Ali Jinnah
(1876–1948)**
Leader of the Muslim League and Pakistan separatist movement from 1935. Co-operated with British during the Second World War. Became Governor-General of Pakistan, 1947.

1. **What difference did the war make to British policy in India?**

2. **Why was India partitioned in 1947?**

3. **How did the Indian parties campaign for nationalism and respond to British policy during the Second World War and after?**

communications and finance were controlled by the centre. However, since 1940, the leader of the Muslim League, Jinnah, had been talking of the impossibility of Hindus and Muslims living together successfully in an independent India, and he feared that the Congress party wanted centralisation to reduce Muslim participation. The League refused to co-operate in making a constitution and decided on 'direct action' to obtain a separate Pakistan. In August 1946 over 5,000 people died in rioting in Calcutta between Hindus and Muslims. The violence continued, and in February 1947. Attlee announced that June 1948 was the date of withdrawal whether or not the League and Congress could reach any agreement, and sent Lord Louis Mountbatten to be the final Viceroy.

Mountbatten tried to get agreement from League and Congress to an all-India federation, but Nehru, the Congress president, was afraid that without a strong centre there would simply be more violence. Mountbatten then proposed partition into two separate Dominions, India and Pakistan. Congress agreed to this, but only if withdrawal was speeded up, and so India and Pakistan became independent in August 1947. They immediately began to dispute the partition of Kashmir. Britain had failed to achieve a government in India with which it would maintain defence links, nor had the rights of minorities such as the Sikhs been guaranteed, but the new Dominions were members of the Commonwealth. This did not however mean they were supporters of British policy – as leader of the Non-Aligned Movement in the 1950s, India continually criticised British imperialism, and moved away from Britain in seeking allies against China. Britain has been criticised for the speed of its withdrawal. In the violence that followed at least 250,000 people died in the Punjab alone.

9.3 How did Britain attempt to make the Empire pay?

The Labour government of 1945 was committed to social policies in Britain, such as the National Health Service, which would be a significant cost to the state. There were fears that continued expenditure abroad might damage Britain's economic stability – in 1946 the Chancellor of the Exchequer was warning that the balance of payments could not stand the cost of the 1.2 million British people serving abroad. In 1947 Britain's dollar reserves were reduced as US prices rose, and in June the Treasury warned that without American aid the dollar shortage combined with convertibility of sterling to dollars (promised to the Americans for July that year) could destroy the British economy. In fact, convertibility lasted just a month before the threat of a complete loss of the pound's value led to the reintroduction of exchange controls. In November 1947 the sterling area had a dollar deficit of £600–£700 million per year.

The sterling area was formed at the beginning of the war and consisted principally of the Empire/Commonwealth countries. After 1945 it was much more controlled, and discriminated against trade with 'hard currencies' – currencies like the US dollar which could be bought and sold anywhere – and became a way for Britain to earn dollars. Exports such as rubber from Malaya and cocoa from the Gold Coast brought dollars into the area. Britain then bought the dollars at a fixed exchange rate, crediting the country with a sterling balance – which could only be spent within the sterling area. Since Britain was unable to produce all the goods that a country like Malaya wanted to purchase, this led to shortages and therefore inflation in countries that earned hard currency. The Commonwealth Colombo Plan of 1950 partly hoped to address this by improving living standards in South-East Asia. This was also meant to prevent communism from being too attractive.

Colonial Development Corporation (CDC): Set up 1948 to promote increased colonial production on an economic and self-supporting basis, especially of food, raw material and manufactures, which would help improve the balance of payments. It could borrow up to £100 million for investment.

East African Groundnut Scheme: In 1946 it was proposed that 1 million acres of Tanganyika be used to grow groundnuts as a solution to the shortage of edible oils and fats. The scheme was approved in January 1947 and the area increased to 3.2 million acres. By 1949 the scheme had to be closed down: almost all of the budget had been spent on clearing 1.4% of the ground.

1. a) What was the sterling area?

b) Why was it important to British imperial policy?

2. How important was the Empire to Britain's economy in the 1940s and 1950s?

3. Could the Empire be made to pay? (Give reasons to support your answer.)

The colonies were vital to the sterling area since Britain had control over them, which it did not over the Crown Dominions, such as Australia. It was feared that if power were transferred to colonial nationalists, they might draw too much on their sterling balances and destabilise the British economy, which was another factor against allowing independence for many at this time.

The British economy was rescued by Marshall Aid. In fact, American assistance, first in 1945 and then in 1948, allowed Britain to postpone a serious reappraisal of its overseas commitments and ability to pay for the Empire. Instead, attempts were made to make the Empire pay. It was a source of cheap food (often bought below market rates) and raw materials, so the aim of British policy was to try to invest in the colonies to make them happy and productive, raising their living standards, benefiting Britain economically and so also presenting colonialism in a more positive way. The Empire also offered a secure outlet for British goods, and developing colonial economies would allow their consumers to buy more of these.

The Colonial Office recruited 4,100 new staff between June 1945 and September 1948; a 45% increase on the whole period 1945–54. Colonial Development and Welfare Acts were passed during the war, intended to help pay for improving living standards in the colonies and developing their economies. The overseas technical departments expanded. The Act passed in 1945 provided £120 million for colonial development. The Cabinet set up a **Colonial Development Corporation** at the end of 1948. Projects such as the **East African Groundnut Scheme** were set up to attempt to exploit imperial economic resources better, and efforts were made to reform agricultural practices in Africa. These attempts, however, were often very unpopular with the local people, and the groundnut scheme was a spectacular failure. Britain never managed to turn Africa into a source of dollars.

The Middle East was of course very important economically to Britain because of oil. In May 1951 the Iranian government nationalised the Anglo-Iranian Oil Company, with its refinery at Abadan, which was owned and run by Britain had usually put pressure on Iran by threatening to intervene in south Persia, but the Americans were afraid that this would lead to the Russians attacking the north and opposed British military action. So Britain was restricted to trying to stop Iranian oil getting to the world market. Although the Iranian regime was overthrown in 1953, with secret help from the US Central Intelligence Agency (CIA), Britain only regained a 40% stake in what was now an international consortium. At the time, however, this was not a disastrous economic blow, because Kuwait and other Gulf states were producing so much oil, helping the balance of payments. Attlee had contemplated withdrawing from the Middle East after the war, because of the expense of building up British bases there again, but was persuaded by the Foreign Office and the military that Britain must stay to contain the Soviet Union, and of course to protect oil interests.

Elsewhere in the Empire Britain tried to attract American investment, but although US industry needed raw materials from the Third World, it was only the Middle Eastern oil industry which attracted serious investment – where of course they were rivals to British firms. Few US companies were willing to risk their capital in an unstable and underdeveloped empire.

Despite these attempts to make the Empire pay, during the 1950s Britain was beginning to trade less with the Empire/Commonwealth and more with other industrialised nations. Economists were also beginning to question the desirability of the sterling area, and of encouraging colonies to build up large sterling balances. The various colonial loans that were floated on the Stock Market in the 1950s were all unpopular. By the end of the 1950s it was clear that the attempt to make the Empire pay had failed: in fact it had contributed to the pressure for decolonisation.

9.4 *What caused the growth of nationalism in so many different colonies in the 1950s?*

The Second World War had an important impact on nationalism in many colonies. Local populations were mobilised to produce war materials, or to serve abroad, and economies were disrupted. Service abroad influenced many people from the colonies, as they came into contact with fellow soldiers and with military organisation, and often developed a sense of their national identity. Wartime measures were accompanied by talk of postwar development and movement towards self-government, as the reward for co-operation during the war. After the war ministers spoke of the mutual benefits that Britons and colonial peoples would derive from

Decolonisation in Africa and the Middle East: the dates of British withdrawal

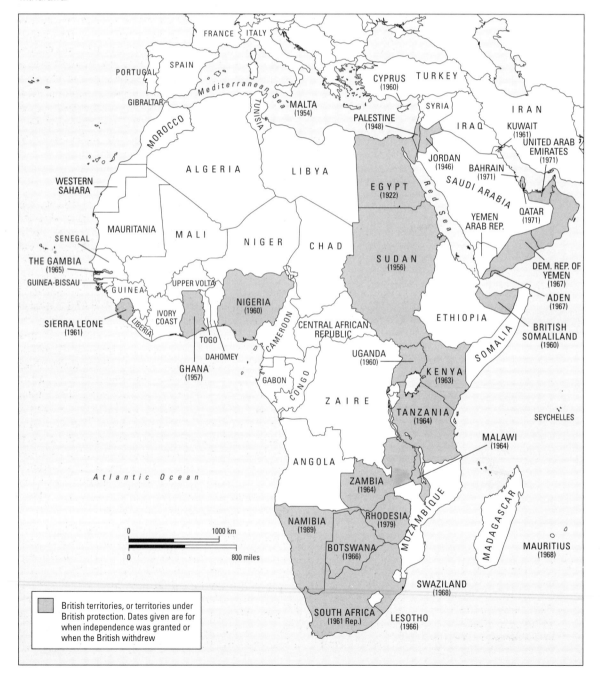

colonial development – Britain might benefit economically, but the colonies would also gain a higher standard of living. As we have seen, attempts to make the Empire profitable were unsuccessful, but they raised expectations among the local populations.

Instead of development, immediately after the war there were shortages, unemployment and inflation in many colonies, such as Nigeria, Kenya and Tanganyika, leading to strikes and protests. When attempts were made, for example to develop agriculture, this often involved unacceptable interference with traditional practices by agricultural officers. They wanted to build terraces to avoid soil erosion, introduce new crops, destroy diseased animals and plants, and backed this up with penalties and compulsory labour. In Kenya, for example, the government believed that such measures would solve the problem of the Kikuyu tribe's claim to the land farmed by the white settlers, by increasing production. Although these measures might have been necessary, in countries that were still being underpaid for their products and experiencing no rise in living standards, they aroused huge resentment. Putting such policies into practice were the increased numbers of European Colonial Office administrators and experts, thus making British rule much more visible and resented. In some countries, such as Southern Rhodesia, these additional officials were accompanied by a new generation of white settlers, for whom peasant African farmers were evicted – a very unwelcome 'second colonial occupation'.

The Gold Coast (Ghana)

The attempts at political development were not always welcome, and often contributed to nationalist feeling. The Gold Coast (now Ghana), where cocoa was the main commercial product (and a major dollar earner), provides an example of this. After the war, a constitution was introduced to give greater representation to local opinion, as a first step on the gradual road to independence. During the war, income tax had been introduced and central control over local government extended. Traditionally government had been operated on a local level in alliance with the local chiefs, but the new constitution proposed to bring the whole country under one legislature. It seemed that local chiefs now needed political influence at the centre to protect local interests. The business community feared that the constitution would entrench the chiefs too closely with the colonial government, and the chiefs were conservative and opposed to western ideas of democracy. The nationalist United Gold Coast Convention (UGCC) was formed in 1947 by a lawyer, J.B. Danquah. Meanwhile, the war had led to inflation and food shortages, making the colonial government unpopular. At the same time the government was enforcing the destruction of cocoa trees attacked by swollen shoot disease, according to the Colonial Office technicians' advice. Farmers resented this – the trees could go on being productive for years – and did not believe they would receive compensation. In early 1948 a demonstration by unemployed ex-servicemen led to riots.

The riots were put down by the British, and a constitutional committee set up, which recommended a larger elected assembly and universal (though usually indirect) suffrage. Meanwhile, Kwame Nkrumah, who had returned from studying in London to help with the UGCC's campaign by mobilising trade unions and local farmers' associations, set up his own party, the Convention People's Party, and began organising strikes and demonstrations. He was imprisoned, but his party still won the election and he had to be let out to take office as chief minister of the new assembly. In fact, once in office, he co-operated happily enough

How does the map on page 202 help explain the British withdrawal from Africa in the 1950s and 1960s?

with the British, and made it clear that he sought self-government within the Commonwealth and the sterling area. Britain accepted this, and the Gold Coast became independent in 1957. The nationalist movement started and developed clear aims partly because of Britain's attempts to draw up a new constitution, uniting the country more firmly, partly because of the shortages and inflation caused by the war, and partly because of the attempts to control the cocoa industry (even if for its own good). All these factors united the different interests in the local population against British rule. Colonial development, once begun, could lead very quickly to independence.

Nigeria

Similarly in Nigeria, initial plans for a gradual move towards self-government did not last. Britain wanted to draw together the very distinct parts of Nigeria – Muslim in the north, more influenced by western Christianity in the south, which was itself divided between the Yoruba in the west and Ibo in the east – into a modern state. When a new constitution was proposed, aiming to draw educated groups in all areas into developing the state, the very difficulty of getting these different groups to agree meant that independence had to be promised as a reward, and was achieved in 1960.

Kenya

British attempts to create large federations also aroused nationalist feelings and fears – part of the motivation for the Mau Mau revolt in Kenya was the proposal for a union of Kenya, Uganda and Tanganyika in an East African Federation. Given the example of the Central African Federation (see below), this did not appeal to their black populations. In Kenya, urban unemployment and housing shortages combined with rural grievances about the new development of agriculture, leading to disturbances and the creation of the underground Mau Mau movement, which was violently resisting British rule by the end of 1952 – though in fact most of its victims (14,000 compared to 95 whites) were Kikuyu. It was a war fought between those who had adopted western ideas or had benefited from colonial rule and those who believed it must be resisted in every way. Britain responded with force, declaring an emergency and eventually suppressing the Mau Mau by the end of 1956. However, at the same time the colonial government attempted to make fundamental agriculture and land reforms, consolidating holdings and creating a new class of conservative farmers. This meant that African representation had to be extended to gain moderate support for these plans, though this was as part of Britain's aim that Kenya should be run by a power-sharing group of Europeans, Asians and Africans.

Tanganyika

Attempts from 1952 to reform the Tanganyika government to fit in with the same multi-racial powersharing model were what led to nationalist resistance there. Locally government had been African, with a British district officer; now it was to include Europeans and Asians. At the same time, efforts were being made to improve agriculture, conserve the soil and raise productivity. The local chiefs used to enforce this had become unpopular, and the Tanganyika African National Union (TANU) had been formed. It became an important force of opposition to multi-racialism and in the 1958 elections, which Britain had intended to produce a multi-racial council, TANU candidates won a majority.

In South-East Asia matters seemed easier to handle. In Malaya, consideration had been given to self-government since the start of the Emergency operation against Chinese communist rebels, which lasted from 1948 until the mid-1950s. The different communities in Malaya – Chinese, Malay and Indian – needed incentives to co-operate with each other and, as elsewhere, Britain hoped for multi-racial parties to emerge. Meanwhile, however, Britain had been left as the only major colonial power in South-East Asia, when France left Indo-China. The United States wanted the end of colonialism in the area to help contain communism in Vietnam. The leaders of two main Malayan parties, allied to each other, were keen to retain their connections with Britain, partly because they needed help in ending the Emergency, and agreed in return to remain within the sterling area. This was precisely the kind of decolonisation Britain wanted – but it was the need for continued security assistance that brought it about.

Nationalist movements were becoming troublesome elsewhere in the Empire. Aden, between Yemen and Oman, which Britain valued increasingly during the 1950s, was coveted by Yemen. Also, within the Aden colony, British rule was resented – more so after the Suez crisis of 1956, which had shown the limits of British power. Attempts to put together the Federation of South Arabia, created in 1963, which would bring together the interior with the Aden peninsula, threatened the power of local tribes, who revolted in 1963.

As we have seen, then, nationalist movements everywhere grew during the 1950s. The economic problems following the war, together with increased controls that had been imposed during it, meant that local populations found British rule increasingly oppressive, while increased numbers of white officials and settlers made it more visible. Attempts to create limited suffrage as a first step on the road to independence gave nationalist parties an opportunity to gain political influence, and overturned programmes for very slow constitutional change moving very gradually towards independence – as in Ghana. Britain would hang on, for example in Kenya, fighting violent nationalist movements, but this was a very expensive option.

1. Why were British governments in favour of federations?

2. How and why did nationalist parties develop in Africa? Give examples from at least two countries.

9.5 The problem of white settlers in Africa

There were particular problems with decolonisation in areas with significant numbers of white settlers. In Central Africa, white nationalism was a strong force – there were 300,000 whites in Southern and Northern Rhodesia, and new settlers began to arrive after 1945. Although, in theory, the British government had to approve constitutional changes and laws that affected the African population of Southern Rhodesia, in fact the country had been internally self-governed since 1923. White Northern Rhodesians aspired to the same independence, and after the war, as Rhodesian copper and tobacco were vital to the sterling area, the British government had to move carefully. White workers in the mining industry had active trade unions, and were afraid of cheap black labourers taking their jobs. Moves towards black majority rule elsewhere in Africa encouraged white nationalism, and the belief that white settlers were beneficial to African development was shared by the British government during the 1950s. The extreme poverty of most of the black Africans in Nyasaland and Northern Rhodesia meant that there was little political organisation or nationalist agitation among the black population. In Southern Rhodesia more Africans had moved to the towns during the war, and trade union and political organisation had developed (there was a strike in Salisbury

Federation: A group of states, which retain equal status but share aspects of central policy making.

Amalgamation: Joining together.

and Bulawayo in 1948) but the white population there had full political control. Opposition from the British government to the white population's desire for unification was abandoned in 1949, partly influenced by fear of Afrikaner domination in the Rhodesias – there were many Afrikaners among the new immigrants, and the National Party had just won control of South Africa. South Africa later adopted a system of apartheid by which the black and white populations were separated in every part of life, education, sport, work, transport and where they lived.

The scheme developed during 1951–53 (with a constitutional review promised for 1959) was for **federation** rather than **amalgamation**, and included Nyasaland, a poor British protectorate. The Colonial Office would continue to supervise Northern Rhodesia and Nyasaland, with responsibility for the political advancement of the Africans and for internal security, and staffed by members of the Colonial Service. However, when in 1957 the African Affairs Board, set up to do so, referred to British legislation that enlarged the Federal Assembly while keeping the number of African representatives the same, the British government approved it. The federal government pressed for further self-government for Northern Rhodesia, and in 1957 the British government began to redraw the constitution (though attempting to include measures encouraging multi-racial politics), but black opposition was by now more effective. Attempts to involve Africans in politics to preserve the constitution had increased their political awareness, but the main force behind African nationalism, uniting rural and urban, chiefs and politicians, was the fear of being trapped in a white Dominion.

Under Kenneth Kaunda, the Zambia African National Congress split from the African National Congress to promote a boycott of the new constitution in Northern Rhodesia, while Dr Hastings Banda of the Nyasaland African Congress (NAC) was leading a campaign for independent majority rule there. By March 1959 an 'emergency' had been declared in Nyasaland and a police and military operation against the NAC begun, on the pretext that the NAC planned to murder government officials, which led to the deaths of about 51 Africans. At the same time in Northern Rhodesia the Zambia African National Congress (ZANC) led by Kaunda was banned and in Southern Rhodesia 500 African political activists were arrested. Instead of crushing opposition to federation, the number of deaths and the disorder in Nyasaland meant there had to be an independent inquiry, and its report condemned the government's actions. The Monckton Commission, set up to review the federal constitution, recommended in 1960 that federation should be retained, but with, for example, parity of representation for whites and blacks in the Federal Assembly and African majorities in the Nyasaland and Northern Rhodesian assemblies. The British government was rapidly repositioning itself away from the white settlers, releasing Kaunda and Banda and pressing the federal premier to accept an African majority in Northern Rhodesia. Britain was not prepared to fight in defence of white settler claims. Attempts to negotiate a new federal constitution in 1960 were deadlocked between white and black nationalists. There were violent disturbances in Northern Rhodesia when a constitution was proposed for Southern Rhodesia weighted to give a white majority in the legislature; by March 1961 the new Colonial Secretary, Reginald Maudling, announced a new constitution that would give an African majority for Northern Rhodesia. Elections in Northern Rhodesia resulted in a majority for independence, and in Southern Rhodesia a new Rhodesian Front campaigned for separate independence there. The Federation was over. Northern Rhodesia became Zambia and Nyasaland Malawi.

Executive power: The power to carry out and enforce laws and decrees.

Jomo Kenyatta (1889–1978)
Leader of the Kikuyu in Kenya, he was one of the moderate Africans who negotiated with Macmillan for independence in the early 1960s, after the cost of suppressing the Mau Mau rebellion became too much for Britain. Became Prime Minister of independent Kenya in 1963 and President in 1964.

Elsewhere, Britain had planned for an East African Federation of Kenya, Uganda and Tanganyika, under governments sharing power between Europeans, Asians and Africans. Kenya had been attracting white settlers since the end of the 19th century, and their community, based on exclusive use of a large area of land, the 'White Highlands', dominated Kenyan politics, sharing **executive power** with the Colonial Office administration. The Mau Mau rebellions horrified the British government and the white settler population, and meant all national organisations for Africans were banned. It appeared that the white nationalists were on the way to achieving similar status as Southern Rhodesia, but in fact, as constitutional concessions were made in Uganda and Tanganyika, it was hard to deny them to Kenya. In addition the agricultural reforms made after the Mau Mau rebellion had developed a class of rural notables who now demanded influence over government policy and were hard to resist, since they had been set up by the government and were important in getting the reform programme implemented. Kenya's white settlers lost their influence. They had had to turn to Britain for the money and men to suppress the Mau Mau. Now Britain ended the ban on African movements and held the Lancaster House Conference on the constitution in 1960, at which it was agreed that Africans would have a majority in the legislature. The Kikuyu leader Jomo Kenyatta was in detention, but the two new African parties, rivals for support at home, were demanding his release and further steps towards independence. Although one of them was considered to have British support, it could not be controlled by Britain, and at the same time its requests were difficult to refuse. Kenyatta was released in August 1961, and independence followed in December 1963.

Southern Rhodesia, normally referred to as Rhodesia, remained a problem for Britain for many years. International pressure – including that from within the Commonwealth – was firmly against giving way to white nationalism. South Africa left the Commonwealth in May 1961, ostensibly because it was a republic but really because of the violent demonstrations at Sharpeville (see section 9.7), which showed clearly Commonwealth opinion on this issue. The Central African Federation had to be ended, and Zambia and Malawi were independent, but Rhodesia was still a white-ruled colony, pressing for independence on those terms. Britain refused independence, not wishing to offend the Afro-Asian Commonwealth, and not finding Rhodesia willing to make any real constitutional gesture towards the black community there. Both the Conservative government and then the new Labour government of 1964 under Harold Wilson tried to negotiate with Rhodesia, where Ian Smith was now prime minister, but unsuccessfully. Rhodesia made a Unilateral Declaration of Independence (UDI) on 11 November 1965. Wilson had already said he would not use force, though economic sanctions were imposed, and, governing with a small majority, was afraid that acting against the white Rhodesians would help the Conservative Party. But in the Commonwealth it became the most important issue between Britain and the African and Asian countries, and continued efforts were made to negotiate a solution. All these failed, even though Britain was not demanding majority rule or any quick approach to it. When the final set of proposals (which might lead to majority rule 30 years later) was put to the African population by a commission of enquiry, independence on such terms was comprehensively rejected.

What brought about black majority rule in Rhodesia were other changes in the area, including independence for Portugal's colonies of Angola and Mozambique. For South Africa, the guerrillas operating from eastern Rhodesia were a serious problem, and they used the economic and military help they gave the Rhodesians to press for a

British Prime Minister, Harold
Wilson, meeting Rhodesian
Prime Minister
Ian Smith

1. Compare
decolonisation policies
in Gold Coast (Ghana)
and Kenya. How far
were any differences
caused by white
settlers?

2. When and why did
Britain come to see
African white settlers
as a problem, and how
did governments
attempt to solve it?

compromise with the black population. By 1976 Ian Smith had
announced majority rule within two years, and reached an Internal
Settlement with some of the African nationalists, which was supported
in the elections by the black population. Bishop Muzarewa became
Zimbabwe-Rhodesia's first black prime minister, but the 'Patriotic Front'
parties, led by Joshua Nkomo and Robert Mugabe, continued to fight a
guerrilla war against the government of Zimbabwe-Rhodesia, acting
from Zambia and Mozambique. Britain might have wanted to accept the
Internal Settlement and recognise Zimbabwe-Rhodesia, but a large
number of other Commonwealth countries were firmly opposed to this.
At the Lusaka Heads of Government meeting in 1979 Britain agreed to a
new constitutional conference to establish an independent Zimbabwe,
and that at new elections the 'Patriotic Front' parties would be allowed
to participate. Commonwealth observers would attend and report on the
fairness of the elections. Additionally, as negotiations continued, a
Commonwealth Monitoring Force was sent to police the ceasefire. In
the elections the Patriotic Front parties, including the one led by
Mugabe, won, and Zimbabwe was finally established as an independent
republic, and a member of the Commonwealth – which had itself
successfully influenced British policy.

9.6 *What difference did the Suez Crisis make to the Empire?*
A CASE STUDY IN HISTORICAL INTERPRETATION

On 26 July 1956 the Egyptian President Gamal Abdel Nasser nationalised
the Suez Canal Company, in which Britain and France had previously had
a majority shareholding. The Suez canal linked the Mediterranean to the
Red Sea and was regarded as an essential strategic asset. Britain had continued to have a military presence in Egypt, even when it was technically
independent, to defend the Middle· East and its oil (which, coming
through the Suez canal from sterling area companies, could be paid for in
sterling, not precious dollars), and the Empire generally. Nasser's regime
was hostile to Britain, and under pressure from the United States, where
Eisenhower was President, Britain had signed a new Anglo-Egyptian
treaty in 1954, which included British withdrawal from the Canal Zone by

June 1956. When Nasser nationalised the canal, therefore, Britain no longer had the enormous Suez military base behind it.

The United States and Britain agreed in spring 1956 to collaborate on a scheme to destabilise Nasser's regime, but only through economic and political pressure, and propaganda. When Eden, after the nationalisation, began to prepare a military expedition to bring down Nasser and install a friendly government, Eisenhower was opposed to this from the start. Efforts were made to establish a negotiated solution between Britain, France and Egypt, but in the October the French and British agreed to attack Egypt, and secretly arranged that Israel would attack also. On 29 October Israel did attack Egypt: Britain and France began to bomb Egypt on 31 October. When Britain and France entered Egypt on 5 November, they presented it as an effort to restore peace between Israel and Egypt in the Middle East.

The Americans, however, refused to support such action. They were mainly concerned with containing the Soviet threat in the Middle East, where Britain was concerned for oil and for its own long-term position there. The Commonwealth did not support Britain while India supported Egypt, and in the United Nations the vote for an immediate ceasefire was 64 to 5. As sterling came under pressure, the Americans forced an end to the invasion by withholding essential loans to prop up the pound until Britain had withdrawn unconditionally, which it did in December.

Peter Hennessy, looking at the government papers relating to the Suez crisis, notes that there were plenty of warnings to the government about the course it was taking. Lord Mountbatten, the First Sea Lord, urged Prime Minister Anthony Eden to accept the UN resolution and 'cease military operations' before the fleet reached Port Said. Sir Edward Bridges, at the Treasury, explained in September 'the vital necessity from the point of view of our currency and our economy of ensuring that we do not go it alone, and that we have the maximum United States support'.

Clearly the military expedition was a failure in its own terms and more generally as a demonstration that Britain's imperial power could not be resurrected and was dependent on US support. Historians have argued whether it was even more important than that. Hennessy said it was 'conventional wisdom' that Suez hastened the end of Empire, but that Alec Douglas-Home, then Commonwealth Secretary, interviewed in 1987, thought it had not – 'it was inevitable that the Empire should dissolve'. Brian Lapping (in *Contemporary Record*) argues that Suez did speed up Britain's withdrawal from Empire, for example in Africa in the 1960s. He points out that Suez had an effect on France as well as Britain. Algerians rebelling against French rule were encouraged by Suez, and without that defeat it is unlikely the French would have so abruptly granted independence in 1960 to colonies such as Senegal and Ivory Coast. This in turn influenced British policy. Lapping also notes that Nasser offered help to many African nationalist leaders, including offices in Cairo and access to radio broadcasts. Egypt turned away from the West, and accepted Russian military and economic advisers. At the same time, the Americans became more interested in Africa, and established their Bureau of African Affairs. Britain reduced its overseas military bases after Suez: the crisis had demonstrated that Britain and France could not make military interventions without US backing, so it was reasonable to cut back on the troops. From 1957, the numbers in the armed services fell from about 700,000 to 375,000.

Lapping argues finally that Macmillan, who succeeded Eden as Prime Minister, at first had to continue with Eden's policies in order to reunite the party, but then, having won a general election, was able to change direction, speed up decolonisation and turn towards Europe. 'Macmillan and Macleod changed policy because they saw that, in the light of all the changes speeded up by Suez, they had no choice.' Suez had shown that the British Empire was no longer supported by a superior military force.

Anthony Low (also in *Contemporary Record*) argues instead that Suez did not make much long-term difference to decolonisation. All political parties were already committed to allowing the colonies self-rule, which had already been promised to Ghana (though it would not take effect until 1957). He argues that African nationalist movements were one of the main causes of the speeded-up decolonisation programme after 1959. After the Suez crisis, in 1959, the dates considered for Kenya, Tanganyika and Uganda to become independent were from 1970 to 1975. Although African nationalists may have been encouraged by Suez, there is no evidence of this, and many other considerations, such as the consequences of Belgium's withdrawal from the Congo, and the fear of white domination in Central Africa, appear far more important.

John Darwin (in *Britain and Decolonisation*) suggests that the influence of Suez was 'subtle and diffuse', and did make clear 'the strength of the new pressures on Britain deriving, especially, from the Commonwealth', which would make themselves felt over Rhodesia. It did not, however, mean Britain was unable or unwilling to make military interventions or commit forces abroad – the Anglo-Malayan Defence Agreement came in 1957, after Suez. The most influential aspect of the Suez crisis was 'the fear that by incautious commitment and inflexible conservatism, Britain might again find herself isolated and friendless'.

1. How far was 1956 a turning point for the Empire? (Use examples from the whole chapter.)

2. Why have historians argued about the importance of the Suez crisis?

9.7 'Winds of Change': Why did decolonisation speed up after 1959?

Imperial preference: A system of import and export tariffs giving preferential treatment to Empire goods, constructed during the 1930s. The United States opposed it in favour of free trade.

In 1954 the Conservative Party Conference rejected **imperial preference** in favour of free trade. It was no longer true that the Empire was Britain's route to economic prosperity and world influence. When Harold Macmillan became Prime Minister in 1957, he asked for a review of the costs compared to the benefits of Empire, which came to the conclusion that Britain could withdraw from the colonies without damaging the home economy. Indeed, where once it had been believed that large transfers of sterling into other imperial countries were beneficial to Britain, the Treasury had come to think that external investment was damaging the ability to invest at home. Rather than exporting manufactured goods to the colonies in exchange for raw materials, economists had begun to look to the trade opportunities offered by other industrialised countries, such as the United States and the members of the European Economic Community (EEC). Britain's first application to join the EEC in 1961 is a key turning point in Britain's shift from imperial to regional economic interests.

Macmillan did not, however, believe that decolonisation was a complete break with the past. In early 1958 he said that in those former colonies that were now independent but members of the Commonwealth, 'though we no longer had authority, we still had great influence'.

Where before maintaining colonies had been seen as a weapon against the Soviet Union in the Cold War, by the early 1960s both the Soviet Union and China were offering moral support to anti-colonialists at the United Nations, and Britain was keen to prevent that turning into military support. Managed withdrawal, giving way to democratic government, was expected to avoid newly-independent colonies coming under Communist influence. The consequences of badly-managed decolonisation were sharply illustrated in the Belgian Congo. In January 1960 the Belgian government decided that it should become independent on 30 June, and by 5 July it had begun to sink into anarchy. The civil war there deeply worried Macmillan, who wrote in his diary that, like the Balkans in 1914, it could trigger a world war as the various nationalist groups looked to the Soviet Union for support. It seemed possible that the trouble in the Congo might extend into the surrounding countries, Uganda, Kenya, Tanganyika and the Central Africa Federation, and Britain came to believe that to pull out sooner rather than too late was the best way of maintaining goodwill towards the west in the former colonies.

The French example was also instructive. The extremely expensive war that the French fought in Algeria led to constitutional change in France itself, where the French colonists had representation. After de Gaulle came to power in 1958 France offered independence to its colonies and achieved this by 1960. There was no parliamentary representation for the white colonists in Britain, so it was under no constitutional threat, but there were of course strong links, particularly with Conservative MPs. Iain Macleod, who was Colonial Secretary from 1959–61, had a brother in the white moderate New Kenya Group, which took part in the 1960 constitutional conference.

Racism at home and the start of pressure for immigration restrictions also contributed to the speed with which Macmillan began to seek decolonisation. If citizenship of the Empire or membership of the Commonwealth meant little, and certainly not freedom of movement within the Empire, this affected Britain's ability to assume a world role. The Commonwealth was also putting pressure on Britain to deal with the problem of white nationalism. Macmillan therefore concluded that Britain needed to take a new attitude towards its colonies, and to speed up change. He appointed Iain Macleod as Colonial Secretary in 1959, and the important decisions about moving quickly towards majority rule were taken in the next two years. Macleod said that any other course would have led to rebellion and civil war, and certainly the example of Algeria, and events in South Africa, where following violent demonstrations at Sharpeville and elsewhere over 70 Africans had been shot by the police, reinforced this view. Official criticism of British actions in Nyasaland (see section 9.5) in the Devlin Report, which said it had become 'no doubt only temporarily, a police state', did the government's image no good either at home or internationally. Meanwhile, the speed of French decolonisation made Britain's ideas on gradual democratisation and independence look ridiculous, while giving France a larger block of allies in the United Nations.

All these reasons combined to change Britain's colonial policy in Africa and most of Britain's black African colonies became independent between 1959 and 1964 (including Nigeria, Tanganyika, Jamaica, Kenya, Nyasaland and Zambia). They all joined the Commonwealth. The Commonwealth was clearly a success, although not simply as a vehicle for continued British influence in the world.

In the Far East, however, events moved more slowly, confirming that Britain had not been suddenly converted to believing it had no further international role. Britain was concerned to preserve its role in the Indian Ocean, as part of opposition to the Soviet Union and communism generally. The confrontation with Indonesia, which was thought to be allied with communist China and therefore a threat to Singapore and Malaysia, absorbed a huge amount of British defence effort and only ended in 1966. At the height of the crisis a fleet of 80 ships was in the Far East, including two aircraft carriers. In January 1962 it was still believed that the main threats to Britain were in Africa and Asia, and therefore that Aden and Singapore were the most important places for British troops to be deployed overseas. The Americans were happy for Britain to maintain its role in the Far East, as part of the attempt to contain communism there.

1. In what ways and why did decolonisation speed up after 1959?

2. How did other European countries manage decolonisation? Compare Britain's situation and response.

Source-based questions: Decolonisation in Southern Africa in the 1960s

SOURCE A

In the twentieth century and especially since the end of the war, the processes which gave birth to the nation states of Europe have been repeated all over the world. We have seen the awakening of national consciousness in peoples who have for centuries lived in dependence upon some other power. Fifteen years ago this movement spread to Asia. Many countries there of different races and civilisations pressed their claim to an independent national life. Today the same thing is happening in Africa and the most striking of all the impressions I have formed since I left London a month ago is the strength of this African national consciousness. In different places it takes different forms but it is happening everywhere. The wind of change is blowing through this continent and, whether we like it or not, this growth of national consciousness is a political fact. We must all accept it as a fact, and our national policies must take account of it.

From a speech by Harold Macmillan, the British Prime Minister, to a joint session of both houses of the parliament of the Union of South Africa in Cape Town, 3 February 1960.

SOURCE B

We shall bring before Parliament a general Enabling bill to deal with the situation. It will, first of all, declare that Rhodesia remains part of her Majesty's Dominions and that the Government and Parliament of the United Kingdom continue to have responsibility for it. It will go to give power to make Orders in Council, to enable us to carry through the policy I have stated.

I think that the solution of this problem is not one to be dealt with by military intervention, unless, of course, our troops are asked for to preserve law and order, and to avert a tragic action, subversion, murder and so on. But we do not contemplate any national action, and may I say any international action for the purpose of coercing even the illegal Government of Rhodesia into a Constitutional posture.

A speech by Harold Wilson, the British Prime Minister, to the House of Commons on the Unilateral Declaration of Independence by Rhodesia, 11 November 1965.

SOURCE C

It is convenient here to mention the Wilson government's wavering over its policy towards South Africa. In Opposition, as Leader of the Labour Party, Harold Wilson had spoken with some eloquence in condemning the apartheid regime of the Republic of South Africa. He had promised that the Labour Party in office would not sell arms to South Africa. In 1963 he said: -

'Under Hugh Gaitskell's leadership we condemned the supply of arms to South Africa as long as apartheid continues. That is the policy of the Labour Party today. It will be the policy of the Labour Party when we are called to form the Government of this country.'

Wilson reaffirmed this stand in June 1964. However he refused to go further, to a general boycott of trade with South Africa. The argument used was that such a policy would hit the black South Africans harder than the white minority. On paper it looked a fairly clear and straightforward policy.

From Britain Since 1945: A Political History, *by D. Childs, 1992.*

---

1. *Study Sources A and C.*

Using information contained within this chapter explain the meaning of the word and phrase highlighted in the sources.

a) Decolonisation (title)

b) Apartheid regime (Source C).

2. *Study Source B and information contained in this chapter.*

Given that this just refers to Rhodesia, how significant is this speech in the history of decolonisation in Southern Africa?

3. *Study Sources B and C.*

Of what value are these two sources to a historian writing about British policy towards southern Africa in the 1960s?

4 *Study Sources A, B and C and use information from this chapter to answer the question:*

'How successful was British policy towards southern Africa during the 1960s?'

9.8 How does the European Union affect the Commonwealth?

Britain first applied for membership of the European Economic Community (now the European Union) in 1961, though at that stage it believed that it would be possible to combine EEC membership with the system of Commonwealth and Empire trade preferences. When it was first planned, in 1955, Britain had not been interested in becoming involved in forming the EEC, though membership of NATO, of the Organisation for European Economic Co-operation and of the European Payments Union meant it had some connection with European integration. It was the most powerful western European nation, with close connections to the United States, but it believed that membership of a European community could not be combined with the Commonwealth. The European Free Trade Area, including Austria, Denmark, Norway, Portugal, Sweden, Switzerland and Britain – was set up in November 1959 as a way of reducing tariffs and promoting trade between these countries, without destroying Commonwealth links.

Economically, however, the Empire and Commonwealth were turning away from Britain, and Britain's exports to other industrialised nations in Europe were increasing. Overall, however, as the western economies recovered after the war, Britain's share of world exports declined (from 29% in 1948 to 13.7% in 1964). The United States and the EEC countries offered the best future markets for British goods. The sterling area, which had kept Commonwealth trade links strong, finally ended in 1972, following the crisis of the pound in 1967.

As we have seen, when Harold Macmillan became Prime Minister he no longer believed that the Empire was essential to Britain's economy, and instead looked to EEC membership to modernise and expand British industry and its markets. He also believed that this could revitalise British influence in European affairs, without which its importance to the United States would start to decline. This did not mean a complete turning away from the Commonwealth, or from world influence – Macmillan was determined to maintain Britain's independent nuclear deterrent – but Britain could no longer afford to remain outside a revitalised western Europe. Commonwealth interests had to be made compatible with membership of the EEC. In fact France vetoed British entry twice, but when de Gaulle was succeeded by President Georges Pompidou, and the Heath administration accepted the Treaty of Rome, Britain was able to join in 1973.

The turn towards Europe also grew out of decolonisation, as it became clear that the Commonwealth was not increasing Britain's international influence as had been expected. South Africa's exit from the Commonwealth was important to Macmillan's decision to look towards Europe. Interestingly, as the Conservative Party became pro-Europe in the late 1960s, many in the Labour Party became more attached to the Commonwealth. It was seen as a promoter of international peace and a third way between capitalism and communism, while it was feared that the EEC would restrict a Labour government's freedom of socialist action in domestic policies.

The other countries in the EEC had withdrawn from their colonies, some extremely abruptly, such as France leaving Africa at the end of the 1950s and Belgian withdrawal from the Congo in 1960. The Netherlands had lost the East Indies, but experienced economic growth in the 1950s. So maintaining colonies in New Guinea and the Caribbean came to seem unnecessary. For Portugal, during the 1950s and 1960s, European markets became more and more important to the economy, and when its dictatorship was overthrown in 1974, the new Portuguese government withdrew from Africa as it too turned towards the EEC.

Although Britain may not have seen membership of the EEC (now the

European Union) as conclusive withdrawal from the Commonwealth, it was a permanent and highly important reorientation of Britain's interests, economy and world role. During the 1970s, the value of all British exports rose about five times: the value of exports to EEC countries rose about eight times. The freedom of movement of people which had once been the characteristic of the Empire was now freedom to move within the European Union. At the end of the 20th century, although Britain was sometimes a reluctant partner in Europe (as over the single currency), it had enthusiastically promoted other areas of integration, such as the Single Market. The European Union will occasionally act to try to protect trade with former colonies, as it did in the 1990s over bananas from the Caribbean, against efforts (in this case by the United States) to open up the European market completely. In recent years it has developed agreements on trade with Commonwealth countries and the former colonies of other nations, as world trade generally has opened up. Nonetheless, the importance of the European Union to Britain, and the relative unimportance of the Commonwealth, would have astonished the politicians of the 1940s and 1950s.

1. Did joining the European Community mean the end of the Empire? Give reasons.

2. Was the Empire a principal reason for Britain not joining the EEC when it was first set up? (Use information from chapter 15 as well.)

9.9 Why did Britain fight the Falklands War?

By the end of the 1970s many of the remaining British imperial territories were on the way to achieving independence. The new Conservative government seemed set to follow the well-established path of continuous shedding of overseas responsibilities over which political consensus prevailed. One of Thatcher's first acts was to move resolutely on the Rhodesian issue: after intensive negotiations in London in September 1979 Zimbabwe was created. However, the government's, or rather the Prime Minister's attitude to withdrawal from the Falkland Islands in the Southern Atlantic proved to be different.

The Falklands had been a British colony since 1833 but Argentina had continuously put forward claims. Britain had long realised the need to solve the problem as the islands were a long way away and needed good relations with the regional powers. One option had been to transfer sovereignty to Argentina in return for a long-term lease to Britain to administer the Islands: this was opposed by both the islanders, who insisted on remaining British, and Parliament. After 1979 the pressure on Britain had increased. By March 1982 there were clear signs of Argentina preparing to overtake the Islands by force, yet no British reaction was registered. What is more, the Ministry of Defence had just proposed the removal of *HMS Endurance,* which patrolled the South Atlantic.

All this was probably interpreted by Buenos Aires as lack of British resolve to fight for the Falklands. However, as soon as the Argentine invasion took place on 1 April, a cross-party consensus that Britain should react emerged. The government sent a naval task force immediately. It reached the Southern Atlantic on 25 April. One of the most controversial British acts was the sinking of the Argentine cruiser *General Belgrano* at the beginning of May. The Islands were recovered after less than two months when the Argentines surrendered on 14 June. Britain had achieved victory with a relatively low level of casualties with 255 killed (around 750 on the enemy side) and six ships from the task force of twenty sunk.

The government was accused of negligence and incompetence in handling the problem before the invasion. Indeed, Lord Carrington resigned as Foreign Secretary, although it may be claimed that he was more of a scapegoat rather than the real culprit. In fact, the Foreign Office had warned that in the spring the Islands had been left defenceless. John Nott, the Defence Secretary, also resigned. However, Thatcher came out as the eventual winner. She had been firmly in favour of war and the victory was portrayed more or less as her personal achievement. She triumphantly proclaimed that Britain had ceased to be a nation in retreat and that Great Britain had become great again. This secured her position as a Prime Minister and almost overnight increased the popularity of the Conservatives. It also raised Thatcher's profile abroad and served as an example of her determination and leadership. In stark contrast to Suez, Britain had secured support from regional powers such as Chile, from the United States and even from the United Nations.

That the Falklands War was an exception was confirmed by the relatively smooth process of negotiations regarding other dependent territories, most notably Hong Kong. The 99-year lease from China upon which it was administered was due to expire in 1997. Initially, some sort of renewed lease had been suggested but China persistently demanded the colony back. In 1984, an agreement was reached that for 50 years after the transfer of sovereignty Hong Kong would retain some **autonomy** as a Special Administrative Region whereby its social and economic system would not be altered to copy that of mainland China. However, it was increasingly difficult to believe that China's leadership would honour any Western concepts of economic and political liberalism especially after the cruel suppression of the pro-democracy movement in June 1989. After that incident, all the British governments of both Thatcher and her successor John Major could do was to broaden and speed up political reform in Hong Kong in the hope that democratic practice would be well-established before the transfer. Little could be said in reply to the criticism that Britain was preparing its colony for the biggest mass return of free people to Communism.

Autonomy: Self-government.

1. Why did Argentina invade the Falkland Islands in 1982?

2. What impact did the Falklands War have on Britain?

9.10 Why has the Commonwealth survived?

One of the main reasons that the Commonwealth has survived is that it has never been defined too closely and has always been flexible. For example, South Africa was expelled in 1961 officially for being a republic (and really for the Sharpeville massacre), but India is a republic and also a member: the rules were changed for it in 1949. The Commonwealth offers an extraordinary combination of countries, which would not normally have an international voice, the chance to meet and have their say. The row over whether or not there should be sanctions against South Africa over its apartheid regime may have seemed to threaten to pull the Commonwealth apart, but in fact offered the former colonies a welcome chance to make Britain listen to their views.

There is no fixed Commonwealth constitution, though now there is the Harare declaration on good government and human rights of 1991, which all members are supposed to adhere to. Decolonisation may have failed to establish democratic self-government everywhere, but the Commonwealth has worked towards this. Nigeria's membership was recently suspended when there was a military coup, and it was welcomed back when elections had been held and a civilian regime re-established. South Africa, having ended apartheid, rejoined in 1994, and the 1999 Commonwealth Heads of Government meeting was held in Durban. Like the UN and the Organisation for Security and Co-operation in Europe, the Commonwealth Secretariat sends observers to elections and attempts to encourage and enforce democracy in the member countries. In the mid-1960s the Commonwealth also kept up pressure on the rebel white minority government in Rhodesia and helped train some 4,500 Zimbabweans in the professional skills they would need on the day of majority rule.

There are economic benefits to being a member of the Commonwealth, which has funds to help its poorer members – for example, the Commonwealth Fund for Technical Co-operation (CFTC), which was set up in 1971. This supports many industrial schemes, improving output and creating jobs. Britain contributes 30% of its budget, which was £25 million in 1996–97. The Commonwealth Development Corporation (CDC) is a public corporation sponsored by the UK to assist developing economies, with £1.2 billion directly invested in over 400 businesses in the 55 countries. Separately, over half of British bilateral aid goes to developing countries in the Commonwealth. The Commonwealth includes 13 of the world's fastest growing economies and 14 of the world's poorest. To help developing states, Commonwealth experts advise on national debt problems, economic restructuring and other macroeconomic questions. Targeting smaller businesses, the Commonwealth Secretariat carries out feasibility studies, transfers know-how and helps with education and training.

By 2000 the Commonwealth was an enormous association, made up of 30% of the world's population. It may be too large to be a trading bloc and too diverse to have a single voice in world affairs, but on some issues – such as Nigeria – it can make its views heard and back them up with sanctions. Connections between its various countries, through educational exchanges, development aid, grants and advisory commissions are encouraged, and it may have developed the links between, for example, different countries in Africa, not least through opposition to white rule in Rhodesia and South Africa. It continues to evolve, and has become a success, though not quite in the way Britain originally envisaged, to the extent that membership is prized and has even been extended to Mozambique, a former Portuguese colony. Part of its success in retaining and improving its functions has been the informal nature of many of the contacts and discussions that go on. The 1999 meeting of Heads of Government believed that the modern Commonwealth, which had then lasted 50 years, remained strong and

The Commonwealth Heads of Government in Durban, South Africa, 1999

1. How far does the present Commonwealth fulfil Britain's aims for it in 1947?

2. Does the present Commonwealth matter? Explain why or why not.

3. Has the Commonwealth influenced British government policies? Give examples to support your answer.

relevant and 'renewed their commitment to the Commonwealth's fundamental political values of democracy, human rights, the rule of law, independence of the judiciary and good governance. They reiterated that fundamental political values and sustainable development were interdependent and mutually reinforcing, and that economic and social progress worked to enhance the sustainability of democracy. They called for increased international co-operation to support democracies in achieving benefits for the poor' and considered that the Commonwealth offered one important way of doing this.

British foreign and defence policy, 1945–2000

Key Issues

● *What factors explain Britain's decline as a world power after the Second World War?*

● *Why has Britain's foreign and defence policy been so closely bound with the United States after 1945?*

● *How far did the collapse of Communism affect Britain's foreign and defence policy?*

10.1 Historical interpretation: What caused a 'cold war' to develop after 1945?

10.2 How did British foreign policy re-adjust to political and military realities after the Second World War in 1945–1951?

10.3 How successful was Britain's search for nuclear capability, 1951–1956?

10.4 Why did Britain's dependence on the United States increase between 1957 and 1964?

10.5 How similar were the foreign and defence policies of the Labour and Conservative governments between 1964 and 1979?

10.6 How important was Margaret Thatcher's policy in 1979–1990 for the end of the Cold War?

10.7 How did the end of the Cold War affect British foreign policy after 1990?

Framework of Events

1945–1947	Installation of pro-Soviet Communist regimes in eastern Europe
1946	Soviet pressure on Iran and Turkey
	August: McMahon Act
1947	February: conclusion of the peace treaties with the former German satellites
	March: Truman doctrine
	March: Dunkirk Treaty between Britain and France
	June: Announcement of Marshall Plan
	September: Formation of Cominform
1948	March: Conclusion of Brussels Treaty
	June: The Berlin blockade (ends May 1949)
1949	April: Conclusion of North Atlantic Treaty
	August: First successful Soviet atomic explosion.
	October: Mao's Communist victory in China
1950	June: Start of Korean War (armistice July 1953)
1952	May: EDC Treaty signed
	October: Britain's own atomic explosion carried out
1954	April – July: Geneva conference
	September: South East Asian Treaty Organisation established
1955	May: West Germany entered NATO
1956	April: Khrushchev's visit to Britain
	July – November: Suez crisis
1957	March: Macmillan and Eisenhower meet in Bermuda
	October: Sputnik launched
	October/November: Macmillan, Eisenhower, Washington meeting. Declaration of Common Purpose
1959	September: Khrushchev makes a tour of the USA
1960	May: Paris summit collapses after U-2 incident
1961	June: Kennedy meets Khrushchev in Vienna
	October: Berlin crisis

1962	October: Cuban missile crisis
1964	October: China tests its own nuclear bomb
1967	Johnson meets Soviet Premier Kosygin
1972	Nixon visits Beijing and Moscow; SALT I signed
1979	December: Soviet troops invades Afghanistan
1981	Martial law declared in Poland
1982	April –May: Falklands War
1983	Strategic Defence Initiative launched
1984	British-Chinese agreement on Hong Kong
1985	March: Mikhail Gorbachev becomes leader of Soviet Union
1986	October: Soviet-US summit in Reykjavik
1987	February: Thatcher's visit to Moscow
1990	October: Re-unification of Germany
1991	January: The Gulf War
	August: Dissolution of the Warsaw Pact and the Soviet Union
1995	May: Paris agreement between NATO and Russia
	November: Dayton accord to restore peace in former Yugoslavia
1998	December: Operation Desert Fox
	Anglo-French agreement on defence co-operation
1999	Hungary, Czech Republic and Poland join NATO

Overview

Marxist-Leninist: Lenin's interpretation of Marx's basic socio-economic theory which claims to take into account the development of European capitalism at the turn of the century and also to adapt it to Russia's specific conditions. It saw the current stage of the development of bourgeois society as the most advanced and therefore the last one before the imminent workers' revolution and accordingly called for the organisation of highly disciplined and militant Socialist parties to educate workers and lead their struggle.

Destabilisation: Undermining the existing order by creating political, social or economic tensions and unrest.

Superpower-proxies: Countries acting on behalf of the Superpowers, e.g. North Korea and North Vietnam for the USSR.

Bipolar: Divided between two different ideologies.

The Cold War was seen as a period of heightened tensions derived from confrontation after 1945 between the opposing ideologies of the supporters of free markets and democracy – the United States, Britain and the Western Allies – on the one hand and the **Marxist-Leninist** communist bloc led by the Soviet Union on the other. It is called the 'cold' war because it was not a 'hot' war fought with weapons. Instead it mainly involved propaganda, subversion and attempts at **destabilisation** of adversaries. A number of hot wars were fought between **superpower-proxies** on the periphery in the third world and never led to armed conflict between the superpowers themselves

Although not a superpower, and seen as being in relative decline since the Second World War, Britain was not a negligible force. It was to become the world's third nuclear power maintaining numerous overseas defence commitments. It is, even now, one of the world's largest economies, with an international currency, and global interests. However, growth in Britain's economy was insufficient to permit the funding of an independent defence policy to underpin responsibilities that derived from Commonwealth relationships and colonial possessions. Therefore Britain chose two strategies to fight the Cold War and to project her interests. One was to operate by means of alliance diplomacy: through the North Atlantic Treaty Organization (NATO), the Baghdad Pact, later the Central Treaty Organisation (CENTO), the Australia, New Zealand and Malayan Defence arrangement (ANZAM) and the South East Asia Treaty Organisation (SEATO). The other strategy was to become the close ally of the United States. The Anglo-American relationship has fluctuated in warmth, but throughout the second half of the 20th century defence and espionage links have been developed and maintained.

In the context of the **bipolar** world of the Cold War, British foreign policy and defence policy formulation were closely related. After the Second World War the British government decided that Britain must retain 'a seat at the top table' in international diplomatic relations. The key to this was nuclear capability. Denied the continuation of nuclear research and development with the United States by the McMahon Act of 1946, a British nuclear capability was developed unilaterally, with the first bomb being detonated in 1952. Anglo-American research and development co-operation resumed from 1957, even though the British government and Chiefs of Staff saw independent nuclear capability as the means to influence American defence (and especially nuclear) policy formulation. Moreover, nuclear capacity was also seen as the means to compensate for the manpower reductions which were an integral part of the cost-cutting 1957 Defence White Paper. Funding problems also led to the 1960 decision to cancel the British *Blue Streak* missile and rely on the United States to provide delivery rockets for British-made nuclear warheads.

The high points of Anglo-American diplomatic co-operation were the Bevin-Truman understanding, the Macmillan relationships with US presidents Eisenhower and Kennedy and the Thatcher-Reagan partnership. It is notable that at other times, Britain's global role has been more low-key. The lowest points of post-1945 Anglo-American relations, the Wilson-Johnson and the Heath-Nixon relationships co-incided with the period when Britain was deemed to be in the greatest decline.

Nevertheless, throughout this period Britain has managed to maintain a significant international profile and has remained one of the world's major military powers.

10.1 What caused a 'cold war' to develop after 1945?
A CASE STUDY IN HISTORICAL INTERPRETATION

The historiography of international relations in the post-war period has been largely preoccupied with the policies of the Three Big Allies towards each other. Historians have been predominantly concerned with a number of political developments, mostly in Europe, trying to assess their importance in the origins of the Cold War. Two schools of thought – traditionalist and revisionist – initially offered opposing views of the causes and nature of the controversy. The former developed after the Second World War and entirely blamed the Soviet Union, which was intent on world domination and motivated by its militant Marxist-Leninist ideology. Soviet behaviour in eastern Europe and the Middle East was given as evidence. This aggressive conduct was variously explained by traditional Russian strategy, the nature of the Communist regime and even Stalin's personality. The traditionalists believed that Britain and the United States only reluctantly conceded Soviet domination over eastern Europe because they recognised their own inability to prevent such a development. The West was credited with continuing to uphold the values of democracy and human rights as outlined in the Atlantic Charter and the Yalta Declaration, even after Western recognition had been granted to the Communist governments.

The revisionists who advanced their theories in the period after the Vietnam War argue that the Soviet Union had a legitimate right to dominate the countries lying to its west. They pointed out two precedents – at the end of the war Britain and the United States did not allow equal Soviet participation in the administration of Italy, and the two also insisted on exclusive control over Japan. The revisionists also argued that the tensions between the two Western Allies and the USSR were made worse by actions such as issuing the Truman Doctrine and the Marshall Plan. These were seen not only to have condemned Soviet behaviour in eastern Europe but also to have been correctly understood by the Soviet leadership as part of a campaign to force the Soviet Union out of eastern Europe.

A later trend in historiography, called 'post-revisionism', challenged both traditionalists and revisionists. It tried to introduce new sources as well as new ideas, mainly the theory of mutual misunderstanding and misconception of each other's objectives. Influential works in this category are those of Vojtech Mastny who discussed Soviet foreign policy during 1941–47 in terms of 'the intricate relationship among Moscow's military strategy, diplomacy and management of international Communism'.

Post-Communist Russian scholars attempting to analyse newly-available documents have interestingly had the same debate. Some come to the conclusion that senior Russian diplomats were guided mostly by geo-strategic considerations rather than desire for communisation of Europe. Others claim that careful examination of the interaction between the ideas of world Communism and Russian imperialism reveals that the two were not necessarily contradictory; in fact it is even possible to perceive them as complementing each other.

As the bulk of historical literature on the Cold War originated from the United States it dealt mainly with the Soviet-US controversy and treated Britain as the junior partner in the Atlantic relationship. Such a view was reiterated by the British historian Elisabeth Barker who in *The British between the Superpowers, 1945–50* (1983) described Britain's position 'between the superpowers' as being motivated by a growing concern for its own weakness and acknowledgement of its limited ability to influence world events and pursue independent policy. In contrast, Anne Deighton in *The Impossible Peace* (1993) traced the roots of British post-war diplomacy back to the patterns of wartime thinking and planning. She claimed that it was vital for the interpretation of British policy to understand that Britain regarded itself as a Great Power able to determine the course of events in Europe. Above all Britain justified its right to do so not by its military or economic strength, but because of its expertise in international affairs.

1. What different interpretations explaining the start of the Cold War have been made by historians?

2. Explain why historians have differed in their views.

10.2 How did British foreign policy re-adjust to political and military realities after the Second World War in 1945–1951?

Mandate: Right or authority given to carry out specific policies.

In July 1945, even before the hostilities in Asia had ended, a general election took place in Great Britain. Returning a Labour majority to the House of Commons, the British public demonstrated a significant swing to the left that became characteristic across Europe. After the deprivations of the war, the Labour Party received an unequivocal **mandate** for a speedy economic reconstruction and above all for a welfare-oriented domestic policy. This caused both domestic and foreign observers to wonder whether the new government might not also follow a socialist foreign policy in tune with its welfare and nationalisation programmes. Stalin was shocked by the British electoral result when Churchill had to step down in the middle of the Potsdam conference of Allied leaders (17 July – 2 August 1945).

Stalin, however, could confirm his distrust of any kind of socialists as both Britain's new Prime Minister Clement Attlee and Foreign Secretary Ernest Bevin were strong opponents of communism. Bevin especially had fought the communists who had tried to overtake the Labour-dominated trade unions and was suspicious of communist methods in international affairs. Both Labour leaders had been members of the wartime National Government and were aware of the tensions rising among the Allies towards the end of the Second World War. They were convinced that Britain should preserve its Empire and the Great Power status associated with it. This belief continued to be the underpinning principle of British foreign policy.

Britain faced a number of problems as a result of the Second World War, most notably economic ones. Even though the country's share in world trade had been continuously declining since the end of the 19th century, the 30% decline in the value of exports between 1938 and 1945 was unprecedented. Almost all foreign assets held in Britain by private individuals and companies had been sold off to finance the war. A debt of £365 million was owed to the Empire for materials supplied in the course of the war but it was small in comparison to the £31 billion Britain owed the United States for deliveries under the Lend-Lease agreement. Combined with the huge domestic spending necessary for the implementation of the welfare reforms all this precipitated a severe **balance of payments crisis** throughout the later 1940s.

This situation added to the pressures for rapid **demobilisation**. Indeed, between 1945 and 1948 the number of armed forces was cut fivefold to under 1 million. The level was well above that of the inter-war period but it had to be kept up as British troops were stationed in over 40 countries across the world. To maintain the size of the army in April 1947 the Labour government introduced 12-month national service; its length was extended to 18 months in 1948 and to two years in 1950.

Balance of payments crisis: When the money earned from exports is less than the money spent on imports a country has a balance of payments deficit. The size or continuation of the deficit can cause a crisis.

Demobilisation: Returning soldiers to civilian status.

> *How does this show how the world was divided by the Cold War?*

Why did Britain and the Soviet Union clash over Eastern Europe?

Britain's wartime dealings with either of its Allies had not been easy. Relations with the Soviet Union had never approached cordiality and there had been a lack of co-operation on anything but military matters.

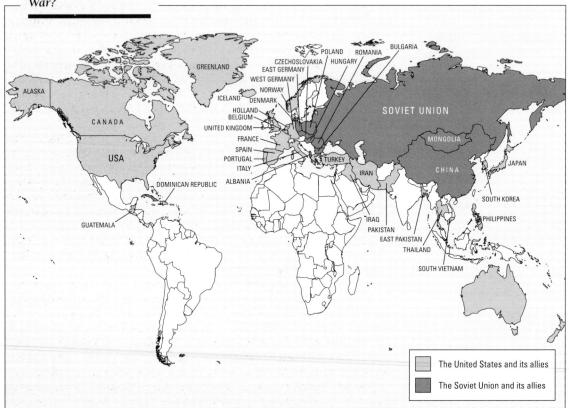

The world during the Cold War.

Big Three: Winston Churchill representing the British Empire, Josef Stalin representing the U.S.S.R. and F. D.Roosevelt representing the U.S.A.

When as early as 1942–43 various British government departments had begun planning for the post-war reconstruction of the world, they had become deeply aware of the need to take into account the global interests of the Soviet Union. Some progress had been made at the **Big Three** conferences at Teheran, Yalta and Potsdam as well as at high-level Anglo-Soviet meetings, notably the one between Churchill and Stalin in Moscow in October 1944. However, after the defeat of Germany, there remained a number of outstanding political questions with Soviet Russia. To those were added new spheres of friction, springing mainly from the Soviet Union's behaviour in its zones of occupation in Europe.

At Yalta (4–11 February 1945) the Allies had signed a joint declaration calling for the establishment of broadly representative governments and the conduct of free elections in all of Germany's ex-satellites. However, at the very moment he was assuring the West of his democratic intentions, Stalin was working towards the elimination of democracy in eastern Europe. One instrument for this was the Allied Control Commissions (ACC) set up to oversee the implementation of armistice terms with Bulgaria, Romania and Hungary: they were headed by high-rank Soviet commanders and used for the promotion of Soviet interests.

Throughout the war Stalin had emphasised the need for the Soviet Union to increase its security through the establishment of friendly governments in the countries along its western borders. The United States and Great Britain recognised this as a legitimate demand. They were prepared to accept an increased degree of Soviet influence over the external relations of its immediate European neighbours but did not consider this incompatible with the application of democratic principles in domestic politics. In contrast, in the view of the Soviet regime security could only result from the establishment of governments that shared its own ideological outlook. In consequence, the Soviet authorities backed the efforts of the local communist parties to secure a leading position in government. Across Eastern Europe, Communists had gained popularity due to their anti-German resistance but nowhere did they hold a parliamentary majority and so had to participate in coalition governments. In direct communication with the Central Committee of the Soviet Communist Party, east European communists used a range of violent methods to gain dominance over the other political parties and gradually eliminate them from effective government.

Coup d'état: An abrupt change of leadership or government, often violent or illegal.

With practically no troops in the region the British government was reduced to watching its worst fears for eastern Europe coming true. In 1945–47 the communists were continuously strengthening their hold over such institutions as the army, the police and the justice system. Already in February 1945, a pro-Soviet **coup d'état** was carried out Romania and in July 1945 a communist-dominated Soviet-backed government was installed in Poland with British and US recognition. The Polish question had been the subject of prolonged controversies between Stalin and Churchill, even though the latter was careful not to jeopardise Soviet-British relations during the war.

The fact that Britain could not stand up to the Soviet Union, even when its traditional allies were involved, demonstrated Britain's declining influence in East European affairs. This was even more clearly shown by Britain's inability to secure the formation of at least broadly representative governments in the former German ex-satellites. In September 1945, Soviet Foreign Minister Molotov went as far as to insist that the Soviet Union had the right to determine unilaterally the political complexion of the post-war governments in Eastern Europe. In Britain's understanding this was a clear breach of the terms of the Yalta Declaration. However, Britain soon realised that any argument on the subject would not change the situation while also straining further overall Anglo-Soviet relations. That is why after the conclusion of the Peace Treaties in 1947, the Labour government chose to recognise the communist regimes in eastern Europe, which effectively meant that Britain was resigned to Soviet dominance in the region.

What was the nature of the Soviet threat?

From the British perspective, the consolidation of Communist power transformed eastern Europe into a Soviet stronghold, which could be used as a springboard for the extension of Soviet influence in the adjoining areas. This raised suspicions as to how far Soviet actions were due to genuine security considerations or by traditional Great Power demands for domination over foreign territories. After 1945, both opinions had supporters in the Foreign Office. Increasingly however, British foreign policy experts subscribed to the view that the Soviet Union was intent on using its strategic gains for the spread of Communism world-wide.

Proof was easily found in Soviet behaviour in the Middle East and the Eastern Mediterranean, both areas of long-term British concern. At the beginning of 1946 Soviet forces were deliberately protracting their withdrawal from the Azerbeijani province of Eastern Persia. After Persia presented the issue for discussion in the first United Nations General Assembly, Soviet troops were finally evacuated in May 1946 but the incident loomed big in British perceptions, not least because of similar Soviet actions in Greece. In that country, historically associated with British influence in the Balkans, elections had been carried out under British supervision in March 1946. The electoral success of the right-wing Populist Party spurred insurgence from Communist-led forces. As in October 1944 Churchill had obtained an undertaking from Stalin not to meddle in Greece, the Soviet Union had no direct involvement in the Greek Civil War. Nevertheless, the Soviet Union continued to voice public criticism of Britain's handling of Greek affairs and even raised the question in the United Nations General Assembly in a move mirroring that regarding Persia. Archival evidence has shown that Stalin had little hope in the victory of the Greek Communists and was therefore reluctant to associate with them.

Simultaneously, just as during the war, the Soviet Union was exerting pressure on Turkey throughout 1945. Soviet demands focused on a revision of the existing friendship treaty between the two countries that would have given the Soviet Union increased influence over the regime of the Straits not only in war but also in peacetime. When Turkey refused, the Soviet Union denounced the treaty and even prepared to invade the country but was dissuaded by the British and US support for Turkey. The Soviet move could be interpreted as nothing but a clear challenge of Britain's strategic interests. This impression was confirmed by a number of subsequent Soviet actions affecting the Eastern Mediterranean such as a demand for a share of Italy's North African territories.

How did Britain react to the Soviet challenge?

Even before the end of the Second World War the British government had realised that it had very limited means with which to counteract growing Soviet domination in Eastern Europe. Therefore, despite frequent public protests to the violent methods of the Soviet-sponsored East European Communists, the Labour government chose not to clash directly with Russia on account of the political developments in the region.

On 6 February 1946 Stalin seemed consciously to exacerbate tensions by declaring at an election rally that capitalism and communism were incompatible and therefore war between the supporters of these doctrines was inevitable. Churchill responded in his speech delivered on 5 March 1946 in Fulton, Missouri, USA, warning that 'an iron curtain' divided the European continent. Churchill's opinion was only that the leader of the British Opposition. However, as nothing was done in London to refute Churchill's accusations against the Soviet Union, Stalin had to believe them to be also representative of British official views.

In the meantime, the British government continued to support the anti-Communist forces in Greece with measures such as the financial maintenance of the Greek Army. However, Chancellor Hugh Dalton demanded that this stop by March 1947 in view of the deteriorating economic situation at home. In the midst of an extraordinarily severe winter, the British government decided to reduce its imperial and foreign commitments, which were a drain on its limited resources. One consequence was that on 21 February 1947 the British government informed the US Department of State that British aid to Greece and Turkey would end in six weeks.

In 1945–46, the American government had itself increasingly recognised the danger to democracy and capitalist economies from the Soviet Union. However, the American demand for quick demobilisation and gradual disengagement from European affairs created uncertainty as to how far the United States would be willing to support Britain in its deepening conflict with Soviet Russia. This was all the more true for areas of traditional British strategic involvement. On the other hand, Soviet actions in eastern Europe combined with the continuing Soviet pressure in the Middle East had led a number of US diplomatic and military officers to express growing fear of the spread of communism. The announcement of Britain's ending of responsibilities alerted the American administration to the need to contain the Soviet Union within its present zone of influence. As a result, on 12 March 1947 President Truman asked the US Congress to approve $400 million in aid to Greece and Turkey and thus 'support free peoples who are resisting attempted **subjugation** by armed minorities or by outside pressures'.

Subjugation: To place under the control of someone.

What was Britain's role in the division of Germany?

Germany was another area where a major confrontation between the Soviet Union and the western Allies occurred in 1947–48. At the Potsdam Conference (17 July – 2 August 1945) the Allies had decided to share the burden of administering Germany after the war and so each of them as well as France had a separate zone of occupation. It was agreed that food deliveries would be made to the western zones from the predominantly agrarian Soviet zone in exchange for industrial goods. The Western Allies had also agreed to reduce the production levels of German industry.

Soviet policy was to extract as much reparations as possible from Germany as compensation for the huge Soviet wartime material losses. Such an approach, although also aiming at reducing Germany's long-term war potential, had the immediate effect of total disruption of what was left of the economy after the devastation of the war. Britain occupied the Ruhr which was the worst damaged part: its maintenance cost the British budget around £120 million in 1946. However reluctantly, Britain and the United States agreed that they should reintegrate their zones and encourage the regeneration of German industry so that Germany could at least partially pay for its needs. On 1 January 1947 the British and American zones were merged into what became known as bi-zonia and later in the year the French zone was added.

The Soviet Union did not approve and accused the West of not honouring its obligations for the treatment of defeated Germany. Moreover,

Checkpoint Charlie. A crossing point between the American and Soviet sectors in Berlin.

Soviet client: A country under the influence of the USSR, e.g. East Germany or Poland.

Soviet actions in the eastern part of Germany aimed at securing a dominating role for the communists: clearly Stalin intended to follow the pattern of political developments in Eastern Europe and transform the country into another **Soviet client**.

The stalemate over Germany's settlement was a major impetus for the declaration of American economic aid to Europe by American Secretary of State General George Marshall on 5 June 1947. This became known as the 'Marshall Plan'. For Ernest Bevin this was 'like a life-line to a sinking man' and within days he had managed to co-ordinate the positive West European response to the US offer. This however accelerated problems with the Soviet Union, which after some initial hesitation decided against participation in the European recovery programme and also imposed the withdrawal from it of the eastern European countries. Eventually, when the scheme began to function in the spring of 1948, Britain received the largest single share, $3.2 billion, of the $12 billion allocated to Europe by the US Congress.

Throughout 1947 and the first half of 1948, the Soviet Union and the western Allies had continued to work at cross purposes in Germany. Each side was supervising the economy and making separate preparations for the establishment of German government while claiming to be following previous wartime agreements. On 18 June 1948 as a step towards the reconstruction of Germany a new currency was introduced in the Western zone; within four days the Soviet authorities introduced their own new German currency. Next, the Russian troops blocked land access to Berlin (itself deeply into the Soviet zone). Realising that the abandonment of West Berlin would have deep political and psychological consequences, without much initial expectation Britain and the United States hastily organised an airlift of essential supplies. It lasted until 12 May 1949 when both sides lifted the blockade.

How did the European and Atlantic circles of British policy interact?

In the final stages of the Second World War, the British Chiefs of Staff had concluded that, although not in the position to begin an immediate

Cominform: The Communist Bureau of Information which existed between 1947 and 1956. In addition to the Soviet Communist Party it included the Communist Parties of the USSR's Eastern European satellites except Albania and those of Italy and France. Yugoslavia was expelled in 1948. This was an instrument for the co-ordination of the domestic and foreign activities of the members and for their subjugation to Stalin's interests.

war, Soviet Russia was the only potential military threat for Britain. Initially this belief had not been fully shared by the Foreign Office, which worried that if the view became known to Stalin this in itself would precipitate hostility. By April 1946 the Foreign Office was convinced that the Soviet Union sought domination of Europe and would put pressure on Western governments, not least through the strong West European Communist parties. This view was sealed by every next Soviet move – the formation of the **Cominform** in September 1947, the Communist coup in Czechoslovakia in February 1948 and the events in Germany later that year.

As it had become increasingly clearer that the post-war world order would not be based on co-operation among the wartime Allies, Britain explored alternative principles for its security. One possibility was to work closer with the West European states, which in the event of Soviet aggression would provide the first line of defence. Another option would be to co-ordinate strategy primarily with the United States, which was the only power capable of facing the Soviet Union on equal terms. In the immediate post-war period the British government had some doubts about the depth of the American commitment to Europe. After the Truman Doctrine and the Marshall Plan, it became more evident that the two circles of British foreign and defence policy – the European and the Atlantic one – were not mutually exclusive. On the contrary, they influenced each other.

In March 1947 Britain signed the Dunkirk Treaty with France: the two countries pledged mutual assistance against Germany and also economic co-operation. After this Bevin continued to seek closer links between the European countries and in March 1948 Britain, France and the Benelux countries signed the Brussels Treaty committing themselves for fifty years to collective defence against any attack. Britain was convinced that the western European countries' initiative to provide for resistance to a possible Soviet attack could only be successful if underwritten by the United States. Days before the conclusion of the Brussels Treaty the US administration began negotiations with a view to placing US involvement in Europe into a definite military and political framework. The United States' growing conviction that its own interest lay in the provision of material support for any regional security organisation in the West which sought to oppose Communism culminated in the conclusion of the North Atlantic Treaty in April 1949. The new alliance, which also included the United States and Canada provided the foundation for British defence policy for the larger part of the next half a century.

British-American post-war relations were already following a particular direction before the formation of NATO. In the economic sphere they had been coloured by the abrupt termination of Lend-Lease in September 1945. However, the US government decided to demand the repayment of only about one-fiftieth of the full amount (£650 million out of £31 billion).

More controversy was caused by the US McMahon Act of August 1946 which put an end to collaboration with Britain on atomic research and development. This was a severe blow to Britain: the atomic bomb had been developed during the war as an Anglo-American project and agreement for consultation and full collaboration had been secured from both Roosevelt and Truman. After the atomic bomb had been used against Japan in August 1945, the very idea of a Great Power was inextricably bound with the possession of nuclear weapons. Immediately after the war, despite its grave economic difficulties, Britain had not lost its self-perception as a world power that had the right to a say in almost every corner of the world. Moreover, unlike the United States, Britain lay within range of Soviet bombers and this was probably the crucial factor that precipitated Britain's decision in January 1947 to develop its own bomb. The necessity for this could only be confirmed when in August 1949 the Soviet Union performed its first successful atomic explosion.

What were the causes and consequences of Britain's involvement in the Korean War?

Containment: A policy aiming to prevent the expansion of Communism and therefore keep Soviet influence within its current boundaries.

The emphasis Britain laid on the US guarantee for the security of Europe presupposed some co-ordination on issues outside that continent. Indeed, the United States retained a generally negative attitude to Britain's ambitions to keep the Empire. In the later 1940s the doctrine of **containment** meant high level of overseas involvement by the United States and its allies. Therefore the United States agreed that Middle East was important. Britain's imperial decline should not allow its former possessions to be infiltrated by Communism: moreover, through its network of military bases from North Africa to Iraq Britain was capable of launching long-range bomb attacks on Eastern Europe and the Soviet Union itself.

In contrast to this understanding was the disagreement on the treatment of China after Mao's communist victory in October 1949. The United States, following a rigid policy of anti-communism refused early diplomatic recognition of the new regime. The British Foreign Office was prepared to shelve its ideological beliefs in the name of good trade with China and also for the benefit of the British colony of Hong Kong. British attitude was additionally shaped by the consideration that normal relations with China could to a degree counter Russian influence there and therefore hinder the enlargement of the Soviet bloc. In January 1950 Britain officially recognised China.

The British-US relationship was finally tested in the Korean conflict of 1950–51. In 1945 Korea had been divided along the 38th parallel where American and Soviet forces had met at the end of the war. In the course of 1949 both the Soviet and the US occupying armies withdrew although the border situation was steadily deteriorating. Additionally, while US attention was preoccupied with developments in Europe and elsewhere in the Far East, in the beginning of 1950 both President Truman and Secretary of State Dean Acheson made speeches implying that South Korea was not included in the American defence perimeter. On 25 June 1950 with Stalin's sanction North Korea invaded the South. South Korea appealed to the UN Security Council. As this body was at the time boycotted by the Soviet Union, American troops were sent in support of the South under UN supervision. Fighting went on for a year and the **38th parallel** was twice crossed first by American and then by Chinese troops, which had entered the war on the side of the North. Although the Soviet Union had not got involved in direct action, it was actively supporting North Korea in the UN Security Council. Although fighting ended in 1951 an armistice was only reached on 27 July 1953.

38th parallel: The political border between North and South Korea.

Western governments believed that the conflict had been started by the Soviet Union and demonstrated Soviet aggressiveness and intention to uproot democratic influences from Asia. Thus, the Korean war assumed the proportions of a clash between communism and liberalism on a global level. In July 1950, British ground and naval troops were sent to Korea. By January 1951 these were more than 10,000-strong, the largest non-American element in the UN force. If Britain strove for continued US involvement in Europe it too had to back the United States in those parts of the world that mattered to the latter. Finally, the British government reasoned that its own participation would have a restraining influence on the United States. Indeed, when in October 1950 the Chinese army overran South Korea, there was a widespread fear that the United States was about to order a nuclear attack. Attlee visited Washington and

1. How did the Cold War develop in the years 1945 to 1953?

2. Explain how the growth and development of the Cold War affected British foreign and defence policy.

received a reassurance from Truman that this would not be done without prior consultation with Britain.

The Korean war started the Labour government's plans for massive rearmament which were announced in early 1951. The Chiefs of Staff made the grim prediction of war with the Soviet Union in 1952 or even in 1951. For the first time since the end of the Second World War the total numbers of the armed forces rose. The cost of defence also increased as there was renewed emphasis on research and development, especially in air defence and anti-submarine combat. As a result, defence spending, which had constituted 8% of GDP in 1950, rose to 14% in 1951. This became one of a number of factors that brought a balance of payments crisis.

10.3 How successful was Britain's search for nuclear capability, 1951–1956?

Peaceful co-existence: The possibility for two opposing systems built on clashing ideologies to exist simultaneously without seeking domination one over the other. This is largely associated with the changes in Soviet foreign policy after the death of Stalin when the new leadership took a less confrontational line towards the West.

In October 1951, the Conservative Party returned to power and once more Churchill became British Prime Minister with Anthony Eden his Foreign Secretary. The problems inherited from Labour in the international field by far exceeded the worst fears of 1945. Not only did it seem that communism was on the rise world-wide but Britain's capacity to carry out an independent foreign policy was reduced. The British position was further complicated when in November 1952 General Eisenhower won the US presidential elections on a anti-Communist Republican agenda. Just two months after Eisenhower assumed office Stalin died on 3 March 1953. When Stalin's successor Malenkov spoke of the possibility for **peaceful co-existence** between different socio-political systems, Churchill saw an opening to present Britain as the mediator between the two super-powers.

What was Britain's contribution to the resolution of the conflicts in Asia?

The immediate concerns of the Conservative administration were those of its predecessor. While Britain was experiencing difficulties in maintaining its imperial positions in Asia, it seemed that this part of the world was at the forefront of the Cold War.

The Korean crisis was still unresolved: in October 1951 armistice talks had begun in earnest but were painful and prolonged as both sides used any excuse to resort to minor shows of force. When in early 1952 Churchill visited Washington, he discussed this situation with Truman and declared that 'prompt, resolute and effective' measures would be taken if either side in Korea broke the truce. It was on 27 July 1953 that finally hostilities ended.

Among the conflicts in Asia those in British Malaya and French Indo-China were similar in that the two imperial powers were struggling against communist insurgents. The United States had already supplied the French with over $1 billion worth of military aid, transport aircraft and military advisers. In early 1954 the militant new Secretary of State, John Foster Dulles, considered the use of nuclear strikes in Vietnam. Such a step however required strong support from the United States' allies and Britain for one was not prepared to extend it. After this opposition, Eisenhower himself decided against using 'those awful things against Asians for the second time in less than ten years'. After the French collapse in Vietnam, Eden became the leading international politician to campaign for a multilateral peace conference on Asia. It never took the

Belligerents: Participants in war.

form intended by him as the **belligerents** and their protectors could not agree on the agenda or even who should be represented. Nevertheless, in Geneva between April and July 1954 some steps were made towards the resolution of the conflicts in Asia. All troops should be withdrawn from Laos and Cambodia: the 17th parallel was confirmed as the line of cease-fire in Vietnam. No solution was found for the political future of Korea. Partly, the success of the conference lay in the fact that it had met at all. On the other hand, the conference was yet another reminder that the issues of the Cold War in South East Asia, the Far East and Europe had become inextricably merged. In the wake of the Geneva conference, in September 1954 the South East Asian Treaty Organisation (SEATO) was established as a defensive alliance, jointly guaranteed by the United States and Great Britain.

How did Britain influence the defence of Europe?

A number of proposals were set in motion towards the strengthened defence of the western part of the continent. The initiative never came from Britain but often the British attitude influenced the outcome. The Labour government had been sceptical towards the Council of Europe – set up in 1949 as a forum for the debate of human rights, individual freedoms and the rule of law – as it had no legislative powers. Britain had more sympathies for the Schuman Plan put forward by the French Foreign Minister in mid-1950 but had not joined the European Coal and Steel Community to which it led in April 1951.

Churchill's peacetime government became more entangled in the fortunes of the Pleven Plan produced in October 1950 by the French Defence Minister. It saw the foundation of an European Defence Community (EDC) with an European parliament and defence minister. The crucial element was that this organisation would have its West European Army which would also include a West German brigade. It had been for some time widely recognised by all European governments, including the French and the British, that because of its rapid economic recovery and central geographic position Western Germany would play an important role in the defence of Europe. Even so, when in May 1952 the EDC treaty was signed by six west European countries, Britain abstained. Britain's reservations towards the process of European economic and military integration sprang from the perception that an overwhelming commitment to Europe might have a limiting effect on British global responsibilities. Furthermore, as the United States was assuming more burdens world-wide and closely guarding its nuclear programmes, Britain was worried about the strength of the US commitment to Europe.

Indeed, it was under US pressure that Britain had to reconsider its decision regarding the EDC. Yet just when Eden had negotiated treaties of British association and agreed to place a British division in the EDC corps, in August 1954 the French National Assembly refused to ratify the EDC treaty and thus effectively put an end to the whole idea. This pleased the Soviet Union which had tried by resuming negotiations over Germany and Austria to slow down if not to prevent their reintegration on the Western sphere. At the same time the United States had made its desire for the rearmament of Germany clear and had reached an agreement with Britain to this effect. In September the British government initiated consultations regarding German rearmament. Eden proposed that after renouncing its right to nuclear weapons West Germany should be admitted to NATO and to a newly constituted Western European Union. Additionally, in November 1954 Britain signed an agreement committing to the defence of Europe through the same framework, immediately assigning 50,000 British troops for the purpose. In May 1955 West Germany entered NATO. The achievement of these efforts was the fact that finally US participation in the defence of Europe was firmly secured with the stationing of more than 300,000 US troops in Europe. In response West Germany entered NATO also in May 1955.

Was there an Alternative to Nuclear Strategy?

Since the final stages of the Second World War the plans for Britain's defence had recognised the importance of the alliance with the United States. However, it was evident that Britain itself was heavily dependent on the United States. Furthermore, while Britain could portray itself as holding the ring between Europe and the United States, it could be argued that for the United States Britain's main value was as a base for European defence.

The Berlin crisis of 1948 had seen the return of American bombers to Britain, some of them with nuclear capability. This made it essential that the air bases in Britain should be used as a result of joint decision and in January 1952 Churchill extracted a sort of a promise from Truman to that effect.

The major issue, however, was related to the production and use of the nuclear deterrent itself. President Eisenhower favoured closer links with Britain but was able to convince Congress to make only minor amendments to the McMahon Act. It seemed that Britain had little choice but to follow an independent nuclear strategy. This had bipartisan support and was obviously enhanced by the first successful test of Britain's own atomic bomb on the Monte Bello islands in the Pacific in October 1952. By then Britain had also acquired its own nuclear strike force as long-range V-bombers came into service.

However, soon afterwards Britain was once again left behind in the arms race by the superpowers: by 1953 both the Soviet Union and the United States had built **H-bombs**. In 1955 Britain announced its intention to produce the new weapon. Defence strategists argued that because it made the stakes so high, the new deterrent significantly reduced the risk of war on a major scale. Churchill and Eden also thought that with the invention of the H-bomb a turning point had been reached and the moment had arrived for practical schemes for disarmament. For this there was also pressure from public opinion increasingly concerned with the possibility of a nuclear accident and the consequences of nuclear tests.

A major factor bearing on the government's defence policy was the strains it placed on the budget. Britain had to commit to funding for NATO's infrastructure such as airfields, communications and headquarters. Throughout the period the cost of defence was steadily rising, and although atomic energy research was mentioned for the first time in a Defence White Paper in 1953 its costs were not included in the announced spending figures. In 1954–55 the cost of rearmament began approaching the levels at the end of the Second World War.

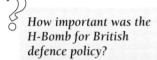

H-bombs: The hydrogen bomb was the second generation of nuclear weapon and was more powerful than the first, atomic bomb.

How important was the H-Bomb for British defence policy?

The explosion of Britain's first H-Bomb near Christmas Island in the Central Pacific, 15 May 1957

Détente: Decline of tensions between generally hostile countries or blocs of countries. Most often this refers to the period of the mid-1960s and 1970s when better diplomatic relations were established between the Soviet Union and the West

Churchill believed that at this stage in the development of the nuclear deterrent *détente* was possible. This seemed all the more likely since the new Soviet leadership had made conciliatory gestures to the West in the late spring of 1953 after Stalin's death in March. In April and May 1953, Churchill called for a conference between the leaders of the rival powers. No doubt he was inspired by the example of the wartime meetings of the Big Three, of whom he was now the only survivor. There was little domestic or international support for the initiative – both the Foreign Office and the US administration disliked it. The Soviet Union replied positively but the conditions it placed on the agenda made the conference impossible. Nevertheless, in January 1954 a four-power meeting took place in Berlin discussing the Austrian and German questions. The outcome was an agreement to convene a conference in Geneva that dealt with the South-East Asian settlement.

This momentum for negotiations was also captured when in early 1954 conferences on disarmament were restarted. Judging by the proposals put forward, each side was treating these occasions more as propaganda forums at which public opinion could be courted. Some relaxation in East-West relations did follow, especially after the conclusion of a Peace Treaty with Austria in 1955.

Churchill did not drop the idea of a summit in July 1954 and even suggested the possibility of a personal visit to Moscow. Finally, a high-level four-power conference was held in July 1955 in Geneva but by then Anthony Eden had become Prime Minister. The views represented highlighted the opposed positions of the major participants regarding the security of Europe. The Soviet Union repeated well-rehearsed propositions for an European security treaty and a disarmament programme: Eisenhower outlined a plan for aerial inspection of each other's territory. Trying to bridge the gap, Eden proposed the progressive limitation of forces in Central Europe and a system for the inspection of forces. Essentially the summit failed as did a Foreign Ministers conference also in Geneva in October the same year. This stalemate did not change when in April 1956 Khrushchev visited Britain. The fact that the Soviet Union was claiming a right to be represented in discussions on the Middle East did little to bring it closer to Britain.

How did Britain embark on the Suez debacle?

The Middle East had a central role in Britain's post-war strategy. Not only did it abound in oil and provide traditional routes for British trade but it also linked the two non-communist parts of the world. Military bases there could threaten the Soviet zone in Europe and the Soviet Union itself. In this respect the Suez Canal Zone was of the greatest value with its network of air and naval bases. Although Egypt had been independent since 1936, around 40,000 British troops were stationed there in 1951. After the war Britain had gradually accepted the necessity to withdraw but prolonged negotiations to that end had yielded little progress as Egypt was reluctant to continue to co-ordinate its defence with Britain.

In October 1954 an agreement for a phased, 20-month British withdrawal from Egypt was reached: the Suez base itself would be maintained in peace and in war Britain had the right to re-enter the country. Britain also hoped to draw Egypt to the Baghdad Pact of Middle Eastern countries signed in April 1955 but Nasser opposed it and discouraged other Arab countries from joining on the grounds that it was an instrument of continued imperial influence. It is also certain that the Baghdad Pact challenged the Soviet Union to pay a closer attention to Middle Eastern politics. Nasser established closer relations with the

Gamal Abdel Nasser (1918–1970)
In 1945 founded the Free Officers movement, which aimed to overthrow the Egyptian King Farouk. Organiser of the successful *coup d'etat* in 1952 and became President of the Interior. In 1954 became President of Egypt.

Warsaw Pact: (1955–91) The military alliance of the Communist countries in Europe and the Soviet Union.

Soviet Union and most significantly began purchasing weapons from the **Warsaw Pact**. In Western eyes this amounted to attempting to turn in the balance of power in the Middle East. Fears of Soviet intentions to make Egypt the starting point for overtaking the whole region resurfaced.

In the long run Egypt's association with the Soviet Union forced the United States and Britain to cancel the Aswan High Dam project, a favourite scheme of Nasser's that they had been funding. In turn Nasser nationalised the predominantly French-owned Suez Canal Company on 26 July 1956. While mediation by Australia and the United States as well as discussion of the question at the UN Security Council failed, urged by Britain and France Israel attacked Egypt on 25 October 1956. When Britain asked each of the two belligerents to withdraw 10 miles of the canal and Egypt did not comply, the British bombarded Port Said and sent parachute troops in. However, on 6 November Britain had to order a cease-fire and on 29 November it withdrew forces. The reasons for this quick change of heart came when the United States refused to support Britain both politically and economically. The United States voted in condemnation of British actions in the UN General Assembly and did even more damage by putting pressure on Britain's gold and dollar reserves. In addition, the negative attitude of the international community to Britain extended even to all members of the Commonwealth except Australia.

The Suez crisis had been largely of Britain and France's own making. Indeed, the policy of intervention in Egypt had been agreed as early as March 1956 and the nationalisation of the Canal Company was only the pretext used to bring the downfall of Nasser. This demonstrated a gross miscalculation of Britain's capacity to influence events in the Middle East. It also had exactly the opposite effect of asserting Nasser's position in Egypt and in the Arab world. The Suez debacle impaired Britain's standing in the United Nations and strained relations with the United States. It alienated the French who claimed that their trust in Britain had been betrayed and questioned the integrity of NATO.

In the long run the Suez adventure came to be seen as the outward expression of Britain's difficulties in accepting the contraction of its empire. Moreover, since there was some Soviet military presence in Egypt the episode could have led to Great-Powers confrontation. The fact that it did not is accepted as a sign that they deliberately restrained themselves. On the other hand, the globalisation of the Cold War was once again highlighted by the unfolding of the Hungarian uprising at the same time as the Suez crisis. The gradual **liberalisation** of the regime in Hungary had taken cue from the Soviet Union's own attempts at **de-stalinisation**. However, when Hungary proclaimed withdrawal from the Warsaw Pact, Soviet tanks rolled into the country to bring it back in line. After the British intervention in Egypt, the West was in no moral position to criticise Soviet actions. The condemnation of the United Nations had no effect whatsoever on the Soviet attitude.

Liberalisation: Relaxation of political control over economic activities and/or freedom of the individual.

De-Stalinisation: The attempts by Stalin's successors, especially Khrushchev, to put an end to the worst atrocities of Stalin's rule.

1. In what ways did British foreign and defence policy change between 1951 and 1956?

2. To what extent did Britain's international position decline in this period?

Source-based questions: The Suez Crisis 1956

SOURCE A

The Cabinet agreed that our essential interests in the area must, if necessary be safeguarded by military action and that the necessary preparedness to this end must be made. Failure to hold the Suez Canal would lead inevitably to the loss one by one of all our interests and assets in the Middle East.

From the minutes of the British Cabinet on the issue of the Suez Canal, 28 July 1956.

SOURCE B

TOP SECRET

I have given you only a few highlights in the chain of reasoning that compels us to conclude that the step you contemplate should not be undertaken until every peaceful means of protecting the rights and the livelihood of great portions of the world had been thoroughly explored and exhausted. Should these means fail, and I think it is erroneous to assume in advance that they must fail, then world opinion would understand how earnestly all of us had attempted to be just, fair and considerate, but that we simply could not accept a situation that would in the long run prove disastrous to the prosperity and living standards of every nation whose economy depends directly or indirectly on East-West shipping.

From a letter from the President of the United States, D. Eisenhower, to Anthony Eden, British Prime Minister, 31 July 1956.

SOURCE C

The Foreign Secretary said that in his judgement the economic considerations were now even more important than the political. We could probably sustain our position in the United Nations for three to four weeks; but, so far from gaining anything by deferring a withdrawal of the Anglo-French force we should thereby risk losing the good will of public opinion, while all countries wished the clearance of the Canal to proceed as rapidly as possible. On the other hand, if we withdrew the Anglo-French force as rapidly as was practicable, we should regain the sympathy of the United States government; we should be better placed to ask for their support in any economic measures which we might need to take.

From the Minutes of the British Cabinet, 29 November 1956, following the Anglo-French attack on the Suez Canal.

SOURCE D

Worldwide Britain, France and Israel were under intense verbal fire – from friends as well as their usual adversaries. Most of the Commonwealth condemned the invasion. Especially severe was India's President Nehru, who was normally counted on as a good friend of Britain.

In any case after such a colossal defeat for [Eden's] personal policy in his central area of interest, it is hard to see how the [Conservative] party could have allowed him to stay on. Britain really needed a new captain on the bridge to convince world public opinion of its renewed sanity. Added to this Eden was a very sick man. After his holiday in Jamaica, he resigned on 9 January 1957. At the end, in the Cabinet, he had broken down in tears and cried 'You are all deserting me, deserting me'. He was in total collapse weeping unashamedly. Then he went upstairs to compose himself. For such is the agony of power when it denies you. Eden's tragedy was that. He was obviously the victim of history, caught between the old Imperial might of the Empire and its total collapse as a world power.

From Britain Since 1945: A Political History, *by D. Childs, 1992.*

---

1. *Study Source A and use information contained in this chapter.*

Why did Britain decide on military action against the Egyptian government?

2. *Study Sources B and C.*

How far do these two sources agree on the likely impact of a military action by Britain and France to take control of the Suez Canal?

3. *Study Sources B and D.*

Which of these sources is more valuable to a historian writing about the Suez Crisis? Give reasons for your answer.

4. *Study Sources B, C and D and use information contained in this chapter.*

To what extent was the Suez Crisis a turning point in British foreign and defence policy in the years 1945 to 2000?

10.4   Why did Britain's dependence on the United States increase between 1957 and 1964?

The Suez affair ultimately removed Eden from office. The Conservative Party, however, retained office under the leadership of Harold Macmillan who became Prime Minister in January 1957. Despite the Conservatives' unpopularity in the wake of the Suez debacle, under Macmillan they consolidated their domestic support and won the October 1959 general election. The new administration certainly felt the effects of Britain's reduced standing in the Middle East, all the more so since Macmillan had previously been Eden's Foreign Secretary. Interestingly enough, Suez did not bring about a major foreign policy review.

That there was no abrupt withdrawal from east of Suez after 1956 did not mean that Suez was an exception or that Britain could hold its imperial positions. However, none of the small regional crises that followed approached the proportions of Suez. Britain's record in the Middle East was chequered. On the one hand, there was a wave towards the termination of general defence agreements or permission to use specific bases, for example in Iraq, Libya and Jordan. The Iraqi government went as far as to suggest publicly that Britain should be expelled from the Baghdad pact, while Syria and Saudi Arabia broke off diplomatic relations with London. On the other hand, British positions in the Persian Gulf were still upheld.

Britain was soon involved in the Middle East again – this time by invitation. During 1957 and 1958, Egypt was successively accused of meddling directly or through Syria in Jordan, Turkey and the Lebanon. The West believed that behind Egypt stood the Soviet Union so when King Feisal of Iraq was overthrown on 14 July 1958, American marines landed in the Lebanon and British troops were sent to Jordan shortly afterwards. Indeed, Khrushchev declared the Middle East to be on the brink of disaster and demanded a summit but his attention was soon diverted elsewhere and at the end of September 1958 the situation had stabilised enough to allow for the Western troops to be pulled out. In 1961 Britain intervened in Kuwait against Iraq but this was a brief expedition that could not overturn the general trend. The logic of the ongoing Cold War demanded that Britain should not voluntarily leave positions which, if transferred to the Communist bloc, would increase its strategic and economic strengths. However, this was accompanied by the belief that caught between domestic difficulties and unable to compete with the economic might of the two superpowers, Britain only stood to benefit from quickly cutting its losses and concentrating on the defence of Europe.

How did Britain's nuclear strategy influence relations with the United States and Europe?

The Suez setback had not occurred because of insufficient military power and after 1956 Britain continued to be an important member of a number of defensive alliances, notably the Baghdad Pact, SEATO, ANZAM (Australia, New Zealand, Malaya) and above all NATO. However, at the time and during the Suez crisis there had been an ongoing controversy around Britain's defence budget. Each of the three services claimed an increased share of the budget, asserting the centrality of its contribution in the event of an armed conflict. The strategic doctrine of the time still attributed an important role to conventional warfare despite increasing attention to nuclear deterrent. In the five years before 1957 defence had accounted for no less than 10% of GDP, engaged 7% of the working population and used around 12% of the output of metal industries.

Macmillan's administration was intent on introducing changes in defence: it justified them with the state of the economy and recent scientific advancements rather than with the trauma of Suez. The new thinking was appeared in the White Paper on Defence, *Defence: Outline of Future Policy*, issued by the new Defence Secretary Duncan Sandys in April 1957. The central proposition was that Britain's military power sprang above all from the possession of nuclear technology, therefore Britain's strategy should also place greater stress on nuclear weapons. The first successful British hydrogen bomb-test had occurred earlier in 1957. As the availability of the new deterrent was also believed to make another global war unacceptable, it was judged that Britain only needed a small central reserve to be able to fight. From the public point of view, the need for conscription and conventional forces was substantially reduced. National service would be gradually phased out by 1960 and the number of troops would be cut by 45% over the next five years, including the British contingent in Germany.

The White Paper pointed out that Britain's economic weakness meant that staying in the arms race would bring bankruptcy. For that reason it considered pooling resources with the continental powers so that a united European force became comparable to both the United States and the Soviet Union. Simultaneously, the centrality of the United States for European defence and above all for British defence was also maintained. President Eisenhower also wanted to mend relations with the British. Both countries expected **rapprochement** with France as well as drawing West Germany closer. However, at the time France was at war against rebels in Algeria and the reduction of British forces on the continent was causing suspicion towards Britain's European loyalties; Franco-US relations had also suffered in the course of the Suez fiasco. Consequently, the strengthening of the Atlantic alliance seemed like the natural first step towards adjusting Britain's international position.

Rapprochement: An increase in friendly international relations.

One lesson of Suez was a need for Britain to retain an independent nuclear deterrent capability which would also enable Britain to influence American defence and foreign policy formulation. In March 1957 Macmillan and Eisenhower met in Bermuda to repair the relationship damaged at Suez. Agreements were signed on intelligence and joint targeting. Sixty American Thor intermediate-range ballistic missiles were to be based in Britain. This had been necessitated by the fact that the V-bombers would become obsolete by 1970 and the supersonic bomber Avro-730, on which the RAF had concentrated, had been cancelled by Sandys. Not only did Macmillan secure the latest technology, he could also claim that Britain had an equal share in the control of the missiles: they would be operated by a dual key, one held by the British, the other by the Americans. Aware of Britain's progress in nuclear fission (nuclear bomb) technology, Eisenhower set up a meeting in Washington. On 3 November 1957 Macmillan and Eisenhower signed agreements providing for exchange of information on design and manufacture of nuclear weapons through the Agreement on Co-operation on the Uses of Atomic Energy for Mutual Defence Purposes, ratified by Congress on 3 July 1958. This had been to a great extent influenced by the successful Soviet launch of Sputnik, the first man-made satellite, on 4 October 1958. This demonstrated that Russia had built intercontinental missiles, a development that had a profound impact on the global balance of power. To drive the message home, in November the Soviet Union launched another larger satellite while a month later an American rocket failed to take off the ground.

The 1957 Washington agreements improved British security. Britain's chief problem was in financing the production of nuclear warhead delivery systems. In 1960 the Blue Streak missile, approved by the 1957

Defence White Paper, was cancelled. Escalating R&D costs did not square with the professed reductions in the defence budget; even more damaging to British confidence was the realisation that the Blue Streak, to be housed in vulnerable land silos, was no longer adequate to improved soviet anti-ballistic missile defences. In March 1960, meeting with Eisenhower again, Macmillan secured the purchase of Skybolt, an air-to-ground missile to prolong the life of V-bombers. Skybolt could be used with Britain's own nuclear warheads (Britain was – and still is – self-sufficient in nuclear warhead production). The President also promised that in a real emergency the British Navy could have Polaris, a submarine-launched missile. In return Macmillan offered a British base for Polaris at Holy Loch on the Clyde. In 1961 the new US Defence Secretary, Robert McNamara, cancelled the production of Skybolt due to the heavy cost and questionable reliability. Macmillan met with the new US President, John F. Kennedy, at Nassau in the Bahamas in December 1962 to warn him that unless the United States provided a substitute for Skybolt, Britain's participation in NATO would be affected. Macmillan secured Polaris but the whole episode showed that Britain's defence would rely heavily on US delivery vehicles (although Blue Streak technological development continued for satellite launcher purposes, thus enabling Britain to make a timely re-entry into large rocket development – at a later stage – for military purposes if necessary). Kennedy insisted on assigning Polaris to NATO but acknowledged Britain's right to use Polaris independently where 'supreme national interests' were concerned.

What was Britain's role in the détente process?

Parallel to the development of its own deterrent and to Anglo-US nuclear co-operation the British government was also determined to pursue a policy of limitation of nuclear arms referred to as *détente*. The 1958 Defence White Paper took the view that while fear of mutual destruction might preserve peace a preferable option was that the nuclear race should not continue. A system of international control and inspection of nuclear weapons was suggested. Even though a resolution had been approved by the United Nations against Soviet objections, the pace of nuclear tests increased in 1958.

In the late 1950s and early 1960s the superpowers were determined not to let a war spark between themselves. Until 1963, however, the test ban negotiations went on slowly and were interrupted by a series of international crises. That they continued at all was due to the dedication and perseverance of Harold Macmillan. This was especially evident with the onset of the Berlin crisis.

After 1957 Britain had continued to adhere to the idea of a summit. Increasingly the Soviet leadership had linked this with its own insistence on the resolution of the German question by handing over West Berlin to East Germany. As in late 1958 there were signs that the Soviet Union was contemplating the occupation of the city, US Secretary of State Dulles gave a guarantee to fight for it. In turn, Khrushchev forwarded a proposal for making Berlin a free city and when this was not accepted he threatened that the Soviet Union would sign a separate peace treaty with East Germany. As the United States prepared for a potentially nuclear war, the alarmed British Prime Minister visited Moscow for ten days in February–March 1959 and agreed to a **communiqué** calling for arms limitations in Europe. Although Macmillan reduced tensions, his visit sparked off hostility from both West Germany and the United States which accused Britain of appeasing the aggressive Soviet Union. The one positive outcome of the Moscow visit was that it led to a conference of the Foreign

Communiqué: An official diplomatic statement, especially one issued to the media.

Nikita Khrushchev, leader of the Soviet Union (centre) in Paris for the peace talks in 1960

Ministers in Geneva, lasting between May and August but totally unproductive. However, it prepared the ground for an exchange of high-level Soviet-US visits – in July Nixon went to Moscow and in September Khrushchev made a tour of the United States. Naturally, this showed some relaxation of East-West tensions and thus corresponded to Macmillan's overall agenda. On the other hand, relations between the superpowers improved. The trend was confirmed when the summit arranged to take place in Paris in May 1960 collapsed after the Soviet Union brought down a US U-2 reconnaissance plane.

In June 1961 Kennedy and Khrushchev met in Vienna but got off to a very bad start and ended up threatening each other with the consequences of a war over Berlin. In the next three months the situation quickly deteriorated. As every week thousands of East Germans were fleeing to the West, the Communist leadership resorted to fencing off West Berlin first with barbed wire and then with a concrete wall. The Soviet occupation troops increasingly obstructed the free movement of Allied personnel across Berlin and the situation worsened until on 27 October Soviet and American tanks faced each other at the line between their sectors. For the 16 hours of the stand-off the danger of a nuclear war was real and although both sides quickly realised that they had overreacted, developments were already under way that precipitated a second nuclear crisis within a year.

In July 1962 the installation of Soviet missiles in Cuba began. Khrushchev's plan was to place short- and medium-range missiles in the United States' backyard and thus create parity with the US long-range weapons. On 22 October President Kennedy informed Khrushchev of a decision to introduce a naval blockade on Cuba in order to prevent the complete equipment of the Soviet nuclear bases there. The US Chiefs of Staff ordered all US forces world-wide to go to a heightened state of nuclear alert, which was substituted to the highest state on 24 October. Khrushchev made it clear that he would resist US actions and was prepared to strike. On 28 October, after an exchange of messages between Kennedy and Khrushchev and after intensive diplomatic activity, the Soviet government announced that it had ordered the dismantling of the sites in Cuba.

Britain's role in the two crises was small. Britain had sought a diplomatic solution to the Berlin question but was forced to follow the United States. At the time of the Cuban crisis, through the British Ambassador Ormsby Gore, Macmillan advised Kennedy to limit the blockade and publish photographic intelligence to prove the Soviet threat to the world. This however cannot obscure the fact that Britain had played only a small part in the overall conduct of the crisis even though Kennedy telephoned Macmillan far into several nights to discuss the issues, regarding Macmillan as his connection to the United Nations and the British Commonwealth. The US decision to remove US missiles from Turkey was again unilaterally taken by the United States even though it directly affected NATO. Nevertheless, Britain remained America's most reliable ally, the third of only four nuclear powers, and with global interests and commitments exceeding those of all states, but the superpowers. Britain and the US co-operated in intelligence operations, foreign and defence policy planning and joint targeting of weapons. Moreover, Britain could claim that throughout 1959–63 it had been the power whose initiative had kept the Geneva negotiations on disarmament going. At the height of the Cuban crisis Macmillan had written to Khrushchev to ask him to reconsider the possibility for a nuclear test ban treaty. Macmillan pursued the treaty with both Kennedy and Khrushchev to the point where, in July 1963, such a treaty was finally concluded.

1. In what ways did Britain's dependence on the United States increase between 1957 and 1964?

2. How successful do you see British foreign policy between 1957 and 1964 as being? Explain your answer.

10.5 How similar were the foreign and defence policies of the Labour and Conservative governments between 1964 and 1979?

How did Britain's withdrawal from east of Suez influence the global balance of power?

When Harold Wilson took office in 1964, he insisted that unless Britain remained a world power it would be 'nothing'. Such a statement was rooted in the understanding that the status of Great Power presupposed the possession of overseas territories. Britain's military presence abroad was justified by obligations undertaken to assist the defence of allies under the Baghdad Pact, SEATO and bilateral agreements with a number of Arab states. The logical outcome of such thinking was that Britain should not give up its role east of Suez. Wilson's views were enhanced by those of the new US President Lyndon Johnson who was keen to maintain Britain's bases east of Suez as the first line of defence for the United States. Indeed, in the summer of 1965 a secret Anglo-American deal was concluded to that effect.

Johnson also hoped for British participation in Vietnam but that was something the British government would not afford. In addition, Britain was faced with a precarious situation in the Far East where in September 1963 68,000 troops had been sent in aid of the Malaysian Federation in its border dispute with Indonesia. The strategic implications of the conflict were immense in view of the rapidly growing threat of Communism in Indochina. Similarly, Britain had been confronted with the serious internal subversion of Bahrain and Kuwait and a prolonged armed insurrection in the South Arabian Federation. If this pattern continued Britain would need to preserve substantial military capabilities overseas. Quite apart from the question of whether Britain's presence was sustainable in the long run in the face of growing nationalism, it was also a constant burden on Britain's financial resources.

The 1966 Defence Review saw the overstretch of Britain's defence capabilities as unjustifiable. It called for a reduction in defence spending from 7 to 6% of GDP. It also emphasised British commitment to NATO as the core of Britain's defence strategy. The first sign was the announcement of a decision to withdraw from Aden within a year. The trend was confirmed by the 1967 Defence Review which stated that a withdrawal from Simonstown was a matter of months, while only core responsibilities would be maintained in the Gulf. However, the government's own schedule was speeded up by the devaluation of the pound caused by the six-day Arab-Israeli war in 1967. Aden was evacuated immediately and it was announced that British forces in Singapore and Malaysia would be halved in 1971 and removed in mid-1970s. As economic problems grew, in January 1968 the Cabinet agreed that spending overseas was the central problem and ruled that defence would suffer further cuts with British forces totally withdrawn from the east of Suez – Singapore, Malaysia and the Gulf – by the end of 1971.

One reason for withdrawal was that it was the end in a long-term process of cutting of imperial engagements caused by rising budgetary pressures. In addition, there was a strong political element reflecting the changes in the government's own attitude. In fact, Britain had turned down the offer of Saudi Arabia and other Arab states to fund continued British presence and the United States had suggested a number of economic measures to support the value of the pound in exchange for continued British commitment. All these proved politically unacceptable.

Heath, as Leader of the Opposition, publicly did not agree with this when in 1969 he pledged himself to maintaining a British presence in the Gulf states, as well as Malaysia and Singapore. This was partly an attempt to distinguish the Conservatives from Labour at least on one issue of foreign policy. Heath believed that he was deriving domestic political benefits by stressing the need to honour international obligations. He also had in mind the threat to stability in the Gulf from the numerous territorial disputes there. Finally, this was the moment when an enormous build-up of the Soviet navy seemed to point to a renewed Soviet militarianism.

The realities of office were however different and having assumed power in June 1970, Heath did not reverse the withdrawal. Indeed, some token commitments were undertaken as for example the sending of a military contingent to Singapore. A presence in Malaysia was also secured and such an arrangement met with the approval of the United States which saw it as an alternative to British involvement in Vietnam.

By 1971 Britain also withdrew from the Persian Gulf. The few remaining facilities were geared towards the protection of Kuwait against Iraq. Until mid-1970 Britain had played the role of a facilitator in exploring the possibility of the smaller states pulling together in some sort of regional defence arrangement. This lost the support of Bahrain and Dubai. In addition, Britain chose to support the United States which preferred Iran as the most reliable local power. This speeded up British withdrawal.

How did defence cuts affect Britain's nuclear deterrent?

Throughout 1964–79 two themes were central in British defence policy: the importance of the nuclear deterrent and the need to control defence expenditure. One of the electoral promises in Labour's 1964 campaign had been that of major reduction on defence spending. Once in government however, Wilson made little change. In turn, the two governments upheld the principles of cost-effectiveness and independent deterrence which had cross-party support in the post-war period.

In Opposition Wilson had called for re-negotiation of the Nassau agreement on terms more favourable to Britain. In December 1963 President Johnson had put forward a proposal for the creation of a multilateral West

European force which would include Britain's deterrent. The new Labour governments reacted with underlined coolness. In November 1964 the British tabled a counter-proposal for an Atlantic nuclear force which would combine the entire nuclear forces of the UK and France with those of US nuclear submarines. This was unacceptable to the United States. So just like Macmillan before him, in 1964 Wilson successfully withstood US pressure for making the Polaris missiles based in Britain a part of a NATO nuclear force. This happened at a moment when the danger of **nuclear proliferation** became especially obvious: in October 1964 China had tested its own nuclear bomb. As China was a Communist state, despite its political and ideological differences with the Soviet Union, its acquisition of nuclear weapons was seen as another aspect of the world-wide clash between Communism and democracy.

Nuclear proliferation: The increase in the number of countries possessing nuclear weapons.

Labour completed the reorganisation of the services merging the War Office, the Admiralty and the Air Ministry into one Ministry of Defence headed by Denis Healey. He attempted to introduce cost-effectiveness to the defence budget. In addition, he aimed to reduce defence spending to 6% of GDP. Coupled with the consequences of inflation that made the production and maintenance of military equipment even more expensive, all this led to the cancellation of three major aircraft programmes – a new fighter and transport aircraft, a new strike and reconnaissance aircraft and a new aircraft carrier. In each case a replacement with the American alternative followed and special importance was given to the purchase of the land-based F-111. As far as the nuclear deterrent was concerned, only one out of the five ordered Polaris submarines was cancelled. Against such a background it was not surprising that Healey announced that Britain would not undertake any major war operations except in co-operation with allies.

To the extent that a number of British commitments overseas were maintained in the latter half of the 1960s, Britain's ability to honour them was seriously limited by the substantial cuts in defence after 1964. Even so, further reductions were in order after the November 1967 devaluation of the pound by 14%. The trend was not altered by the Heath government under which defence spending fell to 5.5% of GDP. As the defence commitments in the Far East and South Africa were abandoned, manpower levels were reduced. The navy – most closely associated with imperial presence – lost about one-seventh of its surface fleet. By 1974–75, Britain's strategy was reoriented towards the protection of the Eastern Atlantic and the English Channel as well as contributing significantly to the European Central front mainly by maintaining the British army in Western Germany. This required new naval equipment and new RAF fighters – partially met by the introduction of mini-carriers for helicopters and vertical take-off jet fighters.

However, in the 1974 Defence Review Labour – striving to devote more resources to health, education and social services – once again supported a cut in the defence budget. The announced target was that defence should account for no more than 4.4% of GDP by 1985. Such control of expenditure clashed with the Labour government's acceptance of the centrality of the nuclear deterrent for British security. The issue presented itself with some urgency as Polaris had become obsolete with the technological innovation in the form of multiple nuclear warheads and especially with the improvement of the Soviet anti-ballistic missile systems. Labour had been pledged not to acquire a new generation of missiles but in secret the government approved an updating programme including the deployment of 96 cruise missiles in Britain, something revealed only in 1980. In effect, Labour's decision also renewed Anglo-American co-operation in testing information. Under Heath there had been some controversy regarding

Britain's position in the defence of West Germany: Britain needed West Germany to absorb more British military equipment while West Germany's needs were fully covered by US deliveries. A proposal for West German payments to the British Army on the Rhine were politically unacceptable as this would turn British soldiers into mercenaries. In addition, Britain was suspicious of the Soviet-American disarmament talks as they might lead to the scrapping of its own forces under a bilateral super-power deal. This was seen to compromise not only Britain's security. In 1979 Prime Minister James Callaghan agreed to increase Britain's contribution to NATO by 3% annually. Accordingly, new tanks and artillery were ordered while manpower cuts were frozen.

Did relations with the United States decline as a consequence of increased attention to Europe?

Coming to office in 1964 Harold Wilson rejected the 'special relationship' and talked instead of merely a 'close relationship' with the United States. Edward Heath in turn insisted on the existence of a 'natural' rather than special link between the two nations, which should not obscure British involvement with Europe. Throughout the period co-operation with the United States continued on such important matters as intelligence and nuclear collaboration.

The most serious issue dividing Britain and the United States was that of the war in Vietnam. After the Geneva agreements of 1954, the country had failed to reunify and the North was governed by communists with Chinese and Soviet help: the South was also under a dictatorship but an anti-communist one. Communist infiltration in the late 1950s and early 1960s led to growing guerrilla activities in the South that appealed for American aid. Just emerged from the Berlin and Cuba crises, the United States was intent on not allowing the establishment of a Communist stronghold in South-East Asia from which the adjoining countries in the region could also be subverted. After 1961, first President Kennedy then President Johnson sent an increasing number of US troops as 'military advisers'. After the Tonkin Gulf incident in August 1964, the US Congress authorised full-scale US involvement in what was a Vietnamese civil war. This continued until 1973 when the United States signed the Paris Peace accords to disengage from Vietnam with the last US advisers pulling out in 1975 practically defeated. Vietnam played a crucial role in the shaping of subsequent US policy. Throughout the war a source of constant American irritation was the fact that the United Kingdom together with the United States' other European allies failed to contribute a single soldier.

In 1965 when the Americans looked set for further deployment in Vietnam, Harold Wilson requested an audience with Johnson to counsel against further US military involvement. His efforts were deeply resented. The United States failed to understand the British government's position. Labour's anti-American constituency and its thin majority in Parliament accounted for its stubborn resistance to American pressure. 'When the Russians invade Sussex, don't expect us to come and help you', was US Secretary of State Dean Rusk's warning to the British.

A further serious blow to Anglo-American understanding was British behaviour in the Middle East. Following the British decision to withdraw from east of Suez the United States had no choice but to step in so that Britain's place would not be filled by a Communist power. The development was best shown when Britain handed over to the United States the extensive military facilities of **Diego Garcia**. Not only did this increase the American burden but the timing was also awkward. As if all this was not enough, Britain and the United States differed with regard to the ongoing

Diego Garcia: Part of the British Indian Ocean territory leased to the United States. It eventually became a US airbase.

Arab-Israeli conflict which in 1973 erupted in a new war. Egypt and Syria attacked Israel on 6 October, the Day of Atonement (Yom Kippur), the holiest day of prayer and fasting in the Jewish calendar. The Arab countries were seeking to reverse the results of the previous war in 1967 when Israel had captured the Sinai peninsula.

Their initial successes were quickly turned back when Israel recovered from the surprise, rallied its forces and received US support. The latter was severely hindered by the firm refusal of Britain – again together with the other European countries – to allow American forces to use British bases or even fly over its territory to supply Israel. Britain was sensitive to the possible effects on its economy of disturbances of the oil imports from the Arab states, an attitude that did not shelter it from the shocks of the quadrupled oil prices in the wake of the war. The British government also considered that the United States had not shown sufficient interest over the previous three years so that a settlement between the opposing sides was reached. But the all-time low point of relations was caused by the order given on 24 October by President Nixon, or rather his National Security Adviser Henry Kissinger to place US forces at a state of high nuclear alert. Indeed, this was done in response to signals that the Soviet Union was preparing to send forces to the Middle East in help of Egypt. However, none of the United States' European allies were consulted even though they would have been the prime target for Soviet retaliation. British Foreign Secretary Alec Douglas-Home was placed in the uncomfortable position of having to defend in the House of Commons the right of the US government to alert its forces without himself being consulted. Finally, the United States and Britain had completely different approaches to the Arab-Israeli settlement after the war: Heath insisted on multilateral talks overseen by the UN, while Kissinger preferred bilateral Arab-Israeli deals overseen by the United States so that the Soviet Union was denied the right of veto.

Britain also played an important secondary role in the continuing process of East-West *détente* in the second half of the 1960s and the 1970s. This was driven by the dual development of improving relations between the United States and China, and West Germany's own **Östpolitik** aiming at rapprochement with Eastern Germany, Poland and Eastern Europe and ultimately the Soviet Union. A complicating circumstance ensued from the fact that in 1966 Charles de Gaulle took France out of the military structures of NATO and tried to pursue a relatively independent policy to the Soviet bloc. Although the successive British governments were strongly in favour of measures that would reduce tensions between the two opposing blocs, Britain could rarely take the initiative in this respect. Indeed, Britain was a willing participant in multilateral negotiations but could not fail to realise that the decisions were taken by the United States and USSR. In 1967 Johnson met with Soviet Premier Kosygin and even though the two states were in conflict over Vietnam, the possibilities for starting an arms control process were sounded. This was underpinned by the increased sense in the US Congress that US troops should pull out of Europe. In order to maintain the US military commitment in Europe Johnson had to seek to reduce it by negotiation with the Soviet Union. This made Britain uneasy about America's continued engagement in Europe.

However, as a nuclear power Britain was genuinely committed to a nuclear non-proliferation treaty. The first Wilson government engaged in considerable efforts both to smoothen differences within NATO and to convince West Germany that such a treaty would not either discriminate against it or endanger its security. It was probably this attitude that made the United States at least consult Britain in the course of the preparation for an anti-ballistic missile treaty under the acronym SALT I (Strategic Arms

Östpolitik: Foreign policy associated with West German Chancellor, Willy Brandt. It involved an attempt to improve diplomatic relations between West and East Germany.

Limitation Treaty). It was signed in May 1972 after Nixon visited first Beijing and Moscow. It limited the deployment of anti-ballistic missiles as well as freezing the deployment of intercontinental ballistic missiles. Britain also played a positive role in the preparation and conclusion of the Helsinki treaties of 1975 which recognised European borders, introduced control of armaments and started a steady growth in trade and cultural links between Communist and democratic countries.

To a great extent the shifts in the Anglo-American relationship were determined by Britain's firm intention to seek increased co-operation with western Europe and aim at entry in the European Community. The process had been influenced by the deteriorating state of the British economy. This was in turn related to a change in defence strategy most evident in the 1969 Defence White Paper which argued that Britain's defence should concentrate on Europe. Moreover, the doctrine of mass retaliation was now being overtaken by that of a flexible response, which in Britain's case required maintenance of small conventional forces, especially in Europe.

Interestingly enough, for its own reasons the United States also approved of Britain's efforts to join the European Community. Both the Johnson and Nixon administrations saw Britain as a useful mediator between Europe and United States. But it was exactly the calculation that made the Europeans, especially France, suspicious of a Britain whose close Atlantic link might disturb the relative harmony of the EEC. In November 1967 de Gaulle made his second veto on British membership in the EEC. That was why Heath, in his successful bid for European membership was doubly careful about the United States. To prove his European credentials Heath responded with caution to Nixon's call in April 1973 for a new Atlantic Charter – he accepted to negotiate only from a common position with the other European powers and was prepared to contemplate French leadership in the matter. He even explored the idea of Anglo-French nuclear co-operation but French abstinence from NATO's integrated command was a hurdle. Therefore, after Britain joined the European Community in January 1973, its foreign policy became more European.

1. In what ways did British foreign and defence policy change between 1964 and 2000?

2. To what extent was British foreign and defence policy still dominated by relations with the United States?

10.6 How important was Margaret Thatcher's policy in 1979–90 for the end of the Cold War?

1979 marked a turning point in British foreign policy with the election of a majority Conservative government headed by Margaret Thatcher. The new Prime Minister with her strong ideological convictions and forceful style had an impact on foreign policy.

Was anti-Communism the focal point of the renewed special relationship?

One of the most distinctive aspects of Thatcher's foreign policy was her dealing with the Soviet Union. In the late 1970s Britain's role in *détente* had diminished while the process itself had also waned. Disarmament had been increasingly handled through bilateral Soviet-American channels but whatever progress had been made lately was abruptly halted by the Soviet Union's invasion of Afghanistan. Military and financial aid had been supplied for months to the indigenous Communists who were themselves divided and faced with serious internal Muslim opposition. Finally, in December 1979, Soviet troops stepped in at the request of local Communists and among Soviet fears that China was involved in the intensifying civil war. In the following years the situation in the Middle East deteriorated further with the outbreak of the Iran-Iraq war in 1980 and the

Israeli invasion of the Lebanon in 1982. To the West all these were cases in which the Soviet Union's expansionist aspirations could be detected.

In response to the Afghanistan crisis, President Carter withdrew the SALT II agreement on arms control, which had been worked out the previous year, from the process of Senate ratification. In addition, the United States imposed trade sanctions on the Soviet Union and even tried to co-operate with China in supporting the anti-Soviet rebels in Afghanistan. Amongst the European Allies, Britain was the only one which stood firmly by the United States. In 1981, the new US President Ronald Reagan went much further in that he made anti-Communism the pillar of his policies. Calling for a new-era crusade against the 'Evil Empire' Reagan set about defeating world Communism by economic and military competition. Reagan's outlook, and pro-active leadership made an immediate connection with Thatcher. She shared all the ideological convictions of liberal capitalism. Moreover, she was convinced that NATO was the linchpin of European and British defence and to strengthen it a revival of the special relationship was necessary. The outcome was – in accordance with NATO's decision to modernise its intermediate nuclear forces in Europe – the purchasing of the American Trident C4 missiles, the next generation after Polaris. When the **Pentagon** decided to develop the D5 version of Trident, Britain had little choice but to accept. This certainly reminded of British nuclear dependence on the United States, a point highlighted by the simultaneous deployment of cruise missiles in Germany in response to the Soviet SS-20s.

The new phase in nuclear rearmament started the recovery of the Campaign for Nuclear Disarmament in Britain, a civil movement that had been dormant since 1960s. It was best known for the women's tent camp at the US air base at Greenham Common. As elsewhere in Europe, where a wave of anti-nuclear movements sprang up, the British protesters adopted a distinctly anti-American outlook. They were also encouraged by the Soviet Union in the hope that the struggle to cope with domestic popular hostility would pose severe strains on the NATO alliance. In Britain, under the influence of the trade unions the Labour Party had already swung far left. In the run up to the 1983 elections Labour made the nuclear issue the central point in its campaign demanding not only the cancellation of Cruise and Trident but also a completely non-nuclear Britain. However, public opinion in Britain was generally less hostile to the deployment than in Europe.

Thatcher also supported Reagan's Strategic Defence Initiative (SDI) launched in 1983. This was a vastly ambitious research project to develop an anti-missile system on the ground and in space to act as a nuclear shield over the United States. The idea was that by intercepting Soviet missiles in space the United States would be able to survive a nuclear attack. The huge resources committed to the programme, known as 'Star Wars', had the immediate effect of increasing the arms race with the Soviet bloc, as the Soviet leadership declared that it would never allow military superiority over the USSR. Thatcher was extremely unhappy about the manner in which SDI had been announced – without consultation with the United States' Allies. After all, the shield over the United States would not extend to the other side of the Atlantic and Britain and Europe would be even more than usually exposed to a Soviet attack. The reservations were publicly expressed by British Foreign Secretary Geoffrey Howe. On her part Thatcher had a stormy meeting with the President at which she secured a joint statement that any stage of implementation of SDI beyond research would have to be negotiated in advance with the Allies. While voicing the worries of the other west European powers, Thatcher again seemed to be demonstrating unique influence over Reagan and such

Pentagon: The headquarters of the US Department of Defense near Washington DC. It takes its name from the outline of the building as seen from above.

closeness with the United States served to complicate Britain's own relations with Europe. Soon afterwards, Reagan's anti-communism brought huge domestic political embarrassment for Thatcher when in October 1983, without consulting Britain, the United States attacked Grenada, a member of the Commonwealth, to overthrow a Marxist regime. Nevertheless, after a furious telephone conversation between Thatcher and Reagan the 'special relationship' was again patched up. It was forcefully illustrated when in April 1986 US F-111s used British bases to bomb Libya.

After the 1983 re-election the Conservative government increased attention to the Soviet zone. Under the influence of the Foreign Office a policy of differentiation between the members of the Soviet bloc was adopted, which aimed at cultivating the more open regimes of Central Eastern Europe. In fact the trend had appeared as early as 1981 when martial law was declared in Poland in a desperate bid from the local Communist leadership to suffocate political turmoil caused by striking workers and prevent a Soviet invasion. Publicly, Thatcher supported Reagan in imposing sanctions on the Polish government but the practical British measures were relatively mild. On the other hand, the British government openly disagreed with the American policy of forbidding companies to participate in the building of a Soviet gas pipeline from Siberia to Western Europe as this encroached on private and public West European economic interests.

Thatcher's dislike of Communism was combined with a practical approach. The Prime Minister approved of the relative liberalisation measures undertaken by the Communist leadership of Hungary and was openly supportive of the anti-Communist trade unions in Poland. Howe was the first British Foreign Secretary to tour all the capitals of the Warsaw Pact countries in 1985–86. Crucially, Thatcher succeeded in establishing a working relationship with Mikhail Gorbachev, who assumed power in the Soviet Union in March 1985. Over the next years there was a lot of Soviet-British activity in the diplomatic and economic field culminating in the Prime Minister's visit to Moscow in February 1987. All this placed Britain in the position of mediator between the

Mr and Mrs Gorbachev meet Mrs and Mr Thatcher, and members of the British Cabinet at Chequers, 1984

United States and the Soviet Union serving Thatcher's need for a higher profile at home and enabling her to be presented as the supporter of peace, successfully negotiating from a position of strength.

However, for the Soviet Union facing multiplying economic and social problems under the burden of all-out competition with the West, the need for resumed *détente* was a matter of survival. It needed to be taken up with the United States, the protagonist of the Western bloc. Reagan and Gorbachev met in Geneva in November 1985 when they agreed in principle to work towards the Strategic Arms Reduction Treaty to cut their nuclear arsenals in half. After a stream of private communications, the Soviet-US summit in Reykjavik in October 1986 confirmed the agreement in principle to scrap all intermediate-range missiles from Europe, both NATO's Cruise and Pershing and the Soviet SS-20s. Further progress was made when attention was turned to the elimination of tactical and battlefield nuclear weapons and eventually conventional forces. The final agreement was reached in Washington in December 1987.

The Reykjavik agreement disturbed the Europeans in that the proposed elimination of all nuclear weapons would expose Europe to the larger conventional Soviet forces. As it would affect missiles deployed in Britain and Eastern Europe, while leaving SDI for the moment it would also make clear the limitations of the British independent deterrent. Meeting Reagan, Thatcher did indeed speak on behalf of all of Europe when she demanded that the reductions would be limited to intermediate-range missile and no more than 50% cut in strategic weapons. Despite this, it was obvious that – as on previous occasions – the momentum of superpower *détente* pushed Thatcher out of the way.

The speed of events on the international scene in the last years of Margaret Thatcher's premiership was breathtaking. One by one the countries of Eastern Europe each underwent their own revolution leading to sweeping domestic changes and an effective end of Soviet domination over them. The process of slow but steady erosion of Communism that had been most notable in the events in Hungary in 1956, Czechoslovakia in 1968 and Poland in the early 1980s reached its culmination in the overthrow of the eastern European regimes within six months in 1989. The commitment of the Soviet Union to disarmament had made certain that it would not intervene to support any of the old Communist guard in Eastern Europe. And one of the crucial elements in the Soviet position was the realisation that the USSR would never be able to outspend the United States in the field of rearmament and technological innovation. By 1991 the Warsaw Pact was dead and the Soviet Union itself ceased to exist with the proclamation of independence by a number of its former republics. Aside from the moral victory that Britain could claim to share with the rest of the NATO countries, this shattered the whole framework of British foreign policy. The disappearance of Communism as the eternal enemy suddenly meant also the dismantling of the stability and security of the bipolar world.

Thatcher's apprehension of what might succeed was demonstrated in her attitude to the transformation of Germany. The changes across eastern Europe had led to the pulling down of the wall around West Berlin in November 1989 after which an unstoppable movement towards the reunification of Germany began. In March 1990 the Christian-Democrats won the elections in East Germany, in July 1990 a currency union between the two German states took place, and that led to a political union in October 1990. Before the announcement of the latter, Gorbachev had struck a deal with Chancellor Helmut Kohl under which, in return for financial help to the struggling Soviet Union, there would be German re-unification and NATO membership for the new country. This was not to Thatcher's liking. Firstly, she feared how the reappearance of a big and strong Germany would affect the European balance of power. Secondly, understanding that it would be difficult to withhold the momentum for reunification, she preferred to see it delayed while political and economic reforms in Eastern Europe were completed.

Did Britain's defence strategy change under the Conservatives?

The Prime Minister's anti-communism meant that in office, just like in Opposition the Conservatives were fully committed to maintaining and enhancing Britain's defence capabilities. The government strove to highlight the importance attached to this issue by making one of its early measures the 33% pay-rise for the armed services in an attempt to arrest decline in morale and shortfall of skilled personnel. As under previous governments, the Conservative's defence strategy focused on Britain's nuclear potential which in turn required a close link with the United States and NATO.

However, the government was soon under simultaneous conflicting pressures. On the one hand, Britain was bound by and undertaking together with the other NATO countries to an annual 3% increase in real terms of contributions to the Alliance's budget. NATO had also decided to modernise its INF in Europe with Pershing II and Cruise missiles, 160 of which were to be stationed in Britain. As a result Britain was spending on defence a proportion of GDP greater than any European power. On the other hand, the state of the domestic economy called for reduction of defence expenditure. In 1981 in the Defence review 'The Way Forward', the Ministry of Defence seemed to have found the solution in savings from a proposed 25% cut of the surface fleet of the Navy, including vessels cruising the Southern Atlantic. This was however overturned by the Falklands War.

Nuclear deterrence was largely unchallenged in government circles. 'The Way Forward' had made a point of maintaining Britain's nuclear submarines and already in December 1980 it had been decided to purchase the Trident submarine-launched missiles. The June 1983 re-election of the Conservatives ensured that the plans would go ahead while the ascendance of Chancellor Kohl in Germany confirmed the deployment of Pershing there. Despite the controversial fashion in which Reagan had announce the SDI, Thatcher acquired a US guarantee that Britain's own nuclear deterrent would continue to be supported through Trident. Their availability to Britain was also confirmed in the wake of the Reykjavik summit. Even when NATO agreed in principle to remove its short-range nuclear forces, it was Thatcher who made sure that only partial changes would take place. As a result, Britain's defence expenditure 1981–86 amounted to an average 5.2% of GDP and registered an overall increase by 21% in real terms. As late as 1990, Trident was one of the few pieces in the British arsenal not suffering continuous reductions.

1. *In what ways did British foreign and defence policy change under Margaret Thatcher?*

2. *To what extent did Margaret Thatcher change Britain's international position?*

10.7 How did the end of the Cold War affect British foreign policy after 1990?

The changes in British foreign policy after 1990 certainly reflected Thatcher's stepping down from government. To a greater extent however, they were a consequence of the radically-altered international situation. With the end of the Cold War, a new British foreign policy had to be found. Britain's position in the world and security at home had to be safeguarded in a way that would not strain further the country's continuously tight resources.

British governments in 1990–2000, both Conservative and Labour, had to lead a cautious foreign policy mainly because this was an extremely volatile period for world affairs in general. The old bipolar system was unexpectedly quickly dismantled unleashing previously suppressed tensions like nationalism. In the meantime, Britain also had to respond to the increased foreign policy integration of Europe and clarify its own view on the link between institutions such as NATO and the European Union in the field of international relations.

How did Britain react to the crises in the Persian Gulf?

One of the major tests for Britain's role in the post-Cold-War world and for the new government of John Major was in January 1991 when it participated in the Gulf War. The previous August Iraq, under its president Saddam Hussein, had invaded Kuwait. Iraq wanted to annex Kuwait because the country's position greatly hindered Iraqi access to the Persian Gulf. Kuwait, which had been under British protection also had the support of the United States and some other Arab states opposed to the Iraqi regime. The United Nations Security Council had called on Saddam to withdraw and had also imposed economic sanctions on him. The Soviet Union did not veto these measures even though it had interests in Iraq and preferred a diplomatic solution. In the following months US military presence in the Gulf region amassed and around 35,000 British troops were also sent to the zone of the conflict.

In accordance with an UN ultimatum for the withdrawal of Iraqi troops from Kuwait, on 15 January 1991 operation Desert Storm began against Iraq. Although under operational US command, it was carried out under the United Nations, the only precedent being the Korean War. Five weeks of air war were followed by a ground campaign until on 28 February 1991 Iraq accepted a cease-fire. Throughout the war, the RAF had played a prominent role on equal footing with the US Air Force and British forces had also been essential in the co-ordination of naval movements. Britain's unequivocal support of the United States through the crisis did a lot to reinvigorate the 'special relationship' for which there had been fears after both Thatcher and Reagan were gone from politics. It proved especially important against the background of limited German involvement and disconcerted response from the European partners among which France was conspicuous with a last-minute initiative to prevent the strikes. One side-effect for Britain was that relations with Syria and Iran were restored leading to the release of a number of British hostages from across the Arab world. Additionally, there occurred better opportunities for the presentation of the British position on the Arab-Israeli conflict: since 1980 Britain had consistently worked for settlement on the basis of guarantees for Israeli security in turn for some sort of a Palestinian homeland.

One of the aims of the United States and Britain had been to eliminate Saddam, but to pursue that to the end meant continuing armed action on Iraqi territory leading to the seizure of the capital Baghdad. The United States did not feel justified in carrying out such an undertaking. President Bush believed it would break up the coalition against Iraq which had been committed to liberating Kuwait only. Moreover, it did not want to challenge either China or the USSR both of whom had reservations. In this Britain again followed the American lead. However, Iraq's effective defeat had increased instability within Iraq. The Iraqi regime turned its full military potential against the Kurds and the Shi'ite Arabs of Southern Iraq. With the humanitarian situation deteriorating steadily, the international community had to step in. Upon largely British initiative, safe havens were created in Northern and Southern Iraq over which non-fly zones for the Iraqi air force were imposed. International troops, including British were sent to monitor Iraqi observation of the rules. Britain was breaching its long-standing policy of non-intervention in other countries' domestic affairs – however just the humanitarian cause. In implementation of this new policy, in 1993 Britain participated in strikes aiming to enforce no-fly zone and secure Iraqi co-operation with the UN observers. In the following years Saddam alternated between co-operation and obstruction, backing down only when western forces were deployed in the Gulf in support of UN resolutions. Such behaviour precipitated the bombing of Iraqi military installations in December 1998 – operation Desert Fox – aiming to reduce Iraq's military capabilities. In this Britain again fully supported the United States.

How did Britain's defence priorities change at the end of the Cold War?

The elimination of the Soviet Union as the main enemy did not mean that relations became smooth and easy. On the one hand, the British government stood for the principle of self-determination and saw its interest in the promotion of democracy and market economy in the former Soviet republics and Russia itself. This determined the positive British attitude to the independence proclaimed by the three Baltic republics in August 1991. On the other hand, Britain – and indeed the other European powers and the United States – were worried in case a number of regional conflicts, similar to those in former Yugoslavia for example, emerged after the withdrawal of Moscow's control. Indeed this was already the case in the Caucasus and Moldavia. So, the UK seemed to agree that Russia should police some of the less stable former republics. Another source of potential threat was the nuclear potential of the former Soviet Union which should not fall in extremists' hands. That is why in an attempt to maintain the status quo Britain continued to support Gorbachev's presidency almost to its end even though Gorbachev seemed unable to carry through the very reforms he had initiated. Once Boris Yeltsin was established in power as the new Russian President, Britain switched support to him spending diplomatic and financial resources to boost him against Communist and nationalist opponents. Even so, on a number of occasions Britain, together with the United States, and Russia emerged on the opposite sides, the most notable example provided by Russian moral support for Serbia in the Kosovo conflict.

Despite the fact that Russia could still create trouble on the international scene, it was economically feeble and demoralised by the loss of its superpower status. Barely in a position to maintain order in the outskirts of its own territory, Moscow could hardly harbour any aggressive intentions. Such reasoning precipitated a major reappraisal of the government's defence policy which had already begun under Thatcher. In 1991 the government brought the level of defence spending to 4% of GDP, the lowest in the whole post-war period. This was improved further in 1992 to 2.7% of GDP. All three services experienced reduction. The biggest cuts occurred in the British European forces which were halved but participated in NATO's Rapid Reaction Force newly created and placed under British command to deal with dangers in Eastern Europe. Upon pressure from the Treasury cuts worth £3 billion over ten years were initiated. One-quarter of the Navy's ships were put into less intensive roles, the number of warheads of the Trident force was to be reduced and the RAF was gradually to be phased out of a major nuclear role. The Army suffered less due to its newly-found peace keeping role but the Territorial Army was to be reorganised for possible use in front-line operations. A new round of reductions was announced by Labour in July 1998 affecting submarines, frigates, aircraft carriers and tank regiments in Germany. All this was based on the two major assumptions that any future fighting would be carried out away from home and that battlefield has given way to battlespace dominated by air force and intelligence. Simultaneously, after 1995 the governments acknowledged that the defence budget should reflect the emphasis on highly flexible forces to meet a peacekeeping role. However, should the need arise, the existing structure of the armed forces should enable them to participate in high-intensity war and should also easily and quickly render to expansion, if necessary.

After 1989 and especially after 1991 Britain was also engulfed in debates about the future structure of European defence. One aspect was the changing nature of the relationship among the NATO countries underlined by divisions during the Gulf War and the tests for the alliance posed by Balkan nationalism in Yugoslavia. At closer inspection this is the old unresolved question of whether Britain should adhere to predominantly Atlantic or predominantly European priorities. A pro-NATO position would benefit from US participation in European defence; simultaneously in the mid-1990s Britain moved to accepting increased co-operation in foreign policy within the European Union. The idea of giving the West European Union some sort of defence identity was also mooted but for Britain this could only be as a bridge between the EU and NATO. Finally in 1995 the Conservative government stated that NATO would continue to be responsible for defence while the EU would increase security. In December 1998, when an Anglo-French agreement was signed on defence co-operation, it seemed that this could be a first step to an EU military structure to take care of occasions such as the Bosnian war where EU-member troops operated under NATO command.

A second aspect of defence policy was that related to the enlargement of NATO to include some former members of the Warsaw Pact. In October 1993 Yeltsin signed an agreement with Polish President Lech Walesa that Russia did not object to Poland joining NATO, but under pressure from the Russian military Yeltsin reversed his attitude. However, in May 1995 in Paris, an agreement between NATO and Russia was signed. This stated that Russian nuclear weapons targeting NATO would be dismantled while attention would be paid by the Alliance to Russia's views without its having a veto. The agreement paved the way for its eastward enlargement starting with negotiations with Hungary, Poland and the Czech Republic in July 1997. NATO also undertook not to deploy nuclear weapons on these territories of former Soviet satellites, which formally joined in 1999 just before the war in Kosovo. Throughout the discussions the position of the British government had been in favour of enlargement.

1. How did the end of the Cold War affect British foreign and defence policy?

2. What do you regard as the most important issues facing British defence policy between 1945 and 2000? Explain your answer.

3. How far have the aims of British foreign policy changed between 1945 and 2000?

4. To what extent has Britain's international position been one of steady decline between 1945 and 2000?

British-Irish relations, 1914–2000

Key Issues

● How did British policy change towards Ireland between 1914–2000?

● Why were Nationalists and Unionists in conflict in Ireland between 1914–2000?

● Why has it been so difficult to find a permanent solution to British-Irish relations?

11.1 Why was Ireland partitioned between 1914 and 1922?

11.2 How did relations between Britain and the Irish Free State/Eire develop between 1922 and 1949?

11.3 Historical Interpretation: Why did civil and political disorder develop in Northern Ireland by 1969?

11.4 How effective was British policy towards Northern Ireland between 1969 and 1985?

11.5 Why was it so difficult to find a political solution in Northern Ireland between 1985 and 2000?

Framework of Events

1914	Home Rule becomes law but its operation is suspended for the duration of the First World War
1916	Easter Rising in Dublin
1917–1918	Irish Convention
1918	General Election: Sinn Fein wins 73 seats
1919	Dail Eireann established in Dublin
1920	Government of Ireland Act
1921	Anglo-Irish Treaty
1922	Irish Free State created
1922–3	Civil War within the Irish Free State
1926	Balfour Declaration on dominion self-government
1931	Statute of Westminster
1932	Fianna Fail win Irish Free State general election
1932–36	Fianna Fail government begins dismantling links between Irish Free State and Britain
1937	New Constitution: Irish Free State becomes Eire
1938	Anglo-Irish agreements: Treaty ports given to Eire
1939	Eire stays neutral in the Second World War
1949	Eire becomes Republic of Ireland and leaves the Commonwealth
1956–1962	IRA Border Campaign
1965	Meetings between Prime Ministers of Northern Ireland and the Republic
1968	Civil Rights Movement develops in Northern Ireland. Civil disturbances begin
1969	British government orders troops into Northern Ireland. Beginning of the 'Troubles'
1971	Northern Ireland government introduces internment
1972	'Bloody Sunday' in Londonderry. Northern Ireland government suspended
1973	Britain and the Republic of Ireland join the EEC Sunningdale Agreement on setting up a power sharing executive in Northern Ireland

1974	Ulster Loyalist strike against power sharing. Sunningdale Agreement collapses
1976	'Peace People' movement against violence. The two leaders Mairead Corrigan (Catholic) and Betty Williams (Protestant) win Nobel peace prize
1981	Hunger Strike by Republican prisoners. One of them, Bobby Sands, is elected MP for Fermanagh and South Tyrone. He and nine other hunger strikers die
1982	Prior's 'Rolling Devolution' Proposals
1984	Margaret Thatcher and members of the Cabinet survive Brighton Bombing by Provisional IRA
1985	Anglo-Irish Agreement: Margaret Thatcher and Garret Fitzgerald, Prime Minister of the Republic of Ireland sign agreement on Northern Ireland
1993	Downing Street Declaration
1994	IRA ceasefire
1996	IRA ceasefire collapses after failure to reach agreement on decommissioning paramilitary weapons
1998	'Good Friday Agreement'
1999	Creation of Northern Ireland Executive

Overview

BRITAIN'S Irish problem, or Ireland's British problem, has been a dominant theme of United Kingdom politics between 1914–22 and since 1969. In September 1914 a political solution to British-Irish relations seemed to have been made. A Home Rule Act, granting limited self-government, was passed by the Westminster Parliament but was suspended for the duration of the First World War. However, by 1922, Ireland was partitioned between Northern Ireland and the Irish Free State. The latter was a state within the British Empire with internal self-government. These political developments occurred mainly because of the effects of a failed armed rebellion against British rule made by extreme Nationalists in Dublin in 1916.

From the founding of the Irish Free State to the creation of the Republic of Ireland in 1949, some Irish politicians attempted gradually to weaken the links with the British Empire. The most notable was Eamon de Valera. From 1932 to 1937 he severed many of these links. In 1937 he introduced a new constitution which created an independent republic 'in all but name'. In addition, he laid claim to Northern Ireland as part of a united Ireland. In 1949 Ireland became a fully independent state outside the Commonwealth.

Northern Ireland did receive Home Rule. From 1921 to 1972 it was dominated by the Ulster Unionist party. This party was predominantly Protestant. It discriminated against Catholics, who were seen as Nationalists who wanted a united Ireland. By 1968 Catholic civil rights had become a major issue in Northern Ireland politics. It sparked off a Protestant unionist reaction which led to major sectarian violence in 1969. The British government first sent troops to Northern Ireland in 1969 in an attempt to maintain law and order. In 1972 the government suspended the Northern Ireland Parliament and ruled the area directly from London.

From 1969 to 1998 Northern Ireland was badly affected by political violence. The Provisional IRA and Loyalist paramilitary groups engaged in guerrilla

Hillsborough Agreement: Hillsborough Castle is the Secretary of State for Northern Ireland's official residence.

Decommissioning: The handing in for destruction of military equipment including rifles and bomb making equipment.

warfare and sectarian murder. Successive British governments, both Labour and Conservative, have attempted to find a political solution. Attempts to involve both Nationalist and Unionists in government failed. In 1985 a new attempt was made with the Anglo-Irish (**Hillsborough**) **Agreement** which involved co-operation between the British and Irish governments. By the 1990s attempts to solve the conflict in Northern Ireland involved a fusion of previous attempts at a political solution: co-operation in government between political parties within Northern Ireland and co-operation between Britain and Ireland. Whether a permanent political solution is to be found will depend on an end to political violence and the **decommissioning** of paramilitary weapons.

Political Parties in Northern Ireland

The Ulster Unionist Party
The main party since the creation of the state in 1921. Wants to maintain the union with Britain. Moderate party, which signed the Sunningdale Agreement and the Good Friday Agreement.

The Democratic Unionist Party
Founded in 1971 by Ian Paisley. Wants the return of a Stormont-style government to Northern Ireland. Completely opposed to any involvement of the Irish Republic in Northern Ireland politics. Opposed to Sunningdale Agreement, Anglo-Irish Agreement and Good Friday Agreement all because of links with the Irish Republic.

The Social Democratic and Labour Party
Founded in 1970 by Gerry Fitt. Originated from the Civil Rights movement. Attracts about two-thirds of the Nationalist vote. In favour of a reunification of Ireland by consent. Main aim: to defend the rights of the Nationalist community.

Sinn Fein
Originally Arthur Griffith's party in 1906. Became associated with the demand for an independent Irish republic after 1916. From 1919 it opposed parliamentary representation of Ireland in the British (Westminster) Parliament. From 1922 it opposed representation in the Irish Free State, which was still part of Britain's Dominions. Present party is the political wing of the Republican movement in Northern Ireland. Initially in favour of the 'armed struggle', it moderated its views in the 1980s to support the twin policy of the political violence and democratic politics (the armalite and ballot box strategy). Received about 40% of the Nationalist vote by 1990s. Now supports representation in the Northern Ireland Assembly and Dublin Parliament.

Paramilitary groups in Northern Ireland since 1969

Provisional IRA
Formed in 1970 through split with the Official IRA. Led armed struggle to expel the British from Northern Ireland since that date. In favour of a united Irish republic. Have adopted various policies such as political assassination; bombing in Northern Ireland and Britain; organising demonstrations such, as the '**Dirty Protest**' for political status in Northern Ireland's prison in late 1970s, and the Hunger Strike of 1981. Well-armed through support from Libya and money from supporters in the United States.

Irish National Liberation Army
A faction which split from the Provisional IRA in 1975. Military wing of Irish Republican Socialist Party. Engaged in campaign of violence which included the murder of Lord Mountbatten and Airey Neave. Also killed 17 people in Dropping Well pub bombing. Nearly fell apart with faction fighting in 1987.

Real IRA
Another faction which split from the Provisional IRA in November 1997. Responsible for the Omagh bombing of 1998.

UDA (The Ulster Defence Association)
Formed in 1972. Contained 40,000 members and remained legal until 1992. Sees itself as defender of Protestant working-class communities. Active in Ulster Workers' Strike of 1974. Mainly engaged in sectarian murders of Catholics.

UVF (The Ulster Volunteer Force)
Originally formed in 1912 to oppose Home Rule. Mainly engaged in sectarian murders of Catholics. For instance in 1992 11 Catholics were murdered by the UVF.

(Of the 3,600 deaths in the Northern Ireland conflict since 1969 43% have been Catholic [1,548]. Most were killed by Loyalist gunmen.)

Dirty Protest: The name given to the protest by Republican prisoners when they refused to wear clothing and 'dirtied' themselves with their own excreta.

11.1 Why was Ireland partitioned between 1914 and 1922?

The Irish Question: The term given to the problem posed by Ireland to British governments.

In September 1914, it seemed that the British government had found a solution to the **Irish Question**. A Home Rule Act was passed. This granted limited self-government to Ireland within the United Kingdom and seemed to be the end of a political process, which had begun with Gladstone's conversion to Irish Home Rule in 1886.

However, within eight years Ireland was partitioned between Northern Ireland and the Irish Free State. Why did the plan to introduce Irish Home Rule fail?

The problem of Ulster

During the political crisis which led to the passage of the Home Rule Act, a political crisis occurred over Ulster. North-east Ireland contained a Protestant/Unionist majority which was opposed to Home Rule. In 1912 100,000 Ulster Unionists formed the Ulster Volunteer Force (UVF) to oppose Home Rule by force if necessary. When the First World War broke out Ireland seemed to be on the verge of civil war. In addition to the UVF,

Nationalists in Ireland formed the Irish Volunteers in 1913 to defend Home Rule. It numbered 200,000 men but was not as well armed as the UVF.

The First World War prevented an armed clash. The UVF and large numbers of the Irish Volunteers volunteered for the British Army. In addition, when the Home Rule Act was passed the Prime Minister, H.H. Asquith, promised to introduce an 'Amending Bill' which would exclude the six north-eastern counties of Ireland from the operation of Home Rule for a period of time.

How did the Easter Rising of 1916 affect British-Irish Relations?

During the early years of the war Nationalist opinion in Ireland was upset by a number of developments. At the outbreak of war the UVF were allowed to form their own division of the British Army (the 36th Division). The Irish Volunteers were not allowed the same privilege. In addition, the son of John Redmond, the leader of the Irish Nationalist Party, was denied a commission to become a British army officer. When a coalition government was formed in May 1915, Sir Edward Carson, leading Irish Unionist and opponent of Home Rule, joined the Cabinet.

Of greater significance was the decision by the **Irish Republican Brotherhood** (IRB) to stage an armed uprising against British rule. Their aim was to create an independent Irish republic. The IRB had infiltrated the organisation of the Irish Volunteers. Around 11,000 men had decided to stay in Ireland and not join the British army. In league with other separatist groups, such as the **Irish Citizen Army**, an uprising involving fewer than 2,000 Volunteers occurred in Dublin at the end of April, 1916. The Rising lasted less than a week and was easily defeated by the British garrison.

Although the Easter Rising was a military failure it did have a profound effect on Irish public opinion. The decision by the British authorities to execute sixteen leaders helped turn the rebels into Nationalist martyrs. However, the Allied powers were hoping the United States would join the war on their side and Britain did not want to alienate Irish-American opinion, so in 1917 several hundred rebel prisoners were released and

Edward Carson (1854–1935)
Carson was educated at Trinity College, Dublin. Irish Solicitor-General from 1892 and MP until 1918 he was a leading Irish Unionist opponent of Home Rule. Carson was a member of British Cabinet 1915–18.

Irish Republican Brotherhood: Originally founded in 1858 the IRB were once known as Fenians. They wanted to create an independent Irish Republic by violent means and engaged in an uprising in 1865–67 and bombing London in the 1880s.

Irish Citizen Army: A small group of socialist trade unionists led by James Connolly who became armed to defend trade unionists during strikes.

Explain the impact of the Easter Rising, 1916, on British-Irish relations.

Dublin City Centre, following the Easter Rising, 1916

allowed to return to Ireland. This created a powerful Republican political force. Finally, in 1918 the British government outraged Nationalist opinion by attempting to introduce compulsory military conscription into Ireland. Irish Nationalist MPs and Republicans campaigned jointly against the plan.

British government policy to solve Irish problems came to nothing. Lloyd George, the Prime Minister, called an Irish Convention of all Irish political groups to discuss problems. It met between 1917 and 1918, but was boycotted by Republicans and Unionists opposed any attempt to introduce Home Rule. A turning-point in British-Irish relations came in the December 1918 general election. The Irish Republicans, now known as Sinn Fein, won 73 out of 106 seats in Ireland. In January 1919, instead of going to Westminster, they set up their own parliament in Dublin, **Dail** Eireann. Between 1919 and 1921 Irish Republicans attempted to create an independent state outside the United Kingdom.

Dail: The Parliament of the Republic of Ireland and historically of the Irish Free State and Eire.

Why was the Irish Free State created in 1922?

In Ireland the years 1919–21 are known as the War of Independence. Armed groups of Republicans, known as the Irish Republican Army (IRA) fought a **guerrilla war** against the armed police force, the Royal Irish Constabulary, and the British Army. IRA activity was masterminded by Michael Collins who was Minister of Finance in the Dail Government.

Guerrilla war: A plan of campaign fought against a regular army by small bands of armed men and women.

British policy towards this problem was two-fold. Firstly, through the Government of Ireland Act (1920), the government tried to find a political solution. Two Home Rule parliaments and governments would be established in Ireland. One would be for the six counties of the north east (Northern Ireland), the other for the remaining twenty-six counties (termed Southern Ireland). Only part of the act was implemented. In the May, 1921 elections in Ireland, Sinn Fein won an overwhelming vote in the South. They refused to accept the Act.

At the same time, the British government attempted to defeat the IRA by military means. The Royal Irish Constabulary was reinforced by two groups of volunteer forces from Britain, the Auxiliaries and the '**Black and Tans**'. These groups engaged in reprisal raids on the civilian population in retaliation for IRA attacks on British forces. This policy was unpopular in the United States and among Liberals and Labour politicians in Britain.

Black and Tans: Volunteers recruited by the British Government after the First World War to supplement the work of the Royal Irish Constabulary and the regular army in countering Irish republican attacks. The Black and Tans became notorious for the violence of their 'reprisals' against the nationalist population. The name is thought to derive from their dark berets and khaki tunics.

In the summer of 1921, Lloyd George, the Prime Minister, changed British policy. He called a ceasefire with the IRA and began political negotiations with Sinn Fein.

In December 1921 an agreement was signed in London. Representatives of Sinn Fein, led by Arthur Griffith and Michael Collins, accepted the creation of a self-governing state, outside the United Kingdom but part of the British Empire. This became the Irish Free State. Initially, the six counties of Northern Ireland were to be excluded. It was

Michael Collins (1890–1922)
Collins was born in Clonakilty, county Cork. He took part in Easter Rising, later becoming President of the IRB. He was Minister of Finance in the Dail Government of 1919, raised the National Loan 1919–21 and organised the IRA. A member of the Irish delegation for Anglo-Irish Treaty talks, he succeeded Griffith as Prime Minister of the Irish Free State, but was assassinated a few weeks later in August 1922.

Arthur Griffith (1871–1922)
Griffith was born in Dublin, and educated by the Christian Brothers. He was a member of the IRB 1893–1910. In 1906 Griffith founded the Sinn Fein Party. He wanted internal self-government for Ireland similar to Hungary's position in Austria-Hungary, and opposed the Home Rule Bill. He didn't take part in the Easter Rising but became Vice-President of the new Sinn Fein party in 1918. He headed the Irish delegation in the Anglo-Irish Treaty talks 1921 and was elected President of the Dail [Prime Minister] in January 1922, but died seven months later.

The partition of Ireland, 1920–21

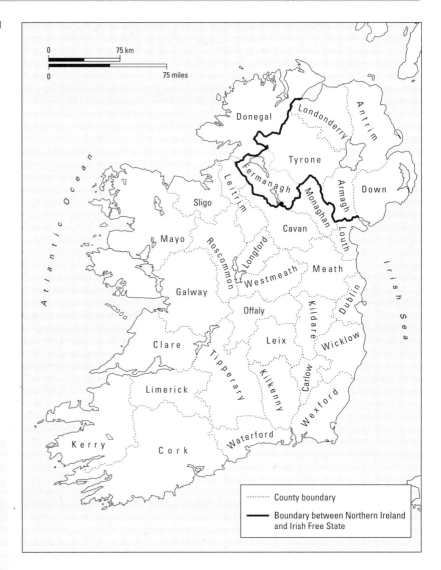

1. How did British policy towards Ireland change between 1914 and 1922?

2. Who benefited most from the Partition of Ireland and the creation of the Irish Free State?

a) The British government?

b) Irish Unionists?

c) Irish Republicans?

Give reasons to support your answer

3. How far did the political settlement of 1920–22 differ from the Home Rule Act 1914?

agreed that a Boundary Commission would study the border between the Irish Free State and Northern Ireland and would recommend changes. Michael Collins believed that the Boundary Commission would give the Irish Free State large parts of Northern Ireland. This would have the effect of forcing Northern Ireland into a united Irish state.

The Anglo-Irish Treaty of 1921 upset extremists on both sides. 'Die hard' Conservatives disliked the breakup of the United Kingdom. Irish republicans, led by Eamon de Valera, were opposed to staying within the British Empire. De Valera's stance seems odd because he had been notified by Lloyd George in secret negotiations in July 1921 that this was the best he could offer. It does explain why de Valera did not lead the Irish negotiating team in London in November and December 1921. The split over the Treaty led to civil war within the Irish Free State. Between June 1922 and 1923, Free State forces defeated Irish Republican forces. The main casualty was Michael Collins, then Prime Minister of the Irish Free State. He was killed in an ambush on 22 August 1922.

11.2 How did relations between Britain and the Irish Free State/Eire develop between 1922 and 1949?

Eamon de Valera (1882–1975)
De Valera was born in New York, USA and raised in County Limerick. He took a leading part in the Easter Rising but escaped execution. Elected President of Ireland in 1919 he opposed the Anglo-Irish treaty of 1921 and sided with anti-Treaty forces in the Irish Civil War 1922–23. He founded the Fianna Fail Party in 1926. De Valera became Prime Minister of the Irish Free State in 1932. Following the creation of Eire in 1937 he became its Prime Minister 1937–49, 1951–54 and 1957–59 and then President of the Republic of Ireland 1959–73. Throughout his life he worked to achieve a united Irish Republic.

Political Parties in Eire/Republic of Ireland

Fianna Fail
Founded in 1926 by Eamon de Valera when he split from the IRA. Entered the Irish Parliament in 1927 and became the governing party in 1932. Has been the largest party in the Republic of Ireland since 1932. In favour of a 32-county independent Irish Republic to be achieved by democratic means. However, in 1971 two leading members of Fianna Fail, Charles Haughey (future Taoiseach) and Neil Blaney, were accused of gunrunning to the Provisional IRA.

Fine Gael
Founded in 1933. Supported the Anglo-Irish Treaty of 1921. A more pro-British party than Fianna Fail. Has taken a more conciliatory line towards cross-border security and extradition.

Prime Ministers of Irish Free State (1922–1937), Eire (1937–1948) and the Republic of Ireland (1948 onwards)

1922–32	William T. Cosgrave (Cumann na nGaedhael)
1932–48	Eamon de Valera (Fianna Fail)
1948–51	John Costello (Coalition)
1951–54	Eamon de Valera (Fianna Fail)
1954–57	John Costello (Coalition)
1957–59	Eamon de Valera (Fianna Fail)
1959–66	Sean Lemass (Fianna Fail)
1966–73	Jack Lynch (Fianna Fail)
1973–77	Liam Cosgrave (Fine Gael)
1977–79	Jack Lynch (Fianna Fail)
1979–81	Charles Haughey (Fianna Fail)
1981–82	Garret Fitzgerald (Fine Gael)
1982 (Mar–Dec)	Charles Haughey (Fianna Fail)
1982–87	Garret Fitzgerald (Fine Gael)
1987–92	Charles Haughey (Fianna Fail)
1992–94	Albert Reynolds (Fianna Fail)
1994–6	John Bruton (Fine Gael)
1996–	Bertie Ahern (Fianna Fail)

In his defence of the Anglo-Irish Treaty Michael Collins claimed that it gave 'freedom to achieve freedom'. By this he meant that the creation of the Irish Free State would be the beginning of a process which would eventually lead to the creation of a completely independent Irish state. Between 1922 and 1949 the Irish Free State did follow this route. However, the chief architect of this development was Collins' political rival Eamon de Valera.

The creation of Eire

Fortunately for Irish nationalists, political developments within the British Empire assisted this change. At the Imperial Conference of 1926 the 'Balfour Declaration' gave the dominions of the British Empire full internal self-government. The dominions were Canada, Australia, New Zealand, South Africa, Southern Rhodesia, Newfoundland and the Irish

Governor-General: The Monarch's representative in Commonwealth countries which regard the Monarch as Head of State. Between 1939 and 1949 Britain was represented in Dublin by the UK Representative in Ireland, Sir John Maffey, later Lord Rugby.

Free State. By the Statute of Westminster (1931) the self-governing dominions were declared independent states within the British Commonwealth. These were all held together by common allegiance to the British monarchy.

In 1932, Eamon de Valera became Prime Minister of the Irish Free State. He used the position to sever the political links with Britain. He abolished the Oath of Allegiance to the British Crown which every Irish MP had to take. The position of **Governor-General** to Ireland was reduced to a position of political insignificance. De Valera nominated an obscure Irish politician, D. Buckley, to the post. Instead of living at the Vice-Regal Lodge, the Monarch's residence in Dublin, he was banished to a small house in the Dublin suburbs. Finally de Valera abolished the right of Irish people to send legal cases to the Judicial Committee of the Privy Council.

In 1937 de Valera introduced a new constitution. The Irish Free State became Eire.

The position of Governor-General was abolished. Instead Eire would have an elected President as Head of State. Eire was a 'republic in all but name'. At the Imperial Conference of 1937 it was declared that the creation of Eire did not substantially change Ireland's links with the British Commonwealth. However, the only constitutional link between Eire and Britain was the External Relations Act. This stated that Irish diplomats abroad were seen as representatives of the British Crown.

Eire and the Second World War

A major development in British-Irish relations was the Second World War. Eire was the only part of the British Empire and Commonwealth to stay neutral in the war. Given Eire's strategic position in the Battle of the Atlantic Irish neutrality created serious problems for Britain. This position had been made worse in 1938 when Neville Chamberlain had signed an Anglo-Irish Agreement with de Valera. Under the Agreement a trade war between the two states, which had existed since 1932, came to an end. Of greater significance was the British decision to hand over to Eire the 'Treaty Ports' of Cork Harbour, Bere Haven and Lough Swilly. These ports could have provided important British naval bases during the War.

On a number of occasions Britain attempted to end Eire neutrality. In June 1940, Malcolm McDonald, former Dominions Secretary and son of Ramsay McDonald, was sent to Dublin on a secret mission. He offered de Valera the reunification of Ireland if Eire entered the War on the Allied side. De Valera refused mainly because the Northern Ireland government had not been consulted. He also believed that the British Prime Minister, Winston Churchill, did not have the political will to honour the agreement.

On two occasions the British considered military intervention to occupy Eire: in June/July 1940, shortly after the fall of France and again in the early summer of 1944, shortly before D-Day. Intervention was ruled out in 1940 because the Cabinet Committee dealing with the issue thought the action would alienate American opinion and lead to guerrilla warfare in Eire. In 1944 intervention was considered because the German and Japanese embassies were still functioning in Dublin. The Allies feared the Germans might find out about the D-Day landings because Northern Ireland was an important staging area for that operation.

By the end of the war Eire's neutrality had greatly distanced it from Britain and the Commonwealth. In his victory speech to the British Empire on V.E. Day, Winston Churchill made specific reference to the problems caused by Irish neutrality in the War. De Valera did not help matters when he signed a book of condolence at the German Embassy in Dublin on the news of Adolf Hitler's death.

The creation of the Republic of Ireland

In 1948, Costello, the Eire Prime Minister, declared, on a trip to Canada, that Eire would become an independent Republic outside the British Commonwealth. This development should have led to a widening of relations between Britain and Ireland. However, under the Ireland Act (1949) Irish citizens still retained considerable rights within the United Kingdom. Unlike any other **aliens** they could stand for the British Parliament and vote in British elections if they were resident in Britain. They could also join the British armed forces and police.

Alien: A person who is not a citizen.

The main reasons behind this British policy concerned other parts of the Commonwealth. Both Australia and New Zealand lobbied the British Government not to change the status of Irish citizens in the United Kingdom: with elections due in 1949 they feared the effects of a change in policy on the large Irish electorates in both these countries. Britain was also concerned about India's relations with the Commonwealth. India had become independent in August 1947, but remained within the Commonwealth. The British government knew that India planned to declare itself a republic. Therefore, in order to keep India, as a republic, within the Commonwealth, relations with Ireland were not changed.

There is another significant aspect of the Ireland Act. The Act stated that no attempt would be made to alter the constitutional position of Northern Ireland without the consent of the people of Northern Ireland. As Unionists had a permanent majority in Northern Ireland (they comprised about 66% of the population) this declaration created the 'Unionist veto'. This had an important impact on British policy in Northern Ireland after 1969.

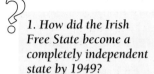

1. How did the Irish Free State become a completely independent state by 1949?

2. Who or what do you regard as most responsible for this political development? Give reasons for your answer.

3. How significant was the Ireland Act, 1949 to British-Irish relations?

11.3 Why did civil and political disorder develop in Northern Ireland by 1969?

A CASE STUDY IN HISTORICAL INTERPRETATION

The outbreak of widespread civil and political disorder between the Nationalist and Unionist communities in Northern Ireland was a constant feature of British politics from 1969 to 1999. The causes of this disorder, known by some as 'the Troubles', is the subject of much controversy. Both sides in Northern Ireland have widely differing interpretations of these events. Such differing perceptions are a major, if not the major reason why a political solution to Northern Ireland's problems has been so difficult to find.

The background

When Northern Ireland received Home Rule under the Government of Ireland Act, 1920, it was a political solution which Irish Unionists did not seek. They wanted to prevent any form of Home Rule for Ireland. As a result of the Irish political settlements made from 1920 to 1922 only a small number of Irish Unionists (around 100,000) lived in the Irish Free State. The majority of Irish Unionists lived in Northern Ireland.

Between 1921 and 1972 Northern Ireland politics was dominated by the Ulster Unionist Party, which held power continuously over this period. The Ulster Unionists at Westminster (there were 12 in this period) usually voted with the Conservative Party.

Nationalists, who made up around one-third of the Northern Ireland population, made very little impact on Northern Ireland politics. Some of their elected representatives abstained from attending the **Stormont** Parliament. More significantly, the electoral system ensured Unionist dominance.

Stormont: The site of the Northern Ireland Parliament, in a Belfast suburb. The name is also used to describe the Northern Ireland government.

Terence O'Neill (1914–1990)
Born in London, and educated at Eton, O'Neill was a Captain in the Irish Guards 1939–45. He was leader of the Ulster Unionist Party and Prime Minister of Northern Ireland 1963–69.

James Chichester-Clark (1923–)
Eton-educated Chichester-Clark was leader of Ulster Unionist Party and Prime Minister of Northern Ireland, May 1969 to March 1971. He resigned because the Heath government would not send more troops to Ulster.

Apprentice Boys' March:
Celebration by a group of men of the apprentices who defended Derry from the troops of James II during the siege of 1689.

How useful is this photograph to a historian writing about the Civil Rights Movement in Northern Ireland in the late 1960s?

Nationalists also felt discriminated against in other fields such as housing and employment. By the 1960s resentment felt against the Northern Ireland government by one-third of the population led to the creation of the Northern Ireland Civil Rights Association (NICRA) and a student organisation called People's Democracy. These groups comprised Nationalists, liberal members of the Unionist community and Churchmen. Inspired by the African American Civil Rights movement in the United States the NICRA called for 'one man one vote' and the end to discrimination in housing and employment. People's Democracy had similar aims. Its origins were similar to the student radicalism which affected much of Western Europe and North America from the mid-1960s.

These groups used similar tactics to the African American Civil Rights Movement. Demonstrations and walks were organised. In 1968 a NICRA march took place at Dungannon, County Tyrone. In October, serious rioting accompanied a Civil Rights march in Derry City. The Civil Rights movement was opposed by the Northern Ireland Government and various Unionist organisations. The latter attempted to disrupt marches and demonstrations. Following the **Apprentice Boys' March** in Derry City, in August 1969, rioting by Nationalists became so serious that the police force, the RUC, was finding it difficult to keep control. In addition, armed Unionist groups began attacking Nationalist areas in Belfast and Derry City.

Following a poor showing in the Northern Ireland general election of 1969, the Northern Ireland Prime Minister Captain Terence O'Neill resigned. He was replaced by another Unionist, Major James Chichester-Clark. Faced with ever-mounting sectarian violence, Chichester-Clark requested the support of the British army to maintain peace. On 15 August 1969 British troops were sent to Northern Ireland in a 'peace-keeping role'.

The events of 1968–1969 were a turning point in British-Irish relations. Until 1968 Northern Ireland issues were rarely discussed at

The Civil Rights March from Coalisland to Dungannon, Country Tyrone, in 1969

Westminster. The Speaker's rules stipulated that Northern Ireland issues be discussed by Northern Ireland ministers at Stormont not in Britain. However, the Civil Rights Movement and the Unionist opposition to it meant that Northern Ireland issues could no longer be ignored by a British government. From 1968 the Northern Ireland problem has been a major issue in British politics.

Northern Ireland terminology

The conflict in Northern Ireland has produced a series of inter-connected and sometimes slightly confusing titles for political groups and place names.

Nationalists are those members of the Northern Ireland community who would like to see a united Ireland. They include moderate democratic politicians and extremists.

Republicans are those members of the Nationalist community most closely associated with the idea of creating a united Irish state by force if necessary. Groups such as Sinn Fein, the Provisional IRA and INLA are republican.

Catholics: In Northern Ireland there is a very strong link between Nationalism and Catholicism. The vast majority of Catholics regard themselves as Nationalist, so much so that the terms Catholic and Nationalist are virtually interchangeable.

Unionists are those who want Northern Ireland to remain part of the United Kingdom. They include moderate democratic politicians as well as extremists who engage in sectarian violence.

Loyalists are those members of the Unionist community who engage in political violence to prevent Northern Ireland becoming part of a united Ireland. They include paramilitary groups such as the UDA, the UFF and the UVF. Most recently they have been associated with political parties such as the Ulster Democratic Party and Ulster Progressive Party.

Protestants: The link between Protestantism and Unionism is very strong; again the terms are virtually interchangeable. An important Protestant/Unionist organisation is the Orange Order. This organisation aims to defend religious liberties and the Union with Britain. It is anti-Catholic.

Place names: The most noticeable split between the Nationalist and Unionist communities is over the name of Londonderry/Derry. The former term is used by Unionists, the latter by Nationalists. Since the 1980s the official use has been Derry City for the county town and Londonderry for the county.

Prime Ministers of Northern Ireland

1921–40	Sir James Craig (Lord Craigavon)
1940–43	J. M. Andrews
1943–63	Sir Basil Brooke (Lord Brookeborough)
1963–69	Capt. Terence O'Neill
1969–71	James Chichester-Clark
1971–72	Brian Faulkner

A Nationalist view of the causes of conflict in Northern Ireland

To most Nationalists, Northern Ireland is an artificial sub-state. It was created in 1920 by Lloyd George as an attempt to solve the Irish problem by providing a political unit within Ireland where there was a built-in Protestant/Unionist majority. The plan was to defend British strategic interests by preventing the unification of Ireland.

This Nationalist view is supported by the failure to create a Council of Ireland. This body was meant to be set up under the Government of Ireland Act. It was to contain representatives from Northern and Southern Ireland. The aim was supposedly to create an All-Ireland political body, which might one day lead to the end of partition. The other failure was that of the Boundary Commission to make any significant changes to the border between the Irish Free State and Northern Ireland. The Commission had been created by the Anglo-Irish Treaty of 1921. When it reported, in 1925, it left large numbers of Catholic/Nationalists within Northern Ireland.

British indifference to Irish Nationalism was confirmed by the failure to stop Unionist dominance of Northern Ireland. Sir James Craig, a leading Ulster Unionist, described Stormont as 'a Protestant Parliament for a Protestant people'. From the moment Northern Ireland was created, Catholics were made to feel like second-class citizens. In 1929 Nationalist fears seemed to be confirmed when the Unionist government changed the electoral system. Proportional representation was abolished. It was replaced by the 'first-past-the-post' system, which ensured Unionist dominance at Stormont.

In local government, votes were given to rate payers rather than all adults. This discriminated against Catholics, because many did not own their own homes. In addition, **gerrymandering** took place. In Derry City, even though Catholics comprised two-thirds of the population, a Unionist city government was in control.

Discrimination against the Catholic minority was also seen in policing. The Royal Ulster Constabulary (RUC) was a predominantly Protestant force. It was supported by a part-time police force known as the 'B' specials – Protestants who harassed the local Catholic community. Both forces possessed considerable law and order powers. These were established under the Civil Authorities (Special Powers) Act, Northern Ireland (1922) and gave the police wide powers to stop, search and detain anyone they believed might be engaged in illegal political activity.

The problem also entered social and employment fields. A government Commission under Lord Cameron was set up to look into the causes of the disturbances of 1968–69. It reported in 1969 that favouritism towards Protestants in the allocation of council housing was rife in Dungannon, Armagh and, most notably, in Belfast and Derry City. In employment Protestants tended only to employ Protestants. As a result, unemployment was over twice as high among Catholics, because Protestants dominated the employer class.

The anti-Catholic/Nationalist nature of the Unionist majority was shown by the reaction to Prime Minister O'Neill's attempts to forge relations with the Republic of Ireland. In 1965, for the first time, a meeting took place between the prime ministers of Northern Ireland and the Republic. This led to opposition to O'Neill within the Unionist community. It created an opportunity for a young Presbyterian cleric, Ian Paisley, to make his political mark by opposing links with Catholics and the Republic.

In February 1969, O'Neill called a general election in Northern Ireland. He narrowly defeated Paisley in the Upper Bann constituency and the election returned a large number of anti-O'Neill Unionists. O'Neill was forced to resign.

James Craig (1871–1940)
Craig was born in Belfast. A Unionist MP for East Down, 1906, he was a leading Ulster Unionist opponent of Home Rule from 1912. He became the first Prime Minister of Northern Ireland in 1921 and held the post until his death. He was made Lord Craigavon in 1927.

Gerrymandering: The deliberate drawing of electoral boundaries in order to manipulate the election result.

Ian Paisley (1926–)
A founder member of Free Presbyterian Church of Ulster in 1951, Paisley was born in County Armagh, educated at Barry School of Evangelism and Bob Jones University, USA. He was imprisoned for obstructing a Civil Rights March, November 1968. In September 1971 he founded the Democratic Unionist party. He as been an European Parliament MP since 1979 and Westminster MP for North Antrim since 1970 and has opposed the Sunningdale, Anglo-Irish and Good Friday Agreements.

To the Nationalists, the causes of the conflict stemmed from Britain, which had a selfish interest in maintaining control over part of Ireland. Successive British governments had allowed a Unionist-dominated government to discriminate against the Catholic minority. When Catholics engaged in legitimate political protest to highlight their grievances they were met by opposition from Unionist thugs, and the RUC and 'B' Specials.

Local government employment in County Fermanagh, March 1969

(County Fermanagh had a Catholic/Nationalist majority)

Jobs	Catholics	Protestants
County Council Administration	0	33
Housing Department	0	10
County Library	1	14
Planning and Tourism	0	5
Public Works Dept	4	60
Education Office	4	120
Health and Welfare Department	21	88
Total	*30*	*330*

Local representation in Derry City, 1966: The problem of gerrymandering

There were 24 local government councillors for Derry city. Each ward elected eight councillors.

South Ward	14,125 anti-Unionist votes	1,474 Unionist votes
North Ward	3,173 anti-Unionist votes	4,380 Unionist votes
Waterside Ward	2,804 anti-Unionist votes	4,420 Unionist votes

Both of the above inserts are from *Divided Ulster* by Liam de Paor (1971)

? *How useful are these two tables in explaining the degree of discrimination against Catholics in Northern Ireland in the 1960s?*

A Unionist view on the causes of conflict in Northern Ireland

The majority of the population of Northern Ireland came from English and Scots stock. They had colonised the north east of Ireland from the end of the 16th century. They regard themselves as British rather than Irish. These colonists faced hostility from the Catholic Irish majority: in 1641 an Irish Rebellion led to the massacre of Protestants in Ulster. In 1688–90 the Catholic James II, in league with Louis XIV of France, attempted to force Catholicism on Britain and Ireland. He was defeated by William of Orange at the Battle of the Boyne in 1690. This victory protected the civil and religious liberties of the Protestant population of Ireland and saved Britain from absolutist government.

The link between north-east Ireland and Britain was strengthened in the 19th century by the industrial revolution. Shipbuilding and textiles industries flourished in north-east Ireland as part of an industrial British economy. The area had much more in common with central Scotland and northern England than the rest of Ireland.

As a minority in the whole of Ireland, Protestants feared domination by what they saw as an alien religion and culture. This was reinforced by the Catholic Church's insistence that in a mixed marriage between a Catholic and a Protestant, all the offspring had to be brought up as Catholics. Fear of the Catholic majority was reinforced during the political instability of 1919–22. Irish nationalists attempted to force the Unionist/Protestants of the north east into a united Ireland against their will. When Michael Collins, the Prime Minister of the Irish Free State, was shot on 22 August 1922, he was planning a major IRA campaign to destroy Northern Ireland.

From the very start of Northern Ireland's existence Catholics were seen as a dangerous **fifth column**. They supported unification with the Republic of Ireland. From 1937, under Articles 2 and 3 of the Eire constitution, the Republic claimed Northern Ireland as part of their national territory. The anti-British position of Irish Nationalists was emphasised by the neutrality of Eire during the Second World War. Between 1956 and 1962 the IRA launched a border campaign of terrorism, attacking border posts and killing RUC officers.

Catholics had also created problems for themselves by opposing Northern Ireland from the start. Many Catholics believed that Northern Ireland wouldn't last long as a sub-state within the United Kingdom. They therefore abstained from participating in government. The Catholic Church refused to co-operate with the creation of a province-wide system of education. It insisted on running its own schools so that from an early age Catholics and Protestants were kept separate, thereby reinforcing the split within Northern Ireland society.

Unlike Nationalists, Unionists do not believe there was any historical justification for a united Ireland. Throughout history, Ulster had a separate identity and the only time Ireland was united as one political entity was under British rule.

The disturbances which occurred in Northern Ireland had their origin in an attempt by Nationalists to push the province into the Republic of Ireland by force. The Official IRA had links with the NICRA and People's Democracy. These were seen as front organisation for this Republican plan. Attempts by the Irish Prime Minister, Sean Lemass, to meet and forge links with Captain Terence O'Neill was seen as part of a broader Nationalist conspiracy to achieve unification.

Protestant fears included the Second Vatican Council of the Catholic Church which began in 1963. Other Christian groups, including Protestants, were invited to attend as observers. This was seen as some as part of a global attempt by Catholicism to dominate Christianity. In *God Save Ulster!* (1989), S. Bruce quoted the Rev. Ian Paisley who stated: 'The aim is a super one-world Church. Rome, of course, already sees herself as that Church'.

There are important social and economic considerations in opposition to an all-Ireland state. Catholic influence in the Republic of Ireland meant that contraception was illegal. The Catholic Church also provided a form of censorship with a list of prohibited books. Northern Ireland, on the other hand, benefited from the National Health Service and the Welfare State, and the standard of living was much higher than in the Republic of Ireland.

Fifth column: Individuals or groups within a country who support an enemy force.

Sean Lemass (1899–1969)
Born in County Dublin in 1899 Lemass was in his teens when he took part in Easter Rising. He was Deputy Prime Minister 1945–49 and Taoiseach 1959–65. He re-established free trade with Britain in 1965 and was the first Irish Prime Minister to visit Belfast. He held talks with Terence O'Neill, Prime Minister of Northern Ireland on improving North–South relations in 1965.

---

1. *What were the main grievances of the Catholic/Nationalist minority towards the Northern Ireland government by the mid-1960s?*

2. *To what extent is the differences between the Nationalist and Unionist views on the causes of conflict based on religion?*

11.4 How effective was British policy towards Northern Ireland between 1969 and 1985?

Between 1969 and 1985, British government policy was affected by a number of factors:

● high levels of political violence, which began in Northern Ireland but spread to both Britain and the Republic of Ireland. Political violence involved assassination, car bombs, and the shooting of police and soldiers. It involved paramilitary groups from the Loyalist and Republican communities (see panel on page 255), the RUC and the British army;

● attempts to find a political solution within Northern Ireland between Unionists and Nationalists;

● attempts to find a political solution between Northern Ireland and the rest of the United Kingdom;

● attempts to find a political solution which would involve the Republic of Ireland.

In trying to develop a coherent British policy, developments such as a change in government (from Labour to Conservative) or a change in the Secretary of State for Northern Ireland would have great significance. In addition, the Northern Ireland problem was affected by public opinion in the United States (in particular Irish-American opinion) and in Europe. (After January 1973 both the United Kingdom and the Republic of Ireland were part of the European Community.)

How did the policy followed by the Labour and Conservative governments towards Northern Ireland develop between 1969 and 1973?

After decades of disinterest and neglect the British government was faced with a major domestic political crisis in August 1969. Normally, the responsibility for maintaining law and order within Northern Ireland lay with the Stormont government. However, in *A House Divided* (1970) the Labour Home Secretary, James Callaghan, expressed his belief that military intervention was required by the British army to protect Catholic areas from attacks by Protestant mobs. This was most apparent in west Belfast. During the disturbances of 1968–69 Catholic areas felt that they lacked protection. Walls in these areas were daubed with slogans such as 'IRA, I ran away' condemning the IRA for its failure to defend them.

Direct British involvement under Labour was welcomed by the Catholic/Nationalist community. Their homes were now protected by the British army. A report by the Hunt Advisory Committee to the British government recommended the disarming of the RUC, the disbanding of the 'B' Specials and a transfer of council-house allocation from local authorities to the Stormont government. In April 1970 the 'B' Specials were replaced by a part-time regiment of the British Army, the Ulster Defence Regiment (UDR). Unfortunately, the UDR contained large numbers of former 'B' Specials.

The Republican reaction to the 1968–69 disturbances led to a split within the IRA. An IRA convention in 1969 saw the creation of the Provisional IRA. This group split from the Official IRA mainly because it wanted to engage in armed defence of the Catholic community. The Provisional IRA leader was Sean MacStiofain.

By the time Edward Heath became Conservative Prime Minister in June 1970 the political situation in Northern Ireland had begun to change. The continued existence of a Unionist-dominated Stormont government meant that the Catholic/Nationalist community began to regard the British Army as defenders of Unionism. This development was made worse by the decision of the Provisional IRA to go on the offensive in early 1971. The first British soldier (Gunner Curtis) was shot dead in February 1971 by the Provisional IRA.

With the escalation of political violence the British Government faced a difficult problem. British policy on the ground in Northern Ireland was determined by the senior army officer (General Officer Commanding – GOC – Northern Ireland) working with the Stormont government. A clash had occurred in October 1969 between the Chief Constable of the RUC and the GOC over security, which led to the GOC's role being restricted to co-ordination, and not overall control, of army and police. However, ultimate control lay with Westminster. In April 1971 the Northern Ireland Prime Minister, Chichester-Clark, resigned because the Heath government refused to increase troop levels in the Province.

In August 1971, the Heath government made a major tactical error by agreeing to the introduction of internment without trial, proposed by the new Northern Ireland Prime Minister, Brain Faulkner. With poor police and military intelligence about who was in the Provisional IRA, British troops and the RUC arrested large numbers of Catholic/Nationalists. They were placed mainly in an old military camp near Belfast known as Long Kesh. (It later became the Maze Prison.) The Catholic/Nationalist reaction to internment led to a large increase in support for the Provisional IRA.

The policy of using the army and police to restore law and order in the Catholic/Nationalist community reached crisis point on 30 January 1972. An illegal Civil Rights march in Derry City was stopped by RUC and the Army. Fourteen marchers were killed by the Army, mainly by members of the Parachute Regiment. To this day the precise circumstances surrounding 'Bloody Sunday' have yet to be revealed. It was, however, a major

Brian Faulkner (1921–1977)
Faulkner was born in County Down. He was leader of Ulster Unionist Party and Prime Minister of Northern Ireland March 1971 to March 1972. He introduced internment, signed Sunningdale Agreement in December 1973 and became Chief Executive of Power Sharing government January–May 1974. He founded the Unionist Party of Northern Ireland 1974.

Why do you think photographs such as this helped bring about the suspension of the Stormont Government?

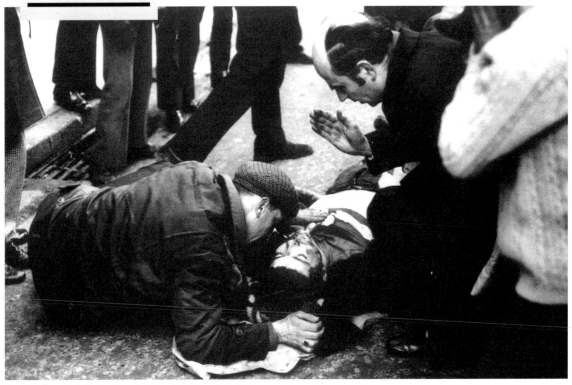

'Bloody Sunday', Derry City, January 1972

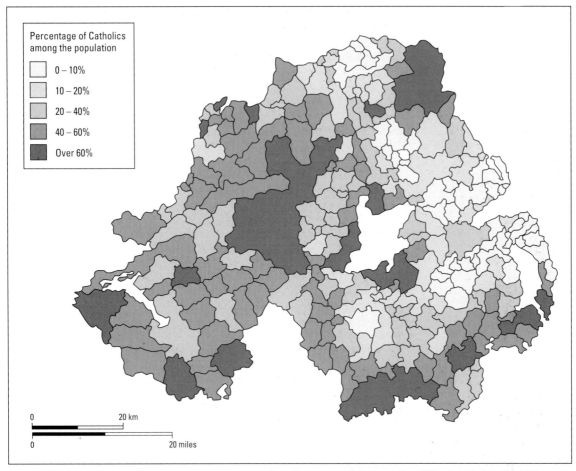

The percentage of Catholics among the population of Northern Ireland in 1971

On the evidence of this map, why do you think the partition of Northern Ireland has not been regarded as a serious political solution to the political and civil disorder since 1969?

SDLP: The Social Democratic and Labour Party – see box on political parties in Northern Ireland, p.254.

The Alliance Party: A non-sectarian political party representing both Catholics and Protestants, and mainly supported by the middle class. It has made very little impact on the Northern Ireland political scene.

setback for British policy. It caused uproar in the Republic of Ireland and the British Embassy was burned down. It also led directly to the Heath government's decision to suspend the Stormont government in March 1972, introducing Direct Rule from Westminster. From 1972 Northern Ireland affairs were under the responsibility of a member of the British Cabinet, the Secretary of State for Northern Ireland.

Under the first Secretary of State, William Whitelaw, the Heath government engaged in a major attempt to find a political solution within Northern Ireland. On 19 August 1969, the Labour Prime Minister, Harold Wilson, had made 'The Downing Street Declaration'. In it he declared British commitment to maintaining Northern Ireland's union with Britain as long as the majority of the Northern Ireland community agreed. Whitelaw took the bold step of opening negotiations with all sides of the conflict. In July, 1972 he even met Sean MacStiofain of the Provisional IRA but these talks came to nothing mainly because of the Provisional IRA's insistence on British withdrawal.

By the end of 1973 Whitelaw had been able to get moderate Unionists, led by Brian Faulkner, and moderate Nationalists of the **SDLP** with the **Alliance Party** to agree to the Sunningdale Agreement. The Agreement involved the passage of two acts of parliament: The Northern Ireland Assembly Act, May 1973, and the Northern Ireland Constitution

Consociational democracy:
Democracy achieved by bringing
together representative groups into
government rather than having a
ballot.

Taoiseach: The Prime Minister of the
Republic of Ireland.

Act, July 1973, and an agreement between the British and Irish governments in December 1973. Direct Rule was to be replaced by
'Power-Sharing'. The government of Northern Ireland was to contain
representatives from both the Unionist and Nationalist communities.
This was a version of **consociational democracy**. It was introduced
because the normal operation of democracy meant that Unionists would
always hold power.

Another important feature of the Sunningdale Agreement was the
inclusion of an All-Ireland dimension. Since September 1971, the
Taoiseach, Jack Lynch, had been conducting talks with Edward Heath
about Northern Ireland. Both prime ministers wanted an end to political
violence. In the course of 1972 the Fianna Fail government in Dublin had
introduced harsh measures against the Provisional IRA within the
Republic. In December 1973 the Irish dimension of the agreement included the creation of a Council of Ireland. This would be an advisory
committee involving political representatives from Northern Ireland and
the Republic with limited executive power. It was a similar institution to
the one proposed under the Government of Ireland Act, 1920.

The Sunningdale Agreement seemed to offer political stability for
Northern Ireland. It was supported by moderate Unionists, moderate
Nationalists, and the British and Irish governments. However, it was
opposed by paramilitary groups on both sides, the Provisional IRA, the
UDA and the UVF. It was also opposed by many Unionists. Most promi-
nent were the Democratic Unionist Party of the Rev. Ian Paisley and the
Vanguard Unionist Party of James Craig, a former Northern Ireland Home
Secretary.

Why did the Sunningdale Agreement fail?

The Power Sharing Executive operated for only four months. The collapse
of the Sunningdale Agreement was brought about by a general strike
organised by the Ulster Workers' Council in May 1974. This group included Unionist politicians, Loyalist paramilitaries and trade unionists.
Although it lasted only 14 days, the strike brought Northern Ireland to a
standstill.

One reason behind the failure was a change in government. In
February 1974 Edward Heath had called a general election over the
miners' strike. He was replaced by a minority Labour government under
Harold Wilson which lacked the political power to act decisively.

Secondly, there was a lack of decisive leadership by the Labour
Secretary of State for Northern Ireland, Merlyn Rees. He allowed the

---

Secretaries of State for Northern Ireland

1972–73	William Whitelaw (Con)
1973–74	Francis Pym (Con)
1974–76	Merlyn Rees (Lab)
1976–79	Roy Mason (Lab)
1979–81	Humphrey Atkins (Con)
1981–84	James Prior (Con)
1984–85	Douglas Hurd (Con)
1985–89	Tom King (Con)
1989–92	Peter Brooke (Con)
1992–97	Sir Patrick Mayhew (Con)
1997–99	Dr Mo Mowlam (Lab)
1999–	Peter Mandelson (Lab)

general strike to become established during the second week in May although he could, for instance, have used troops to operate power stations. Instead of supporting the Power Sharing Executive he allowed it to fail and suggested a Constitutional Convention to discuss other ways of finding a political agreement. In elections for the convention, in May 1975, anti-Power Sharing Unionists did well. By November 1975, when the Convention reported, it was split between Unionists who wanted a return of the Stormont government and a minority in favour of Power-Sharing. The Convention was dissolved, a failure, in March 1976.

Did Labour Policy towards Northern Ireland achieve anything between 1974 and 1979?

Diplock Courts: Special courts in Northern Ireland for trying terrorist cases. They were named after Lord Diplock, whose report in 1973 suggested that terrorists should not be tried by jury, because of widespread evidence of intimidation of jurors by paramilitaries.

Birmingham Pub Bombings: On 21 November 1974, the Provisional IRA placed bombs in two city centre pubs – the Tavern in the Town and the Mulberry Bush. Nineteen people were killed and 182 wounded.

Although Rees has been criticised over the failure of Power Sharing he did bring an end to internment. By 1976 the prisons contained convicted criminals, many tried by **Diplock Courts**. The Labour Government also introduced the Prevention of Terrorism Act in November 1974 following the **Birmingham Pub Bombings** by the Provisional IRA. This Act gave the British police powers of arrest and detention for anyone they suspected of terrorist offences. It also allowed the government to prevent people in Northern Ireland travelling to the mainland if they were suspected of being a security threat.

When Rees was succeeded by Roy Mason as Secretary of State in 1976, Mason abandoned attempts to find political agreement. Instead he concentrated on making Direct Rule work by attempting to reduce the level of political violence. He gave greater responsibility to the RUC for security, and used the SAS for counter-insurgency operations against the Provisional IRA.

Unfortunately, the success of Mason's policy forced the Provisional IRA to reorganise itself into cells, a structure which was impossible for the

Deaths due to political violence and terrorism in Northern Ireland

1969–1998

1969	13	1977	112	1985	54	1993	90
1970	25	1978	81	1986	61	1994	68
1971	174	1979	113	1987	93	1995	9
1972	467	1980	76	1988	93	1996	21
1973	250	1981	101	1989	62	1997	23
1974	216	1982	97	1990	76	1998	30
1975	247	1983	77	1991	94		
1976	297	1984	64	1992	84		

Deaths due to terrorism associated with Northern Ireland but occurring in the Republic of Ireland, Britain and Europe

1970–1992

1970	3	1977	4	1984	6	1991	3
1971	3	1978	1	1985	4	1992	6
1972	11	1979	9	1986	0		
1973	8	1980	6	1987	6		
1974	2	1981	4	1988	9		
1975	17	1982	13	1989	16		
1976	6	1983	10	1990	6		

British Army to break. A secret government report, the Glover Report, in 1968, declared that the Provisional IRA could not be defeated militarily. In his book *Final Term, the Labour Government 1974–1976* (1979) Harold Wilson declared that Labour policy seemed negative and almost defeatist in character. He declared that the political solution to Northern Ireland's problems lay within Northern Ireland. However, after Margaret Thatcher's victory in the 1979 general election British policy took a more dynamic turn.

How far did British policy change under Margaret Thatcher between 1979 and 1985?

Political violence associated with Northern Ireland reached a new intensity in 1979. Airey Neave, the Conservative Shadow spokesman on Northern Ireland, was murdered by the INLA in the House of Commons car park. In the Republic of Ireland INLA murdered Lord Mountbatten, a close relation of the Queen. At Warrenpoint, County Down, close to the border with the Republic 18 members of the Parachute Regiment were blown up by a large bomb detonated by the Provisional IRA.

However, the main problem facing the Thatcher government during its first term was the Hunger Strike by Republican prisoners in 1981. They were demanding the status of political prisoners. This crisis came to a head when a hunger-striker, Bobby Sands, was elected as MP for Fermanagh and South Tyrone. Sands' subsequent death from starvation, and the deaths of nine other hunger strikers, led to a major rise in support for the political wing of the Provisional IRA, Sinn Fein. It also gained considerable international publicity, particularly with the Irish-American community.

Throughout the period 1979 to 1985 the Conservatives tried a number of political initiatives to break the political deadlock. The Secretary of State in 1982, James Prior, tried 'rolling devolution'. This meant political power would be handed back to Northern Ireland gradually if political violence subsided. More significant were the continued links between the British and Irish governments. These discussions, however, were affected

Garret Fitzgerald (1926–)
Fitzgerald was born in Dublin and educated at University College, Dublin where he was a lecturer in Political Economy from 1959–73. He was leader of Fine Gael 1977–87, and Taoiseach June 1981 – March 1982 and again December 1982 – March 1987. He signed the Anglo-Irish Agreement of 1985.

Why was the Anglo-Irish Agreement of 1985 significant in the development of British-Irish relations?

Margaret Thatcher and Garret Fitzgerald, the architects of the Anglo-Irish Agreement of 1985 by political changes in the Republic of Ireland. When the Fine Gael Taoiseach, Garret Fitzgerald, was in power relations were cordial. When Fianna Fail Taoiseach, Charles Haughey, held power relations were more difficult. These difficulties were made worse during the Falklands Conflict of 1982, when Haughey failed to support Britain. However, by 1985 a new departure in British policy occurred with the Anglo-Irish (Hillsborough) Agreement. It was jointly signed by Margaret Thatcher and Garret Fitzgerald.

To what extent was the Anglo-Irish Agreement of 1985 a turning point in British Irish relations?

The agreement established an Inter-Governmental Conference between the British and Irish governments. This would contain representatives from both governments. It would discuss Northern Ireland and the relations between Northern Ireland and the Republic of Ireland. Matters to be discussed involved cross-border security arrangements and justice. The latter involved the issue of extradition, the returning of terrorist suspects either to Britain or the Republic by the other state to face trial.

This was a major new departure. It formally involved the Republic of Ireland in the affairs of Northern Ireland for the first time. However, the Agreement also recognised that no change in the political status of Northern Ireland would occur without the consent of the majority. This meant that, for the first time, the Republic of Ireland officially recognised the existence of Northern Ireland. This went against Articles 2 and 3 of the Eire Constitution of 1937.

From the British point of view this agreement was driven by increasing concerns about the growth in support for Sinn Fein. By 1985 the Republican movement had altered its strategy. It now followed a policy of 'the armalite and the ballot box'. This involved continuing the 'armed struggle' against the British but at the same time seeking election to local government and the Westminster parliament. The Anglo-Irish Agreement, by adding an 'Irish dimension', was a political strategy to stunt the growth of Sinn Fein's political power.

According to Paul Norris in 'Northern Ireland, the Long Road to Peace', published in *Talking Politics* (1998): 'The Anglo-Irish Agreement was a watershed in that it established the Irish government as a legitimate player in the internal affairs of Northern Ireland. The agreement sparked a sustained expression of a sense of absolute betrayal in the unionist community and among its political leaders. The agreement was a political boost for the SDLP who were seen to have top level access to British ministers at a time when Sinn Fein had entered politics and were capturing up to 40% of the nationalist vote.'

1. What reasons can you give to explain why British policy changed towards Northern Ireland between 1969 and 1985?

2. What do you regard as the main obstacles to finding a political settlement in Northern Ireland between 1969 and 1985?

3. Who was more effective in dealing with the problems of Northern Ireland between 1969 and 1985: the Labour governments or the Conservative governments? Give reasons for your answer.

11.5 Why was it so difficult to find a political solution in Northern Ireland between 1985 and 2000?

Although the Anglo-Irish Agreement was a major new departure in Northern Ireland affairs, obstacles to peace still remained.

- **The continuation of political violence.** In 1987 the SAS virtually wiped out the East Tyrone Active Service Unit of the Provisional IRA at Loughgall. In November 1987 the Provisional IRA exploded a bomb at the Remembrance Day service at Enniskillen killing 11 and injuring 63. On 22 September 1989, 11 British servicemen (musicians) were killed by a the Provisional IRA bomb in Kent, England.

- **The continued political success of Sinn Fein.** The Agreement failed to stem the advance of Sinn Fein. They continued to win about 40% of the nationalist vote. They also ended their boycott of elections in the Republic of Ireland in 1986.

- **The Unionists were politically divided.** Since the 1960s the once-united Unionist community had split into many factions. The largest group was the Official Unionist Party. However, Ian Paisley's Democratic Unionist Party usually represented three Westminster constituencies. Ian Paisley also topped the poll in last three European Union elections. Other Unionist groups have appeared over the past 30 years. The UK Unionist Party held the North Down constituency in the 1997 general election. Both the DUP and the UK Unionists have been completely opposed to links with the Republic of Ireland.

- **The existence of paramilitary groups on both sides.** The commitment of paramilitary groups to violence created a wider gap between two communities. Any attempt by democratic politicians to exclude them from a political agreement meant that it would be difficult to find a lasting peace.

- **Limited support for a lasting peace involving both communities.** Between 1976 and 1977 there was a brief but popular attempt to try to bring the two communities in Northern Ireland in a bid to create a climate for peace. It followed the deaths of three children after the Provisional IRA bank raid in August 1976. Under the cross-community leadership of Mairead Corrigan and Betty Williams, a women's movement both North and South of the border led a campaign for peace. The 'Peace People' gained international publicity and the two leaders won the Nobel Peace Prize but their movement produced nothing tangible.

What changes were made by the Downing Street Declaration of 1993?

A major move towards peace came on 15 December 1993 with a joint statement by the British and Irish governments. It declared that Britain had no selfish strategic or economic interest in Northern Ireland. It stated that a political settlement should be based on 'the right of the people on both parts of the island to exercise the right of self-determination on the basis of consent north and south to bring about a united Ireland, if that is their will'.

The declaration occurred for a number of reasons.

- Firstly, as in 1976, there was public indignation about political violence in Britain and Ireland. On 20 March 1993 two boys had been killed by a Provisional IRA bomb in Warrington, England. It was followed by bombing in both Britain and Northern Ireland.

- Secondly, the United States government was putting pressure on the British government to find a solution. The Clinton administration was sympathetic to Irish nationalist opinion in the United States. The president appointed a pro-nationalist ambassador to the Republic in 1993, Jean Kennedy-Smith. Congress had already accepted the '**MacBride Principles**' in the mid-1980s concerning trade with Northern Irish companies.

- Thirdly, Albert Reynolds had become Taoiseach in February 1991. His diplomatic skill was important in persuading the Major government to made a political statement.

MacBride Principles: Passed by Congress in 1984. This was an attempt to end religious discrimination in Northern Ireland. US government firms could only agree contracts with Northern Ireland firms if the latter was proved not to discriminate against Catholics.

● Finally, John Hume, leader of the SDLP, had several secret talks with Gerry Adams, leader of Sinn Fein. The aim was to bring Sinn Fein into the peace making process.

Following the Downing Street Declaration, the Provisional IRA declared a ceasefire on 31 August 1994, claiming that 'an opportunity to secure a just and lasting settlement had been created'.

Why did the Downing Street Declaration fail to bring an all-round peace agreement?

In 1995 and 1996 progress towards a peace agreement seemed possible. The Twin Track Initiative by the British and Irish governments on 28 November 1995 attempted a bridge-building exercise between the two communities. It established an International Commission led by ex-US Senator George Mitchell to investigate the issue of decommissioning paramilitary weapons.

The Downing Street Declaration failed to produce an all-round peace agreement in advance of the 1997 general election. The major obstacle to peace was the decommissioning of paramilitary weapons. The Conservative government was heavily dependent on Ulster Unionist support to stay in power and the Ulster Unionists demanded decommissioning before Sinn Fein should be allowed into talks.

This impasse led to the end of the Provisional IRA ceasefire with the Canary Wharf bombing of 9 February 1996. Even though elections took place for a Northern Ireland Forum to discuss peace on 30 May 1996, any genuine attempt at a peace settlement was still-born until after the election.

Will the 'Good Friday Agreement' of 10 April 1998 bring lasting peace?

Following Blair's landslide victory in the 1997 general election the Provisional IRA announced a new ceasefire on 20 July 1997. Under the guidance of a new Secretary of State, Mo Mowlam, all sides in the Northern Ireland conflict were invited into a peace process. This included Sinn Fein and representatives of the Loyalist paramilitaries. The DUP and the UK Unionists boycotted the talks.

The Good Friday Agreement proposed change in the constitutions of Britain and the Republic of Ireland to include the principle of consent for the place of Northern Ireland within the United Kingdom. It also recognised the identity and aspirations of the Nationalist minority.

The Agreement created a Northern Ireland Assembly, a Power-Sharing Executive and a Council of Ireland between North and South. In many ways it seemed to be similar to the Sunningdale Agreement of 1973. However, this time the agreement included representatives from the paramilitaries. Sinn Fein, the Ulster Democratic Party and the Ulster Progressive Party signed up to the agreement. In return paramilitary prisoners were to be released. The Agreement was also backed by a Referendum in Northern Ireland and the Republic which supported the agreement. It was also supported by the Clinton administration in the United States. However, a number of obstacles remain:

● There is opposition from within the Unionist community. Both the DUP and the UK Unionist Party oppose the Agreement. Even within the Ulster Unionist Party, David Trimble the leader has faced criticism mainly from Jeffrey Donaldson MP.

● The Agreement and the Provisional IRA ceasefire resulted in a further split in the IRA. The Real IRA was formed in November 1997. On

15 August 1998, the worst atrocity since 1969 occurred in Omagh, County Tyrone when a car bomb planted by the Real IRA killed 29 people and wounded a further 200. Even though the Real IRA declared a ceasefire on 8 September 1998 there is still the possibility of breakaway groups within the IRA returning to political violence.

● Punishment beatings and murders continue in Republican and Loyalist areas. These have been so frequent that in August 1999 Mo Mowlam investigated the possibility that the Provisional IRA had broken its ceasefire.

● One of the last acts of the Major government was to establish a Parades Commission in January 1997. This organisation has had to deal with the issue of parades, usually Orange parades. Flashpoints since the Agreement have been Drumcree Church, Portadown, the Lower Ormeau Road, Belfast and Derry City. The banning or re-routing of Parades has caused considerable resentment in the Unionist community.

● The issue of paramilitary decommission has proved to be a major problem. As part of the Mitchell Review of the Good Friday Agreement, in December 1999, the IRA has appointed a go-between to discuss decommissioning with Canadian General de Chastelan.

● Linked with the decommissioning issue was the resentment felt by some members of the Northern Ireland Community about the early release of paramilitary prisoners. Many of them had been convicted of multiple murders.

By the end of December 1999 the prospect of permanent peace seemed possible. Former US Senator George Mitchell's review of the Good Friday Agreement had led to the creation of a Northern Ireland Executive containing members of Sinn Fein. Martin McGuiness of Sinn Fein became Minister of Education. However, although two DUP members are part of the new Executive they have stated that they will not attend meetings with Sinn Fein ministers present. In addition, the government of the Republic of Ireland agreed to change articles 2 and 3 of the 1937 Irish Constitution, which laid claim to Northern Ireland. Finally, the 'Council of the Isles' containing representatives of the British and Irish governments and representatives from the devolved governments of Scotland, Wales and Northern Ireland also met for the first time. For his efforts in trying to achieve permanent peace in Northern Ireland, George Mitchell was nominated for the Nobel Peace Prize.

1. What have been the major obstacles to finding a permanent peace in Northern Ireland since 1985?

2. To what extent is the Good Friday Agreement of 1998 different from the Sunningdale Agreement of 1973?

3. Answer using information from the whole of this chapter:

'Why has the Irish problem been such a difficult problem for British government to deal with from 1914 to 2000?'

Source-based questions: The Peace Process, 1992

SOURCE A

The problem we have to resolve in relation to Northern Ireland is the notoriously difficult one of two sets of conflicting rights. There is no argument for the self-determination of the unionist community that cannot be applied, with at least equal force, to the nationalist community in Northern Ireland. That community sees itself locked into a political entity it bitterly opposed. Its aspirations to independence were denied. It was cut off from the rest of Ireland and consigned to minority status which repeated itself at every level of politics and society. The symbols of the state, like the working of majority rule, might be neutral in Great Britain. They were, and are, both far from neutral in Northern Ireland.

From the opening statement by the Representative of the Republic of Ireland at the British-Irish Round Table talks, 6 July 1992.

SOURCE B

As to British constitutional arrangements 'Her Majesty's Government reaffirms their position that Northern Ireland's present status as part of the United Kingdom will not change without the consent of a majority of its people'.

Though perhaps not everyone will agree, I believe that the Anglo-Irish Agreement would give effect to any wish that might in future be expressed by a majority of the people of Northern Ireland for any alternative status.

As to Articles 2 and 3 of the Irish constitution, HMG fully accepts the sincerity with which the unionist delegations argue that any successful outcome from the talks process must include the repeal or amendment of those Articles.

From a statement by the Secretary of State for Northern Ireland, Sir Patrick Mayhew, on British-Irish Talks, 18 September 1992.

SOURCE C

British propaganda now claims that while 'preferring' to keep the Six County Statelet within the 'United Kingdom' it has no selfish strategic or economic reason for doing so. British preference in relation to matters internal to Ireland holds no validity against the preference of the clear majority of the Irish people for national independence as expressed for generations.

Moreover, there are multiple democratic and practical reasons why partition should go:

It defies the wishes of the Irish people as a whole.

It rejects the wishes of the population in Britain as expressed in opinion poll after opinion poll.

It flouts international law.

It is undemocratic

It is permanently abnormal and can only be maintained by extraordinary means.

It has created a generation of casualties in the Six Counties.

It cannot produce lasting peace.

From 'Towards a Lasting Peace in Ireland' a Sinn Fein publication, 1992.

SOURCE D

Commitment to the Army is total belief in the Army, in its aims and objects, in its style of warfare, in its methods of struggle, and in its political foundation.

Commitment to the Republican Movement is the firm belief that its struggle both militarily and political is morally justified, that war is morally justified and that the Army is the direct representatives of the 1918 Dail Eireann parliament, and that as such they are the legal and lawful government of the Irish Republic, which has the moral right to pass laws for the whole geographical fragment of Ireland and all its people regardless of creed or loyalty.

From 'The Green Book', the Provisional IRA Training Manual.

---

1. From information contained within this chapter explain the meaning of the following phrases underlined in the sources above.

a) 'Articles 2 and 3 of the Irish Constitution' (Source B)

b) The 'Republican Movement' (Source D)

2. Study Sources C and D and use information in this chapter.

How far do the points raised in these Sources reflect the view of Irish nationalists?

3. Study the Sources above and use information contained in this chapter. 'The failure to produce a lasting settlement to British-Irish relations since 1914 was the creation and maintenance of Northern Ireland within the United Kingdom.'

Assess the validity of this statement.

12 The Labour Party, 1945–2000

Key Issues

- *How successful were the post-war Labour Governments?*

- *What problems did the Labour Party experience while in opposition?*

- *What has been the influence of the left of the party on policy-making?*

Framework of Events

1940	Labour enters wartime coalition with Clement Attlee as Deputy Leader
1945	Labour wins general election: Clement Attlee becomes Prime Minister
	Economic loan negotiated with the Americans
1947	Nationalisation of coal mines
	Grant of independence to India and Pakistan
1948	Nationalisation of railways
	Foundation of National Health Service
1949	Devaluation of the pound
1950	General election: Labour returned with a small majority
1951	Festival of Britain
	General election: Conservatives win under Winston Churchill
1955	General election: Conservatives increase majority under Anthony Eden
	Hugh Gaitskell becomes leader of the Labour Party following Attlee
1956	Publication of Anthony Crosland's *The Future of Socialism* arguing for a revision of policy and attitudes within the Labour Party
	Suez Crisis
1959	General election: Conservatives increase majority under Macmillan
1960	Labour Party adopts a policy opposing British possession of nuclear weapons
1961	Hugh Gaitskell fails in his attempt to revise Clause 4 of the party's constitution defining aims and objectives
1963	Hugh Gaitskell dies, replaced by Harold Wilson as leader
	Wilson's speech to party conference on 'the white heat of technology'
1964	General election: Labour win with small majority
1965	Rhodesia unilaterally declares independence
1966	General election: Labour returned with large majority
	Emergency budget: government spending cut to preserve pound
1967	Pound devalued. Abortion legalised
1968	Commonwealth Immigration Act restricts immigration to Britain
	Attempt to reform House of Lords abandoned in view of opposition within House of Commons
1969	White Paper 'In Place of Strife' tries to modernise industrial relations practises. Opposed by trade unions and backbench MPs
1970	Equal Pay Act establishes the right of equal pay for women workers
	General election: Conservatives win under Edward Heath

1972	Minority of Labour MPs support Heath to get bill allowing Britain to join the European Economic Community through Parliament
1973	Publication of 'Labour's Programme 1973' disowned by party leadership
	Miners' strike. Oil crisis
1974	February: Labour forms minority government after general election
	October: Labour wins general election with small minority
1975	Referendum on Britain's membership of European Economic Community overwhelmingly endorses membership
1976	Harold Wilson resigns as leader, replaced by James Callaghan
	Government applies for loan from International Monetary Fund (IMF) to help solve economic crisis
	Government spending cut in order to meet IMF loan conditions
1978–9	'Winter of discontent' as public sector workers strike for more money
1979	General election: Conservatives under Margaret Thatcher win
1980	James Callaghan resigns as leader, replaced by Michael Foot
1981	Denis Healey narrowly beats Tony Benn in contest for deputy leadership
	Departure of 25 MPs under Roy Jenkins and David Owen to form Social Democratic Party
1983	General election: Conservatives increase majority under Margaret Thatcher – worst result for Labour since 1935
	Michael Foot resigns as leader, replaced by Neil Kinnock
1985	Neil Kinnock attacks influence of Militant Tendency within party in speech at Labour Party Conference
1986	Peter Mandelson appointed as Director of Communications
1987	General election: Conservatives returned with slightly reduced majority under Margaret Thatcher
1988–9	Policy review fundamentally modernises Party policies
1992	General election: Conservatives win under John Major, but with a much reduced majority
	Neil Kinnock resigns as leader, replaced by John Smith
1994	John Smith dies suddenly, replaced as leader by Tony Blair
1995	Party membership overwhelmingly approve a new set of Party values and objectives to replace the old Clause 4 of the Party Constitution.
1997	General election: Labour wins with large majority

Overview

Post-war consensus:
Many contemporary commentators have argued that between the late 1940s and mid 1970s the main political parties shared common beliefs and policies in the field of economic, social and foreign policies. Historians are now beginning to question whether this was so. (See the case study in historical interpretation, chapter 13, section 8.)

Few observers looking at the result of the 1945 general election, in which Labour had a massive parliamentary majority, would have guessed that in the following 55 years, Labour would be in power for only 20 of them. Indeed the post-war record of the Party has been exceptionally patchy.

Nobody would deny the achievements of Attlee's administration between 1945 and 1951 that radically changed society, with nationalised industries and the National Health Service, and a start made in repairing the neglect of centuries in housing and education. Abroad Labour began the disengagement from Empire and established Britain very firmly as a key member of the Atlantic alliance during the Cold War.

Perhaps the greatest achievement was the creation of a **post-war consensus** that lasted 30 years, in which Labour and Conservative parties alike were committed to Keynesian economic policies of high public spending in order to keep unemployment under control. This led to a period of prosperity the like of which had never been experienced before – even if neither party were able to reverse Britain's decline as an economic, political or military world power.

Yet the achievements of the Wilson and Callaghan administrations of the

1960s and 1970s are much less certain. Improvements were certainly made to the lives of the poorest in society, but for all that there is a feeling that they could have done much more. The 1964–70 government particularly promised much and delivered little. A decade later the Wilson and Callaghan administrations between 1974 and 1979 were constrained by a precarious parliamentary majority. The decisions made at the time of the International Monetary Fund (IMF) Loan crisis in 1976 were a precursor to the policies of Margaret Thatcher and her successors, including Tony Blair.

The internal history of the Labour Party has not been a happy one. For much of the period under discussion the Party was split to varying degrees between left and right. In the 1950s the split was mainly (but not exclusively) between MPs in the **Parliamentary Labour Party**. Even though the election in 1963 of Harold Wilson, perceived as being on the left of the Party, brought about a truce between the two factions, their rivalry continued throughout the 1964–70 government and to a lesser extent between 1974–79. A much greater threat, indeed one which nearly destroyed the Labour Party, came with the rise of unrest among ordinary members in the 1960s and 1970s. MPs were less involved, although the leader of movement, Tony Benn, was a prominent and important cabinet minister. The Party nearly tore itself apart during a period of self-inflicted infighting between 1980 and 1983. It took the 1983 election result, the worst for 50 years, to persuade people at all levels within Labour that things had to change. Even so it took nearly a decade and a half, and an almost total revision of everything the Party ever stood for, for Labour to become re-electable.

The fate of Labour governments has also depended on co-operation with all parts of the labour movement, particularly trade unions. The embarrassing climb down by Harold Wilson and Barbara Castle over mild plans to reform trade unions damaged the standing of the government with the electorate. In 1979 the government's inability to control union militancy during the 'Winter of Discontent' directly led to the election of the Conservatives.

Of course in 2000 the jury is still out on the Blair administration, although there are signs that he has learnt many of the lessons from previous administrations. The Labour Party that he leads is very different to the Party at any time in the past. Although there is grumbling at the slow pace of change, the Party is both disciplined and united behind the government. Two of the problems that plagued previous leaders have largely disappeared: the left hardly exists any more and relations with the trade unions are distant. Whether New Labour has finally discovered the magic formula for perpetual Labour government remains to be seen.

Parliamentary Labour Party (PLP): Organisation of Labour MPs and representatives of Labour peers. Until 1982 alone elected leader and deputy leader of the Party. Elects members of shadow cabinet, but not cabinet ministers who are appointed by the Prime Minister.

Anthony Wedgwood Benn 'Tony Benn' (1925–)
A peer, Benn succeeded in renouncing his peerage in 1963 to sit in the Commons. He held the post of Minister of Technology 1966–70, Minister of Trade and Industry 1974–75, and Minister of Energy 1974–79. He contested Deputy Leadership in 1981 and 1988.

12.1 'Quite a day' – Labour and the election of 1945

The election of the Labour Government in 1945 was probably the greatest British political upset of the 20th century. Politicians of all parties and the press were united in their belief that the British people would reward Winston Churchill for his leadership during the recent war with a renewed mandate to prepare the country for the post-war world. Opinion polls, however, which politicians had yet to learn to rely on, had long told a different story.

Labour's victory was convincing. It had a majority of 146 seats over all other parties. For the first time it broke out of its industrial heartlands of the north to win seats in southern England; such as High Wycombe and

Winchester, as well as suburban areas such as respectable Wimbledon. The party even won a few rural seats, mainly in Norfolk.

On the knocker: Going house to house finding out how residents would be voting at the election.

For party members the victory was an event they would always remember. Fifty years on, in 1995, Donald Matheson in Liverpool recalled: 'We went **on the knocker** and we leafleted and whatnot. We didn't expect to win. Everybody quoted Wordsworth "Bliss was it in that dawn to be alive". It was like that. It really was. We really thought "Everything is going to be all right now".' (*Generating Socialism*, 1995) Even the normally cautious Attlee, the new Prime Minister, noted in his diary that election day 'had been quite an exciting day'.

The Labour victory was even more impressive considering the Party's dismal electoral performance since its foundation as the Labour Representation Committee in February 1900. The number of Labour MPs had risen to 154 in the 1935 general election – the last before the outbreak of war – but even so they were considerably outnumbered by the Conservatives and their allies in the National Government.

The 1930s saw a revision of Labour's aims culminating in *Labour's Immediate Programme* published in 1937. Many of the points in the Programme would find their way into the manifesto put to the country in 1945, such as the nationalisation of the Bank of England and the coal mines. Labour's leaders were also able to capitalise on the growing interest in left-wing politics, as well as concern over the appeasement policies of the Conservatives under Neville Chamberlain. In the years before the outbreak of war in 1939 the party campaigned hard against the appeasement of Nazi Germany. As a result the party attracted an increasing number of intellectuals and academics. Hugh Gaitskell, Anthony Crosland and Douglas Jay became members in the 1930s. Barbara Castle and Harold Wilson, among many others, joined during the War. They helped to ensure that for the first time the party had carefully thought-out proposals.

Herbert Morrison (1888–1965)
Morrison joined the wartime coalition as Home Secretary 1940–45. He served in the postwar Labour government as Deputy Prime Minister and Lord President 1945–51, and Foreign Secretary during 1951. He was Deputy Leader of the Labour Party 1951–55.

In the difficult days of May 1940, Labour entered the new Coalition government led by Winston Churchill. The price for their entry was full partnership in running the war. Many of the Labour's leaders became ministers: Clement Attlee became Deputy Prime Minister, Ernest Bevin Minister of Labour, and Herbert Morrison Home Secretary. Labour ministers tended to be responsible for domestic matters, as Churchill was uninterested in the **Home Front**. The effective way in which the ministers handled their responsibilities encouraged confidence in the belief that a Labour government would be run sensibly. Of the senior ministers in the first Labour Cabinet only Aneurin Bevan had not held government office before.

Home Front: Aspects of the Second World War that directly affected civilians.

For many, their experiences during the war transformed their political outlook. It quickly became accepted that Britain was fighting for a better post-war world, breaking the circle of poverty and unemployment that had so blighted the inter-war period. As Queen Elizabeth, wife of George VI, wrote to her mother-in-law Queen Mary during the Blitz in October 1940, 'the destruction is so awful, and the people so wonderful – they deserve a better world'.

The most influential book published during the war was the Beveridge Report, called *Social Insurance and Allied Services* (December 1942). Steve Fielding, in *From Blitz to Blair* (1997), concludes that 'this proved to be the most significant political event of the war, establishing the parameters of the debate on post-war Britain and placing party differences in stark relief'. Beveridge prefaced his report with the statement that 'a revolutionary moment in the world's history is a time for revolution not patching'. Much of the report was, however, far from revolutionary, proposing to unify pre-war social security schemes. What it did offer was a vision of a world free from what Beveridge called the 'five giants on the road to reconstruction': Want, Disease, Ignorance, Squalor and Idleness.

Aided by careful publicity the report became astonishingly influential in thinking about the post-war world. It eventually sold some 630,000 copies. Opinion polls showed that 86% of the population were in favour of the report. One worker said, 'it will make the ordinary man think that the country at last has some regard for him as he is supposed to have regard for the country'. The Conservatives, however, were distinctly cool about the proposals. Churchill himself felt that Beveridge had fostered 'a dangerous optimism' out of step with the 'hard facts of life'. The Labour Party in contrast was generally supportive, but the need to sustain the wartime coalition meant that their support was muted in public.

There were many reports and proposals published during the war years, from town and country planning to health. However, only one measure was passed, the 1944 Education Act put forward by the Conservative R.A. Butler, which raised the school leaving age to 15 and introduced secondary schooling for every child.

Mobilisation of labour:
Conscription of men and women and sending them to work where there were shortages of labour.

From the summer of 1940 the state quickly became involved in spheres of activity that would have been unthinkable a few years before. Rationing, economic controls, and the **mobilisation of labour** all became acceptable. This use of state power was very much in tune with the electorate, who had seen that life had become very much fairer, and conditions for the poorest in society improved. It became accepted that the state should play a major role in post-war reconstruction. The two main political parties had radically different views of the state, with Labour accepting that government power could be used to better the lives of the people. Douglas Jay, a senior Labour minister, wrote in 1947 that 'the gentleman in Whitehall really does know better what is good for the people than the people know themselves'.

It was clear that the electorate did not want a return to the miseries of the 1920s and 1930s. As James Callaghan, a newly-elected MP in 1945, points out, 'the pervading sentiment was no return to 1919 ... it was the memory of the ex-servicemen with no legs displaying their medals on street corners, combined with unemployment in the thirties, that made us all say we are not going back there' (*Election '45,* 1995). The election campaign itself largely resolved round the need for reconstruction. The Conservatives fought a lack-lustre campaign around Churchill urging the electorate to 'let him finish the job'.

In contrast, Labour had a very clear idea of the post-war world that it wanted to create. In an election broadcast Clement Attlee, the Party leader, argued, 'we have to plan the broad lines of our national life so that all may have the duty and the opportunity of rendering service to the nation ... and that all may help to create and share in an increasing material prosperity free from the fear of want'. Candidates stressed a better future under Labour. As Michael Foot told voters in Plymouth, 'We shall not have won the peace until every citizen in Devonport [a district of Plymouth] and every citizen of England has a good roof over his head, the chance to marry and bring up his children, safe from the fears of unemployment, sickness and worry'.

Although Labour's intentions were not as radical as commonly believed today, they were very much in tune with what voters felt needed to be done to create a new and better Britain. The title given to the manifesto said it all, 'Let us face the future'. In retirement Attlee summed up the result, 'I think the general feeling was that they [the electorate] wanted a new future. We were looking towards the future. The Tories were looking towards the past.' Kenneth O. Morgan argues, in *Labour in Power, 1945–1951* (1985), that Labour's victory can be understood in the context of the war years, backed by the new realism of Labour domestic and foreign policies in the 1930s. Labour was uniquely identified with a sweeping change of mood and with the new social agenda emerging during the war years.

1. How important do you think the Beveridge Report was in Labour's election victory in 1945?

2. Why do you think the Conservatives did so badly in this general election? Give reasons

12.2 Building Jerusalem – How successful was the Labour government of 1945?

Clement Attlee (1883–1967)
Attlee was Leader of the Labour Party, 1935–55, Deputy Prime Minister, 1940–45, and Prime Minister 1945–51.

The Attlee administration can readily be divided into two distinct periods. The vast majority of the radical initiatives, such as the nationalisation of the coal mines and the introduction of the welfare state, were implemented before late 1947. By the end of 1947 this radicalism died away, as Britain's economic circumstances worsened and the major parts of the party's policy had been implemented. It was to be replaced by a much more cautious, pragmatic approach.

This is particularly true of Attlee's second short-lived administration between February 1950 and October 1951. The small majority – only six MPs over the other parties (see table 1) – and the illness or evident tiredness of many of the senior ministers (many of whom who had been in office continuously since 1940) led to the feeling that, in Hugh Dalton's words, Labour was in office, but was 'without authority or power'.

Historians are divided on the achievements of the 1945 government. Generally, those on the left have argued that the Labour government did not move sufficiently far down the path towards socialism. Trevor Blackwell and Jeremy Seabrook in *The Politics of Hope* (1988) wrote, 'the role of Labour was twofold. First of all to provide illusions that the new beginning actually represented a radical break from the past. The will to create a new society which would articulate the hopes and desires of their own people. And secondly, and more prosaically, to provide a scaffolding of welfare services which would both support and shroud the restoration of the old structures.'

Meanwhile, many on the right believe that Attlee should have devoted scarce resources to building up industrial recovery rather than on the welfare state – as Correlli Barnett put it in *The Audit of War* (1986), 'to them [the voters] victory in the war merited a rich reward, and they meant to have it: for the high-minded a reward in the shape of an ideal society, and for the humbler in the shape of free welfare and a secure job'.

The position lies somewhere between these two extremes. Most historians would agree with Kenneth O. Morgan's conclusion in *Labour and Power* (1984) that the Attlee government was undoubtedly the most effective of Labour governments and possibly perhaps among the most effective of all British governments.

The Labour Cabinet 1945: Prime Minister Clement Attlee is sixth from the left in the front row. On his right is Ernest Bevin and on his left Herbert Morrison (grandfather of Peter Mandelson). On the left hand side of the back row is Aneurin Bevan.

Table 1 Election results 1935–97

	1935		1945		1950		1951	
	No. seats	% vote	No. seats	% vote	No. seats	% vote	No. seats	% vote
Conservative	432	54	213	40	298	44	321	48
Liberal	20	6	12	9	9	9	6	3
Labour	154	38	393	48	315	46	295	49
Others	9	2	22	3	3	1	3	1
Total	615	100	640	100	625	100	625	101

	1955		1959		1964		1966	
	No. seats	% vote	No. seats	% vote	No. seats	% vote	No. seats	% vote
Conservative	344	50	365	49	304	43	253	42
Liberal	6	3	6	6	9	11	12	9
Labour	277	46	258	44	317	44	363	48
Others	3	1	1	1	0	1	2	1
Total	630	100	630	100	630	100	630	100

	1970		1974 (Feb)	1974 (Oct)		1979		
	No. seats	% vote	No. seats	% vote	No. seats	% vote	No. seats	% vote
Conservative	330	46	297	38	277	36	339	44
Liberal	6	8	14	19	13	18	11	14
Labour	287	43	301	37	319	39	269	37
Others	7	3	23	6	26	7	16	5
Total	630	100	635	100	635	100	635	100

	1983		1987		1992		1997	
	No. seats	% vote	No. seats	% vote	No. seats	% vote	No. seats	% vote
Conservative	397	42	376	42	336	42	165	31
Liberal	23	25	22	23	20	18	46	17
Labour	209	28	229	31	271	35	419	43
Others	21	5	23	4	24	5	28	9
Total	650	100	650	100	651	100	658	100

Source: adapted from David and Gareth Butler, *British Political Facts 1900–1994*, 1994.

Ernest Bevin (1881–1951)

A manual worker, Bevin had left school at 11. He became an official of the Dockers' Union. He organised the amalgamation of 18 unions into the Transport and General Workers Union and was its General Secretary, 1921–40. Elected to Parliament for the first time in 1940 he went straight into the Cabinet as Minister of Labour. He was Foreign Secretary from 1945 until a month before his death in 1951.

Harold Wilson (1916–1995)

Wilson was President of the Board of Trade 1947–51 in Attlee's Administration. He was Leader of the Labour Party 1963–76, during which time he served two terms as Prime Minister, 1964–70 and 1974–76.

What were the pressures on the 1945 Labour government?

Governments are subject to pressures and constraints, either of their own making – for example from party members or the resignation of ministers – or due to external forces, such as economic trends or an international incident. The Labour government of 1945 suffered as much as any other.

Internal factors

Clement Attlee was lucky in that the party was generally supportive of his administration. Unlike ministers in the Wilson and Callaghan Cabinets of the 1960s and 1970s, personal relationships were generally good. There was however deep personal animosity between Ernest Bevin and Herbert Morrison. It was once suggested to Bevin that Morrison was his own worst enemy. 'Not while I'm alive, he isn't', Bevin growled.

To an extent this unity was the result of careful party management. As Kenneth O. Morgan in *Labour in Power* argues that 'the Cabinet and leadership were in control at all levels of the party hierarchy'. Complaints from local parties, particularly about Labour's defence and foreign policies and the expulsion of MPs for Communist sympathies, such as Konni Zilliacus and John Platts-Mills, were brushed aside. Indeed these protests only came from a small number of constituencies; most members remained happy with their government's policies and achievements.

Despite some grassroots complaints about wage restraint, the trade unions remained very supportive of the government. The leaders of the big three unions, Arthur Deakin (Transport and General Workers Union), Tom Williamson (General and Municipal Workers Union), and Will Lather (National Union of Mineworkers) were all firmly on the party's right and were aggressively hostile to the left and the Communists. They ensured that the Trades Union Congress (TUC) remained supportive of the government's work.

Only during 1950 and 1951 was there a hint of the divisive left-right split which would so damage the Party in years to come. This mainly centred around the massive rearmament programme proposed by the Chancellor of the Exchequer, Hugh Gaitskell, as a result of the outbreak of the Korean War in June 1950. The programme led to the introduction of prescription charges and other cuts to the welfare state, causing the resignation of three left-wing cabinet ministers Aneurin Bevan, Harold Wilson, and John Freeman in April 1951.

For all its radicalism it should be remembered that the majority of ministers were essentially conservative figures. Paul Addison in *The Road to 1945* (1975) called them 'moderate social patriots'. They had come to political maturity in the inter-war period, and their responses were conditioned by their experiences then. This helps to explain why they were relatively uninterested in constitutional reform or in regenerating British industry, yet keen to maintain Britain's position as a great world power. They preferred to address the very real evils of poverty that they and their constituents had experienced during the 1930s, rather than plan ahead for a post-war world.

In education the ministers responsible, Ellen Wilkinson and George Tomlinson, were happy to accept the arguably socially divisive **tripartite division of secondary education** and resisted demands from teachers and educationalists for comprehensives, which indeed had been party policy since 1942. Instead Wilkinson persuaded the Cabinet to raise the school leaving age to 15 in 1944 and to maintain the expensive programme of rebuilding schools and training new teachers, undoubtedly considerable achievements at a time of economic difficulty. Kenneth Morgan, however, concludes that 'it is hard to avoid the view that education was an area where the Labour Government failed to provide any new ideas or inspiration'.

Economic circumstances

If Attlee was lucky in having a united party and experienced and disciplined ministers behind him, he was much less lucky with the economic circumstances. The Second World War bankrupted Britain. Victory had been achieved at enormous economic cost. In particular, Britain had become dependent on American loans to keep fighting. Within a week of the surrender of the Japanese in September 1945, the Americans abruptly ended their financial support, thereby destroying British hopes for a lengthy transition from war to peace – and putting the implementation of the policies of the new government in jeopardy. As Lord (John Maynard) Keynes, the government's financial adviser, wrote, Britain was facing an 'economic Dunkirk'. After tough negotiations a further loan of $3.75bn for five years was secured, albeit with many uncomfortable strings attached. Despite these problems the government remained committed to its programme. Hugh Dalton, the Chancellor of the Exchequer, declared in November 1945 that Labour ministers were 'determined to advance along the road to economic and social equality.'

The next economic crisis occurred two years later with a rapidly worsening **balance of payments crisis** and the outflow of British gold reserves. Eventually the introduction of import controls and other tough measures in August 1947 improved matters. Although the crisis was dangerous in

Tripartite division of secondary education: The Education Act 1944 proposed to divide secondary education into three types of school – grammar (for academically minded children), technical (for the scientifically minded) and secondary modern (for the rest).

Hugh Dalton (1887–1962)
Dalton joined the war-time coalition as President of the Board of Trade 1942–45. Under the Labour Government he became Chancellor of the Exchequer 1945–47, and was later Minister of Town and Country Planning, 1950–51.

Balance of payments crisis: A situation when a country imports more than it can export thus causing a loss of confidence in its finances by the international markets.

the short term, it probably did most harm to the self-confidence of the government and the reputation it had built up for financial management. This reputation was to be tested again in the crisis over the devaluation of the pound sterling: in September 1949 a further 'dollar drain' from Britain forced a 30% devaluation against the dollar from $4.03 to $2.80 to the pound. (The exchange rate in August 1999 was $1.60 to the pound.) This was accompanied by much dithering by ministers. The cumulative effect of these crises was pressure on social spending such as on the National Health Service, and to give credence to the accusations of incompetence levied by the Conservative opposition. However, historians such as Kenneth O. Morgan give credit to devaluation for reinvigorating the economy as devaluation meant that British goods were increasingly competitive in a world slowly recovering from the effects of the war.

Domestic circumstances

By the late 1940s British people were becoming increasingly restive. They had endured nearly a decade of rationing, shortages, and intrusive state control. This feeling is perhaps best summed up by the **Ealing Comedy** *Passport to Pimlico* released in 1949, where a London community discovers itself to be part of Burgundy, thus enabling the residents to free themselves of rationing that 'perfectly caught the public mood'. (The message of the film was, however, that they were better off as part of Britain.)

1946 saw the rise of the British Housewives League campaigning against rationing, which at its peak claimed to have 100,000 members. Although it received much attention in the newspapers the League had little effect on ministers. Indeed the League soon became discredited in the public eye because of suspected links to the Conservative Party.

Knowing the economic knife-edge on which Britain teetered the government reacted cautiously to the new mood. The new President of the Board of Trade, Harold Wilson, announced 'a bonfire of controls' in November 1948 to a broad welcome. During 1949 and 1950 rationing was gradually relaxed. Bread rationing, which had been introduced in May 1946 at the worst time in Britain's economic fortunes, was ended in July 1948. Rationing of clothes finished in March 1949, and a month later saw the freedom to buy sweets and chocolate.

The government also encouraged the **Festival of Britain**, which was held on London's South Bank in 1951 to show how the nation had

Ealing Comedies: A series of films made at the Ealing Studios between 1948 and 1952. The best known films were *Kind Hearts and Coronets* and *The Man in the White Suit*.

Festival of Britain: Like the Great Exhibition of 1851, the centenary of which it marked, aimed to show the world British technological and artistic skills.

In what ways was the Festival of Britain similar to the Millennium Dome of 2000?

The Festival of Britain, 1951, on the South Bank of the Thames recovered from the war and was ready to face the challenges of the future. Herbert Morrison sold the idea to the Cabinet by saying 'we ought to do something jolly … we need something to give Britain a lift'. Although ridiculed by the press and the Conservatives it proved immensely popular with the public and had major impact on many fields, especially design, for nearly two decades.

What were the achievements of the Attlee administration?

Despite at times desperate economic circumstances the achievements of the 1945 government are astounding. Apart from the many new initiatives, some of which are discussed below, it should not be forgotten that the government was faced with a shattered economy and in many places a physically shattered environment as well. During the war 750,000 houses were destroyed or damaged as well as hundreds of schools and hospitals. Yet the government set about with a will to repair this damage and to build new homes and schools of a quality better than anything seen before the war. It also successfully achieved the demobilisation of the armed forces and the reintegration of ex-servicemen into the economy. Indeed, the demand for labour was so great that the period saw the first arrivals of migrants from the West Indies to fill vacancies, with the arrival of the *Empire Windrush* from Jamaica in May 1948.

The welfare state

The greatest achievement of Attlee's government was undoubtedly the National Health Service, which offered free health care. Before July 1948, health care had to be paid for by individuals, private insurance or charities. About half the male workforce were entitled to free treatment through various insurance schemes, although their wives and dependents did not qualify. Many families had no such insurance and in times of illness had to rely for support on friends and neighbours or local charities. Hospitals also varied tremendously. There were few modern hospitals. Most had begun as either Victorian workhouse infirmaries – totally unsuited for the sick – or charity hospitals, which increasingly were unable to meet needs. It was generally agreed, both before and during the war, that health provision was unsatisfactory.

> **Aneurin Bevan (1897–1960)**
> A miner's son, Bevan was Minister of Health, 1945–51, Minister of Labour 1951. In 1959 he became Deputy Leader of Labour Party and held the post until 1960. He and his wife, Jenny Lee, (also an MP) were considered by some to be the socialist soul of Labour.

Clement Attlee chose Aneurin Bevan, a leading left-wing rebel who had spent the war years on the backbenches, to be Minister of Health with responsibility for establishing the new health service. Bevan became an exceptional minister, combining considerable charm with a steely determination to succeed. His first act was to take local and charity hospitals into public ownership. This seemed a natural development, because by the end of the war, some 90% of their finance came from the state. Bevan's problems, however, began when he began to establish the new National Health Service. He faced increasing opposition from the British Medical Association, representing doctors who feared that their livelihoods would be threatened by the new system. One doctor wrote in 1946 that 'I have examined the bill and it looks to me uncommonly like the first step, and a big one, towards National Socialism as practised in Germany'. As the start of the new Service approached, the doctors intensified their opposition. Eventually their fears were eased when Bevan agreed that doctors could remain outside the salaried structure of the rest of the Health Service. For the first time everybody was now entitled to free health care.

The new service was rapidly overwhelmed by the demand. The extent of health problems among the population had not been realised. It would soon have very serious consequences because the NHS budget rose from the £134 million predicted for its establishment in 1948 to £228 million in 1949, and £356 million in 1950. With increasing total NHS costs, and other demands on the national budget (such as rearmament) the principle of a free service was breached in 1949 with the introduction of a charge of one shilling (5p) per prescription. Bevan resigned from the Cabinet in 1951 over the principle of cuts to the service he had created, although by then he was no longer Minister of Health. For all the changes since 1948 it remains his memorial because as Kenneth O. Morgan says, it is the finest of monuments to his talents and his beliefs (*Labour in Power*, 1984).

Related to the National Health Service was the establishment of the welfare state to provide support to those who needed it. The minister, James Griffiths, simplified existing provisions, abolished the hated 'means testing' whereby people seeking assistance had to prove their eligibility, and introduced family allowances paying allowances for children to their mothers. The key principle of assistance for people of working age was its universality; as Griffiths later said 'it was to be all in: women from sixteen to sixty and men to sixty-five'. Pensions and allowances were also increased, in some cases for the first time in many years. In 1946 the old age pension for a single person rose to 26s (£1.30) a week, the first increase since 1920 when it had been fixed at 10s (50p).

Housing

Bevan was also responsible for housing policy. It came first among concerns of the British electorate, many of whom could remember the promise made by Lloyd George, the Prime Minister at the end of the First World War, of 'Homes fit for Heroes', which was broken in the inter-war years. This concern was not surprising because not only had some many hundreds of thousands of houses either been destroyed or damaged during the war, but many millions of people lived in slum dwellings without even basic amenities. A White Paper published in March 1945 estimated that 750,000 new houses would be needed after the war 'to afford a separate dwelling for every family desirous of having one'. During the campaign Ernest Bevin promised 'five million homes in quick time.'

To meet Bevin's target would have required a supply and organisational miracle. Even the White Paper's estimate turned out to be beyond the reach of Attlee's administration. Raw materials were in short supply. The problem was compounded by a bureaucratic nightmare. *Picture Post* magazine in 1946 estimated that it took ten ministries in Whitehall to approve any new building project from the Ministry of Health to the Board of Trade and Ministry of Works.

Two short-term solutions were adopted to cure the housing shortage. The first was the provision of pre-fabricated houses (prefabs). By the end of 1948 nearly 125,000 had been produced largely by aircraft factories as the demand for their usual output eased. The second was squatting. Incited and encouraged by the Communists, the homeless occupied many empty properties, especially army bases. By October 1946 it was estimated that nearly 50,000 people were occupying over a thousand military properties. The authorities generally turned a blind eye, glad to have some kind of safety valve that eased the pressure on housing stock.

New council houses were slowly being built: 55,400 in 1946 rising to 217,000 in 1948. Thereafter there was a slow decline as the economic crisis further affected the provision of raw materials. Even so a million houses were built by 1951, of which four out of five were built by the state. Building private housing almost stopped as priority for scarce resources was given to council houses. Bevan insisted on good quality, well-designed houses, arguing that 'we shall be judged for a year or two by the number of houses we build. We shall be judged in ten years time by the type of house we build'. He increased the space allocated to each family from 750 square feet to 900, with lavatories upstairs as well as down.

Nationalisation

Some 20% of British industry, much of it suffering from years of neglect and under-investment, was nationalised (see table 2). Nationalisation of the coal mines had long been a central plank of Labour's programme as the result of pressure from the mining unions, although resolutions in favour of the takeover of other industries by the state was passed at the 1944 party conference despite opposition from the leadership.

Nationalisation: The taking over and subsequent control of an industry by the state.

Nationalisation, however, has long been proclaimed as being one of the key successes of the Attlee government. Kenneth Morgan in *Labour in Power* argues that nationalisation was essential to sustain the morale and impetus of the 1945 Labour government. To members of the party and the movement nationalisation was the government's ultimate justification. It was a defining moment of the administration when on 1 January 1947, signs appeared outside the mines declaring, 'This colliery is now managed by the National Coal Board on behalf of the people'. In many industries – coal, electricity, gas and the railways – it made sense to establish a national monopoly rather than the patchwork of municipal and private companies that had existed before the war. Some industries, particularly coal and the railways, had suffered decades of poor management and bad labour relations. Only the nationalisation of the iron and steel industry provoked much opposition.

Yet looking at the subsequent history of these industries it is easy to query the reasons behind nationalisation. The government was often uncertain about what the nationalised industries should do, except to act as non-profit-making utilities. It was hoped that nationalisation would encourage efficiency and investment as well as improve working conditions. Critics, such as Correlli Barnett in *The Lost Victory* (1995), have claimed that 'nationalisation turned out in all respects to be not so much a revolution as a prolonging of the *ancien regime* by bureaucratic means'.

In certain cases, particularly with the mines and railway, nationalisation was probably the only solution to the otherwise certain collapse of these industries. The record of the nationalised industries proved to be patchy, but most turned out to be competently if conservatively run.

Table 2 Nationalisation measures 1945–1951

Industry	2nd reading of bill	Vesting day	Numbers employed
Bank of England	29 October 1945	1 March 1946	6,700
Coal	29 January 1946	1 January 1947	765,000
Civil aviation	6 May 1946	1 August 1946	23,300
Cable and Wireless (telecommunications)	21 May 1945	1 January 1947	9,500
Transport (railways, canals, road haulage)	16 December 1946	1 January 1948	888,000
Electricity	3 February 1947	1 April 1948	176,000
Gas	10 February 1948	1 April 1949	143,500
Iron and steel	15 November 1948	15 February 1951	292,000

Source: Kevin Jeffrey, *The Attlee Government*, 1992.

What were the failures of the 1945 Labour government?

Certainly the 1945 'revolution' was curiously patchy, reflecting the interests of the Cabinet and to a lesser degree the wider party. In nationalising the mines, railways and other industries, the government was generally content to leave the existing managers in charge, and resisted attempts to appoint representatives of the workforce to their boards. Attempts to plan the economy were less than successful, and this from a party that had proclaimed the benefits of planning before the outbreak of the Second World War. This anomaly may be due in part to the fact that very little work had been done on the practicalities of actually implementing these measures. Planning was virtually still-born, as ministers and their advisers adopted a voluntary approach towards industry, which had been commonplace during the war, encouraging rather than directing effort.

In foreign and defence policy the Attlee administration was also very conservative. In this they received considerable criticism from the Labour Party and backbench MPs. Attlee and his ministers had grown up at a time when the British Empire was at its height. One of his colleagues described Ernest Bevin, the Foreign Secretary, as a man who 'at heart was an old-fashioned imperialist keener to expand than contract the Empire'. The departure from the Indian sub-continent, although often portrayed as a great triumph, actually came about as ministers realised that British forces could no longer control mounting communal strife, which indeed occurred with great ferocity in the months after the granting of independence to India and Pakistan in August 1947.

Closer to home the need to remain a great power distorted economic recovery. This desire persuaded the government in 1946 to build the atomic bomb. At the Cabinet meeting that decided to proceed with the development of the new weapon, Bevin exclaimed, 'we've got to have this thing over here, what ever it costs … We've got to have a bloody Union Jack flying on the top of it.' The financial crisis of 1947, caused largely by a drain on Britain's financial reserves, was in part due to the burden of a world role that in the view of many observers 'obviously exceeded the country's economic capacity'. Four years later the ambitious rearmament programme, designed to help the United Nations in Korea, derailed Britain's economic recovery, at the very time when the Germany and Japan were successfully rebuilding theirs. According to Kenneth O. Morgan the budget of April 1951, which announced this plan, was a political and economic disaster (*Labour in Power*, 1984). The Conservatives had to scale down the rearmament programme once they took power in October 1951 for they could see the danger it was doing to the economy.

Conclusion

There is no doubt that Attlee's administration was one of the great reforming administrations of the 20th century. It succeeded despite tremendous economic problems and an increasingly fraught international situation, not forgetting the frailties of the members of the government themselves.

The 1945 Labour government was effective in three important ways. Firstly, in contrast to Lloyd George and the Conservative administration between 1918 and 1922, it successfully saw the return of the nation to a peacetime economy with no dislocation of industry or mass unemployment. Secondly, it achieved a transformation of British society which improved the lives of millions of people, male and female, young and old. For the first time the uncertainties caused by unemployment and serious illness were banished by the welfare state, and a start was made in providing decent housing and education for everyone. Thirdly, and perhaps most importantly, many of the policy assumptions, particularly

1. What do you think the greatest achievement of the Attlee administration was? Explain whether you think the government was successful and why.

2. What constraints were there on Attlee's government? Of these which do you think was the most important?

the central importance of the mixed economy, containing both state controlled and privately-owned industries, and the need to maintain the welfare state and the National Health Service, were wholeheartedly adopted by politicians of all parties. Certainly Winston Churchill's incoming Conservative government in October 1951 made no attempt to reverse any of the achievements of the previous administration. With the exception of the return to the private sector of the iron and steel industry, the nationalisation of which in February 1951 had been widely opposed even within the Labour Party, they left well alone.

This 'post-war consensus' built around a shared belief in Keynesian economics, the welfare state and the mixed economy would remain until the economic difficulties of the mid-1970s forced the rethinking of ever-increasing state spending. However, it took the election of Margaret Thatcher in 1979 to rigorously challenge these beliefs by privatising the nationalised industries and shaking up the National Health Service. Even today no politician could seriously call for the National Health Service to be broken up and welfare provisions to be totally abandoned.

12.3 Lessons in failure? – The Labour governments of 1964–70 and 1974–79

Labour under Harold Wilson and then James Callaghan was in power between 1964–70 and 1974–79. Historians have long been critical of the performance of the administrations. The left bemoans the lack of progress towards social equality. Critics like Ralph Milliband in *Parliamentary Socialism* (1973) felt that 'the government could have had all the support it required from trade unionists had it been genuinely engaged in the creation of a society marked by greater social justice'. The left-wing MP and NEC member, Ian Mikardo, thought '1974–9 was a greater disappointment than 1964–70. The rich got richer under Callaghan.' While the right, both in business and within the Conservative Party, were confirmed in their prejudices that Labour was incapable of running the economy.

In discussing these governments however it is important to remember that they were constrained by three factors:

● Between October 1964 and March 1966, and for the whole duration of the 1974–79 administrations, Labour either had a very small majority (six in 1964; three in October 1974) or no majority at all (February to October 1974 and 1977 to 1979). This meant that ministers could have difficulties in getting measures through Parliament.

● Both governments suffered major economic crises. Harold Wilson during 1966 and 1967 had to grapple with problems brought about by an over-valued pound. Ten years later his successor James Callaghan had to accept large cuts in public expenditure as a condition of a loan from the International Monetary Fund (IMF) to prop up the economy.

● Dissension was growing within the party and the wider Labour Movement. Party members increasingly became frustrated at the ineffectual performance of both governments. Between 1964 and 1970 150,000 members left the party. A decade later party activists were much more confident about using the machinery at their disposal, especially the **National Executive Committee** (NEC), which the left controlled, to make their feelings known. Trade unions were also increasingly estranged from the party by the actions of Labour governments, particularly perceived attacks on living standards of members, and attempts to curtail wage increases.

National Executive Committee (NEC): 'The administrative authority' of the Party, made up of trade unionists, constituency delegates (mostly MPs), as well as the leader and deputy leader. It is responsible for both administrative and election organisation, and also with much policy research.

The Labour Governments, 1964–70

The new Labour government was swept into office in October 1964 in a wave of enthusiasm. Harold Wilson was, at 47, the youngest Prime Minister since 1812. He contrasted well with the patrician Conservative leader Sir Alec Douglas-Home. Peter Shore, later a senior figure himself within the Party, says, 'what Harold Wilson offered was not just an image but to some extent also the reality of a modern man, a competent man – none of the old Labour business of lumbering along … He was on the move. He knew what the modern world was all about.' Harold Wilson played on this image by talking about the need for planning and the opportunities offered by, in his phrase, 'the white heat of technology'. In this the Party had caught the mood of the moment.

In practice neither planning nor new technology received a high priority within the new administration. Responsibility for planning was given to the mercurial George Brown at a new ministry – the Department of Economic Affairs. Although industry, the trade unions and the government signed what was grandly called the National Plan in September 1965 it was clear, as Kenneth O. Morgan comments in *The People's Peace* (1990), that it had no real regulation or procedure for raising production or exports. The Department itself suffered from the hostility of the Treasury, which resented another ministry having influence over economic matters.

Investment in research and development of new products was largely swallowed up by the arms industry. What remained tended to be used for a few high-profile projects such as **Concorde** or **nuclear energy**. The government, however, encouraged the merger of companies to enable British industry to compete worldwide. One of these new companies was International Computers Ltd (ICL), still a leader in computing today.

What dominated the government for the nearly six years of its existence was the economy. When the new Chancellor of the Exchequer, James Callaghan, arrived at the Treasury in October 1964, he was greeted with the news that the economic position of the country was much worse than the previous administration had let on. The need to maintain the pound's strength in the international money markets, encourage exports and restrict imports limited what the new administration could do. As a result, certain key manifesto pledges had to be abandoned or curtailed. In particular the government failed to build as many houses as had been promised, the raising of the school leaving age to 16 in 1968 was postponed, and ambitious plans to restructure state pensions had to be abandoned.

As a reaction to the economic situation the government cut back public spending and increased taxes in an emergency budget in July 1966. Many observers see this as a turning point in the government's life. The severity of the cuts stunned the party and helped to fuel the growing atmosphere of distrust among party members and the public in general about the resolve of the government.

The real problem faced by the government was the high value of the pound against foreign currencies, particularly the dollar. This made British exports very expensive while imports, in comparison, were cheap. Despite mounting pressure, particularly on the money markets, the government refused to devalue the pound until November 1967. The delay in **devaluation** was largely due to the opposition of Harold Wilson to the measure. There are three reasons for this: he had been a key part of the decision to devalue the pound under Clement Attlee in 1949; he believed that devaluation would damage Britain's prestige in the world; and lastly there were good economic arguments for why Britain need not devalue. Peter Shore witnessed the Prime Minister's private response when the decision to devalue had been made, 'that was terribly damaging to him

---

George Brown (1914–1985)
Brown occupied several minor government posts under Attlee. He was Deputy Leader of the Labour Party 1960–70 but lost his seat in the 1970 election. He held the posts of Secretary of State for Economic Affairs 1964–66 and Foreign Secretary 1966–68.

Concorde: Anglo-French supersonic aircraft that made its first flight in April 1968. It was a financial disaster as only the state airlines of Britain (British Airways) and France (Air France) bought aircraft.

Nuclear energy: Electricity produced by harnessing atomic or nuclear power. Britain's first atomic power station opened at Calder Hall in May 1956. Fears over safety and the high cost of development has hindered the growth of nuclear power in Britain.

James Callaghan (1912–)
Callaghan led the Labour Party 1976–80. In the course of his political career Callaghan held all the highest offices of state: a unique record. He was Chancellor of the Exchequer 1964–67, Home Secretary 1967–70, Foreign Secretary 1974–76 and Prime Minister 1976–79.

Devaluation: The decision to reduce the value of a currency against other currencies. Devaluation can often stimulate an economy because exports then become cheaper and thus more competitive in the world market than they previously were.

Roy Jenkins (1920–)
Jenkins held the posts in Labour governments of Home Secretary 1965–67, Chancellor of the Exchequer 1967–70, and Home Secretary 1974–76. He was Deputy Leader of the Labour Party 1970–72 and, following his split with the Labour Party, was Leader of Social Democratic Party 1982–83.

Barbara Castle (1911–)
Castle was Minister of Overseas Development 1964–65, Minister of Transport 1965–68, Secretary of State for Employment 1968–70, and Secretary of State for Health, 1974–76.

Anthony Crosland (1918–1977)
Crosland held the posts of Secretary of State for Education 1965–67, President of the Board of Trade 1967–69, Secretary of State for Local Government 1969–70, Secretary of State for the Environment 1974–76, Foreign Secretary 1976–77.

personally. He felt it, and it was damaging to him politically as well, and to the whole coherent reputation and authority of the Labour government.'

Devaluation and careful management of the economy by the new Chancellor of the Exchequer, Roy Jenkins, however, led to a much better position by the time of the general election in June 1970.

Another difficulty faced by the government was industrial relations. Paradoxically as Kenneth O. Morgan points out, in *The People's Peace* (1990), this was the government's particular claim to understanding and authority, and in the end its most disastrous failure. Relations with the trade union movement soon became strained as the new government continued the Conservative freeze on pay increases. Matters were made worse by a rash of strikes, of which perhaps the most extraordinary was the seamen's strike between May and July 1966. On 20 June Harold Wilson startled the House of Commons when he attributed the strike to sabotage perpetuated by 'a tightly knit group of politically motivated extremists', although there is little evidence of such a group.

In 1968 Wilson appointed Barbara Castle as Secretary of State for Employment and Productivity. Although on the left of the Party, Castle had long believed that order was needed in industrial relations. With the support of Wilson and Roy Jenkins she published a White Paper, optimistically entitled 'In Place of Strife', in January 1969 in which she proposed fairly mild controls, by the standards of legislation in the 1980s and 1990s, over unions and their right to strike. She called it a 'charter of trade union rights'. Although popular with the public it met a lot of opposition not just from within the trade unions but across the Labour Party. James Callaghan, the Home Secretary, led much of this opposition. Even with a majority of a hundred it soon became clear that there was no chance of getting the legislation through Parliament. Eventually Wilson and Castle had to back down and signed a 'solemn and binding undertaking' with the Trades Union Congress (TUC) in June 1969 that stated that the Congress would monitor strikes and attempt to mediate in industrial disputes.

The whole episode was a humiliation for the government and the Prime Minister in particular. Philip Whitehead, in the *Writing on the Wall* (1985), noted that 'The government had lost both trade union support for being too tough and some public support by appearing in the last analysis to be too weak'.

The government had many achievements to its name. It may not have had the impact of those of the Attlee administrations, but Clive Ponting in *Breach of Promise* (1989) believes that it 'had a significant impact on social attitudes and the lives of ordinary individuals'. The one that Wilson himself had most time for was the establishment of a 'University of the Air' (or Open University as it became known) to enable working adults to receive a university education at home. Meanwhile Anthony Crosland, as Secretary of State for Education, began to introduce comprehensive schools, replacing grammar and secondary modern schools.

The 'swinging sixties' and 'the permissive society' had an effect on ministers and resulted in some notably liberal measures. Theatre censorship and the death penalty were abolished in 1965. Two years later came the legalisation of abortion and homosexual acts between consenting adults in private. And 1968 saw the granting of votes to 18-year-olds.

The Equal Pay Act, 1970, although not fully introduced until 1975, secured the principle of equal pay for equal work. It is an important step on the path towards equality for women, because up to that time women were generally paid less for doing the same work as men. Race relations acts in 1965 and 1968 established the Race Relations Board and made illegal many forms of racist behaviour. To a certain extent this work was made harder by the Commonwealth Immigration Act 1968, which restricted the right of entry of certain groups, particularly Asians from East Africa, who had been granted British passports in the early 1960s.

Possibly the greatest achievement of all, and one in the words of Clive Ponting that was achieved 'in the face of an awful economic legacy, economic difficulties throughout the period and considerable opposition from the Treasury' was a narrowing of the gap between the richest and poorest in society. This was largely achieved by an increase in benefits, rather than in direct redistribution of wealth through higher income tax. When taking the broadest measure of disposable income (after tax but including benefits) individuals on the highest incomes suffered a fall of a third, whereas lowest incomes went up by 104% (see table 3).

Table 3 Increase in spending 1964–70
% of Gross Domestic Product (GDP) spent on

	1964	1970	% increase
Education	4.8	6.1	12.7
Health	3.9	4.9	12.6
Social security	16.0	23.0	14.3

There has always been an air of failure attached to the Labour government of 1964 to 1966. The achievements are overlooked and perhaps too little is made of the economic problems which the government tackled and overcame. Labour had been elected in October 1964 with such high hopes and yet few of these hopes had come to fruition. David Marquand in *The Progressive Dilemma* (1991) feels that 'no modern British government has disappointed their supporters so thoroughly'. He sums the period up as being one of 'lost innocence and of hopes betrayed'.

Much of the blame must be laid at the feet of the Prime Minister himself. Harold Wilson was a consummate politician, but it soon became clear that he did not believe in anything very much. This was coupled with an almost paranoid belief in plots and threats against him, which destroyed much of his credibility not just among his colleagues, but in the country in general. According to Denis Healey, one of his closest colleagues as Minister of Defence, between 1964 and 1970, 'he had no purpose of direction, and rarely looked more than a few months ahead. His short-term opportunism, allied to a capacity for self-delusion which made **Walter Mitty** appear unimaginative, often plunged the government into chaos. Worse still, when things went wrong he imagined every one was campaigning against him. He believed in demons, and saw most of his colleagues in this role at some time or other.'

The government went into the 1970 general election campaign with a clear lead in the opinion polls. But weeks of complacent campaigning and a poor set of economic figures a few days before the election secured victory for Edward Heath. Harold Wilson put the Conservative victory down to the weather, 'I think what really did us in was the heat. It was very hot weather … the combination of the heat and the opinion polls did us.' Tony Benn, however, was shrewder when he pointed at voter apathy, 'power slipped through our fingers because we were saying nothing very useful to people'.

Walter Mitty: A character in a short story by the American humorist James Thurber who lives his life in ever greater daydreams.

The Wilson and Callaghan years, 1974–79

Unlike in 1964 few people had high expectations of the Labour government which came to power in February 1974. The election produced an inconclusive result (Labour 301, Conservatives 297, see table 1 page 284). After a half-hearted attempt by Edward Heath to form a coalition with the Liberal Party, Harold Wilson, who (just) had the largest number of seats, became Prime Minister. The immediate cause of the election, the Miner's Strike, was settled within two days of Wilson becoming Prime Minister. The October 1974 election produced the narrowest of majorities: three seats, which were soon whittled away in a series of poor by-election results for the government.

The new administration was in some ways very different from the one that left office in 1970. Wilson himself was happier to take less of a leading role, acting as he described as a 'deep-lying centre-half' encouraging rather than leading ministers. His cabinet reflected the increasing left-right split within the Party. The veteran left-winger Michael Foot was appointed as Secretary of State for Employment, a popular choice with the trade union leadership. Tony Benn became first Secretary of State for Industry, where his attempts to introduce radical policies were effectively blocked by Wilson and departmental civil servants, and from July 1975 Minister for Energy. The great offices of state were however reserved for those on the right of the Party: Denis Healey became Chancellor of the Exchequer, James Callaghan Foreign Secretary, and Roy Jenkins returned to the Home Office where he had been Home Secretary a decade before.

Wilson remained as Prime Minister, until he suddenly resigned in March 1976. Subsequently there has been much speculation as to the reasons why. The answer simply seems to be that he had long promised his wife that he would leave politics when he reached sixty. His birthday occurred a few days before he resigned. In the leadership contest James Callaghan easily beat Michael Foot. Callaghan was a rather different leader to Wilson. He had close personal links with the trade unions and had an avuncular, common-sense approach which a number of commentators have compared to the Conservative inter-war Prime Minister Stanley Baldwin. Kenneth O. Morgan in *The People's Peace* argues that he was the most effective Prime Minister since Harold Macmillan. One of his colleagues, William Rogers, (referring to Callaghan's wartime service in the Navy) thought that Callaghan saw himself as 'the able seaman, the man who understands the common man'.

The most important task of the government, under Wilson or Callaghan, was to survive, because it could be defeated at almost any time in the House of Commons. It had to endure many amendments to legislation that it would have preferred not to accept. Joe Ashton, a Labour **Whip**, recalled, 'the 1974–79 government did a magnificent job with hardly a majority … You had to be in government to know how thin the thread was. We never revealed the wheeling and dealing to secure a majority.'

For 18 months from the spring of 1977 a lifeline was thrown to the government in the form of a pact with the 13 MPs of the Liberal Party. At the time both Labour and the Liberals were doing badly at by-elections and the pact brought a respite for both sides. In practice, however, it made little difference to the running of the government, as the Liberals asked for very little in return for their support.

The 1974–79 government's achievements were pretty modest. In part this stems from the precarious situation in which it found itself, but also the October 1974 party manifesto was a pretty cautious affair. Their achievements, however, do include the Health and Safety Act (1974), which aimed to make the workplace a far safer place. Race discrimination and equal opportunities legislation was also strengthened.

Referendums to set up regional assemblies in Scotland and Wales were held in March 1979, but support for devolution did not meet the 40% of the total population threshold required by the Act. The threshold was inserted by rebellious backbench MPs opposed to devolution, including

---

Michael Foot (1913–)
Foot was Secretary of State for Employment 1974–76, Lord President 1976–79. During this time he was also Deputy Leader of the Labour Party 1976–80. He became Leader in 1980 and was succeeded by Neil Kinnock in 1983.

Whip: MPs of a party responsible for ensuring MPs support that party's position in the House of Commons.

Referendums (or referenda): National vote on whether a policy should be adopted or approved. In 1997 referendums were held in Scotland and Wales to approve the establishment of a Scottish Parliament and Welsh Assembly.

Neil Kinnock (1942–)
Leader of the Labour Party
1983–92, European
Commissioner 1993–.

Denis Healey (1917–)
Deputy Leader of the Labour
Party, 1980–83, Healey's earlier
career had been as Minister of
Defence 1964–70 and
Chancellor of the Exchequer
1974–79.

Capitalism: The economic system
prevalent in Britain and western
society, sometimes called the free
market or private enterprise
economy. Economic decision-making
is highly decentralised with a large
number of companies selling goods
and services and consumers
choosing which services and goods
most suits their needs.

Keynesian economics: Argued that
a government could spend its way
out of an economic crisis.

Tam Dalyell and Neil Kinnock, into the legislation. This is an example of
the weakness of the government in Parliament.

Possibly the greatest achievements relate to the economy. Callaghan
bequeathed to the Conservatives a more promising inheritance than the
utter disaster that Harold Wilson had inherited from Edward Heath.
When Labour was returned to power in 1974, inflation was running at
30%, but by mid-1978 this had been reduced to 7%. Although unemployment undoubtedly rose over the five years that Labour was in power, and
despite a memorable Conservative policy claiming that 'Labour isn't
working' (see page 328) the unemployment rate in May 1979 was 5.5%.
No government of the 1980s or 1990s could claim so few unemployed.

One reason for this was that the revenue from the North Sea oilfields
was beginning to flow into the Treasury. By the end of 1978 Britain was
well on the way to becoming self-sufficient in oil and gas, thus reducing
imports considerably.

The defining moment of the government was the International
Monetary Fund (IMF) loan crisis of the autumn of 1976. As so often in
the past the crisis was caused by a run on the pound, leading to a drain
in Britain's foreign reserves. Foreign bankers, especially from America,
put increasing pressure on the British Government to make severe cuts
in public spending to satisfy the markets. Despite measures taken in July
designed to satisfy the markets it was not enough. By the end of
September 1976 the situation had deteriorated. In a dramatic move the
Chancellor, Denis Healey, on his way to Heathrow Airport for a meeting
in the Philippines, received a message that the position had worsened.
He went instead to Blackpool where the Labour Party was having its
conference. There Healey discussed the position with the Prime Minister
and, in his words, 'decided the only thing to do was to announce we
were going to the IMF [for a loan] because that was the only thing that
would hold the markets, which it did'. They decided to ask for a loan of
$3 billion.

The IMF insisted on severe terms in return for the loan, including large
cuts in public expenditure. This was resisted by many of the Cabinet, not
just left-wing members. Tony Benn put forward an alternative strategy to
Cabinet, but Healey remembered, 'he didn't have alternative proposals. I
think on many of the big issues of the time he was simply agin it'. During
a series of 23 Cabinet meetings in the autumn of 1976, Anthony Crosland,
Tony Benn and other critics were persuaded that the very severity of the
crisis made the loan essential. According to Benn, Crosland eventually
told Cabinet, 'it is mad but we have no alternative'. The Cabinet agreed
the terms and announced £2.5 billion of cuts in public spending.

Ironically it seems that the loan wasn't actually needed. The whole
exercise was done on false figures. Healey concluded, 'the virtue of the
whole thing, even though it wasn't necessary, is the sentiment internationally completely switched round'. Ultimately, as Martin Holmes, in
The Labour Government 1974–1979 (1985), suggests 'both Healey and
Callaghan knew that the IMF medicine, while tasting foul, would
benefit the patient in economic terms'. However there was a price to pay.
Many within the Labour movement were disgusted by what they saw as
a sell-out to international **capitalism**. Martin Holmes believes 'the most
valuable contribution of the 1974–79 government was arguably not in
any specific policy at all but in the change of intellectual direction in the
latter months of 1976 away from **Keynesian economics** towards what is
known as monetarism'.

Part of the medicine administered by the IMF was the slow abandonment of Keynesian economics, which no longer seemed applicable for
the position Britain found itself in. James Callaghan sounded the death

knell of the old ways when he told the 1976 conference, 'we used to think you could spend your way out of a recession and increase employment by cutting taxes and boosting spending. I tell you in all candour that the option no longer exists, and in so far as it ever did exist, it only worked by injecting a bigger dose of inflation into the system.' The public expenditure cuts of 1976 and the subsequent recovery in the economy demolished the post-war consensus, and showed the way for Thatcher and the Conservative governments of the 1980s and 1990s.

For many people the abiding memory of the Callaghan administration was the so-called 'Winter of Discontent'. Three years of agreed pay deals between unions and the government had cut many workers' living standards. The 5% maximum pay rise proposed by Callaghan did not please the unions or their members, as they felt entitled to greater increases to make up lost ground. Alan Fisher, leader of the health service union **NUPE**, complained, 'you know what percentages do for the lower paid. It gives least to those who need it most and most to those who need it least.'

NUPE: National Union of Public Employees now part of the union UNISON.

Government ministers repeatedly ignored warnings from friends in the labour movement that the figure proposed was too low. Denis Healey remembers, 'I'm convinced now that if we had said we wanted settlements in single figures, we'd have probably come out with something like 12% overall and retained the support of the unions, avoided the Winter of Discontent, and won the election. But **hubris** tends to affect all governments after a period of success, and by golly it hit us.'

Hubris: A feeling of self-confidence, that nothing can go wrong.

The TUC, with the support of many within the Labour Party, decided to ignore the government's recommendation. The round of pay settlements began with the Ford workers receiving a rise of 15%. This set the pattern for other rises. When the government tried to enforce moderate pay rises it found it couldn't. Callaghan was reluctant to take on the unions, with whom he had had close links for many years. By the end of January 1979, however, many public sector workers were on strike.

Why did scenes such as this discredit the Labour government of the time?

Uncollected rubbish in Leicester Square, London, during the 'Winter of Discontent', 1978–79

Tabloid press: Mass circulation newspapers such as the *Sun*, *Daily Mirror*, *Daily Express* and *Daily Mail*. Only the *Daily Mirror* was traditionally a Labour-supporting newspaper.

Roads went ungritted, rubbish uncollected, and in one macabre twist the dead on Merseyside were left unburied. The **tabloid press**, most of which supported the Conservatives, had a field day with screaming headlines 'Has Everyone Gone Mad?' 'No Mercy' 'Target for Today – Sick Children' with graphic photographs of picket lines, unoccupied graves and closed hospitals. NUPE, many of whose members were the least well paid in the country, were at the forefront of the action. Eventually many pay deals were signed with employers giving rises far higher than had been anticipated.

The damage, however, had been done. In the short term the images of militancy were a gift to the Conservatives under Margaret Thatcher. The government was finally put out of its misery when it lost a vote of no confidence in March 1979. The memory of picket lines and unfilled graves would linger for many years, damaging Labour's electoral prospects and the reputation of the unions themselves.

The resulting election marked a decisive break in British history. Callaghan himself recognised this when during the campaign he confided to a friend that he sensed 'a sea change' in British society, as great as the one that had first taken him to Parliament in 1945. Yet to an extent, with the adoption of monetarist policies and severe cutbacks in public spending, Callaghan had already anticipated Thatcherism.

How successful was the Labour government between 1974 and 1979? Eric Shaw, in *The Labour Party since 1945* (1996), feels that 'one is left with the impression of a government struggling to do its best in extremely bleak conditions, where the familiar landmarks were vanishing and where few of the levers used in the past to control events any longer worked'.

Although the record of the government has long been attacked within the Labour Party, and indeed its perceived failure fuelled the civil war which engulfed the Party after 1979, it is difficult not to come to the conclusion that – unlike the 1964–70 government – it did its best under nearly impossible circumstances. Economically it left the country in a much healthier position than it inherited. Despite cuts it did its best to protect the least well-off. Ultimately it failed however because it could not control its own supporters, particularly within the trade unions. It would take almost 20 years for the lesson to be learnt by the Party.

1. How successful do you think the Labour governments of 1964–70 and 1974–79 were?

2. Identify the constraints on Harold Wilson and James Callaghan as Prime Ministers. Why do you think they acted as they did?

12.4 Why did the Labour Party spend so much time in opposition after 1951?

A CASE STUDY IN HISTORICAL INTERPRETATION

Many political commentators in the 1940s and late 1960s predicted that the Labour Party was the 'natural party of government'. The reality however has been very different, with the party in opposition for 35 of the 55 years since the end of the Second World War. The reason for being in opposition for so long depends not just on the effectiveness of Conservative governments, but also on the failure of Labour in opposition to modernise its policies and to present a united face to the electorate.

The 1950s and 1960s

Cast into opposition in 1951 Labour went through a similar, if unfinished, period of modernisation of its policies. As James Cronin wrote in *Labour and Society in Britain 1918–1979* (1984), 'in the 1950s the Labour Party's problem was not that it had become the natural party of government but that it seemed incapable of presenting a sufficiently coherent face to the electorate to recapture power at all'.

Hugh Gaitskell (1906–1963)
Gaitskell was Chancellor of the Exchequer 1950–51. He was Leader of the Labour Party from 1955 until his sudden death in 1963. Many regarded him as the great lost leader of the Party.

Revisionist or revisionism: In this context the term given in the 1950s to those who wished to revise the Party's policies, and ultimately its aims and objectives. In some ways they were not dissimilar to the modernisers of the 1990s.

Richard Crossman (1907–1974)
Crossman published a diary of his time as a Labour minister, during which he was Minister for Housing 1964–66, Lord President 1966–68, and Secretary of State for Social Services 1968–70.

Platform: The policies on which a party stands.

The left-right split was mainly centred within the Parliamentary Labour Party and was fuelled by intense personal rivalry. The left wing was led by Aneurin Bevan, and the right by Hugh Gaitskell. Ideologically the left, always in a minority, called for a fresh extension of the public sector, while the right supported Herbert Morrison's call for a period of 'consolidation' to digest the accomplishments of the post-war administration and concentrate on administering the new welfare state.

Renewal within the party began with the election of Hugh Gaitskell as leader after the 1955 general election, and his cautious rapprochement with Aneurin Bevan. Gaitskell was an enthusiastic **revisionist**, believing that it was vital that the party should be educated in the new realities of post-war Britain and that its programme should accordingly be renewed.

In this Gaitskell was helped by Anthony Crosland, his close friend and ally. During 1956 he published *The Future of Socialism* described by Eric Shaw in *The Labour Party since 1945* (1996) as 'the most important work of post-war British social democracy since the war'. In it Crosland argued that the need for public ownership and the replacement of the market economy was outdated. Socialism was about values – above all, equality and social justice, in Crosland's words 'the most characteristic feature of socialist thought'.

The high point of revisionism was Gaitskell's failed attempt to remove Clause 4 at the 1961 Party conference. He urged the party to accept that there had been 'a significant change in the economic and social background in politics' that required Labour to abandon its old doctrines and slogans. He told the conference, 'let us remember we are a party of the future, not of the past … It is no good waving the banners of a bygone age.' Gaitskell failed to persuade the conference and the wider party of the advantages of making the change, largely because he could not provide a satisfactory alternative. A chance was missed to update Labour's core doctrine to meet the aspirational needs of those in the newly 'affluent society'.

A decade of internal debate and bitter factional rivalry was in the end remarkably unproductive in terms of revising and updating the party programme. A saviour, however, appeared in the form of the scientific revolution, which was, as James Hinton argues in *Labour and Socialism* (1983) 'a compromise based more on torpor than on genuine agreement'. The claim that Labour would revive the economy by harnessing science emerged as a major theme with the party's 1960 document 'Signposts to the Sixties'. Scientific managerialism was an idea that both right and left could agree on. As Crossman put it, 'here was an new creative socialist idea needed to reconcile the revisionists of the right with the traditionalists of the left'.

Harold Wilson, who was elected leader of the party in early 1963 on the sudden death of Hugh Gaitskell, enthusiastically took this theme up. Wilson played on the image by talking about the need for planning and the opportunities offered by new technology. It was best expressed in Wilson's speech to the 1963 Party conference, in which he talked about 'the white heat of technology' The idea of the scientific revolution was popular with the electorate. The experience of the 1964 and 1966 Labour governments, however, was disillusioning. The emphasis on the scientific revolution was largely forgotten in the economic crises that beset the new administration.

Neither Gaitskell nor Wilson saw fit to really challenge the post-war consensus because it largely grew out of the achievements of the Attlee administration to which they had contributed. Gaitskell did not have the support successfully to challenge the consensus, while Wilson was uninterested in doing so. A wholesale reform of the party's **platform** had not been made and this would considerably damage the Party in the decades to come. As Keith Middlemass in *The Politics of Industrial Society* (1979) said, 'what really occurred … resembled the dosing of a malarial patient with quinine: the symptoms disappeared, but the Party wasn't really strengthened, nor were its ideological fevers cured'.

The rise of the left 1970–87

The 1970s and early 1980s saw the rise of grassroots activism, which moved the Labour Party considerably to the left. The reasons for this grassroots revolt are threefold:

- **Dissatisfaction** within the party at the performance of the Labour governments of 1964 and 1974, which promised much but seemingly delivered very little in the way of socialist measures let alone reduce the inequalities within society;

- **Frustration** at the unresponsiveness of MPs and ministers to the concerns of ordinary members;

- **A changing membership** which brought into the party younger, better educated people, largely from the public services such as teaching and social work, who were less prepared to be deferential to senior figures within the party.

Matters were made worse by an antiquated party structure. In particular there was conflict and uncertainty over the powers of conference, the National Executive Committee (NEC), the Parliamentary Labour Party (PLP), and the Leader. Michael Foot, leader of the party between 1980 and 1982, pointed out in *Another Heart and other Pulses* (1984) that 'many of the internal rows … have revolved around this theoretically impractical constitutional arrangement'.

Until the 1960s the system worked reasonably well, partly because the membership was in general in agreement with the policies of the party promulgated by the leadership. The leadership could usually also count on the support of the trade unions at conference, where their voting strength would defeat motions with which the leadership disagreed. Trade union support became less certain in the late 1950s as a new generation of left-wing trade union general secretaries, notably Jack Jones (Transport and General Workers Union) and Hugh Scanlon (Amalgamated Engineering Union) was elected. The trade unions were also increasingly estranged from the party by the actions of Labour governments, particularly attempts to curtail wage increases through prices and incomes policies.

The party machinery in the country was also increasingly in a poor way. In the mid-1950s Harold Wilson described it as being 'a penny-farthing machine in the jet age'. Membership in particular declined dramatically. In the early 1950s there were about a million members of the party. By the early 1980s this had declined to 250,000. (In 1997 it was about 400,000.) The loss of members was due in part to disillusionment with Labour government. The decline was particularly steep between 1964 and 1970 when 150,000 people left the Party. The party leadership, however, remained complacent, believing that as election campaigns were increasingly fought on television, the need for local electioneering and other activities were, in the words of Anthony Crosland, 'now largely a ritual'.

It was easy for small groups of left-wing activists to take control of moribund local parties. The real importance was that control of local parties gave influence to **Trotskyist** and other extremist groups, way beyond their actual strength within the Labour movement as a whole. The most active group engaged in these activities was the Revolutionary Socialist League, better known as the Militant Tendency. In 1975 Militant

Trotskyists: As the name suggests, they follow the teachings of Leon Trotsky (1879–1940) one of the leaders of the Russian Revolution who increasingly became critical of the development of Communism in the Soviet Union under Joseph Stalin. They seek to use working-class organisations, particularly trade unions, in order to ferment socialist revolution.

Constituencies: The Constituency Labour Party (CLP) is the organisation of the Labour Party locally. Its boundaries are identical to those of a parliamentary constituency. Each constituency is divided into a number of smaller wards, based on local authority ward boundaries. CLPs are run by General Committees comprising delegates from local trade union branches and ward branches. Until 1992 the General Committee also selected the Parliamentary candidate.

stated, 'we must consciously aim to penetrate every **constituency** in the country … A citadel in every constituency, a base in every ward'. The influence these groups exerted is not clear. According to Eric Shaw in *The Labour Party since 1945* (1996) 'the influence [of Militant] was often wildly exaggerated'. Many party officials, however, were less sure.

The pain of Labour's dismissal from office in 1970 was not eased – as it had been 20 years previously – by pride in its accomplishments. Indeed the mood was one of disillusionment. This made party members resentful of the leadership who had been ministers in government. As Clive Ponting suggests in *Breach of Promise* (1989), 'the 1964–70 government sowed the seeds of much of the grassroots revolt in the 1970s with its demands for greater accountability within the party'.

The early 1970s saw Anthony Wedgwood Benn's (Tony Benn as he increasingly wished to be known) move to the left. Kenneth O. Morgan, in *Labour People* (1987), says, that having been a centre, even right-wing member of Labour cabinets, Benn became the pied piper of almost every available left-wing cause. In opposition, Benn increasingly felt that the Party's defeat in 1970 had been brought about by the government's drifting too far from the wisdom of its supporters.

By 1974 Benn was increasingly perceived as leading the left and articulating the views of many party members. His Cabinet colleague, Peter Shore, thought that Benn 'had a special claim to be architect and custodian of Party policy' at this time. Benn was helped by the fact that the NEC was dominated by the left, which initiated a number of policy reviews leading to the adoption of left-wing policies, particularly in connection with planning and nationalisation. The result of this work appeared in the 1973 policy paper *Labour's Programme 1973*, parts of which significantly were rejected by Harold Wilson and other senior Labour figures. Wilson denounced the adoption of the proposal to nationalise 25 key British companies, telling reporters, '… the shadow cabinet would not hesitate to use its veto … It is inconceivable that the party would go into the general election on this proposal'. Activists, however, were horrified by the way in which the leader ignored the democratic will of the party. Attitudes like this by senior ministers would come back to haunt them in years to follow.

The election of a Labour government in February 1974 curtailed feuding within the party. The truce was not to last long. The perceived poor performance of the government, particularly relating to the International Monetary Fund (IMF) loan negotiated in the autumn of 1976 and continuing industrial relations problems, led to renewed criticisms. In particular the government's handling of the various public sector industrial disputes which made up the 'Winter of Discontent' during the winter of 1978–79 was heavily criticised by many within the Party. Peter Hain, a leading political activist in the 1970s, was one critic: 'above all [the government was] not seen by party members such as myself as really seriously putting forward a socialist economic strategy. They were seeking to manage capitalism in crisis … So I think there was tremendous disillusionment and a feeling of betrayal. That was a word often used – that lots of these Labour leaders didn't actually believe in the policies upon which they had been elected.'

Peter Hain and his fellow critics failed, however, to take into account the precarious position of Harold Wilson and James Callaghan, who found themselves without a workable Parliamentary majority for most of the five years Labour were in power. This severely hampered the government's room for manoeuvre and ability to introduce controversial legislation.

Much of the infighting, which erupted from 1979, concerned internal party matters, particularly how the Party Leader should be elected, the mandatory reselection of MPs, and who was responsible for the election manifesto. These measures, it was argued, should ensure that activists had some control over the Parliamentary Labour Party and Shadow Cabinet that had so often ignored the views of the membership. The left's triumph over reselection and the election of the leader, Benn recorded in his diary in January 1981, had wrought 'an enormous change because the PLP, which has been the great centre of power in British politics, has had to yield to the movement that put members there'.

Much of the campaign to introduce these policies was masterminded by the Campaign for Labour Party Democracy. It was always a small body with only 1,200 members at the height of its influence in 1982. But what it lacked in size the Campaign more than made up for in its skill in using internal party procedures to forward its agenda.

Callaghan stepped down as Party leader in November 1980, and Michael Foot was elected as his replacement. Foot had impeccable left-wing credentials and was widely respected within the party as a man of honour. But he was no match either for opponents of the Labour leadership, or his Conservative opponents in Parliament and the media. Eric Shaw, in *The Labour Party since 1979* (1994) argues that 'Foot proved to be an ineffectual leader who lacked either the power base or the political gifts to stamp his authority on the party'.

The turmoil eventually led to the first major split within the party since 1931 as Roy Jenkins, David Owen, William Rogers, and Shirley Williams – four former cabinet ministers – left in January 1981 to form the new Social Democratic Party (SDP). Eventually 25 Labour and 1 Conservative MPs joined the new party. They believed that the SDP could replace Labour as the party of the centre-left. In the words of the Limehouse Declaration, which launched the SDP, 'we believe that a realignment of British politics must now be faced'. This realignment resulted in an alliance with the Liberal Party in 1982. The two parties formally merged after the 1987 general election to become the Liberal Democrats.

The greatest battle of the civil war within the Labour Party was the election for the Deputy Leadership in 1981. Tony Benn launched a challenge for this largely honorific post against Denis Healey. It was perceived as being a battle for the soul of the Party, and the campaign was conducted with increasing vehemence. In the end Healey won, but his margin of victory was less than 1%, and was largely secured by the fact that four MPs, including Neil Kinnock, abstained in the final vote.

The left also became increasingly influential in the policy-making procedures through its control of the National Executive Committee. As a result the party adopted **unilateral disarmament**, agreed to withdraw from Europe, and proposed further nationalisation of industry. These policies, especially nuclear disarmament, were used by the media, especially newspapers, to portray Labour as an extremist party, out of touch with the needs of ordinary voters. The myriad policies were combined into the 1983 election manifesto, subsequently memorably described by Peter Shore as being 'the longest suicide note in history'.

The 1983 general election was a disaster for the Labour Party. Its campaign was amateurish and largely irrelevant, especially when compared with the slick media-friendly Conservative performance under Margaret Thatcher. The result showed deep disillusionment with Labour and its policies, especially among the expanding social groups of skilled workers and white collar workers and the south east. As Philip Gould, in *The Unfinished Revolution* (1998) writes, 'the point could not be clearer – there was a new majority in Britain – new working class, new middle class voters. And yet Labour and this new majority were parting company. Labour dragging its feet, they surging ahead. Labour had lost its purpose.'

David Owen (1938–)
Becoming Foreign Secretary at the age of just 38, Owen held the post 1977–79. Disillusioned with the Labour Party he was one of the 'gang of four' to leave and set up the Social Democratic Party. He was Leader of the SDP from 1983 until its demise in 1990.

Roy Hattersley (1932–)
Hattersley was Secretary of State for Prices 1976–79, later becoming Deputy Leader of the Labour Party 1983–92.

Unilateral disarmament: A policy abandoning Britain's nuclear weapons. The Labour Party had famously adopted nuclear disarmament for a short period in the early 1960s. Increased fear of nuclear war in the late 1970s saw the rebirth of the pressure group Campaign for Nuclear Disarmament (CND) and increasing demands for the Labour Party to get rid of Britain's nuclear weapons when it returned to power.

Table 4 Election of leaders and deputy leaders of the Labour Party 1980–83

1980 – Election of Leader
Electorate: MPs

1st ballot

Michael Foot	83
Denis Healey	112
John Silkin	38
Peter Shore	32

2nd ballot

Michael Foot	139
Denis Healey	129

1 September 1981 – Election of Deputy Leader
Electorate: electoral college with trade unions having 40% of the vote, constituency parties and the Parliamentary Labour Party 30% each

	Trade unions	Constituencies	MPs	TOTAL
1st ballot	%	%	%	%
Tony Benn	6	23	7	36
Denis Healey	25	5	15	45
John Silkin	9	1	8	18
2nd ballot	%	%	%	%
Tony Benn	15	24	10	50
Denis Healey	25	6	20	51

1983 – election of leader
Electorate: electoral college with trade unions having 40% of the vote, constituency parties and the Parliamentary Labour Party 30% each

	Trade unions	Constituencies	MPs	TOTAL
	%	%	%	%
Roy Hattersley	11	1	8	19
Eric Heffer	0	2	4	6
Neil Kinnock	29	27	15	71
Peter Shore	0	0	3	3

Source: David and Gareth Butler, *British Political Facts, 1900–1914*, 1994.
All discrepancies in percentages are due to rounding.

Explain how the election of Michael Foot and Neil Kinnock affected the development of the Labour Party.

The total vote and number of MPs were the lowest since 1935 (see table 1). It just avoided coming third behind the Liberal-SDP Alliance in the popular vote. Michael Foot resigned shortly after the election. A much younger man, Neil Kinnock, replaced him. Kinnock was on the left of the party, but was essentially a pragmatist who was determined to rebuild Labour as a credible political force whatever the cost.

Neil Kinnock was helped by the fact that Tony Benn had lost his seat at the general election and so could not contest the leadership. Even when he was returned to Parliament in a by-election in 1984, observers such as Kenneth O. Morgan, in *Labour People*, sensed that Benn seemed more and more marginalised and was a spent force. In addition the left-wing coalition, which dominated the party up until the deputy leadership contest, slowly disintegrated, as members preferred to engage in internal disputes rather than unite for further potential gains.

Even so Kinnock did not have an automatic majority in the National Executive Committee, let alone at conference, so he had to tread very carefully, and such reforms as he made were necessarily piecemeal. He soon discovered that he could not rely on loyalty to the leader, but had to build convincing majorities for change. His first task, as advisers told him, was to establish unquestionable control. That finally came in 1985 with his conference speech attacking the Militant-run council in Liverpool for its dogma, reminding them, 'you can't play politics with people's jobs and with people's services and their homes'. Neil Kinnock was praised by the media: *The Guardian* commented that it was 'the bravest and most important speech by a Labour leader in a generation'.

During 1986 Peter Mandelson was appointed the Party's Director of Communications, significantly under the leader rather than the NEC. He made various changes to the presentation of the Party, but it was not enough to prevent an election defeat in 1987 almost as bad as that of 1983. This time, in the words of Colin Hughes and Patrick Wintour, in *Labour Rebuilt: the new Model Party* (1990), 'it was the defeat with excuses: there had been no winter of discontent, no Falklands War, no ageing leader, on which to blame the electorate's refusal to embrace Labour'. It was increasingly difficult to avoid the conclusion that the party was out of touch with the electorate.

The triumph of New Labour, 1987–1997

The 1987 election made it clear that the party could not remain as it was. Policies had to be updated to meet the challenges of the 1980s and 1990s. The instrument to change these policies was the Policy Review that took place during 1988 and 1989. Its conclusions formed the basis of a policy document, *Meet the Challenge Make the Change*, published in 1989, which in turn formed the basis of the platform upon which the Party fought, and lost, in 1992. The review led to the party gingerly embracing market forces, abandoning most public ownership, general acceptance of the industrial relations legislation introduced by the Conservatives, and, most controversially of all, the abandonment of a unilateral defence policy. The critics, left and right, proclaimed that the Party had deserted its socialist roots. Ivor Crew claimed that the Review was the 'least socialist policy statement ever to be published by the Party'. Others, like David Marquand in *The Progressive Dilemma* (1991) argued that the Review had been 'opinion-survey-driven' rather than 'doctrine-driven.' But Tudor Jones in *Remaking the Labour Party* (1996) is surely right in saying that 'it offered more modest, if arguably more realisable objectives and aspirations and as a result lower aspirations'.

Organisationally the party was becoming much more professional, increasingly focused on presentational matters and preparation for the forthcoming election. Much power and influence was increasingly centred around the leader taking control of policy-making. In this Kinnock and his advisers hoped to by-pass the NEC and other potential centres of opposition to the modernisation that was sweeping the party. Considerable improvements were made to Labour's relations with the media, and in the campaigns conducted in the country, professional marketing and advertising techniques were being used.

Yet, all this was not quite enough to win the 1992 general election campaign (Conservatives 336, Labour 271, see table 1). It was clear that further change had to be made. As one of the key modernisers, Philip Gould described in *The Unfinished Revolution: How the modernisers saved the Labour Party* (1998), 'Labour had failed to understand that the old working class was becoming a new middle class … They had outgrown crude collectivism and left it behind in the supermarket car park.'

It was clear, as David Hill, communications director of the Party, told the NEC in December 1992, that the Labour Party had no clear identity with the electorate, which still associated it with a poor economic record, trade union dominance, and the so-called 'loony left'. He concluded that 'the greater the prospects of a Labour government the more fearful the public were of that prospect'.

John Smith, who took over from Neil Kinnock in July 1992, was sceptical of the need to alter to any great degree party policy. However, he pressed ahead with reforms within the party, giving ordinary members a greater role in electing the leader and parliamentary candidates.

Tony Blair, who became leader on the sudden death of Smith in May 1994, had no such doubts about the need for change. He and his supporters believed that the party had not adapted sufficiently rapidly or wholeheartedly to new social, and economic realities. Since 1994 the Labour Party has portrayed itself as being almost a new political movement, distancing itself from the policies and many of the politicians who had made the party unelectable over the previous 20 years. In his speech to the Labour Party conference in October 1995, for example, Blair used the word 'new' on 59 occasions, 16 with reference to 'New Labour'. In contrast he referred to socialism just once and to the working class not at all.

The pace of change in the policies and structure of the party was bewildering. Symbolically Blair started with Clause 4 of the party's constitution, which Hugh Gaitskell had failed to replace 35 years previously. A referendum of members overwhelmingly approved a more modern statement of the party's aims. Labour increasingly focused on the aspirations of the floating voters, reassuring them about the party's tax and economic plans which had caused doubt among many in 1992.

> **John Smith (1938–1994)**
> Smith was Secretary of State for Trade, 1978–79. He was Leader of the Labour Party 1992–94.

> **Tony Blair (1953–)**
> Leader of Labour Party 1994–. Prime Minister 1997–

1. What message is this photograph attempting to give about Tony Blair?

2. How far do you think Blair's victory in 1997 was due to an effective media campaign by the Labour Party?

Tony Blair, at the final Labour Party Conference before the 1997 general election

> **Gordon Brown (1951–)**
> Brown became Chancellor of the Exchequer in the Blair Cabinet in 1997.

In particular, economic policy was rather different than before 1992. Gordon Brown, the Shadow Chancellor, made it clear that 'spending is no longer the best measure of the effectiveness of government action in the public interest'. Unlike in 1945, New Labour was not offering the public a radically new political economy. Thatcherite policies and assumptions would remain in place. The 1997 election manifesto, *New Labour, New Britain*, stressed that 'we are pledged not to raise the basic or top rates of income tax throughout the next Parliament'.

The work of Blair and his allies came to fruition with general election of 1997. The result (Labour 419, Conservatives 165, see table 1) gave the Labour Party its biggest majority ever; indeed the biggest majority for any political party in Parliament since 1832. The result is in part a reflection of the poor performance of the Conservative government under John Major, but it was also an emphatic sign that after nearly 20 years in the political wilderness the electorate finally trusted the Labour Party to provide policies that met its needs and concerns.

Conclusion

No political party likes being in opposition. The Labour Party's experience has been particularly horrendous. Tony Blair put his finger on the problems between 1979 and 1997 when he wrote in the *Daily Mirror* in 1996 that 'the Tories didn't win four elections. We lost them'. His sentiments could be extended to the other elections that Labour failed to win.

In particular the party has suffered self-inflicted splits between the left and right, which led to vicious amounts of infighting for no long-term gain. The history of the party since 1951 has been one of learning time and again to appeal to voters at the centre of British politics. Labour, in contrast with the Conservatives, has found it difficult to jettison out-of-date policies and adopt new ones likely to appeal to floating and undecided voters.

The lesson was finally learnt after the 1992 election, which against all predictions Labour did not win. The party that Tony Blair shaped after unexpectedly becoming leader in 1994 is one that offers a genuinely united face to the electors, where dissent is ruthlessly eradicated. It is a party that is very much in tune with the aspirations and needs of the middle classes who now make up Labour's core vote.

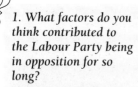

1. What factors do you think contributed to the Labour Party being in opposition for so long?

2. Of these which do you think was the most important? Give reasons to support the answer.

Source-based questions: Labour Party manifestos

SOURCE A

Britain's coming election will be the greatest test in our history of the judgement and common sense of our people. The nation wants food, work and homes. It wants more than that – it wants good food in plenty, useful work for all, and comfortable labour-saving homes that take full advantage of the resources of modern science and productive industry. It wants a high and rising standard of living, security for all against a rainy day, an educational system that will give every boy and girl a chance to develop the best that is in them … The nation needs a tremendous overhaul, a great programme of modernisation and re-equipment of its homes, its factories and machinery, its schools, its social services. All parties say so – the Labour Party means it. For the Labour Party is prepared to achieve it by drastic policies of replanning and by keeping a firm constructive hand on our whole productive machinery; the Labour Party will put the community first and the sectional interests of private business after … the Labour Party is a Socialist Party and proud of it. Its ultimate purpose at home is the establishment of the Socialist Commonwealth of Great Britain – free, democratic, efficient, public spirited, its material resources organised in the service of the British people.

From the Labour Party's 1945 Manifesto,
Let us Face the Future.

SOURCE B

The world wants it and would welcome it. The British people *want* it, *deserve* it, and urgently *need* it. And now, at last, the general election presents us with the exciting prospect of achieving it. The dying months of a frustrating 1964 can be transformed into the launching pad for the New Britain of the late 1960s and early 1970s. A New Britain:

Mobilising the resources of technology under a national plan;

Harnessing our national wealth in brains, our genius for scientific invention and medical discovery;

Reversing the decline of thirteen wasted years*;

Affording a new opportunity to equal, and if possible surpass the roaring progress of other western powers while Tory Britain has remained sideways, backwards but seldom forwards.

The country needs fresh and virile leadership. Labour is ready. Poised to swing its plans into instant operation. Impatient to apply the New Thinking that will be the end of chaos and sterility …

The Labour Party is offering Britain a new way of life that will stir our hearts, rekindle an authentic patriotic faith in our future, and enable our country to re-establish itself as a stable force in the world today for progress, peace and justice.

From the Labour Party's 1964 Manifesto,
Let's Go with Labour for the New Britain.

*****Thirteen wasted years**: The Conservative administrations between 1951 and 1964.

SOURCE C

I [Tony Blair] believe in Britain. It is a great country with a great history. The British people are a great people. But I believe Britain can and must be better: better schools, better hospitals, better ways of tackling crime, of building a modern welfare state, of equipping ourselves for a new world economy.

I want a Britain that is one nation, with shared values and purpose, where merit comes before privilege, run for the many not the few, strong and sure of itself at home and abroad. I want a Britain that does not shuffle into the new millennium afraid of the future, but strides into it with confidence …

The Conservatives' broken promises taint all politics. That is why we have made it our guiding rule not to promise what we cannot deliver; and to deliver what we can promise. What follows … is not the politics of revolution, but of a fresh start, the patient rebuilding and renewing of this country – renewal that can take root and build over time …

We have modernised the Labour Party and we will modernise Britain. This means knowing where we want to go; being clear-headed about the country's future; telling the truth; making tough choices; insisting that all parts of the public sector live within their means; taking on vested interests that hold people back; standing up to unreasonable demands from any quarter; and being prepared to give a moral lead where government has responsibilities it should not shirk.

From the Labour Party's 1997 Manifesto,
New Labour because Britain deserves better.

---

1. Study Sources A, B and C.

What are the similarities and differences between the three manifestos? Explain your answer.

2. Study Sources A and B.

Of what value are these sources to a historian writing about the Labour Party after 1945?

3. Study Sources A, B and C and use information contained in this chapter.

How far did the Labour Party achieve its electoral aims between 1945 and 2000?

The Conservative Party, 1945–2000

Key Issues

● **What factors have affected the success of the Conservative Party since 1945?**

● **To what extent did Conservative policies change between 1945 and 2000?**

● **How important were Conservative Party leaders to the development of Conservatism after 1945?**

13.1 What factors explain the revival of Conservatism after the general election defeat of 1945?

13.2 To what extent does the affluence of the 1950s account for the Conservative election victories in 1955 and 1959?

13.3 Why did the Conservative Party lose the general election of 1964?

13.4 To what extent is it fair to criticise Edward Heath's government of 1970–1974 for its 'U-turns' on policy pledges made in opposition?

13.5 What factors account for Margaret Thatcher's election to the leadership of the Conservative Party in 1975?

13.6 How far did Margaret Thatcher achieve the aims of 'Thatcherism' between 1979 and 1990?

13.7 What factors account for the decline of Conservatism in the final decade of the 20th century?

13.8 Historical Interpretation: The myth of consensus

Framework of Events

1945	July: Conservative defeat under Winston Churchill
1947	Publication of *The Industrial Charter*
1951	October: Conservative victory returns Churchill to power
1955	Churchill retires, Anthony Eden becomes party leader
	May: Conservative victory under Eden
1957	Eden resigns over Suez, succeeded by Harold Macmillan
1959	October: Conservative victory under Macmillan
1962	'Night of the Long Knives' – Cabinet reshuffle
1963	Macmillan resigns
1964	October: Conservative defeat under Sir Alec Douglas-Home
1965	July: Edward Heath becomes first elected leader of the Conservative Party
1970	June: Conservative victory brings Heath to power
1974	February: general election returns Heath to power in minority government
	October: Conservative defeat under Heath
1979	May: Conservative victory brings Margaret Thatcher to power
1983	June: Conservative victory under Thatcher
1987	June: Conservative victory under Thatcher
1990	Thatcher resigns as Prime Minister and party leader
1992	April: Conservative victory under John Major
1997	May: Conservative defeat under Major
	William Hague defeats Kenneth Clarke to become Conservative Party leader
1998	Conservatives make gains in local government and EU elections
1999	Criticism of Hague's leadership and policies leads to defection of Shawn Woodward, MP, to Labour Party. Conservatives still trail the Labour Party badly in opinion polls
2000	Michael Portillo joins the Shadow Cabinet as Shadow Chancellor of the Exchequer

Overview

THE years covered in this chapter begin and end with a landslide defeat for the Conservative Party. In both 1945 and 1997 the rules of politics seemed to have shifted significantly in favour of the Labour Party. But there were important differences in the circumstances of these elections. In 1945 the mood of the country had swung decisively towards the left and in favour of socialism. Influenced by the sacrifices of the war and the desire to build a new and better society, voters in 1945 were primarily interested in social reform and welfare. Labour was widely viewed as more likely to deliver these objectives. This was especially the case given memories of the interwar years. Conservative dominated governments had retreated from promises of social reform after the First World War, and led the country during the Depression years. Few people wanted to see a return to that era, and the Conservatives after 1945 had to convince the electorate that they could be trusted with this new set of priorities.

The defeat of 1997 was quite a different matter. This time it was Labour that had shifted towards the right. Bruised and battered by the popular successes of the Thatcher administrations of the 1980s, New Labour under the leadership of Tony Blair set a very different agenda from Labour under Clement Attlee. Whereas the Conservatives after 1945 could gather a broad base of support, particularly from middle-class voters grown weary of high taxation and rationing, in the late 1990s Labour had managed to capture and hold the middle ground of political debate with an agenda that bore a close resemblance to Conservatism in the 1950s. It proved more difficult in these circumstances for the Conservatives to find their feet again.

Paradox: A statement that sounds absurd but is nevertheless true.

The **paradox** of the situation in which the Conservative Party found itself at the end of the century was that it was largely the victim of its own success. The intervening years had seen two long stretches of successful and popular Conservative rule. Between 1951 and 1964, and again between 1979 and 1997 the Conservatives had set the agenda of British politics. At times slowly and at times rapidly, the party in government shifted the country away from the values of 1945. So many Conservatives and political commentators have highlighted the contrast between the Conservatism of the 1950s and the 1980s, that the differences between these eras have been exaggerated. In fact, the continuity in the party's policy has been far more significant than its differences. While it is true that tactics and strategy have changed with different circumstances, the general determination to promote widespread property ownership and to challenge the socialism of the left have been the

---

Conservative Party Leaders since 1940

Date became leader

9 October 1940	Winston Churchill	(Prime Minister 1940–45 and 1951–55)
21 April 1955	Sir Anthony Eden	(Prime Minister 1955–57)
22 January 1957	Harold Macmillan	(Prime Minister 1957–63)
11 November 1963	Sir Alec Douglas-Home	(Prime Minister 1963–64)
2 August 1965	Edward Heath	(Prime Minister 1970–74)
11 February 1975	Margaret Thatcher	(Prime Minister 1979–90)
28 November 1990	John Major	(Prime Minister 1990–97)
19 June 1997	William Hague	

overwhelming and consistent goals of Conservatism, not only since the war, but since the beginning of the 20th century. In these objectives the party has been strikingly successful. The question at the end of the century was: how can the Conservative party find a new role in a post-socialist age?

Groups within the Conservative Party

- The **1922 Committee** was founded in 1923 to assist and inform backbench Conservative MPs. It meets weekly and provides a forum for the frank exchange of views between the backbenches and the party leadership.
- The **Bow Group** was founded in 1950 by former Conservative students to provide a forum for new ideas from young members of the Conservative Party.
- The **One Nation Group** was founded by a small number of new Conservative MPs in 1950 to promote a progressive and modern approach to policy-making.
- The **Suez Group** was formed in 1954 to protest against the government's decision to withdraw from British military bases in Egypt.
- The **'No Turning Back'** group of MPs was founded in 1985 to support Thatcherism.

13.1 What factors explain the revival of Conservatism after the general election defeat of 1945?

The outcome of the general election of 1945 should not have come as a complete surprise to the leaders of the Conservative Party. There had been clear indications in opinion polls taken during the latter stages of the war, that social and economic reform at home would be a key issue. Most voters believed that Labour was better at domestic issues like housing, health care and maintaining full employment than the Conservatives. Furthermore, the Conservative-dominated National Governments after

Churchill addressing the 1945 Conservative Party Conference

1931 were associated in many people's minds with the mass unemployment and hardship of the Depression. While Winston Churchill was universally agreed to have been a great war leader, attention was now focused on rebuilding Britain.

But the defeat came as a crushing blow. Labour won an overall majority of 146 seats in the House of Commons and won 8% more votes than the Conservatives. The Conservative share of the vote had dropped by 5.9% from that of the last election, which had been held in 1935. There seemed to be an enormous job to do in reorganising the party's structure and policies to have a fighting chance when the time came to go back to the polls, and few would have predicted that the party would recover as quickly as it did. But by 1948 the Conservatives had regained their confidence and were looking like a serious party of Opposition. In the general election of 1950, the Conservatives gained 85 seats, and the Labour Party's overall majority was reduced to only five. Over the following year, the party's front and backbenchers tirelessly harassed the exhausted and increasingly divided Attlee administration. When a new election was called for October 1951, the Conservative Party was fighting fit, only six years after its humiliating defeat.

How was this recovery accomplished so quickly? There are four basic factors that contribute towards an answer: structural reorganisation and recovery, policy development and propaganda, domestic economic problems, and the political and cultural atmosphere that accompanied the Cold War.

Structural Reorganisation and Recovery

Lord Woolton (1883–1964)
Became a household name during the war as Minister of Food 1940–43 and Minister of Reconstruction 1943–45. He served as Chairman of the Conservative Party 1946–55 and is credited with the revival of the party's organiation and finances after the war. As a member of the 1951–55 Churchill government he served as Lord President of the Council 1951–52 and Chancellor of the Duchy of Lancaster 1952–55.

Patron: A financial supporter.

The professional and efficient local and national organisation of the Conservative Party, which had set it apart from other parties in the interwar years, had disintegrated during the war. The 1945 campaign had been run on a shoestring with almost no professional staff. After the election, the party had to be built up again almost from scratch, and much of the first 18 months was spent recruiting new staff for the Central Office in London as well as in the regions. Even the most basic tools of a political party, such as lists of members, or handbooks for party workers, had to be reconstructed, and it was not until 1947 that these basic operations had been restored. Lord Woolton's appointment as Party Chairman in July 1946 was an important step in this process, although important steps had been taken by his predecessor. Between 1945 and 1950 nearly 300 people qualified as constituency agents for the party, and many more than that began their training.

The membership and fundraising drives initiated by Lord Woolton were very successful. By the beginning of the 1950s the party in England, Wales and Scotland had a combined membership approaching 3 million, making it easily the largest organisation of its kind before or since. Woolton's Fighting Fund restored the party's depleted finances through small member donations, as well as sponsorship from industry and wealthy **patrons** in Britain and abroad. This money enabled him to expand the party's staff and public relations machinery.

The party attempted after the war to project a more youthful and democratic image. The Young Conservative movement, which got underway in 1946 and grew rapidly, operated in many communities as a social club rather than as a political movement, but was nevertheless a key aspect of the revival of the party's grass roots. Democratisation of the party's structure was the main aim of the Maxwell-Fyfe Report of 1949, which attempted to open and democratise the party's selection procedures. By 1950 the party had been fully restored and had the finances and the organisation to fight from a position of strength.

Richard Austen ('Rab') Butler (1902–1982)

Remembered as one of the most influential Conservative politicians of the century, and came close on three occasions to becoming Prime Minister. He was responsible for the development of Conservative policy after the defeat of 1945, and served as Undersecretary of State at the Foreign Office 1938–41; President of the Board of Education 1941–45; Minister of Labour 1945; Chancellor of the Exchequer 1951–55; Lord Privy Seal 1955–59; Home Secretary 1957–62; First Secretary of State 1962; and Foreign Secretary 1963–64.

Enoch Powell (1912–1998)

Served as Minister of Health 1960–64 but is chiefly remembered for his increasingly inflammatory right-wing political views on issues such as European integration and immigration, which ultimately led to a break with the Conservative Party in 1974.

Iain Macleod (1913–1970)

Remembered for his efforts to adjust Conservative policy after the war to the changing nature of British power and society. He served as Minister of Health under Churchill 1952–55; Minister of Labour 1955–59; Colonial Secretary 1959–61; Chancellor of the Duchy of Lancaster 1961–63. He resigned from government in protest over the undemocratic way in which a new leader was chosen to replace Macmillan. When Heath came to power in 1970, Macleod served briefly as Chancellor of the Exchequer before his sudden death in July.

Laissez-faire: French for 'let do': used to mean that the economy works best when governments leave it alone.

Manifesto: A written statement of a party's policy.

Policy development and propaganda

The second factor in explaining the party's recovery after the war involves policy-making and presentation. The Labour government's domestic programme stressed the nationalisation of key industries and the implementation of a welfare state which was *universal* (social services for everybody rather than just for the poor). The Conservatives opposed all of this, but had to face up to the fact that much of Labour's programme was very popular. Devising an effective Opposition policy was therefore no easy matter. That is one reason why Winston Churchill, who remained leader of the party after 1945, initially opposed making any specific policy commitments.

By the end of 1945, however, there were already signs of life in the party's policy-making machinery. Richard Austen ('Rab') Butler, author of the 1944 Education Act and chairman of the party's wartime policy committee, was appointed leader of a new Advisory Committee on Policy and Political Education in November 1945. This was served by a Conservative Political Centre to promote policy education and propaganda. Early the following year Butler became chairman of the revived Conservative Research Department, which acted as a think tank on policy development. Under Butler's leadership, these organisations attracted a number of talented young and ambitious Conservatives, including Reginald Maudling, Enoch Powell, and Iain Macleod. Gradually, some meat was put into party policy and strategy as these bodies became established. Catchy but rather vague phrases such as 'property-owning democracy' became increasingly well defined around the notion of individual ownership and enterprise.

Churchill was forced to approve further policy development when a resolution calling for a clear statement of policy was passed almost unanimously at the October 1946 Party Conference. This led to the establishment of a committee, also chaired by Butler, to consider industrial policy. The ownership and structure of industry was given first priority because of the strength of feeling aroused by Labour's programme of nationalisation. The committee's work resulted in the publication of *The Industrial Charter* in 1947, which is seen as a landmark in the party's road to recovery. *The Industrial Charter* was not by any means a revolutionary document. Nor did it mark a dramatic break with past policy. It placed great emphasis on the need for cooperation within industry, and acknowledged the valuable role that trade unions had to play in a democratic society. It called for the reduction of taxation and public expenditure, but conceded that government economic policy should be used to encourage high levels of employment. It attacked monopolies and restrictive practices and supported schemes of 'co-partnership' and profit sharing in industry on a voluntary basis. The document was written in a style that seemed progressive and in tune with the aspirations of individuals and people of all class backgrounds. Above all, *The Industrial Charter* made it clear that Conservatism did not stand for *laissez-faire* as many people believed, but rather for a reduction in the role of the state and a greater part for individual enterprise in society.

The Industrial Charter was followed up with a series of charters on other aspects of policy including women and agriculture. In 1949 the first general statement of party policy was produced under the title *The Right Road for Britain*. This acted as the basis for the **manifesto** in the 1950 campaign, and stressed that the Conservatives would protect the welfare state and not undo the reforms of the Attlee years. In subtle ways, however, the party did not conceal its desire to lower taxes and make people in work responsible for a greater share of the cost of services such as health care and housing. At the Party Conference in 1950, a resolution was passed which pledged a future Conservative government to building 300,000 houses a year, which was claimed to be possible in free market conditions.

This was a powerful weapon with voters, many of whom had been waiting for new homes for many years.

Domestic economic problems

The third factor that contributed to the rise of Conservatism after the war concerns the continuing economic problems faced by the Labour government after 1945. In spite of the fact that Britain was a victor in the Second World War, this was accomplished at an enormous cost, and the country was virtually bankrupt by the end of hostilities. Although still much wealthier than its neighbours on the continent of Europe, the country's spending commitments were also far greater – in defending and developing the Empire and Commonwealth, in paying for the occupation of Germany, in undertaking to construct a welfare state, and in the costs of rebuilding ravaged city centres and damaged housing.

The Labour government was determined that the 'fair shares' policy which had characterised the war years should not be abandoned in peacetime. Indeed this was extended in some respects. This was the postwar **'age of austerity'**. Labour hoped that by restricting individual consumption money could be diverted into industrial production as well into the new social services. Many middle-class voters, women in particular, soon became tired of this. It was one thing to put up with queuing during the war, but quite another once the war was over. The Conservatives took advantage of these circumstances by promising that if elected they would drastically reduce the controls and bureaucracy that had grown during the war.

Age of austerity: The period after 1945 when rationing was still in force.

The impact of the Cold War

A final factor which contributed to the postwar recovery of Conservatism was the changing political climate at home and abroad which accompanied the early Cold War. Conservatives had been placed on the defensive when life during the war seemed to justify socialist claims that the state could provide efficiently and more fairly the employment and services which had been so conspicuously absent during the Depression. The Soviet Union, after all, was a wartime ally, and wartime propaganda had portrayed socialist approaches to the economy and society more favourably than had been the case before. The opposition to Labour which emerged after the war was in essence an anti-Socialist alliance. Not only Conservatives, but Liberals too were disturbed by the apparent ease with which wartime high taxation and expansion of the role of the state seemed to have been continued into peacetime.

When the Cold War began to emerge in the spring of 1946, the language of politics began to change. This was true first and foremost of course, in Britain's dealings with the Soviet Union and communism. That debate stressed freedom and democracy versus repression and dictatorship; enterprise and opportunity versus planning and bureaucracy; individualism and justice versus collectivism and injustice. This language with which Britain, the United States and their allies attacked the Stalinist Eastern bloc, fed usefully into domestic debates at home. Even though Labour's version of socialism bore little resemblance to the Soviet system, the same language could be and was adopted by the Conservatives to persuade voters to reject policies aimed at increasing equality in society. Capitalist free enterprise no longer had the negative associations linked with the 1930s that it had in 1945. By 1950 such concepts had gained a far more positive meaning as a result of the changing international climate.

1. Why do you think that so many women voted for the Conservatives in 1950s and 1951?

2. Why is the Industrial Charter remembered as a milestone in postwar Conservative history?

3. To what extent did the Cold War assist the Conservative recovery after the war?

Source-based questions: The recovery of the Conservative Party after the 1945 general election

SOURCE A

In my opinion, we owe our defeat not to anything which happened during the election campaign itself, but to a persistent and ably-conducted campaign of socialist propaganda which extended from the last general election in November 1935 until July 1945 with no let-up whatsoever during the war.

We Conservatives (wrongly I think) interpreted the political truce as barring us from all propaganda efforts. The Socialists, on the other hand, interpreted it as a by-election truce only … It would require a good deal of investigation to assess the value of the various forms of Socialist propaganda, but there can be no doubt that the following had their part:

● The appointment of a prominent member of the Workers' Educational Association to direct the Army Bureau of Current Affairs, and the clever use made by the Socialists of many of the lectures. Many paid lecturers were Socialists, and made full use of their opportunities.

● The persistent use of the BBC broadcasting service granted to prominent left-wing writers and politicians, and the left bias of many of the news reports and talks.

● Widespread newspaper propaganda in the columns of left-wing national daily papers, such as the *Daily Herald*, *Daily Mirror*, *News Chronicle*, *Daily Worker*, *The Star*.

● On top of this widespread press campaign, we had regular week-end speeches by leading Socialists, invariably well reported not only by the press but also by the BBC.

From The Next General Election *by Sir Joseph Ball, acting Chairman of the Conservative Party, 1940–45. He was acting Chairman during the 1945 general election.*

SOURCE B

The organisation of the Conservative Party was the most topsy-like* arrangement that I had ever come across. It had grown up amidst conflicting and – it seemed – almost irreconcilable claims. I faced up to the fact that whilst as the Chairman of the Party I had received an enthusiastic welcome from the associations, I had, on paper, no control over their activities; they selected their candidates; they selected their agent and employed him … I depended on their goodwill, I relied on Central Office earning the goodwill and confidence of all these diversified bodies which troubled my business instincts.

I rejected caution and decided to ask for a fund of one million pounds, thereby demonstrating my faith in the willingness of the Party to make sacrifices in order to convince the electors of the country of the rightness of the Conservative approach. These were shock tactics. This bold demand created an infectious and compelling enthusiasm. People went out for this apparently unassailable goal, and the stimulation of this widespread effort among all grades of society of which the Conservative Party is composed not only produced the millions of pounds that I asked for, but it gave the Party a sense of accomplishment. Their hopes revived; they found that people believed in them in spite of the recent electoral defeat.

From the Memoirs of Lord Woolton, *1959. Lord Woolton was Chairman of the Conservative Party from 1946 to 1955.*

* Topsy-like – it just grew.

SOURCE C

At the age of 77 Churchill returned to power, and his own instincts and the narrowness of the margin ensured that his ministry followed a moderate line in home affairs. The Conservative dominance of 1951–1964 was founded upon this and three other factors which remained constant until the early 1960s: the public appeal of successive moderate Conservative leaders, the growth of consumer affluence over which they presided, and the persistent disunity in the Labour opposition. An effective combination of 'progressive' Tory domestic policy and 'world power' foreign policy characterised the governments of Churchill and his successors from 1951 to 1964. Only after this did a different agenda emerge in part under Heath, with 'Selsdon Man' and the entry into Europe, and later and more completely with Thatcher's crusade to roll back the state and shatter the post-war 'consensus'.

From The Conservative Party and British Politics, *1902–1951, by Stuart Ball, 1995.*

Source-based questions: The recovery of the Conservative Party after the 1945 general election

SOURCE D

The reasons for this considerable success must be analysed. Some of it was certainly the result of favourable economic circumstances that the Conservatives had been able to exploit to party advantage; whatever government had been in power through the 1950s such factors would have helped them to give a great measure of prosperity to the electorate. But it is not as easy as that. It was the consistent policy of Conservatism, at least since Disraeli, to improve 'the condition of the people' in the sure knowledge that such a policy was both wise and popular. Macmillan in the 1950s portrayed his party as the believers in material well-being and other parties as believers in moral changes and structural reforms. It has been a Conservative belief that politics is not the whole of life but that economics is much nearly so.

From The Conservatives *by John Ramsden, 1977. He refers to the reasons for Conservative electoral success in the 1950s.*

1. Study Sources B and C.

Using information contained within this chapter explain the meaning of the phrases highlighted as they applied to the Conservative Party 1945–2000.

a) 'Chairman of the Party' (Source B)

b) 'Selsdon Man' (Source C)

c) 'The post war consensus' (Source C)

2. Study Source A.

How reliable is this source as evidence for the Conservative defeat in the 1945 general election? Explain your answer.

3. Study Source B.

Of what value is this source to a historian writing about the Conservative revival after the 1945 general election defeat?

4. Study Sources B, C and D, and use information contained within this chapter.

Do the three sources fully explain why the Conservatives were able to recover from their electoral defeat in 1945 to dominate national politics between 1951 and 1964? Give reasons to explain your answer.

13.2 To what extent does the affluence of the 1950s account for the Conservative election victories in 1955 and 1959?

Indian Summer: A period of very warm, summer-like weather when in fact autumn is about to begin. In this context a final success in a long career.

The Conservative Party won the general election of 1951, bringing Winston Churchill back to power for an '**Indian Summer**' period of office. But the circumstances of that victory were by no means comforting for the party's leadership. The overall parliamentary majority was less than 20. The economic crisis sparked by the costs of the Korean War made it seem for the first year that things could only get worse. The Cabinet was under constant pressure to cut back expenditure, and yet feared that unpopular cuts in education or the housing programme would lead to defeat and another long period of Labour government.

The end of austerity

The fortunes of the government began to change by the end of 1952. Improving economic conditions and relatively rapid rates of growth in the middle of the 1950s undoubtedly helped to ensure the party's re-election in 1955, and again in 1959. The health of the economy was claimed to be the work of Butler, who served as Chancellor of the Exchequer between

---

1951 and 1955. In fact, the turnaround was largely the product of international economic conditions after the war in Korea had ended. The economy grew fast enough for Butler to reduce taxes and increase spending on welfare at the same time, keeping voters happy. Full employment continued to characterise this period, spreading the gains of growth widely throughout society. Harold Macmillan, who served as Minister of Housing between 1951 and 1954, was able to fulfill the '300,000' houses a year pledge in 1953, a year earlier than promised. Although this was accomplished largely through the local authority housing programmes (and partly by reducing the size of council houses) the government made a concerted effort to encourage home ownership and made it much easier to purchase a home in the private sector. The housing drive was a big source of popularity for the government, and contributed towards Macmillan's personal rise to power later in the decade.

The Churchill administration was able to end rationing and many of the controls which had characterised the war and early postwar years. Britain moved from an era of austerity into an era of affluence.

The primary source of disquiet within insider circles of the party and the government after 1951 was actually Winston Churchill's leadership. The Prime Minister's disintegrating health (he suffered at least two strokes in this period) accentuated his already eccentric behaviour. Churchill's almost mythical stature at home and abroad was established in these years, making it especially difficult to ease him out of office. This was a source of frustration for his expected successor, Anthony Eden. Finally, he resigned in April 1955; a new election was held at the end of May.

It was, on the whole, a quiet campaign. The Conservatives made the most of prosperity, contrasting 'socialist meddling and muddling' with the improved conditions since 1951. Divisions in the Labour Party between the Bevanites and Gaitskellites was a further factor in explaining the party's poor performance. There was never much doubt that the Conservatives would win the election. The only question in 1955 was the size of the majority. That was increased to a much safer 58 seats, while the Conservative share of the vote rose by nearly 2%. Perhaps the most interesting aspect of the entire campaign was the extent to which television was used in addition to radio broadcasts. 1955 was indeed the first election fought on television, although it was not until 1959 that television took the place of radio as a medium of communication for the parties.

Eden and Suez, 1956

Eden had been confirmed as premier by the voters, but those around him in the party had deep reservations about his fitness for the job from the outset. He was emotionally unsuited for leadership, nervous and prone to sudden mood swings. Eden certainly did not have the confidence of his colleagues and it did not take long for these doubts to be confirmed. He was an indecisive and interfering Prime Minister. Conservative fortunes were flagging well before the Suez Crisis. Butler's famous quip to journalists that he was 'the best Prime Minister we have' summed up the lukewarm support he commanded in the party by the beginning of 1956.

Signs of discontent were evident as well among the voters by this time, allowing the Liberals to make surprising inroads in by-elections. Middle-class frustration over taxes and inflation was particularly evident, as shown by several short lived lobby groups that sprang up in this period such as the Middle Class Alliance. Higher interest rates hit homeowners hard at the same time that employers seemed to be raising industrial wage packets above the rate of inflation. This is the kind of atmosphere in which resentments were bound to arise, and furthered Eden's image problems.

The end was in sight, therefore, by the time that the Suez Crisis erupted in the autumn of 1956, and in fact Eden's weak position may well have influenced his decision to take such a risky course of action. This worked while the country was at war, and the party regained its sense of unity during the crisis. The American response to the Anglo-French invasion of Egypt made it inevitable, however, that Britain would have to withdraw. This simply capped the impression of Eden as a Prime Minister without authority or sound judgement. On the advice of his doctors, he flew to Jamaica for a rest on 23 November. There was no question that, having been unable to stand the strain of defeat, he would be allowed to resume office upon his return.

The question that remained was who would succeed him, Butler or Macmillan. Butler was the senior figure in the party, but Macmillan had several advantages over him. Butler was viewed within the party as a rather academic and aloof figure. He had been an appeaser before the war, and a bad arm had prevented him from serving in the armed forces after 1940. As Chancellor he had started out strongly, but after the 1955 election the economy had dipped, and he bore the blame. Moreover, Butler had kept quiet during Suez. Macmillan was the more confident of the two. He had built up a solid portfolio of ministerial posts after 1951 and during Suez had at least been a strong supporter of action, even if he was one of the first to advocate pulling out. There was no formal mechanism for the selection of the Conservative Party leader at this time. When Eden resigned on 9 January, Lord Salisbury, the **Lord President of the Council**, invited Cabinet Ministers into his office one by one to get their view. Almost all selected Macmillan. This advice was passed to the Queen, and he was summoned to the Palace the following day.

It is remarkable that the Suez Crisis made such a small impression on domestic politics in Britain. Compared to France, for example, where the colonial wars of the 1950s in Indochina and Algeria were to cause upheaval leading to the fall of the regime in 1958, in Britain the retreat in Egypt did not even occasion a general election. This can partly be explained by the fact that Conservative leaders were defiant in the face of defeat – there was no apology for the events of November, and indeed, the crisis was not even mentioned in the 1959 election manifesto. Part of Macmillan's genius as leader in these years was in the way that he managed to turn his back on these events, and focus the country's attention around a new agenda.

'Supermac' and the affluent society

The years 1957–59 tend to be remembered as the high point of the decade's affluence, while in fact it was only in the particular circumstances of the first half of the decade that the party was able to deliver lower taxes and higher public spending without serious consequences. When Macmillan delivered his well-known speech in Bedford in July 1957 declaring that 'most of our people have never had it so good' he was not welcoming an age of affluence but trying to warn the country that high public spending, rising standards of living, full employment and low inflation were not simultaneously possible. The economic difficulties which had begun in the second half of 1955 had made the Cabinet acutely aware of the underlying problems in the economy.

In fact, the harsh realities of economic management would soon culminate in an argument within the government which led to the resignation of the entire Treasury ministerial team at the beginning of 1958. The Chancellor, Peter Thorneycroft felt so strongly on the principle of economic orthodoxy that he resigned over his colleague's refusal to cut the last £50 million off the budget reduction targets that he had

Lord President of the Council: The title given to the member of the Cabinet who is leader of the Privy Council (all former members of the Cabinet).

A cartoon published following Macmillan's victory in the 1959 general election. He is surrounded by consumer items: a fridge, car, washing machine and television.

MACMILLAN: Well gentlemen, I think we all fought a good fight.

What is the message the cartoonist is trying to get across about the reasons for the 1959 Conservative electoral victory?

believed necessary to deflate the economy. The resignations, followed by a series of by-election defeats in the spring, were the low point of the administration.

But the tide turned for the government in the spring, as Macmillan became more confident, and as the government faced down the unions in the London Bus Strike. Furthermore, in 1958 the economy entered into another period of boom. In spite of the foreign and colonial record of doubt and uncertainty – as Britain lost her empire and sense of purpose in the world order – the domestic record was the one that mattered to most voters in the run-up to the election. This created a feeling of affluence and well-being sufficient to carry the party through the general election of 1959. But the concerns which had been identified by Thorneycroft had not gone away and would soon resurface.

These were the years of 'Supermac', the nickname coined by the cartoonist Vicky, and cultivated by the Prime Minister. Macmillan was a clever politician. He mastered television and understood the importance of addressing his own image in the age of visual media. His personal approval ratings rose steadily in the polls: from less than 40% at the beginning of 1958 to nearly 70% when the election was called. During the chairmanship of the popular Lord Hailsham between 1957 and 1959, the party adopted new methods of campaigning in the late 1950s which paid far more attention to opinion polling and modern methods of public relations. Campaigns in the national press designed by commercial advertising firms signalled a new standard in political communication.

1. What were the main domestic reforms made by the Conservatives in the 1950s?

2. What factors explain Harold Macmillan's rise to the leadership of the Conservative Party in 1957?

3. Why did the Conservatives win the general election of 1959?

The party was thus well prepared for the election, when it was called for October 1959. In spite of Suez and the internal divisions of only two years previously, the Conservatives entered the campaign with an advantage in the polls which dipped slightly over the first two weeks, only to recover by the end of the campaign. This was to be the third successive victory, which saw the Conservative majority in the House of Commons increase to 100 seats. It was unprecedented in modern politics, and Macmillan's star continued to rise in 1960. No Prime Minister at least, had ever had it so good.

13.3 Why did the Conservative Party lose the general election of 1964?

Sir Alec Douglas-Home (Lord Home) (1903–1995)
Served briefly as Prime Minister 1963–64 following the resignation of Harold Macmillan and was an influential figure in British politics for a remarkably long time, first entering Parliament in 1931 as MP for South Lanark, and still taking an active role in the House of Lords after Margaret Thatcher came to power.

Old Etonians: Men who had been educated at the privileged public school at Eton.

The Establishment: The ruling elite.

The success of the Conservative administrations of the 1950s rested in large part on the material conditions of those years. With hindsight the 1950s have been criticised as a period of missed opportunity and growth that was sluggish by comparison to its competitors. At the time, the record of the party in office was strong. But with great speed, the party lost its way after 1959. By 1964 no one was surprised when Labour came back to power. The Conservatives now looked out-of-date and uncertain. How did this happen so quickly?

The establishment factor

For one thing, Macmillan was tired. Sixty-five in 1959, he had spent ten years in Cabinet and led the party and the country through the tense international and economic climate surrounding Suez. He also seemed to be increasingly out of touch with the socially mobile affluent age that the party had been at pains to cultivate in the previous decade. Half of his Cabinet after 1959 were fellow **old Etonians**. The promotion of a peer, Lord Home, to the Foreign Office in 1960 was criticised as highly undemocratic, and in general Macmillan did not hesitate to use politicians from the Lords to an extent that was difficult to reconcile with a modern democracy. He and his government were thus easy targets for satire, as shown to devastating effect by the young comedians of the day. Suddenly, the Conservative leadership became labelled as 'the **Establishment**'.

Educational background of Conservative MPs

Year	Public School followed by Oxford or Cambridge University
1945	48%
1955	50%
1964	48%
1974 (Feb)	48%
1983	42%
1992	32%

Source: *Dod's Parliamentary Companion, 1945–1992*

Equally worrying was the extent to which the party's organisation lost its sense of momentum after 1959. Lord Hailsham was not reappointed by Macmillan (who found his popularity something of a threat). Butler took on the Chairmanship, but as Leader of the House and Home Secretary as well, could not spend the time necessary to keep on top of the party. After so many years in office it would in any case have been difficult to maintain the sense of passion for doing voluntary work for the party that is needed for a healthy grass roots organisation. Macleod replaced Butler as Party Chairman in the autumn of 1961, and he proved to be a more dynamic and younger-minded leader. But by that time the government's downturn had become more obvious, and that made the job of rescuing the party organisation far more difficult to achieve.

The problem of affluence

Affluence too brought its own problems for the government. Party officials sensed that the voters had come to expect too much and grew angry when these objectives could not all be met. And it was becoming increasingly clear in the early 1960s that the country's economic performance was hitting some serious problems. Selwyn Lloyd, who became Chancellor of the Exchequer in July 1961, imposed an unpopular series of deflationary policies over the following months, which contributed to the poor local and by-election results at this time. At a broader level, Britain seemed to be losing a sense of purpose and place in the world. Decolonisation in Africa was speeding up and the days of empire were ending quickly. There was increasing disquiet on the right of the party and among many voters over West Indian and Asian immigration to Britain, forcing the government to pass the Commonwealth Immigration Act in 1962. Factors such as these, combined with economic problems, contributed to a sense of unease in British society in these years.

Macmillan fights back

Swing: The shift in votes between two elections when comparing the results for each party in percentages, i.e. an increase in votes from 45% to 50% is a 5% swing.

In politics, these problems were reflected in a series of by-elections from the middle of 1961. The Liberal Party benefited most from the government's problems, and in March 1962 actually won the previously safe Conservative seat of Orpington, Kent, on a **swing** of 27%. Conservative Party strategists became preoccupied with winning back 'Orpington Man'. There were several strands to the recovery strategy that emerged in response to these problems.

The Cabinet's decision to apply for membership of the EEC in July 1961 should be seen in this context, for example. European integration, it was hoped, would set a new and modern agenda in British politics and economic policy which the Conservatives could take a lead on. This would force a cold shower of modernisation and competition on industry that the government could not impose in isolation. In the meantime, Macmillan was convinced that economic policy was the basic problem for most voters. He told his Cabinet in May 1962 that trying to maintain full employment, low inflation, the balance of payments and high rates of growth all at the same time was like trying to juggle too many balls. Under his direction the Cabinet agreed an economic strategy in the early summer of 1962 that was far more interventionist than anything the Conservatives had ever tried previously, hoping that voters could be convinced that the government was back in control. Macmillan gambled on the idea that controlled expansion of the economy could revive the party's fortunes in the following year, and that the prospect of membership of the European Community would inspire and rejuvenate the party's fortunes at the next general election.

The 'Night of the Long Knives'

If this 'New Approach' to economic policy was the first element in Macmillan's plan to regain popularity, a radical reshuffle of the Cabinet was the second. In July 1962 he announced abrupt and radical changes to the composition of the government, which involved alterations to 39 out of the total of 101 ministerial posts. This move, which is remembered as Macmillan's 'Night of the Long Knives', was intended to create the impression of having appointed virtually a new government in an attempt to inject an air of freshness into an administration which had come to seem old and stale. But it proved to be an enormous miscalculation. Macmillan caused great offence by dismissing so many of his colleagues without adequate warning or ceremony. This only served to make the low morale in the party worse, as there was widespread anger at the way so many loyal and experienced Conservatives had been treated. The affair did little to enhance Macmillan's personal reputation. The Liberal MP, Jeremy Thorpe, famously quipped afterwards that the Prime Minister had 'laid down his friends for his life'.

The night of the long knives is often cited as an important example of the Prime Minister's prerogative, or power. By dismissing so many senior members of the government simultaneously, he was wielding one of the most important tools that the executive has in the British system of government. It was clear, however, that Macmillan was not acting from a position of strength, but rather out of an increasing sense of political desperation. On the other hand, the long-term damage that the reshuffle caused has probably been exaggerated. It is true that the Conservatives failed to recover sufficiently to win the election in 1964. But it could be argued that the defeat might have been worse had such radical action not been taken. Significantly, the reshuffle cleared the way for Macmillan's economic ideas to be implemented. Expansion after 1962 was certainly an important factor in drawing votes back to the party, even in numbers insufficient to retain overall control of the House of Commons.

> **Why did Macmillan decide to reshuffle his government so drastically in July 1962?**

Europe, scandal and the fall of Macmillan

Macmillan's New Approach took a series of beatings in 1963. In January, General de Gaulle famously said '*non*' to the British EEC application. Party strategists had not planned for this possibility, and the Conservative case for voters had depended heavily upon the ability to contrast the efficiency and modernisation of EEC membership that they promised, in contrast to Labour's increasingly anti-European, insular line. Moreover, in the same month Harold Wilson was elected to lead the Labour Party following Hugh Gaitskell's sudden death. At 46, Wilson found it easy to contrast his youth with the old and 'square' Macmillan (and also his successor, Alec Douglas-Home).

The news on Europe left the government reeling for several months. By the late spring, however, there were signs of renewed confidence. The new Chancellor, Reginald Maudling, unveiled his 'dash for growth' budget, attempting to implement the New Approach developed the previous summer. There were signs that expansionist policies were beginning to bear fruit. By May, the Conservatives were back on their feet, planning for the forthcoming election campaign in a style reminiscent of 1958.

Meanwhile, however, the government was rocked by the Profumo scandal, and by June, the Prime Minister was fighting for his political life. John Profumo, the War Minister, was rumoured in the press to have had an affair with a woman named Christine Keeler in 1961. She was in turn said to have also had an affair with a Russian diplomat. The government had had to handle a spy scandal in the autumn of 1962, which had been the subject of hysterical press coverage. At first, Macmillan was determined to face down this new round of gossip. In March, the Cabinet backed Profumo, who denied the rumours in the House of Commons. But the scandal would not go away. Profumo, it emerged, had lied about his actions. In June, he was forced to admit this and resign. The Profumo scandal certainly weakened Macmillan's already battered position as premier.

The 'changing of the guard'

In these circumstances, it was inevitable that speculation grew about Macmillan's position as leader of the party. Macmillan himself was undecided about whether to resign in time for a new leader to take charge of the general election campaign. Part of this indecision was due to the fact that the succession was uncertain. These questions were brought to a head in a sudden and dramatic fashion, when Macmillan was taken ill at the beginning of the week of the Conservative Party Conference in early October. On the advice of his doctors, Macmillan resigned, and, in an fit of bad judgement, made that decision known while the Conference was in full-swing. The week degenerated into one of undignified jostling between the contenders. Macmillan, who initiated a process of formal consultation to find a successor in the week following the Conference, was sobered by this performance. As the opinions of Cabinet Ministers, MPs and peers, and the constituencies were canvassed over the next several days, it became clear that opinion was sharply divided between Butler and Hailsham. It was in this context that Lord Home emerged as a compromise candidate, even though he was hardly anyone's first choice. It was for this reason that Macmillan advised the Queen to invite Home to form a government.

The selection process in 1963 was highly controversial. Macleod, in particular, would later charge that it had been undemocratic, governed by a 'magic circle' of old Etonians around the Prime Minister. In the short term, the bitter aftertaste of the selection process gave a public impression of division within the party which would be a further hindrance in the election campaign. In the longer term the episode demonstrated how important it was to have an open and clearly democratic leadership selection process.

Sir Alec Douglas-Home (who renounced his peerage upon becoming Prime Minister) was never going to have enough time to stamp his mark in office before a general election had to be called. He was hampered from the outset by his aristocratic background, at a time when the Conservative Party was already vulnerable to the charge of being led by the upper class and out of touch with the concerns of middle- and working-class voters. Wilson's Labour Party had a soft target against which to offset its modernising agenda. In spite of the Conservative Party's attempt to run an effective and sophisticated campaign along the lines of 1959, these were handicaps which proved difficult to overcome.

1. Why was Sir Alec Douglas-Home's appointment as Conservative leader controversial?

2. What 'image problems' had the Conservative Party developed by 1964?

The timing of the election was postponed as long as possible to give the government the maximum amount of time to gather support in 1964 and to recover from the series of disasters of the previous year. Finally, in September the vote was announced for 15 October. Home did not prove to be an effective campaigner. He was no good on television, and did not handle hecklers well. In the circumstances, it was almost surprising that the defeat was not more convincing. Although the Conservative vote dropped by around 1.75 million, Labour was sent to power with a majority of only four seats.

13.4 To what extent is it fair to criticise Edward Heath's government of 1970–1974 for its 'U-turns' on policy pledges made in opposition?

Edward Heath, who led the Conservative Party for the decade 1965–75, has often been condemned for failing to carry through the promised tough programme of economic and industrial reform on which the Conservatives had won the general election of 1970. These charges were highlighted particularly by the Thatcherite wing of the party that rose to prominence following the fall of Heath in 1975. Indeed, Margaret Thatcher deliberately and effectively contrasted her leadership of the country when she famously declared that 'the Lady's not for turning'. Were the actions of the 1970–74 government the product of weak leadership or of the extraordinary and unstable domestic and international problems with which it was faced?

Heath in opposition

Edward Heath (1916–)
He became an MP in 1950 and joined a group of Conservatives with an interest in social policy. As chief whip held the party together during the Suez crisis in 1956. Minister of Labour 1959. At Foreign Office from 1960 and involved in negotiations to join Common Market. Became leader in 1965 while party were in opposition. First leader to be elected. Lost 1966 election but came to power in 1970. Led the opposition from 1974 until the election of Thatcher in 1975.

Edward Heath became leader of the Conservative Party in July 1965. The first leader to be elected democratically by a ballot of Conservative MPs (Home had introduced this new system in February), he was judged to have the tough, bullish qualities required of an Opposition leader. Unlike his predecessors, moreover, he was a product of the state education system, and came from a solid middle-class background. Heath was from the outset viewed as a professional, technocratic moderniser, devoted to the cause of good and efficient government. He proceeded to promote a generation of younger politicians, many of them, like himself, from suburban, middle-class backgrounds. This was an important departure in the character of the Conservative Party, which was no longer perceived to be dominated by products of a privileged, upper class elite. But Heath was, nevertheless, a difficult personality. He was never an easy-going leader, and his abrasive character led him to become an isolated party leader, particularly in the years after he became Prime Minister.

The party's top priority after the election defeat of 1964 was to undertake a complete review of its policies, initially at least in preparation for the next generation which was bound to come quickly in view of the narrow majority of the Wilson government. Already by the time that a new election was called in 1966, a new emphasis was noticeable in British Conservatism. In its manifesto of that year, the party stressed tax reform, competition, trade union reform, and more means testing in the welfare system. All of these policies were designed to increase competition and efficiency in the British economy in order to prepare it for membership of the European Economic Community of which Heath was, throughout his career, a strong advocate.

'Powellism' and 'Selsdon Man'

These policies were developed further between 1966 and 1970, as the party prepared for an election which it stood a reasonable chance of winning. As the Wilson administration faced a whole series of crises – from the failure of trade union reform to the devaluation crisis of 1967 (see chapter 12) – the Conservative Opposition moved steadily to the right. This can be partly explained by the success of Enoch Powell's increasingly extreme pronouncements, beginning with his vocal advocacy of the free market in the mid-1960s, and reaching a climax with his infamous series of speeches on race relations and immigration beginning in 1968. This latter development led to his sacking from the front bench, and the beginning of his role as maverick outcast on the right fringe of British politics. But Heath, in spite of the fact that he personally detested Powell, could not ignore his views, which had strong support within the party and among a significant section of the electorate. The rise of the right was a foretaste of the Thatcherite movement which would emerge in the following decade. In the second half of the 1960s, it could be traced by the growth of organisations such as the **Monday Club**, whose membership grew to around 2,000 by 1970. Heath had to take this influence into account in formulating policy, as it was his duty to maintain party unity in the run-up to the election.

Monday Club: The extreme right-wing Conservative group founded in 1961 to protest against the loss of Empire.

The Conservative shift to the right got a big publicity boost as a result of the weekend strategy meeting of the Shadow Cabinet held at the Selsdon Park Hotel just south of London in January 1970. Harold

Wilson's subsequent jibes about 'Selsdon Man' – meant to poke fun at Heathite policies – had the effect of giving coherence to the Conservative platform, which it had not previously had. In the public mind, Selsdon Man stood for a return to free enterprise and values of hard work, for a tough approach to the trade unions, and a more efficient and independent industry independent of government control. None of this was a new departure for the party in 1970, but by the time that the general election was called for 18 June, there was a widespread perception that the Conservatives were offering a new alternative to Wilson.

Heath in power

Heath started out determined to carry through a Conservative 'quiet revolution' by reducing the scale of the public sector and government intervention in the economy. But as premier, he was always better at the details of policy and the business of government than at communicating a message to the public or at keeping focused on the 'big ideas'. He also became quite isolated in office, and unwisely dependent upon the advice of his civil servants. The Heath Administration was beset with a series of problems from the outset, but it must be said that these were compounded by tactical errors of judgement. It is easy to forget, however, that the government was learning bitter lessons that the next Conservative administration did not repeat. For example, in industrial relations, Heath, in his determination to get the trade unions under control, made the mistake of legislating too quickly, without sufficient consultation. The **Industrial Relations Act 1971** was so broad in scope that it became an obvious target for the hostility of the labour movement. The good aspects of the Act became lost in the general bitterness over the method of its passage. The general refusal to comply with its terms meant that it never became a credible part of the legal culture of Britain, and was inevitably repealed by the next Labour government, in spite of the fact that a large majority of the voters continued to approve of its basic provisions.

It is also true that the Heath government was beset by a series of problems not of its own making. The Ugandan Asian Crisis of 1972, for example, inflamed public hostility towards New Commonwealth immigration. Politics in Northern Ireland were an added problem, because Heath continued to rely upon the support of the Unionist MPs in the House of Commons. Rising violence in Northern Ireland led inevitably to the imposition of direct rule from London in March 1972. This precipitated the loss of Unionist support, and hampered Heath's political position at a critical moment.

But in other respects, the Heath administration made determined efforts to carry through its manifesto commitments. Taxes were cut, and radical reform of the tax and benefits system was well advanced by the time that the government fell. The government stopped subsidising house-building and increased council rents in face of strenuous opposition. It also continued and extended the rights to buy council houses – although as in the 1950s this was obstructed by Labour local authorities. Again, this was a lesson learned by Margaret Thatcher, who understood that an extensive sell-off of public housing would depend upon central government control of local housing policy.

The U-turns

Heath's policy reversals of 1972 are what the government has been chiefly criticised for. Although Rolls Royce had been nationalised in

Industrial Relations Act 1971: The basic terms of the act were: unions had to register; secret ballots had to be held of union members to agree to a strike; the National Industrial Relations Court ensured that the Act was obeyed; the Commission for Industrial Relations would iron-out conflicts between unions.

Barber boom: The name given to Anthony Barber's policies as Chancellor of the Exchequer under Heath.

1. *What was different about Edward Heath's rise to the leadership, compared with previous Conservative leaders?*

2. *Why did Enoch Powell and Edward Heath dislike each other?*

3. *Why was the Heath government forced to reconsider its policies in 1972?*

1971, this could be explained as a special circumstance for a firm on the brink of bankruptcy with an international reputation and operations of strategic importance to the country. The decision, after a year of refusal, to bail out the Upper Clyde Shipbuilders in the spring of 1972, on the other hand, was a climb down in the face of the threat of public disorder. Rising unemployment, combined with the determination to speed the rate of growth before entry to the EEC led to deliberate economic expansion – 'the Barber boom' – which flew in the face of Heath's previous commitment to solve the problem of inflation. Voluntary wage control proved impossible to maintain in the face of rising inflation, and when tripartite talks between the government, employers and the unions broke down in 1972, Heath announced that prices and wages would be controlled by law. This was the ultimate U-turn, and no amount of qualification and explanation from the Prime Minister could get away from the fact that the government had strayed far away from its claims at the Selsdon Park Hotel. By the end of its period in office then, the Heath government had failed dramatically in its attempt to impose a quiet revolution.

13.5 What factors account for Margaret Thatcher's election to the leadership of the Conservative Party in 1975?

Powellism: The ideas associated with Enoch Powell.

Margaret Thatcher's emergence as party leader in 1975 was a landmark in the history of British Conservatism. As a supporter of the New Right thinking that had become increasingly influential since the appearance of **Powellism** in the previous decade, it was clear even at the time that her leadership would mark a real break with Heath and the moderate pragmatism for which he stood. Moreover, in the history of gender politics, this was also a milestone. Thatcher had been only the second woman to achieve a position in a Conservative Cabinet. Her election to lead the party thus took nearly everyone by surprise. No one had considered her campaign as a serious one until it was all over.

Why Thatcher hated Heath

In order to explain her rise to power, it is important to recall the increasingly bitter divisions in the party which had emerged after 1970. The U-turns of 1972 had caused widespread disillusionment at a grass roots level. The get-tough policies associated with 'Selsdon Man' had fizzled out, and by the beginning of 1974 Heath was involved in a miners' strike that threatened chaos. The February election, called on the issue of 'who governs Britain?' did not, as Heath had hoped, indicate that the country wanted strong government action. Within the party, the election brought out even further some of the simmering resentment that had been building for several years. Enoch Powell, a strong opponent of EEC membership, was so disgusted that he resigned his seat in the House and announced his intention to vote Labour, which was also anti-Europe. That election resulted in a hung Parliament, and the lowest number of votes for the Conservatives since the 1920s. Heath clung on for several months, even though the Conservatives actually had fewer MPs than Labour. The election called in October returned a small Labour majority. It had become clear that Heath's days as party leader were numbered. But Heath was reluctant to give up the position.

Changes in the party

The general gloom within the party at this point was evident on a number of levels. Membership levels had fallen dramatically since the 1950s, and once thriving organisations such as the Young Conservatives had almost collapsed. Meanwhile, the character and profile of the party was changing. Whereas in the days of Macmillan, the typical Conservative MP had been to a public school, had a private income, and a paternalist sense of civic responsibility, by the mid-1970s a Conservative backbencher was far more likely to have been educated at a grammar school, to come from a middle-class suburb, and to have a more professional and ideological approach to politics. There was an increasing frustration among this group with the Front Bench approach to economic and social policy. As British society became characterised by industrial militancy and rising levels of social discontent, many Conservatives began to question the moderate approach which the party had adopted since the 1950s. Heath and the 'Heathmen' seemed to be following a kind of domestic appeasement when what was needed was a strong and principled leadership.

It was in this atmosphere that the ideas of the right-wing thinkers began to gain widespread support. Whereas Powellism had been confined to a marginal group, by the mid-1970s New Right thinking was becoming far more respectable – and as traditional approaches to governing Britain seemed to fail, this radical alternative seemed increasingly plausible. In March 1974, two Cabinet Ministers, Keith Joseph and Margaret Thatcher, founded the Centre for Policy Studies, a party research unit to promote these ideas. Joseph was at this point the senior figure, and a series of high profile speeches in these months attracted much publicity. Joseph, Thatcher, and those around them were arguing for what they believed to be an entirely new approach, which would break with the 'consensus politics' that had dominated public life since 1945. In their view, past Conservative governments had compromised their principles in order to reach a consensus with Labour on broad areas of policy. Joseph argued famously that this had led only to a 'ratchet effect', as Labour's demands moved further to the left.

Margaret Thatcher's coup d'état

Heath was reluctant to resign the leadership after the October election defeat, on the grounds that he would be delivering the Conservative Party into the hands of right-wing extremists. But in November, bowing to the inevitable, he called a leadership election for February. The exercise became, in effect, a vote of confidence in Heath. In spite of the fact that there was a widespread feeling in the Parliamentary Party by this time that Heath had to go, there was no obvious contender for the job. Joseph himself was too prone to making gaffes, and ruled himself out; Enoch Powell had given up his chance during the February election, just as the party had begun to move firmly in his direction; other possible candidates were either too inexperienced or otherwise inappropriate.

It was in these circumstances that Margaret Thatcher put herself forward. With the benefit of hindsight, it is difficult to appreciate how extraordinary this situation seemed at the time. She had a personal score to settle with Heath, who had patronised her in Cabinet. The two clearly disliked each other from the moment that they had to start working together. Heath, along with many others, underestimated her chances essentially on the grounds that the party would never elect a woman to be leader. But although Thatcher had been kept down in Heath's Cabinet before 1974, she had made a strong impression as Minister for the

Keith Joseph (1918–1994)
Senior Conservative Minister in the Heath and Thatcher administrations. He served as Minister of Health and Social Security 1970–74; Minister of Industry 1979–81; and Minister for Education and Science 1981–86.

coup d'état: An unexpected change of leadership.

1. Why was Conservative morale so low by the beginning of 1975?

2. What factors explain the increasing influence of the right wing of the Conservative Party by the middle of the 1970s?

3. In what ways did Margaret Thatcher's gender affect the leadership election of 1975?

Environment from February, and as Shadow Finance Minister in the autumn. Thatcher was clearly a fighter, with strong and passionately-held Conservative beliefs. Her conduct in these weeks soon took on a legendary significance. It had taken a woman to stand up to Heath, and Thatcher had shown the courage and determination that her male colleagues lacked. In this way, she gathered admirers and was able throughout her subsequent career, to turn her gender to her political advantage.

Her success was not entirely due to luck and grit, however. Thatcher's campaign was skilfully managed by the MP Airey Neave, who came on board in January. Neave's tactics, which deliberately fostered the impression that Thatcher would not get enough votes to challenge Heath's leadership sufficiently to go to a second ballot, was effective in persuading wavering backbenchers to vote for her. When the votes were counted on 4 February, she came a wholly unexpected first with 130 votes to Heath's 119. Heath withdrew immediately. In the second ballot several substantial candidates entered the fray. But Thatcher was in a strong position, and admiration for her grew dramatically as a result of her stand against Heath. It was in these circumstances that she won the second ballot and was elected leader of the party. Heath's fear that the party would be taken over by his enemies had come to pass.

13.6 How far did Margaret Thatcher achieve the aims of 'Thatcherism' between 1979 and 1990?

Margaret Thatcher stands apart from other modern leaders of the Conservative Party to such an extent that many commentators have argued that she was not really a Conservative at all. Conservative government has traditionally placed stress on 'conserving' the status quo, and on reforming only where it is necessary to preserve and strengthen British society and its institutions. Baldwin, Chamberlain, Churchill, Macmillan and Heath were all party leaders in that mould. Thatcher, by contrast, embarked upon a series of reforming measures which seemed so radical that by the middle of the 1980s the term 'Thatcherism' was commonly used to describe her approach.

Thatcherism

'-Isms' – Marxism, Socialism, Fascism – are normally associated with a coherent set of ideas or an ideology. The term Thatcherism would therefore imply that Margaret Thatcher entered office with a clearly thought out plan of action for putting into practice her deeply-held beliefs. This assumption is misleading, however, because there is little evidence that this was the case in 1979. Much of what we have come to associate with Thatcherism was not part of a premeditated plan, but rather a set of responses that evolved as a pragmatic reaction to circumstances as they arose. In that sense, it is not strictly accurate to think of Thatcherism as an ideology. It is more useful to think of Thatcher's outlook as one based upon a set of moral values accompanied by her belief in strong and authoritative leadership. These values included a faith in individual responsibility, the importance of hard work and the right to enjoy the fruits of success, the central importance of the traditional family, the need to limit the role of the state, the importance of patriotism, and an utter revulsion against socialism. All of these beliefs were firmly held from the time that she became active in politics. Upon becoming Prime Minister, Thatcher was determined to *restore* these moral values to the centre of

British political culture. In that sense, she was not a radical reforming Prime Minister. Rather than introducing new ideas, her premiership represented a period of *reaction* against the reforms of the previous generation. This is what she believed would be required to rescue Britain from what she saw as an economic and moral decline, the roots of which went back to the Second World War.

Thatcher comes to power

When she came to power Thatcher's more moderate colleagues hoped that she would be tamed by the pressures of office. There were several grounds for this. The election manifesto of 1979 was not particularly extreme. It was based on the promise to reduce inflation through the introduction of 'monetarist' economic policy, trade union reform, the sale of council housing, the reduction of taxation and public spending, the firm handling of immigration, a stress upon law and order, and a strong defence policy. These policies had a widespread popular appeal, and proved to be particularly successful with skilled workers – who swung to the Conservatives in high numbers. It was not a particularly extreme agenda.

Secondly, the Conservatives came to office with a majority of 30 in the House of Commons. It was enough to govern comfortably, but not sufficient to survive great controversy. In Cabinet, moreover, she was surrounded by Conservative 'grandees' of the moderate centre. Between men like William Whitelaw, Jim Prior, Ian Gilmour, and Peter Walker and the moderating influence which the civil servants generally have on policy-making, there did not seem to be any great danger that the right wing of the party would gain the upper hand.

By 1983, however, it had become clear that Thatcher had outmanoeuvred her opponents, and was not prepared to countenance the policy U-turns that had characterised the Heath years. This was particularly surprising given the deep recession of 1979–82, which saw

How important was the role of advertisers such as Saatchi and Saatchi and other 'image' makers in British politics during the 1980s and 1990s?

A woman and her little boy walk past a Conservative Party poster during the run up to the August 1979 general election (which the Conservatives went on to win)

unemployment rise to 3 million and the collapse of the manufacturing sector. The Prime Minister's refusal to shift was a reflection of her extraordinary determination and utter belief in the policies she had endorsed. That she was able to impose her views was the result of both the power of the office of Prime Minister, and the powers conferred on the leader of the Conservative Party. As premier, she wasted no time demoting or sacking the 'wets' in her Cabinet, and promoting supporters like Norman Tebbit, Nigel Lawson and Cecil Parkinson. As party leader she, like Heath, could claim to have support for her approach to an extent that had not been true before electoral reform had been introduced in the party in 1965. Thatcher's domineering style of leadership was both criticised and admired. Her conduct of the Falklands War, in 1982, exemplified her approach to leadership. She took the decision to challenge General Galtieri herself, by-passing the Cabinet Committee system by conducting the war with the aid of a hand-picked group of advisers. It was in this period that she secured her own domination of the government and the party. Cabinet met less often and became less of a team. By the mid-1980s she had surrounded herself with her own supporters, isolating or dismissing her opponents.

Thatcherism in practice

Thatcher's strong image, assisted by the Falklands victory and the signs of an economic upturn helps to explain her decisive victory in the 1983 election. The enormous Conservative majority of 144 can only be fully explained by the weaknesses of the Opposition, and the structure of the British 'first past the post' electoral system, however. With such a large majority, Thatcher's dominance and freedom to legislate was finally secured. But it had been achieved on only 42.4% of the vote. In political terms, Britain was now clearly divided geographically, and increasingly by wealth and poverty. Those areas which had been hardest hit by the recession – the north of England, Scotland and Wales – had become impregnable Labour strongholds. More prosperous areas of England went to the Conservatives, with the Social Democratic Party often taking second place.

This was evident in the second Thatcher government, when most analysts, such as Peter Riddell in *The Thatcher Decade* (1989), have traced the beginnings of what is generally understood to be 'Thatcherism'. It was

Election night 1987: Margaret Thatcher becomes the only 20th century British Prime Minister to serve three consecutive terms of office

Ringfenced: Identified as being kept for a particular purpose.

Windfall profits: An unexpectedly large profit. The shares of privatised business rose in value soon after issue and investors could then sell them on for a very quick and substantial profit.

Poll Tax riots: Violent public demonstrations against local tax reform in the spring of 1990.

Eurosceptic: Opposed to further European integration.

Michael Heseltine (1933–)
Served as Environment Secretary 1979–83 and Defence Secretary 1983–86 under Margaret Thatcher, and came closer than any other senior Conservative figure to bringing her down, when he resigned in January 1986. While on the surface, this decision concerned his disagreement with the Cabinet's decision to allow the sale of the ailing Westland helicopter company to an American firm, Heseltine was frustrated by her increasingly autocratic and anti-European approach.

---

in this administration that privatisation became a central feature of government policy. The revenue raised by selling nationalised industries such as British Airways and British Gas, was, like the revenue from North Sea oil and gas, absorbed into general government spending rather than **ringfenced** for a planned programme of investment. In spite of this, privatisation was a popular programme, largely because of the **windfall profits** available for investors. The government attempted to encourage more popular support for capitalism through widespread share ownership, in a similar fashion to the extension of home ownership to low income earners through the sale of council housing. Easy credit policies and the deregulation of the City contributed to a boom centred on the south of England. For the 'haves' of the mid 1980s, real wages outstripped inflation. By the time that the next election was called in 1987, Thatcher seemed to be delivering an economic miracle in the prosperous parts of the country where the Conservative vote was already focused. That victory was on a similar scale and for similar structural reasons, led to a majority of 101 seats on just 42.3% of the vote.

Beneath this veneer of success, however, there were profound and troubling failures associated with the Thatcher years. For those who did not directly benefit from the government's economic policies, these were years of increasing social exclusion. This was evident as early as 1981, as social unrest erupted in Brixton, south London, soon to be followed in other cities. The problems of the inner city were compounded in those parts of Britain where unemployment hit levels not seen since the interwar years as a result of industrial decline. Thatcher's handling of the miners' strike in 1984–85 may have won admirers from among those who believed that the trade unions needed to be confronted. But the extent of police powers used during the strike, and the evident weakness of the miners as a result of the new reforms convinced many that the Conservatives had tipped the balance too far in the other direction. Thatcher's Britain had little regard for civil liberties, and by the latter years of the decade, the Prime Minister seemed increasingly distant from these concerns. The disaster of the Local Government Finance Act 1988, culminating in the '**Poll Tax riots**' of the following year, was a crucial turning point. Thatcher, previously the strongest Conservative Party leader of living memory, suddenly seemed an electoral liability.

Margaret Thatcher's off-hand treatment of her senior colleagues had made her many powerful enemies by the end of the 1980s. Her judgement on a range of issues, from the Poll Tax to her **Euroscepticism** had led to increasing unease within the party. In November 1989, she became the victim of the same amended rules which she had used against Heath. Sir Anthony Meyer, a relatively obscure pro-European backbencher, challenged her for the leadership. In the ballot, it became clear that she had lost the support of one-fifth of Conservative MPs. The following November saw a more serious challenge from Michael Heseltine, openly supported by Geoffrey Howe and Nigel Lawson. This time the revolt was large enough to go to a second ballot. When it became clear that she had lost the confidence of most of her Cabinet colleagues, Thatcher had no option but to resign.

The impact of Thatcherism

How successful was Thatcherism? The answer depends upon the criteria used to measure that success. In many ways her policies had failed. It proved far more difficult to roll back the state than had been foreseen. In 1980 government spending accounted to 43.2% of GDP; in 1995 the same figure was 42.5%. Indeed one of the key paradoxes associated with

Thatcherism was that, under Thatcher's leadership, the authority of the government became increasingly centralised and interventionist at a number of levels. Because so many of the local authorities remained Labour controlled, the governments of the 1980s imposed a series of entirely new powers over local government spending and policy-making. In education policy, the Conservatives introduced a national curriculum that set clear limits on the freedom to choose subjects and methods of teaching in state schools. The privatisation of industry was accompanied by the introduction of a bewildering series of regulatory bodies and '**quangos**' staffed by unelected officials.

At other levels, Thatcher's accomplishments were more impressive, however. The power of the trade unions was drastically reduced, to an extent undreamed of a decade previously. The density of trade union membership in the total workforce dropped by nearly 10% between 1981 and 1991, from 43.7% to 34.3%. The number of working days lost to strikes declined steeply, from nearly 30 million in 1979 to just under 2 million in 1990. The pattern of housing ownership was also dramatically changed, in spite of the disastrous collapse of the housing market in the late 1980s. The Housing Act 1980, which gave council tenants the right to buy at substantial discounts, meant that council house sales completed rose from 1,342 in 1980 to a high of 202,558 in 1982, settling down to an average of over 100,000 for the rest of the decade. Local authorities were barred from ploughing these profits back into public housing, insuring that the structure of the market was shifted towards the private sector.

At a broader level, it could be argued that Thatcher succeeded in changing Britain's political culture. Labour's political wilderness of the 1980s was a powerful argument in favour of policy modernisation on the left. Socialism as a force in domestic politics was finished off by the clear popularity of the Thatcherite agenda, not only among middle-class voters but also with skilled workers. By the time that Tony Blair won the general election of 1997, it had become clear that her aim of killing off a socialist alternative in British politics had been surprisingly successful in the long term. The implications that this would have for Conservative fortunes, however, were bleak.

Quango: A quasi autonomous non-government organisation. Although not a government organisation these were funded by government departments and, to a certain extent, were responsible to those departments to oversee aspects of government work.

1. Explain what was meant by the term 'Thatcherism'.

2. What was distinctive about Margaret Thatcher's style of leadership?

3. Why did the Conservatives secure such large majorities in 1983 and 1987?

13.7 What factors account for the decline of Conservatism in the final decade of the 20th century?

John Major succeeded Thatcher as leader of the party and Prime Minister at the end of November 1990. His rise to power was sudden. He had only served as a Cabinet Minister since 1987, and he benefited from being untainted by the bitterness of those years. Initially it was hoped that he could unite the party and provide a period of consolidation. His style of leadership was far more conciliatory than his predecessor's, and he had a reputation for integrity and decency that earned him the nickname 'Honest John'. For a time this formula worked. By December 1990 the polls showed a swing of around 9% in favour of the Conservatives. Moreover, Major's personal rating in the polls far exceeded Thatcher. In spite of the fact of an economic recession that he inherited (and as Chancellor of the Exchequer, was partly responsible for), Major managed to win the general election of 1992. Voters still seemed to trust the Conservatives to handle the economy more competently than Labour, and there were clear signs of recovery in the months before polling day. The tabloid press was savage in its portrayal of Neil Kinnock as untrustworthy and incompetent. Major's homespun campaigning style was popular with many voters.

The collapse of Conservatism

This victory was followed by the disintegration of Conservative fortunes, however. A series of local, European and by-elections beginning in 1993 recorded the worst results experienced by any modern British political party. In May 1993, for example, a Conservative majority of more than 12,000 turned to a Liberal Democrat margin of over 22,000. In 1994 the news was even worse than that. By the end of 1995 the Conservative Party had been wiped out in local politics throughout Great Britain. Only 13 councils in England retained a precarious Conservative majority. What factors explain this dramatic reversal of fortunes?

First of all, the Major administration lost the traditional public confidence in Conservatives being better at managing the economy than Labour. This was partly the result of 'Black Wednesday', 16 September 1992, when Britain was forced to pull out of the European Exchange Rate Mechanism and to devalue the pound (see chapter 14, section 1). The Cabinet's uncertain leadership during that crisis cost the country billions of pounds, and the consequences were clearly reflected in the opinion polls. The Labour lead grew by around 14% in the weeks that followed. This disaster was compounded by unpopular tax increases, particularly the proposal to impose of VAT on fuel in 1994. Higher taxes seemed particularly hypocritical in view of Conservative warnings of Labour tax plans in the 1992 election.

Secondly, the Major government was plagued by a 'sleaze factor' which easily surpassed the scandals which plagued the final years of the Macmillan government. A series of sexual revelations involving both ministers and backbenchers contrasted sharply with the government's moralizing postures on subjects like single motherhood and 'back to basics'. In November 1992 Major announced the formation of the Scott Inquiry into the sale of arms to Iraq between 1984 and 1990, against government guidelines. Most damaging of all, in October 1994, the Nolan Committee on standards in public life was established in response to a 'cash for questions' scandal which implicated a number of MPs in the improper acceptance of money and other perks from wealthy individuals

1. How does the information in the source below highlight the lack of fairness in the single majority system of voting which is used in British general elections?

2. In what ways did John Major's Conservative government differ from Margaret Thatcher's last administration?

Conservative general election performance 1945–2000

Date	No. of Conservative Candidates	Conservative MPs Elected	Total votes for Conservative Party	Conservative Share of Vote (%)
1945	618	210	9,972,010	39.6
1950	619	298	12,492,404	43.5
1951	617	321	13,718,199	48.0
1959	625	365	13,750,876	49.3
1964	630	304	12,002,642	43.4
1966	629	253	11,418,455	41.0
1970	628	330	13,145,123	46.4
(Feb) 1974	623	297	11,872,180	37.9
(Oct) 1974	622	277	10,462,565	35.8
1979	622	339	13,697,923	43.9
1983	633	397	13,012,316	42.4
1987	633	376	12,760,583	42.3
1992	645	336	14,092,891	41.9
1997	611	165	9,602,989	30.7

Michael Portillo (front) hearing that he had lost his seat for Southgate to a Labour candidate (behind) in the 1997 general election

The Murdoch press: The group of newspapers owned by the Australian tycoon, Rupert Murdoch, including *The Times* and the *Sun*.

1. Why should the Conservatives not have been surprised by their loss of the 1997 election?

2. What factors account for the popularity of John Major between 1990 and 1992?

3. Why did the Conservative Party become so divided after 1992?

4. What impact did the shift to the right of party policy under Hague's leadership have on the party's performance after 1997?

and corporations in return for political favours. The party seemed to have been corrupted by its years in power, and even Major's personal high standing could not overcome that impression.

Thirdly, the Conservative Party, which traditionally presented a unified public face, was split throughout the 1992–97 Parliament. Europe was the most divisive issue, and as Euroscepticism swept through the party and the Cabinet, it became increasingly difficult for Major to maintain party discipline. He was forced to contend with a small but defiant group of Eurosceptic rebels on the backbenches who wielded power out of proportion to their numbers as a result of the slim majority on which the government depended. The debate on Europe hardened over the ratification of the Treaty of Maastricht (see chapter 15, section 8) and policy towards a single currency. By 1995 only 12% of the public identified the Conservatives as a unified party.

Major's problems took place in the context of the revival of the Labour Party, which was transformed under the leadership of Tony Blair from 1994 into a unified, confident and disciplined party. For once, the voters had a clear and convincing alternative to vote for by the time that the election was called for 1 May 1997. Certainly, the press was convinced. The hostility of traditionally pro-Conservative newspapers towards the government from the mid-1990s was wholly unprecedented in modern history. In particular, the **Murdoch press** swung in favour of New Labour – providing the greatest election publicity for any party at the time.

In spite of the evidence of a likely heavy Conservative defeat, the extent of Labour's victory in the May 1997 election was unanticipated. In what is likely to be remembered as the worst defeat in Conservative election history, the party lost 178 seats, retaining only a rump of 165 on a swing of 10% towards Labour. Major seemed relieved to hand over the burden of managing a disintegrating party. At the end of the century, William Hague, who succeeded Major as leader, did manage to manufacture greater unity in the party. He proved to be effective and confident in Parliamentary debate, but lacked the charisma necessary to provide a convincing alternative to Blair with the voters. Unable to challenge the Blair ascendancy on law and order, the economy, or foreign policy – traditional Conservative strengths – Hague took the gamble of playing to the public's fear of deepening European integration. By the end of the century, the party had become marginalised on the right wing of British politics, effectively a single issue campaigning group. This process occurred against the advice of many of the party's most experienced politicians, many of whom – like Michael Heseltine and Kenneth Clarke – had more in common with Labour's European policy. The shift to the right of Hague's Conservative Party MP was highlighted on 18 December 1999, when Shaun Woodward MP defected to Labour shortly after his sacking as junior environment spokesman over his support for gay rights. By the end of 1999 the Conservatives were becoming more disciplined than under Major, but seemed increasingly out of touch with mainstream British politics.

13.8 *The myth of consensus*
A CASE STUDY IN HISTORICAL INTERPRETATION

When contemporary historians began to write about early postwar British society and politics the theme that emerged was one of 'consensus'. The war, it was argued, had led to an unusual degree of agreement between politicians, civil servants, and people of all classes over the shape of postwar Britain. This common agenda for the future was characterised by support for a number of goals. In economic terms, there should be a mixed economy, in which key industries – such as coal or the railways – should be nationalised, but alongside a large private sector which allowed scope for free enterprise and competition. The ideas of the economist John Maynard Keynes on the government's role in maintaining economic stability and relatively high employment levels were broadly accepted as well. In industrial relations, there emerged a broad commitment to collective bargaining between the trades unions and the employers with minimal intervention by the state. In respect of social policy, there grew a marked acceptance of the construction of a 'welfare state' that would guarantee a minimum income, access to adequate health care, education through the secondary level, decent housing, and social insurance in case of hardship to every individual, regardless of background. Taken together, these aims and objectives formed a broad common vision of the future, which was intended to establish a new Britain, more efficient and productive, more just and compassionate than that of the interwar years.

The origins of this supposed consensus have been traced most persuasively by Paul Addison, whose influential book *The Road to 1945* was published in 1975. Addison argued that a combination of factors accounted for a new sense of purpose in British politics emerging from 1942. The popular unity engendered by the shared hardship of war, the experience of coalition government, the popular pressure for social reform following the publication of the *Beveridge Report* in November, the growing power of the trades unions in the midst of labour shortages, the example of high productivity which resulted from the war economy, and memories of mass unemployment and poverty during the Depression era – all were factors in the development of consensus politics.

According to supporters of this interpretation, a basis for policy was forged during the war that was adhered to by both Labour and Conservative governments for many years afterwards. Thus the period from the late 1940s until the mid-1970s has often been described as the era of consensus. This was indeed the heyday of the mixed economy, full employment and the welfare state. But it was also a period in which Britain's economic performance was slipping relative to its competitors abroad. By the 1970s Britain was beset by a series of grave problems: widespread industrial unrest, inflation, growing unemployment, disaffected youth, and urban decay.

'Wet' Conservatism: Inclined to compromise.

The period of consensus is widely perceived to have ended when Margaret Thatcher became leader of the Conservative Party in 1975. Thatcher was highly critical of the postwar consensus, accusing **'wet' Conservatism** of collaborating with the left in a series of weak policy compromises and unrealistically high levels of public welfare spending. For her, consensus meant mismanagement, and her policy advisers deliberately chose to criticise the concept in order to highlight the new approach that her brand of Conservatism could offer to cure the British 'disease'. Many commentators have argued that Thatcherism ultimately replaced the postwar Keynes/Beveridge consensus with a new set of broadly shared beliefs and attitudes that were subsequently taken up by the New Labour of Tony Blair.

The 'consensus' view of postwar Britain came under increasing scrutiny from the mid-1980s. As historians gained access to the official archives and began to test the consensus model, it became clear that there was far more division and debate both during and after the war than this interpretation allows for. Moreover, both Labour and Conservative governments pursued economic and social policy agendas that were sharply at odds, even in the forties and fifties. In simple terms, Labour was determined to develop a universal welfare state, paid for through direct taxation, and a greater degree of planning in order to deliver a broader range of social services, and less social inequality, arguing that only a society which delivered a social as well as a political basis for citizenship could remain stable and prosperous. The Conservatives wanted to limit nationalisation, reduce taxation, encourage the private sector, and reorient the welfare state to target those in genuine need, arguing that only a system that rewarded hard work and ingenuity could remain productive and successful. In other words, the war did little to shift the fundamental axis of British politics from its familiar poles of individualism versus collectivism. Unsurprisingly therefore, historians in recent years, such as Kevin Jeffreys in *Retreat from New Jerusalem* (1997) have begun to stress the continuities in British politics between the interwar and postwar periods, and have become increasingly sceptical of the idea that the war led to significant or sharp change.

Consensus, in the sense that it has been applied to the postwar era, seems increasingly simplistic as an historical explanation, and shows part of the celebratory tone that is typical of British memories of the war. The explanation for policy convergence on issues like welfare and full employment seems to owe more to international economic and political circumstances and constraints rather than to any deliberate series of agreements on domestic policy. Full employment, for example, was widespread throughout the West, not just in Britain. Welfare states all over Western Europe at this time are increasingly understood as having been a response to the need to stabilise capitalist economic systems during the Cold War. Labour and Conservative policies in this period were inevitably limited by the circumstances to which they were responding.

1. Why have some historians argued that there was an unusual degree of 'consensus' in Britain after 1945?

2. How have the views of historians on the question of a postwar consensus changed since the 1970s?

3. Is it possible to have a stable democracy without some sort of policy consensus between the major political parties?

14 Social and economic history, 1945–2000

Key Issues

● How far did British society change between 1945 and 2000?

● How far did the British economy experience change between 1945 and 2000?

● What impact did the arrival of migrants from the Caribbean, Africa and Asia have on Britain?

14.1 Historical interpretation: How successful has the British economy been since 1945?

14.2 In what way did British society change between 1945 and 2000?

14.3 Has Britain become a multi-cultural society between 1945 and 2000?

14.4 What impact did changes in the mass media have on Britain between 1945 and 2000?

14.5 The rise and fall of the British trade union movement, 1945–2000

Framework of Events

1947	Nationalisation of the coal industry and railways
	Sterling crisis
1948	Establishment of National Health Service
1949	Economic crisis forces devaluation of pound
1951	Festival of Britain
1953	Coronation of Queen Elizabeth II
1955	Start of commercial television
	Introduction of frozen food to Britain
1956	Rock and roll comes to Britain
1958	Race riots in Notting Hill, London
1960	Trial of Penguin Books for obscenity for publishing *Lady Chatterley's Lover*
1961	First issue of *Private Eye*
1962	Commonwealth Immigration Act introduces first controls on migrants to Britain
1963	The Beatles have three number 1 hits
1964	Start of BBC2
1965	Abolition of the death penalty
1966	England win soccer World Cup
1967	Start of colour television transmissions
	Devaluation of pound as a result of the economic crisis
	Abortion legalised
	Homosexuality 'between consenting adults' legalised
	Pirate radio banned as Radio One is launched.
1968	Commonwealth Immigration Act restricts immigration, particularly Kenyan Asians, to Britain
	Abolition of theatre censorship
1969	White Paper 'In Place of Strife' proposes controls over strikes and trade unions
	Divorce Reform Act liberalises divorce
1970	Equal Pay Act introduces legal enforcement of equal pay for women

1971	Immigration Act effectively ends non-white immigration
	Industrial Relations Act gives government broad powers of intervention in strikes
1972	Miners' strike
1973	Britain joins Common Market (European Economic Community)
	Oil crisis
	Beginning of commercial local radio
1974	Miners' strike
	First commercial flight of Concorde
1975	Referendum confirms Britain's membership of Common Market (EEC)
	Sex Discrimination Act establishes Equal Opportunities Commission
1976	IMF crisis
	Establishment of Commission for Racial Equality
	Introduction of public expenditure cuts
1977	Queen Elizabeth II's Silver Jubilee
	Sex Pistols reach number 2 in the charts with the banned record 'God save the Queen'
1978	Government introduces 5% pay norm for wage increases – rejected by the unions
	Unemployment rises above 1 million for the first time since 1945
1979	'Winter of Discontent': widespread industrial action in the public sector
	Margaret Thatcher elected Prime Minister
1980	Unemployment rises above 2 million for the first time since 1939
1981	Employment Act outlaws secondary picketing in industrial disputes
	Social Democratic Party splits from Labour Party
	Widespread riots in Brixton (London), Toxteth (Liverpool) and Moss Side (Manchester)
1982	Start of Channel 4
1984	Miners' strike
	First major privatisation with sale of British Telecom
1985	Live Aid concert for famine relief
1986	Privatisation of British Gas, the largest of the decade
	Serious riots outside Wapping headquarters of Rupert Murdoch's News International after 5,000 printers dismissed over dispute about introduction of new technology
1989	Introduction of Poll Tax in Scotland
1990	Introduction of Poll Tax in England and Wales: widespread riots
1992	Start of national commercial radio with Classic FM
	'Black Wednesday' departure of Britain from the Exchange Rate Mechanism
1996	Sale of the railways: the last major privatisation scheme
1999	Start of the European Single Currency
	Inflation at lowest level since 1963

Overview

Capitalism: The economic system prevalent in Britain and western society, sometimes called the free market or private enterprise economy. Economic decision-making is highly decentralised with a large number of companies selling goods and services and consumers choosing which services and goods most suits their needs.

WHY the extraordinary economic and social changes that have taken place since 1945 happened is by no means clear, especially as to many contemporary observers the economic depression of the 1930s had proven that the **capitalist** system had failed. Even historians as eminent as Eric Hobsbawm remain baffled. In his *Age of Extremes: a history of the world, 1914–1991* (1994) he confesses 'there are no really satisfactory explanations for the sheer scale of the "great leap forward" of the capitalist world economy and consequently for its unprecedented social consequences'.

Professor B.W.E. Alford, however, is more certain. He argues in *British Economic Performance, 1945–1973* (1988) that the 'combination of elements

Economic growth: The expansion (or decline) of the real output of an economy usually measured by percentage increase or decline annually to the Gross Domestic Product (GDP) the total size of the economy.

Welfare transfer payments: Taxation spent on the welfare state.

General Agreement on Tariffs and Trade: An international organisation established in 1947 to promote the expansion of international trade through the removal of tariffs and other restrictions on cross-frontier trade. Now called the World Trade Organisation.

World Bank: The World Bank, or International Bank for Reconstruction and Development, also set up in 1947 to provide economic aid to member countries – mainly developing countries – to strengthen their economies.

Oil crisis: In the autumn of 1973 the Organisation of Petroleum Exporting Countries (OPEC) forced up the price of oil, a commodity upon which many countries in the west (including Britain) were heavily dependent for fuel, and as the raw material of plastics and other items.

Productivity: Increase in the efficiency of making goods or operating services.

Cartel: A group of producers or companies who agree to maximise profits by artificially raising the price of their goods to consumers.

Inflation: An increase in the general level of prices that is sustained over time. The annual increase may be small or gradual (creeping inflation) or large and accelerating (hyper-inflation). Inflation can be caused by an increase in the cost of raw materials which is then passed on to the consumer, or by a shortage of goods the demand for which pushes prices up.

favourable to **economic growth** in the major economies ... were post-war reconstruction, a production gap between the USA and the rest which drew American dollars and know-how into Europe and Japan, a sharp upward shift in peacetime levels of public expenditure (caused by defence needs and **welfare transfer payments**) and the absence of general synchronisation in the down-swings which took place in the major economies from time to time. Arising out of these conditions, and at the same time reinforcing them, was a widespread and buoyant expectation of economic growth which was powerful enough to ride out random shocks.'

There is no doubt that the leaders of the western world, guided by economic advisers such as John Maynard Keynes, learnt well the lessons of the 1930s. By the end of the Second World War they had set up an international monetary system guided by the International Monetary Fund (IMF), the **General Agreement on Tariffs and Trade** (GATT), and the **World Bank** to prevent such a slump occurring again. Governments also accepted that they had a duty to intervene more heavily in the running of national economies. The White Paper on employment policy, published in 1944, committed the post-war government to a 'high and stable' level of employment. Hugh Dalton, Chancellor of the Exchequer in Clement Attlee's Labour government, set the tone by announcing in 1946, 'twice in our lifetime we have banished unemployment in wartime. Now we must banish it in peace. I will find, with a song in my heart, all the money necessary for sound constructive schemes.' As well as this commitment to full employment, the government was committed to the provision of a welfare state, and close links to both trade unions and industry itself.

The period between 1945 and the onset of **oil crisis** of 1973 was a 'golden age'. Unemployment, which had hit 22% during the depression of the 1930s, stayed well below 500,000. Economic growth rose by 3% per annum, as did **productivity**, and investment grew by around 6% a year from 1950 until the 1960s, when it tailed off to stagnate during the 1970s. The position became more difficult after 1973 when the **cartel** of oil-producing nations quadrupled petroleum prices. In any case the relentless rise of **inflation** was making a mockery of government spending plans as well as the real wages of millions of working people. The Labour governments between 1974 and 1979 were caught between this new economic reality and the expectations of its supporters which led to the 'Winter of Discontent' in early 1979 and the election of the Conservatives under Margaret Thatcher. Her victory was seen by most com-mentators to spell the end of state spending to achieve full employment, state-subsidised welfare and the power of the trade unions.

The early years of the new economics were hardly encouraging. While other economies grew by 6.3% between 1979 and 1981, Britain's fell by 2.5%. Unemployment rose to 13.3%, the highest in western Europe. However the stern economic policy of Margaret Thatcher and her successors eventually began to work. These policies of rigorously controlling public spending and the encouragement of business were adopted by the 'New Labour' administration of Tony Blair.

The changes dealt with in this chapter have not been without their critics. In particular there have been increasing concerns about:

Acid rain: Pollutants, produced especially by coal and oil power stations, which are found in rainfall and which kill trees.

Global warming: The warming of the earth as a result of greenhouse gases, including carbon dioxide, produced by industry and motor vehicles.

Nuclear family: A household consisting just of mother, father and two children.

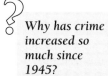

Why has crime increased so much since 1945?

Magneto: The ignition switch for the combustion engine.

- The environment, pollution and the increasing use of the motor car. Economists and environmentalists, such as Fritz Schumacher in *Small is Beautiful* (1974), have warned of the consequences of uncontrolled economic growth on the planet. During the 1980s great concern was shown about **acid rain**, and by the 1990s scientists were presenting a convincing case for **global warming**.

- **The supposed breakdown of society**, which many conservative commentators argue has resulted in rising crime, the rise of divorce, and the break down of the **nuclear family** There is no doubt that Britain is a much less law-abiding place: crime has risen more than tenfold since 1945 (see table 1).

TABLE 1 Indictable offences

	Total offences (000s)	Rate per million of population
1945	478	12,705
1955	438	11,235
1965	1,134	28,259
1970	1,556	38,031
1997	4,595	88,350

- **The spiritual, rather than the material, impoverishment of society.** George Orwell saw this danger in pre-war society, which he described in his essay *The Lion and the Unicorn* (1941) as being 'a civilisation in which children grow up with an intimate knowledge of the **magneto** and in complete ignorance of the Bible'. Other observers have pointed out the paradox that despite an ever-increasing array of machines to help us manage our lives society seems to be running faster and faster to keep up.

Source-based questions: Statistical analysis

	1956–7	1998–9
Average weekly income (women)	£6.16 (equivalent to £80)	£303.70
Average weekly income (men)	£11.89 (equivalent to £155)	£420.30
Average hours worked (women)	41.5	37.6
Average hours worked (men)	48.5	41.7
Unemployment rate	1.3%	4.5%
Trade union membership as percentage of workforce	41.5%	24.8%
Annual rate of inflation	3.7%	1.1%
Percentage of income spent on food	35%	16%
Price of pint of beer	9p	£2.00
Percentage of households owning a television	27%	98%

Look at the table above and others in this chapter.

1. Outline the major changes which have taken place since the end of the war to both the British economy and society in general.

2. Make suggestions as to how and why these changes have taken place.

14.1 How successful has the British economy been since 1945?
A CASE STUDY IN HISTORICAL INTERPRETATION

1945–1951

In 1945 Britain had just fought and won the greatest war in its history, at great cost to both the economy and the people themselves. The Labour government under Clement Attlee, which had been swept to power in July 1945, was pledged to rebuild the country. Attlee was determined not to repeat the mistakes that had been made after 1918 that had led to high unemployment and low economic growth for most of the inter-war period. The Labour Party, whose 1945 manifesto stated that the people 'deserve and must be assured of a happier future than so many of them faced after the last war', shared this determination.

In this task both the Labour government, and its Conservative successor under Winston Churchill, were largely successful. The decade after 1945 was one of rapid growth, low inflation, and full employment. The welfare state and the National Health Service guaranteed better living standards and health for everybody, rich and poor. About 20% of British industry was nationalised.

But there were considerable problems along the way. Almost as soon as Attlee came to power, the Americans ended the Lend-Lease system that had supported the British war effort. Officials negotiated a further loan of $3.5bn in December 1945, but the whole incident showed the weakness of Britain's economic position. Further crises in 1947 and 1949 forced the devaluation of the pound, which had the effect of boosting Britain's exports as they were now cheaper to buy, but cast doubts on the handling of the economy by Labour.

In order to repay wartime debts, and to finance the necessary imports for recovery, exports had to be rapidly increased (see table 2). 'Export or die' was the dramatic slogan used by the government. Britain was helped, but perhaps in the long term hindered, by the fact that apart from the United States her economic competitors were still rebuilding after the war. There was high demand for almost everything that British industry could make. But in concentrating on manufacturing for export, Britain failed to modernise its industry. This hampered its ability to effectively compete in the post-war world.

TABLE 2 British trade and payments, 1946–52 (£ million)

	1946	1947	1948	1949	1950	1951	1952
Exports	900	1125	1550	1790	2221	2708	2836
Imports	1100	1574	1768	1970	2374	3497	2927
Balance of trade	−200	−449	−218	−180	−153	−789	−91

Why do you think the balance of trade worsened in 1951?

American–European Recovery Programme: Universally called Marshall Aid, after the American Secretary of State, George C. Marshall, who introduced it.

During the late 1940s, Britain as well other countries in western Europe was considerably helped by the **American–European Recovery Programme**. Marshall Aid was designed to kick-start war-torn European economies, by supplying financial aid and allowing access to American technology and production methods. It was also thought that this would reduce the likelihood of a Communist takeover. The British received $2.7 billion, the largest amount of any country. West Germany received $1.7 billion. Aid helped to reduce Britain's dollar deficit rather than rebuild its industry.

On the outbreak of the Korean War Britain supported the United Nations by sending troops to South Korea. This was accompanied by a massive rearmament programme introduced by the Chancellor of the Exchequer, Hugh Gaitskell, in April 1951 that would have doubled armaments production within two years. Cuts were made to the welfare state to pay for the programme, and it slowed down economic recovery by directing scarce resources away from the export drive to the armaments industry at a time when industries of Britain's main European rivals, France and Germany, were finally recovering from wartime devastation. This meant that Britain lost important export markets that were difficult to recapture. It also led to a sharp increase in inflation as the price of imports also rose. On coming to power in October 1951, the Conservatives quickly scaled down the rearmament programme. The economist Alec Cairncross concludes that 'rearmament in Britain probably did less harm to the economy in the short run at least than the rise in import prices that resulted from rearmament elsewhere'.

Commentators are divided about Labour's economic record between 1945 and 1952. One of the most critical is Correlli Barnett, who argues in *The Lost Victory* (1995) that Britain was 'in need of being rebuilt from the keel upwards, she had instead only undergone a superficial refit, with items of new technology bolted on to her Victorian structure'. Other historians recognise the achievements and difficulties that Clement Attlee and his ministers had to face. Catherine Schenk, in *Twentieth Century Britain* (1994), concludes 'The transition from wartime production and distribution had been accomplished within a short period of time and the seemingly insurmountable problems posed by the war were overcome'.

1951–1973

Gross Domestic Product: The total money value of all final goods and services produced in an economy over a one year period.

1. Why was British economic growth slower than its main economic rivals?

2. Why did Britain's share of world trade decrease?

Many commentators, such as Larry Elliott and Dan Atkinson in *The Age of Insecurity* (1998), have argued that the period between about 1951 and 1973 was a 'golden age'. There was high economic growth, low unemployment and inflation, and a constantly rising standard of living. Yet the picture was not all golden. In particular Britain's economic growth lagged consistently behind that of its European competitors.

Between 1951 and 1973 the British economy, in terms of **Gross Domestic Product** (GDP) grew at a rate of 2.8% per annum, a third higher than in the inter-war period and double that of the pre-1914 rate. In the same period, however, the economies of Britain's economic rivals grew rather faster (see table 3). Britain's share of world trade declined from a quarter in 1950 to just over 10% in 1970 (see table 4). This decline caused great anguish. According to Alford in *British Economic Performance, 1945–1975* (1988), 'Britain's poor economic performance has been the dominant theme of political debate and economic discourse since the 1950s'.

TABLE 3 Growth rates of real Gross Domestic Product per head, 1913–89 (%)

	1913–50	1950–73	1973–89
France	1.1	4.0	2.8
Germany	0.7	4.9	2.1
Japan	0.9	8.0	3.1
United Kingdom	0.8	2.5	2.8
United States	2.6	2.2	2.6

TABLE 4 UK comparative trade performance 1950–88: Percentage shares of world exports of manufactures

	1950	1960	1970	1988
United Kingdom	25.5	16.5	10.8	8.3
France	9.9	9.6	8.7	9.1
Germany	7.3	19.3	19.8	20.6
Japan	3.4	6.9	12.7	18.1
United States	27.3	22.6	18.5	14.9

Many reasons for this general economic decline have been advanced including government policies towards industry, the strength of the trade unions, inadequate management, and low levels of investment. According to Sean Glynn and Alan Booth in *Modern Britain: An economic and social history* (1996), however, 'no single answer can fully explain the timing and pattern of the British slide'.

An important element was the decline of industries in which the British had traditionally been strong. By the 1980s the shipbuilding industry, for example, had almost totally collapsed. British shipbuilding declined between 1945 and 1975, the time of the most rapid and sustained expansion in the history of world shipbuilding. Britain had a head start after the war: in 1950 it had a 37% share of the market measured in tonnage launched. However, by 1974 Britain's share had slumped to 3.7%. Companies remained small and yards were troubled by **restrictive industrial practices**. Both factors kept productivity low by international comparisons. But companies were very reluctant to consider specialisation or expansionist investment programmes to meet international competition head on. British shipbuilders were therefore unable to take advantage of the new market for tankers and container ships, preferring to build general cargo ships for which there was a declining demand. As a result, according to Glynn and Booth, the industry suffered 'a slow and painful death'.

The car industry, perhaps the most important modern industry in postwar Britain, also had serious problems. The industry expanded rapidly after 1945, accounting in 1966 for 7.5% of manufacturing output. The effects of the war on European and Japanese car makers allowed British and American firms to dominate the world markets until the mid-1950s. West Germany overtook British annual output in 1956, and the productivity in British car factories soon fell behind that of Europe or Japan. In 1973 *The Economist* magazine revealed that British factories needed between 67% and 132% more labour than German or Belgian producers to make apparently identical vehicles. In addition, by the late 1960s British cars had an increasing reputation of poor reliability, which helped fuel imports of foreign vehicles and reduced exports. The number of new foreign cars registered increased from 5% in 1964 to 31% by 1973 and 62% by 1979. Nowhere is there a better example of this decline than British Leyland (renamed Rover in 1985). In 1968 it was the largest British car company (and the fifth largest in the world), building approximately 1 million vehicles, accounting for just under 40% of total UK production. In 1991 it had barely 13% of the British market representing an output of 400,000 vehicles.

Industry was naturally heavily affected by economic policies dictated by the government, in which politicians and their advisers tried to juggle competing interests of industry, the consumer in the context of the wider economic position. The 1950s saw the emergence of the 'Stop-Go Cycle'. In the 'Go' phase the domestic economy grew, reducing unemployment, and increasing spending, which increased demand and fuelled inflation. The government used tax increases and credit restrictions to curb demand. As demand fell, economic growth slowed down and unemployment would rise – the 'Stop' phase.

The Stop-Go Cycle was particularly important between 1951 and the devaluation of the pound in 1967. In July 1961 there was a 'Stop' budget increasing taxes, imposing new controls of overseas investments and introducing a pay-freeze for public sector workers. Two years later with an election looming, the Conservatives attempted to boost the economy to reduce unemployment and encourage consumer spending, under policies that became known as 'the dash for growth'.

Restrictive industrial practices: Curbs placed on production by inter-union rivalry or out of date working practices.

Economists are divided about the effects of the policy on economic growth. Many argue that Stop-Go created an unstable climate that hindered long-term growth of the economy. Its cumulative effect was to harm long-term objectives, such as full employment, growth and structural changes to the economy. Industry was thus often unable to plan ahead and make the necessary investment because it was uncertain whether a change in economic policy would curtail demand for its products. The lack of new investment made it harder to increase productivity through new technology, which in turn meant that British goods were over-priced compared with those produced in other countries. The economic historian Sidney Pollard, for example, argued in *The Development of the British Economy* (1983) that the cycle helped to encourage imports at the cost of exports and thus created a downward spiral that made Britain's continued relative decline inevitable.

Other economists, such as Michael Surrey, are supportive of the policy and point out that the cycle actually provided a stable policy framework which was committed to full employment, a stable exchange rate and economic growth. Indeed the effect of the policies may be exaggerated, for all the changes made seem to have had relatively little impact on underlying growth. Alford concludes, 'comparisons with other economies suggest that stop/go was not the problem – rather it was the weakness of the underlying trend of growth which exaggerated the effect of stop/go phases'.

Other reasons often put forward for Britain's relative economic decline in the 1950s, 1960s and even afterwards, have been poor management and poor labour relations. Glynn and Booth argue that 'British managers have been notably ill-equipped' both in terms of training and in vision. Most British firms did not recruit graduate managers before the 1950s. The engineering industry was especially reluctant to recruit graduate engineers. Even by the late 1980s only 24% of senior British managers were graduates, compared with 85% in the United States and Japan.

During the 1960s the small businessman was often, in the words of Larry Elliott and Dan Atkinson in *The Age of Insecurity* (1998), portrayed as being 'hidebound and reactionary, as much an enemy of economic progress as he was of social progress'. There is certainly an element of truth in this assertion, for managers were often cautious and unwilling to invest in new processes or to take opportunities, making Britain weaker than its major competitors. These problems were identified by the Labour government that came to power in 1964. Its solution was to encourage the merger of smaller companies into larger ones, under a general business ethic that 'big was beautiful'. Through a government agency, the Industrial Reorganisation Corporation (IRC) the government acted as a marriage-broker for mergers between Leyland Trucks and the British Motor Corporation to form British Leyland, English Electric and General Electric, and various smaller companies into International Computers Ltd (ICL).

A particular feature of the 1950s and 1960s was low unemployment, which meant that there was much competition, particularly for skilled labour (see table 5). In the spring of 1956, there were 216,000 registered unemployed and some 400,000 unfilled vacancies. Governments regarded unemployment figures of 500,000 or more as being a major catastrophe. Historically these figures were remarkable considering the high unemployment of the inter-war period, where in the 1930s it had averaged 13% compared to an average of 2% between 1951 and 1973. Such low unemployment had an impact in two ways on people's lives, particularly those of the working classes: it became very easy to switch jobs and it also forced wages up as employers competed for workers.

Why have there been increases and decreases in unemployment?

TABLE 5 United Kingdom Unemployment rates, 1937–98 (percentage)

1937	1951	1964	1973	1979	1986	1989	1992	1998
10.1	1.3	1.7	2.0	4.7	12.3	7.9	13.3	6.2

Women also had an increasingly important part to play in the workforce (see table 6). Before the war, middle-class women in most occupations, such as teaching and the civil service, were expected to give up work when they married. Many working-class women, however, continued to work even after marriage as their families needed the extra income. Women were encouraged to enter the labour market during the war and nearly 8 million were in paid work in June 1943. Many however returned to the home once the war had ended and only 6 million were working by June 1947. During the 1950s and 1960s women, particularly among the middle classes, returned to work once they had had their children. Others turned to part-time working as a way of juggling family commitments. The percentage of part-time women workers rose from 12% in 1951 to 34% of the female workforce by 1972.

TABLE 6 Women in the labour force, 1951–81

	1951	1961	1971	1981
As % of total labour force	31	33	37	40
As % of women aged 20–64	36	42	52	61
Part-time as % of total labour force	12	26	35	42
% of all married women aged 15–59 in labour force	36	35	49	62

Why did more women work part-time during the period under consideration?

What did not change was the work that women undertook. Most remained concentrated in lower-status, poorly-paid white collar, service and industrial occupations. While women were increasingly employed in the expanding service sector such as banking or the civil service, it was often as clerks or secretaries. Few women entered the professions: in 1961 women made up only 15% of doctors and just 1,031 (3.5%) of the whole legal profession. However, women increasingly turned away from that mainstay of pre-war employment – domestic service. In 1921 there had been 2.4 million servants: in 1962 there were only 362,000.

What also remained unchanged was the fact that women were paid less than men, often for doing exactly the same work. In January 1945 the average earnings of women in industry was 53% of those of men. The issue was a contentious one. Women and trade unionists in the public sector continued to press the government – their employer. In 1955 the government began to introduce equal pay into the civil service, local government and teaching.

Pressure for equal pay throughout industry mounted during the 1960s. One of the last accomplishments of the 1964–70 Labour governments was to introduce the Equal Pay Act that established equal rates of pay for the same work. The Act, however, did not fully come into effect until 1975. It has helped close the gap between men's and women's pay, with women's full-time earnings rising from approximately two-thirds to nearly three-quarters of the average male rate.

1973–2000

If with hindsight the period between 1955 and 1973 was a period of smooth growth and a gentle progression towards prosperity, then changes in British life between 1973 and 2000 have been more of a roller-coaster ride. Since the early 1970s the British economy, and British industry in particular, has experienced two major depressions and several shorter periods of growth. The 1970s, however, were largely a period of stagnation in the economy. The economy grew roughly at about 2.5% per annum while there was little or no growth in manufacturing itself.

Government economic policies have increasingly played a part in the management of the economy, for better and for worse. Edward Heath came to power in 1970 with a determination to let industry 'stand on its own two feet'. He initially adopted what might be called proto-Thatcherite policies, abolishing price and income controls, refusing to get involved in strikes, and cutting public expenditure. But his administration was soon overwhelmed by events. Some were of the government's own making, particularly the failure to regulate the trade unions, 'U-turns' on incomes and prices policies and providing support for failing industries such as Upper Clyde Shipbuilders and Rolls-Royce Engineering. The early refusal to introduce wage and price curbs led to a rapidly rising rate of inflation. Huge rises in commodity prices during 1973 also help fuel inflation. Non-oil prices rose by 62% during the year, the largest recorded annual increase.

But other events, especially the end of fixed exchange rates in 1972 and the oil crisis of late 1973, were outside the control of the government. The ending of a fixed rate badly hit oil exporting countries because their prices were in dollars, which had effectively been devalued. But they found they could flex their muscles and through the Organisation of Petroleum Exporting Countries (OPEC) raised prices dramatically. During the year oil prices quadrupled from $2.50 to over $12.50 a barrel.

The Labour governments of 1974 to 1979, under Harold Wilson and his successor James Callaghan, had their own economic problems. With the co-operation of the trade unions, wage rises were gradually reduced. Industrial production, however, remained static, and unemployment slowly rose, reaching 1 million in 1978 for the first time since the 1930s.

The real problem facing Labour was the lack of confidence in the government felt by the financial markets. In early 1976 the pound began a seemingly endless slide against the dollar from $2.00 in March to a low of $1.64 in October. The government decided that its only course of action was to buy time, using a loan from the International Monetary Fund (IMF) to create a breathing space secure from outside pressure. The IMF were willing to help, provided cuts were made to public expenditure. Denis Healey, the Chancellor of the Exchequer, negotiated a loan of $3.9 billion worth of credit in exchange for a £2.5 billion cut in government expenditure. In the end little of the credit was actually taken up, but great damage was done to Britain's reputation and led to much speculation about Britain as 'the sick man of Europe'. The *Wall Street Journal* commented 'Goodbye Britain, it was nice knowing you'.

There was, however, modest economic recovery between 1976 and 1978, helped by the arrival of North Sea oil. The balance of payments and the inflation position both improved, while the pound rose to nearly $2.00. The government increasingly abandoned its belief in Keynesian economic policies in favour of more orthodox economic strategies. Writers such as Larry Elliott and Dan Atkinson in *The Age of Insecurity* have argued that 'Callaghan provided the overture for Thatcherism, pioneering many of her themes'.

Margaret Thatcher came to power with a radically different agenda to any previous Prime Minister. Chief among her policies was the adoption of monetarist policies along the lines advocated by the American economist Milton Friedman. Unfortunately, the effect of these new policies spelled disaster for the economy, which in any case was plunging into recession at the time of her election. Output and employment plummeted. The worst effects were felt in manufacturing, with output falling by 17% in 21 months. The loss of jobs in industry was substantial: 2 million manufacturing jobs were lost during the 1980s, of which three-quarters disappeared between 1980 and 1982. High interest rates (rising to nearly 16% in 1980) and the effects of North Sea oil led to a rapid rise in the exchange rate (reaching $2.45 in October 1981). All this devastated British manufacturing industry, driving firm after firm to the wall in sectors like engineering and textiles.

Although many of the monetarist policies were quietly abandoned, the effects of the recession lingered. In 1983, for the first time since the mediaeval period, Britain imported more manufactured goods than it exported. Thereafter the United Kingdom was kept in the black by earnings from the service sector of the economy, especially the financial services in the City of London.

The economy began to recover during 1983 and growth rates rose to about those during the 1950s and 1960s, (about 2.5% per annum). In particularly productivity grew quickly during the whole of the 1980s. In 1977 German manufacturing productivity was 46% above Britain's: by 1989 it was 15%. Yet British manufacturing found it hard to recover from the slump of the early 1980s. Despite the shedding of labour, new factory building and re-equipment by industry during the latter part of the 1980s, British firms still had difficulty competing with foreign rivals. Indeed, as demand for goods rose in the boom of the late 1980s, British industry lacked the capacity to meet it and imports rose to meet the demand.

Manufacturing output only grew by 1% or less per annum. The share of manufacturing in gross domestic product declined from 27% in 1973 to 20% in 1990. Britain's share of world trade continued to decline (see table 7). The long, increasingly inflationary, upswing of 1982 to 1990 eventually collapsed into a deep protracted slump that the economy only pulled out of in 1993 and 1994 (see table 8).

?

1. Using table 7 and information in this section, has Britain done better than its economic competitors during this period?

2. From figures in table 8 explain whether people were getting better off during the period under consideration. What other factors would you take into consideration to make a reasoned judgement?

TABLE 7 *Average annual growth rate of Gross Domestic Product (percentages)*

	1965–80	1980–90	1991	1992	1993	1994	1995
Japan	6.4	4.1	4.3	1.1	0.1	0.6	0.5
US	2.7	3.4	–0.7	2.6	3.0	4.1	2.9
Germany	3.3	2.1	2.0	2.1	–1.2	2.9	2.8
Britain	2.3	3.1	–2.2	–0.6	1.9	3.8	2.7

TABLE 8 *Selected indicators of economic performance, 1960–89 (percentages)*

	1960–73	1973–79	1979–89
Real earnings increase (average growth per annum)	2.1	0.5	2.8
Inflation (retail price index average annual increase)	4.8	14.7	8.0
Unemployment rate (percentage of workforce unemployed average)	1.9	3.4	9.1

As industry faltered, unemployment became a significant problem for the first time since the 1930s. In the first recession of the early 1980s this unemployment fell disproportionately on northern England, South Wales and Scotland. The recession of the early 1990s affected the south-east as well: *The Guardian* called it the 'nightmare on Acacia Avenue' because it affected prim suburban streets in Streatham and Shenfield as much as terraced rows in Salford or Sedgley. The government, however, accepted unemployment as a necessary evil in order to control inflation. Despite the costs to the economy, unemployment never became a political issue: political parties preferred to focus their attentions on the employed. The unemployed became a marginalised group, increasingly seen to be themselves responsible for their situation.

Margaret Thatcher also began privatising many of the industries that the Labour government had nationalised in the late 1940s. Initially **privatisation** formed only a small part of Conservative policy, but as the 1980s and 1990s progressed it became increasingly important (see table 9). The first major privatisation was of the medical research group Amersham International in 1982. British Telecom and British Airways followed in 1984 and British Gas in 1986.

Privatisation: The act of transferring an industry from public ownership to the private sector.

TABLE 9 *Total revenue from privatisation: financial years 1982/3–1991/2 (£m)*

1982/3	1983/4	1984/5	1985/6	1986/7	1987/8	1988/9	1989/90	1990/1	1991/2	1992/3
455	1139	2050	2706	4458	5140	7069	4226	5346	7923	7962

When do you think privatisation became an important source of income for the government?

The government argued that privatisation could enable these industries to benefit from the rigours of the private sector and would be able to manage their affairs without interference from the state. In general however the privatised utilities became private sector monopolies with very little competition. The public was generally in favour, largely because they could make gains by buying shares when they were first issued and then selling them for considerable profits a short time later. By the end of the 1980s the government was making £5 billion a year from privatisations. The money, however, was not invested in long-term capital projects, such as the modernisation of the crumbling transport system, but was largely frittered away on current spending. In effect this income was given back to the electorate as a tax cut.

The Major administration from 1990 was in many ways a continuation of Thatcherite policies. John Major's record for economic competence was mixed. He won the 1992 election during a deep slump, but lost the 1997 contest at a time when the economy was booming. His government will mainly be remembered for the fiasco of the **European Exchange Rate Mechanism** (ERM), which, although offering the prospect of stability, was entered at too high a rate for sterling and the British economy to benefit. Above all there was the extraordinary

European Exchange Rate Mechanism: A system whereby many countries in the European Community agreed fixed exchange rates with each other. It was a forerunner to the Euro.

TABLE 10 *Changes in gross domestic product (1990 = 100)*

	1985	1990	1993	1995	1998
USA	87	100	104	111	127
Japan	80	100	105	107	111
France	86	100	101	105	113
Germany	87	100	104	108	115
Britain	85	100	99	109	115

From this table say whether Britain has done as well as its economic competitors during the 1990s.

1. What have been the major changes to the British economy since 1945?

2. What do you think are the major factors that have caused these changes?

3. How important do you think government policy has been in British economic development?

4. Why have historians and economists offered different interpretations of Britain's economic performance since 1945?

episode of 'Black Wednesday', 16 September 1992, when Britain left the ERM in considerable confusion. Outside the ERM the government was able to cut interest rates sharply and allow the pound to fall. Recovery began almost immediately. Both unemployment and inflation began to decline. 'Black Wednesday', however, largely destroyed the public's faith in the Conservatives' economic policies and contributed to their humiliation at the polls in May 1997.

The late 1990s has seen a sustained boom, accompanied by slow falls in unemployment towards the 1 million level. Inflation too has fallen away, so by the middle of 1999 it was as low as it had been in July 1963. According to at least one commentator, the economy had been remarkably stable, with few signs of the 'boom and bust' cycle of the 1970s, 1980s and early 1990s. As a result, British economic growth has matched that of its main economic competitors. Yet many structural problems still remain. In particular there remains a lack of the highly-trained, highly-skilled workers that are increasingly needed to run modern industry.

Tony Blair and his chancellor, Gordon Brown, have largely followed their predecessors' policies, keeping a tight rein on public expenditure and a close interest in controlling inflation. Policies such as the 'University for Industry' and encouragement of the City to invest in industry may over time help solve some of the problems manufacturing industry has endured for a hundred years and more.

14.2 In what way did British society change between 1945 and 2000?

1945–1951

As well as damaging the economy, the Second World War had impoverished people's lives. The British in 1945 may have shared common interests, and endured common problems, but life was drab and heavily regulated. Extensive rationing addressed the shortages in food, in clothing and in consumer goods. The amount of consumer expenditure subject to rationing rose from about 25% in 1946 to 30% in 1948, before dropping away to 12% in 1949. Most foods remained rationed for many years after the war, as did clothing until 1949.

It was clear by 1950 that Britain was slowly emerging into what Tony Benn later called 'a decade of hope'. One sign of this new confidence was the Festival of Britain, held on London's South Bank. The Festival was to be a showcase for all that was best about British industry and innovation. It was also a designed to be in the slogan of the period 'a tonic to the nation': a celebration of the fact that the country was confidently looking towards a better future.

1951–1973

The Conservative administration that came to power in 1951 made few changes to its predecessor's policies. It was to remove the remaining restrictions. This philosophy was summoned up by Churchill in a broadcast in 1952, 'we think that it is a good thing to set the people free, as much as possible in our complicated modern society, from the trammels of state control and bureaucratic management'. The result was the first of many consumer booms. It was encouraged by cuts in taxation. Income tax was reduced by sixpence ($2\frac{1}{2}$p) to nine shillings (45p) in the pound [today the basic rate is 22p] and purchase tax was also cut. As a result there was a dramatic rise in the sale of consumer goods (see table 11). As Catherine Schenk in *Twentieth Century Britain: Economic, Social and Cultural Change* (1994) suggests, 'the British people seemed finally to have been rewarded for their earlier sacrifice as the era of mass consumption arrived'.

TABLE 11 *Consumption of selected consumer durables*

	1949	1950	1951	1952	1953	1954	1955	1956	1957
New car registrations (000s)	13.8	11.1	11.4	15.7	24.7	33.7	41.9	33.4	35.5
TV sets (000s)	17.4	43.4	57.6	65.3	95.4	104.2	140.5	119.4	151.3

Why did consumption of these items increase?

By 1957 the new Prime Minister, Harold Macmillan, was famously able to assert in a speech at Bedford that 'Most of our people have never had it so good. Go around the country, go to the industrial towns, go to the farms and you will see a state of prosperity such as we have never had in my lifetime – nor indeed ever in the history of this country.'

There is no doubt that living standards improved considerably during the period. Consumer goods that once only the rich could afford were increasingly becoming available to the middle and working classes. The Conservative Home Secretary R.A. Butler, in an election broadcast during the 1959 general election suggested, 'we have developed … an affluent, open and democratic society in which the class escalators are continuing moving and in which the people are divided not so much between the "haves" and the "have-nots" as between "haves" and "have-mores".'

This rise can be seen by the rise in the average weekly earnings: the average male factory worker saw his weekly earnings rise from £7.83p in 1950 to £41.52p in 1973 (see table 12). At the same time the average number of hours he worked fell slightly from 48 to 45 a week. Women's earnings, however, lagged behind men, even so as more women worked, their wages were an increasingly important part of household budgets.

TABLE 12 *Average annual wage*

	Average annual wage £	Average annual wage index 1935–6 = 100
1935–6	134	100
1955–6	469	350
1960	581	434
1970	1,289	962
1978	3,827	2,856
1991	12,220	9,119

Have wages increased more than prices during this period?

Modest increases in inflation reduced some of the effect of the rapid rise in wages (see table 13). Between 1955 and 1960 retail prices rose by 15%, by 1969 they were 63% higher than in 1955. When overtime is taken into account average weekly earnings rose 130% between 1955 and 1969. This almost exactly matched the 127% rise in earnings by middle-class salaried earners during the same period.

TABLE 13 *Increases in earnings and retail prices 1981–1997 index*

	1981	1995	1997
Average earnings (1990=100)	125	336	386
Retail prices (1987=100)	75	149	157

A kitchen in the 1950s

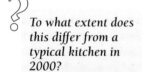 *To what extent does this differ from a typical kitchen in 2000?*

The most obvious sign of this increased affluence was in the ownership of consumer durables. In 1949 only 7% of adults owned a car, but by 1966 over half the adult population had a vehicle of some kind. Many goods, such as television sets and washing machines, cost less year by year and so became more affordable. During the 1950s and particularly during the 1960s an increasing proportion of households had central heating. By 1970, houses were on average 5°C warmer than they had been in 1950. There was an increasing array of household consumer goods, which either entertained, such as televisions and transistor radios, or were labour-saving such as washing machines and frozen food. By 1968 over 90% of households had televisions (see table 14).

TABLE 14 Consumer durables: availability in households (%)

	1955	1975	1995
Vacuum cleaner	51	90	96
Washing machine	18	70	91
Refrigerator	8	85	98
Freezer	n/a	15	79
Television	35	96	98
Telephone	19	52	92
Central heating	5	47	85
Dishwasher	1	2	12
Microwave oven	n/a	n/a	47
Video recorder	n/a	n/a	70
CD-player	n/a	n/a	63
Home computer	n/a	n/a	20

(n/a – not available)

How could households afford the increasing array of consumer goods on sale?

By the mid-1960s the children born in the baby-boom of the mid- and late-1940s had become teenagers. There were more young people around than before and they increasingly had more disposable income. By the late 1950s this was 50% higher than it had been pre-war. There were now goods for them to spend it on, clothes, transistor radios, and records. The writer Colin MacInnes suggested in 1958 that 'the great social revolution of the past fifteen years may not be the one which redivided wealth amongst among adults in the Welfare State, but the one that has given teenagers economic power'.

With the slow decline in working hours, teenagers had time to enjoy their new found affluence in milk and coffee bars or, for the well-off, jazz clubs. Above all it was rock and roll which summed up the period. The music arrived in Britain with the film *Rock around the Clock* (1956). The broadcaster Ray Gosling, then a teenager in Northampton, remembers, 'it was like an electric shock, and we all stood on our chairs and the aisles and howled'. As a result of the film there were riots in Croydon and the Elephant and Castle in London. In Northampton, however, Gosling 'remembered no aggro – it was just the experience of our lives'.

Teenage rebellion seemed more extreme in a society which was dull and conformist. Post-war austerity had been replaced by a natural desire to make up for the privations of a decade and a half. Britain during the 1950s was backward-looking, uncertain of its role in a very different world. Britain in the 1950s and early 1960s was increasingly criticised for its greyness.

For many the first break in this dull conformity was the prosecution and acquittal of Penguin Books in 1960 for obscenity in publishing *Lady Chatterley's Lover* by D. H. Lawrence, a book not available in Britain since the 1920s. It was then possible for books containing explicit material to be published.

What many called the 'permissive society' finally arrived between 1963 and 1966, when as Arthur Marwick noted, 'British society seemed to have broken out of the straitjacket of dullness and conformity'. In practice, however, the sexual and other freedoms excitedly talked about in newspapers and magazines, such as the contraceptive pill, hardly touched most ordinary people. By 1970, for example, only 8% of women used the Pill. London was singled out as 'Swinging London' for a reason. Many of the changes in social mores began in the capital and only slowly filtered out to the provinces.

The middle and late 1960s saw legislation passed by the Labour government that significantly relaxed the old Victorian code. Politicians, however, were reacting to events of the time, rather than taking a lead. Among acts passed during this period were:

- The abolition of hanging for criminal offences in 1965.

- The legalisation of abortion in 1967.

- The legalisation of homosexuality in 1967.

- Local authorities were allowed to set up family planning clinics in 1967, which in effect made these clinics legal for the first time.

- Abolition of theatre censorship in 1968 and a notable relaxation in cinema censorship which took place during the period.

- Divorce was made easier with the passing of the Divorce Reform Act, 1969.

Britain in the early 1970s was very different from 20 years before.

1973–2000

Post-war affluence had given people goods their parents could not have imagined, let alone afforded. Until the mid-1970s, affluence was almost universal, but although for many the rise in prosperity continued at an ever increasing rate, for the first time since 1945 this prosperity was not universal. The gap between rich and poor increased more dramatically than at any time in the 20th century (see table 15). This gap was encouraged by government policy offering tax cuts for the affluent and cuts in benefit for the poorest.

? *From this table indicate whether or not Britain has become a more equal country in the period 1977 to 1992.*

TABLE 15 Share of income by household group, 1977–92

	Bottom 20%	Bottom 40%	Top 40%	Top 20%
1977	4	14	69	43
1979	2	12	70	43
1985	3	10	74	47
1992	2	8	76	50

Individualism: The concept that individuals, and individual rights, are more important than society as a whole.

This has also been accompanied by what Elliott and Atkinson describe as 'a gradual erosion of the collectivist element that held the West together in the era of Beveridge and the Beatles'. Politicians, both of left and right, are increasingly committed to encourage **individualism** and individual achievements. The Conservative Prime Minister Margaret Thatcher summed up this new belief when she once declared in a speech that 'there is no such thing as society', meaning that individuals and their families were more important than society as a whole. 'New Labour' too has largely abandoned the collectivist traditions of the Labour Party.

Yet Britain has not really become an individualistic society, generally remaining resistant to official encouragement to become more entrepreneurial and go-getting. Nowhere is this truer than in attachment to the National Health Service, the greatest collective achievement. Even at the height of her powers, Thatcher time and again had to repeat that the 'National Health Service is safe in our hands'. Although reforms were made, neither Thatcher nor John Major attempted to abandon the principle of free medical care.

Inevitably changes had led to a much more divided society. The groups hardest hit by the changes have been the ethnic minorities, particularly the black and Muslim communities. Men in general were also badly affected. In the 20 years since 1979, men's employment rates fell while women's rose. In 1975 more than 92% of working-age men had a job, but by 1998 this had fallen to 81%, while for women over the same period the figure rose from 59% to 69%.

Women in 2000 were also earning more, thus beginning to close the gap on their male colleagues. By the end of the 20th century one in five women earned more than their working partners, compared with only one in fourteen in the 1970s. In 1998 women earned on average 75% of the average male hourly wage, compared with only 62% in 1974. Women were increasingly being accepted in management and professional circles, despite complaints of a 'glass ceiling' preventing them from progressing beyond a certain point. The share of women in senior positions rose from 7% in 1989 to 14% in 1998.

During the 1970s and 1980s the moral revolution launched in the mid-1960s finally percolated down throughout society. It was increasingly easy for people to adopt a lifestyle that suited them without fear of persecution. Homosexuality, finally legalised in 1967, for example, has become more widely tolerated. Gay scenes developed in many cities, like Canal Street in Manchester. Finally after a long campaign the age of consent for homosexual men was first lowered to 18 and then attempts were made to lower it to 16 as the century ended.

Among the British population as a whole there was increasing sexual freedom. By the late 1990s about 95% of couples had slept together before marriage, whereas in the early 1970s the figure was perhaps 30%. Young people were becoming sexually active at a younger age. In part this was due to the wide availability of contraceptives, especially the pill. As the result of legislation in 1967, many local authorities and hospitals set up family planning clinics making it very much easier for people of all ages to get both advice and contraceptives themselves. The acceptance of the contraceptive pill by women took rather longer than has commonly been supposed, largely because of fears over side-effects. In 1971 only 19% of married women were taking the pill, while two-fifths of couples were taking no precautions at all. By the 1990s the pill, closely followed by condoms, was the favourite means of contraception.

The period from the 1970s saw a decline in the institution of marriage. Increasingly couples preferred to live together before marriage, or not get married at all. In 1992 those **cohabiting** without actually getting married amounted to 18% of the total number of unmarried adults. By the end of the decade this figure was almost certainly higher. The number of marriages declined from 396,000 in 1984 to 318,000 in 1996; about a third of these marriages were people marrying for a second or subsequent time. Divorce too became more common, partly because legislation made divorce easier and as social taboos against it relaxed (see table 16). By the late 1990s a third of marriages ended in divorce.

Cohabit: To live together as a couple.

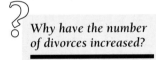

Why have the number of divorces increased?

TABLE 16 *Decrees made absolute (000s)*

1930	1950	1960	1970	1980	1990
4	33	26	62	159	166

Opposition to these changes has been surprisingly quiet. Mrs Mary Whitehouse, through her National Viewers and Listeners Association, campaigned with some success during the 1970s and 1980s to reduce the amount of sex and violence shown on television. Legislation was passed in the late 1980s controlling what could be taught about homosexuality in schools. Conservative politicians in particular have tried to reverse the trend, stressing 'family values' and the need to 'return back to basics.'

By and large the political parties were unable and unwilling to halt the social changes which were taking place, indeed they increasingly sought to mould their appeal to the new social groups and their aspirations. Politicians increasingly crafted their appeal to what became known as Middle England – the middle classes and the prosperous working classes. From the late 1970s the Tories owed a lot of their electoral success to their appeal to 'Essex woman' and 'Mondeo man'. It took over a decade for the Labour to realise that they had to do the same.

Judicious tax cuts and cheap privatised shares ensured that incomes remained buoyant. A constant stream of new goods appeared on shop shelves to tempt consumers: videos, microwaves, home computers and mobile phones. The rapid pace of technological developments ensured that prices kept falling while the machines themselves were more efficient and effective. The memory and speed of the first home computers in the early 1980s were a mere fraction of what is offered by even the most modest computers by 2000.

Another effect of affluence was that people began to travel more. The package holiday had started in the late 1950s, first to Spain and Italy and then to Greece, Cyprus and Turkey. In the early 1970s, 7 million people travelled abroad for their holidays. These figures grew dramatically during the 1980s and 1990s as fares, particularly across the Atlantic and to Australia fell. By 1998 39 million visits a year were being made abroad (see table 17). Young people especially could benefit from cheap flights to go on holidays clubbing in Ibiza or to more exotic locations during 'gap years' between school and university.

Why did more Britons travel abroad?

TABLE 17 Leisure visits abroad (millions)

1951	1961	1971	1978	1986	1997
2	4	7	9	22	39

1. What have been the main changes in British society since the war?

2. How has the role of women changed?

3. What changes have there been in what people can buy?

Has material wealth made Britain a happier place? At the end of a traumatic century there seems a sense of unease about the future, in contrast with the optimistic predictions that began the century. What is clear however is that life at work and at home has become much less secure than it was in the decades after the end of the Second World War. There are predictions that workers will have five to nine jobs in a career where welfare provision and the protection offered by trade unions will be minimal. In *The State We are In* (1995) and other writings, the journalist and economist Will Hutton argues that the net effect of these changes has been to shrink to just 40% of the population those who could be said to be secure in their work and homes. A further 30% were unemployed or economically inactive and a middle 30% were in 'structurally insecure' employment.

14.3 Has Britain become a multi-cultural society between 1945 and 2000?

Before the Second World War there were very few West Indians and even fewer Asians in Britain. Outside the dock areas of London, Liverpool, Cardiff and South Shields (where there was a lively Somali community) it would have been rare to have seen a black face, except for an occasional student. Black people were often objects of curiosity. It was not uncommon for migrants from the West Indies in the 1940s and 1950s to be touched for luck, while some small children were threatened by the warning, 'If you don't behave yourself the black man's going to get you'.

The Second World War saw the arrival of large number of black troops from the United States. The authorities in Britain were reluctant to accept them, fearing racial problems, although in general they were warmly received. Volunteers also came from the West Indies, Africa and the Indian sub-continent to serve in British forces. Large numbers of people, particularly from Ireland, were recruited to work in factories. They included several parties of men from the West Indies, the first 155 of whom came over in 1942 and worked in power stations in north-west England.

During the 1950s shortage of labour meant that the government, and to a lesser degree private employers, encouraged migration into Britain. Migrant workers were attracted from the Caribbean and the Indian sub-continent in increasing numbers, beginning with the 492, mainly young men, who travelled from Jamaica on the *Empire Windrush* in 1948. One of the 'pioneers', as he described himself was Dan Lawrence who remembers, 'I wanted to see the country that influenced my education very greatly and my values in life. Most of us were young men who just came over on a wave of excitement to try life in a new country. There were a few older men who had worked in England during the war. They went back home to Jamaica and they couldn't settle down there so they came back on the boat with us.' (BBC Radio WM, *The Century Speaks*, 1999).

Men from Jamaica arriving at Tilbury on the *Empire Windrush* in 1948.

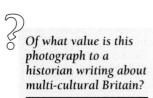

Of what value is this photograph to a historian writing about multi-cultural Britain?

Immigration from the West Indies and the Indian sub-continent ran at about 14,000 a year during the 1950s, but in 1961 there was a large rise prompted in part by fears that the government planned to introduce restrictions on immigration (see table 18). There were a number of limited schemes recruiting West Indian workers (such as those for London Transport and regional hospital boards) to carry out jobs for which they had difficulty finding British workers. Most migrants, however, came independently, seeking to better themselves and their families. There were also substantial inflows of Irish throughout the whole period, and Poles in the late 1940s and Italians in the 1950s and 1960s.

Do the numbers arriving in Britain show any decline as result of the Commonwealth Immigrants Act, 1962? What figures should be included to show fully the effect of the Act?

TABLE 18 New Commonwealth immigration into Britain, 1956–62

	West Indians	**Indians**	**Pakistanis and Bangladeshis**	**Total**
1956	26,400	5,600	2,100	34,100
1957	22,500	6,000	5,200	33,700
1958	16,500	6,200	4,700	27,400
1959	20,400	2,900	900	24,200
1960	52,700	5,900	2,500	61,100
1961	61,600	23,750	25,100	110,850
1962	35,000	22,100	24,900	82,000

The 'Mother Country' turned out to be far less welcoming than migrants had been led to expect. Mohammed Ayyub remembers arriving in Birmingham from the Punjab in December 1961, 'I tried to find a job, but I couldn't get a job at all. I ultimately applied in the West Midlands Transport for a conductor's job. My degree from Punjab wasn't recognised so it was useless. Being a graduate I didn't want to do that job but I was forced. Most of the people who turned us away from the gate, they said "no jobs". It was a surprise because we had heard stories that the English were very decent.' (*The Century Speaks*).

Official attitudes to migration from the **New Commonwealth** ranged from mild hostility to indifference. Half-hearted attempts were made to dissuade passengers on the *Empire Windrush* from coming to Britain,

New Commonwealth: Those members of the Commonwealth of Nations who were either still dependencies or had gained independence from Britain after 1947.

although once the ship had docked at Tilbury work was quickly found for most people. Administrations, both Labour and Conservative, were keen to avoid alienating Commonwealth governments, but they were also sensitive to mounting calls for immigration controls within Britain itself. In effect during the 1950s they neither controlled migration into the country, nor did they attempt to combat the rising tide of racism. The first attempt to control immigration came with the clearly racist Commonwealth Immigrants Act 1962 that placed restrictions for the first time upon entry of people from the New Commonwealth who were overwhelmingly black, but not on people from the Irish Republic, which had left the Commonwealth when it became a Republic. Further legislation controlling immigration was enacted in 1968 and 1971, which effectively reduced the number of migrants so that by 1973 only 4,000 were arriving each year.

What do you think accounts for the decline of migrants from the New Commonwealth?

TABLE 19 *Acceptances for settlement in the United Kingdom, 1963–91 from the New Commonwealth*

1963	1968	1973	1978	1983	1988	1991
56,071	60,620	32,247	30,514	27,550	22,800	27,930

TABLE 20 *New Commonwealth immigrants in the United Kingdom (defined as living in households whose head was born in the relevant area according to census returns) (000)*

	West Indian	Indian sub-continent	Total for whole of Commonwealth
1961	173	116	597
1971	302	462	1,294
1981	295	629	1,666
1991	434	1,296	2,635

From which other Commonwealth countries did sizeable numbers of migrants come?

Tackling racism was more difficult. Although increasingly aware of the problem, the government initially took little action preferring to rely on voluntary measures. Even racist riots in Nottingham and Notting Hill in London during 1958 and overwhelming evidence of discrimination against migrants failed to make the government act. A number of industries operated an unofficial colour bar, refusing to employ black or Asian workers, while other employers took on migrants from the New Commonwealth as long as they were never seen in public.

The new migrants tended to settle in inner-city areas, leading to tension with the established working-class communities. This was particularly the case in the West Midlands and parts of London (such as Indians in Southall and West Indians in Brixton) where a third of all immigrants settled. A lot of these tensions came to the fore in the Black Country constituency of Smethwick during the 1964 election campaign, where the openly racist Conservative candidate, Peter Griffiths, defeated the sitting Labour member Patrick Gordon-Walker. Slogans such as 'If you want a nigger for a neighbour vote Labour' appeared throughout the constituency.

Matters were not helped by a speech made by a senior Conservative politician, Enoch Powell, at Birmingham in April 1968 in which he called for the repatriation of black and other Commonwealth immigrants. Powell was immediately dismissed from the **Shadow Cabinet**, but his views attracted much sympathy among white working-class people in

Shadow Cabinet: A collective term for the opposition front bench spokespeople.

inner city areas. There was for example a march of dockers to the Houses of Parliament in Westminster in his support.

The position of the Labour government elected in 1964 was in practice little different to their Conservative predecessors. Politicians were split between the anti-racism of the political classes, and the concerns of Labour's working-class supporters. The liberal-minded Home Secretary, Roy Jenkins, was determined to stamp out racism and established the Race Relations Board in 1965 and helped prepare the Race Relations Act (1968). On the other hand the government quickly acted to stem the flow of Kenyan Asians forced to leave Kenya in the late 1960s. Legislation was hurriedly passed in early 1968 to restrict the entry of these people, despite their having British passports and a legal right to settle in Britain. The result was misery for many of the 125,000-strong community as well as for the smaller Ugandan Asian community forced to flee neighbouring Uganda by Idi Amin in 1971 and 1972.

During the 1970s the first generation of 'Black Britons' grew up. In 1976, Mark Bonham-Carter, Chairman of the Community Relations Commission, warned that Britain's black community, 40% of whom were now born in the country, would not settle for second-class citizenship. He said that they take 'the phrase "equality of opportunity" for what it means. I have no doubt that we have not kept pace with the expectations of British-born blacks'. The Race Relations Act 1976 tried to tackle these problems by making discrimination unlawful in employment, training and education, and in the provision of goods and services. The Act also made it an offence to stir up racial hatred.

Even so racist attacks and discrimination continued. Occasionally the frustrations of the black communities at the poor conditions in which they lived and their lack of opportunities had vented themselves in outbreaks of rioting during the early 1980s. They began in the St Pauls district of Bristol in 1980, followed by riots in Brixton in London, Toxteth in Liverpool, and Moss Side in Manchester in 1981. These protests were more than race riots, for they were often joined by whites equally frustrated at the conditions they lived in. The **Scarman Report** on the Brixton riots spoke eloquently of the despair of unemployed young blacks and their sense of alienation from the community and especially from the police, whose intolerance and insensitivity were deplored.

The Scarman Report: The result of a committee investigation by Lord Scarman, a senior Law Lord with a liberal reputation.

What reasons can you give to explain why unemployment was higher for ethnic minorities rather than for whites?

TABLE 21 *Unemployment rates by ethnic origin (%)*

	1979	1990	1998
White	5	7	6
Black	10	13	15
Indian	6	10	9
Pakistani/Bangladeshi	11	20	20
Mixed and others	3	12	13

Despite depressingly high levels of racial attacks and accusations of institutional racism in the police force during the 1970s and 1980s the West Indian and Asian ethnic minorities were slowly being integrated into the mainstream of society. The first Labour Asian and black MPs were elected in 1987 and the first Conservative one in 1992. Perhaps the greatest sign of assimilation has been the popularity of Asian food, even if the dishes served at Indian restaurants bear little resemblance to native Indian cuisine. In 1950 there were only six Indian restaurants in Britain. By 1970 there were 2,000 and in 1994 there were 7,500 Indian restaurants nationwide. Chinese food was equally popular. A national catering survey in 1970 found that of those who ate out regularly or occasionally, 31% had eaten at Chinese restaurants, while only 5% had eaten at French restaurants.

There is much to be done however, as the Stephen Lawrence case in 1993 showed, particularly in tackling the 'institutional racism' which the report into the affair found to be prevalent in the police and some other public services. At the end of the 1990s, one in ten London Asian or Afro-Caribbean households had suffered racial harassment in or near the home and one in three felt threatened by the existence of racism. Arthur Marwick however concludes that 'the levels of integration achieved by Britain in the mid-1990s were better than might well have been predicted ten years earlier; at the bottom of the scale black youths were suffering disproportionally, but this (as in America) was becoming more of a class, than a purely racial, issue – in the "enterprise culture" all the poor were getting poorer (while some small businessmen, particularly Asian and Chinese were doing well.)'

1. What problems do you think these migrants encountered in Britain?

2. Have these communities become assimilated?

14.4 What impact did changes in the mass media have on Britain between 1945 and 2000?

BBC: British Broadcasting Corporation founded in 1922 (as the British Broadcasting Company) as the national broadcaster.

Since 1945 Britain has seen an explosion in the choice in what we watch and hear. In 1948 less than 10% of the population had a television set, but within 15 years over 90% of households had television. Newspapers are bigger, cheaper and full of colour compared with their counterparts in 1945. At the end of the war the **BBC** operated just two radio stations, whereas now there are five national radio stations and a network of local radio stations as well as many national and local commercial broadcasters. Numbers going to the cinema declined dramatically with the introduction of television, but films still remain popular and, indeed, audience numbers have risen steadily since 1985 (see table 22).

TABLE 22 Cinema attendance 1960–1998

	Screens	Admissions (000s)	Average visits per person
1960	3,034	501	9.6
1970	1,529	193	3.5
1980	1,715	101	1.8
1990	1,715	91	1.6
1998	2,581	136	2.3

Why do you think the number of visits to cinemas increased in the 1990s?

The programmes and other services offered by the media itself have changed, reflecting British society more closely than they did in the 1940s and 1950s. The 1960s in particular saw the media begin to tackle subjects that had previously been taboo, notably sexual relations, and take a much more critical view of politicians. New forms of popular music, particularly rock and roll in the 1950s and 1960s, showed the spending power that teenagers now had and emphasised a dissatisfaction with the place young people had in society.

Until the 1970s the media was, however, generally a unifying force. Choice was limited to two or three TV channels and three or four radio stations. People tended to watch and listen to the same programmes. During the 1980s and particularly the 1990s this changed with a proliferation of channels on **terrestrial**, **satellite** and **cable** television. Video recorders meant that people could record and watch programmes when it suited them. Popular music too split into various types, such as rap, drum

Terrestrial: Television broadcast through the air and available to everyone with a television aerial.

Satellite: Television broadcast via satellites in space and picked up by special receivers.

Cable: Television broadcast through special cables and picked up with decoders.

and bass, and reggae, whereas previously people had not much choice outside the Top Forty hits.

The media in 1945

In 1945 the British people got much of their news from newspapers and the radio (then called the wireless). For entertainment they turned to the wireless and cinema. The media had played a major part in the war effort keeping up morale with films like *In Which we Serve* (1942) and *Henry V* (1944), while the radio entertained with programmes such as *Bandwagon* and particularly *ITMA* (*It's That Man Again*) that gently satirised the bureaucracy and shortages of Britain in the 1940s.

Because of the shortage of paper, newspapers generally consisted of four or eight pages. Despite being heavily censored – no weather reports, for example, were carried during the war for fear of giving information to the enemy – they still remained extremely popular. Two newspapers were especially important. The Labour-Party-supporting *Daily Mirror* was the firm favourite of servicemen, who particularly followed the 'Adventures of Jane' a daily strip cartoon featuring a scantily clad heroine. The middle classes generally preferred the conservative *Daily Express*, owned by Lord Beaverbrook, a friend of Winston Churchill and a minister in the wartime government.

The most popular form of entertainment, however, was the cinema. In 1946 about a third of the population went to see a film at least once a week and one in eight twice a week or more. Cinemas were warm and comfortable and the films themselves offered an escape for an hour or two from the dreary existence of wartime and post-war Britain. Newsreels provided by Pathé and Movietone were shown between films and proved an important source of news for audiences.

However the most important source of both news and entertainment was the BBC. At the outbreak of war in September 1939 there were some 9 million wireless sets, about one for every four members of the population. As with British films the BBC reinforced a cosy image of a Britain at peace with itself. The Corporation rigorously censored programmes and even the lyrics of popular songs. The BBC maintained that it had the duty, in the words of its Director-General Sir William Haley, to 'use ... broadcasting to develop true citizenship and the leading of a full life'.

The rise of television

The BBC broadcast the first commercial television programmes in the world from Alexandra Palace in North London on 2 November 1936. Transmission ceased on the outbreak of war in September 1939 and resumed on 7 June 1946. Most viewers lived in the south-east. Hours were limited and the new service closed down for a period in the early evening to allow parents to put their children to sleep. There were fears almost from the first programme that television would corrupt the young and bring unhealthy American influences.

What made television really popular was the Coronation of Queen Elizabeth II in 1953, which was watched by half the British population, and also the launch of Independent Television (ITV) on 22 September 1955. The new service was to be funded by advertising and was seen as dangerous by people such as the Archbishop of York. Fears over the quality of programmes shown on the new channel were unfounded. An American commentator observed, 'the British have decided to paint the gaudy thing a sombre grey to blend with the general fog'.

What set ITV apart from the BBC was an innovative news service provided by Independent Television News (ITN) which the BBC was soon forced to emulate. The resulting competition for viewers between the two channels led in general to the development of many more popular television programmes. As a result the numbers of television sets in people's homes soared (see table 23). The television set in the front room was the symbol of the affluent society that Britain had become by the late 1950s. Sets may have been plentiful, but the choice of viewing remained limited and until 1967 was entirely in black and white. The third television channel, BBC 2, was not launched until April 1964.

Why do think there was an increase in TV licences?

TABLE 23 Television licences (thousands)

1947	1950	1955	1960	1965	1975	1985
15	344	4504	10,470	13,253	17,701	18,716

The 1960s, however, have often been seen as being a golden age of broadcasting with the combination of well-funded broadcasting companies with increasingly liberal and permissive attitudes. There were certainly ground-breaking programmes such as the satirical series *That was the Week that Was* (broadcast in 1963 and 1964) and later *Monty Python's Flying Circus* (broadcast between 1969 and 1972). Controversial television plays such as *The War Game* on the effects of a nuclear warhead dropped on Chatham (which the government banned in 1965) and *Cathy Come Home* (broadcast in 1966), which exposed the plight of single mothers, kept television very much in the public eye. These were combined with popular and long-running series like *Steptoe and Son, Dr Who,* and especially *Coronation Street,* which has been running since 1960.

There had long been pressure for a second commercial channel. Channel 4 went on air in November 1982 aiming to provide programmes designed to appeal to minority audiences. In this it has generally been both commercially and artistically successful. Terrestrial television was completed in March 1997 with the appearance of Channel 5.

But the big challenge to broadcasters from the mid-1980s has been satellite and, to a much lesser extent, cable television. In 1999 subscribers could receive 50 or more different channels. In particular Sky TV, which went on air in February 1989, posed a big threat. The major share-owner in the company, News International, controlled by Rupert Murdoch, realised that it could only prosper by buying up the rights, previously owned by terrestrial television, to show sporting fixtures, particularly football. To watch these events people had to subscribe to British Sky Broadcasting (as it is now called). Both ITV and, particularly, the BBC were unable to compete with the money offered by BSkyB to the various sporting federations.

Radio

At the end of the war the BBC had two radio stations – the Home Service (now Radio 4) and the Forces Programme which was renamed the Light Programme (now Radio 2) in July 1945. It was soon joined by the Third Programme (now Radio 3) in September 1946, intended to serve the intellectual elite. The programmes broadcast were listened to by millions of people from *Dick Barton: Secret Agent* and *Children's Hour* for the young, to *Have a Go* and *Mrs Dale's Diary* for the middle-aged.

Radio listening soon declined in popularity with the growth of its great rival, television. During the mid-1960s the BBC also faced increasing competition from pirate radio stations broadcasting pop music from ships moored outside British territorial waters in the North Sea. Radio Caroline, set up in 1964, was the most popular. Eventually the BBC bowed to pressure and set up its own pop music radio station – Radio 1 – in 1967. At the same time legal action closed down the pirate stations. The BBC effectively had a monopoly of radio broadcasting until 1973 when the first commercial local radio stations were licensed. The first national commercial radio station, Classic FM, started broadcasting in September 1992.

Newspapers

Newspapers have changed out of all recognition since 1945. In particular the number of pages have increased in each issue, expanded the coverage of subjects such as sport and travel, and used technological developments to improve the layout of the paper and (especially during the 1990s) colour photography. National newspapers have generally prospered at the cost of provincial and local newspapers. Many provincial daily and evening papers have closed, while local newspapers contain more national and less local news. The numbers of people buying and reading national newspapers have remained very high despite the challenge of television (see table 24).

TABLE 24 Newspaper circulation (000)

	1939	1951	1960	1970	1980	1990	1999
Daily Express	2,486	4,193	4,130	3,607	2,325	1,585	1,091
Daily Herald	2,000	2,071	1,467				
Daily Mail	1,510	2,245	2,084	1,917	1,985	1,708	2,357
Sun				1,509	3,837	3,855	3,701
Daily Mirror	1,367	4,567	4,545	4,697	3,651	3,083	2,341
Daily Sketch	850	777	1,152	806			
Daily Star					1,033	833	613
Daily Telegraph	640	976	1,155	1,402	1,456	1,076	1,044
Guardian	51	140	190	303	375	424	393
Independent						411	224
News Chronicle	1,317	1,586	1,206				
The Times	213	254	255	402	316	420	727
Today						540	
TOTAL circulation	10,434	16,809	16,184	14,643	14,978	13,935	12,491

From the table what do you think have been the main trends in newspaper circulation since the war? Explain your answer.

Since 1945 the national newspaper scene has remained remarkably consistent. Three new national daily newspapers have been launched – the *Sun* (1964), *Daily Star* (1978) and the *Independent* (1986), while newspapers that closed include the *Daily Sketch* (1971), the *News Chronicle* (1960), and the *Daily Herald* (1964).

The freedom of the press as against the privacy of the individual has remained a constant issue. Newspapers, especially the tabloids, have always included many stories about celebrities, but until the 1970s the lives of the royal family and politicians were generally left alone. This changed, however, largely as a result of the massive media interest in the life of Lady Diana Spencer who married Prince Charles in 1982. Stories about her filled many pages in the newspapers. The private lives of politicians also increasingly came under the scrutiny of the press and a succession of minor Conservative ministers resigned from office during the 1990s when their stories hit the front page.

This has increasingly led to calls for regulation of the press to ensure the private lives of people in the public eye and particularly lives of ordinary citizens are respected. Back in 1949 a royal commission on the press recommended the establishment of a press council to act as a forum for the industry. The Press Council was duly set up in 1953 and could hear complaints about invasion of privacy. It was later re-established in 1991, as the

Press Complaints Commission, Both the Council and the Commission have proved unable to regulate the press to prevent abuses happening.

There has also been considerable debate about the influence of newspapers in politics. Most newspapers in the 1980s and early 1990s were firmly behind the Conservative government and used their pages to denigrate the Labour Party, its policies and its leaders. The *Sun* after the 1992 election which saw the Conservatives unexpectedly returned to power, proclaimed, 'It was the Sun wot won it'. By 1997, however, most newspapers had switched their allegiance to 'New Labour' reflecting their readers' views that the Conservatives were out of touch with the concerns of the voters.

Film

The common language and, very largely, culture with America has meant that the British film industry has found it difficult to survive. Many of the most talented producers, directors and actors have been lured to Hollywood or, from the 1950s, preferred to work in television. In addition the government has been reluctant to support the film industry in the way that is common on the continent.

Even so a number of notable films have been made and shown to both critical and public acclaim. The late 1940s probably saw the peak of the British film industry, supported by the '**Eady Levy**' and heavy import duties on American films. The best films were probably those made by Ealing Studios, such as *The Lavender Hill Mob* (1951) and *Passport to Pimlico* (1949).

Eady Levy: A tax levied on cinema tickets in order to provide grants to the British film industry. Named after Sir William Eady, Chairman of the National Film Production Council.

British films of the period in general tended to avoid controversial issues, preferring to follow the traditional stereotypes in presenting a familiar, reassuring, tolerant, kindly British people to itself. There was no new artistic form as seen on the continent. There was a resurgence of British film-making during the 1960s, beginning with a series of films looking at working-class life of the period, unkindly dubbed 'kitchen sink dramas' by critics. Notable examples were *Saturday Night and Sunday Morning* (1960) on the life of a factory worker in Nottingham and *This Sporting Life* (1963) about a rugby league player. Later in the decade came the first of the James Bond films and *The Italian Job* (1969) which celebrated a newly modernised, confident Britain. The 1960s also saw the heyday of the *Carry On* films, particularly *Carry on Cleo* (1965) and *Carry on up the Khyber* (1967).

1. What changes have happened to the mass-media since the end of the Second World War?

2. Why do you think these changes have occurred?

Subsequent decades have not seen the same number of films being made, but a few highly popular films are still released. They include *My Beautiful Laundrette* (1985), *Gandhi* (1982), *Four Weddings and a Funeral* (1994) and *The Full Monty* (1997).

14.5 The rise and fall of the British trade union movement, 1945–2000

The trade union movement has played an important part in shaping post-war Britain. The experience however has not been a happy one for the unions because, particularly after 1979, they have seen most of their power and much of their influence disappear.

1940–1968

The place of trade unions in the war effort was recognised by the appointment of Ernest Bevin, the leader of Britain's biggest union, the Transport and General Workers Union (TGWU), as Minister of Labour in 1940 with responsibility for ensuring war factories got the workers they needed.

Bevin fully mobilised the trade union movement in this work. In turn the unions had insisted on the reintroduction of pre-war working practices after the war.

The trade unions emerged after 1945 as powerful partners with government and the employers in the management of the economy. Nearly half the working population were members of unions (see table 25). The unions naturally enjoyed warm relations with the Attlee administration. The union leadership in particular did much to contain protests from members about working conditions and ensured that wage rises remained low, thus helping to keep inflation low. In return they ensured that the government took into consideration their concerns, particularly over nationalisation. Clement Attlee also repealed the Trades Disputes Act, 1927 which had done much to shackle union activity during the 1930s.

TABLE 25 Membership of trade unions, 1936–93

	Members of trade unions (000)	% union members as proportion of workforce
1938	5,842	30
1951	9,289	44
1961	9,897	43
1970	11,179	48
1974	11,756	50
1981	12,947	44
1993	7,762	28

Why do think union membership declined in the 1980s and 1990s?

The Conservatives elected in 1951 were determined to continue this close relationship. A symbol of this was the appointment of Sir Walter Monckton as Minister of Labour. 'So conciliatory was Monckton,' John Charmley remarks in *A History of Conservative Politics, 1900–1996* (1996) that 'there were many who wondered whether he was the minister *for* labour'. What lay behind this was a recognition that Conservative politics were constrained to operate within the framework of Labour's post-war settlement that had brought significant benefits to working class voters.

Even so there was an increasing belief that poor industrial relations were affecting industrial growth. A stream of press and television stories encouraged this impression, although most strikes were concentrated in one or two industries. A Department of Employment study showed that, between 1971 and 1973, some 98% of manufacturing establishments had no strikes at all (see table 26).

TABLE 26 Industrial disputes 1931–97 (n/a – not available)

	Working days lost		Number of stoppages in year	
	(000s)	1931 = 100		1931 = 100
1931	6,983	100	420	100
1946	2,158	31	2,205	525
1951	1,694	24	1,719	409
1956	2,083	30	2,648	630
1961	3,046	44	2,686	640
1966	2,398	34	1,937	461
1970	3,906	56	10,980	2,614
1975	2,282	33	6,012	1,413
1980	11,964	171	830	198
1985	6,402	92	903	215
1990	1,903	27	630	150
1995	400	6	211	50
1997	200	3	n/a	n/a

Why have there been dramatic increases and decreases in industrial action as shown by this table?

Where they occurred in industry, strikes were often short 'wildcat' strikes over minor job demarcation or manning levels. Over time these had serious long-term effects on output, quality, delivery dates, and labour costs, all of which contributed to the loss of markets at home and abroad. The shipbuilding, car and newspapers industries, which had a large number of competing craft unions, were particularly prone to strikes of this kind.

Strikes increased during the 1960s. There were a number of well-publicised strikes particularly in the docks. The best known of these was probably the seamen's strike during the summer of 1966, which caused immense damage to Britain's export trade and resulted in heavy pressure on sterling. Governments seemed powerless to act, although ministers were well aware of the damage to the economy.

One strategy to curb the unions would have been a change in economic strategy to end the policy of full employment, for the demand for labour and the ease of changing jobs gave unions considerable leverage in arguing for wage increases. But to do so would have struck at the very heart of the consensus that governments, of both left and right, were striving to build. During the 1960s and 1970s many politicians still had vivid memories of the misery that mass unemployment caused between the wars and had no wish to see this happen again. It would take the Conservatives under Margaret Thatcher, and the end of full employment in the late 1970s and early 1980s, to control the unions effectively.

1968–1979

In 1965 the government decided to set up a royal commission, under Lord Donovan, to look at industrial relations. When the commission reported in 1968 it advised against sanctions to curb union power. Barbara Castle, the Secretary of State for Employment, however proposed stiffer measures to regulate industrial disputes in the White Paper *In Place of Strife* (1969). These fairly moderate proposals were overwhelmingly rejected by the trade union movement, as well as by the Labour Party itself, forcing a humiliating retreat by the government. In the end the Trades Union Congress (TUC) and the government agreed a weak compromise.

The Conservative government in 1970 took a rather different approach. It passed the Industrial Relations Act 1971, which introduced unprecedented legal regulation of union activities in an attempt to stop wildcat strikes. This was bitterly resisted by the trade union movement, which refused to register, as the Act directed. This largely rendered the legislation ineffective. In addition the government's approach was also condemned by the **Confederation of British Industry** (CBI). The Act was abolished in 1974 after Labour was returned to power.

The Heath government collapsed in early 1974 as the result of a bruising clash with the National Union of Miners. Between 1971 and 1972 the miners had, in the first national strike in the coal mines since 1926, successfully gone on strike for a large pay rise. The strike had caused widespread disruption to industry, including power cuts and compulsory short-term working known as 'the three day week'. The miners, and other trade unions, angered by the falling behind of wages, threatened industrial action. Heath's reaction was to call an election for late February, specifically on the question 'Who governs Britain?' The electorate inconclusively decided that the Conservatives didn't, returning a minority Labour government that resolved the dispute with the miners within days of the election.

Like Heath, James Callaghan would eventually fall foul of the trade unions, though this is more surprising considering Callaghan's background in the trade union movement. Initially relations were warm. Many

Confederation of British Industry: Represents industry in dealings with the government. Formed in 1965.

of the long-standing demands of the unions were met, such as the Health and Safety At Work Act (1974), which improved conditions in factories and offices across Britain. Unions also fully co-operated in attempts to reduce inflation. A voluntary code was introduced in 1976 which lasted for nearly two years; far longer than most observers had predicted.

By the middle of 1978 the pressure on trade union leaders from members after several years of wage restraint was almost irresistible. The government, however, decided to ignore the warning signs when it introduced a 5% pay rise limit in October 1978, without consulting the unions. The figure was rejected first by the Labour Party conference and then opposed by various key groups – firemen, lorry drivers, and Ford workers – who obtained substantial settlements well into double figures. Public sector workers, always poorly paid, tried to follow suit. Months of sporadic industrial action followed which became known as the 'Winter of Discontent'. Eventually the government caved in and awarded a 9% pay rise. The damage, however, had been done. The feeling that the trade unions had got out of control greatly benefited the Conservatives at the general election in 1979.

1979–2000

The new Thatcher government had no qualms in taking on the trade unions. In this the government was helped by the economic slump, which had seen a massive increase in unemployment including many hundreds of thousands of former union members. The government also learnt from the mistakes made by Edward Heath and avoided a full frontal attack, instead preferring a piecemeal approach with a series of acts restricting union activities. Chief among them were requirements for ballots before strike action and restrictions on picketing. Union opposition was muted, partly because it was clear that this legislation was popular among members; a majority of whom had indeed voted for the Conservatives in 1979. Days lost due to industrial disputes fell from 6.2 million days in 1981 to 528 in 1982.

The last great act of union resistance was the miners' strike of 1984–85, in which the National Union of Miners under Arthur Scargill was comprehensively defeated by a determined government, who perhaps remembered the bruising contests with the miners in 1972 and 1974. Although the strike attracted considerable public sympathy, it was badly-led by Scargill. As Neil Kinnock told the Labour Party, the miners were 'lions led by donkeys'. However popular the strike might have been it was ultimately doomed to failure, for British industry was no longer as dependent on coal as it had once been. Indeed stocks had been increasing for some months before the strike in anticipation of industrial action.

The defeat of the strike allowed the Conservatives to pass further laws controlling the unions and the power of industrial action. As a result strikes fell to an all-time low.

New Labour has an ambivalent relationship with the unions. Although it is willing to take the union money to help fund the party, the leaders have been keen to be seen to be keeping unions at arm's length. This has led one union leader to complain that the unions are treated as if they were 'embarrassing elderly relations at a party'. The Blair administration has introduced a number of reforms including the introduction of a minimum pay rate – something which the unions long campaigned for – and a relaxing of a few of the more draconian laws passed by the Conservatives. Even so Tony Blair is very wary of unleashing union power which caused so much trouble to his predecessors and to Britain as a whole.

1. Why were the unions so powerful after the Second World War?

2. Why was there so much industrial unrest in the 1960s and 1970s?

3. How did the Conservative and Labour governments tackle industrial relations in the 1980s and 1990s?

Britain and Europe, 1945–2000

15.1 Why did Ernest Bevin reject the idea of a European 'Third Force' in 1949?

15.2 How did Anthony Eden deal with the problems of West German rearmament in 1954?

15.3 Historical Interpretation: Did Britain 'miss the bus' in Europe, 1950–1957?

15.4 Why did Harold Macmillan decide to apply for membership of the EEC?

15.5 Why was Britain not able to join the EEC until 1973?

15.6 Why did the Labour governments have so many concerns about Britain's membership of the EEC in the 1970s?

15.7 Did Margaret Thatcher's attitude towards her European partners help or harm Britain's standing in Europe?

15.8 Why was the Conservative Party so divided over the question of European integration in the 1990s?

15.9 How European were the British at the end of the 20th century?

Key Issues

● Why did Britain fail to take the lead in Europe at the end of the Second World War?

● Was British membership of the EEC inevitable?

● Why did the idea of a United States of Europe still divide parties and public opinion in Britain at the end of the 20th century?

Framework of Events

1947	Dunkirk Treaty signed. Marshall Aid
1948	Brussels Pact. Council of Europe
	Communist coup in Czechoslovakia
	Berlin Airlift
1949	NATO. Division of Germany
1950	Schuman Plan for European Coal and Steel Community
	Pleven Plan for European Defence Community
1954	French fail to ratify EDC
1955	Western European Union set up
	Talks begin at Messina for a European Economic Community
1956	Talks begin on Free Trade Area – Plan G
	Suez Crisis
1957	Treaty of Rome signed, creating EEC
1958	Free Trade Area talks fail
1959	European Free Trade Area (EFTA) set up
1961	Macmillan applies for membership of the EEC
1963	General de Gaulle vetoes British application
1967	Harold Wilson applies for membership of the EEC
1972	Edward Heath successfully takes Britain into the EEC
1975	British referendum on Common Market membership
1985	The EC agrees the Single European Act
1988	Jacques Delors reports on Economic and Monetary Union and Social Chapter
1990	Thatcher 'deposed' by pro-European Conservatives. Britain enters ERM
1992	Maastricht Treaty on European Union
	Britain leaves Exchange Rate Mechanism and devalues pound
1999	Eleven countries launch Euro as trading currency.
	Britain does not join the single currency

Overview

THE Second World War devastated the continent of Europe. Millions lost their lives, homes and families. Whole cities were destroyed. There were drastic shortages of food and fuel. Unlike many European nations, Britain had not been occupied by the Nazis. The war confirmed British policy-makers' belief in Britain's role as a great power: Britain had her empire, and a tradition of parliamentary government unbroken since the 17th century. British policy-makers believed that Britain would be the key player in shaping post-war Europe.

However, the war had only been won with the help of the United States and the Soviet Union. This determined the political geography of mainland Europe: the Allies decided to divide Germany, and govern it among themselves. By 1948, Marshall Aid, the Czechoslovakian coup and the Berlin Airlift showed that co-operation between west and east would not be possible. Communist regimes were established in eastern European states and in East Germany. Western European nations accepted American aid and moved towards liberal capitalist systems. The Cold War, characterised by two superpowers straddling a divided Europe, had begun.

In western Europe, France, West Germany, Italy, the Netherlands, Belgium and Luxembourg responded by creating, in 1957, a European Economic Community, to strengthen their own economic and political power. The EEC aimed to create a political **federation** in Europe, housing France and Germany under one roof and so preventing another war. It also aimed to benefit European trade. Britain declined to participate because British politicians did not want British **national sovereignty** to be challenged. However, by 1961, the British had realised the importance of membership of such a European group, for economic benefit, and to bolster Britain's flagging political influence. However, in 1963, and again in 1967, the French leader General de Gaulle refused Britain entry to the European Economic Community. Entry was only achieved after his death in 1972.

Britain has often been seen as an awkward partner in the EEC. British politicians found it difficult to adjust to Britain's new role; and they saw Europe as a useful question over which to fight for their own political ends. In 1975, the Labour government held a referendum on continued membership of Europe. The people voted overwhelmingly in favour, but the Labour party moved towards a position of withdrawal from the EC, causing pro-European Labour party members to leave in 1981.

Under the Conservative Prime Minister Margaret Thatcher after 1979, Britain appeared to be moving towards a more constructive relationship with the EC. However, the EC wanted deeper integration and increasing political unity. Thatcher supported the developing **single market** in Europe, but was not in favour of the **supranational** institutions that accompanied it. When the Community began to debate economic and monetary union in 1988, she began to withdraw her support. The result was that Britain again found itself on the outskirts of European decision-making. The Conservative Party were driven into civil war as they failed to agree on a sensible policy towards Europe.

The political landscape of post-war Europe changed again dramatically in 1989 when the Soviet Union collapsed and the Berlin Wall came down. Germany was reunified, and increased German strength encouraged the continental states to integrate further. Europe could also expand outwards into eastern Europe,

Federation: A 'federal' Europe would have a European government, consisting of the European nations, but acting in the interests of Europe as a whole.

National sovereignty: The power and independence of the British nation, Parliament and people.

Single market: The idea that all Europe should be one single economic unit.

Supranational: 'Above the nation'. Nations agree to give some national sovereignty to European institutions.

raising questions about the sort of institutions Europe needed. The Treaty of European Union, signed at Maastricht in 1991, developed European unity, adding intergovernmental structures to the existing supranational ones. The British, however, found it difficult to come to terms with the new European reality.

15.1 Why did Ernest Bevin reject the idea of a European 'Third Force' in 1949?

Ernest Bevin was one of the most brilliant politicians in Churchill's war cabinet. When the Labour government won the 1945 election, Bevin became Foreign Secretary. He was one of the more powerful members of the cabinet. A former trade union leader, Bevin was to the right of the Labour Party, and some historians believe that he was strongly anti-communist.

Did Bevin ever support the idea of a Third Force Europe?

Third Force: The idea that western Europe could act as a powerful international political force alongside the USA and USSR and independent from them..

The traditional view of historians like Lord Bullock is that Bevin was never interested in a **Third Force** Europe. Bullock argued that his whole foreign policy was aimed to attract the United States to defend Europe. Revisionist historians, however, have argued that Bevin was interested in a Third Force before 1948.

The problem facing Western Europe was how to secure a lasting peace settlement. The Versailles Peace Treaty in 1919 had clearly failed. The French wanted to crush German industrial power so Germany could not start another war, but Britain and America believed that Germany should be allowed to recover. A Third Force Europe would be one way of controlling Germany's recovery, and would offer a way of defending Western Europe if America refused to participate. It would also help to create prosperity, and so prevent the spread of communism. In 1944 the Foreign Office believed Germany to be a greater threat to peace than the Soviet Union and wanted to create a Third Force Europe. The left wing of the Labour Party also supported the idea because it would enable Europe to be independent of the capitalist United States and to pursue a co-operative arrangement with the Soviet Union.

Bevin was certainly interested in the idea of a Third Force Europe. He spoke to his Foreign Office officials in 1945 about the possibility of close commercial, political and economic links with Europe, including Greece, Italy, France, Belgium, the Netherlands and Scandinavia. He also considered taking the industrial Ruhr from Germany and placing it under international control. In 1947, Bevin insisted that the Foreign Office study the possibility of a **customs union** in Europe. In 1948, he told the House of Commons of his vision to unite Europe with the Commonwealth. The Commonwealth's raw materials, food and resources would help to strengthen Europe. Bevin also committed British troops to the continent for the first time ever in peacetime in the Treaties of Dunkirk and Brussels in 1947 and 1948. However, Third Force proposals were only discussed once in Cabinet in 1947, and Bevin's ideas were never translated into concrete plans.

Customs union: Nations in the union agree to remove customs duties on goods traded within the union. There is a tariff on imports into the customs union from other countries.

Economic recovery in Western Europe

In order to secure peace in Western Europe, it was essential that Europe's economies should recover . The immediate problem was reconstructing economic infrastructures - housing, roads and railways - which required investment of capital. After the war, Britain thought that it could provide for British and Western European recovery. However, by 1947 it was clear that Britain's economy was not strong enough, and European recovery was not possible without American help. In 1949, the Labour government had to devalue the pound, and this convinced the European countries that they could not rely on Britain to provide economic stability. It also convinced the Americans to allow Britain to concentrate on its world role in Commonwealth and Empire as the United States saw the maintenance of sterling as essential.

The British government's economic departments, the Board of Trade and the Treasury, were strongly opposed to a Third Force Europe because of Britain's economic weakness. They did not think that Britain would benefit from a customs union in western Europe because of the weakness of Europe itself. A European trading bloc would also be contrary to the doctrine of free trade throughout the world, popular in the United States. They predicted that there would be a world shortage of raw materials and food, and so thought that Britain's interests lay in preserving her trading links with the Empire and Commonwealth. Furthermore, the Treasury and the Board of Trade wanted to maintain **sterling** as a world trading currency. As well as generating revenue, sterling's world role provided Britain with international prestige, and confirmed her position as head of the Commonwealth and the Empire.

Sterling: The British currency.

Economic weakness meant that Britain had to seek economic help from the United States. In 1947, the United States offered economic aid to Europe with the Marshall Plan. The Plan had far reaching consequences. The Soviet Union refused participation for itself and for its eastern European satellites. This divided Europe into two hostile blocs, with western Europe accepting **liberal capitalism**, and eastern Europe communist ideals. Marshall Aid also forced the issue of western European co-operation, as it was necessary to set up a body to manage the four-year economic recovery programme. The French and the Americans wanted a supranational authority and customs union in western Europe. Bevin refused, and the weaker intergovernmental Organisation for European Economic Co-operation (OEEC) was set up. Bevin realised that, economically, an independent third force in Europe was impossible. Marshall Aid showed that Europe needed American money. Bevin now wanted to illustrate British strength by bridging the gap between America and Europe.

Liberal capitalism: The political and economic system based on democracy and the private ownership of businesses.

British policy towards the Soviet Union

The other main factor causing Bevin to reject the idea of a Third Force Europe was that he saw the Soviet Union as the main threat to peace in Europe. If the Soviet Union attacked, western Europe would be powerless against its superior might. America was the only power with enough resources to challenge the Soviet Union. America also had an atomic bomb, used for the first time to devastating effect in Japan in 1945. Bevin realised that only the American nuclear threat could deter the Soviet Union, and keep Europe at peace.

Historians have different views on when Bevin realised this threat. Anne Deighton, in *The Impossible Peace* (1993), argued that Bevin and the Foreign Office believed from soon after the war that the Soviet Union, not Germany, would prove to be the main threat to mainland Europe. However, the Soviet Union was an ally, and the Soviets had shown bravery and suffered huge loss of life in defeating the Germans. Bevin therefore had to hide his suspicions, while secretly working in the Council of Foreign Ministers meetings between the British, Americans, French and Russians, to attract America out of isolationism. Bullock saw the Treaties of Dunkirk and Brussels as **'a sprat to catch a mackerel'**. Europe had to show that it could defend itself, to encourage American involvement.

'A sprat to catch a mackerel': A saying where bait is used to force someone into action.

On the other hand, Sean Greenwood argues that Bevin was not completely sure until 1948 that American involvement was vital to contain the threat of the Soviet Union. That year was certainly crucial in consolidating the division of Europe: the Soviet leader Josef Stalin reacted to Czech interest in Marshall Aid by staging a coup, replacing the Czech's democratically-elected government with a pro-Soviet, communist government. He then directly threatened the west by cutting off road and rail links to west Berlin, which lay within the Soviet zone of Germany. For a whole year, the Allies had to airlift food and fuel into West Berlin to prevent the citizens from starving. In 1949, the **NATO** treaty was signed, committing America to defend western Europe. The USA promised to regard an attack against any NATO country as an attack against itself.

NATO: Established by the USA, Canada, UK, France, Iceland, Italy, Belgium, Luxembourg and the Netherlands.

1. What evidence is there to suggest that Bevin sought to establish a European Third Force after the war?

2. How important was the Soviet Union in the formation of Bevin's foreign policy?

Europe and federalism

British involvement with the United States both in the devaluation crisis, and in joining NATO, left France with the initiative to develop plans for western Europe. In France, ideas for a federal Europe gathered force. In 1948, at a special Congress in the Hague, the French advanced plans for a federal Europe, run by a European Parliament. Churchill raised expectations that Britain would get involved when he declared that Britain wanted a 'United States of Europe'. Bevin had no intention of joining, however, as he did not want any loss of British national sovereignty. Instead he set up the Council of Europe, with a looser, intergovernmental structure. Even Churchill did not believe that Britain should surrender national sovereignty. His idea of the United States of Europe had Britain guiding Europe from the outside.

15.2 How did Anthony Eden deal with the problem of West German rearmament in 1954?

West German rearmament

After the war, an Allied Control Commission of Britain, France, the United States of America and the Soviet Union governed Germany. After Stalin annexed the eastern zone of Germany in 1948, Britain, France and America agreed to set up a German government in the west. West Germany would be allowed to govern itself: a vital step on the road to **national autonomy**. In 1950, the United States began to call for the rearmament of West Germany. The immediate reason for this was because America was fighting the communists in Korea. They saw the Korean War as evidence of Soviet aggression, which could turn next to Europe. West Germany had the potential to develop into the strongest state in Europe, and so could contribute a great deal to the defence of the continent. Britain agreed with the Americans, because of the cost of British troops in West Germany. France, however, was horrified that only five years after the end of the war, the West Germans would again be given their own army.

National autonomy: National self government, national independence.

The French solution

The French responded to this problem with the Pleven Plan for a European Defence Community (EDC). The economist Jean Monnet, who drafted the Plan, proposed a supranational army. Both France and Germany would contribute troops and military resources, which would be commanded by a joint body containing both French and German personnel. Bevin was opposed to this plan, because he thought it was militarily naïve and because it could threaten the NATO alliance. However, if the British and Americans agreed to study the Plan, the French would then agree to the principle of West German rearmament, which the British and Americans wanted.

Jean Monnet (1889–1979)
French economist and architect of European integration. Believed in supranational integration to help the French economy. One of the leading figures setting up the European Economic Community in 1957.

The British reaction to the Pleven Plan

Bevin's initial reaction was hostile, but he allowed studies of the plan to begin. Herbert Morrison, who became Foreign Secretary when Bevin died in 1950, realised that Britain would have to support the plan in order to secure West German rearmament. He believed that Britain's role should be to watch as other states moved towards supranationalism. Britain could bridge the gap between the European nations and America. In 1951 there was another change of Foreign Secretary as Anthony Eden took the post when the Conservatives won the general election. His policy has been described by John Young in *Britain and European Unity, 1945–1992* (1993) as 'benevolence towards, but non-involvement in' supranationality. Eden was anxious to see the EDC succeed, but refused absolutely to consider British participation in a supranational community. Nobody in Britain thought Britain should join a supranational community at this point. Churchill, the Prime Minister, who had been thought to have 'pro-European' attitudes, described the EDC as a **'sludgy amalgam'**.

Sludgy amalgam: Badly formed mixture.

Did the British try to wreck the EDC?

The British have been accused of trying to sabotage the EDC. The evidence for this is that Eden proposed alternative plans. For example, France, Germany, Italy, and **Benelux** – or the 'Six' – signed a treaty in May 1952 agreeing the establishment of the EDC. Eden responded with the Eden Plan for a 'bridge' to be built between the Six and those countries such as Britain, Scandinavia, Austria, Switzerland and Greece who preferred intergovernmental organisations to the Six's supranationality. Again, in 1954, Eden proposed an institutional link between Britain and the Six called the 'Council of Association'. Britain promised to commit troops to the continent: roughly the same amount as demanded by the Pleven Plan. The difference, of course, was that Britain retained national control over the use of these forces. Some Conservatives, including Churchill, said in Cabinet meetings that they hoped the EDC would fail. However, records of Cabinet meetings also show that Eden appreciated the importance of the EDC to retain French goodwill in NATO, and to rearm Germany. He was concerned that Britain would appear to be trying to sabotage the EDC and worked hard to prevent this. He wanted the EDC to work, but was eager to avoid tying Britain to it. When the EDC failed, the speed with which Eden outlined his alternative proposals also raised suspicions that Britain had tried to wreck the EDC all along.

Benelux: Belgium, the Netherlands and Luxembourg.

The failure of the EDC

In 1954, the French National Assembly failed to **ratify** the EDC treaty. There were many reasons for the change of French heart. Some French politicians had been opposed to the Pleven Plan from the start because they did not want to 'surrender' French forces to the Germans for nationalist reasons. Some, including the communists, still rejected any form of German rearmament. More importantly the international climate had changed. The Korean War ended in July 1953, which meant that the need for continental forces to defend Europe was lessened. In March 1953, the Soviet dictator Joseph Stalin died. This led to a relaxation of world tension, and a belief that **détente** would follow. Furthermore, the French were now fighting a colonial war in French Indochina. The involvement of their forces there meant the German army in Europe would certainly be bigger than the French one. The French did not like the thought of being weaker than the Germans in a joint army.

Ratify: Pass into law.

Détente: Relaxing of tense relationships.

Eden's proposal for West German rearmament

The British had been studying alternative plans to the EDC, and when the EDC unexpectedly failed, the opportunity was ripe for making proposals.

Eden's proposal was to extend the Brussels Pact of 1948 to West Germany and Italy as well as to France and Benelux. This involved Britain further in the defence of the continent. The Brussels Pact troops would be managed in the Western European Union (WEU), set up in 1955. This was an inter-governmental organisation, meaning that forces would not be merged under one supranational authority. In return for British involvement in European defence, West Germany would be rearmed under NATO guidance, and, most importantly, West Germany was to regain national sovereignty and be allowed to sit in the NATO Council. Eden therefore ensured the completion of West German recovery, which was what the Americans and British wanted. In the absence of any alternative proposals, the Six agreed to Eden's plan. Robert Rhodes James, Eden's biographer, called the WEU a triumph of Eden's policy.

The consequences of Eden's solution

The acceptance of the WEU by the Six was a success for Anthony Eden. He managed to secure West German rearmament in the way the British wanted, and avoided participation in supranational organisations without too much criticism of sabotage. The WEU was an example of the success of the 'three circles', with Britain mediating between the Atlantic Alliance and the European nations. However, this success may well have lulled the British into a false sense of security about their bargaining power and international role. The success of Eden's policy, and the belief that the British could get their own way in international affairs, contributed directly to Britain's failure to participate in talks to set up the European Economic Community, the most important development in European relations since the Second World War.

1. What was Anthony Eden and Winston Churchill's attitude to supranationalism?

2. Did the British try to wreck the EDC?

15.3 Did Britain 'miss the bus' in Europe, 1950–1957?
A CASE STUDY IN HISTORICAL INTERPRETATION

In 1951 the 'Six' signed the Treaty of Paris establishing the European Coal and Steel Community. In 1957, they signed the Treaty of Rome, setting up the European Economic Community, the result of talks begun at Messina two years earlier. The ECSC, originating from a Plan by the French Foreign Minister Robert Schuman, arranged supranational institutions for the Six's

Of what value is this cartoon to a historian looking at Britain's relations with the EEC in the 1960s?

"IF THEY WANT US THEY WILL HAVE TO MAKE IT EASY FOR US" —MR. MACMILLAN

coal and steel industries. The EEC was an economic customs union, in a supranational political structure.

The traditional view among historians is that Britain 'missed the bus' on Europe at some point between 1945–57. The Conservative MP, Anthony Nutting, in *Europe Will Not Wait* (1964), argued that Britain threw away the opportunity to take the leadership of Europe, which was its for the taking, after the war. British policy towards Europe always developed a few years too late. For example, Britain realised only in 1961 that it would have to apply for membership. If it had realised in 1955, it could have been part of the Messina talks and the Rome Treaty. An earlier development of European policy would have been better for British interests, because it could have moulded Europe to suit itself.

Missing the bus at the Schuman Plan

The case for

● Edmund Dell, an historian and Labour MP in the 1970s, argued that Britain 'missed the bus' when Bevin failed to participate in the Schuman Plan talks. He argued that officials and ministers had a responsibility to understand events on the continent, and should have appreciated the drive towards integration. Even if ministers could not accept supra-nationality, they should have worked to encourage '**rapprochement**' between France and West Germany. Ministers should have had the imagination to sell the idea of 'Europe' to the public. Furthermore, he shows that France did want Britain to participate in the Schuman talks. Jean Monnet was frequently on the phone to Britain to ask it to join, and the French ambassador Rene Massigli was also very pro-British. The failure to participate in the ECSC, Dell argues, made failure to participate at Messina inevitable. The Six learnt they could forge ahead without Britain, and the British saw that the Six were developing in ways they did not like.

Rapprochement: Establishment of a good relationship.

The case against

● Dell and Nutting have been criticised because they assume that Britain could have taken the leadership of Europe at any point after the war. There is nothing to prove that this was the case. Britain did make initiatives in Europe, such as the Council of Europe in 1949, or the Eden Plan in 1952. Bullock shows that Britain did establish leadership, through the OEEC and NATO. However, the French preferred to pursue supranationalism in 1950 through the Schuman Plan, and the Eden Plan was ignored.

● Revisionist historians like John Young in *Britian and European Unity* show that Whitehall did not just dismiss the Schuman Plan out of hand, but seriously contemplated it, and decided that membership was not in British interests. The Plan demanded that participants agree to lose sovereignty before they began discussing the Plan. This was contrary to the British desire to develop political structures slowly. Accepting supranationality in advance would be, in Bevin's words, 'putting the roof on before you have built the house'. The Foreign Office also thought that the Schuman Plan, without British participation, had only a limited chance of success.

● The British also had domestic political reasons for not getting involved. Foreign Secretary Herbert Morrison told the Cabinet that 'the Durham miners won't wear it'. Britain had the strongest coal and steel industries in Europe and saw no reason to share this around. Coal and steel were also politically important to Labour. British industrialisation had been built on the back of coal and steel, and Labour had only recently nationalised the industries, a popular socialist policy.

● Roger Bullen argued that the French made it hard for the British to participate. They did not inform the British when Schuman first developed the plan, although they had undertaken to do so. In May 1950, Bevin wanted more time to consider the British position and whether or not Britain could 'associate' with the ECSC. Schuman, however, gave Britain twenty-four hours to decide whether or not to attend the talks. This attitude persuaded the British to say no. Whether or not the French invited the British, it was clear that the Schuman Plan did not require British membership. Bevin may have felt snubbed. He told the junior MP James Callaghan that Britain could not join because 'the French don't want us'.

Missing the bus at Messina

The case for

● Bevin's biographer Lord Bullock argued that real opportunities were not missed until Messina. John Young agreed. Young argued that when the Six were discussing the EEC, the British fully understood the dangers of exclusion from a successful customs union on the continent. Ministers should therefore have re-evaluated the importance of Europe, and should have appreciated that federalism would not harm British interests. They knew by 1955 that the Commonwealth trade preference was less important to British interests than it had been, and they were no longer preoccupied by the Soviet threat. However, they failed to think seriously about Britain's future role in the world. Britain should have had the foresight to re-evaluate its world position.

The case against

● A second main criticism of the school of thought that says that Britain 'missed the bus' is that it judges British policy from a pro-European viewpoint. Both Nutting and Dell were strongly pro-European. They therefore assume that supranational, political integration was the correct and natural course for Europe to take after the war. During the war, resistance movements fighting the Nazis dreamed that federalism would replace nationalism. If nation states were dead, another nationalist war would be impossible. Nutting and Dell assumed that the EEC was a bus that Britain should have caught.

● Revisionist historians have suggested that perhaps Britain did not want to catch the bus. Firstly, the economic historian Alan Milward examined the nature of the EEC in *The Reconstruction of Western Europe 1945–51* (1984), and concluded that the Six joined the EEC because it was in their national interests. France wanted to share in the strong German industries, and control the development of the German state, to ensure that Germany could never again invade France. The West Germans wanted to prove their peaceful intentions by accepting limits on their national sovereignty. They could then rebuild the German economy and state. For the smaller states, membership of the EEC would give them privileged access to the large German economy, as well as increasing their political voice. Britain did not have such an obvious reason for joining the EEC.

● Miriam Camps in *Britain and the European Community 1955–1963* (1964) shows that the British felt that the EEC was against their national interest in some ways. The Foreign Office did not want join a supranational community in 1957, as it did not want to surrender national sovereignty. The Treasury and the Board of Trade still felt that British interests lay in trading with the world at large. They also thought that western European economies were weak, and could adversely affect the British economy. Politicians were also wary that the public would not support the idea of going into Europe. The idea of Empire and Britain's Great Power status was popular. As Lord Douglas-Home said, 'the British public was still too near to the glory of Empire to accept the role for Britain of just another country in Europe'. Wolfram Kaiser argued that politicians deliberately clung onto the myth of Britain's Empire and greatness, in order to emphasise how different from Europe Britain was. They used patriotic language because it was popular with the public, and so helped their own interests by helping them stay in power.

● A further criticism of the 'missed the bus' school of thought is it concentrates on what British policy should have been, rather than on what British policy actually was. James Ellison shows how Britain tried to influence the course of European integration. In 1955, Britain tried to sabotage the EEC by encouraging the Six to use the intergovernmental OEEC. The Six refused. The Treasury and Board of Trade realised that if a customs union developed on the continent, it would not be in Britain's national interests to be stuck outside. In 1956, Britain developed Plan G proposals for a **free trade area**. Between 1957 and 1958, Britain negotiated with the Six to develop a free trade area alongside the customs union. Britain therefore had a sensible response to the Messina proposals. If the free trade area talks had succeeded, Britain would not have appeared so isolated in Europe. The question was therefore less whether Britain missed the bus, but why Britain failed to change its direction.

It was not inevitable that the free trade area talks would fail. The West Germans were interested in free trade to increase markets for their exports, and there was opposition in France to supranationality. Firstly, Plan G failed because the British overestimated their bargaining power, and underestimated the strength of feeling among the Six for supranational integration. Secondly, as Miriam Camps showed, the free trade area talks failed because of the **Suez Crisis**. Suez destroyed good feeling between the French and the British. Both countries realised that they could not act alone in the world. Britain turned to America to rebuild their special relationship which would enhance Britain's power. France realised that the best way to build up its own power base was through the EEC. France could only lead in Europe in the absence of Britain. The French were therefore determined that the EEC would work, and without Britain. In 1958, the formidable French war hero General de Gaulle returned to power. He had no time for diplomatic niceties, and immediately vetoed the free trade area talks.

Free trade area: Britain wanted to encourage free trade throughout Europe, including Scandinavia. A Free Trade Area would allow preferential trade with the Commonwealth, and would not include agricultural produce. It would have intergovernmental, not supranational governance.

Suez Crisis: Conflict between the British, French and Israelis against the Egyptian leader Colonel Nasser, October–November 1956. The British, French and Israelis secretly agreed to stage Egyptian aggression in order to give them an excuse to attack Nasser. Britain could not sustain military involvement because its economy was not strong enough. It had to withdraw, internationally humiliated. The Americans were furious because they had not been consulted (see Chapter 10, section 3).

1. Why have historians taken different views about Britain's policy towards European integration in the 1950s?

2. Why did Bevin reject participation in the Schuman Plan talks?

3. Why did Britain fail to create a free trade area in Europe?

15.4 Why did Harold Macmillan decide to apply for membership of the EEC?

Harold Macmillan became Prime Minister in 1957. He had been one of the Tory pro-Europeans under Anthony Eden, calling for a more constructive role with the EDC. He believed that Britain must enter the EEC, because he realised that Britain's days as a Great Power were over. Macmillan presided over some of the most radical foreign policy changes since the war. As well as the application to the EEC, he accelerated Britain's withdrawal from empire. At a famous speech in Africa, he claimed that the 'winds of change' were sweeping over that continent. By 1963, many of Britain's colonies had been granted independence. These huge changes have led historians to see Macmillan as a radical Prime Minister. Miriam Camps claimed that Macmillan's application to the EEC marked a considerable evolution in British attitudes to Europe.

It could, however, also be seen as inevitable that Britain should apply to join the EEC. The British understood, when the Messina talks began, that if a political and economic group did develop on the continent, it would not be in British interests to be excluded from it. When the free trade area talks ended in failure, Britain was left with Sweden, Denmark, Norway, Austria, Switzerland and Portugal, with whom it formed the European Free Trade Association (EFTA). EFTA could never be the political and economic force that the EEC became. Britain could not afford to remain outside the EEC, a fact it had always known.

There were several basic economic reasons pushing Britain towards the EEC. The Six were enjoying economic growth, stimulated by the removal of tariff barriers to trade among themselves in 1960. By contrast, British economic growth was slowing, and for the first time since the war, discontent was growing at home over Britain's economic policies. The weakness of the Commonwealth to provide for Britain's trading needs was also exposed as Britain's trade with Western Europe grew far faster. From 1954–60, Britain's exports to the Common Market rose by 29%, compared to 1% to the Sterling Area countries. EFTA did not help promote British trade, as Britain was the largest market among the EFTA countries. Big business in Britain was now in favour of British membership of the EEC, to provide a stimulus to competition, and to encourage investment.

The political reasons, however, were stronger. The Suez Crisis in 1956 dealt a severe shock to British policy makers, revealing in no uncertain terms that Britain was no longer a Great Power. The Americans were

The growth of the European Union

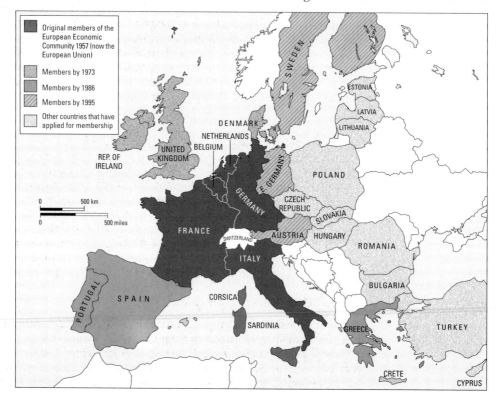

**General de Gaulle
(1890–1970)**

When France surrendered to
the Germans in 1940, General
de Gaulle led the French
resistance movement, the 'Free
French', setting up government
in England. He returned to
power in 1958, forming the
Fifth Republic, and remained
President until 1969.
Formidably powerful.

*To what extent was
Macmillan's policy
towards Europe a
radical change?*

annoyed because Britain had not consulted them. Macmillan wanted to restore the 'special relationship' with the Americans, fearing that if the EEC developed into a strong political bloc, that the Americans would prefer to deal with Germany than Britain. Britain's traditional policy in the Commonwealth was also in trouble. Economic weakness in Britain meant that the Commonwealth countries were looking to other markets to export goods and the Commonwealth was not politically cohesive. It was possible that Commonwealth countries could seek association with the EEC, as Nigeria did in 1962. Macmillan therefore saw EEC membership as a means of boosting British power and influence in the world. Rather than a radical change in attitude, Macmillan's policy could be seen as a continuation of traditional British policy. He wanted to retain British influence in the world, and wanted to use the EEC to achieve this.

Wolfram Kaiser in *Using Europe, Abusing the Europeans: Britain and European Integration 1945–63* (1963) has emphasised the positive aspects of Macmillan's policy. He argued that Macmillan's application was not just an inevitable attempt to claw back British power. Rather, the application solved some of Macmillan's short-term problems. Firstly, and most importantly, the United States wanted the British to apply for membership. When John F. Kennedy became President in 1961, he pressurised Macmillan to join the EEC. Kennedy thought it vital that the EEC developed in line with American political and security interests in Europe, and British membership would help achieve this. Britain and America wanted to avoid an independent Europe led by General de Gaulle. Such a 'Third Force' Europe could turn away from NATO. Macmillan and Kennedy wanted to keep Europe looking outwards to the Atlantic. In order to retain the 'special relationship', and to ensure that Britain retained her own nuclear capability, provided by the Americans, Macmillan had to apply to the EEC. He needed to show Kennedy that he was interested in membership, even if the application was likely to fail.

Kaiser also argues that an application would have helped Macmillan control the division in the Conservative Party over Europe. Kaiser sees this as the beginning of the problems caused by Europe in British party politics. With leading Cabinet ministers like Edward Heath, Duncan Sandys and Lord Douglas-Home now in favour of membership, Macmillan had to apply in order to show them that he too, was a 'pro' European. Influential groups in the City of London and business also wanted to join. Therefore, the application had some short-term political advantages for Macmillan.

15.5 Why was Britain not able to join the EEC until 1973?

Macmillan's application was vetoed by General de Gaulle in 1963, after two years of negotiations. In 1967, the Labour government led by Harold Wilson once again applied for membership. De Gaulle vetoed it six months later, before negotiations had even begun. This time, however, Wilson left the application 'on the table'. In 1970, the Conservatives won the general election again, now led by the pro-European Edward Heath. General de Gaulle resigned as French leader in 1969, and died a year later. However, even without de Gaulle, British entry was far from inevitable.

Harold Macmillan's application

De Gaulle's vision for Europe stood in the way of British entry, and this was the fundamental reason preventing Britain from achieving entry in 1961 and 1967. Firstly, de Gaulle wanted France to lead Europe. If Britain was allowed in, Britain would also want to lead Europe, so from de Gaulle's point of view, it was better to keep her out. Secondly, he wanted

Europe to be strong, and independent from American influence. He wanted French culture and language to flourish. Politically, he saw Europe as a 'Third Force' between the superpowers. Thirdly, de Gaulle was interested in pursuing détente by developing an independent French force, and by making friends with the Russians. This policy developed in the later 1960s, when de Gaulle decided he no longer wanted to participate in NATO. With these goals in mind, it is not surprising that he did not want British interference, still less did he want American influence strengthened by British membership.

Most historians agree that there was little Macmillan could do to secure British entry into the EEC in 1961–63. However, some, such as Piers Ludlow, have stressed that British policy contributed to the failure of the application. Macmillan's application said that Britain would negotiate to find out whether membership would be compatible with Britain's commitments to the Commonwealth and with British systems of agriculture. The negotiations dealt at great length with Commonwealth exports and the Community's Common Agricultural Policy (CAP). Britain would only enter 'if the conditions were right'. There was plenty of opposition in the Conservative government to the application and the Labour Party were against it. Britain did not seem to be a European nation, and this made it easier for de Gaulle to veto.

Furthermore, there was a dispute in the Community itself about the value of supranationalism. The Five – West Germany, Italy, the Netherlands, Belgium and Luxembourg – wanted to increase supranationality and move towards greater integration. France, however, preferred a 'Europe des Patries': a Europe of independent states. This, of course, appealed to the British. In 1961, with the Fouchet Plan, the French suggested moving towards political co-operation between national governments, which would strengthen the political role of the EEC while reducing the supranational element. Macmillan believed that it was possible to put pressure on de Gaulle by emphasising that Britain could help reduce supranationality in the Community. The problem with this approach was that the Five, who supported British entry, also supported supranationalism. This again made it easier for de Gaulle to claim that Britain was not 'European' enough to join the Community.

Macmillan's main tactic, however, was to offer the French political incentives. France did not have her own nuclear weapons, and wanted them to build up French power. At a meeting at Chateau des Champs in June 1962, it is possible that Macmillan offered de Gaulle a nuclear deal with the British. After this meeting, there was some hope among French officials that de Gaulle would allow Britain to come in. However, the British were reliant on the Americans for nuclear weapons. At a meeting in Nassau, Macmillan agreed with the American President John F. Kennedy that Britain would buy Polaris missiles from the United States. Macmillan needed to do this in order to retain Britain's independent nuclear deterrent. Macmillan told de Gaulle at a meeting at Rambouillet in October 1962 that France could have these Polaris missiles as well. However, the last thing de Gaulle wanted was help from the Americans, and this gave him a further excuse to veto the application.

Harold Wilson's application

In 1967 the new Labour Prime Minister Harold Wilson decided that it was worth another attempt, and applied for membership. The economic and political reasons compelling Macmillan to take this step in 1961 were now even more urgent. Britain now had severe problems with the economy and the strength of sterling. Wilson's tactics showed that the lessons of the first application had to some extent been learnt. He kept the issues for negotiation to a minimum, mainly involving the CAP, and tried to play down the conditions for Britain's entry. Most importantly, Wilson stated that Britain was prepared to accept the Treaty of Rome. In saying this, Wilson agreed to the supranational principle behind the EEC.

Like Macmillan, Wilson may well have believed he had a chance of persuading de Gaulle to let Britain in by arguing that de Gaulle would prevent the development of Europe into a great force if he refused to let Britain in. However, he had even less bargaining power than Macmillan, and in practice had to rely on the persuasion of the Five. But it was clear that in the last resort, the Five were not willing to risk breaking up the Community and losing France just to let Britain in. When de Gaulle finally vetoed in November 1967, he stressed Britain's economic weakness, claiming that Britain only wanted to get in to help her economy. Wilson countered by leaving the application open, ready to be taken up again at the earliest opportunity. This opportunity arrived when de Gaulle resigned in early 1969.

Edward Heath's application

However, Britain could not just then enter the Community, as Britain still had certain problems with the EEC system. At an EEC meeting in 1969, the principle to negotiate for Britain was agreed, but the French insisted that agriculture must be settled first. The agricultural system then agreed was harmful to British interests, because Britain would have to pay more into it, and would get less back, than the other EEC countries. In 1970, Wilson created more obstacles by saying on television that British entry would have to be on the right terms, especially regarding agriculture. Despite his earlier concessions, he also said that there must be no federal constitution. The Europeans could see his comments as an attempt to change the nature of the Community.

In 1970, the Conservative government under Edward Heath was elected into government. Edward Heath was a committed pro-European. He even played down Britain's 'special relationship' with the United States, in order to appeal to the EEC. This was very important in the forthcoming talks. Negotiations, as set up under Wilson, began straight away. However, the talks got into difficulties in October 1970 over the question of agriculture, and the fact that the French now wanted to discuss the world role of the pound sterling. Edward Heath intervened and went to talk to the new French President Georges Pompidou. Because of Heath's pro-European attitude, Pompidou believed he could trust Heath, and it was down to these talks that British membership of the European Community was agreed.

1. How did Macmillan and Wilson attempt to achieve Britain's membership of the EEC?

2. To what extent was Edward Heath responsible for taking Britain into Europe?

3. Was French opposition the only factor keeping Britain out of Europe between 1961 and 1973?

15.6 Why did the Labour governments have so many concerns about British membership of the EEC in the 1970s?

Harold Wilson was a master politician and tactician. In his early political career, he sided with the left wing of the Labour Party. The left were mainly anti-European. When he was Prime Minister, he betrayed the left by applying to join the EEC. He continued to pretend to his left-wing allies that he did not want to go into the EEC, and told them not to worry because de Gaulle would veto the application anyway. He also outwitted the left wing. When he first considered applying to join Europe, early in 1966, he spoke about the terms and conditions Britain would have to arrange to safeguard her essential interests. The party therefore did not debate whether or not to go in, only how they would do it. The pro-Europeans, mainly on right wing of the party, led by Roy Jenkins and George Brown, were pleased with the decision to go into

Europe. However, they saw Wilson as untrustworthy, using Europe for domestic political reasons. When the Labour government fell in 1970, both sides of the party decided to give vent to their built-up anger.

Left-wing attitudes to Europe

Many left wingers, and some right-wingers such as Douglas Jay, had objections to Britain's membership of the EEC. Led by Tony Benn and Michael Foot, the left thought that Britain's national sovereignty would be threatened by the EEC. There were two threads to this fear. Firstly, and this was a fear shared by the Conservative right wing, that the EEC would erode the power of British Parliament to make law. Secondly, as more policy would be made by the government with its European partners in Brussels, rather than in London, parliament would lose the ability to keep an effective check on policy-making. Benn saw this as a threat to democracy. The left also saw the EEC as a danger to socialism. They saw the EEC as a capitalist trading bloc, which would stop Britain planning the economy. The EEC's protectionist common external tariff would also prevent international socialism and development of Third World countries in the Commonwealth. As well as these fundamental objections, the left also had specific fears. EEC membership would push up the cost of food, and harm the 'ordinary housewife'. Increased industrial competition would encourage development in the wealthy south and east, to the detriment of the poorer north and west. Farmers in the north and west would also suffer. EEC membership impeded the left's vision of a socialist solution to Britain's increasing economic problems.

The struggle between the left and right of the party to lead Labour also contributed to the strength of feeling about Europe. The right's vision for the future was much more in line with moderates in the Conservative Party. They saw that Britain had to be in Europe, and did not champion a socialist-style planned economy. Both left and right wanted to capture the hearts and minds of party members and the public, and so gain power within the party. In 1971, Heath's application was debated in the House of Commons. Heath only had a small majority, and so there was a chance to defeat the government. But the right of the Labour party – 69 MPs – voted with Heath to take Britain into Europe. The left could not believe that the right preferred to take Britain into Europe than defeat a Conservative government. The right realised that siding with the Tories over Europe was one way of ensuring that the left did not gain too much power within the Labour Party.

The question of personal political ambitions must also be taken into account. Europe was a vital issue for Britain's national interests. It was also an emotional one, and one where it was possible to influence public opinion because the public were relatively ignorant about European affairs. Tony Benn, in 1967, was moderately in favour of Britain's membership of the EEC. His conversion to anti-Europeanism could be seen as a calculation to bring maximum personal benefit. As the Labour Party became more dominated by the left in the 1970s, the best way to gain power was to support left-wing causes. Benn was the highest profile anti-European on the left, and this was a challenge to the Labour Party's leadership. The left's concerns about Europe in the 1970s therefore must be seen as a mixture of ideology and political ambition.

Wilson's response to Labour attitudes to Europe

To keep the party together, and to preserve his position, Wilson decided he had to present a more anti-European image. It is important that he never said that Britain should withdraw from Europe. Rather, he said that Edward

Heath had not managed to secure satisfactory terms to safeguard Britain's national interests. Wilson now said that if he were back in power, he would renegotiate those terms with the EEC. The left, however, was not satisfied. Tony Benn claimed that Britain should have a referendum on whether or not to remain a member of the EEC. As all three of the main parties were in favour of European membership, an anti-European voter did not have the opportunity to vote for an anti-European policy. On an issue of vital national importance, Benn saw this as undemocratic. A referendum would solve this problem by allowing the public to vote. More importantly, it provided the Labour Party with a solution to their internal disputes. If the public were to decide whether or not to stay in Europe, Wilson did not have to.

Renegotiation and referendum

When Wilson was returned to power in 1974, he set about renegotiating the terms under which Britain was a member of the EEC. This has widely been regarded as a waste of time, contributing to the lack of business in the Community in the 1970s and creating bad will between Britain and Europe. Wilson did manage to slightly reduce Britain's contributions to the agricultural budget, and to extend the arrangements for importing New Zealand's butter for a further three years. These concessions did little to dampen the left's fears, and did much to annoy the right.

The referendum was a unique constitutional experience. It was the first referendum in British history. It was also the first time in British history that the Cabinet had been allowed to disagree in public. Wilson thought that this would clear the air and allow the 'pro' and 'anti' Europeans to all have their say. However, the sides were not particularly evenly matched. On the side of the pros were the leaders of the Labour party, Conservative party and Liberals, and many centre-right, moderate politicians. The pros also had the backing of big business and so their campaign was better funded. The antis on the other hand were the extremists from both parties. Left-wingers Benn and Foot campaigned with virulent right-wingers led by Enoch Powell. Powell was by this time notorious for his racist 'rivers of blood' speech, and so did not have the support of moderate opinion. The result of the referendum was a 67% vote to stay inside the EEC. This was a resounding backing for British membership, but the problems causing the referendum in the first place were far from over.

The consequences of the referendum

The left wing felt hard done by because Wilson had thrown in his lot with the pro-Europeans. They saw that they had lost the centre ground of British politics and determined to win it back. Their programme was far broader than just Europe. At a time of increasing economic and industrial unrest, they wanted increased nationalisation of industries and greater welfare spending. The right wing, on the other hand, led by Roy Jenkins, saw in the referendum that they had more in common with moderate conservatives and liberals than they did with members of their own party. The referendum therefore set the scene for the split of the Labour party in 1981. Labour lost the 1979 election, and, in reaction to the right-wing Thatcher government, rising unemployment and economic recession, moved further to the left. Michael Foot was elected leader. The pro-European right, under Roy Jenkins, decided to leave the Labour party and form a new party, the Social Democratic Party (SDP).

The referendum also had long-term consequences in the development of the debate in Britain about European membership. The left did have some legitimate fears. There was a threat to British parliamentary democracy, and membership would necessitate some fundamental changes to Britain's trade and agriculture systems. However, Wilson did nothing to

1. Was Harold Wilson a pro or anti European?

2. Why was the left wing of the Labour party so anti-European in the 1970s?

address these fears head on. Rather, the pro-European argument during the referendum campaign asserted that there was no alternative for Britain if it wished to retain influence in the world. While the left argued that EEC membership would increase food prices and unemployment, the right simply said that these fears were unfounded. The pro-Europeans were afraid to address the question of national sovereignty, in case it made EEC membership unpopular in the country. Pro-Europeans were anxious to play down the fact that in future, British law could be over-ridden by European legislation. Therefore, there was no serious debate about what British membership of the European Economic Community actually meant, and what changes it could bring. This had a long-term effect on Britain's ability to play a positive and constructive role in the Community.

15.7 Did Margaret Thatcher's attitude towards her European partners help or harm Britain's standing in Europe?

Margaret Thatcher was a strong-willed, determined character, sometimes called the 'Iron Lady'. She introduced sweeping changes to Britain's society, economy and politics. Her attitude towards Europe was something of a paradox. In private, she was hostile towards the Europeans. She believed in British strength and national pride. However, in practice, she took Britain further into Europe. By the end of her 11-year rule in 1990, Britain had signed the Single European Act for a single European market, and withdrawal from the EC (as the EEC was later called) was unthinkable.

The British budgetary question

From 1979–84, Community business was dominated by the question of the amount of money Britain contributed to the Community budget. Thatcher believed that Britain paid too much money to the EC and determined to get some of it back. She fought for this for four years to the exclusion of other Community business. At the Fontainebleau Summit in 1984, the Community agreed that Britain should have two-thirds of its money returned each year.

Stephen George in *An Awkward Partner: Britain and the European Community* (1990) argued that Thatcher's negotiations over the budget made Britain 'a skilful and normal actor in the Community game'. Her policy could be described as 'pragmatic involvement'. The budget question also helped British standing in Europe because Thatcher's fighting style was popular with the public. However, her style, characterised by her banging her handbag on the table and demanding 'our money' back, annoyed the Europeans. She failed to develop a good relationship with the new French and German leaders, Francois Mitterand and Helmut Kohl. They stored up hostility against her, which inevitably meant that Britain would not get its own way all the time in the future. In the 1970s the Community had developed along intergovernmental lines with the European Council. The British Budgetary debate gave France and Germany the will to overcome this 'Euro-paralysis' and continue with supranational economic integration.

The Single European Act

In 1985, Margaret Thatcher signed the **Single European Act** (SEA). This committed Britain to greater institutional integration and to a single market. Thatcher actively contributed to the Single European Act because she was strongly in favour of a single market. A single market was consistent with her ideological belief in free market economics, and therefore

The Single European Act: At the Luxembourg Intergovernmental Conference 1985–86 the European Community agreed to move to a single market by 1992. The SEA stated that Europe would 'make concrete progress to closer integration'. However, the actual provisions for deeper integration were not very radical, strengthening the role of the European Parliament and European Court of Justice, and making it harder for nations to veto decisions for themselves.

she could use Europe to advance 'Thatcherism'. This was the first time since 1973 that a British leader had outlined a positive role for Britain in Europe, and a positive image for the European project in British politics. She circulated her proposals to the EC in 1985, entitled 'Europe: The Future'. She regarded the Single European Act at the time as a success for her single market ideas.

The second main reason for signing the SEA was because she wanted to retain influence in Europe. The French President Mitterand told the European Parliament that Europe could develop in 'two tiers'. Those states that did not want greater federalism could remain outside in the second tier. Thatcher realised that Britain would have no influence in the second tier. She signed the SEA because she realised that Britain had to be at the heart of European decision-making. However, she was not willing to tell the public that this was what she had done. Instead she later claimed that the Europeans had deceived her over the SEA, pretending they wanted a single market when really they intended to move to deeper federalism.

The Social Charter

The SEA promised progress to closer integration. In 1988, the President of the Commission, Jaques Delors, set up a committee to study economic and monetary union. The Delors report, submitted in 1989, recommended three stages to Economic and Monetary Union. Stage one was membership of the Exchange Rate Mechanism. Stage two was currency alignment. Stage three was a single currency and a Central European Bank. Delors also recommended social provisions for minimum conditions of education, employment and social security. Thatcher had ideological objections to the Social Charter. It was at odds with her doctrine of a free market, and of lessening state intervention in social policies. The Labour Party, however, liked the Social Charter because it supported their ideas of social welfare. Under Neil Kinnock Labour moved back in favour of European membership, from its position of total withdrawal in 1983.

Thatcher initially reacted to development in Europe by continuing with pragmatic involvement in European negotiations. In 1987, she blocked changes in Community funding that would have helped to develop the social policy. But in 1988, the Community again threatened to leave her outside if she did not join with them, and she had to agree to double the amount of money in the Community's social fund. She then made a speech in Bruges which the Europeans saw as hostile. She emphasised the extent to which Britain was a part of Europe, but then attacked Community policies.

The Bruges speech marked a turning point in Thatcher's policy towards Europe. It is possible that she was continuing with the pragmatic involvement of the budget negotiations. In this interpretation, she recognised that Britain must become involved with deeper integration, but wanted to emphasise the British vision of integration, creating the impression that Britain could still 'win' in Europe. Alternatively, Hugo Young described the Bruges speech as the moment when Thatcher could keep her personal hatred of Europeans to herself no longer. She knew Europe would integrate further, and wanted to make British opposition to this clear. In this analysis, the Bruges speech ended Britain's pragmatic involvement with Europe. This analysis seems more likely, because Thatcher initially wanted to deliver a much more hostile speech in Bruges. The Foreign Office, however, forced her to change it.

Source-based questions: Britain and Europe

SOURCE A

Over wide areas a vast quivering mass of tormented, hungry, care-worn and bewildered human beings gape at the ruins of their cities and homes, and scan the dark horizons for the approach of some new peril, tyranny or terror. The remedy ... is to recreate the European family, and provide it with a structure under which it can dwell in peace, in safety and in freedom. We must build a United States of Europe. ... We all know that the two world wars through which we have passed arose out of the vain passion of a newly united Germany to play the dominating part in the world. ... The first step in the recreation of the European family must be a partnership between France and Germany. In this way only can France recover the moral leadership of Europe ... France and Germany must take the lead together. Great Britain, the British Commonwealth of nations, mighty America, and I trust Soviet Russia, must be the friends and sponsors of the new Europe and must champion its right to live and shine.

Winston Churchill, speech in Zurich,
September 1946.

SOURCE B

Britain applied to join the Common Market after refusing to participate earlier, creating a Free Trade Association, and 'putting some pressure on the Six to prevent a real beginning being made in the application of the Common Market ... The nature, the structure, the very situation of England differed profoundly from the countries of the six'. She is insular, maritime, linked to distant countries, essentially industrial and commercial and with slight agricultural interest. The whole question is whether Britain can place herself 'inside a tariff which is genuinely common', renounce all Commonwealth preference, give up agricultural privileges, and 'more than that', regard her EFTA engagements as 'null and void' .... The defence of Europe has become of secondary importance to the United States. Cuba illustrated this .... This has led to the French determination to equip themselves with their own atomic force .... The Polaris offer is of 'no apparent interest to France.'

Summary of de Gaulle's Press Conference,
14 January 1963.

SOURCE C

Britain does not dream of some cosy isolated existence on the fringes of the European Community. Our destiny is in Europe, as part of the Community. That is not to say that our future lies only in Europe. But nor does that of France or Spain or indeed any other member .... Willing and active co-operation between independent states is the best way to build a successful European Community .... We have not rolled back the frontiers of the state in Britain only to have them reimposed at European level, with a European super-state exercising a new dominance from Brussels .... The Treaty of Rome was always intended as a Charter for Economic Liberty .... And that means action to free markets, action to widen choice, action to reduce government intervention ... Europe should not be protectionist ... Europe must continue to maintain sure defence through NATO.

Margaret Thatcher's speech in Bruges,
20 September 1988.

---

1. Look at Source A.

a) What did Winston Churchill mean when he said 'we must build a United States of Europe'?

b) What were Churchill's intentions in making this speech?

2. Look at Source B.

a) How reliable is de Gaulle's account of his motives in vetoing Macmillan's application?

b) Was de Gaulle justified in his criticisms of British policy?

3. Look at Source C.

a) Was Margaret Thatcher right to see the Treaty of Rome as a charter for economic liberty?

b) Was Thatcher pro or anti-European?

c) What was Thatcher's intention in making the Bruges speech?

4. Study Sources A, B and C and use information from this chapter. To what extent were the British 'Reluctant Europeans' after 1945?

French farmers' tractors form a blockade during an agricultural dispute

Economic and Monetary Union

The most important step for the European Community towards greater integration was economic and monetary union (EMU). Britain and Denmark opposed moving towards a union (which would involve supranationality) rather than increased co-operation. The first stage of EMU was membership of the Exchange Rate Mechanism (ERM), established without British participation in 1979. The Chancellor of the Exchequer Norman Lamont, and the Foreign Secretary Geoffrey Howe, both thought that if Britain joined the ERM, it would then be possible to prevent the development of EMU. Outside ERM, however, Britain had no influence. Howe and Lawson forced Margaret Thatcher to tell the European Community at the Madrid summit in 1989 that Britain would join the ERM. Thatcher then sacked Howe from the Foreign Office (although he then became Leader of the House of Commons) and Lawson resigned. Later, Howe also resigned from the government, and his resignation speech in the House of Commons in November 1990 sparked off events leading to the end of Margaret Thatcher's premiership.

Europe and Thatcher's legacy

By the end of Margaret Thatcher's years as Prime Minister, Britain was committed to Europe to a far greater degree. Her fighting talk hid the extent of Britain's involvement with Europe, creating the impression that Britain had to 'win' in Europe. More seriously, in 1989, the Cold War ended and changed the context of British foreign policy completely.

Thatcher attempted to resist the reunification of East and West Germany. She could not, and Britain was left in 1989 facing the prospect of a dominant, wealthy Germany taking Britain's place in the 'special relationship' with America, as well as the prospect of the ex-communist states becoming members of the European Community. British foreign policy was ill-equipped to deal with these new challenges.

1. **Was Margaret Thatcher pro or anti European?**

2. **To what extent was Britain a fully involved member of the European Community in 1990?**

3. **Did the European leaders deceive Thatcher over the Single European Act?**

15.8 Why was the Conservative Party so divided on the question of European integration in the 1990s?

Margaret Thatcher was deposed by pro-Europeans in her Cabinet in November 1990. In the leadership election, the pro-European Michael Heseltine stood against her, but failed to win. The post of Prime Minister instead went to the relatively unknown John Major. Major did not have a large following in the party, and won the election more because he did not have any enemies. A weak character who liked to compromise rather than fight, he came to be seen by the media as grey and uninteresting.

Europe after the Cold War

The end of the Cold War posed three main challenges to European integration. The first was the reunification of Germany, which would make Germany the undisputed dominant partner in the European Community. The British and the French did not want Germany to reunify. However, like the aftermath of the Second World War, the French wanted to control

German dominance and wealth through increased integration in EMU. French support for EMU led to the agreements at the Maastricht negotiations in 1991 for a single currency (the Euro). The United States wanted German reunification, because it would help American trade, and because Germany was wealthy enough to pay for European defence. Britain risked losing her 'special relationship' with the United States as the United States preferred to deal with Germany.

The second challenge was enlargement of the Community to incorporate the eastern European countries. Western Europe and America regarded it as important to attract eastern European states to help ensure stability and prosperity, and to prevent the re-emergence of communism. The prospect of enlarging the Community led to a debate at Maastricht about whether the Community should be more supranational, or more intergovernmental. The Dutch proposed supranational decision making for foreign policy and for home affairs. Britain and France both rejected this, preferring intergovernmental decision-making instead.

The third challenge was to defence policy. Economic collapse in the Soviet Union meant that the Soviet Union was no longer likely to invade Europe, or start a nuclear war against the United States. The United States, under President Bill Clinton, therefore wanted to withdraw its troops from Europe, meaning that Europe would have to organise, and pay for, its own defence policy. The European Community realised that the main threat to European stability was regional conflict in the new states of Central and Eastern Europe, for example the ongoing war in the former Yugoslavia. At Maastricht, the Europeans agreed to hold intergovernmental meetings to decide on common foreign and defence policies, although there was little agreement on what those policies should be. Without common defence policies, it was difficult for the European Community to claim to be a major world power.

Conservative policy towards the Maastricht negotiations.

The Maastricht negotiations decided the future of Europe. From the European Community, the European Union (EU) was born, with powers over a larger number of policy areas, such as foreign policy, and home affairs and justice. John Major, keen to put Britain at the heart of Europe, committed Britain further to the EU by agreeing these changes. The victory of intergovernmental decision-making over supranational decision-making meant that it was easier for Britain to accept the European way of making policies. Influential pro-European Conservatives like Michael Heseltine and Kenneth Clarke thought that increased British participation in Europe was inevitable. The end of the Cold War meant that Britain had no other role to play in the world, and furthermore, as Europe expanded, Britain would be unable to survive without European trade.

Anti-Europeans like John Redwood, Michael Portillo (whose father was Spanish) and Michael Howard, however, reacted against British participation in Europe partly because it was inevitable, and because it was becoming more acceptable. They saw it as their last chance to alter Britain's destiny. Anti-European pressure meant that Major opted out of the EU's Social Chapter. He, like Thatcher, tried to create the impression that Britain was winning in Europe, declaring a complete British victory at the Maastricht negotiations.

Economic and Monetary Union (EMU)

The most serious question about which the Conservative Party divided was that of EMU. The first stage of EMU was membership of the ERM, which Britain had joined in 1989. In 1992, however, Britain was forced to pull out of the ERM and devalue the pound. The Bank of England lost £4 billion in one day. The ERM crisis confirmed anti-Europeans' belief that the EMU was not in Britain's economic interests. The ERM crisis was caused by high interest rates in Germany, and anti-Europeans thought that the Germans would use EMU to take over Europe. Pro-Europeans thought that if Britain had entered the ERM earlier, the pound would not have been so weak in the first place, and so could have influenced German interest rates. They also thought that non-participation in EMU would relegate Britain to the 'second tier' of European decision-making.

Domestic party politics

Most of the Conservative anti-Europeans were on the right wing of the Conservative Party. Part of the reason behind their opposition to Europe was that it was one way of attacking John Major, whom they hated for winning the leadership election in 1990. Margaret Thatcher herself became increasingly anti-European, claiming she had been deceived by European federalists when she signed the Single European Act in 1985. Her opposition led other MPs who had supported the SEA, for example Kenneth (now Lord) Baker, to turn against Europe and against Major. In 1995, the right-wing John Redwood tried to take over directly by standing against Major in a leadership election that Major narrowly won.

Anti-Europeans were also encouraged because Major's small parliamentary majority gave them a chance to influence matters. In 1992, anti-Europeans voted against the Maastricht Bill, and nearly managed to stop it coming into law. In Cabinet, anti-Europeans bullied Major. In 1995, they forced the government to change its policy on enlargement of the EU, although Britain had been in favour of enlargement for years.

Anti-Europeans saw opposition to the Euro (the end result of EMU) as the only way to win the 1997 election, and also thought that opposition to the Euro would win support for themselves. In 1994, Major expelled eight 'Euro-rebels' from the party. They gained more publicity than ever before in their political careers. The ERM crisis and the crisis over British beef in 1996 made Europe increasingly unpopular with press and public opinion. The *Sun* led the anti-European tabloids, for example with its famous headline 'Up Yours Delors'. In the 1997 election, the maverick businessman Sir James Goldsmith created a new political party, the Referendum Party, to campaign for a referendum on the Euro. As with the Labour Party in the 1970s, hostility to Europe mixed with domestic and personal political ambitions.

The consequences of the Conservative split over Europe

The Conservative civil war on Europe contributed to the Conservatives' heavy defeat in the 1997 election. Back in Opposition, the Conservative Party rejected a pro-European leadership, voting for a right-wing, but weak, figure, William Hague. Hague's policy was 'in Europe, but not run by Europe', which the pro-Europeans saw as meaningless. Anti-Europeans moved towards a policy of complete withdrawal from the EU. The party threatened to split totally in 1999, with pro-Europeans Kenneth Clarke and Michael Heseltine joining the Labour leader Tony Blair to campaign for 'Britain in Europe'.

1. Why did the anti-Europeans argue that Britain should be 'in Europe, but not run by Europe'?

2. What changes did the pro-Europeans think that Britain had to make to her foreign policy after the end of the Cold War?

3. Which was the most important in creating Conservative divisions on Europe, hostility to the EU or domestic political considerations?

15.9 How European were the British at the end of the 20th century?

Society and culture

The influence of European culture could be seen throughout British society. Every British citizen was a 'citizen of the union'. They carried European Union passports, and could travel and work freely throughout Europe. Many British people took holidays in Spain – Tenerife or Majorca – or Greece. For young people and students, European holidays became commonplace, and initiatives such as InterRail train tickets possible because of increased co-operation between EU member states. The development of the Channel Tunnel and the Eurostar made travel to the continent even easier: from London, it was quicker to get to Brussels than to Edinburgh.

Food, also was one area in which the British were becoming increasingly 'European'. The fact that Europeans could also travel and work here improved the quality and variety of restaurants enormously. Pizza and pasta from Italy was the most obvious example of European food becoming as common as British 'national' dishes, like fish and chips. Supermarkets were full of food imported from Europe. Products like yoghurt, pizza, salami and wine were hardly available in Britain before membership of the EEC in 1973. In schools, the National Curriculum originally made the teaching of one foreign language obligatory up to the age of 16. The result was that most British pupils left school with at least a rudimentary grasp of French, Spanish or German, and many had travelled to the continent on school exchanges. Improved education made growing links with the continent easier.

Football was another element of British society where European membership had a large, visible effect. The free movement of workers made it possible for footballers to move to any other club in Europe once their contracts expired. European footballers played in virtually all Premier League and First Division teams. Britain's heroes were Europeans: Eric Cantona, Dennis Bergkamp and Gianluca Vialli became household names. By the end of the 20th century, Europe was a fact of British life.

Trade, business and economics

In 1999, over half of all British trade was conducted with the European Union. This made the EU far too important to markets and business to seriously contemplate withdrawal. Europe was likely to expand into eastern Europe. The Czech Republic, Estonia, Poland, Hungary, Cyprus and Slovenia were involved in enlargement talks in 1999, with suggestions for talks to be extended to Bulgaria, Latvia, Lithuania, Malta, Romania and Slovakia. This would create a market of 500 million people. It would simply be inconceivable for Britain to sustain itself as a trading nation outside this gigantic union.

Membership of the EU meant that business was attracted to Britain in order to take advantage of the huge market. Non-EU countries, like Japan and America, were encouraged to invest in Britain because of the market opportunities. The Japanese car company, Nissan, was one of the largest employers in the north-east, and late in 1999 was part-bought by the French company Renault. Huge continental companies like Siemens and Phillips had bases in Britain, employing British people. British companies like the drugs company SmithKline Beecham could use the opportunities presented by the European market to expand into Europe. London Electricity and SWEB were owned by a French company, which in turn was part owned by the French government. The abolition of customs

Eurostar, the passenger train service that uses the Channel Tunnel

How does this photograph explain the increased involvement of Britain in Europe?

duties meant that British people could take cheap crossings to France, stock up on alcohol and cigarettes, which were much cheaper in France because of lower taxes, and take them back to Britain without additional charges. European economies were intertwined.

European law

The importance of the EU as a law-making body was still not widely appreciated by the end of the 20th century. In fact, British law could be overridden by EU law. The EU provided half of all national legislation, including 80% of economic and social legislation and 70% of business legislation.

The European Court of Human Rights also had an important bearing on the everyday life of the British. The Court was not part of the EU, but arose from the Council of Europe, and was expected to ensure that the United Nations' Universal Declaration of Human Rights was upheld throughout Europe. The Court was used increasingly by British citizens by the end of the 20th century, as the Convention on Human Rights was incorporated into British law. For example, the Court ruled it illegal for the army to exclude gays and lesbians. The parents of the murdered teenager Stephen Lawrence used the Court to rule that the police could not be exempted from charges of negligence. British citizens also used the European Court of Justice, which upheld European law. Female pensioners over the age of 60 got payments from the government towards their fuel bills, whereas male pensioners were not eligible until they were 65: a 63-year-old postman used the Court of Justice to win the same right for male pensioners.

Politics and Europe

Government civil servants spent up to a third of their time dealing with European affairs. The EU extended into policy-making for home affairs and justice, as agreed at Maastricht. European politics were absolutely central to the everyday running of British politics, yet the political debate about Britain's future in Europe was underdeveloped. The Labour government was still, in 1999, reluctant to come out in favour of a single currency, saying instead that Britain would join the Euro if the conditions were right, and if the people voted 'yes' in a referendum. The Conservative Party became more anti-European, with some right-wingers arguing that Britain must never join the Euro and should withdraw from the EU.

The Labour government declared it wanted to be at the heart of Europe. However, Britain did not participate in the first wave of the Euro in 1999. This meant that Britain was excluded from the Euro-committee of European politicians, who made important decisions about European finance. Labour did make some changes that suggested that eventually the British would go into the Euro, such as allowing companies to sell shares in Euros, and giving the Bank of England control over interest rates. However, Labour has been criticised by the Europeans for failing to educate the public in favour of the Euro.

Tony Blair also adopted the Social Chapter in 1997, and initiated policies on job creation and environmental protection. Blair was the first British Prime Minister to speak French to the Europeans, at the French National Assembly. Labour also made proposals for a more co-ordinated European foreign and defence policy, and agreed to participate in creating the 'Euro-fighter' military plane. However, Britain's support of America's bombing of Iraq in 1997–98 seemed to indicate that Britain still attached much importance to the 'special relationship'. During the Kosovo crisis in 1999, Britain sided with America in calling for NATO to bomb Yugoslavia, although other NATO partners were more reluctant.

Press and public opinion

The media in Britain were also on the whole opposed to closer monetary union. The tabloid press believed that Britain should 'save the pound' and did not want to see the Queen's head removed from national currency. They believed this would appeal to their readers, capitalising on nationalism and on a latent dislike of foreigners in the public, in particular stereotyping the Germans.

An opinion poll in 1998 showed that 60% of the public were opposed to joining the single currency. The elections to the European Parliament in 1999 showed also that Europe was not a popular issue. The turn-out of the electorate was very small, averaging around 23% with the smallest ever recorded turnout in Sunderland, at 1.5%. Labour lost seats, and the sceptic Conservatives gained. The 'UK Independence Party', in favour of withdrawal, and with alleged links to the fascist British National Party, gained three seats. 'Saving the pound' seemed to be popular among the public at large. The battle for the hearts and minds of the people over Britain's future relations with Europe was therefore far from won.

1. In what ways had Europe influenced British society by 2000?

2. Did Tony Blair's policies suggest that Britain was really 'at the heart of Europe'?

3. Why was Europe so unpopular in Britain at the end of the 20th century?

Further Reading

CHAPTER 2 *The political, social and economic impact of the First World War, 1914–1918*

Texts designed specifically for AS and A2 students

The Deluge by Arthur Marwick (Bodley Head, 1967) – classic interpretation of effects of First World War.

There is a collection of essays in The *First World War in British History*, edited by S. Constantine, M. Kirby and M. B. Rose (Edward Arnold, 1995).

Impact of war on women and on politics

The Making of Modern British Politics by Martin Pugh (Blackwell, 1982)

Women's Suffrage in Britain, 1867–1928 by Martin Pugh (Historical Association, 1980)

Testament of Youth by Vera Brittain (Gollancz, 1978).

Articles in Modern History Review

A. Marwick on the impact of the Two World Wars (September 1990)

K. O. Morgan on Lloyd George (February 1994)

CHAPTER 3 *Social and economic history, 1918–1939*

Articles in Modern History Review

'The General Strike' by Margaret Morris and R.A. Florey (Vol.2 No.3)

'The General Strike: a bluff which was called?' by Joyce Howson (Vol.8 No.1)

'The Locust Years? Britain's inter-war economy' by D.H. Aldcroft (Vol.5 No.2)

'Perspectives: the 1930s – Britain in the Slump' by Ben Pimlott and John Barnes (Vol.1 No.3)

'Unemployment in inter-war Britain' by Joyce Howson (Vol.9 No.1)

Texts designed specifically for AS and A2 students

Britain: Industrial Relations and the Economy 1900–39 by Robert Pearce (Access to History series, Hodder and Stoughton, 1992)

The British Economy since 1914 by Rex Pope (Longman Seminar Studies, 1998)

Unemployment in Britain between the Wars by Stephen Constantine (Longman Seminar Studies, 1980)

For more advanced reading

Britain in the Depression: society and politics 1929–39 John Stevenson and Chris Cook, 2nd ed., (Longman, 1994)

British Society 1914–1945 by John Stevenson (Penguin, 1984)

The Development of the British Economy 1914–1990 by Sidney Pollard, 4th ed., (Edward Arnold, 1992)

War and Progress: Britain 1914–1945 by Peter Dewey (Longman, 1996)

The Working Class in Britain 1850–1939 by John Benson (Longman, 1989)

Documentary coverage

Democracy in a Depression: Britain in the 1920s and 1930s by Malcolm Smith (University of Wales Press, 1998)

CHAPTER 4 *The Conservative Party, 1918–1939*

Articles in Modern History Review

'The Conservative dominance 1918–1940' by Stuart Ball (Vol.3 No.2)

'Ditching the Goat: the fall of Lloyd George' by Graham Goodlad (Vol.10 No.4)

'Stanley Baldwin and the Conservative Party' by Derrick Murphy (Vol.9 No.4)

Texts designed specifically for AS and A2 students

Britain: Domestic Politics 1918–1939 by Robert Pearce (Access to History series, Hodder and Stoughton, 1992)

The Conservative Party and British Politics 1902–1951 by Stuart Ball (Longman Seminar Studies, 1995), also contains a useful selection of documentary extracts

Stanley Baldwin and the Search for Consensus by Duncan Watts (Personalities and Powers series, Hodder and Stoughton, 1996)

For more advanced reading

An Appetite for Power: a history of the Conservative Party since 1830 by John Ramsden (HarperCollins, 1998), Chapters 9 to 11

Baldwin by Philip Williamson (Cambridge University Press, 1999)

Bonar Law by R.J.Q. Adams (John Murray, 1999)

The Conservative Party from Peel to Major by Robert Blake (Heinemann, 1997), Chapter 7

How Tory Governments Fall: the Tory Party in power since 1783 edited by Anthony Seldon (Fontana, 1996), Chapters 6 and 7

The Making of Modern British Politics 1867–1939 by Martin Pugh (Blackwell, 1982), Part 4

CHAPTER 5 *The Labour Party, 1918–1939*

Articles in Modern History Review

'The political career of Ramsay MacDonald' by Adrian Smith (Vol. 3 No. 4)

'Perspectives: the 1931 crisis' by Andrew Thorpe and Philip Williamson (Vol. 5 No. 2)

'The challenge of Labour: class conflict in interwar Britain' by Rodney Lowe (Vol. 6 No. 1)

Texts designed specifically for AS and A2 students

Britain: Domestic Politics 1918–1939 by Robert Pearce (Access to History series, Hodder and Stoughton, 1992)

The Rise of the Labour Party 1893–1931 by Gordon Phillips (Lancaster Pamphlets, Routledge, 1992)

The Rise of the Labour Party 1880–1945 by Paul Adelman, 3rd ed., (Longman Seminar Studies, 1996) – also contains a useful selection of documentary extracts

For more advanced reading

Arthur Henderson by Chris Wrigley (University of Wales Press, 1990)

The Evolution of the Labour Party 1910–1924 by Ross McKibbin (Oxford University Press, 1974)

A History of the British Labour Party by Andrew Thorpe (Macmillan, 1997)

Labour and the Left in the 1930s by Ben Pimlott (Cambridge University Press, 1977)

Labour People: Leaders and Lieutenants: Hardie to Kinnock by Kenneth Morgan (Oxford University Press, 1987)

The Making of Modern British Politics 1867–1939 by Martin Pugh (Blackwell, 1982), see Parts 3 and 4

Politicians and the Slump: the Labour Government of 1929–1931 by Robert Skidelsky (Penguin, 1970)

Ramsay MacDonald by David Marquand (Cape, 1977)

CHAPTER 6   British foreign and imperial policy, 1918–1939

Texts designed specifically for AS and A2 students

Britain: Foreign and Imperial Policy 1918–1939 by Alan Farmer (Hodder and Stoughton, 1992)

British Foreign Policy in the Twentieth Century by C.J. Bartlett (British History in Perspective Series, Macmillan, 1989)

Europe 1870 to 1989 by Terry Morris and Derrick Murphy (Collins Educational, 2000)

The Origins of the Second World War by Richard Overy (Longman Seminar Studies, 1987)

The Origins of the Second World War by Ruth Hening (Routledge Lancaster Pamphlets, 1985)

Versailles and After by Ruth Hening (Routledge Lancaster Pamphlets, 1984)

For more advanced reading

Britain in the 20th Century, Parts One and Two by Lawrence Butler and Harriet Jones (Heinemann, 1994)

Chamberlain and Appeasement by R.A.C. Parker (Macmillan, 1993)

The Evolution of the Modern Commonwealth by Denis Judd and Peter Slinn (Macmillan, 1982)

Origins of the Second World War by Philip Bell (Longman, 1997)

CHAPTER 7   The Liberal Party, 1918–2000

Texts designed specifically for AS and A2 students

The Decline of the Liberal Party 1910–1931 by Paul Adelman (Longman Seminar Studies, 1981) – contains documents

The Liberal Party: Triumph and Disintegration: 1886 to 1929 by G. R. Searle (British History in Perspective, Macmillan, 1994)

Lloyd George by Stephen Constantine (Routledge Lancaster Pamphlets, 1992)

For more advanced reading

The Age of Lloyd George 1890 to 1929 by Kenneth O. Morgan (Allen and Unwin, 1978) – contains documents

A History of the Liberal Party 1895 to 1970 by R. Douglas (Sidgwick and Jackson, 1971)

The Liberal Democrats edited by Don McIver (Prentice Hall, 1996)

Lloyd George by Chris Wrigley (Historical Association Studies, Blackwell, 1992)

The Making of Modern British Politics 1867–1939 by Martin Pugh (Blackwell, 1992)

Third Party Politics since 1945, Liberals, Alliance and Liberal Democrats by John Stevenson (Institute of Contemporary British History, Blackwell, 1993)

SDP The Birth, Life and Death of the Social Democratic Party by Ivor Crew and Anthony King (Oxford University Press, 1995)

CHAPTER 8   The road to 1945: the impact of the Second World War

Texts designed specifically for AS and A2 students

The Attlee Governments 1945 to 1951 by Kevin Jeffreys (Longman Seminar Studies, 1995), opening section on 'Labour and the Road to 1945'

The British Welfare State : A Critical History by John Brown (Historical Association Studies, Blackwell, 1995)

The Conservative Party 1902 to 1951 by Stuart Ball (Longman Seminar Studies, 1995)

Empire to Welfare State 1906–1985 by T.O. Lloyd, 3rd ed., (Oxford University Press, 1986)

The Shaping of the Welfare State by R.C. Birch (Longman Seminar Studies, 1974)

War in Europe 1939–1945 by Anthony Wood (Longman Seminar Studies, 1987)

War and Society 1899 to 1948 by Rex Pope (Longman Seminar Studies, 1991)

All the Seminar Studies books have a document section.

For more advanced reading

The Road to 1945: British Politics and the Second World War by Paul Addison (Cape, 1975)

The Churchill Coalition and Wartime Politics 1940–1945 by Kevin Jefferys (Manchester University Press, 1991)

The People's War, by Angus Calder (Pimlico, 1992)

War and Reform: British Politics during the Second World War edited by Kevin Jefferys, (Manchester University Press, 1994)

The Second World War by Martin Gilbert (Fontana, 1989)

The Oxford Companion to the Second World War, I.C.B. Dear (Oxford University Press, 1995) – a good book for dipping into with short pieces on a wide variety of topics

CHAPTER 9   From Empire to Commonwealth, 1945–2000

Articles

'Controversy: Did Suez Hasten the End of Empire?' *Contemporary Record*, (Vol. 1 No. 2, Summer 1987), Institute of Contemporary British History

'Suez – What the Papers Say', by Peter Hennessy and Mark Laity, *Contemporary Record*, (Vol. 1 No. 1 Spring 1987), Institute of Contemporary British History

For more advanced reading

Britain and Decolonisation by John Darwin (Macmillan, 1998)

British Decolonisation, 1946–97 by David McIntyre (St. Martin's Press, 1988)

Decolonisation and the British Empire 1775 to 1997 by D. George Boyce (Macmillan, 1999)

Decolonisation: The British Experience since 1945 by Nicholas J. White (Longman, 1999)

Industrialisation and the British Colonial State by
Lawrence Butler (Cass, 1997)

The Lion's Share 1850–1995 by Bernard Porter
(Macmillan, 1996)

*The Pursuit of Greatness: Britain and the World Role
1900–1970* by Robert Holland (Fontana, 1991)

CHAPTER 10   British foreign and defence policy, 1945–2000

Article
'The Cold War 1945–49', by Derrick Murphy, *Modern
History Review*, Vol. No. 10, 4, April 1999

Texts designed specifically for AS and A2 students
The Cold War by Hugh Higgins, 3rd ed., (Heinemann,
1993)

The Cold War 1945–1965 by Joseph Smith (Historical
Association Studies, Blackwell, 1989)

The Cold War 1945–1991 by John W. Mason (Routledge
Lancaster Pamphlets, 1996)

The Origins of the Cold War, 1941–49 by Martin
Macauley, 2nd ed., (Longman Seminar Studies, 1995)

Russia, America and the Cold War 1949–1991 by Martin
Macauley (Longman Seminar Studies, 1998)

The USA and the Cold War by Oliver Edwards (Hodder
and Stoughton, 1997)

More advanced reading
Britain and the Cold War 1945 to 1991 by Sean
Greenwood (Macmillan, 2000)

Cold War Europe 1945–1989 by S. Young (Edward
Arnold, 1991)

The Cold War: The Great Powers and the Allies by J.
Dunbabin (Longman, 1994)

The Cold War 1947 to 1991 by S. J. Ball (Hodder
Headline, 1998)

The Cold War, 1945–87, by R. Levering (Harlan
Davidson, 1988)

The United States and the Cold War, 1945–53 by R.
Crockatt (The British Association for the
Advancement of Science, 1989)

CHAPTER 11   British-Irish relations, 1914–2000

Texts designed specifically for AS and A2 students
The Irish Question in British Politics 1868–1986 by
D.G. Boyce (Macmillan, 1988)

Ireland 1828–1923 by D.G. Boyce (Historical Association
Studies, Blackwell, 1992)

Politics UK edited by B. Jones (Prentice Hall, 1998)

The Ulster Question 1603–1973 by T.W. Moody (Mercier,
1974)

Understanding Northern Ireland by D. Quinn (Baseline,
1993)

More advanced reading
Modern Ireland 1600–1972 by R.F. Foster (Allen Lane,
1988)

The Origins of the Present Troubles in Northern Ireland by
C. Kennedy-Pipe (Longman, 1997)

The Northern Ireland Question in British Politics edited by
P. Catterall and S. McDougall (Macmillan, 1996)

Northern Ireland since 1968 by P. Arthur and K. Jeffrey
(Blackwell, 1988)

CHAPTER 12   The Labour Party, 1945–2000

Texts designed specifically for AS and A2 students
The Attlee Government, 1945–1951 by Kevin Jefferys
(Longman Seminar Studies, 1992)

*The Labour Party since 1951: 'Socialism' and Society since
1951* by Steve Fielding (Manchester University Press,
1997)

Never Again: Britain 1945–1951 by Peter Hennessy
(Jonathan Cape, 1992)

The People's Peace: British History 1945–1990 by Kenneth
O. Morgan (Penguin, 1990)

More advanced reading
Breach of Promise: Labour in Power 1964–70 by Clive
Ponting (Penguin, 1989)

Election '45 Reflections on the Revolution in Britain by
Austin Mitchell (Fabian Society, 1995)

From Blitz to Blair: A new history of Britain since 1939
edited by Nick Tiratsoo (Weidenfeld and Nicolson,
1997)

*Generating Socialism: Recollections of life in the Labour
Party* by Daniel Weinbren (Sutton Publishing, 1997)

The Labour Party since 1945 by Eric Shaw (Blackwell,
1996)

The Labour Party since 1979: crisis and transformation by
Eric Shaw (Routledge, 1994)

Labour in Power 1945–1951 by Kenneth O. Morgan
(Oxford University Press, 1985)

Labour People: Leaders and Lieutenants Hardie to Kinnock
by Kenneth O. Morgan (Oxford University Press,
1987)

Remaking the Labour Party: From Gaitskell to Blair by
Tudor Jones (Routledge, 1996)

The Writing on the Wall: Britain in the Seventies by Philip
Whitehead (Michael Joseph, 1985)

In addition Tony Benn, Barbara Castle and Richard
Crossman have all published diaries of their time as
ministers. They offer illuminating insights into the
Labour governments of the 1960s and 1970s.

CHAPTER 13   The Conservative Party, 1945–2000

Texts designed specifically for AS and A2 students
British Domestic Politics 1939–1964 by Paul Adelman
(Access to History series, Hodder & Stoughton,
1994)

The Conservative Party and British Politics 1902–1951 by
Stuart Ball (Longman Seminar Studies, 1995),
chapters 7 and 8

Politics UK by B. Jones and others (Prentice Hall, 1998),
chapter 14

Articles
The *Modern History Review* regularly has articles on this
topic

Politics Review also has articles on this topic on a regular
basis including:

'Labour and Conservative Members compared' by P. Seyd
and P. Whitely (No. 4, April 1998)

'The Conservative Leadership Contest, 1997' by
P. Norton (Vol. 7, No. 4, April 1998)

Talking Politics also has regular articles including:

'The 1997 Election and the Conservative Party's Prospects'
by D. Nicholson (Vol. 10, No. 3, Spring 1998)

For more advance reading

The Conservative Party since 1945 edited by Stuart Ball (Manchester University Press, 1998)

The Conservative Party from Peel to Major by Robert Blake (Heinemann, 1997)

How Tory Governments Fall: The Tory Party in Power since 1783 edited by Anthony Seldon (Fontana, 1996)

Conservative Century: The Conservative Party since 1900 edited by Athony Seldon and Stuart Ball (Oxford University Press, 1994

CHAPTER 14   *Social and economic history, 1945–2000*

Texts designed specifically for AS and A2 students

British Society since 1945 by Arthur Marwick (Penguin, 1996)

From Blitz to Blair: A New History of Britain since 1939 edited by Nick Tiratsoo (Weidenfeld and Nicolson, 1997)

The People's Peace by Kenneth O. Morgan (Oxford University Press, 1990)

Twentieth Century Britain: Economic, Social and Cultural Change edited by Paul Johnson (Longman, 1994)

More advanced reading

The Age of Insecurity by Larry Elliott and Dan Atkinson (Verso, 1998)

British Economic Performance since 1945 by B.W.E. Alford (Macmillan, 1988)

Modern Britain: an Economic and Social History by Sean Glynn and Alan Booth (Routledge, 1996)

Websites

A useful site giving basic statistical information about the United Kingdom is the Office for National Statistics http://www.statistics.gov.uk

CHAPTER 15   *Britain and Europe, 1945–2000*

Britain and European Unity 1945–1992 by John Young (Macmillan, 1993)

Britain and European Co-operation Since 1945 by Sean Greenwood (Blackwell, 1992)

From Reconstruction to Integration, Britain and Europe since 1945 edited by Brian Brivati and Harriet Jones (Leicester University Press, 1993)

An Awkward Partner: Britain in the European Community by Stephen George (Oxford University Press, 1990)

Index

Glossary terms